Special Edition
Using

Corel® WordPerfect®
Office 2000

NEW AND IMPROVED
WORDPERFECT OFFICE FEATURES

Install-As-You-Go   Installs noninstalled items, asking you whether you would like to install the item; the hard disk drive isn't cluttered with features you don't use (located throughout the book)

AutoScroll tool   Gives you functionality of IntelliMouse with a regular mouse; you can quickly scroll in any direction in a document; automatically scrolls through the document for you; use AutoScroll tool with a Microsoft IntelliMouse or a conventional mouse, p. 32

Browse document   New Back button and Forward button on the toolbar allow you to browse backward and forward in your document, just like you browse through Web pages on the Internet, p. 84

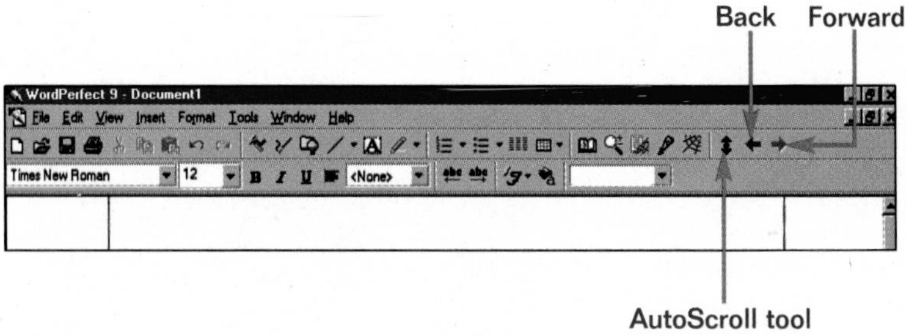

Back   Forward

Figure 1
Browse document features

AutoScroll tool

WordPerfect menus   Restructured menus for access to most frequently used features; right-click a menu to select a menu similar to one used in a previous version of WordPerfect, p. 80

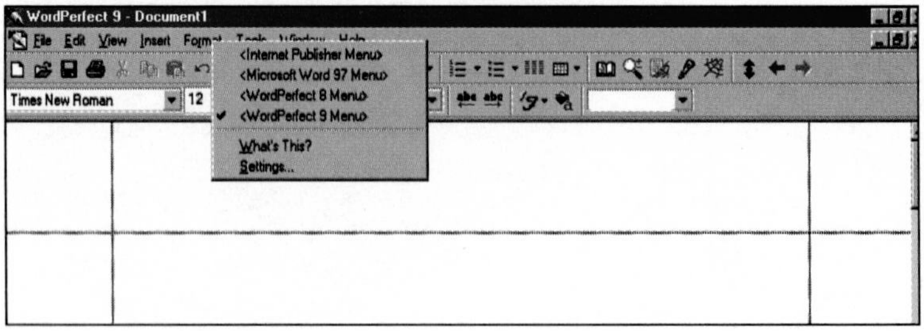

Figure 2
Restructured WordPerfect menus

Browse   New Browse button on the vertical scrollbar lets you select the document element you want to browse through, such as page (default), table, box, footnote, endnote, heading, edit position, or comment. The labels on the Previous and Next buttons on each side of the Browse button change, depending on what the Browse button is set to browse. For example, if you choose Browse by Table using the Browse button, you will see Previous Table and Next Table buttons (the double Up and Down arrows on each side of the Browse button), p. 80

Figure 3
Browse button on the vertical scrollbar

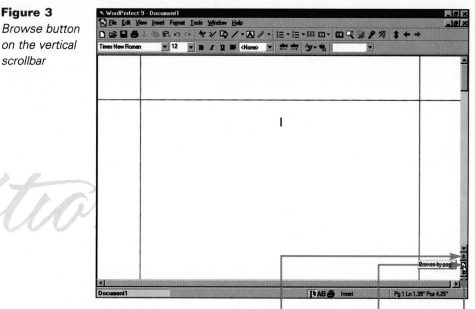

Previous button   Browse button   Next button

Opening a document   WordPerfect 9 documents use the same file format as WordPerfect 6, WordPerfect 6.1, WordPerfect 7, and WordPerfect 8; open and use documents from previous versions, p. 93

File conversion   Enhanced file conversion retains the same file format of Lotus Ami Pro, Lotus Word Pro, and Microsoft Word documents, p. 91

RealTime Preview   Lets you experiment with formatting, such as font and font size, and preview formatting before you apply it to the document, p. 109

Figure 4
Formatting with RealTime Preview

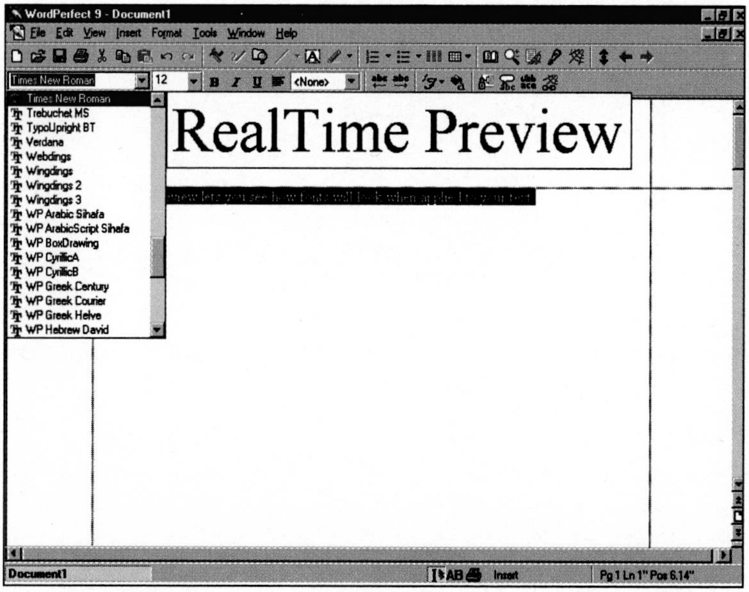

Make It Fit   Enhanced Make It Fit expands or condenses a document in a user-defined space, p. 135

Multiple languages   You can choose from a wide variety of multiple languages for use with Spell Checker, Thesaurus, and Grammatik, p. 163

Previewing a document   Now Print Preview is fully editable; you can use editing commands to make changes to your WordPerfect document directly in Print Preview, p. 170

PerfectPrint   Enlarge or reduce a document to fit any paper size without changing the format of page, p. 171

Printing an envelope   The Print Upside Down feature allows you to print return addresses closer to the edge of the envelope on a DeskJet printer, p. 173

Skewed table cells   Now you can slant (skew) table cells and the text in the skewed cells on the top row or the left or right column of a table, giving the cells a three-dimensional look; you can even specify a skew angle, p. 242

Figure 5
Skewed table cells

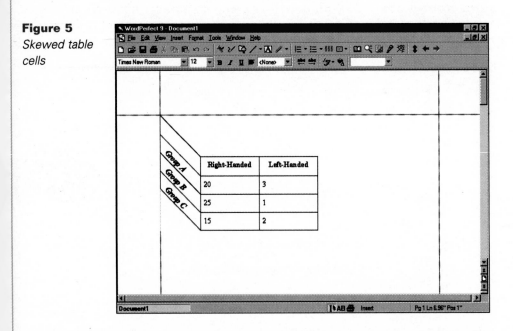

Graphic objects   More than 100 new shapes; Text In Shapes lets you add text to fancy shapes, p. 265

Scrapbook   The Scrapbook has been redesigned and enhanced to provide you with clip art, photos, sounds, and movies; lets you search and preview images, drag and drop, copy and paste; organizes images by category; create your own category; view automatic updates of thumbnails; preview sounds, movies, and bitmap images, p. 275

Figure 6
Redesigned and enhanced Scrapbook

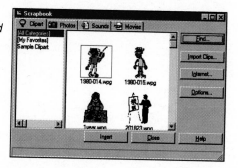

Editing graphics objects   In-place editing allows you to edit a graphic object in the view you're currently in; when you click an object, QuickSpot provides a Property bar that displays buttons for graphics editing tools, p. 271

Adding images from the Web   Now you can add images from the Web into your Scrapbook, p. 277

Importing images from earlier versions of WordPerfect   You can import images you created or used from WordPerfect 7 and WordPerfect 8, p. 277

Moving around in a Notebook   New Browse buttons; enhanced Go To dialog box; lets you search for formulas, values, named cells, and comments, p. 336

3D Notebooks   Increased notebook size; more rows, columns, and sheets, p. 350

Notebook file compatibility   Compatibility settings ensure file compatibility with Microsoft Excel 97, Lotus 1-2-3, and earlier versions of Quattro Pro, p. 353

Editing cell entries   Enhanced cell-editing enables you to edit a cell; for example, Quattro Pro shows numeric formatting, such as 50% instead of 0.5, and a date value instead of a Julian value, p. 356

Formulas   Formula marker (blue triangle) now appears to identify which cells contain formulas; QuickTip shows formula in a QuickTip box near a cell that contains a formula, p. 359

Figure 7
Formula markers and QuickTips

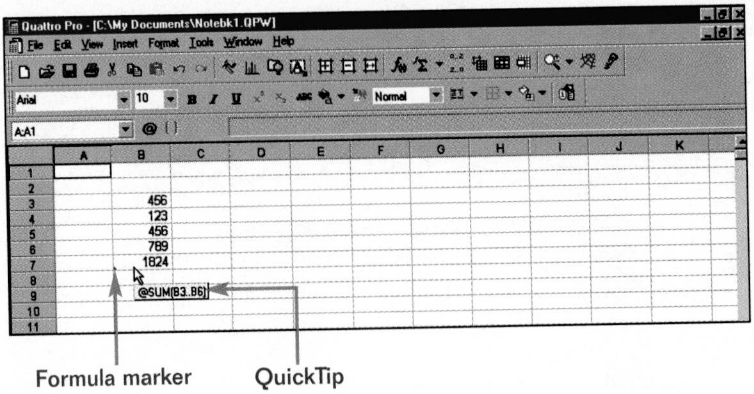

Formula marker   QuickTip

Saving Notebook files
Notebook files are now saved automatically in a smaller file size; saved files are compressed to save disk space, p. 367

Quattro Pro menus
Restructured menus for access to the most frequently used features; right-click a menu to select a menu similar to one used in a previous version of Quattro Pro, p. 374

SpeedFunctions
Frequently used functions, such as @SUM, @MIN, @MAX, and @AVG, are readily available on the toolbar, p. 400

Figure 8
SpeedFunctions on the toolbar

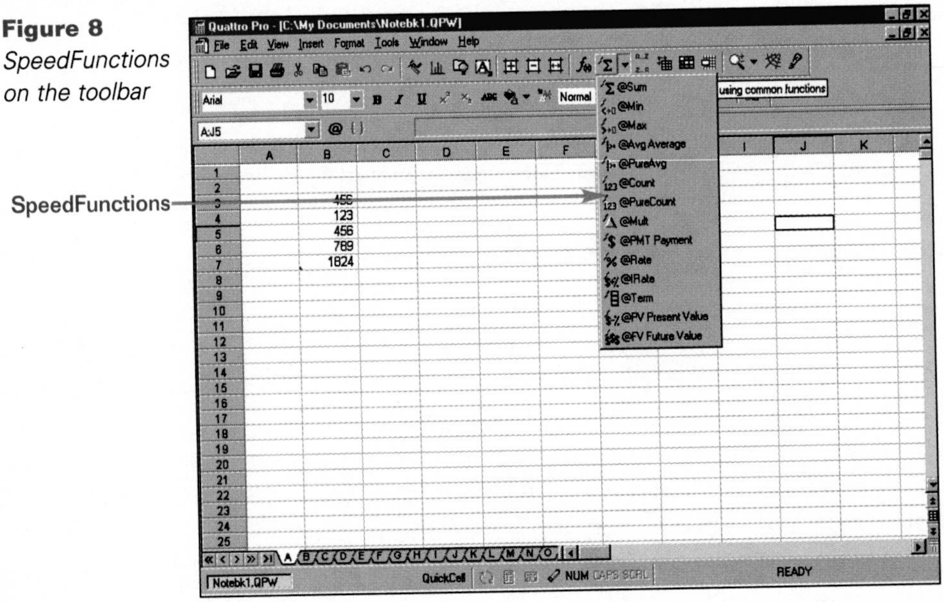

SpeedFunctions—

Formula tips   Quattro Pro now displays a tip for each value requested by a function as you type the function, p. 401

Row height   Row height is automatically adjusted after you enter data in the row, p. 406

Numeric formats   The Euro has been added to the currency numeric format, p. 415

Custom numeric formats   There are more options for custom numeric formats, including font attributes, cell attributes, and conditional formatting, p. 426

RealTime Preview   Lets you experiment with formatting, such as font and font size, and preview your formatting before you apply it to spreadsheet data, p. 426

Page Breaks view   Shows where page breaks will appear in the spreadsheet when printed, allows you to change the margins in this view by simply dragging borders, p. 485

Figure 9
Page Breaks view in the spreadsheet

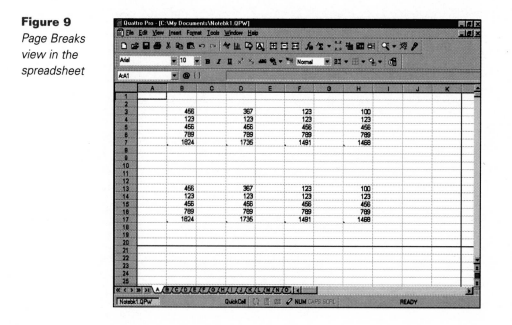

Property Bars   Redesigned Property Bars in Corel Presentations give you quick and easy access to the features you use most frequently; many features that could be accessed only through menus in previous versions of Corel Presentations can now be accessed through the Property Bar, p. 504

Adding text to a slide   QuickFonts have been removed since Corel Presentations 8, p. 511

Shapes   Shapes are displayed in RealTime Preview to show you how they will look when inserted into the slide; image tools let you apply special effects to shapes with Brightness, Contrast, Watermark, Coloring Book, Outline All, Transparent; convert shapes to polygons; add 3D effects; use QuickWarp to bend or twist a shape; contour text to a shape; combine a polygon with another object with the Combine tool, p. 544

SpeedLinks   Lets you create hyperlinks in a Web document or electronic document; automatic creation of a hyperlink when you type text beginning with www, ftp, http, or mailto, p. 593

Dragon NaturallySpeaking   A speech recognition and dictation application that allows you to dictate at about 160 words per minute; your words are transcribed on the screen and into your document; you can access Dragon NaturallySpeaking menus and buttons in WordPerfect, p. 644

Special Edition

Using

Corel

WordPerfect®

Office

2000

Trudi Reisner

A Division of Macmillan Computer Publishing, USA

201 W. 103rd Street

Indianapolis, Indiana 46290

CONTENTS AT A GLANCE

Special Edition Using Corel WordPerfect® Office 2000

Copyright ©1999 by Que® Corporation

International Standard Book Number: 0-7897-1731-X

Library of Congress Catalog Card Number: 98-86951

Printed in the United States of America

First Printing: August 1999

00 99   4   3   2   1

Trademarks

Warning and Disclaimer

Executive Editor
John Pierce

Development Editor
Nancy Warner

Managing Editor
Tom Hayes

Project Editor
Karen S. Shields

Copy Editor
Julie McNamee

Indexer
Becky Hornyak

Proofreader
Maribeth Echard

Technical Editors
Darralyn McCall
Gary Krakow

Interior Design
Ruth Lewis
Nathan Clement

Cover Design
Dan Armstrong
Ruth Lewis

Copy Writer
Eric Borgert

Layout Technicians
Brandon Allen
Timothy Osborn
Staci Somers

TABLE OF CONTENTS

ABOUT THE AUTHOR

Trudi Reisner is a computer technical writer, specializing in writing and developing books and courseware based on microcomputer software applications. Trudi has also taught and written extensively on WordPerfect. She is the author of more than 35 computer books, including Que's *10 Minute Guide to Windows 95*, *Easy Microsoft Office 97*, and *Easy WordPerfect 6 for Windows*, *WordPerfect 6 Solutions* published by John Wiley & Sons, Inc., and *Sams Teach Yourself Excel 2000 in 24 Hours*. Other computer books she has written include *Excel 97 Exam Cram* published by Coriolis, *Outlook 97 One Step at a Time*, *Word 97 One Step at a Time*, and *Word 2000 One Step at a Time* published by IDG Books Worldwide.

DEDICATION

My gratitude to Karen Giventer for her support, encouragement, and humor that kept me going during this project.

ACKNOWLEDGMENTS

An acknowledgment to author Bill Bruck and coauthors for their hard work on the previous editions of this book, which formed the basis for this edition.

I would like to extend my thanks and acknowledgment to my literary agent, David Fugate; Acquisitions Editor, Jamie Milazzo; Development Editor, Nancy Warner; and Technical Editor, Darralyn McCall. Also, many thanks to the Que staff for proofreading and producing the entire book.

TELL US WHAT YOU THINK!

As the reader of this book, *you* are our most important critic and commentator. We value your opinion and want to know what we're doing right, what we could do better, what areas you'd like to see us publish in, and any other words of wisdom you're willing to pass our way.

As a Publisher for Que, I welcome your comments. You can fax, email, or write me directly to let me know what you did or didn't like about this book—as well as what we can do to make our books stronger.

Please note that I cannot help you with technical problems related to the topic of this book, and that due to the high volume of mail I receive, I might not be able to reply to every message.

When you write, please be sure to include this book's title and author as well as your name and phone or fax number. I will carefully review your comments and share them with the author and editors who worked on the book.

Fax: 317-581-4666

Email: office_que@mcp.com

Mail: John Pierce
          Que Publishing
          201 West 103rd Street
          Indianapolis, IN 46290 USA

INTRODUCTION

Corel WordPerfect Office 2000 is the most popular retail software suite of desktop applications you can buy. Its powerful, integrated software set includes many best-of-class applications, including the latest versions of WordPerfect for word processing, Quattro Pro for spreadsheet analysis, and Presentations for drawing and presentation graphics. In addition, you receive tools such as fonts, clip art, and QuickFinder to help integrate and publish your work.

With the power of Corel WordPerfect Office 2000 come both ease of use and sophisticated features. Individuals can load it on their standalone machines at home and let PerfectExpert guide them through sending correspondence, making family budgets, and maintaining a holiday list. Multinational corporations can load the Corel WordPerfect Office 2000 on LANs, and conduct enterprise computing via the Internet and corporate intranets through the suite's built-in Internet features. Businesses can also maintain corporate documents electronically through Envoy, keep corporate financial spreadsheets in Quattro Pro, and create custom interfaces and automated tasks.

WHO SHOULD USE THIS BOOK?

Corel has created an easy-to-use and easy-to-learn product in WordPerfect Office 2000. However, the sheer number of included applications, richness of features, variety of short-cuts, and power of its automation functions imply that both the new and experienced user will be unable to take full advantage of the suite by mere experimentation. *Special Edition Using Corel WordPerfect Office 2000* can increase understanding and decrease learning time for everyone using Corel WordPerfect Office 2000.

For newcomers, this book offers a conceptual overview of the suite, step-by-step instructions for common functionality, and a thorough introduction to each of the included applications.

More experienced users will appreciate coverage of the new features offered by suite applications, along with the sections on suite customization and integration. Discussion of creating and moving files from and onto the Internet will also be of great value.

Many readers will find that they use one application extensively and the others occasionally. For these users, this book will be their only point of reference for those applications used occasionally. It will also serve as a first point of reference for the major application.

HOW THIS BOOK IS ORGANIZED

Special Edition Using Corel WordPerfect Office 2000 is organized into seven major parts that take you from the basic design of WordPerfect Office 2000, through using each application, and into advanced integration and customization of the suite:

> Part I: Working with Corel WordPerfect Office 2000
>
> Part II: Using Corel WordPerfect 9
>
> Part III: Using Corel Quattro Pro
>
> Part IV: Using Corel Presentations
>
> Part V: Web Publishing with Corel WordPerfect Office 2000
>
> Part VI: Using the Bonus Applications

Part I, "Working with Corel WordPerfect Office 2000," provides a conceptual overview of the suite. It shows you how to perform simple functions, explains how common tools such as the Desktop Application Director and help system work, discusses common file management issues, and shows you how to create and edit toolbars and custom menus.

Parts II through IV are devoted to the specific applications that make up Corel WordPerfect Office 2000. The main focus is on WordPerfect 9. You can turn directly to these sections if you have specific questions to answer or tasks to accomplish.

If you will be working with the Internet, Part V is for you. You'll learn all about how to publish documents on the Web from each of the main suite applications.

Part VI discusses the bonus applications. In it, you'll learn how to use Dragon NaturallySpeaking, a voice recognition and dictation application, CorelCENTRAL to manage your schedule and tasks, and Address Book to maintain your contact list.

CONVENTIONS USED IN THIS BOOK

The conventions used in this book have been developed to help you learn to use Corel WordPerfect Office 2000 quickly and easily. Most commands can be entered with a mouse, the keyboard, or toolbar buttons. Commands are written in a way that enables you to choose the method you prefer. For example, if the instruction says "Choose File, Open," you can click the File menu, and then click the Open option. Alternatively, you can press

Alt+F to access the File menu, and then press O; or use the arrow keys to highlight Open, and then press Enter. Finally, you can use the mouse to click the Open file button on the toolbar.

When you need to hold down the first key while you press a second key, a plus sign (+) is used for the combination:

Alt+F or Ctrl+M

The Shift, Ctrl, and Alt keys must all be used in this way.

When two keys are pressed in sequence, they are separated with a comma. For instance, the Home key is never held down while simultaneously pressing another key, but it is often pressed before pressing another key. "Press Home, up arrow" means to press and release the Home key; then press and release the up-arrow key.

When a letter in a menu or dialog box is underlined, it indicates that you can press the Alt key plus that letter (or that letter alone in submenus and dialog boxes) to choose that command. In "Choose File, Open" you can access the menu by pressing Alt+F; then with the File menu selected, you can choose Open by pressing the letter O. Often, the underlined letter is the first letter in the word; at other times it is not. For instance, to choose Tools, Settings, you would press the Alt key and hold it down while you press T; then you would press the N key (for Settings).

If there are two common ways to invoke a command, they are separated with a semicolon (;). For instance, you can access the Print dialog box in two ways, as indicated by these instructions: "Choose File, Print; or press Ctrl+P."

Many times, the quickest way to access a feature is with a button on the toolbar. In this case, the appropriate toolbar button is shown in the margin next to the instructions.

Bold text is used to indicate text you are asked to type. Italic text is used for new terms. UPPERCASE letters are used to distinguish filenames. Onscreen messages appear in monospace type.

Note

Notes provide additional information that might help you avoid problems or offer advice or general information related to the current topic.

Tip #1001 from
Trudi Reisner

Tips provide extra information that supplements the current topic. Often, tips offer shortcuts or alternative methods for accomplishing a task.

Caution

Cautions warn you if a procedure or description in the topic could lead to unexpected results or even data loss or damage to your system. If you see a caution, proceed carefully.

I'm having a specific problem with a WordPerfect feature. Look for troubleshooting elements to help you identify and resolve specific problems you might be having with WordPerfect, your system, or network.

Practical projects show you how to make better Corel WordPerfect Office 2000 documents, be a more effective communicator through your documents, and how to streamline the process of creating professional documents. Some practical projects even show you how to combine features to accomplish results you may not think of.

What About Sidebars?

Sidebars are sprinkled throughout the book to give you the author's insight into a particular topic. The information in a sidebar supplements the material in the chapter.

Cross-references such as the following direct you to related information in other parts of the book.

→ **See** "Starting Corel Quattro Pro," **p. 334**

Inline cross-references, such as *functions (page 437)*, direct you to the part of the book where the topic is explained.

I, the author, hope you enjoy using *Special Edition Using Corel WordPerfect Office 2000*, and hope that you find this book to be a valuable tool, as well as an ongoing reference to assist you in the learning process.

WORKING WITH COREL WORDPERFECT OFFICE 2000

CHAPTER

1

INTRODUCING COREL WORDPERFECT OFFICE 2000

In this chapter

WHAT IS COREL WORDPERFECT OFFICE 2000?

Corel WordPerfect Office 2000 is a collection of applications for common home and office tasks, integrated with the Desktop Application Director, which includes a scripting language for cross-program applications.

WHAT'S INCLUDED IN THE SUITE?

The Corel WordPerfect Office 2000 Suite is designed for the Windows 95 operating environment and it ships with the following applications:

- WordPerfect 9
- Quattro Pro 9
- Presentations 9

In addition, you get a number of bonus applications with WordPerfect Office, including

- Dragon NaturallySpeaking
- Desktop Application Director
- CorelCENTRAL 9
- Fonts
- Clip art and Photos

Corel also publishes WordPerfect Office 2000 Professional, which is targeted to a more specialized audience. The Professional suite includes the same core applications as the standard version and adds applications, such as Paradox, targeted toward business users.

You can use *Special Edition Using Corel WordPerfect Office 2000* to learn the core applications common to both the Standard and the Professional versions.

WHAT ARE THE OPERATING REQUIREMENTS?

To use WordPerfect Office 2000, Corel recommends the following minimum system requirements:

- Windows 95, Windows 98, or Windows NT 4.0
- 486/66 processor
- 16MB RAM
- 300MB hard disk space
- CD-ROM
- VGA or higher monitor

UNDERSTANDING THE DESIGN GOALS

WordPerfect Office isn't just a bunch of standalone applications bundled and marketed together. It is a true suite of products that is integrated together and aimed at home and business functionality.

Therefore, understanding WordPerfect Office 2000 isn't merely a matter of learning the features of individual applications. In fact, before you learn about the functions of all the applications, it's important to understand the basic design goals of WordPerfect Office. These may be divided into the following areas:

- Ease of learning and use
- Integrated working environment
- Extension of your desktop

UNDERSTANDING EASE-OF-USE FEATURES

The WordPerfect Office 2000 suite has been developed with extensive input from WordPerfect's usability testing procedures. Two features that have been incorporated into the suite as a result of this research are a consistent user interface and the extensive availability of help in a variety of formats.

CONSISTENT INTERFACE

A consistent interface means that the way you work in one application should parallel how you work in another. In WordPerfect Office, this can be seen in several areas:

- Menu similarity—As you can see in Figure 1.1, menus are similar in WordPerfect Office 2000 applications. Not only are the names on the menu bar similar, the selections within each menu item parallel one another as much as possible, taking into consideration the differences in each application's features.
- Toolbar similarity—In menus that are parallel within each application, the same buttons are used for basic tools across applications. These buttons are shown in Table 1.1.
- Dialog box similarity—In addition, similar dialog boxes are used wherever possible throughout WordPerfect Office. For instance, the same Open dialog box is used in WordPerfect, Quattro Pro, and Presentations.

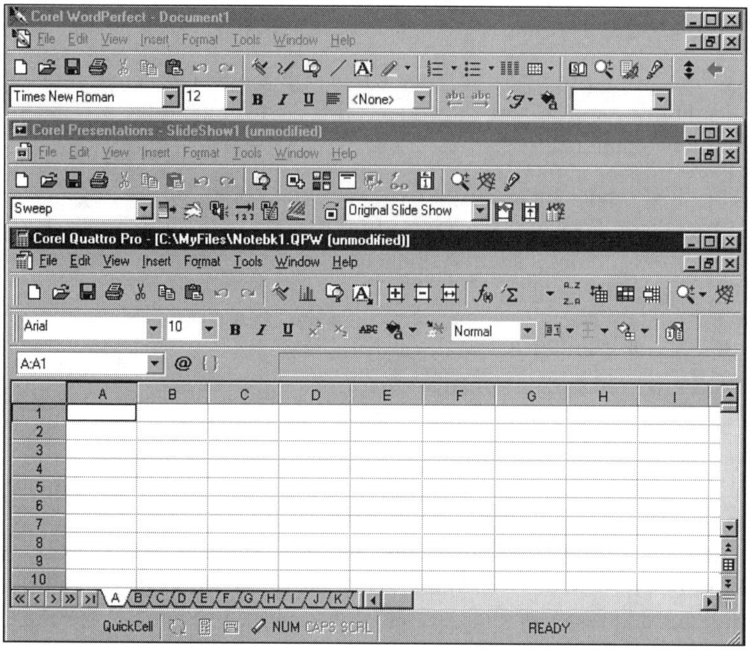

Figure 1.1
Menus are similar in
WordPerfect Office
applications.

TABLE 1.1 COMMON WORDPERFECT OFFICE 2000 BUTTONS

Icon	Name	Function
	New Blank Document	Creates a blank document in a new window
	Open	Opens an existing document in a new window
	Save	Saves the current document
	Print	Prints the current document
	Cut	Moves the selection to the Clipboard
	Copy	Copies the selection to the Clipboard
	Paste	Inserts the Clipboard contents at the insertion point
	Undo	Reverses the last change
	Redo	Reverses the last undo
	Bold	Turns on/off bold
	Italic	Turns on/off italic
	Underline	Turns on/off underline
	Corel Web Site	Launches your default Web browser and goes to the Corel Web site
	PerfectExpert	Displays the PerfectExpert for assistance

Some of the buttons aren't on the default toolbars, but they can be added by customizing a toolbar to easily get to the tools you want.

→ To learn how to customize toolbars, **see** "Customizing Toolbars and Property Bars," **p. 58**

ASK THE PERFECTEXPERT

WordPerfect Office's Ask the *PerfectExpert* helps you do everyday tasks in a number of ways.

PerfectExpert provides help from the Ask the PerfectExpert tab in the Help Topics dialog box. In this tab, you can ask questions in plain English, and the PerfectExpert finds the help topics most closely related to your request. For example, Figure 1.2 shows the question "How do I create page numbers?" PerfectExpert shows the help topics most likely to relate to the question. You see this dialog box when you choose Help, PerfectExpert.

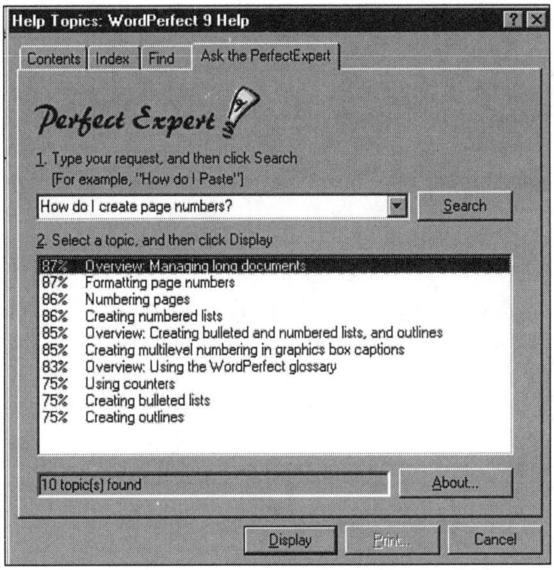

Figure 1.2
The Help Topics dialog box contains an Ask the PerfectExpert tab that permits you to ask your questions in everyday English.

→ To learn more about WordPerfect Office Suite's Help features, **see** "Using Help," **p. 20**

PerfectExpert guides you through tasks. When you display the PerfectExpert pane in suite applications, you see buttons for common tasks that apply to the type of document you are working on. For example, Figure 1.3 shows the PerfectExpert pane in a normal WordPerfect document. Buttons take you through everything from prewriting tasks (such as creating an outline) to finishing tasks (such as saving, faxing, or printing your document).

Figure 1.3
The PerfectExpert pane in WordPerfect provides assistance for every phase of creating a document.

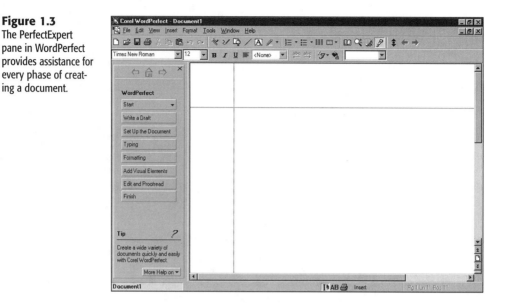

PERFECTEXPERT

PerfectExpert has predesigned projects. The PerfectExpert pane in Figure 1.3 shows the steps for creating a simple WordPerfect document. Creating a simple WordPerfect document is a project. Projects are included for WordPerfect, Quattro Pro, and Presentations. These range from creating simple documents and spreadsheets to complex projects that assist you in calculating seven-year balloon payments in Quattro Pro, or making a calendar in WordPerfect. You can see a partial list of projects in Figure 1.4.

Figure 1.4
PerfectExpert projects assist you in accomplishing even sophisticated tasks such as creating an annual report or an asset inventory.

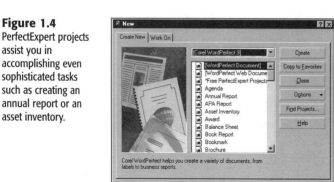

→ To learn more about how to use PerfectExpert Projects, **see** "Learning About PefectExpert Projects," **p. 138**

→ To find out more on how to manage PerfectExpert Projects, **see** "Managing PerfectExpert Projects," **p. 152**

UNDERSTANDING THE INTEGRATED WORKING ENVIRONMENT

Perhaps WordPerfect Office's most powerful feature is the integrated working environment it provides. With WordPerfect Office 2000, you can concentrate more on the tasks you need to do and less on the application(s) in which you need to do them.

Of course, part of an integrated working environment is the common look and feel of the applications. However, with WordPerfect Office 2000, this is only the beginning. WordPerfect Office 2000 offers features that include

- PerfectExpert Projects (discussed in the previous section)
- Common tools for file management and writing
- The Desktop Application Director (DAD)

COMMON FILE MANAGEMENT TOOLS

File management is the art of creating an organized electronic filing system that enables you to store files securely and find files quickly. WordPerfect Office 2000 offers you tools to assist you in your electronic filing tasks:

- Common file-management dialog boxes—WordPerfect Office applications have common file management dialog boxes (see Figure 1.5). These dialog boxes all have file-management capabilities built in. From these dialog boxes, you can copy, move, rename, print, and change file attributes, plus create, remove, and rename folders.

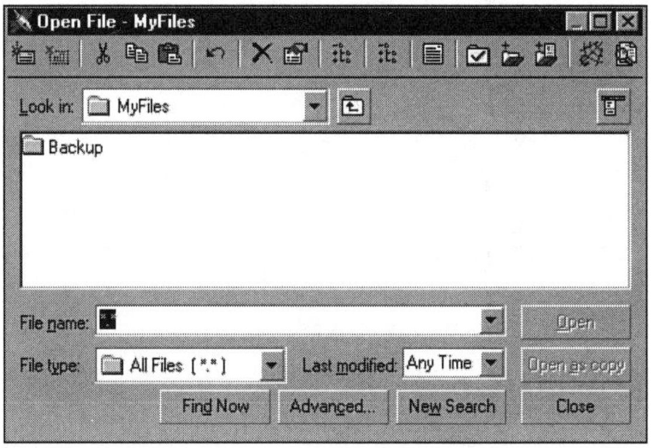

Figure 1.5
WordPerfect Office applications use common file-management dialog boxes for file management.

- QuickFinder—WordPerfect Office 2000 also includes the powerful QuickFinder indexing program. It enables you to build indexes of your data files. Using these indexes, you can search for files with specific words in them (for example, "Wilson Accounting Group"). Almost immediately, all files with these words are listed. You can even search for files containing synonyms of target words (accounting, budgeting), word forms (account, accounted, accounting), and common misspellings (acount).

You can access QuickFinder from any suite file-management dialog box. It is also available to you from any Corel or non-Corel application by clicking the Start button on the taskbar, and then choosing Programs, Corel WordPerfect Office 2000, Utilities, Corel QuickFinder 9 Searcher.

→ For more information on the QuickFinder indexing program, **see** "Using QuickFinder," **p. 52**

COMMON WRITING TOOLS

WordPerfect Office 2000 also provides you with writing tools that make the art of writing easier, and make your document more professional-looking. These tools are not only available in WordPerfect, but also in Presentations. They include

- Speller—The speller (also available in Quattro Pro) corrects common spelling errors and catches irregular capitalization, words containing numbers, and repeated words. The speller also remembers words you have told it to ignore in a document so that future spelling checks of that document will continue to ignore the words.

→ For more information on Corel's speller, **see** "Checking Spelling," **p. 158**

- Thesaurus—The Thesaurus provides you with synonyms and antonyms of selected words. It groups synonyms according to the word's meaning and part of speech (noun, adjective, verb).

→ For more information on how to use the Thesaurus, **see** "Using the Thesaurus," **p. 163**

- Grammatik—Grammatik is WordPerfect Office's grammar checker. Not only does it flag more than a dozen types of errors; it will actually rewrite sentences for you! You can select from among predefined checking styles, depending on the style of writing you use, or you can create your own.

→ For more information on how to review your grammar, **see** "Checking Grammar," **p. 164**

- QuickCorrect—QuickCorrect can correct your spelling as you type and automatically expand common abbreviations as you type, such as expanding LKSB to your firm's name of Luskin, Brankowitsch, Serrandello, and Buskin. Not only can QuickCorrect correct spelling and abbreviations; it can also automatically capitalize the first word of sentences, correct irregular capitalization, and place the correct number of spaces between sentences. QuickCorrect is also available in Quattro Pro.

→ To learn how to use QuickCorrect, **see** "Using QuickCorrect," **p. 161**

Because these writing tools are used most when you are using a word processing program, they are discussed in the Using WordPerfect section. However, they work similarly throughout the WordPerfect Office.

DAD

The Desktop Application Director, DAD, provides convenient access to the WordPerfect Office 2000 applications. DAD installs application icons called the Tool Tray, directly on the Windows 98 taskbar (see Figure 1.6).

Figure 1.6
DAD allows you to access WordPerfect Office applications from the Tool Tray.

WordPerfect Office
icons Tool Tray

You can read more about DAD Bars in Chapter 2, "Getting Started with Corel WordPerfect Office 2000."

EXTENDING YOUR DESKTOP

Although WordPerfect Office 2000 is a powerful desktop tool, its power is increased when you extend your desktop to your network, corporate intranet, or the Internet. The suite's capability to extend your desktop can be seen in many areas, including

- Performing common network tasks within applications
- Internet integration
- Data sharing
- Integrated code

PERFORM COMMON NETWORK TASKS

Whether you are running Novell, Banyan, Windows 95, Windows 98, Windows 2000, Windows NT, or another common network operating system, WordPerfect Office 2000 enables you to perform common network tasks, such as attaching to file servers, from any file-management dialog box.

DOCUMENT PUBLISHING

As time goes on, companies are publishing more and more documents electronically. For instance, master copies of personnel manuals or technical manuals can be maintained electronically on a corporate intranet. They can then be updated as needed by responsible parties, and the updated information is available instantly to all users.

WordPerfect Office 2000 includes Envoy—a powerful document-publishing application that allows you to distribute documents across LANs, intranets, the Internet, or on disk. Files can contain bookmarks and hypertext links to assist users in jumping to areas of interest. Documents are *bonded* so that users cannot change them but can highlight or add notes to areas of interest. Envoy even includes a runtime viewer, so documents can be read and annotated by others who don't have Envoy on their computer.

The suite also includes Corel's Barista technology. Barista enables you to create documents that can be published on the World Wide Web by making Java applets out of them. This enables the documents to include much more sophisticated formatting than is usually supported in HTML—the *lingua franca* of the Web.

INTERNET INTEGRATION

WordPerfect, Quattro Pro, and Presentations are all able to convert files directly to *HTML format* for publishing on the World Wide Web. You can add links to Internet files in your documents so that a reader can click them and go immediately to a related file on the Internet. The suite even extends the Help system to access help files that are maintained by Corel on the Internet.

DATA SHARING

You can also extend your desktop by sharing data between applications with three WordPerfect Office applications. Data sharing features include

- *Shared file formats*—Whether you need to bring a WordPerfect outline into a Presentations slide, or clip a memo graphic from Presentations and insert it into a Quattro Pro notebook, you will find it easy to do.
- OLE 2.0—The latest version of Microsoft's Object Linking and Embedding (OLE) is available in WordPerfect, Quattro Pro, and Presentations. OLE 2.0 enables you to drag and drop objects, such as drawings or charts, from one application window to another. It also enables you to edit objects, such as Presentations drawings, from within WordPerfect by merely double-clicking the object.

→ For more information on ways to link and embed in WordPerfect Office Suites, **see** "Learning Techniques for Linking and Embedding," **p. 324**

CODE INTEGRATION

The WordPerfect Office 2000 suite uses the concept of shared code to maximize performance and minimize use of system resources. Common tools such as the Speller, Thesaurus, Grammatik, QuickCorrect, and QuickFinder are shared among applications, thus saving disk space. Moreover, no matter which application calls them, they are loaded only once, saving system resources.

CHAPTER **2**

GETTING STARTED WITH COREL WORDPERFECT OFFICE 2000

In this chapter

INTRODUCING DAD

DAD is the Desktop Application Director that enables you to launch Corel WordPerfect Office 2000 programs easily from the taskbar. In learning to use WordPerfect Office, it is appropriate that you start by learning how to use DAD to launch the Office applications. Using DAD involves three aspects:

- Ensuring that DAD appears on your taskbar
- Launching applications with DAD
- Adding or removing applications from DAD

DISPLAYING DAD

When DAD is installed, you see icons for various WordPerfect Office tools in the Tool Tray area of your taskbar, as shown in Figure 2.1.

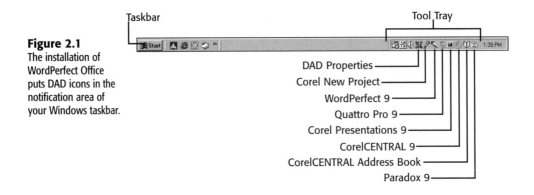

Figure 2.1
The installation of WordPerfect Office puts DAD icons in the notification area of your Windows taskbar.

Taskbar

Tool Tray

DAD Properties
Corel New Project
WordPerfect 9
Quattro Pro 9
Corel Presentations 9
CorelCENTRAL 9
CorelCENTRAL Address Book
Paradox 9

If you do not see any of these icons, DAD is probably not installed or isn't in the startup folder.

STARTING DAD

If the DAD icons don't appear on the taskbar and you want to start DAD, click the Start button on the taskbar, and then click Programs, WordPerfect Office 2000, Utilities, and Desktop Application Director 9. The WordPerfect Office DAD icons appear on the taskbar.

If you want to ensure that DAD starts automatically whenever you start Windows, do the following:

1. Start DAD as described in the previous paragraph.
2. Right-click any DAD icon.
3. Choose Display DAD on Startup.

The next time you start Windows, DAD is loaded automatically.

⚠ *If the DAD icons do not appear on the Windows 98 taskbar, see "DAD Icons" in the Troubleshooting section at the end of this chapter.*

EXITING DAD

Under normal circumstances, you should never need to close DAD. You will need to close DAD, however, if you want to add or remove WordPerfect Office components using the Office Setup program.

PART

I

CH

2

To close DAD, do the following:

1. Right-click one of the WordPerfect Office icons on the Windows taskbar.
2. Choose Exit DAD from the pop-up menu shown in Figure 2.2. The Office icons disappear from the taskbar, and you have exited DAD.

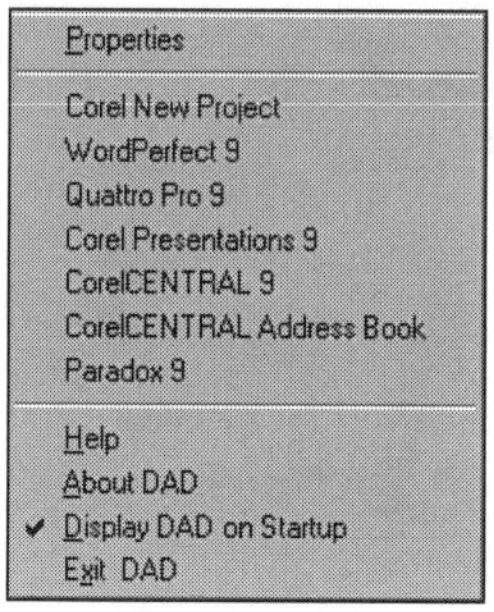

Figure 2.2
Exit DAD by right-clicking a WordPerfect Office application on the Windows taskbar.

Properties
Corel New Project
WordPerfect 9
Quattro Pro 9
Corel Presentations 9
CorelCENTRAL 9
CorelCENTRAL Address Book
Paradox 9
Help
About DAD
✓ Display DAD on Startup
Exit DAD

LAUNCHING APPLICATIONS WITH DAD

To launch a WordPerfect Office application from DAD, click the appropriate icon for the desired application on the Windows taskbar.

Tip #1 from
Trudi Reisner

Occasionally, you may not know what application a button will launch. If you rest your mouse pointer on an icon for more than a second or so, you will see a pop-up QuickTip that tells you the name of the application.

You can also use DAD to switch between Office applications that are already open. For instance, if you click the WordPerfect icon on the DAD Bar, and then click the Presentations icon, both WordPerfect and Presentations will be open. If you click the WordPerfect icon again, you will switch back to WordPerfect.

ADDING AND REMOVING APPLICATIONS FROM DAD

You can easily add or remove WordPerfect Office icons from the taskbar by following these steps:

1. Right-click any WordPerfect Office icon you see on the taskbar, and then choose Properties. The DAD Properties dialog box appears as shown in Figure 2.3.

Figure 2.3
Add or remove
WordPerfect Office
applications from the
taskbar with the DAD
Properties dialog box.

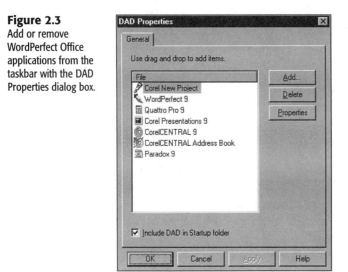

2. To add an application, choose Add and the Open dialog box appears. Double-click the application to be added.

3. To remove an application, highlight it and then choose Delete. The application is removed from the application list.

4. Click OK. You return to the Windows desktop and see the changed set of icons on the taskbar.

USING HELP

The WordPerfect Office suite offers many different ways to provide help to you, including

- Help Topics
- Ask the PerfectExpert
- PerfectExpert
- Corel Web Site
- Microsoft Help
- Context-sensitive help
- Reference manuals

USING HELP TOPICS

WordPerfect Office uses a standard Windows help system; in other words, WordPerfect Office Help works the same way as it does in any other Windows application.

To access the Help system, choose Help Topics from the Help menu; or press F1. What you see differs somewhat depending on the application you are in, but is similar to the WordPerfect Help dialog box shown in Figure 2.4. Five different types of help are offered: Contents, Index, Find, Ask the PerfectExpert, and Corel Knowledge Base.

Figure 2.4
The Help Topics: WordPerfect 9 Help dialog box provides tabs offering five different types of help.

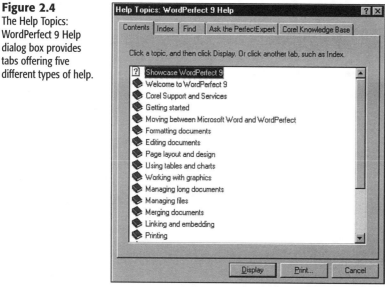

PART

I

CH

2

> **Note**
>
> Some slight differences exist between the Help features in the main Office applications and the bonus applications. If you understand the Help options in this section, however, you will easily be able to obtain help in the other applications.

CONTENTS

The Contents tab of the Help dialog box acts like a table of contents for your help system, displaying major categories of help topics. For instance, as shown in Figure 2.5, you see help for Merging Documents, which provides specialized help with creating and performing merges. You also see help for Merge and help for Macros, which provide specialized help with creating merges, recording macros, and programming them in WordPerfect.

To use the Contents help, do the following:

1. Choose Help, Help Topics, and be sure that you are in the Contents tab.

2. Double-click the major topic (such as Merging Documents), and then double-click the desired subtopic (such as Working with Form Documents).

3. You may see further subtopics (denoted by a book icon), or help documents (pieces of paper with a question mark on them). Double-click the subtopic or document you want to see (such as Creating Form Documents).

Figure 2.5
Help for Merging
Documents, which is
available in the Help
Topics: WordPerfect 9
Help dialog box,
provides help with
mass-producing
merged form letters.

INDEX

If the Contents tab is like a table of contents for your help system that lists major topics, the
Index tab works like the index you might find in the back of a book. It lists keywords that
you find throughout the help system and enables you to quickly go to the help you need,
even if it isn't a major help topic. The Index for WordPerfect is shown in Figure 2.6.

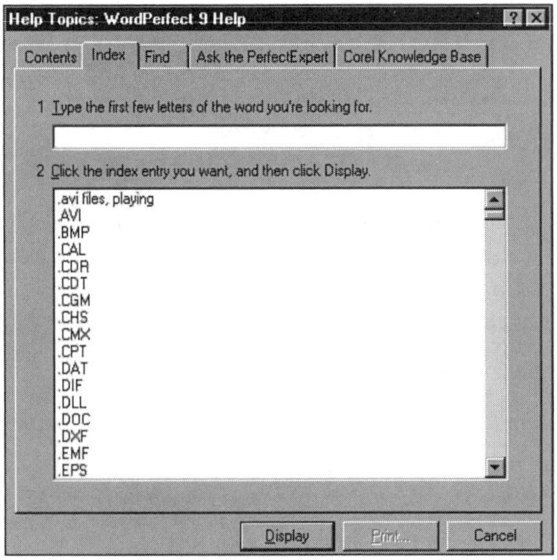

Figure 2.6
The Help Index
alphabetically lists all
the keywords in the
help system of each
application, such as
the one shown here
for WordPerfect.

To use the index feature, choose <u>H</u>elp, Help Topics, and be sure that you are in the Index tab. Type the word you're looking for in the <u>T</u>ype the First Few Letters of the Word You're Looking For box. You see topics related to the desired term in the Index Entry box. Select the appropriate term, and then click <u>D</u>isplay.

Tip #2 from	Sometimes you might want to print the information you find in a Help dialog box. A fast
Trudi Reisner	way to print a help topic is to right-click anywhere on the text in the dialog box. From the QuickMenu, choose <u>P</u>rint Topic, and click OK.

FIND

The Find tab uses another Windows help feature—an indexed list of every word in the help system. The first time you use the Find feature, a wizard asks you a few questions, and then all the words in the help file are indexed. After this is done, a word list is created, and you can search for any word in the help file—not just the ones the help file authors included in the index. The WordPerfect Help Find tab is shown in Figure 2.7.

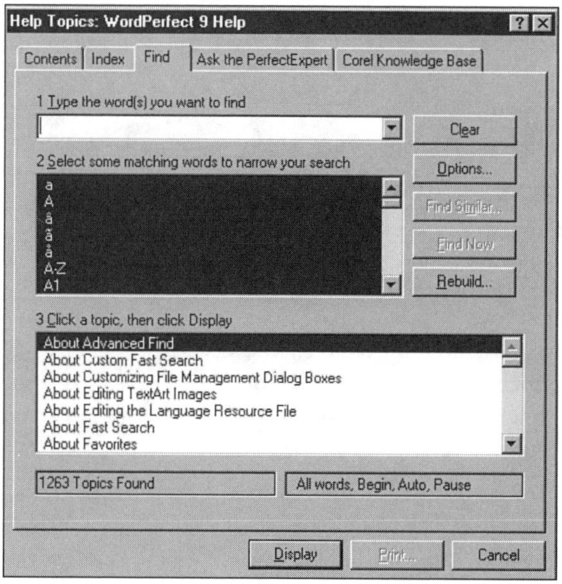

Figure 2.7
Use the Find tab in your application's Help Topics dialog box when the topic you want is not in the Contents or Index.

To use Find, choose <u>H</u>elp, <u>H</u>elp Topics, and be sure that you are in the Find tab. Type the word you want to find in the <u>T</u>ype the Word(s) You Want to Find box, and then select the term that best fits what you're looking for. You see a list of related topics in the Topic box. Select the most appropriate topic, and then click <u>D</u>isplay.

ASK THE PERFECTEXPERT

The Ask the PerfectExpert feature allows you to formulate queries in plain English. The PerfectExpert interprets your question and displays a number of help topics that may assist you.

To use the PerfectExpert, choose Help, Help Topics, and then select the Ask the PerfectExpert tab; or select Help, Ask the PerfectExpert. You see the Ask the PerfectExpert tab (see Figure 2.8).

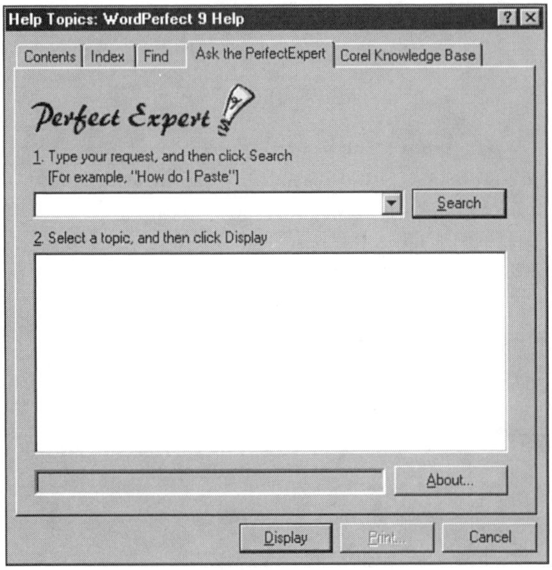

Figure 2.8
Ask the PerfectExpert allows you to frame queries in plain English in the Ask the PerfectExpert dialog box.

Type your question in the 1. Type Your Request, and Then Click Search box just as you would ask a help desk person. For example, type How do I create page numbers? When you click the Search button, you see a number of topics that may assist you, as displayed at the bottom of the dialog box in Figure 2.9. Select the one that addresses your question most directly, and then choose Display.

COREL KNOWLEDGE BASE

The new Corel Knowledge Base feature gives you a way to search for help on common problems that occur in WordPerfect Office. This features lets you search for solutions to common problems on the Internet. You must be connected to the Internet before you begin using Corel Knowledge Base. After you're connected, click the Corel Knowledge Base tab in the Help Topics dialog box (see Figure 2.10). Enter a keyword or two keywords with "AND" or "OR" to search for common issues. For example, type "merging AND error" to find solutions to WordPerfect merging errors. Then, click the Search button. You are taken to the Web site where there is a list of common issues based on the keyword(s) you entered.

Figure 2.9
After you ask the
PerfectExpert your
question, you see a
number of topics that
may assist you.

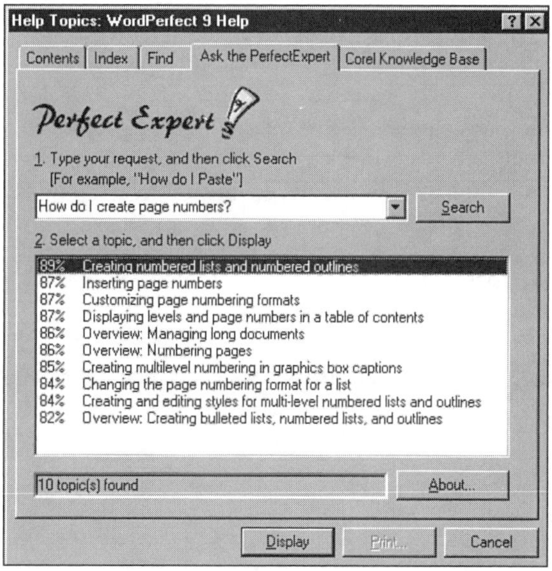

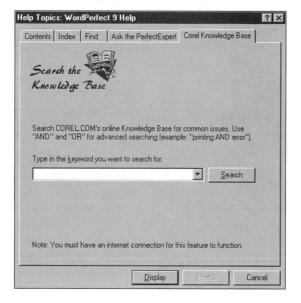

Figure 2.10
Corel Knowledge
Base lets you search
the Internet for
solutions to common
problems that occur
when you use
WordPerfect Office.

USING THE HELP MENU

There are several other useful WordPerfect Office Help features on the Help menu that
include PerfectExpert, Corel Web Site, Corel on the Web, and Microsoft Word Help.

PERFECTEXPERT

The WordPerfect Office Suite has another expert feature called the PerfectExpert. It provides templates with patterns for shaping a document and guides you through the process of creating it. A PerfectExpert template is also referred to as a project. PerfectExpert gives you extra step-by-step help in creating almost any kind of document: agendas, brochures, calendars, auto expense reports, or balloon loan payments. PerfectExpert projects are included in WordPerfect, Quattro Pro, and Presentations.

Choose Help, PerfectExpert, and the PerfectExpert pane appears for creating a simple WordPerfect document, as shown in Figure 2.11.

Figure 2.11
The PerfectExpert pane in WordPerfect provides assistance for every phase of creating a document.

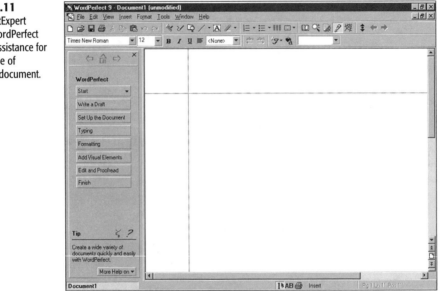

Click the Start button in the PerfectExpert pane and choose New Project/Existing File. In the New dialog box, be sure the Create New tab is selected, and then choose the PerfectExpert project you want. For example, you can create a PerfectExpert document by using the project for creating an annual report in WordPerfect. You can see a partial list of the WordPerfect PerfectExpert projects in Figure 2.12.

Figure 2.12
PerfectExpert projects assist you in accomplishing even sophisticated tasks such as creating an annual report or balance sheet in WordPerfect.

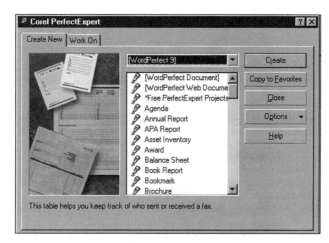

→ For more information on using Help, **see** "Using Help," **p. 20**

→ For detailed information on using PerfectExpert projects, **see** "Learning About PerfectExpert Projects," **p. 138**

→ For additional information on working with PerfectExpert projects, **see** "Managing PerfectExpert Projects," **p. 152**

COREL WEB SITE

You can immediately access the Corel documentation site on the Internet by choosing Help, Corel Web Site.

The Corel Internet site contains links to the Reference Center, from which you can download manuals and system administration information. You can also follow links to Corel Technical Information Documents, as well as tips and tricks for using the WordPerfect Office effectively. To link to the Corel Internet site, you must have an Internet connection via your network or a dial-up connection, and a Web browser, such as Netscape Navigator (included with Office).

Your ISP or other Internet connection takes you to the users' forums that discuss the use of WordPerfect Office 2000. To link to the Internet, you must have an ISP account or other gateway to the Internet.

Tip #3 from
Trudi Reisner

If you are attached to a network that has an ISDN or T1 connection to the Internet, you will find Help Online especially valuable, because you can access it almost as quickly and easily as the Help files that are on your local hard disk or network.

To access Help Online, do the following:

1. Choose Help, Corel Web Site. If you're not already online, you see the Dial-Up Connection dialog box.

2. Choose Connect. Your Web browser or online software starts, and you are connected to the appropriate online service, such as the Netscape connection to Corel's Web site, as shown in Figure 2.13.

Note

Even when you are already connected via modem to your ISP and your computer has pre-loaded ISP software, clicking the icon for Corel's Web site displays the ISP setup screen. In this case, you need to enter the URL for the Corel site, which is www.corel.com.

Figure 2.13
The Netscape connection to Corel's Web site gives you access to online Help.

COREL ON THE WEB

To get to specific areas on the Corel Web site and access helpful information, you can choose Help, Corel on the Web, and select Technical Support, Tips and Tricks, Learning and Certification, and Approved Service Bureaus.

MICROSOFT HELP

If you are upgrading from a competitive product—Microsoft Word, Microsoft Excel, or Microsoft PowerPoint—you may find Microsoft Help useful. When you are in WordPerfect, access Microsoft Help by choosing Help, Microsoft Word Help. In Quattro Pro, choose Help, Microsoft Excel Help. In Presentations, choose Help, Microsoft PowerPoint Help. You see a Help dialog box that contains information on conversion features, conversion losses, and upgrading from a Microsoft product.

In case you haven't bought your software yet, you need to know that Corel considers a switch to WordPerfect Office to be an upgrade, even when you had the *latest and greatest* suite from one of Corel's competitors.

USING CONTEXT-SENSITIVE HELP

Context-sensitive help is available throughout the WordPerfect Office applications. In many dialog boxes, you will see a Help button such as the one shown in the WordPerfect Styles dialog box in Figure 2.14.

Figure 2.14
Help buttons appear in many dialog boxes.

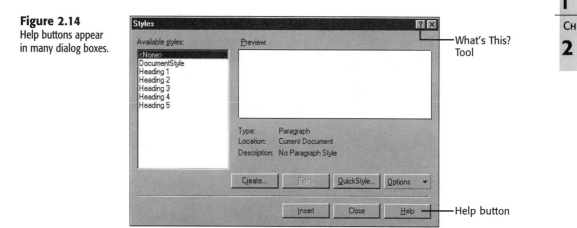

PART

I

CH

2

What's This? Tool

Help button

Choosing Help displays assistance for the function you are working on. In addition, even when there is no Help button, you can often receive context-sensitive help by pressing the Help key (F1).

Many dialog boxes also have a What's This? tool. If you click this tool, your mouse pointer changes into a pointer with a question mark. You can point at different objects in the active window or dialog box and click them to receive help on that specific object.

> **Note**
>
> One other way that you can get context-sensitive help when you are not in a dialog box is to right-click an area of the active window to bring up the QuickMenu. The QuickMenu often has a What's This? choice.

REFERENCE MANUALS

If you loaded WordPerfect Office 2000 from the CD, you have reference manuals online in the Reference Center. You may have even installed them to your local hard drive or network workspace.

To access the Reference Center, put the Corel CD in your drive (if you didn't install the Reference Center to your hard drive), and choose Start, Corel WordPerfect Office 2000, Setup & Notes, Reference Center. You see the Corel Reference Center dialog box shown in Figure 2.15.

Figure 2.15
The Corel Reference Center provides reference materials for Office applications.

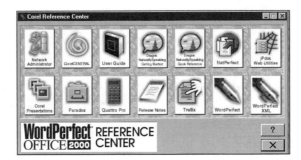

Double-click any icon. The reference book is brought up in Adobe Acrobat. You can click items in the table of contents to go to the area of interest, read the book cover to cover (if you do that sort of thing), or even search for specific keywords throughout the electronic manual.

USING THE INTELLIMOUSE

The Office suite is compatible with the Microsoft IntelliMouse. The IntelliMouse looks like a regular two-button mouse, but it has a small wheel located between the two buttons. You can turn the wheel or click it.

If you are at the main editing window of an Office application and see a vertical scrollbar, when you turn the wheel, the scroll-down function is performed. In other words, turning the wheel is like clicking and holding the mouse button on the up or down arrow of the vertical scrollbar.

If you click the wheel, the vertical scrollbar changes its appearance, such as the one shown in Figure 2.16.

Figure 2.16
When you click the
IntelliMouse wheel,
you can move the
mouse up and
down to scroll
your document.

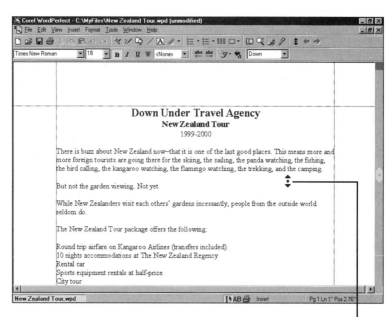

AutoScroll tool

PART

I

CH

2

As you move your mouse up and down, your document scrolls smoothly. Stop moving the mouse to stop scrolling the document, and click the wheel again to return to the normal mode of operation.

To scroll horizontally, hold down the Shift key and turn the wheel up to move left or down to move right.

You can also zoom in and out with your IntelliMouse to change magnification levels in a document. Hold down the Ctrl key and rotate the wheel backward to zoom in or forward to zoom out. The magnification levels vary depending on the Office application you're working in.

Tip #4 from
Trudi Reisner

You must install the IntelliMouse software that comes with the mouse for the wheel to work. This software also provides many other options for efficiently using the mouse. Access these options by choosing Start, Settings, Control Panel, and then double-clicking the Mouse icon.

WordPerfect Office 2000 has a new feature called AutoScroll that lets you quickly scroll in any direction in a document. AutoScroll automatically scrolls through the document for you. As you move the mouse pointer farther away from the AutoScroll tool, the scrolling speed is faster. If you move the arrow closer to the AutoScroll tool, the scrolling speed slows down. You can use AutoScroll with a Microsoft IntelliMouse or a conventional mouse.

USING AUTOSCROLL WITH MICROSOFT INTELLIMOUSE

To set up WordPerfect Office 2000 to work with your Microsoft IntelliMouse, click the Start button on the Windows taskbar. Choose Settings, Control Panel, and double-click the Mouse icon. In the Mouse Properties dialog box, click the Wheel tab. In the Wheel Button section, make sure the Turn On the Wheel Button check box is checked. From the Button Assignment list box, choose Default.

Now you need to determine the AutoScroll central point, which is the direction and speed of the AutoScroll. Click the IntelliMouse wheel anywhere in the document to position the Auto Scroll central point.

To scroll up or down, turn the wheel on the mouse in the direction you want to scroll. To scroll left or right, hold Shift while turning the wheel up or down. The document scrolls in the direction you move away from the central point. Notice the speed increases as you move the mouse away from the AutoScroll central point. To stop AutoScroll, press any key or click any mouse button.

USING AUTOSCROLL WITH A CONVENTIONAL MOUSE

You can use AutoScroll with a conventional mouse to scroll around a document, instead of using the arrow keys or the scrollbars. To use this feature in WordPerfect, click the AutoScroll tool on the WordPerfect toolbar. The mouse pointer changes into a large double arrow. To scroll through your document, do one of the following:

- To scroll up, move the mouse to the top of the page. Notice the Up Arrow appears with the AutoScroll tool.
- To scroll down, move the mouse to the bottom of the page. Notice the Down Arrow appears with the AutoScroll tool.
- To scroll left, move the mouse to the left side of the page. Notice the Left Arrow appears with the AutoScroll tool.
- To scroll right, move the mouse to the right side of the page. Notice the Right Arrow appears with the AutoScroll tool.

To stop AutoScroll, press any key or click any mouse button.

PRACTICAL PROJECT

If you want to get some great tips and hints on using WordPerfect Office 2000, you can find them on the Web. Just go directly from WordPerfect Office to the Web by choosing Help, Corel on the Web, Tips and Tricks.

TROUBLESHOOTING

DAD ICONS

WordPerfect Office 2000 is on your machine, but the DAD icons do not appear on the Windows taskbar.

Someone has removed the necessary files from the Startup folder in the Windows directory. Start DAD from the Windows menu to see the icons on the Tool Tray.

CHAPTER 3

MANAGING FILES

In this chapter

SAVING, OPENING, AND CLOSING FILES

When you create a Corel WordPerfect document, Corel Quattro Pro spreadsheet, or Corel Presentations slideshow, you are working with a file. Files can exist in your computer's memory and on disks. You can think of these electronic files like their paper counterparts.

Your computer's memory is like the surface of a desk that, for security reasons, is cleared off at the end of the day and everything on it is put into the shredder. You can work on files while they are on your desktop. You can create files, add information to them, or send them to other people. But at the end of the day, unless you put them away, they will be destroyed. In many companies, paper files can't stay on the desktop after hours. Similarly, electronic files are destroyed when you turn off your computer, or exit the program that creates them.

Note

For those of you who aren't computer techies, memory is the working area of your computer. Memory is also the generic term for Random Access Memory, or RAM. When you are using programs, they are loaded into memory. When you open a file, it is loaded into memory. The programs and data that are in memory are lost when you turn off your computer.

Disks, whether they are floppy disks, local (in your own computer) hard disks, or network drives, are storage areas. You do not *run* programs from the disk. You load a program from the disk into memory when you open it. Then, when it is in memory, you can use it. Similarly, you load data from your disk into memory to access it. Data on disks is maintained even when you turn off your computer.

Your disk is like your file cabinet. You can keep files in it indefinitely—that is, until it gets full. Then, you can add another file cabinet, until your office gets full of cabinets! The better idea is to purge files in your file cabinet periodically, so that you keep only the ones you need. However, until you take a file from the file drawer and put it on your desk, you can't work on it. Similarly, electronic files can stay on a disk indefinitely, but until you load them into memory, you can't work on them.

In fact, the analogy can be carried further; you can think of each disk drive as a file cabinet. Each disk can contain folders—as file cabinets contain file drawers. Each drawer can contain hanging folders or loose sheets of paper; likewise, electronic folders can contain subfolders or files. Each hanging folder can contain manila folders or sheets of paper; likewise, electronic subfolders can contain other subfolders or files.

Note

In Windows, the term *directories* that was used in previous versions of Windows and DOS has been changed to *folders*. Users of previous versions can think of folders just as they used to think about directories.

Thus, whether you are working in WordPerfect, Quattro Pro, Presentations, or other WordPerfect Office 2000 applications, you need to save your work if you want to be able to access it after you turn off your computer. You also need to be able to retrieve it from the disk into memory when you want to edit it again.

> **Note**
>
> In most applications, files exist only in memory until they are saved. If you add 100 rows of information to a spreadsheet without saving your work and then the power goes off, you will lose that work. This is true in WordPerfect, Presentations, and Quattro Pro. Databases work somewhat differently. After the database is created, each record is saved on the disk as it is created or edited. Thus, the most information you would lose in a power failure would be changes to the current record. CorelCENTRAL and Paradox are databases. Each record is saved as it is created or edited.

SAVING FILES

Saving a file is like taking a copy of it from your desktop and putting it into a file drawer. To save a file means storing it on a disk—a floppy disk, your local hard drive, or a network drive. After you save a file, it exists in two places—in memory and on the disk—until the program you used to create it is exited or the machine is turned off. Then you have only the file that you saved.

In all WordPerfect Office 2000 applications, you can save the file you are working on by choosing File, Save. If the toolbar is displayed, you can also click the Save button.

> **Note**
>
> A path plus a filename (the drive, folder, and filename) can be up to 255 characters long and can have an optional extension of up to three characters. The name can contain any combination of letters and numbers except the following:
>
> / \ : * ? < > | "
>
> Don't use any other special characters, such as commas or backslashes. Also, don't use any of the following names, which are reserved by DOS for its own use: CLOCK$, COM1, COM2, COM3, COM4, CON, AUX, LPT1, LPT2, LPT3, LPT4, NUL, or PRN.

> **Caution**
>
> Be careful in using long filenames. Many network operating systems do not support filenames longer than eight characters. Consider using no more than eight characters in your filenames and no spaces, if you are using such a network.

The first time you save a file, you see a Save dialog box such as the Presentations one shown in Figure 3.1. Type the name of the file in the File Name box and click Save to save your work.

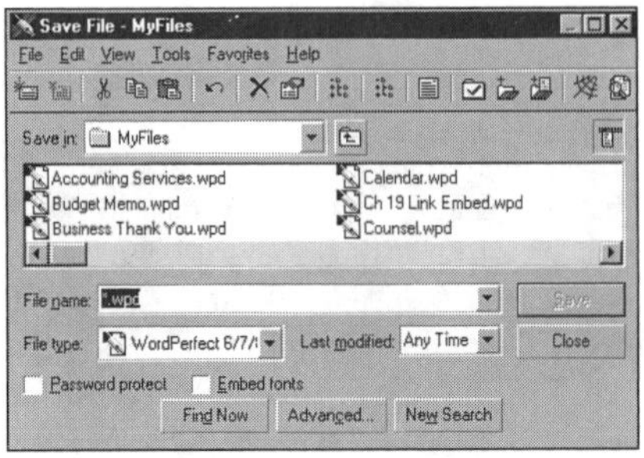

Figure 3.1
The first time you save a file, you see the Save File dialog box, enabling you to give the file a name.

Tip #5 from
Trudi Reisner

As you start saving more and more files, you'll need to create electronic folders to organize your files. If you don't choose a folder, your files are saved in the default folder at first. If you change the folder you are saving your files in, additional files will continue to be saved to that new folder until you exit the application. Then, the next time you open the application, files will be saved in the default folder again.

You can also save the file on a different drive or in a different folder as explained in the section "Using File Management Dialog Boxes" later in this chapter.

When you continue working in the same document and want to save your work again, choose File, Save, or click the Save button on the toolbar again. You do not see a dialog box. The operation happens immediately. When you resave your work in this way, the first version is replaced on the disk by the second; thus, the earlier file is gone.

To save both versions, you need to either save the second one with a different name, or in a different folder. You cannot have two files with the same name in the same folder. Choose File, Save As to rename the latter version. You will see the Save As dialog box, and you can rename the document or specify a different folder prior to saving it.

OPENING FILES

Opening a file is like taking a copy of it from your file drawer and putting it on your desk. It then exists in two places—in the file drawer and on your desk. When you make changes to it, the original is still safely in the file drawer. The original copy in the file drawer is changed only when you save the edited version again.

Thus, when you open a file, you are retrieving a copy of the file from the disk to your computer's memory. In all WordPerfect Office 2000 applications, you can open a file by choosing File, Open. If the toolbar is displayed, you may also click the Open button. In either case, you see an Open File dialog box similar to the one shown in Figure 3.2. Instructions for choosing files from this dialog box are found in the section "Using File Management Dialog Boxes" later in this chapter.

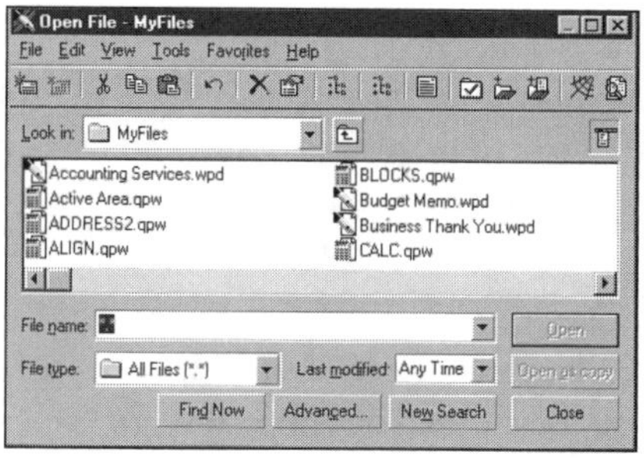

Figure 3.2
Choose files to open from the Open File dialog box, which also provides many file management capabilities.

![Open File - MyFiles dialog box showing a file listing including Accounting Services.wpd, Active Area.qpw, ADDRESS2.qpw, ALIGN.qpw, BLOCKS.qpw, Budget Memo.wpd, Business Thank You.wpd, and CALC.qpw]

> **Note**
>
> The title bar of file management dialog boxes includes the current folder name, Open File - MyFiles or Save File - Backup. What you see on the title bar depends on your default folder. Furthermore, Presentations uses the name Save for the Save dialog box, although WordPerfect and Quattro Pro uses Save File. To prevent confusion, this book refers to file management dialog boxes only by their function—for example, Open File or Save File.

PART

I

CH

3

CLOSING FILES

Closing a file is like taking it off your desktop and shredding it. If you have saved it prior to closing it, it is in your file cabinet (or stored electronically). Otherwise, it is gone for good.

Therefore, when you close a file, you are erasing it from your computer's memory. In WordPerfect Office 2000 applications, you close a file by choosing File, Close. If the file has been edited since it was last saved, you are prompted to save it prior to closing it. Unless you want to lose your work, it's a good idea to save it.

> **Note**
>
> When you close an application, you will also close any open files in that application. Therefore, when you close an application that has modified, open files, you will be prompted to save them before the application closes.

 If there isn't a button to close a file as there is to save or open a file on the toolbar, see "Using the Close Button" in the Troubleshooting section at the end of this chapter.

→ For more information on working with toolbars and menu bars, **see** "Creating and Editing Toolbars and Menu Bars," **p. 65**

CREATING A FILE MANAGEMENT SYSTEM

File management dialog boxes enable you to manipulate files and folders with ease. Before learning how to do this, however, it's a good idea to think through several issues:

- Which drive should you save your files on?
- What folders should you have?
- How should you name your files?

CHOOSING A DRIVE

You will generally have up to four choices for types of disk drives to save your files on: the floppy drive(s), local hard drive(s) (the hard drive(s) in your computer), network drives (if you're on a network), and the Internet or a corporate intranet (if you are so connected).

FLOPPY DRIVES

In the past, most people saved their work on floppy disks. Many people are still used to doing this. It seems reasonable; you use a different floppy disk for each subject, and it's easy to stay organized. If someone else needs the file, you hand him/her the disk. This process keeps the hard disk from filling up.

A piece of advice: Stop thinking this way.

If you exchange files often, you should be working on a network. Hard disks hold 10 to 20 times more than they used to; if your hard disk keeps filling up, you should either have a high-capacity hard disk, or better yet, archive and purge your files periodically as you do with your paper filing system. If you want to stay organized, use folders on your hard drives rather than individual floppy disks.

Several reasons to use hard drives rather than floppy disk drives are given in the sections that follow. Floppy disk drives are good in three circumstances:

- Taking files offsite to work on them
- Archiving old files when you don't have access to a tape backup or other mass storage devices for archiving purposes
- Creating backup copies of critical data that can be stored elsewhere and retrieved if necessary in a disaster-recovery situation

LOCAL HARD DRIVES

A local hard drive operates 10 to 20 times faster than a floppy disk drive, and has the advantage that all your files are available whenever you want them. As you become more familiar with working electronically, this latter advantage becomes more important. You will find yourself bringing up old files often, and cutting pieces out of them for your new work. Or, you may use them as the basis for template and style creation. You can also use your old files as a knowledge base, accessing work done by you or others in your workgroup to learn from what you've done before, or to track the history of a project.

The other reason you will want to save your work on a hard drive is that the QuickFinder indexing system discussed later will then index all your files. That way, you can immediately find all documents by specifying any text that is in them—no matter what folder you put them in on your hard drive.

Local hard drives are an excellent place to store documents when

- You are working on a standalone computer
- Your network administrator limits the amount of storage you have for documents
- The files will only be used by you, and you regularly back up your hard drive

NETWORK DRIVES

Saving files on network drives has all the advantages of saving them on local hard drives, but a couple of other considerations must be taken into account.

First, the network almost invariably is backed up regularly, often daily. (Ask your system administrator for details.) Because most people don't back up their local drive regularly, this may be reason enough to save files on the network.

Second, if you work in a workgroup, saving files on a network is the best way to start creating a *learning organization*—a team of people who can build on one another's work.

There are three disadvantages to saving files on the network. First, if the network goes down, you will not have access to your files. Second, if you don't archive and purge your files regularly, the network drive fills up rapidly. Third, some companies' network drive purge policies are time-based, meaning that if a certain file has not been actively used for a certain time period, that file is archived. If it is archived, it may still be accessible by request, but may require time or papers work for you to have the network administrator retrieve it; you will not have direct access to it.

Tip #6 from
Trudi Reisner
Saving files to a shared workspace on a network is one of the best ways to get workgroups to start sharing files electronically.

→ To learn more about sharing notebooks, **see** "Understanding Shared Notebooks," **p. 491**
→ For more information on how to review changes you make to a notebook, **see** "Reviewing Changes in a Shared Notebook," **p. 492**

INTERNET SERVERS

You can also save files on an Internet server, if you have a Web site and sufficient permissions. This gives people throughout the world access to the files.

The WordPerfect Office 2000 suite can assist you in creating Web pages (files that can be viewed with Web browsers such as Netscape Navigator); however, the suite does not have programs designed for uploading such files to the Internet.

→ For information on how to publish WordPerfect Office Suite documents, **see** "Publishing HTML Documents," **p. 605**

→ To learn how to publish Quattro Pro spreadsheets, **see** "Publishing Corel Quattro Pro Spreadsheet Data," **p. 614**

→ To find out how to load individual Presentations to your Web site, **see** "Uploading Your Presentation," **p. 637**

Ask your Internet service provider or network administrator for procedures to be used in uploading your files to the Internet. Be aware, however, that when you upload files to an Internet service provider, there may be fees attached for storage of those files.

UNDERSTANDING ELECTRONIC FILING SYSTEMS

After you have decided which drive(s) to save your files on, you need to create a filing system—a set of folders and subfolders—in which to save your files.

If you are saving files on a network drive, you have a workspace that contains only your data files. If you are working on a standalone computer, consider creating a main folder for all your data files. When you install the WordPerfect Suite, the folder MyFiles is created. This can serve admirably as a main folder. If all your other folders are created as subfolders of MyFiles, you can easily back up your data files because they are all in one place. You can also keep all your data files separate from program folders so that you can more easily search them.

Note

Your electronic filing system should mimic your paper filing system. Therefore, if you have different filing cabinets or file drawers that are organized by type of business, client, or employee, your main subfolders should be organized the same way.

Create subfolders under the main subfolders that mimic your hanging files, and if needed, create an additional layer of subfolders that mimic your manila files. You probably don't want to have more than four or five layers of folders, because navigating through them becomes time-consuming. Coordinate your folders with your file-naming conventions, as described in the next section.

SETTING FILE-NAMING CONVENTIONS

Just as you wouldn't want your office manager or employees to randomly put stickers on manila folders, you should also systematically think about how to name your files. Keep in mind that you can now make use of long filenames with spaces.

Consider the following when creating file-naming conventions:

- Agree on file-naming conventions within the office—Assign one person to be responsible for periodically checking filenames in public workspaces, renaming files as needed, and notifying the owner of the file that the name has been changed. Create a document that outlines the file-naming conventions and distribute it to present and new employees.

- Coordinate filenames with folders—If you have a folder for each client, with subfolders for letters, briefs, and legal memos, you do not need to have the word "letter" or the client name in the filename, because a letter will be saved in the appropriate client folder and letters subfolder.

- Remember alphabetization—Have the first word(s) of the filenames be keywords that you can alphabetize your files by. This may be type of file (letter), client name (Smith John), or subject.

A typical file management dialog box is shown in Figure 3.3. In this case, the filing system is set up in such a way that all letters (to anyone) are in a Letters folder. Thus, the file-naming convention calls for the client's last name, followed by the number of the letter, followed by a few words describing the subject of the letter.

Figure 3.3
A good file-naming system enables anyone in your office to quickly find a file you have saved.

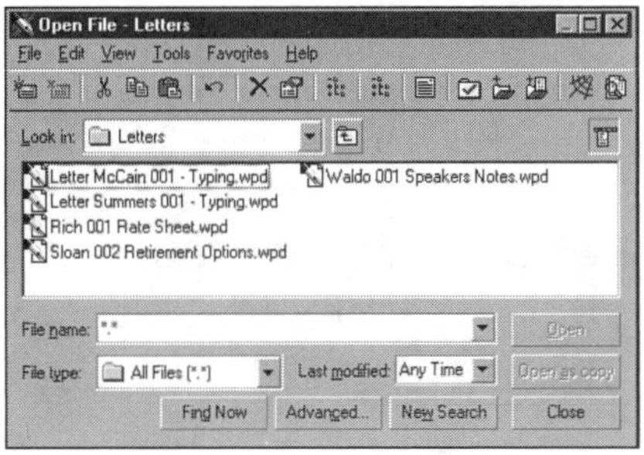

PART
I

CH
3

USING FILE MANAGEMENT DIALOG BOXES

WordPerfect Office 2000 offers extremely powerful file management features through file management dialog boxes. You see a file management dialog box whenever you use any feature that offers you options while saving or retrieving files (for example, File, Open; File, Save As; Insert, File; Insert, Object; and so on). In fact, any time you can select a file using the Go Back One Folder Level button, you are taken to a file management dialog box, such as the Save File dialog box shown in Figure 3.4.

Figure 3.4
All file management dialog boxes have options similar to the file management options shown in this Save File dialog box.

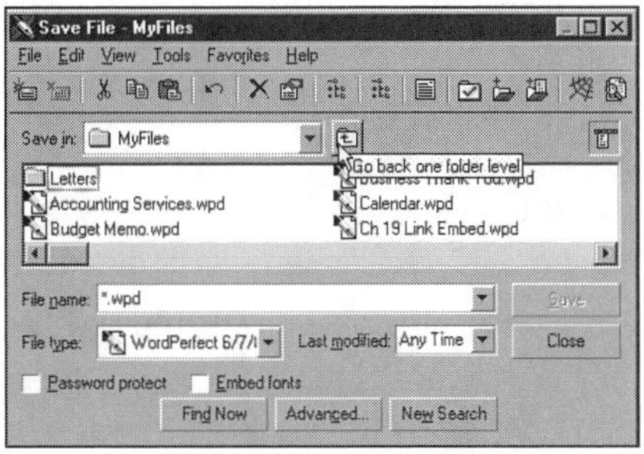

Note

Your dialog box may not resemble the one shown, because the way files may be displayed is determined by options that you can set, as explained in the next section.

File management dialog boxes enable you to quickly navigate throughout your filing system. More importantly, however, they enable you to manage your drives, folders, and files.

SETTING FILE MANAGEMENT DIALOG BOX OPTIONS

Depending on their function, file management dialog boxes have slightly different options. However, some options are common to all file management dialog boxes.

You can use the menu bar or the toolbar to change file management dialog box options. By default, the menu bar is not displayed. If you click the Toggle Menu On/Off button, you see the menu bar.

The toolbar is an excellent way to set dialog box display options. If the toolbar is not displayed, choose View, Toolbar. A check mark appears by the Toolbar entry (see Figure 3.5).

Figure 3.5
File management dia-log boxes have their own toolbars that you can display or hide.

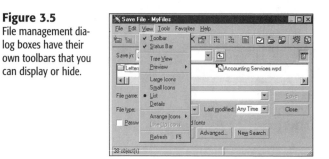

You can split the main window that shows your folders and files into two or three separate windows:

- If you click the Toggle Tree View On/Off icon, you see your folders in the left window and the subfolders and files contained in the selected folder in the window to its right. Using the Tree View is the easiest way to navigate through your filing system.

- If you click the Toggle Preview On/Off icon, you see a window on the right that shows you the contents of the selected file.

- You can also display the files in the selected folder in four ways: as large icons, small icons, a list of filenames, or a single list of filenames with details.

    Large and Small Icons show you what type of file each file is (Quattro Pro, WordPerfect, and so on). They are not terribly useful if you store files of only one type in a folder. Moreover, they don't permit as much of the filename to show.

    The filename List can be a useful view because you see several columns of files in one screen, and can often locate your file much more quickly. The Details view shows only one column of filenames, but it does display the file size and date it was last saved, which some users prefer to see.

Tip #7 from
Trudi Reisner

When you are viewing file details, click a column, such as Filename or Modified, to put the files in alphabetical order based on that column. Click again for descending alphabetical order.

NAVIGATING THE FILING SYSTEM

After you've used the suite for a while, you will want to put your files in different folders to organize them. You can switch between drives and folders, and select one or more files with file management dialog boxes.

SWITCHING BETWEEN DRIVES AND FOLDERS

You navigate through your filing system in two directions: up and down. Navigating down is easy; the subfolders of the currently selected folder display in the window. For example, if the MyFiles folder has a subfolder called Letters, the Letters subfolder displays if the MyFiles folder is selected.

To navigate down to a subfolder, double-click it. For example, to navigate from the MyFiles folder shown in Figure 3.6 to the Letters subfolder, you would double-click it.

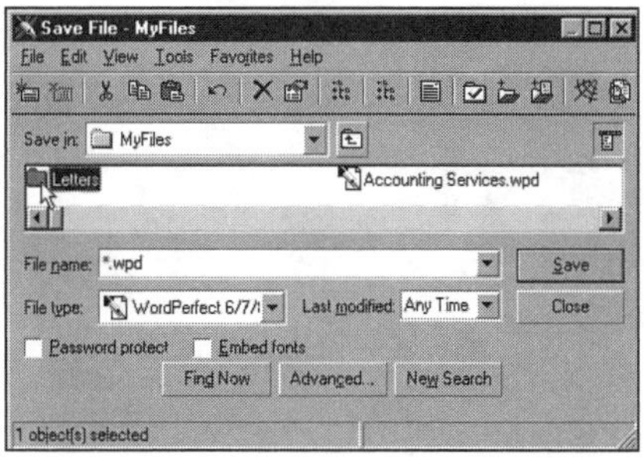

Figure 3.6
Navigate down to a subfolder such as Letters in the example shown by double-clicking it.

PART
I
CH
3

To go to a folder that is not a subfolder of the currently selected folder, navigate up, and then (possibly) down again, by navigating up to a common point.

For example, say the MyFiles folder has several subfolders, including Letters and Memos. You are in the Letters subfolder and want to go to the Memos subfolder. You must first navigate up to the common folder, MyFiles, and then back down to the Memos subfolder. It may sound complicated, but it's actually easy after you've done it a few times.

If you continue to navigate up, you will reach the drive itself. One level up from the drive is My Computer. From My Computer, you can see all the drives on the computer, as well as folders for the Control Panel and Printers.

One level up from My Computer is the Desktop, from which you can see your computer, the Network Neighborhood, Recycle Bin, and your Briefcase (if it is installed).

To see the folder, drive, or computer above the selected object, click the Go Back One Folder Level button. For example, to navigate from a local hard drive to a network drive, you continue to click the Go Back One Folder Level icon until you reach the Desktop. Double-click Network Neighborhood, and then double-click the appropriate workgroup and the network computer you are navigating to.

SELECTING FILES

After you have navigated to the appropriate folder, you can type in the name of the file to be saved, or double-click the file to be opened.

On occasion, however, you might want to select more than one file—either to open multiple files or to perform file management tasks.

To select multiple adjacent files, click the first file to be selected, and then hold down the Shift key and click the last file. To select nonadjacent files, click the first file to be selected, and then hold down the Ctrl key while you click any additional files. The selected files are highlighted, as shown in Figure 3.7.

Figure 3.7
You can select multiple files, whether they are adjacent to one another or not, as shown in this example.

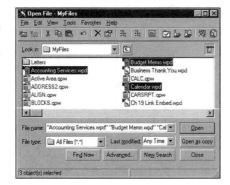

MANAGING DRIVES

You can map and disconnect network drives from WordPerfect Office 2000 file management dialog boxes. This can be useful if you work on a large network, and are not normally connected to all the available servers. When you need to open a file on a server you are not connected to, you can map to that server, and then disconnect from it when you are finished.

Tip #8 from
Trudi Reisner

Mapping to a network drive assigns a letter to the drive. This makes the drive accessible to opening and saving files, and makes it possible to log on to the drive.

To map to a network drive, first be sure you are connected to a network and then access any file management dialog box. Click the Map Network Drive button. You see the Map Network Drive dialog box shown in Figure 3.8. Select the letter for the Drive you want to map to, and then type the Path to the drive and click OK.

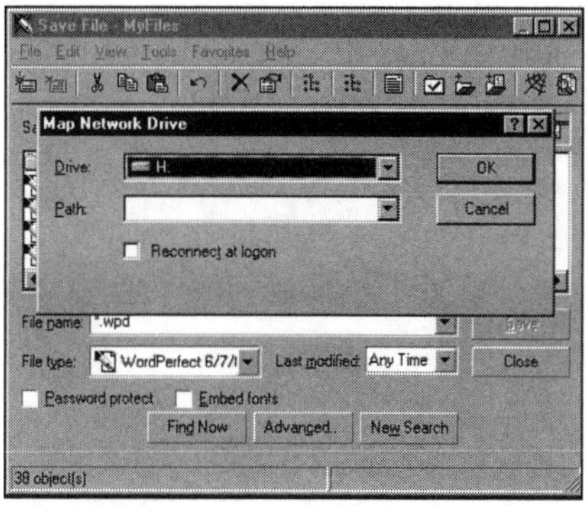

Figure 3.8
You can map to network drives from the Map Network Drive dialog box, which can be accessed through any file management dialog box.

When you are finished, you can disconnect from the drive by using the Disconnect Net Drive button.

Tip #9 from
Trudi Reisner

The Reconnect at Logon option causes Windows to automatically remap the specified drive when you log into the system the next time. This is handy if you use your network drive frequently. Keep in mind, however, that other people might have access to this information; check with your network administrator.

MANAGING FOLDERS

If you remember our original analogy, folders and subfolders are like the drawers, hanging folders, and manila folders in a file cabinet (disk drive). They are used to organize your work, and enable you to create a system for maintaining your files.

To manage the directories that make up your electronic filing system, you need to be able to create, remove (delete), and rename directories (folders). To create a new folder, do the following:

1. Access a file management dialog box.
2. Navigate to the folder that will be the parent of the new folder.
3. Click the Toggle Menu On/Off button, if menus are not displayed. Choose File, New, Folder. You see the new folder named New Folder under the original folder, with its name highlighted, as shown in Figure 3.9.

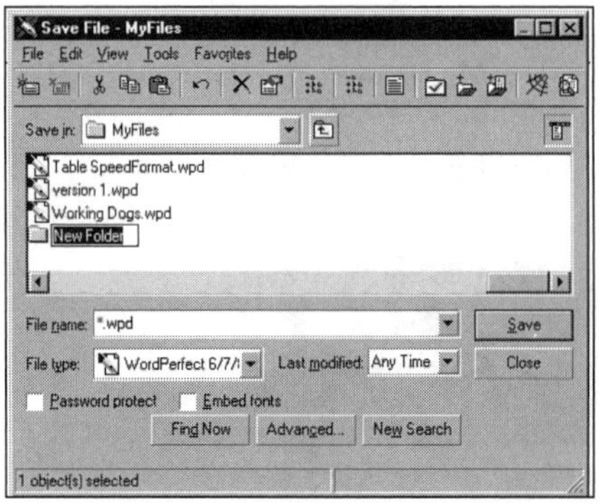

Figure 3.9
You can create new
folders in any file
management dialog
box.

4. Type the name for the new folder and press Enter.

Tip #10 from
Trudi Reisner

You can access these options to manage folders via a QuickMenu by right-clicking the folder.

To rename a folder, select it, and then choose File, Rename. The folder name is highlighted; type the new name and press Enter.

To remove a folder, select it, and then choose File, Delete. The folder and its contents are deleted, and its contents are moved to the Recycle Bin.

You can also use the Rename and Delete commands that appear on the QuickMenu when you right-click a file or folder name.

Caution

Removing a folder with files in it deletes the files from the disk and puts them in the Recycle Bin. Although they can be recovered, they will not automatically be put back into the right folder, even if you re-create it. Use this command with care.

You can also view and set the properties for a folder, including whether it is hidden, read-only, or shared (on a Microsoft network). To do so, select the folder, and choose File, Properties or right-click and choose Properties from the context menu. You see the Letters Properties dialog box shown in Figure 3.10.

MANAGING FILES

When you have the backbone of your filing system—the folders—created, you can finish creating your filing system by renaming and moving files into your new filing system. Periodically, you should archive and purge your filing system by moving files out of the folders and onto floppy disks or a tape backup unit.

With WordPerfect Office 2000 dialog boxes, you can do these tasks and more. You can copy, move, rename, and delete files, and you can set their properties.

Figure 3.10
You can view or set properties and file-sharing options of a file from file management dialog boxes.

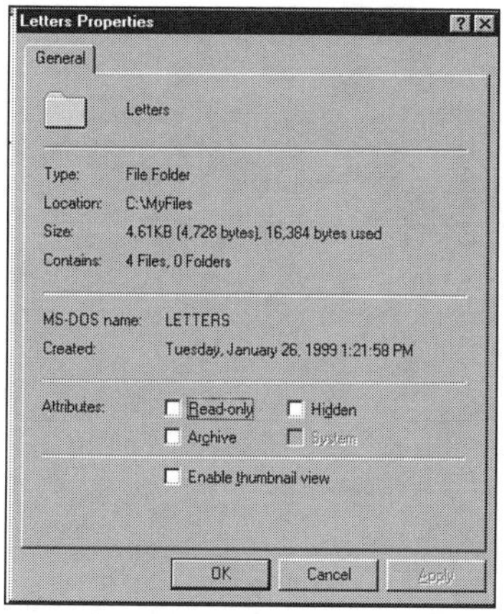

PART

I

CH

3

Tip #11 from
Trudi Reisner

If you hold down the Shift key while you delete a file, it will not go into the Recycle Bin. However, after a file is deleted in this way, it is gone and the safety provided by the Recycle Bin is not there.

COPYING AND MOVING FILES

The easiest way to copy and move files is by using the Tree view. In this view, you can copy and move files just as you would with Windows Explorer.

From any file management dialog box, click the Toggle Tree view On/Off button. Navigate through the folders in the left window until you see the folder containing the source file(s) you want. Double-click this folder, if necessary, so that you see the desired file(s) in the right window.

Navigate to the destination folder until you can see it in the left window. If you need to open folders to see subfolders, click the plus sign to the left of the folder icon rather than double-clicking the folder itself. This ensures that the contents of the right window do not change.

When you can see the destination folder in the left window, select the file(s) you want to move or copy in the right window. Drag them from the right window to the icon for the destination folder in the left window.

Dragging files from one folder to another on the same drive moves them by default. Dragging files from a folder in one drive to a different drive copies them by default. To copy files instead of moving them from one folder to another on the same drive, hold down the Ctrl key while you drag them. You see a plus sign on the icon as they are moved, as shown in Figure 3.11, indicating that the files are being copied.

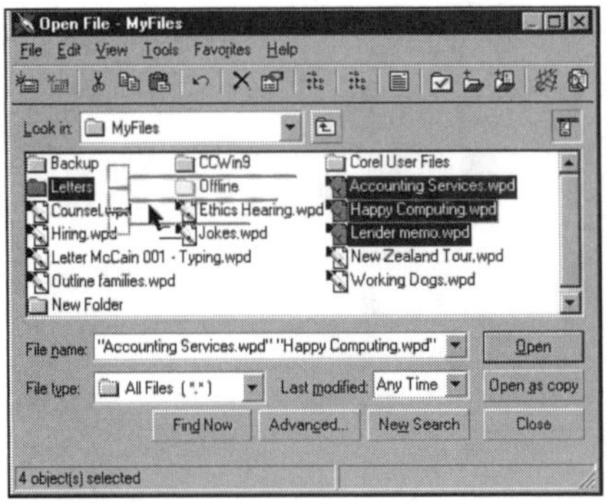

Figure 3.11
Holding down the Ctrl key while dragging files is indicated by a plus sign in a box next to the cursor, and forces the files to be copied rather than moved.

Note

To move files from one drive to another, drag them by using the right mouse button rather than the left. When you drag the file to the new drive and release the mouse button, you see a pop-up menu, and you can choose whether to move or copy the file.

You can also move or copy files by selecting them, and then choosing Edit, Cut or Edit, Copy. Then navigate to the destination folder and choose Edit, Paste. If you copy a file to the same directory, its name has "Copy of" appended to the front of it.

SETTING FILE ATTRIBUTES

You can make a file hidden, read-only, or see when it was created, last modified, and last accessed. To do so, select the file, and then choose File, Properties; alternatively, right-click the file and choose Properties. You see the Accounting Services Properties dialog box shown in Figure 3.12. Set the properties as desired, and then click OK.

Figure 3.12
You can set file properties or see when a file was created, modified, or last accessed in the file's Properties dialog box.

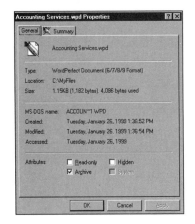

RENAMING FILES

To rename a file, select it in a file management dialog box, and then choose File, Rename; alternatively, you can right-click the file, and then choose Rename. The filename is highlighted with a box around it. Type the new name and press Enter.

DELETING FILES

To delete one or more files, select them in a file management dialog box, as described previously. Press the Delete key or click the Delete button. You see the Confirm File Delete dialog box shown in Figure 3.13. Confirm that you want to delete the files, and they are moved to the Recycle Bin.

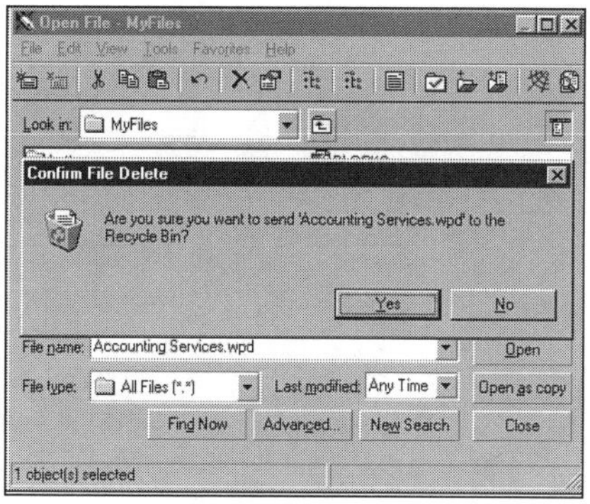

Figure 3.13
When you delete files, they go to the Recycle Bin, where you can undelete them if you need to.

PART
I

CH
3

FINDING FILES

Sometimes, even with the powerful file management tools at your disposal, you forget where you have filed an important document. Or, someone else in your office comes to you and says, "Can you get that memo that I did sometime last month? It was about Providence National Bank." In the past, this could have been a full-day job, but not anymore!

Corel provides you with two powerful tools to make finding files a snap: Favorites and QuickFinder.

> **Caution**
>
> Your files might not go to the Recycle Bin if the Recycle Bin properties have been modified. To check your Recycle Bin settings, right-click the Recycle Bin icon on the desktop, and then choose Properties.

USING FAVORITES

The WordPerfect Office 2000 suite integrates tightly with the Favorites folder contained in Windows.

The Favorites folder contains shortcuts to your most-used folders and files. The Favorites folder is common to all Windows applications, so if you add a file to your Favorites folder while you are in a non-Corel application, you will see it when you access Favorites in Corel Suite applications as well.

Note

A shortcut is a small file that, as the name implies, is a shortcut to another folder or file. It merely tells Windows where the actual folder or file is located. When you double-click a shortcut, it has the same effect as double-clicking the actual folder or file.

To access your Favorites folder, you can be in any file management dialog box. Click the Go To/From Favorites button. You see the contents of the Favorites folder. If you click the button again, you return to the folder you were previously in.

To add an item to the Favorites folder, select it, and then click the Add Selected Item(s) to Favorites button. You are given the choice of adding the selected item, or the folder in which it resides.

To delete an item from the Favorites folder, go to the Favorites folder, select the item, press the Delete key, and confirm the deletion.

Note

Deleting an item from the Favorites folder merely deletes the shortcut to the item that resides in the Favorites folder and leaves the item untouched.

USING QUICKFINDER

QuickFinder is a utility that helps you quickly find the files you need. It can look through every file on your disk and find just the files that contain the words you specify. This can be a lifesaver when you can't remember what you named a file. It can also enable you to create knowledge bases by saving old documents that you can quickly look through to find other work on a subject of interest.

QuickFinder can even index your files by examining them during off hours, and making a list (index) of words that your files contain. That way, when you look for files containing "providence," you find them virtually instantly!

You can access QuickFinder from any file management dialog box by clicking the Find Now button. When you click the Find Now button, you see QuickFinder Search Results in the Look In box, as shown in Figure 3.14.

Before you start conducting searches, however, you should configure the QuickFinder to create index files of the folders you commonly store documents in.

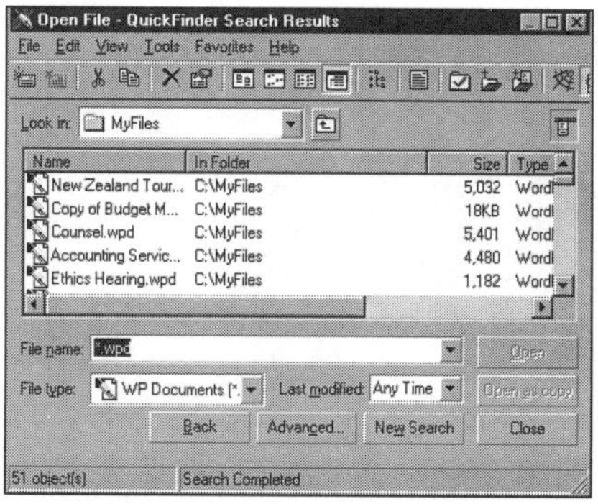

Figure 3.14
QuickFinder is used to index your files, enabling you to search for files by the text they contain, and finding resulting files almost instantly.

CONFIGURING QUICKFINDER

QuickFinder can search for files in two ways. If you configure QuickFinder to index specific folders, an index file is created containing an alphabetical list of words and the files they are in. Then, when you search for text, QuickFinder searches this index and finds appropriate files rapidly. This is called a Fast Search. If an index is not created, QuickFinder searches through files one by one, which is a slow process.

To configure QuickFinder, do the following:

1. Choose Start, Programs, Corel WordPerfect Office 2000, Utilities, Corel QuickFinder 9 Manager. You see the QuickFinder Manager dialog box shown in Figure 3.15.

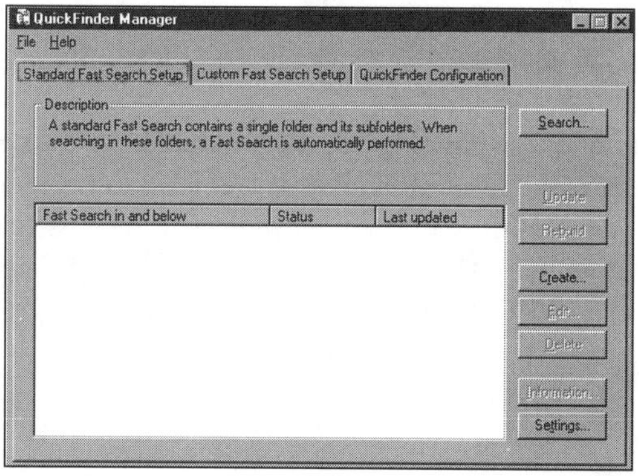

Figure 3.15
Configure QuickFinder in the QuickFinder Manager dialog box to do Fast Searches on your documents.

2. Any QuickFinder Fast Searches (indexes) are listed in the QuickFinder Manager dialog box. If you want to index additional drives or folders, click the Create button. You see the QuickFinder Standard Fast Search dialog box shown in Figure 3.16.

PART

I

CH

3

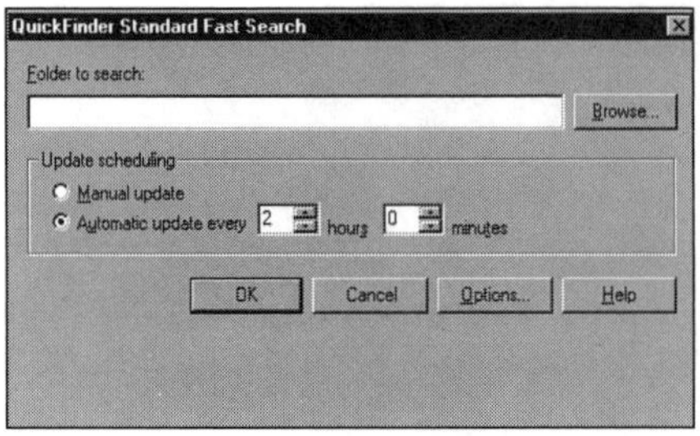

Figure 3.16
Configure QuickFinder to search through multiple drives or folders by creating new indexes in the QuickFinder Standard Fast Search dialog box.

3. Type in the drive and folder you want to search; or click the Browse button, navigate to the desired folder, and then double-click it.

4. Choose Manual Update, or choose Automate Update Every, and specify how often the index should be updated. If you choose Automatic Update, you will see a warning dialog box informing you that automatic update is disabled by default. Confirm that you want to enable Automatic Update before proceeding.

5. Click the Options button to specify whether the search should include the full document or just the document summary; then choose OK to return to the QuickFinder Standard Fast Search dialog box.

Tip #12 from
Trudi Reisner

Automatic updating is most convenient, but it may slow down your computer dramatically during the time it takes to update the index.

6. Close the dialog box when you are finished.

If you have set your options for manual update, you can update a Fast Search by accessing the QuickFinder Manager dialog box, highlighting the index to be updated, and choosing Update. Periodically, you will want to delete your index and reconstruct it completely. This makes sure that you don't get false "hits" from files that have been deleted. You can do this by selecting an index and clicking Rebuild instead of Update.

Tip #13 from
Trudi Reisner

You can edit a Fast Search to change the schedule by which it is updated, or delete one entirely, if desired.

FINDING FILES

You can find files by using the QuickFinder from any Open dialog box, or by choosing Start, Corel WordPerfect Office 2000, Utilities, Corel QuickFinder 9 Searcher.

To search for a file with a specified word or phrase in it, access an Open dialog box. Type the text you want to find in the Filename box, and specify the folder in which you want to look in the Look In box. Click the Find Now button. The files containing the desired text appear in the file list, and you see QuickFinder Search Results in the Look In box.

To toggle back to your original file list, click the Back button.

PRACTICAL PROJECT

You probably have a lot of documents you create in WordPerfect and you may be storing them in one folder. However, you can organize them in an easy fashion. Just create several new folders in the Save File dialog box and move the files to their respective new folder. For example, name the folders in the following way: Letters, Memos, Reports, and Misc., or you can create a folder for each person in your department or by project.

TROUBLESHOOTING

USING THE CLOSE BUTTON

Why isn't there a button to close a file as there is to save or open a file?

There is—but it's not on the toolbar. The Close button is the button with the X on it in the upper-right corner of the menu bar. You can also put a button on your toolbar to close a document in most WordPerfect Office 2000 applications.

CHAPTER 4

CUSTOMIZING TOOLBARS, PROPERTY BARS, AND MENUS

In this chapter

CUSTOMIZING TOOLBARS AND PROPERTY BARS

Corel WordPerfect, Presentations, and Quattro Pro all enable you to customize your toolbars to display the tools you use most frequently. They do so, however, in slightly different ways. To effectively customize your toolbars, you need to know how to

- Display and hide toolbars
- Select different toolbars
- Access the Toolbar Preferences
- Control toolbar display options
- Position the toolbar in the window

DISPLAYING AND SELECTING TOOLBARS AND PROPERTY BARS

You can choose among several toolbars in each WordPerfect suite application. Additionally, there are Property Bars that offer more features for the task you are working on in WordPerfect and Presentations.

In WordPerfect and Quattro Pro, you can display multiple toolbars simultaneously. In Presentations, you can display only one toolbar at a time. In all applications, only one Property Bar can be displayed at a time.

You can control the display of toolbars and Property Bars by choosing View, Toolbars to access the Toolbars dialog box. Check or uncheck the toolbar(s) or Property Bar to display or hide them.

Tip #14 from
Trudi Reisner

To quickly hide a toolbar or Property Bar, right-click it and then choose Hide Property Bar, or uncheck the toolbar or Property Bar entry.

To select a different toolbar to display, ensure that a toolbar is displayed, and then right-click it. Click the name of the toolbar that you want to display from the QuickMenu that appears. In Presentations, the selected toolbar replaces the original one. In WordPerfect and Quattro Pro, the selected toolbar is displayed in addition to the original one.

CUSTOMIZING TOOLBARS

To control toolbar display options in WordPerfect, Quattro Pro, or Presentations, or to create, edit, copy, rename, or delete a toolbar, use the following procedure:

1. Make sure that a toolbar is displayed, and then right-click it.
2. Select Settings from the QuickMenu. The Customize Settings dialog box opens in WordPerfect (see Figure 4.1). Ensure that the Toolbars tab is selected.

Figure 4.1
You can select different toolbars, as well as create and edit new ones, from the Customize Settings dialog box.

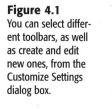

Note

In Quattro Pro, choosing Customize from the QuickMenu displays the Customize Settings dialog box; in Presentations, choosing Settings opens the Customize dialog box. These have similar functionality to the options in the WordPerfect Customize Settings dialog box discussed in this procedure. Some of the buttons will be different in Quattro Pro and Presentations.

PART

I

CH

4

3. Highlight the toolbar that you want to select, edit, copy, rename, or delete.

4. Choose an option from the following list:

- Create—Creates a new toolbar (see "Creating Toolbars and Menu Bars" later in this chapter).

- Edit—Edits an existing toolbar (see "Editing Toolbars and Menu Bars" later in this chapter).

- Copy—Copies an existing toolbar. The option works slightly differently, depending on the application (see "Copying Toolbars" later in this chapter).

- Rename—Renames an existing toolbar. (You may not be able to rename certain toolbars that ship with the product.)

- Reset—Resets the toolbar to its factory-installed condition. This button appears only in WordPerfect and Quattro Pro when you select a toolbar that ships with the suite.

- Delete—Deletes a toolbar. Certain default toolbars cannot be deleted. In WordPerfect, the Delete option appears only when toolbars you have created are selected.

- Options—Sets display preferences, as described in "Setting Toolbar Display Preferences" later in this chapter.

- Help—Provides context-sensitive help.

5. When you finish with whichever option you have selected, click OK. You return to your application.

> **Note**
>
> By default, when you edit the toolbar in Presentations, you are prompted to make a copy of the <Drawing> toolbar, which is the only toolbar available, and cannot be directly edited. You can, however, edit the copy of the drawing toolbar that you made, and save it with a different name.

SETTING TOOLBAR DISPLAY PREFERENCES

You can specify options regarding the appearance and location of your toolbars, although the exact options differ in WordPerfect, Quattro Pro, and Presentations. The selections you make affect any toolbar that you select and are retained in future work sessions until you reset them. To set display preferences, use the following procedure:

1. Access the Customize dialog box as described in the previous section, by right-clicking a toolbar, and then choosing Settings.

2. Choose Options. An options dialog box similar to the Toolbar Options dialog box appears as shown in Figure 4.2.

Figure 4.2
The Toolbar Options dialog box enables you to change the appearance and location of your toolbar.

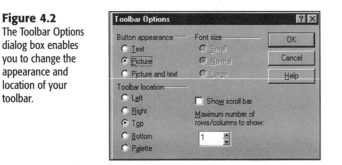

3. Select display preferences (not all preferences are available in all applications):

   • Button Appearance—Toolbars can display Text (text only), Picture (icon only), or Picture and Text.

   • Font Size—Choose the text size for toolbars that display text.

> **Tip #15 from**
> *Trudi Reisner*
>
> If you choose Text or Picture and Text, display your toolbars at the left or right side of the window; otherwise, you won't have room for many buttons.

   • Toolbar Location—You can specify that toolbars display to the Left, Right, Top, or Bottom of the window, or as a floating Palette.

- Sho<u>w</u> Scroll Bar—Click this check box to have a scrollbar appear on the toolbar so that you can have more buttons than appear in the window.

- <u>M</u>aximum Number of Rows/Columns to Show—You can display more than one row or column of buttons by entering a number greater than 1 in this option.

Tip #16 from	If you are setting options for a toolbar that is displayed as a floating palette, the <u>M</u>aximum Number of Rows/Columns to Show option is grayed out.
Trudi Reisner	

4. When you are finished selecting preferences, click OK. You return to the Toolbar Preferences dialog box.

5. You can now set further toolbar preferences or choose <u>C</u>lose to return to the application.

MOVING TOOLBARS WITH THE MOUSE

Another easy way to position toolbars is by moving them with the mouse, as outlined in the following steps:

1. Ensure that the toolbar is visible onscreen.

2. Position the mouse pointer in an area of the toolbar that does not contain buttons—either in the space between buttons or below or after the buttons. The mouse pointer changes into a four-headed arrow.

3. Drag the toolbar to the desired edge of the window. Alternatively, display the toolbar as a palette by dragging it into the middle of the window.

4. When you release the mouse button, the toolbar moves to its new position.

PART

I

CH

4

Tip #17 from	You can also move a toolbar that appears as a palette in the middle of the screen by dragging its title bar, or close it by double-clicking its Control button.
Trudi Reisner	

COPYING TOOLBARS

Copying a toolbar is handled differently by Presentations and WordPerfect. (In Quattro Pro, you do not copy toolbars; you merely create new ones.) In Presentations, a Copy Toolbar dialog box asks you for the name of the new toolbar.

In WordPerfect, toolbars are stored in templates. To copy a toolbar, do the following:

1. Display the Toolbar Preferences dialog box as described previously.

2. Choose Cop<u>y</u>. The Copy Toolbars dialog box appears (see Figure 4.3).

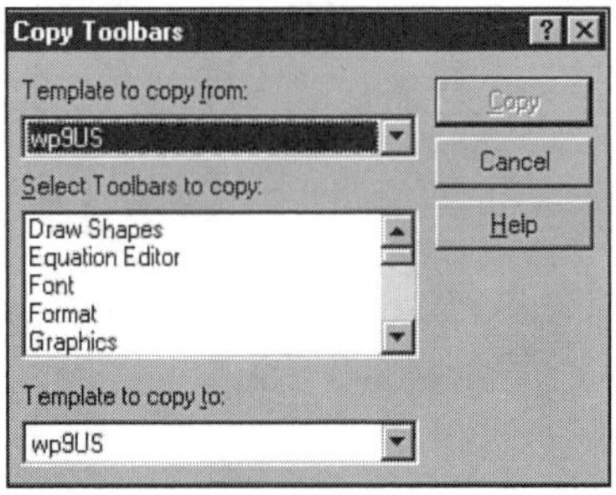

Figure 4.3
In WordPerfect, you copy a toolbar from one template to another using the Copy Toolbars dialog box.

3. Specify the template containing the toolbar you want to copy.

4. Specify the toolbar in that template to be copied.

5. Specify the template to copy the toolbar to.

6. If the copying operation results in overwriting the name of an existing toolbar, you are prompted to overwrite the toolbar or provide a new name for it. (You see this prompt, for instance, when you copy a toolbar to the same template it comes from.)

7. Click the Copy button to copy the toolbar.

CUSTOMIZING PROPERTY BARS

The procedures for customizing Property Bars parallel those for customizing toolbars in WordPerfect and Presentations. By right-clicking a Property Bar, you can choose Settings, and see the appropriate customize dialog box, such as WordPerfect's Customize Settings shown in Figure 4.4.

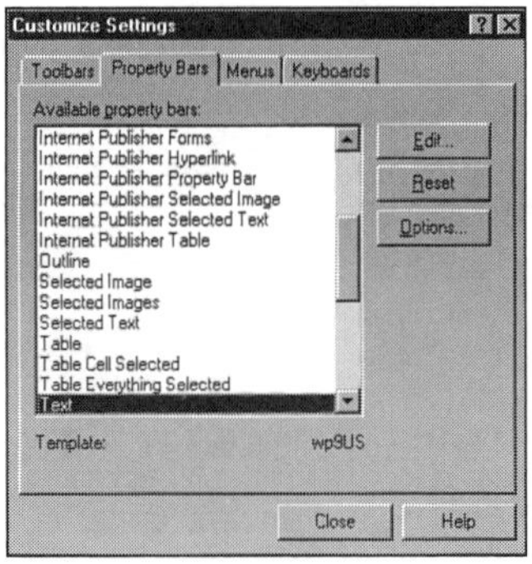

Figure 4.4
You can customize Property Bars just like you customize toolbars, except that you have fewer customization options.

The only three options you have are Edit (as discussed later in "Editing Toolbars and Menu Bars," Reset (which resets the default settings for the Property Bar), and Options (which controls how the Property Bar is displayed).

CUSTOMIZING MENU BARS

In WordPerfect and Presentations, you can create multiple menu bars and edit their contents—just as you can with toolbars.

To effectively customize your menus, you need to know how to

- Select different menu bars
- Access the Menu Preferences dialog box
- Create and edit menus

SELECTING MENU BARS

To select a different menu bar to display, right-click the current menu bar. A QuickMenu appears that displays the names of available menu bars (see Figure 4.5). Click the menu that you want to display.

Figure 4.5
When you right-click a menu bar in WordPerfect or Presentations, a QuickMenu appears enabling you to choose different menus or to set menu preferences.

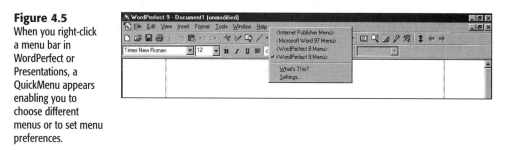

PART

I

CH

4

SETTING MENU PREFERENCES

To create, edit, copy, rename, or delete a menu, you must access the Menu Bar Preferences dialog box. To do so, use the following procedure:

1. Right-click the menu to open a QuickMenu.
2. Choose Settings. A Customize Settings dialog box like the one in WordPerfect appears (see Figure 4.6) or in Quattro Pro, or a Customize dialog box in Presentations that offers similar functionality.
3. Highlight the menu that you want to select, edit, copy, rename, or reset.

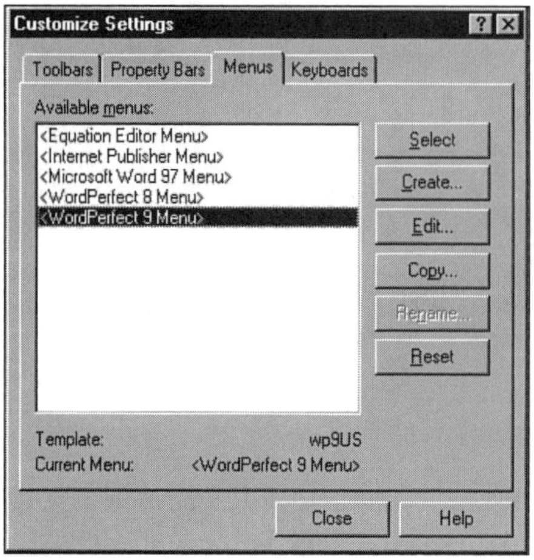

Figure 4.6
The Customize Settings dialog box enables you to customize menus just as you customize toolbars.

Tip #18 from
Trudi Reisner

Menus that are enclosed in angle braces (<>) are default menus that cannot be renamed or deleted. You can copy these menus, however, and then edit the copies.

4. Choose an option from the following list:

- Select—Displays the selected menu.

- Create—Creates a new menu. See the section "Creating Toolbars and Menu Bars" later in this chapter for details.

- Edit—Edits an existing menu. See the section "Editing Toolbars and Menu Bars" later in this chapter for details.

- Copy—Copies an existing menu. The option works slightly differently depending on the application. See the section "Copying Menu Bars" later in this chapter for details.

- Rename—Renames an existing menu.

- Reset—Restores the selected menu to its original commands.

- Delete—Deletes a menu from the list of available menus. The Delete button is available if you selected a menu you created, not a default menu.

- Help—Provides context-sensitive help on menus.

5. When you are finished with whichever option you have selected, choose Close. This option completes any operations you have made and returns you to the application.

COPYING MENU BARS

Copying menu bars is handled differently by Presentations and WordPerfect. In Presentations, a Copy Menu Bar dialog box appears that asks you for the name of the new menu. By default, the new menu has the same entries as the menu selected in the Menu Bars list.

In WordPerfect, menus are stored in templates. To copy a Menu Bar, do the following:

1. Access the Customize Settings dialog box as described previously. Choose Copy. The Copy Menu Bars dialog box appears (see Figure 4.7).

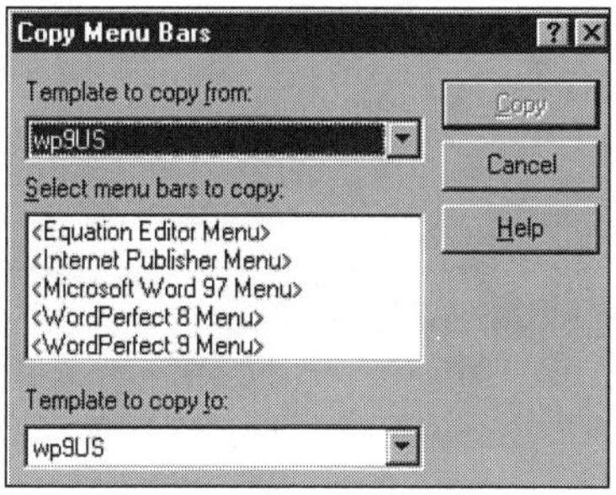

Figure 4.7
The Copy Menu Bars dialog box in WordPerfect enables you to copy menus from one template to another.

2. Specify the template containing the menu you want to copy.

3. Specify the menu in that template to be copied.

4. Indicate the template to copy the menu to. If the copying operation will result in over-writing the name of an existing menu, you are prompted to overwrite the menu or provide a new name for it. (You see this prompt, for instance, when you copy a menu to the same template it comes from.)

5. Click the Copy button to copy the menu.

PART

I

CH

4

CREATING AND EDITING TOOLBARS AND MENU BARS

The process of creating and editing toolbars is almost identical to creating and editing menus. This is because the same elements can be added to toolbar buttons as to menu items.

CREATING TOOLBARS AND MENU BARS

Creating a new toolbar or menu bar involves two basic steps: giving the toolbar or menu bar a name, and then adding buttons or items to it. To create a new toolbar or menu bar, follow these steps:

1. Right-click the menu bar or toolbar to open a QuickMenu.

2. Choose Settings. The Customize Settings or Customize dialog box appears.

3. Choose Create. The Create Toolbar or Create Menu Bar dialog box appears as shown in Figure 4.8.

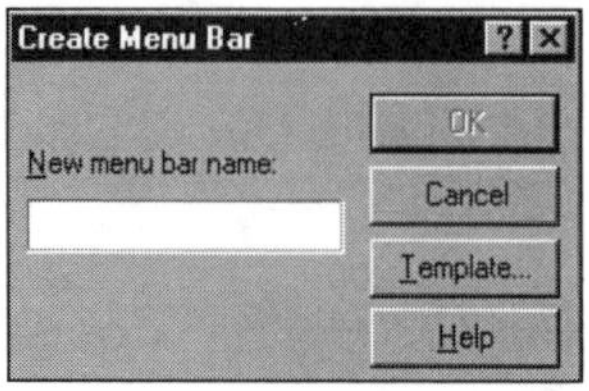

Figure 4.8
The Create Menu Bar dialog box is used to create menu bars.

4. Give the toolbar or menu a descriptive name, and then click OK.

Note

In WordPerfect, toolbars and menu bars are saved in a template rather than as a separate file on the disk. You can specify which template the new toolbar or menu will be saved in by choosing Template from the Create Toolbar or Create Menu Bar dialog box. In the resulting Toolbar or Menu Bar Location dialog box, you can specify either the current document's template or the default template. If you choose the latter, your toolbar or menu will be available in all documents.

5. A Menu Editor (or Toolbar Editor) dialog box similar to the one in Figure 4.9 appears.

Figure 4.9
After you create a toolbar, you can add buttons to it by using the Menu Editor dialog box.

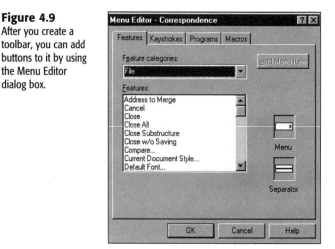

6. Add, move, and delete buttons as described in the section "Editing Toolbars and Menu Bars" later in this chapter.

7. When you are finished, click OK. You return to the Toolbar or Menu Bar Preferences dialog box. Your new toolbar or menu is on the appropriate list.

8. You can set further preferences or choose Close to return to the application.

⚡ *Sometimes you don't know what the toolbar buttons in WordPerfect mean. Your officemate's machine gives a little yellow prompt when she puts her mouse pointer on a button. If you want to know how you can do that, see "Using QuickTips" in the Troubleshooting section at the end of this chapter.*

EDITING TOOLBARS AND MENU BARS

Editing a toolbar or menu bar involves adding, deleting, moving, and customizing buttons or items. To edit an existing toolbar or menu bar, follow these steps:

1. Access the Customize Settings or Customize dialog box as described in the previous section.

2. Select the toolbar or menu to be edited.

3. Choose Edit. A Toolbar or Menu Bar Editor dialog box appears, similar to the one shown in Figure 4.10. (The Menu Editor has similar functionality.)

Figure 4.10
By using the Toolbar Editor dialog box for a specific toolbar, you can add, move, delete, or customize buttons.

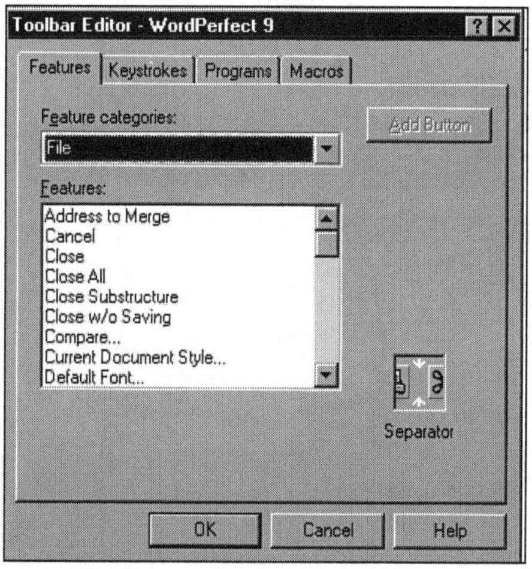

4. Edit the toolbar or menu bar as follows:

   • Add buttons to the toolbar or menu items as described in "Adding Toolbar Buttons and Menu Items" later in this chapter.

   • Move toolbar buttons or menu items by dragging them to a new position on the toolbar or menu.

   • Delete buttons or items by dragging them off the toolbar or menu.

   • Customize buttons and items as described in "Customizing Toolbar Buttons and Menu Items" later in this chapter.

5. When you are finished editing the toolbar or Menu Bar, click OK. You return to the Customize Settings or Customize dialog box.

6. You can now set further preferences or choose Close to return to the application.

ADDING TOOLBAR BUTTONS AND MENU ITEMS

Toolbar buttons and menu items are extremely powerful. One of their simplest uses is to invoke program features. Toolbar buttons and menu items can perform four different types of tasks:

- Activate a feature—Each application has specific features that can be assigned to a toolbar button or menu item. These are the features seen on the default menus of the application. This option enables these menu items to be assigned to toolbar buttons and permits menus to be rearranged to your liking.

- Play Keystrokes—You can use a keyboard script to store a sequence of keystrokes. These keystrokes are played back when you click the button or choose the menu item that contains the keyboard script. Keystroke sequences can contain text and extended characters. They can also contain function key and hotkey keystrokes. Thus, you can record simple macros that do anything that can be done by a sequence of keystrokes (but not mouse movements or mouse clicks).

- Launch a program—Toolbar buttons and menu items can launch any application on your disk—both WordPerfect Suite and non-WordPerfect Suite programs.

- Play a macro—You can also create a button or menu item that runs a macro. (The macro must already have been created and saved on the disk.)

To add a button or item to your toolbar or menu, access the Toolbar or Menu Bar Editor dialog box by creating or editing a toolbar or menu as described in the last section. What you do next depends on what type of button or menu item you want to add.

ADDING A FEATURE

To add a button or menu item that calls a feature, follow these steps:

1. From the Toolbar Editor or Menu Editor dialog box, choose the Features tab. The dialog box shows options for Feature Categories and Features.

2. Select Feature Categories, and click the down arrow to the right of the Feature Categories text box. A list of available Feature Categories appears (see Figure 4.11). These parallel the main menu options. Some applications may have additional feature categories.

3. Depending on the category you select, a different list of features appears. Select the feature you want to associate with the button, and then choose Add Button (or Add Menu Item, if you're editing a menu).

> **Note**
>
> Quattro Pro doesn't have the Add Button option in the Customize Settings dialog box. You can add buttons to the toolbars by locating the button in the dialog box and dragging it to the toolbar outside the dialog box.

Figure 4.11
In the Toolbar Editor, you can assign buttons or menu items to application features that parallel default menu items.

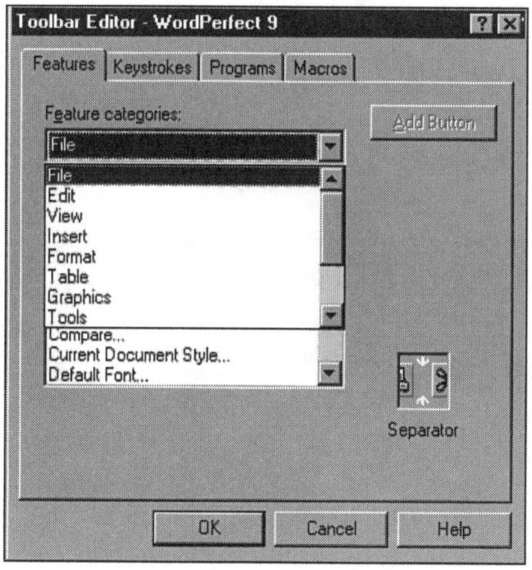

4. A new button or item appears on the toolbar or menu, and you remain in the Edit Toolbar or Menu Editor dialog box so that you can make further additions or accept the change you have made and exit the dialog box by clicking the OK button.

Tip #19 from
Trudi Reisner

New menu items are added as main selections on the menu bar. Move them by dragging them to their appropriate place on a menu.

ADDING A KEYSTROKE SEQUENCE

If you want a button or menu item to play a keystroke sequence, follow these steps to create it:

1. From the Toolbar or Menu Bar Editor dialog box, choose the Keystrokes tab. The Keystrokes tab of the Toolbar or Menu Editor dialog box shows a text box for the keyboard script (see Figure 4.12).

2. Choose Type the Keystrokes This Button (or menu item) Plays. An insertion point appears in the text box.

3. Type the keystrokes that the button should play. Function keys are entered with braces—for example, {Shift+F7}.

4. When you are finished, choose Add Keystrokes. A new button or item appears on the toolbar or menu, and you remain in the Toolbar or Menu Editor dialog box so that you can make further additions.

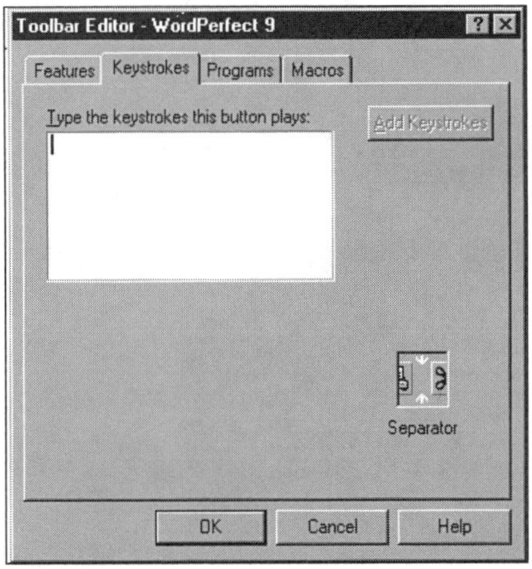

Figure 4.12
In the Toolbar Editor dialog box, you can enter the keystroke sequences that create Toolbar buttons and menu items for text, function keys, or menu choices.

Tip #20 from
Trudi Reisner

By default, a new keyboard sequence item has the name of the first word in the script. To change this name, double-click the menu item while you are editing the menu bar.

LAUNCHING A PROGRAM

To create a button or menu item that launches a program, you must know the name of the program file and the folder in which it resides. Then, create the button or item as follows:

1. From the Toolbar or Menu Editor dialog box, choose the Programs tab.

2. Click the Add Program button. The Open File dialog box appears (see Figure 4.13).

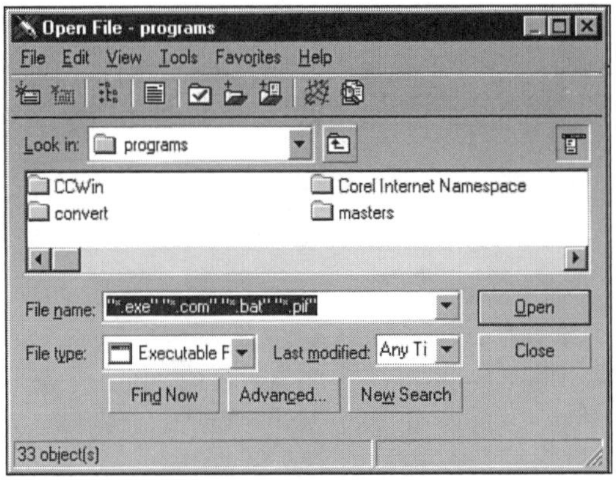

Figure 4.13
Assign an application to a toolbar button or menu item using the Open File dialog box.

3. Navigate to the folder containing the program, and double-click the appropriate program file.

→ For more information on opening files, **see** "Saving, Opening, and Closing Files," **p. 36**

A new button or item appears on the toolbar or menu, and you return to the Toolbar or Menu Editor dialog box so that you can make further additions.

Tip #21 from	By default, a new application launch menu item has the name of the application. To change this name, open the Menu Editor dialog box and double-click the menu item. The Edit Menu Text dialog box opens. Change the Menu Item name and click OK.
Trudi Reisner	

RUNNING A MACRO

If you want to assign a macro to a toolbar button or menu item, use the following steps:

1. From the Toolbar or Menu Editor dialog box, choose the Macros tab.

2. Click the Add Macro button that now appears in the dialog box. The Add Macro or the Select Macro dialog box appears (see Figure 4.14), enabling you to choose the macro to be assigned to the button or menu item.

Figure 4.14
Through the Select Macro dialog box, you can access macros which you can also assign to toolbar buttons and menu items.

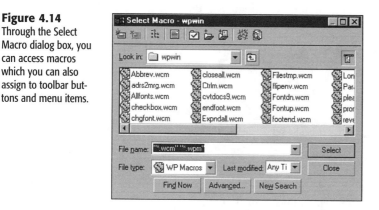

Note	In WordPerfect, you can also choose Add Template Macro. This adds a macro that is stored in a template to a button or menu item, as opposed to one stored on the disk. In this case, you see a list of macros stored in the current template, and you can choose a macro from this list.

3. Navigate to the appropriate folder, and then double-click the macro file. A new button or item appears on the toolbar or menu, and you return to the Edit Toolbar or Menu Editor dialog box so that you can make further additions.

Note	If you see the prompt "Save Macro with Full Path," choose Yes to assign the macro to the toolbar button or menu item.

CUSTOMIZING TOOLBAR BUTTONS AND MENU ITEMS

You may customize a button or menu item by double-clicking it while you are editing or creating a toolbar or menu bar.

If you double-click a toolbar button, the Customize Button dialog box appears (see Figure 4.15).

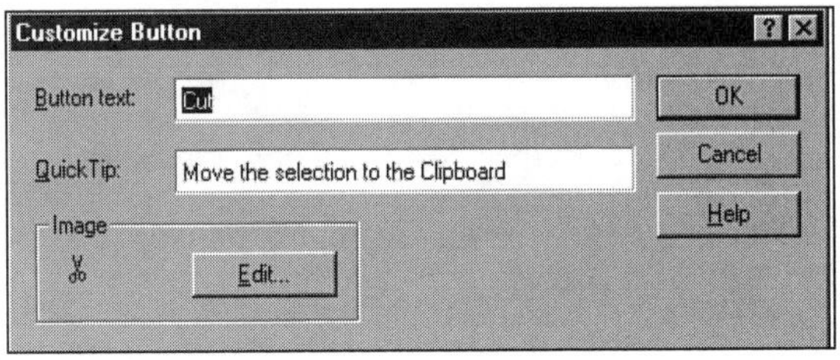

Figure 4.15
The Customize Button dialog box enables you to change the properties of specific buttons on the toolbar.

If you double-click a menu item, the Edit Menu Text dialog box appears (see Figure 4.16).

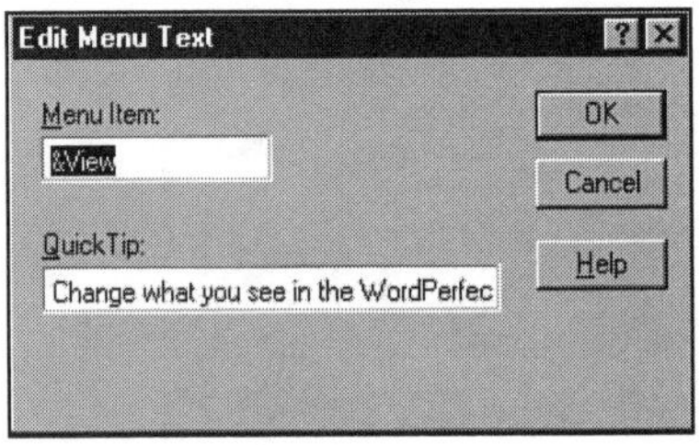

Figure 4.16
The Edit Menu Text dialog box enables you to change the text of the menu item QuickTip.

These dialog boxes provide many options, including

- Button Text and QuickTip (for toolbar buttons)—The text that pops up when you hold the mouse pointer on a toolbar button.
- Menu Item (for menu items)—The text of the menu item.
- Edit (toolbar buttons)—Enables you to edit the image of the button. Choosing Edit displays an Image Editor dialog box (see Figure 4.17).

If you use the Bitmap Editor to change the appearance of your toolbar button, you see the following options:

- Select the colors that you can paint with the left and right mouse buttons by clicking the appropriate colors with the respective buttons.
- If Single Pixel is selected, click either button to fill small rectangles with the appropriate color, one at a time.

- If Fill Whole Area is selected, click a cell to change the color of that cell and all contiguous cells of the same color.

- You can also use the Copy and Paste commands to copy images from one button to another.

Figure 4.17
WordPerfect Suite 9 includes a Bitmap Editor that enables you to change the appearance of toolbar buttons.

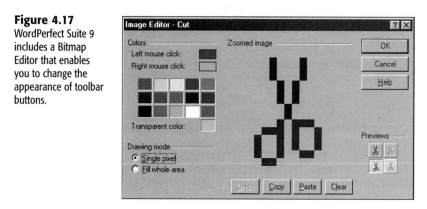

SETTING ADDITIONAL PROPERTIES

When you edit toolbars and menu bars, and double-click a button or menu item, you may see a Properties button.

This Properties option enables you to change certain aspects of the command invoked by the button or menu item. How it works depends on what the button or menu item does:

- For buttons or menu items that invoke a feature, no Properties option is available. There is also no Properties option available for WordPerfect toolbar buttons that invoke macros stored in the template.

- If the button or menu item plays a keyboard script, choosing Properties displays a Script Properties dialog box that enables you to edit the script.

- Choosing Properties for buttons or menu items that launch a program displays an Application Launch Properties dialog box. You can use this dialog box to specify the Command Line, Working Folder, and whether to Run the program minimized.

- Choosing Properties for buttons that launch macros located on the disk enables you to edit the path and name of the macro.

PRACTICAL PROJECT

Create a custom toolbar for changing your settings. For example, put buttons on a toolbar that you would frequently use for editing, printing, and saving a document. Or add buttons for Redline, Strikeout, and reviewing a document with revision marks (as explained in Chapter 13, "Using Revision Tools").

TROUBLESHOOTING

TOOLBAR BUTTONS IDENTIFIED

Sometimes you don't know what the toolbar buttons in WordPerfect mean. Your officemate's machine gives a little yellow prompt when she puts her mouse pointer on a button. How can you do that?

Turn on QuickTips by choosing Tools, Settings, Environment, and then checking the Display QuickTips option in the Interface tab.

PART **II**

Using Corel WordPerfect 9

CHAPTER **5**

GETTING STARTED WITH COREL WORDPERFECT 9

In this chapter

UNDERSTANDING THE WORDPERFECT SCREEN

When starting WordPerfect, you see certain screen elements (as shown in Figure 5.1), including the title bar, menu bar, the WordPerfect 9 toolbar, the Property Bar, guidelines, the Application Bar, and the scrollbars. Because toolbars can be customized, the icons shown in the figure may be different from what you have on your toolbar.

→ To learn about customizing toolbars, **see** "Customizing Toolbars and Property Bars," **p. 58**

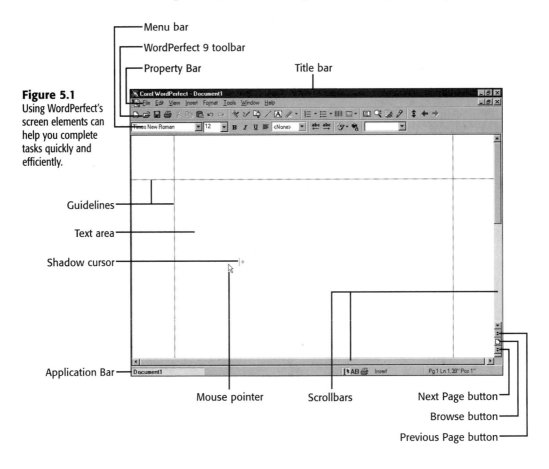

Figure 5.1
Using WordPerfect's screen elements can help you complete tasks quickly and efficiently.

→ For more information on Help, **see** "Using Help," **p. 20**

Screen elements provide information on your document and allow you to quickly complete common tasks. They are listed as follows:

- Title bar—The title bar identifies the WordPerfect application window and the name of the document in the current document window.

- Menu bar—The menu bar gives you access to the most commonly used WordPerfect features. Each menu contains a specialized list of related commands. Choose commands from the Format menu, for example, to specify fonts, change margins, create a header or footer, and so on.

WordPerfect 9 menus have undergone some significant changes. The differences between earlier versions of WordPerfect and WordPerfect 9 menus are listed in Table 5.1.

- Toolbars—By default, the WordPerfect 9 toolbar is displayed just beneath the menu bar. When you point to a button, its name is displayed beneath the pointer and its function is described in the pop-up QuickTip window. Toolbars contain buttons you can use to perform common tasks, such as opening an existing document, saving a document, copying text, and spell checking. When scroll arrows are displayed at the right end of the toolbar, you can use them to see other buttons. You can switch between toolbars whenever you like, and even choose where they appear on the screen.

- Property Bar—The Property Bar consists of a series of buttons that give you easy access to common text-editing and text-layout features. When performing specialized tasks, a specialized Property Bar designed to help you with that task appears. For example, when you're working with a table and have a cell selected, you will see the Table Cell Selected Property Bar.

→ For detailed information on customizing toolbars, **see** "Customizing Toolbars," **p. 58**

- Margin Guidelines—Guidelines are the gray lines you see onscreen that indicate where your margins are. You will see other guidelines from time to time in addition to the gray guidelines you see when you first enter WordPerfect. You will see guidelines around headers and footers, around cells in tables, and around columns. Not only do these nonprinting guidelines show you where various elements will appear, you can also drag them to change the element's formatting. For instance, you can drag the gray guidelines to set margins in your document.

- Text area—The text area consists of a blank "page" in which you can enter text or place pictures, graphics, and so on. By default, the text area is displayed in Page Mode—as it would appear on the printed page—including the margin space at the top of the page (depending on the zoom percentage, you may not see a full page of text at once). The insertion point is a blinking vertical line that indicates the position where text would be inserted if you were to type text.

PART

II

CH

5

Note

You can switch between ways of looking at your document, called views. The Page view is most commonly used; it shows the page as it will print. The Draft view hides headers, footers, and watermarks. Because it does not show a space between one page and the next, some people prefer to use this view when reading long text documents. The Two Pages view shows two complete pages, and is useful when examining your entire page layout. The Web Page view shows how the document would look if it were converted into a Web page. Switch between views by choosing View, and then selecting Draft, Page, or Two Pages, or Web Page. When you switch to Two Pages view, WordPerfect may warn you that the size may be inadequate. Switching to Web Page view may cause WordPerfect to warn you that formatting can be lost permanently.

- Application Bar—The Application Bar informs you of the status of many WordPerfect features. Use it to quickly identify whether you are in Insert or Typeover mode, to note the currently selected printer, and to locate the page, line, and position of your insertion point. You can also use the Application Bar to turn the display of the Shadow Cursor or Caps Lock on or off, and to print your document. The names of all open documents display as buttons on the Application Bar, and you can easily switch between documents by clicking the appropriate button.

- Scrollbars—Use the scrollbars to move quickly to another area of the document. Previous Page and Next Page buttons appear at the bottom of the vertical scrollbar and are used to move to the previous or next printed page of the document. The Browse button appears at the bottom of the vertical scrollbar and is used to select the document element you want to browse through, such as page (default), table, box, footnote, endnote, heading, edit position, or comment. The labels on the Previous and Next buttons on each side of the Browse button change, depending on what the Browse button is set to browse. For example, if you choose Browse by Table using the Browse button, you will see Previous Table and Next Table buttons (the double Up and Down arrows on each side of the Browse button).

- Shadow Cursor—As you move your mouse pointer over white space in your document, a bar with a right arrow appears. This is called the shadow cursor, and it indicates where your insertion point will be if you click the mouse button.

TABLE 5.1 WORDPERFECT 9 MENU CHANGES

Menu	Change
File	The File, Publish As and File, Send commands in WordPerfect 8 appear in the File, Send To menu; Initial Document Style is renamed and appears in the File, Document, Current Document Style menu; Initial Document Font is renamed and appears in the File, Document, Default Font menu.
Insert	The Outline and Bullets & Numbering features are consolidated in the Insert, Outline/Bullets & Numbering command.
Tools	The abbreviations feature is renamed QuickWords and appears as Tools, QuickWords.
Help	Help, Online, which you use to obtain additional Corel technical and product information, is renamed Corel Web Site on the Help menu.
Tables and Graphics	The Tables and Graphics menus are gone from the WordPerfect menu bar and the Tables and Graphics editing commands for tables and graphics are now available on the Property Bar. When you click a table or graphic, the Tables or Graphics Property Bar appears.

You can display or hide many of these elements to suit your working style. To display or hide the toolbar, Property Bar, or Application Bar, do the following:

1. Choose View, Toolbars and the Toolbars dialog box appears as shown in Figure 5.2.

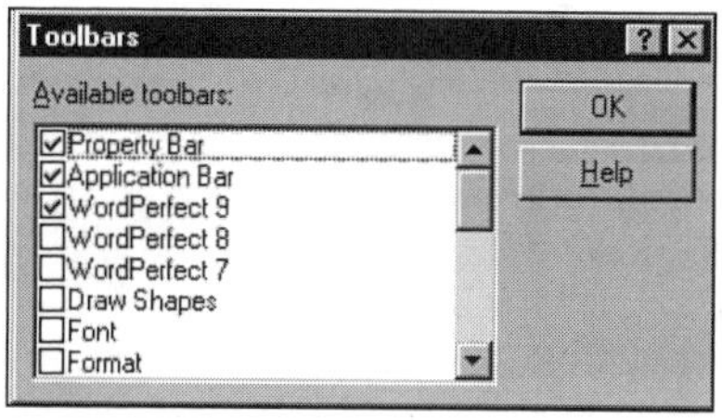

Figure 5.2
You can easily display or hide screen elements to provide more assistance, or give you the "clean screen" look.

2. Check or uncheck the appropriate element to display or hide it.

3. Click OK.

Tip #22 from
Trudi Reisner

You can quickly hide the display of the Property Bar and Application Bar by right-clicking them, and then choosing <u>H</u>ide Property Bar or <u>H</u>ide Application Bar. You can hide the display of various toolbars by right-clicking a toolbar, and then clicking the check-marked toolbar on the menu that appears.

To change the display properties of the scrollbars or the shadow cursor, do the following:

1. Choose <u>T</u>ools, Settings, <u>D</u>isplay, and then choose the Document tab. The Display Settings dialog box appears as shown in Figure 5.3.

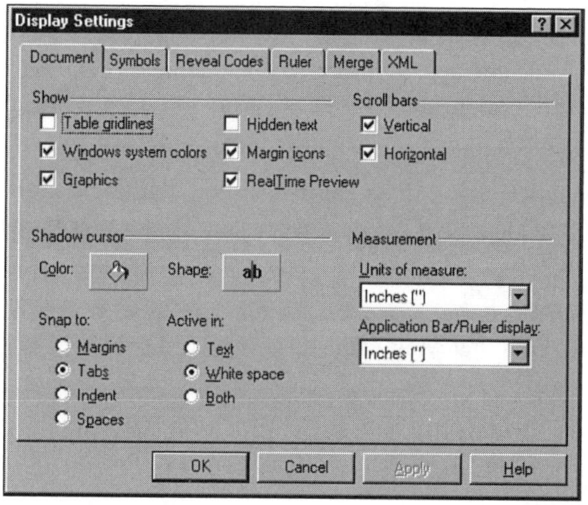

Figure 5.3
You can change the display of scrollbars and the shadow cursor to suit your working style.

2. Check <u>V</u>ertical or Hori<u>z</u>ontal to display the appropriate scrollbar.

3. Select shadow cursor options from the Shadow Cursor group as described in the following note.

4. Click OK, and then choose <u>C</u>lose when you are finished.

Note

You can change the way the shadow cursor operates, to give you more or less assistance with placing your insertion point. From the Display Settings dialog box, choose whether you want your shadow cursor to be Active in the Text, Active in White Space, or Active in Both. The shadow cursor automatically moves to the nearest margin, tab, indent, or space, depending on which option you select. This is called snapping to the element. You can also choose the Color or Shape of the shadow cursor.

ENTERING TEXT

When starting WordPerfect, you are supplied with a new, empty document window named Document1 in the title bar. You can begin to type at the blinking insertion point, initially positioned just below the top margin. As you type, text is entered at the insertion point.

This section describes the basic techniques of entering text, moving through a document, and selecting text for editing.

TYPING TEXT

When typing text, type as you would in any word processor. WordPerfect automatically wraps the text at the end of a line, so you don't have to press Enter to begin a new line. It does so by inserting a soft return at the end of the line. A soft return is a line break that appears as needed.

Press Enter only to start a new paragraph or create a blank line. Pressing Enter inserts a hard return into your document. A hard return is a line break that stays where you put it, even if the line of text does not extend to the right margin. WordPerfect defines a paragraph as text that ends with a hard return, a hard page break, or a hard column break.

As you type, certain keys that you press—such as Enter, Tab, and spacebar—create nonprinting characters at the insertion point. You can view these nonprinting characters by choosing View, Show.

Figure 5.4 illustrates nonprinting characters, with a document containing lines that wrap with hard returns and lines that wrap with automatic word wrap.

The words underlined in red are words the "Spell As You Go" feature doesn't have in its dictionary, and are seen by WordPerfect as misspelled words. Words underlined in blue are flagged as possible grammatical errors.

As you type, follow these guidelines:

■ If you make a mistake, press the Backspace key to erase the character immediately preceding the insertion point.

■ Alternatively, you may press the Delete key to remove the character immediately following the insertion point.

- When you're typing a sentence or phrase that extends past the end of the line, let the words wrap to the next line automatically (do not press Enter when you get to the end of the line, but rather only when you get to the end of the paragraph).

- Use the Tab key to indent the first line of a paragraph; don't use the spacebar.

- Press the Insert key to use Typeover mode, in which the text you type replaces existing text. Press Insert again to switch from Typeover mode to Insert mode. You can tell whether Typeover or Insert mode is active by looking at the Application Bar at the bottom of the screen.

Figure 5.4
Paragraph marks and spaces are nonprinting characters; they do not print, whether or not they are displayed.

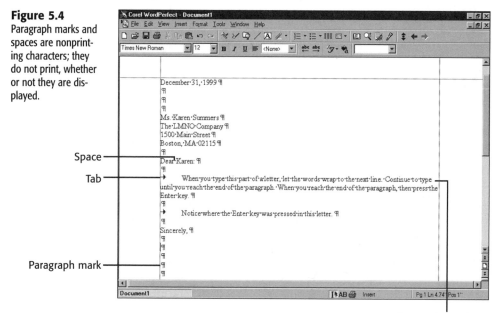

Automatic word wrap

POSITIONING THE INSERTION POINT

To move the insertion point, move the mouse pointer to the new location, noting the position of the shadow cursor as you move the mouse. When the shadow cursor is where you want it, click the left mouse button. You can position the insertion point anywhere in the text area, even if the insertion point lies past the end of the current text.

Tip #23 from
Trudi Reisner

> If you don't see the shadow cursor, choose View, Shadow Cursor to make it visible or click the Shadow Cursor On/Off button on the Application Bar.

To move the insertion point to a place that you don't see onscreen, use the scrollbar(s) to move to a new location. When the new location is visible onscreen, place the mouse pointer where you want to position the insertion point and click the left mouse button.

Another way to move the insertion point is by pressing keys on the keyboard. Sometimes, especially when you're already using the keyboard to type text, it's easier and faster to move the insertion point by pressing the cursor-movement keys than by using the mouse. Table 5.2 lists common keys that you can use to move around in your document.

TABLE 5.2   KEYBOARD KEYS TO EASILY MOVE AROUND IN A DOCUMENT

Key	Moves Insertion Point
→/←	Next/Previous character
↑/↓	One line up/down
PgUp/PgDn	One screen to the top or bottom
Ctrl+→/←	One word to the right or left
Ctrl+↑↓	One word up or down
Home/End	Beginning or end of line
Ctrl+Home/End	Beginning or end of document

A fast way to move the insertion point backward and forward through a document is to use WordPerfect's new Back and Forward buttons on the WordPerfect 9 toolbar. Click the Back button to browse backward, moving the insertion point to its previous position. Click the Forward button to browse forward, moving the insertion point from its previous position. These buttons are similar to the Back and Forward buttons in a Web browser.

Tip #24 from
Trudi Reisner

If the Forward button is not available, it means you have not previously browsed. Click the Back button on the WordPerfect 9 toolbar to make the Forward button available.

SELECTING TEXT

After you enter text, you may want to delete a word, sentence, paragraph, or other section of text, or you may want to boldface the text or change its font or size. Before you can perform many formatting or editing actions on existing text, you first must select the text. Selecting the text shows WordPerfect where to perform the action.

You can select text with the mouse, the keyboard, or a combination of both. Some of the most useful ways to select text include the following:

- To select a section of text of any length, click and drag over the text.
- To select a word, position the shadow cursor anywhere in the word and double-click.
- To select a sentence, position the shadow cursor anywhere in the sentence and triple-click.
- To select a paragraph, position the shadow cursor anywhere in the paragraph and quadruple-click.

- To select a sentence, position the mouse pointer in the left margin area. When you point the mouse in the left margin area, the pointer changes into a right-pointing hollow arrow, as shown in Figure 5.5. Click to select a single sentence; to select multiple sentences, keep holding down the left mouse button after you click and drag through the sentences or drag the mouse pointer in the left margin.

Figure 5.5
To select text, position the mouse pointer in the left margin and click once.

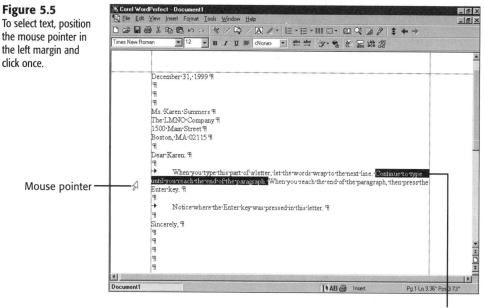

Mouse pointer

Selected sentence

- To select a paragraph, position the arrow pointer next to the paragraph in the left margin area. The arrow pointer should be pointing to the right. If it isn't, move it farther into the left margin area until it points to the right. Double-click to select the paragraph. To select multiple paragraphs, keep holding down the left mouse button after you click and drag through the paragraphs.

- For multiple selection options, position the right-pointing arrow pointer in the left margin area and right-click. Next, make a choice from selection options on the QuickMenu.

- To select a section of text of any length, position the insertion point at one end of the text. Next, position the shadow cursor at the other end of the text and hold down the Shift key while you left-click.

- To select text with the keyboard, position the insertion point at the beginning of the text, and then press and hold down the Shift key while you press the appropriate cursor-movement keys. To select from the insertion point to the end of the line, for example, hold down Shift while you press End. To select the character immediately following the insertion point, hold down Shift while you press the right-arrow key.

If you type text and it doesn't appear where you intended, see "Typing Text Where You Want It to Appear" in the Troubleshooting section at the end of this chapter.

To control a selection when you drag through text with the mouse, see "Controlling Your Selection" in the Troubleshooting section at the end of this chapter.

If you selected some text, typed over it, and your text disappeared, see "Typing Over Selected Text" in the Troubleshooting section at the end of this chapter.

Note | You can use the Shift key to extend (or shrink) a selection. Hold down Shift while you press an arrow key to extend (or shrink) the selection. To deselect text, click the mouse anywhere in the text area, or press any of the arrow keys.

EDITING TEXT

You can easily make changes and corrections to your document. You can select any text and delete it, copy it, or move it. You can even undelete text you accidentally deleted, or undo other editing operations you do by accident. This section shows you how to make basic editing changes quickly and easily.

DELETING TEXT

To delete a small amount of text to the right of the insertion point, press the Delete key. Hold the Delete key to continue deleting text. Similarly, to delete a small amount of text to the left of the insertion point, press the Backspace key. Hold the Backspace key to continue deleting text.

To delete larger amounts of text, select it as described previously, and then press the Delete key.

Tip #25 from | If you delete text by mistake, you can restore it by using the Undelete or Undo commands.
Trudi Reisner

COPYING AND MOVING TEXT

One task you'll do frequently as you edit documents is copy and move text. Copying text leaves the text in its original location, but makes a copy of it in another place. When you move text, it is deleted from the original location and inserted at the new location.

If you're going to copy or move the text to another location, you can use one of two methods: the "cut-and-paste" method or the "drag-and-drop" method.

USING THE CUT-AND-PASTE METHOD

To copy or move text from one area of the document to another area that is not visible onscreen, it is easiest to use the three-step, cut-and-paste method.

In the first step, you select the text and then move or copy the text to the Windows Clipboard. Moving the text to the Windows Clipboard deletes it from its original location, and is thus called cutting the text. The text stays in the Windows Clipboard until you exit Windows or place something else in the Clipboard. (Thus, you can paste text from the Clipboard into your document any number of times, until you put something else in the Clipboard.)

To cut selected text, choose Edit, Cut, or press Ctrl+X. Alternatively, click the Cut button. To copy selected text, choose Edit, Copy, or press Ctrl+C. Alternatively, click the Copy button. The text is placed in the Windows Clipboard.

Tip #26 from *Trudi Reisner*	You can also right-click the selected text, and then choose Cut or Copy from the QuickMenu.

After you move text to the Clipboard, show WordPerfect where you want to place the text by clicking where you want the text to appear in your document.

Paste the text from the Clipboard to the document by choosing Edit, Paste, or pressing Ctrl+V. Alternatively, click the Paste button or right-click at the insertion point and choose Paste from the QuickMenu. The text is copied from the Windows Clipboard to your document.

Note	Copying text—or other elements in your documents, such as pictures and charts—is a way to share data between applications. The Windows Clipboard is common to all applications running under Windows. You can, for example, create text in WordPerfect, copy it, and paste it in Presentations. You can also copy a spreadsheet from Quattro Pro and paste it into WordPerfect.

→ For more information on moving and copying, **see** "Understanding Moving and Copying," **p. 320**

PART

II

CH

5

DRAG-AND-DROP EDITING

Another technique for moving and copying text is called drag and drop. Drag and drop is especially handy for moving or copying selected text a short distance—a location, say, that is already visible onscreen. Drag and drop can also be used to move graphics.

To move or copy text using drag and drop, take the following steps:

1. Select the text you want to move.
2. Point to the selected text and hold down the left mouse button.
3. Drag the pointer until the insertion point is at the new location. The drag-and-drop pointer shown in Figure 5.6 appears. When you are at the new location, release the mouse button.

Figure 5.6
Use the drag-and-drop pointer to drag the selected text or graphic to a new location. When the insertion point is correctly placed, release the mouse button.

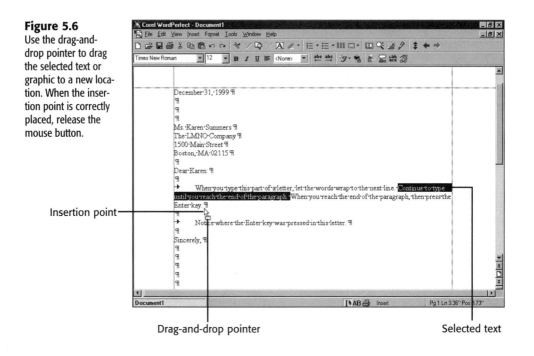

Insertion point

Drag-and-drop pointer   Selected text

Tip #27 from
Trudi Reisner

To copy the text instead of moving it, hold down the Ctrl key before you release the mouse button at the new location. When you hold down Ctrl, the drag-and-drop pointer includes a plus (+) sign.

CONVERTING CASE

WordPerfect includes a useful command that you can use to change the case of selected text. Suppose you type a heading with initial caps at the beginning of each word and then decide that it would look better in all uppercase. You can use Convert Case to convert it to uppercase.

To change the case of existing text, follow these steps:

1. Select the text.
2. Choose Edit, Convert Case.
3. Choose Lowercase, Uppercase, or Initial Capitals.

CORRECTING MISTAKES

Unless you're one of those people who fills out crossword puzzles with a pen, you'll find the Undo command one of your best friends.

Many mistakes can be reversed with the Undo command. Suppose that you move text to the wrong place. You can undo the move operation with Undo. Click the Undo button on the WordPerfect 9 Toolbar to undo your most recent action, or choose Edit, Undo. Click the Undo button or choose Edit, Undo repeatedly to undo previous actions.

WordPerfect also provides a Redo command that you can use to reverse the last Undo. Click the Redo button on the WordPerfect 9 toolbar to reverse your most recent undo action, or choose Edit, Redo.

WordPerfect provides a history of your edits and Undo actions. You can undo a series of actions by choosing Edit, Undo/Redo History.

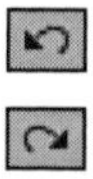

Figure 5.7 shows the Undo/Redo History dialog box displaying the most recent actions. To undo the last four actions, click the fourth item from the top of the Undo list (this selects the first four items that are listed in the illustration) and then choose Undo.

Figure 5.7
The Undo/Redo History lists a series of the most recent actions that you can undo (or redo).

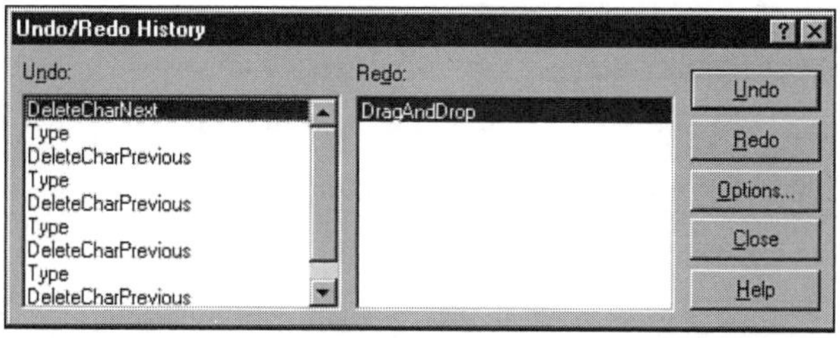

If you want to restore deleted text that you didn't intend to delete, see "Restoring Deleted Text" in the Troubleshooting section at the end of this chapter.

If you pasted text in the wrong place, see "Pasting Text in the Correct Location" in the Troubleshooting section at the end of this chapter.

If you accidentally get the drag-and-drop pointer when you don't want it, see "Canceling Drag and Drop" in the Troubleshooting section at the end of this chapter.

If you tried to move selected text to another page with drag and drop, but it was cumbersome to position the insertion point while dragging the selection, see "Knowing When to Use Drag and Drop" in the Troubleshooting section at the end of this chapter.

PART

II

CH

5

SAVING, CLOSING, AND OPENING A DOCUMENT

As you work on your document, you'll want to save it to the disk so that your work won't be lost if you turn off your computer or lose power. This section shows you how to save and close a document, open an existing document, and start a new one.

→ For more information on saving, opening, and closing files, **see** "Saving, Opening, and Closing Files," **p. 36**

SAVING A DOCUMENT

As in other WordPerfect Office 2000 programs, you save a WordPerfect document by assigning it a name and a location in your drive and folder list. After naming the file, you can save changes to the document without renaming it, or rename it to save both the original and new versions.

NAMING A DOCUMENT

You can save a file to a hard drive, floppy disk drive, or network drive. You can give your file a name that has up to 255 characters and includes spaces. If you need to exchange files with someone using a different word processor, you can even save your file in another format (such as WordPerfect 6 or Microsoft Word).

> **Caution**
>
> Some programs and versions of network operating systems cannot use long filenames. You need to think about where this file will be going in the future. If there is any chance that the document might be going through or to a system that doesn't handle long names, you might consider using the older "8.3" file-naming conventions. Keep your filename to eight characters or fewer, with an optional period and up to three more characters; and don't use spaces in the filename.

When you're ready to save your document for the first time, do the following:

1. Choose File, Save; press Ctrl+S; or click the Save button on the toolbar. WordPerfect displays the Save File dialog box shown in Figure 5.8.

Figure 5.8
The Save File dialog box enables you to save your file to the disk.

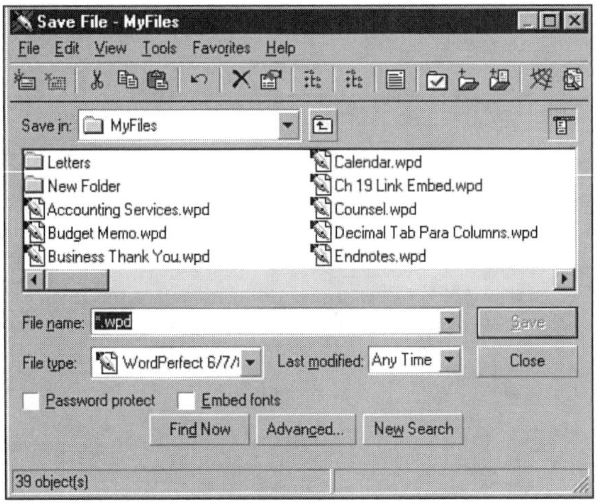

2. If you do not want to save your document in the default folder, navigate to the appropriate drive and folder by clicking the Save In box, and then select the drive and folder you want.

3. If you want to save your file in another format, click the File Type box, and select the desired format.

4. Type the name of the file in the File <u>N</u>ame box, and then click the <u>S</u>ave button. Your file is saved, and you return to the editing window. Notice that the title bar displays the file's location and name, and that it is unmodified.

→ For specific information on file management dialog boxes, **see** "Using File Management Dialog Boxes,"
p. 43

> **Note**
>
> You can specify the default folder in which your documents are stored and the default file-name extension. To do so, choose <u>T</u>ools, Settings, <u>F</u>iles, and then select the Document tab. Enter the default folder in the <u>D</u>efault Document Folder box. To use a default extension, check the Use Default E<u>x</u>tension on Open and Save box, and then enter the appropriate extension. Click OK, and then choose <u>C</u>lose when you finish.

→ For more information on customizing file settings, **see** "Customizing File Settings," **p. 311**

SAVING CHANGES TO A NAMED DOCUMENT

When you've saved your document by assigning it a name and a location on the disk, you can continue to work on it. The changes you make are not saved, however, unless you tell WordPerfect to save them.

 After modifying or editing an already-named document, choose <u>F</u>ile, <u>S</u>ave, or click the Save button on the WordPerfect 9 toolbar. WordPerfect saves the changes and you are ready to proceed.

Tip #28 from	Consider clicking the Save button whenever you are using your mouse to click a button on
Trudi Reisner	the toolbar just to be safe. It's a particularly good idea to save your document before doing large-scale editing such as a global search and replace.

PART

II

CH

5

⚡ *If you want to save a file in a different folder, but that folder isn't listed in the folder list, see "Selecting the Desired Folder" in the Troubleshooting section at the end of this chapter.*

RENAMING A DOCUMENT

Occasionally, you will want to rename your document. This is particularly useful when you are making a new document (such as a proposal or a letter to a customer) that is based on an old one. In this case, you want to keep both the old and new documents, so they need separate names.

Tip #29 from	In previous versions of WordPerfect, you would also rename documents to keep track of
Trudi Reisner	versions of the file. In WordPerfect 9, you do this with the version control feature.

→ For additional information on tracking document versions, **see** "Using Document Compare," **p. 217**

To rename your document, do the following:

1. With the document onscreen, choose File, Save <u>A</u>s. The Save As dialog box appears as shown in Figure 5.9.

Figure 5.9
You can rename your document using the Save As dialog box.

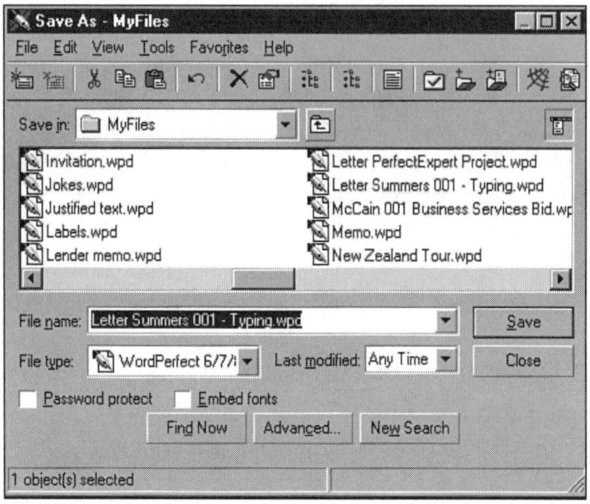

2. If you do not want to save your document in the default folder, navigate to the appropriate drive and folder by clicking the Save <u>I</u>n box, and then select the drive and folder you want.

3. If you want to save your file in another format, click the File <u>T</u>ype box, and pick the desired format.

4. If you want to change the name of your document, type the new name of the file in the File <u>N</u>ame box.

5. Click the <u>S</u>ave button. Your file is saved, and you return to the editing window. Notice that the title bar displays the file's location and name and that it is unmodified.

> ⚠ *If you want to save a file with a new name, but when you click the Save button, you don't have a chance to change the name, see "Saving a File with a New Name" in the Troubleshooting section at the end of this chapter.*

CLOSING A DOCUMENT

When you finish working with a document, you can choose File, <u>C</u>lose. The document is removed from the screen. If there are changes that haven't been saved, WordPerfect asks whether you want to save them before closing the document.

If you intend to exit WordPerfect after working on the document, you do not need to close the document first. The document is closed automatically when you exit WordPerfect, and you are prompted to save the document if there are unsaved editing changes.

OPENING A DOCUMENT

When you open a document, a working copy of it is made from the disk onto the screen and your computer's memory. You can open up to nine documents at once, which can be helpful when you need to bring information from several old documents into a new document.

If you prefer, you can open the document as a copy. If you do this, the document opens as a read-only file and you are unable to accidentally modify the original document. You are able to save the document, however, if you rename it.

Tip #30 from	If you open a document that has been saved in another format, such as a previous version of WordPerfect, Microsoft Word, Lotus Ami Pro, or Lotus Word Pro, the document is converted automatically. WordPerfect keeps the same file format from the file you saved in a different format. That way, you can retain the most document data from opening the document to saving it.
Trudi Reisner	

⚠️ *If you want to save a file in a different file format, see "Saving a File in a Different File Format" in the Troubleshooting section at the end of this chapter.*

To open a document, do the following:

1. Choose File, Open, or click the Open button on the WordPerfect 9 toolbar. WordPerfect displays the Open File dialog box shown in Figure 5.10.

Figure 5.10
Select the file from the list of files, and then choose Open to open the document.

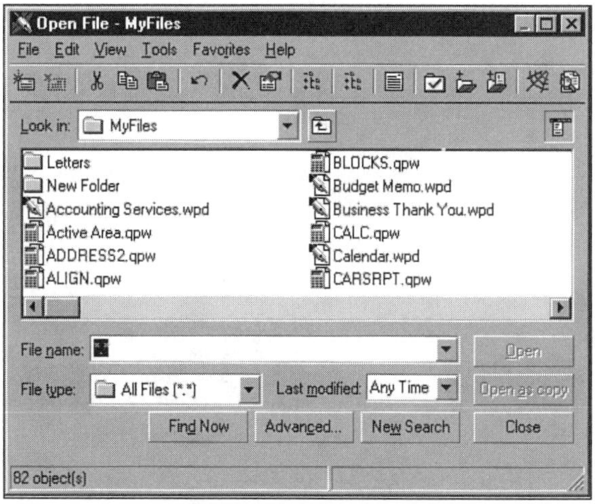

2. In the Open File dialog box, select the filename from the list of files, if you saved it in the default folder. Otherwise, you can change the drive and folder by clicking the Look In box to navigate to the desired folder, and then select the appropriate filename.

3. Click the Open button or the Open As Copy button, as desired; or double-click a filename from the list. The document appears in the editing window with its name on the title bar.

Tip #31 from
Trudi Reisner

To open several files at once, hold the Ctrl key down while selecting each file you want to open. To open several adjacent files, click the first file, and then hold the Shift key and click the last one.

If the file you want to open was recently edited, it is listed at the bottom of the File menu. You can select it from the File menu without accessing the Open dialog box. WordPerfect can display a maximum of nine documents at the bottom of the File menu.

STARTING A NEW DOCUMENT

All documents are based on templates. A template is a master document that contains formatting information, and can also contain text, macros, styles, and keyboard definitions. The standard template is where you save default formatting settings for future documents. The Standard template has the following characteristics:

- Uses an 8 1/2- by 11-inch portrait-oriented page
- Includes 1-inch top and bottom margins and 1-inch left and right margins
- Uses the initial printer font for the currently selected printer
- Uses left justification
- Supplies five heading styles that can be used to format different levels of headings in your document

In the next two sections, you learn how to start a new, blank document, and specify a template.

STARTING A NEW, BLANK DOCUMENT

You can start a new document at any time. To start a new, blank document based on the standard template, click the New Blank Document button, or press Ctrl+N. You see a new, blank document in the editing window.

Note

You do not need to close your old document before starting a new document because WordPerfect can have up to nine documents open at once. If you cannot create a new document, check to see whether the maximum number of documents is already open, or whether your insertion point is currently in a substructure, such as a graphics box.

If you can't open a file and New and Open are grayed out on the File menu, see "Opening Too Many Files" in the Troubleshooting section at the end of this chapter.

STARTING A DOCUMENT AND SPECIFYING A TEMPLATE

A template is a basic document design that can include text as well as formatting. You can save time and work by using templates for your standardized documents, such as letters, memos, and fax forms. Many templates prompt you for information when you use them;

this saves you the work of positioning the insertion point manually to fill in the information. Many templates for common office tasks ship with WordPerfect.

→ For detailed information on templates and projects, **see** "Introducing Templates and Projects," **p. 138**

PRACTICAL PROJECT

Suppose you need to create a press release for your company. Take a look at the Press Release PerfectExpert project, as shown in Figure 5.11. After you create the project document, type the text for the press release, proofread your work, and make any necessary changes by editing the text. Use Insert, Typeover, Delete, Copy, and Move to make your changes. You might want to use the Convert Case feature to emphasize important text with all uppercase letters. Finally, save the document with a meaningful name, close the document, and then open the document whenever you need it again. You can use the File, Save As feature to create other press releases from the original one.

Figure 5.11
The Press Release
PerfectExpert project.

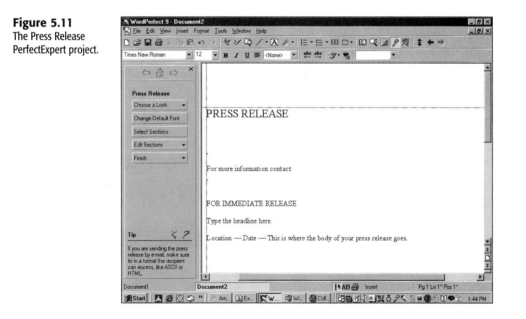

TROUBLESHOOTING

TYPING TEXT WHERE YOU WANT IT TO APPEAR

You began typing the text, but it didn't appear where you expected it to appear.

Text that you type appears at the insertion point, not at the mouse pointer. Before you type text, position the insertion point by clicking where you want the text to appear.

CONTROLLING YOUR SELECTION

You have trouble controlling the selection when you drag through text with the mouse.

It takes practice to control the mouse when you select text by dragging through it. Consider using this method only when all the text you want to select is visible onscreen. When it is not, click at the start of the selection, use the scrollbars to move to the end of the selection, and then hold down the Shift key while you click at the end of the selection for maximum control.

TYPING OVER SELECTED TEXT

You selected some text and made it bold, but when you started typing afterward the text disappeared.

When text is selected, whatever you type replaces the selected text. It's a good idea to deselect text as soon as you finish performing any action(s) on the selection. To deselect text, click anywhere in the typing area. To recover your "lost" text, choose Edit, Undo or click the Undo button on the WordPerfect toolbar.

RESTORING DELETED TEXT

You accidentally deleted text that you didn't mean to delete.

Restore the text by choosing Edit, Undo or click the Undo button on the WordPerfect toolbar.

PASTING TEXT IN THE CORRECT LOCATION

You pasted text in the wrong place.

Before you place anything else in the Clipboard, click the Undo button, and then position the insertion point in the correct location and press Ctrl+V, or choose Edit, Paste.

CANCELING DRAG AND DROP

You accidentally get the drag-and-drop pointer when you don't want it.

Press Esc before you release the mouse button. If it's too late, and the text has already been moved, use the Undo command to correct the mistake.

KNOWING WHEN TO USE DRAG AND DROP

You tried to move selected text to another page with drag and drop, but it was cumbersome to position the insertion point while dragging the selection.

Try using cut and paste rather than drag and drop when moving or copying to a distant location.

SAVING A FILE WITH A NEW NAME

You wanted to save a file with a new name, but when you clicked the Save button, you didn't have a chance to change the name.

To change the name, storage location, or file type of the document in the active document window, choose File, Save As. In the Save As dialog box, you can change any of these options.

SELECTING THE DESIRED FOLDER

You wanted to save a file in a different folder, but that folder isn't listed in the folder list.

You may need to select a folder above the selected folder before you can see the desired folder name. For example, if C:\Myfiles\WPDOCS is the selected folder and you want to look at the files in C:\Myfiles\MEMOS, first you must select C:\Myfiles. Then, you can see (and select) the C:\Myfiles\MEMOS folder. Remember that you should double-click a folder to select it.

SAVING A FILE IN A DIFFERENT FILE FORMAT

You opened a document that was created in another file format, and now you want to save it.

Choose File, Save As. WordPerfect displays the Save File dialog box.

OPENING TOO MANY FILES

You can't open a file; in fact, New and Open are grayed out on the File menu.

You already have nine documents open, which is the maximum WordPerfect allows at once. Close an open document, and then try again. If this isn't the problem, your insertion point may currently be in a substructure, such as a header, footer, or graphics box. Click in the main body of the document, and then try again.

CHAPTER **6**

FORMATTING TEXT

In this chapter

CHANGING SCREEN APPEARANCE

WordPerfect enables you to change your screen appearance in several ways to suit your working style. These include

- Displaying or hiding screen elements
- Specifying viewing modes
- Setting the screen magnification
- Working with the Reveal Codes window

The display or removal of screen elements, view modes, and magnification options are all set from the View menu. To select your view mode, choose View, and then select Draft, Page, or Two Pages. To work with the Reveal Codes window on, choose View, Reveal Codes.

DISPLAYING SCREEN ELEMENTS

You can remove or display various screen elements, such as the toolbar, Property Bar, Ruler, Application Bar, and nonprinting characters to customize the way your screen appears.

To remove or display the toolbar, Property Bar, or Application Bar, choose View, Toolbars. You see the Toolbars dialog box shown in Figure 6.1. Check the elements you want to display, and then choose OK. To toggle the display of the Ruler, choose View, Ruler. The Ruler displays when there is a check mark next to Ruler in the View menu.

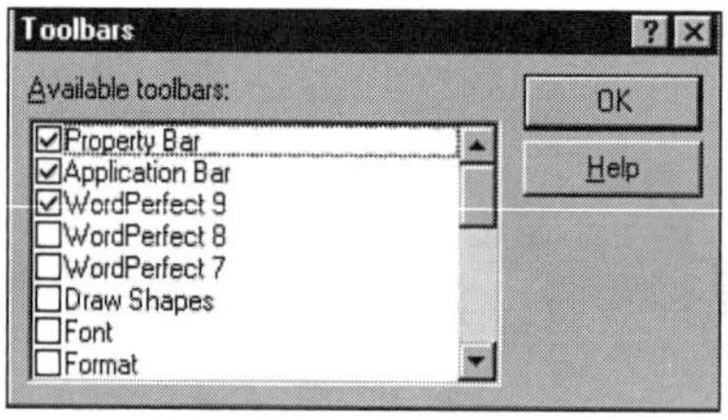

Figure 6.1
You can display or remove screen elements to customize the look of WordPerfect in the Toolbars dialog box.

To provide a totally "clean screen" look and remove all bars (including scrollbars and the title bar), do the following:

1. Choose View, Hide Bars. Unless the display of this dialog box has been suppressed, you see a Hide Bars Information dialog box that tells you the effect of this command and how to restore the screen to its original look.

2. Suppress the future display of this dialog box, if desired, by checking Do Not Show This Message Next Time I Hide Bars.

3. Choose OK. Your screen will look like the one in Figure 6.2.

Figure 6.2
You can produce a completely clean screen look by choosing View, Hide Bars.

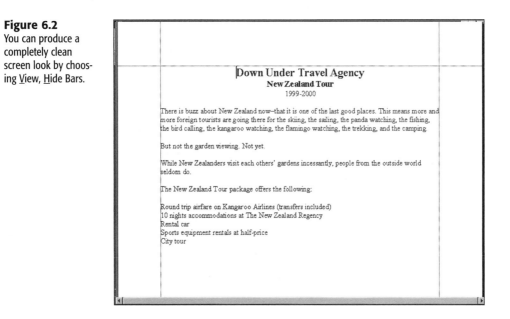

4. Press the Esc key to restore the original look of the screen.

You can also modify the viewing options to display nonprinting characters, such as spaces, hard returns, tabs, indents, and so forth, on the current and a new document. You may not want these characters to show onscreen, because they can become distracting and take your eye away from the text you are typing. On occasion, however, it may be useful to know where spaces and tabs are—especially at the "blank" end of a line. To show these elements, use the following steps:

1. Choose Tools, Settings, Display.

2. Select the Symbols tab. You see the Display Settings dialog box (see Figure 6.3).

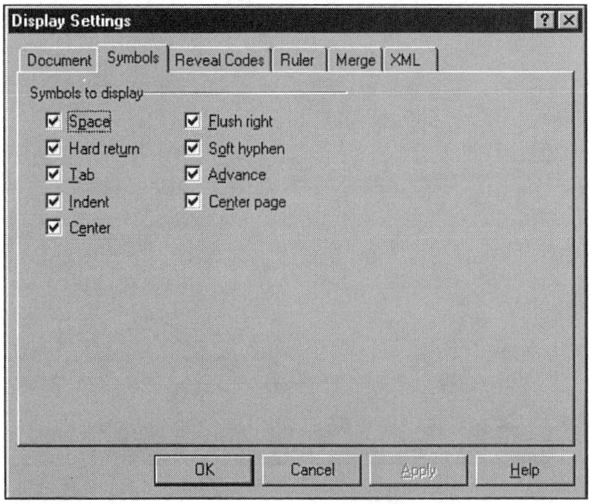

Figure 6.3
You can specify which nonprinting characters should display on your screen in the Display Settings dialog box on the Symbols tab.

3. Check the specific symbols you want to display.

4. Click OK to exit the Display Settings dialog box.

5. Click Close to exit the Settings dialog box and return to your document.

USING VIEW MODES

WordPerfect offers three different viewing modes that you can use while you are editing your document: Page view, Draft view, or Two Page view. Each view offers its own advantages for text editing and formatting. Changing the view affects the onscreen appearance of the document; it doesn't affect the actual formatting of the document or the way it will print out.

Tip #32 from	To quickly toggle the display of nonprinting characters, choose View, Show ¶.
Trudi Reisner	

When you work in a document, you're working in Page view by default. You can use the View menu to switch to another view whenever it suits you.

PAGE VIEW

In Page view, you see the page onscreen just as it will print, as shown in Figure 6.4. This is a true WYSIWYG (What You See Is What You Get) view of your document. Page view displays headers, footers, page borders, top and bottom margins, and footnotes. Page view is well suited for applying finishing touches to the text and page layout, although many people like to use this view for entering and editing text as well. Working in Page view is slightly slower than working in Draft view; on faster computers, however, this difference may be imperceptible.

Figure 6.4
Page view shows you everything on the page just as it will print; this is a true WYSIWYG view.

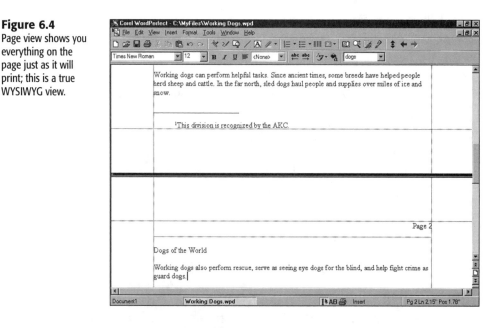

DRAFT VIEW

Entering and editing text is faster and easier when you work in Draft view. In Draft view, you see *text* just as it will print, including variations in font face, font size, and graphics elements, as shown in Figure 6.5. You can scroll smoothly from the bottom of one page to the top of the next page without jumping past the gap between the bottom margin of one page and the top margin of the next page. Whenever you want to see *everything* on the page just as it will print, including margin space, headers, footers, page numbering, and page borders, you can switch from Draft view to Page view.

Figure 6.5
Draft view enables you to enter and edit text smoothly and easily.

If it takes too long to scroll through a document, see "Scrolling Too Slowly" in the Troubleshooting section at the end of this chapter.

If it's difficult to get a continuous view of the text from one page to the next, see "Continuous View of Pages" in the Troubleshooting section at the end of this chapter.

TWO PAGE VIEW

Use Two Page view when you want to see two pages onscreen at the same time. Two Page view is best suited for looking at facing pages (when you're printing on both sides of the paper) and for seeing more of the document layout than you can see in Page view. You can see where text will fit on a page best with the Two Page view and determine how much whitespace exists on each page.

You can edit your document in Two Page view just as you can edit it in Draft view or Page view, although the text is extremely small. Working in Two Page view is even slower than working in Page view.

CHANGING THE VIEW MAGNIFICATION

In addition to the choice of views, WordPerfect provides various magnification options for viewing a document. You can adjust the view magnification from 25 to 400 percent when you are in Draft or Page view. If you have a 15-inch or larger monitor, you may want to use a smaller magnification. The letters on the screen are still readable, but you can see more of the page.

Setting magnification does not affect the way the document is formatted or how it will print out; it affects only its onscreen display.

 To change magnification, click the Zoom button on the toolbar. You see a drop-down menu such as the one in Figure 6.6. Choose your zoom setting from the menu, or select Other to specify a setting that does not appear.

Figure 6.6
Using the Zoom button on the toolbar, you can change the magnification of the screen without affecting the document format or the way it prints out.

When you select Other, the Zoom dialog box appears, as shown in Figure 6.7. This same dialog box appears when you choose View, Zoom from the menu bar. You can click one of the preset magnification levels in the box, or you can set your own level from 25 to 400 percent by clicking the up or down arrow in the spin box at the bottom of the Zoom dialog box.

Figure 6.7
In the Zoom dialog box, you can change the magnification factor of the screen to preset levels or set your own level.

 If you can't see all the text on a line onscreen at once, see "Changing the View Magnification" in the Troubleshooting section at the end of this chapter.

WORKING WITH THE REVEAL CODES WINDOW

The Reveal Codes window gives you a behind-the-scenes look at your document. Unless you have formatting problems, you don't need to look at the Reveal Codes window. Working with Reveal Codes turned on, however, is an excellent method of becoming familiar with codes and formatting. That way, when something does appear onscreen differently than you expected, you can spot the problem code immediately. Remember that WordPerfect records your formatting commands in the form of embedded codes. The Reveal Codes window shows you those embedded codes along with your text. Sometimes, the most efficient way to solve a formatting problem is by working in the Reveal Codes window and by removing the code that causes a problem. This section shows you how to work in the Reveal Codes window.

ACCESSING THE REVEAL CODES WINDOW

The position of the insertion point determines the placement of codes and where their formatting takes effect. When you select a subtitle and make it bold, for example, bold codes are embedded at both ends of the subtitle. When you change tab settings anywhere in a paragraph, however, a tab set code is embedded at the beginning of that paragraph.

To display the Reveal Codes window, choose View, Reveal Codes; press Alt+F3; or drag one of the Reveal Codes bars up or down. The editing screen is split into two windows, as shown in Figure 6.8.

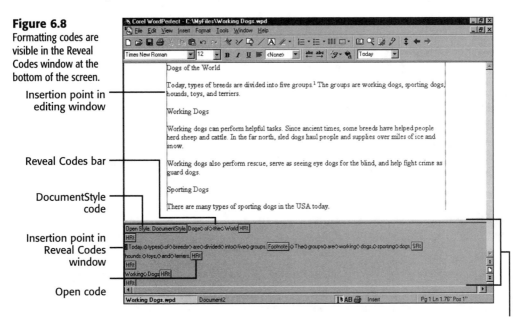

Figure 6.8
Formatting codes are visible in the Reveal Codes window at the bottom of the screen.

Insertion point in editing window

Reveal Codes bar

DocumentStyle code

Insertion point in Reveal Codes window

Open code

Reveal Codes window

PART

II

CH

6

Note

Every document contains an `Open Style: DocumentStyle` code at its beginning. This code cannot be removed, but it can be edited. Formatting in the DocumentStyle is a reflection of formatting in the DocumentStyle for the current template.

The following pointers will help you work in Reveal Codes:

- To remove a code, drag it out of the Reveal Codes window, or position the insertion point in front of the code and press Delete. You can also position the insertion point before the code and then press Backspace.

- There are two kinds of codes: open and paired. Open codes are contained in rectangular boxes. Paired codes are contained in boxes with points at the right (for a Start code) or left (for an End code). Open and paired codes are discussed more fully in the following section.

- To edit a code (so you can change the value it contains), double-click the code in the Reveal Codes window. To edit a margin code, for example, double-click the code. You are taken to the Margins dialog box, where you can specify a new value.

OPEN AND PAIRED CODES

Most character formatting commands are inserted as paired codes—they always have a Start and an End code—for example, a Start Bold and End Bold code. When you select text and then apply the formatting, you are inserting a Start code at the beginning of the block and an End code at the end of it. When you set your insertion point without selecting text and then apply the formatting, you are inserting a Start code immediately followed by an End code, with your insertion point between them. The End code is pushed ahead as you type new text and the specified formatting attribute is applied to the new text.

Some formatting codes, such as typeface and size, are open codes. If you set your insertion point and apply the formatting without selecting text, an Open code is placed in the document, and all text from then on takes that attribute. If you select text before inserting one of these open codes, WordPerfect puts the open typeface or size code at the beginning of your blocked text, and then automatically also puts an open code for the original typeface or size at the end of that text. Therefore, the text after the selected text returns to the original typeface or size.

Note

When you format a document, WordPerfect records your commands in the form of embedded codes. You can avoid formatting problems if you remember to check the position of the insertion point before you make a formatting change. Unless you want to remove specific formatting manually (by removing the code that causes the formatting–discussed later in this chapter), you don't need to concern yourself with embedded codes. You can, however, see embedded codes whenever you want by choosing View, Reveal Codes.

FORMATTING CHARACTERS

With WordPerfect, you can format your text with a variety of font attributes, such as font face, size, and appearance. The most frequently used features can be easily accessed via the WordPerfect toolbar and the Property Bar.

Tip #33 from
Trudi Reisner

Another way to format characters is with the WordPerfect Style feature, discussed in Chapter 11, "Organizing and Formatting Large Documents."

FONT ATTRIBUTES

Font attributes that you can specify include the following:

- Font Face—The font face is the typeface of text. Common faces are Times New Roman and Courier. Choose the font face that suits your work. For an informal flyer, you could choose a light italic font, such as Brush. For a more formal effect, you could choose Shelley or Caslon Openface.

- Font Size—Font size is measured in points. A smaller point size results in a smaller print; a larger point size results in a larger print. All text you enter in a new document that is based on the Standard template is in your printer's initial typeface and size. Most font faces are scalable, meaning that you can change the font size.

Note

Font size points and picas are typesetters' measurements used for measuring spacing, line thickness, and other font attributes. There are 12 points to a pica and 6 picas to an inch; therefore, there are 72 points to an inch. Standard 12-point text has 6 lines per inch—the same as a normal typewriter.

- Appearance—WordPerfect allows you to specify common appearance attributes such as bold, italic, underlined, and double-underlined. You can also specify attributes including outline (letters appear with a clear fill), shadow, small caps, redline (for new text), strikeout, and hidden (text that will not normally appear when the document is printed).

- Position—Text can be normal, superscript (text set slightly above the line—r^2 for example), or subscript (text set slightly below the line, as with H_2O).

- Relative Size—You can specify that text be normal, large, extra large, small, or fine. This enlarges or reduces the text proportionally to the base font size you have selected.

- Text Color—You can choose the color of the text. Text displays in color and, if you have a color printer, also prints in color; the display color and the printer color shade or tone may be somewhat different from each other.

- Shading—You can also specify the darkness of the color you have chosen. 100 percent black is black; 50 percent black is gray.

- Underline Options—You can specify whether the underline feature underlines spaces and tabs, or just the words.

You can apply formatting commands via the toolbar and Property Bar, or via the Font dialog box.

FORMATTING EXISTING TEXT

The easiest way to change the appearance of existing text is to select it, and then click the Bold, Italic, or Underline buttons on the Property Bar; or click the Font Face or Font Size buttons on the Property Bar.

Tip #34 from
Trudi Reisner

For faster formatting with font attributes, press Ctrl+B to boldface text, Ctrl+I to italicize text, and Ctrl+U to underline text.

When you point to a font face or font size in a pull-down menu on the Property Bar, WordPerfect shows a preview of your font selection in two locations. You see a Preview window beneath the Property Bar with all or a portion of the selected text. WordPerfect displays the font change for the text in the Preview window each time you select a font face or font size. You also see a preview of the font change on the page before you apply it. Selecting a font face is shown in Figure 6.9.

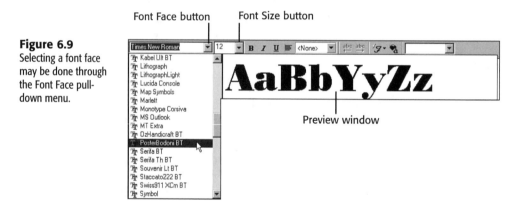

Figure 6.9
Selecting a font face may be done through the Font Face pull-down menu.

If you need more control over your text appearance, or to access features that are not on the toolbar and Property Bar, select the desired text, and then access the Font dialog box by choosing Format, Font. You see the Font Properties dialog box shown in Figure 6.10.

FORMATTING NEW TEXT

You format new text by positioning the insertion point, making the formatting changes with the toolbar or Font dialog box, and then typing the text. All text typed from that point on is formatted according to your specifications, until you change the formatting again. In addition, if you change the typeface or size, the old text starting from the insertion point takes on the new attributes you specify.

When you format text, you put hidden control codes in your document. You can see these by selecting View, Reveal Codes.

Figure 6.10
You can set a variety
of text appearance
attributes by using
the Font Properties
dialog box.

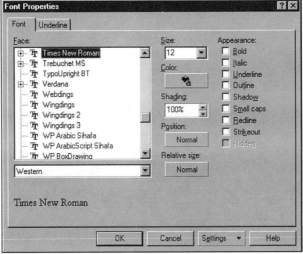

⚠️ *If you changed the font and font size of the text, and the text doesn't look right, see "Undoing Formatting Changes" in the Troubleshooting section at the end of this chapter.*

CHOOSING THE DOCUMENT DEFAULT FONT

To select the font that you want for all elements of a document, including headers, footers, footnotes, and graphic box captions, do the following:

1. Choose Format, Font.
2. Make your selections in the Font Properties dialog box.
3. Click Settings, and then choose Set As Default for This Document (see Figure 6.11).
4. Choose OK.

You can change the document default font for the selected printer while you are in the Font Properties dialog box. To do so, select the desired font, click Settings, and then choose Set as Default for All Documents. When you change the default font for the selected printer, that font becomes the default font for the standard template, and is the default font for all new documents created based on the standard template.

PART
II

CH
6

Tip #35 from
Trudi Reisner

An easy way to reuse font attributes you have recently used is by selecting the text to be changed, and then clicking the QuickFonts button. The last fonts you have used, along with their appearance attributes, are saved on the QuickFonts list; you can pick the one you want to reuse.

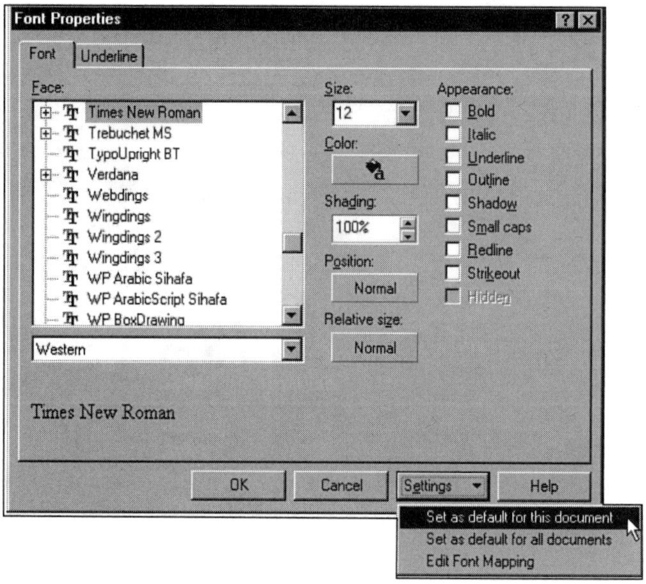

Figure 6.11
Set a variety of text appearance attributes by using the Font Properties dialog box and the Set As Default for This Document setting.

FORMATTING LINES AND PARAGRAPHS

Use Line and Paragraph formatting features for many of the appearance changes that you want to make in a document. For example, you can change line spacing, center text on a line, indent paragraphs, or change margins and justification.

Line and paragraph formatting features are available through the Format menu, and some additional ones are also available on the Property Bar and the WordPerfect 9 toolbar. If you're going to be doing a lot of document formatting, however, you might want to display the Format toolbar. It provides many other options for formatting the lines and paragraphs. To do so, right-click the toolbar, and then choose Format from the drop-down menu or choose View, Toolbars, check the Format toolbar, and click OK. You see the Format toolbar in Figure 6.12. The use of buttons from this toolbar is discussed throughout this section.

Tip #36 from
Trudi Reisner

Use QuickFormat to quickly copy text formats, as discussed later in the "Copying Formats" section.

ADJUSTING SPACING

You can adjust the spacing between lines of text within a paragraph when it suits your work, or you can adjust the spacing between paragraphs. Unless you change the defaults, or unless you're using a specialized template, you'll be using single spacing between lines and between paragraphs.

Figure 6.12
The Format toolbar provides buttons for many paragraph and line formatting tasks.

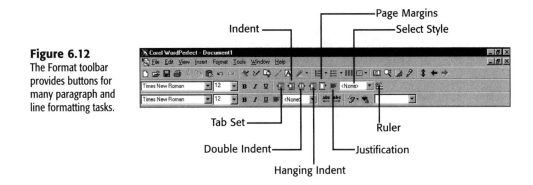

Page Margins

Indent ——— ————— Select Style

Tab Set ——————

Ruler

Double Indent———— ————Justification

Hanging Indent

LINE SPACING

Line spacing refers to the space between the baseline of one line of text and the baseline of an adjacent line of text, as shown in Figure 6.13. WordPerfect adjusts line spacing automatically to allow for the height of the largest font on a line (the line height). Enough extra whitespace is added to make the text readable.

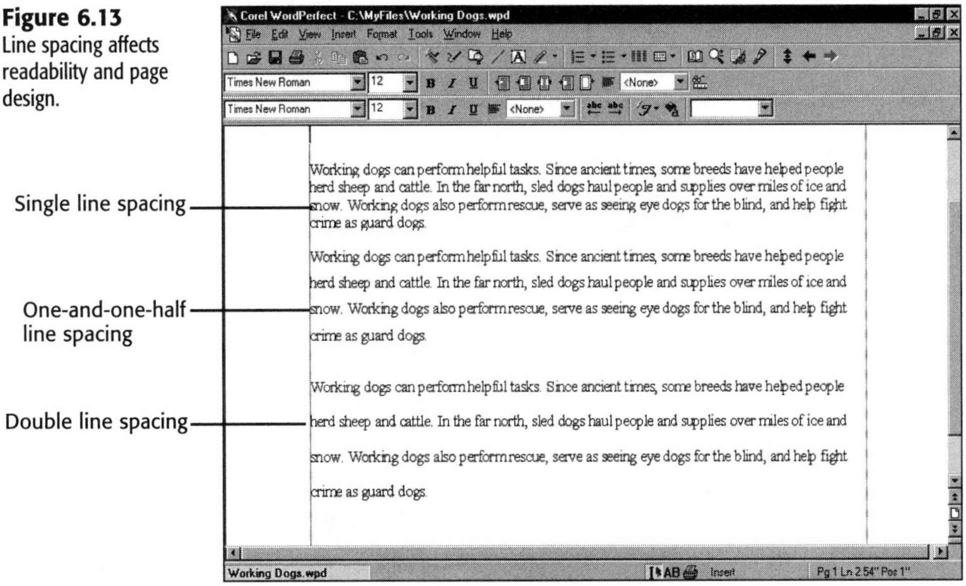

Figure 6.13
Line spacing affects readability and page design.

Single line spacing ———

One-and-one-half line spacing

Double line spacing———

WordPerfect's default line spacing is set to single spacing. When you specify a new number for the line spacing value, the current line height is multiplied by that number. If you choose a value of 1.5 for line spacing, for example, the height of a single-spaced line is multiplied by 1.5.

Note

Line spacing refers to the spacing between lines that are separated by automatic word wrap. Paragraph spacing (discussed later) refers to lines that are separated by a hard return (an Enter keystroke).

To adjust line spacing, do the following:

1. Place your insertion point where the new line spacing should begin, or select the text to which it should be applied.

2. Choose Format, Line, Spacing. You see the Line Spacing dialog box shown in Figure 6.14.

Figure 6.14
Change the line spacing in the Line Spacing dialog box.

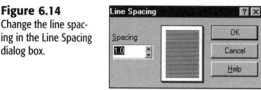

3. In the Line Spacing dialog box, enter a new value in the Spacing text box or click the up or down arrow in the spin box.

4. After entering the value you want for line spacing, choose OK.

Tip #37 from
Trudi Reisner

You can specify the line spacing to two-decimal accuracy (for example, .98 or .35) for total control of your document appearance.

Note

Line spacing is inserted as a paired code if text is selected and as an open code otherwise.

PARAGRAPH SPACING

Adjust the spacing between paragraphs rather than lines when you want to adjust the whitespace between paragraphs (wherever there is an Enter keystroke). In single-spaced text, for example, a blank line often separates paragraphs. Pressing Enter twice can produce this appearance. However, when you set paragraph spacing to 2.0 and press Enter (once) at the end of the paragraph, you achieve the same effect. Not only does this save keystrokes, but also you can ensure consistency in your document's appearance because all paragraphs will have the same spacing.

To adjust the spacing between paragraphs, choose Format, Paragraph, Format. The Paragraph Format dialog box appears (see Figure 6.15). Enter a new value for Spacing Between Paragraphs and choose OK. You see the way the paragraph will look in the sample box within the dialog box. Text with paragraph spacing adjusted to 1.5 is shown in Figure 6.16.

Figure 6.15
In the Paragraph Format dialog box, add extra spacing between paragraphs for readability.

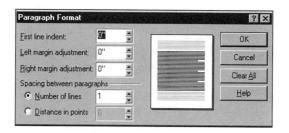

Figure 6.16
With paragraph spacing set at 1.5 in the Paragraph Format dialog box, you just press Enter once between paragraphs to get a result that looks like this.

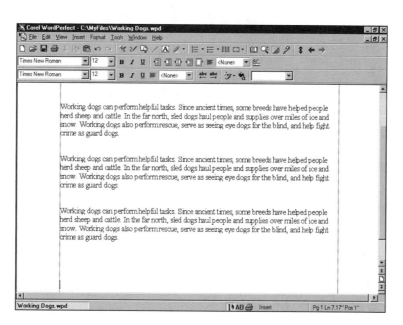

CENTERING AND FLUSH RIGHT

You can position specific text on a single line with the Center or Flush Right command. Centered text is centered between the left and right margins. Title lines are commonly centered. Text that is flush right aligns at the right margin; it extends "backward" to the left.

To apply Center or Flush Right, follow these steps:

1. Position the insertion point immediately before the text that is to be centered or flush right. (To center or flush right the entire line, position the insertion point at the beginning of the line.)

2. Right-click with the mouse, and then choose Center or Flush **R**ight from the QuickMenu.

→ For more information on using context-sensitive Help, **see** "Using Context-Sensitive Help," **p. 29**

PART

II

CH

6

When you apply Center or Flush Right, text following the insertion point is formatted with that feature. Therefore, you can easily have some text on the same line that is at the left of the line, another few words that are centered, and some others that are flush right. To do so, position your insertion point before the text to be centered, choose the Center command, position your insertion point before the text to be flush right, and then choose the Flush Right command.

| Tip #38 from | To create text that is centered or flush right with a dot leader (a series of dots) before it, |
| Trudi Reisner | choose Format, Line, Tab Set, and then select the Tab type, which would be Dot Center or Dot Right. |

The Center and Flush Right commands apply only to text on a single line. To make all text after the insertion point centered or flush right, use the Justification button on the Property Bar.

For more information on aligning text, see the later section "Setting Justification."

| Tip #39 from | To quickly set the justification from the keyboard: Press Ctrl+R for right, Ctrl+L for left, |
| Trudi Reisner | Ctrl+E for center, and Ctrl+J for full justification. |

INDENTING TEXT

You can indent one or more paragraphs to emphasize the text, format a long quotation, or create subordinate levels. There are four common types of indents that you can see in Figure 6.17.

Figure 6.17
You can emphasize text with four types of indents.

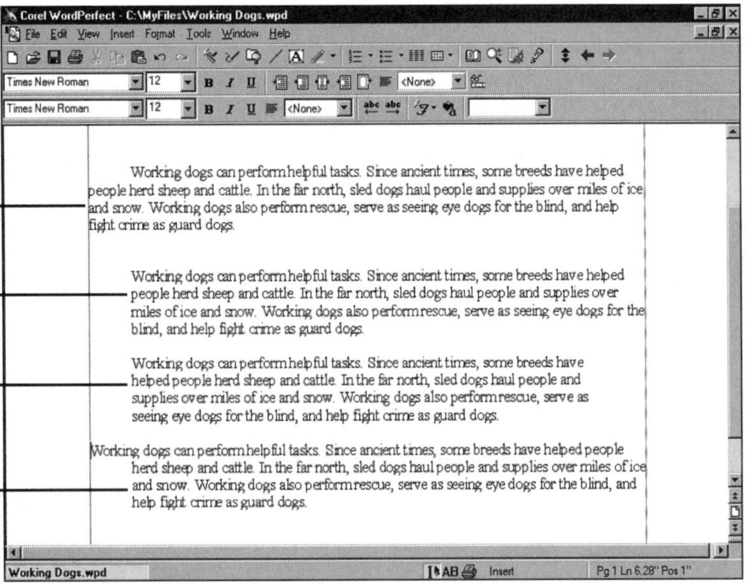

First-line indent

Indent

Double indent

Hanging indent

- First-line indent—The first line of text is indented one tab stop from the left, as when you press the Tab key at the beginning of a paragraph. This is most often used for double-spaced text.

- Indent—This is WordPerfect's term for moving the entire paragraph one tab stop in from the left. This is often used to set off points you are making.

- Double Indent—The entire paragraph is moved in one tab stop from both the left and from the right. This is often used for long quotations.

- Hanging Indent—The first line extends to the left margin, but successive lines are indented in from the left by one tab stop. This is often used in bibliographies.

All these indents affect the text from the insertion point through the end of the paragraph.

If you used a Double Indent to indent text, but the text isn't indented enough, see "Double Indenting Text" in the Troubleshooting section at the end of this chapter.

To create a first-line indent, you can press the Tab key at the beginning of each paragraph. You can automate this process by using the paragraph formatting feature; this is often done in conjunction with setting paragraph spacing. This ensures that all your paragraphs look the same and have the same first-line indent. Position your insertion point before the paragraphs to be indented, and then choose Format, Paragraph, Format. The Paragraph Format dialog box appears (refer to Figure 6.15). Enter a new value for First Line Indent, such as .5, and choose OK.

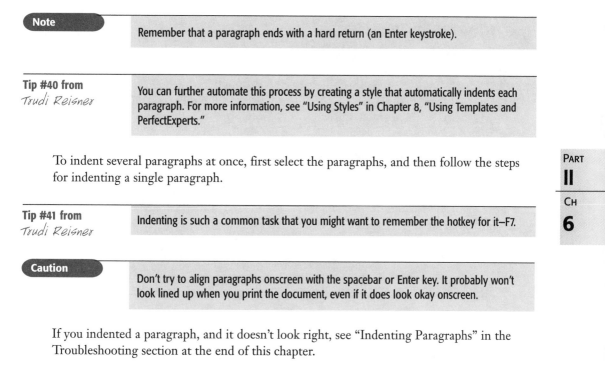

Note

Remember that a paragraph ends with a hard return (an Enter keystroke).

Tip #40 from
Trudi Reisner

You can further automate this process by creating a style that automatically indents each paragraph. For more information, see "Using Styles" in Chapter 8, "Using Templates and PerfectExperts."

To indent several paragraphs at once, first select the paragraphs, and then follow the steps for indenting a single paragraph.

Tip #41 from
Trudi Reisner

Indenting is such a common task that you might want to remember the hotkey for it—F7.

Caution

Don't try to align paragraphs onscreen with the spacebar or Enter key. It probably won't look lined up when you print the document, even if it does look okay onscreen.

If you indented a paragraph, and it doesn't look right, see "Indenting Paragraphs" in the Troubleshooting section at the end of this chapter.

PART
II

CH

6

SETTING AND USING TABS

Unlike indents, which affect all text lines until the next hard return, tabs affect only the current line of text. Tabs are used primarily to indent the first line of a paragraph, to indent one-line paragraphs, and to line up columns of text or numbers.

By default, tabs are set at half-inch intervals across the page. When you use a feature that positions text at the next tab stop (Tab, Indent, Hanging Indent, or Double Indent), the insertion point moves to the next tab stop to the right. You can customize tab stops to suit your work. For example, if you want less space between the bullets in a bulleted list and the text following the bullets, move the tab stop that aligns the text closer to the bullet. You can also set customized tabs to type in columns of text or numbers.

Note

By default, tabs are measured relative to the left margin, not from the left edge of the page. This means that when the left margin is changed, tab settings remain at the same distance from the margin. You can optionally set tabs in absolute measurements, from the left edge of the paper. This feature is used primarily to maintain compatibility with past versions of WordPerfect.

Another way to align columns of text or numbers is with a table. Tables make it easy to align text, and you can use many formatting features to enhance the appearance of tables.

→ For more information on tables, **see** "Working with Tables," **p. 240**

SETTING TABS WITH THE RULER

You can quickly set tabs using the Ruler. New tab settings take effect at the beginning of the current paragraph. If you have selected text, the new tab settings apply only to the selection. If you have not, new tab settings apply to all text from the paragraph the insertion point is in until a different tab setting code is reached. Be sure to position the insertion point properly (or to select the text for which you want customized tab settings) before you adjust tab settings.

→ For more information about displaying the Ruler, **see** "Displaying Screen Elements," **p. 100**

Tab settings on the Ruler are indicated by markers that hang down in the bottom area of the Ruler. The shape of the marker indicates the type of alignment (left, center, right align, decimal align) and whether the tab stop has a dot leader. Figure 6.18 shows the Ruler with customized tab settings for several types of alignment.

Figure 6.18
Setting different types
of tabs is easy on the
Ruler. Just drag a tab
to a new position to
move it, or drag a tab
below the Ruler to
remove it.

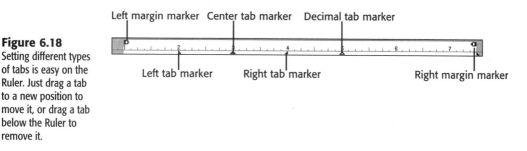

Important items to remember about setting tabs include

- Before you set new tabs, position the insertion point and clear all existing tab stops by right-clicking the bottom of the Ruler and choosing Clear All Tabs.
- To move a tab, drag it to a new position. As you drag, the original position is indicated on the Application Bar.
- To insert a new tab (of the current type), click in the Tab area of the Ruler beneath the numbered ruler scale where you want the marker to appear.
- To set a different type of tab, right-click in the Tab area on the bottom portion of the ruler and choose a type from the QuickMenu. For example, to set a tab that aligns a column of numbers, first right-click in the Tab area. Choose Decimal, and then left-click at the desired position on the ruler scale.
- To remove a tab, drag it below the ruler. To remove all tabs, right-click in the Tab area and choose Clear All Tabs from the QuickMenu.

SETTING TABS FROM THE TAB SET DIALOG BOX

The Tab Set dialog box enables you to set tabs precisely and to specify options that aren't available from the Ruler. Before you adjust tabs, be sure to position the insertion point in the paragraph where you want the new tab stops to take effect, or select the text that you want formatted with new tab stops.

To display the Tab Set dialog box, choose Format, Line, Tab Set, or right-click in the Ruler and choose Tab Set. WordPerfect displays the Tab Set dialog box (see Figure 6.19).

It is best to clear out old tabs before setting the new ones.

To clear a single tab setting, specify the setting in the Tab Position text box, and then choose Clear or Clear All to clear all tabs. To clear existing tab stops and restore the default tabs, choose Default.

To set a tab using the Tab Set dialog box, take the following steps:

1. Select a tab type from the Tab Type drop-down list.
2. Specify a position (in fractions of inches) that you want in the Tab Position box.
3. Choose Set.
4. Click OK when you finish working in the Tab Set dialog box.

PART

II

CH

6

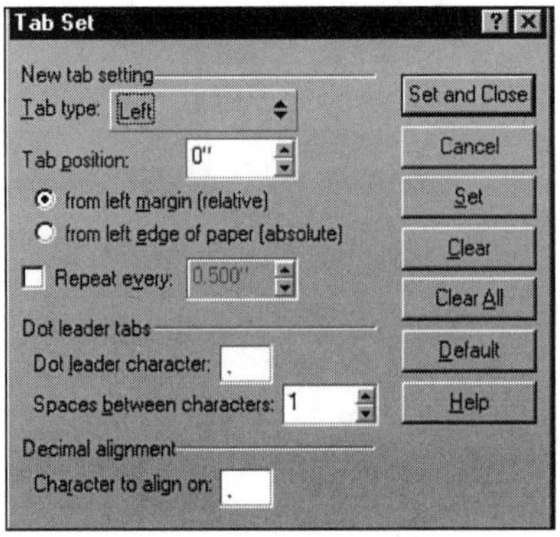

Figure 6.19
After positioning the insertion point, use the Tab Set dialog box to position tabs in precise positions. Positions in this box and on the Ruler are set in inches by default.

→ For more information on creating an outline, **see** "Outlining a Document," **p. 181**

→ For additional information on working with styles, **see** "Using Styles," **p. 186**

⚠ *If you try to adjust the customized tab settings for columns of text, but your columns don't line up evenly, see "Adjusting Customized Tab Stops" in the Troubleshooting section at the end of this chapter.*

If you set customized tab stops for columns of text and at the end of the document, your bulleted list doesn't look right, see "Restoring Default Tab Stops" in the Troubleshooting section at the end of this chapter.

SETTING MARGINS

You can change the margins at any point in a document. You may want to make the left and right margins smaller to add more room for text in columns, or you may want to set one-half inch top and bottom margins when you use page headers and footers. WordPerfect's Standard template uses 1-inch top and bottom margins and 1-inch left and right margins. Left and right margins can be set by dragging margin markers on the Ruler; all four margins can be set from the Margins dialog box or with the guidelines, as described in the next section.

→ For more information on headers and footers, **see** "Using Headers and Footers," **p. 129**

> **Note**
>
> To make your margin change affect all elements of the document—including text, page headers, and footers—choose Format, Styles. Within the Style List dialog box, highlight DocumentStyle and click Edit. Within the Styles Editor dialog box, choose Format, Margins, and set the Margins you want. Click OK. Click the Use As Default check box before you click OK to close the Styles Editor, and then click Close to close the Style List dialog box.

If no text is selected when you set left and right margins, changes take place from the beginning of the current paragraph. Similarly, when you set top and bottom margins, changes take place from the beginning of the current page. Margin changes apply to all following text until another margin code is reached. Alternatively, if text is selected when you change margins, margin changes apply only to selected text.

SETTING MARGINS USING GUIDELINES

You can optionally see gray lines in your editing window that show you where the margins are. They are called *guidelines*. You can turn the display of guidelines on and off by choosing View, Guidelines.

You can quickly adjust all four of the margins by using the guidelines, as follows:

1. Select text or position your insertion point as needed.

2. To adjust the left or right margin, drag the appropriate guideline to the desired position. As you drag the guideline, you will see the margin setting in a tiny pop-up window, as shown in Figure 6.20.

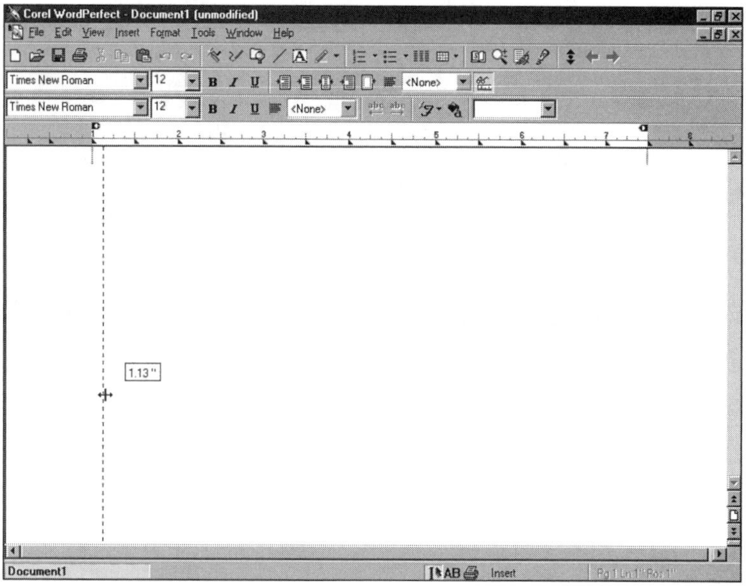

Figure 6.20
You can drag the guidelines to set margins. When you do, the margin setting appears in a small pop-up window.

SETTING MARGINS WITH THE RULER

If you prefer, you can also quickly adjust left and right margins by using the Ruler:

1. Select text or position your insertion point as needed.

2. If it is not already displayed, choose View, Ruler to display the Ruler.

3. To adjust the left or right margin, drag the appropriate margin marker to the desired position (symbols for the margin markers are identified earlier in Figure 6.19). The left margin marker is the outside marker at the left end of the whitespace in the Ruler. The right margin marker is the outside marker at the right end of the whitespace. As you drag a marker, its position is indicated on the Application Bar and a vertical dotted line marks its position.

SETTING MARGINS FROM THE PAGE SETUP DIALOG BOX

You can specify precise margins from the Page Setup dialog box by using the following steps:

1. Select text or position your insertion point as needed.

2. To access the Page Setup dialog box, choose Format, Margins. You see the Margins/Layout tab (see Figure 6.21).

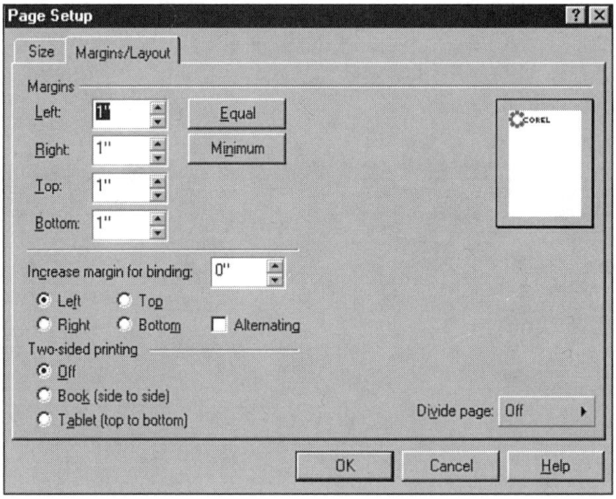

Figure 6.21
Specify precise margins from the Page Setup dialog box.

3. Enter the new settings in the appropriate text box areas.

4. When you finish adjusting margins, choose OK.

SETTING JUSTIFICATION

Justification is the way that text is aligned relative to the left and right margins on the page. The way you justify text can make the text easy to read, decorative, eye-catching, formal and sophisticated, or casual and flexible. WordPerfect provides five main types of justification: Left (the default), Center, Right, Full, and All (see Figure 6.22).

Note

Full and All both produce text that is aligned with both the left and right margins. The difference is in how spaces are inserted. Full justification inserts spaces between words; All inserts spaces between words and between letters within words. All also aligns all lines of text including the last line, which ends with a hard return.

Figure 6.22
WordPerfect offers five types of justification: Left, Center, Right, and Full are pictured here.

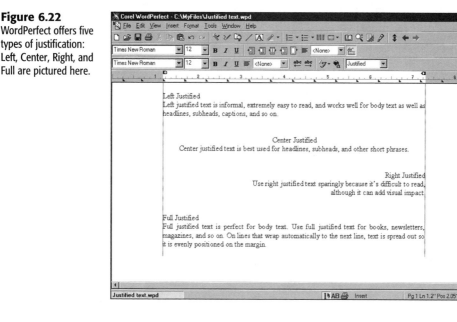

If you have text selected when you set justification, the justification applies only to the selected text. Otherwise, it applies from the paragraph the insertion point is in until it reaches another justification command. To set justification, follow these steps:

1. Select text or position your insertion point as needed.

2. Click the Justification button on the Property Bar, and choose the justification style you desire.

> **Note**
>
> If you want all your new documents to use a justification that is different from the default, change the default justification. Choose Format, Styles. Within the Style List dialog box, highlight DocumentStyle and click Edit. Within the Styles Editor dialog box, choose Format, Justification, and select the justification that you want. Click the Use As Default check box before you click OK to close the Styles Editor. Click Close to close the Style List dialog box.

If you use full justification and there are big gaps between words, see "Full Justification and the Big Gaps" in the Troubleshooting section at the end of this chapter.

COPYING FORMATS

QuickFormat makes it easy to copy formats from already formatted text without respecifying each format instruction. Suppose that you took pains to apply several font changes to a subtitle to make it look just right. Now you want to give the same look to other subtitles. Just show QuickFormat where to copy the formats, and it does all the work for you. When you choose to format headings, WordPerfect automatically updates all related headings formatted with QuickFormat. If you change your mind about the typeface in your heading, for example, you can change the font in one of the headings, and your change is instantly reflected in the others.

You can apply more than one set of QuickFormat formats in the same document.

To use QuickFormat, first select the text that contains the formats that you want to copy, or place the insertion point in the paragraph whose formats you want to copy. Next, click the QuickFormat button on the WordPerfect 9 toolbar, or choose Format, QuickFormat. The QuickFormat dialog box appears (see Figure 6.23).

Figure 6.23
Choose Headings from the QuickFormat dialog box to copy paragraph formatting as well as fonts and attributes. Choose Selected Characters to copy fonts and attributes only.

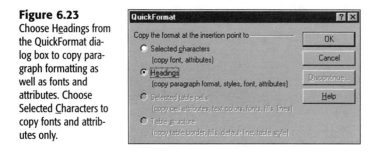

Select Headings to copy fonts and attributes as well as paragraph formatting. When you choose OK, the mouse pointer changes into a paint roller or a paintbrush, depending on whether you chose to format characters (brush) or headings (roller). Figure 6.24 shows you the paint roller pointer while QuickFormat is active.

Figure 6.24
Use QuickFormat to copy formats from one text area to other text areas.

Copy formatting from here...

...to here, using QuickFormat.

Paint Roller pointer

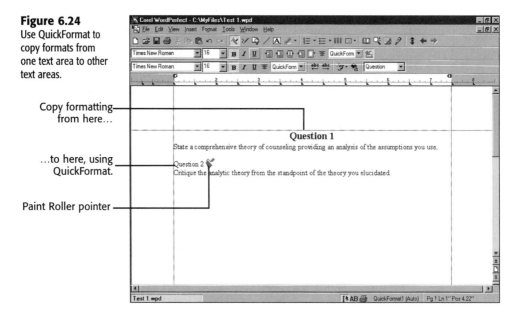

While QuickFormat is active, select any text to which you want to copy formats, or click in a paragraph to which you want to copy formats. Repeat this step as often as desired. When you finish copying formats, click the QuickFormat button to deactivate the feature. The new format is applied to all of the selected paragraphs and the pointer returns to its I-beam appearance.

If you accidentally copied formats to an extra place using QuickFormat, see "Copying Formats with QuickFormat" in the Troubleshooting section at the end of this chapter.

PRACTICAL PROJECT 1

If you have a large section of text in all capital letters, you can make it easier on your reader's eyes by using small caps instead. The Small Caps option is in the Appearance section of the Font Properties dialog box. First turn on the Small Caps option, and then type the text you want to appear in small caps. Figure 6.25 shows a product announcement in all capital letters and in small capital letters.

Figure 6.25
Make your text easier to read by using the Small Caps option.

PRACTICAL PROJECT 2

To draw more attention to words that are boldfaced, italicized, or underlined, you can, for example, show boldface words in red, italic words in blue, and underlined words in yellow. Use the Font Color button on the Property Bar to color your words.

PRACTICAL PROJECT 3

Sometimes you might want to create white text on a dark background, which is known as reversed text or reverse-video text. This feature is useful for optimal readability. Contrasting white text on a black background makes it easy to read; using a lighter background makes it difficult to read. To create reversed video, you need to use the Paragraph, Border/Fill and Font Color features.

To reverse text, select the block of text you want to display as white text on a black background. Choose Format, Paragraph, Border/Fill, and click the Fill tab. Choose 100% Fill and click OK to apply the black background to your text. Click the Font Color button on the Property Bar and choose White. Click anywhere to see the reversed text, as shown in Figure 6.26.

Figure 6.26
Contrasting white text on a black background improves readability.

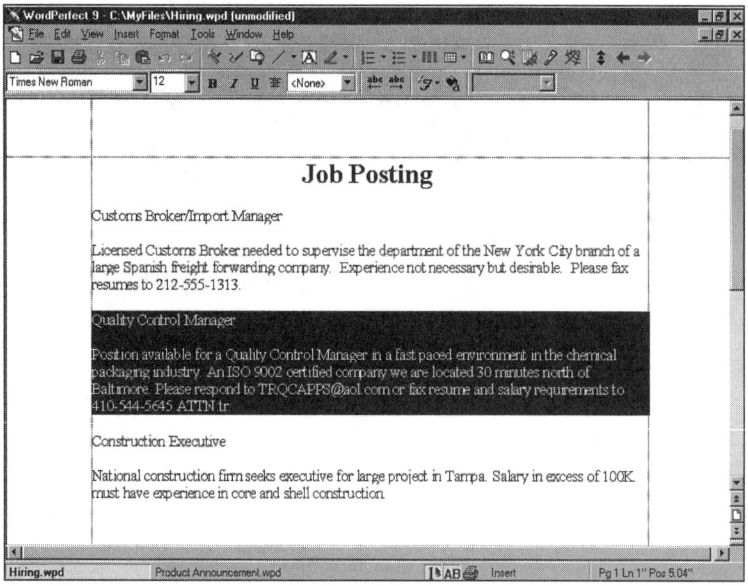

TROUBLESHOOTING

SCROLLING TOO SLOWLY

It takes too long to scroll through a document.

Maximize the speed at which you're working by using Draft view mode (open the View menu to change the view mode).

CONTINUOUS VIEW OF PAGES

When I scroll from the bottom of one page to the top of the next page, the screen takes a big jump and it's difficult to get a continuous view of the text from one page to the next.

Choose View, Draft to change from Page view to Draft view.

CHANGING THE VIEW MAGNIFICATION

I can't see all the text on a line onscreen at once.

Change the level of magnification with the Zoom button or after choosing View, Zoom. Experiment with 100 percent, Margin Width, and Page Width to see what best suits the situation.

UNDOING FORMATTING CHANGES

I just changed the font and font size of the text, and now I want to return it to its original format.

Choose Edit, Undo repeatedly to undo the changes.

DOUBLE INDENTING TEXT

I used a Double Indent to indent a quotation in my document, but I want the text to go farther in from the margins.

Position the insertion point in front of the indented text and create another Double Indent. This indents the text by one more tab stop.

INDENTING PARAGRAPHS

I indented a paragraph, but it doesn't look right.

Remember that you should use Indent only once at the beginning of the paragraph to indent the entire paragraph. If you used Indent again anywhere else in the paragraph, this may be what caused your problem. Either delete the paragraph and retype it, or remove any extraneous [Hd Left Ind] codes (choose View, Reveal Codes to turn on Reveal Codes).

ADJUSTING CUSTOMIZED TAB STOPS

I tried to adjust the customized tab settings that I created for columns of text, but now the columns don't line up evenly.

You can undo the damage with the Undo button. Before you adjust tab settings again, be sure to position the insertion point on the first line of the text that you want to adjust.

RESTORING DEFAULT TAB STOPS

I set customized tab stops for columns of text and now, at the end of the document, my bulleted list doesn't look right.

Position the insertion point at the end of the columns of text and restore the default tab settings (choose Format, Line, Tab Set, Default, OK).

FULL JUSTIFICATION AND THE BIG GAPS

I used full justification in my document, and now there are big gaps between words.

Try using All rather than Full justification, because All will put spaces between letters as well as between words. Another way to alleviate the problem is to turn on Hyphenation by choosing Tools, Language, Hyphenation, Turn Hyphenation On. For more information on using hyphenation, see Hyphenation in the WordPerfect online Help.

COPYING FORMATS WITH QUICKFORMAT

I used QuickFormat to copy formats to text in several locations, but after I finished, I accidentally copied them to an extra place.

When you choose Headings at the QuickFormat dialog box, it's easy to copy formats; simply click in the paragraph that you want to format. However, it's also easy to click inadvertently and to format text unintentionally before you remember to turn off QuickFormat. Clicking the Undo button easily reverses the damage, even after you've turned off QuickFormat.

CHAPTER 7

FORMATTING DOCUMENTS

In this chapter

FORMATTING THE PAGE

When you work with multiple-page documents, you may be concerned with the position of page breaks. You also probably want to use page headers or footers, and you might want to number pages. These topics can all be thought of as elements of page formatting. Page size is also an element of page formatting, although this topic can just as easily apply to a single-page document as to a multiple-page document.

WordPerfect's page-formatting features are flexible and easy to use. You can change the appearance of the page to fit your text so that you present the most professional-looking document possible.

WORKING WITH PAGE BREAKS

WordPerfect automatically divides your document into pages based on the formatting choices you make. These automatic page breaks are called soft page breaks. The position of a soft page break adjusts automatically as you edit a document and cannot be deleted.

Because it's often important to break a page at a specific location, WordPerfect offers ways to control where pages are divided. The simplest method for ensuring that a page break falls where you want it to fall, regardless of format changes, is to use the Page Break feature. A page break created with the Page Break feature is called a hard page break.

To create a hard page break, position the insertion point at the beginning of the first line that is to start on a new page, and press Ctrl+Enter, or choose Insert, New Page. All text following a hard page break automatically repaginates.

In Draft view, a hard page break appears as a double line across the screen; a soft page break appears as a single line across the screen. In Page view, soft page breaks and hard page breaks look exactly alike; each appears as a heavy line across the page.

Tip #42 from
Trudi Reisner

When you remove hard page breaks from a document, start at the beginning of the document and work your way toward the end of the document. When you remove a page break, all text from that position on repaginates automatically, and you can adjust subsequent page breaks accordingly.

Caution

When you use hard page breaks too often, your document cannot easily be edited because the page breaks wind up in the wrong position. Use hard page breaks only when pages should always end at the hard page break—at the end of chapters, for example.

A hard page break can be removed. To remove a hard page break, position the insertion point just in front of the page break and press Delete, or position the insertion point just after the page break and press Backspace. The Make It Fit feature is a good way to avoid using hard page breaks (see "Using Making It Fit" later in this chapter).

 If you created a hard page break, and have too many page breaks, see "Too Many Page Breaks" in the Troubleshooting section at the end of this chapter.

USING HEADERS AND FOOTERS

A header or footer is information that appears at the top or bottom of every page (or just on odd or even pages). You can save yourself a lot of work by creating headers and footers in multiple-page documents.

WordPerfect's headers and footers are easy to use and flexible. A header or footer can include one or more lines of text, automatic page numbers, the document path and filename, graphic lines, and other graphic elements, as well as formatting such as tables or columns.

The amount of whitespace at the top or bottom of the page changes only when you change the top or bottom margin, not when you use headers or footers. When you use headers and footers, there is less room on the page for body text. Soft page breaks adjust automatically to allow room for headers and footers.

Headers and footers are visible onscreen in Page view or Two Page view. Even though you can't see a header or footer onscreen in Draft view, it will print.

WordPerfect provides two headers, Header A and Header B, and two footers, Footer A and Footer B, in case you want different headers or footers on odd and even pages. Unless you're printing on both sides of the paper, you need only one header or footer. The instructions that follow refer to Header A, but are the same as the instructions for Header B, Footer A, or Footer B. To create Header A, perform the following steps:

1. Position the insertion point on the page where you want the header to begin.

2. Right-click in the top margin, and then choose Header/Footer; or choose Insert, Header/Footer. The Headers/Footers dialog box is displayed. Select Header A, if it's not already selected.

3. Choose Create. You are placed in a special editing screen for Header A (indicated in the title bar at the top of the screen). The Header/Footer Property Bar replaces the Main Property Bar that you usually see, and provides extra features for creating your header. If you're working in Page view or Two Page view, you can see the body text onscreen while you're working with your header. The insertion point is placed at the beginning of the header area, as shown in Figure 7.1.

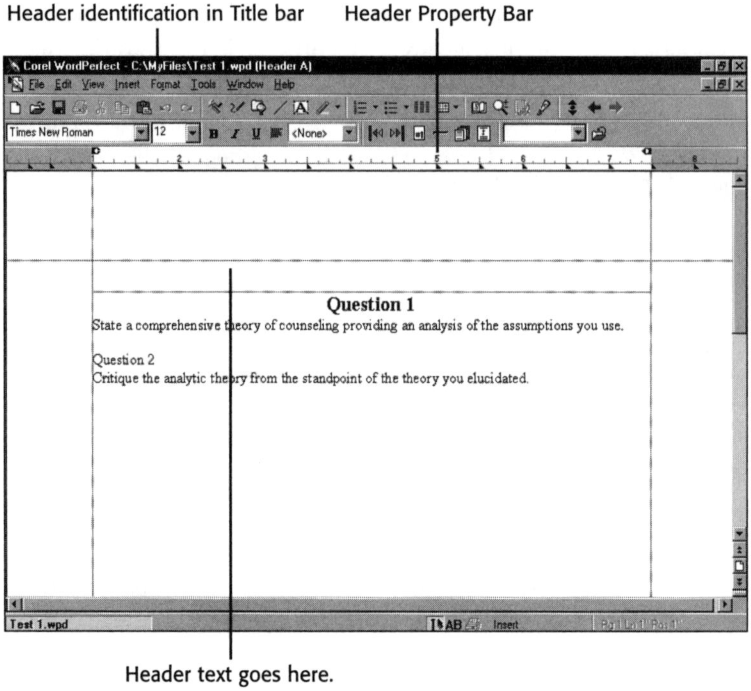

Header identification in Title bar
Header Property Bar
Corel WordPerfect - C:\MyFiles\Test 1.wpd (Header A)
File Edit View Insert Format Tools Window Help
Times New Roman
12
<None>
Question 1
State a comprehensive theory of counseling providing an analysis of the assumptions you use.
Question 2
Critique the analytic theory from the standpoint of the theory you elucidated.
Test 1.wpd
Insert
Header text goes here.

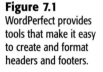

Figure 7.1
WordPerfect provides tools that make it easy to create and format headers and footers.

While you are creating a header or footer, you can insert a number of codes that provide information about your document:

- Choose Insert, Other, Path and Filename to insert the path and filename.
- Use the Center or Flush Right feature to place information appropriately within the header by clicking before the text, and then choosing Format, Line, Center or Format, Line, Flush Right.
- To insert the current date, choose Insert, Date/Time. You see the Date/Time dialog box. Highlight the Date/Time format you prefer. To insert a date that always displays the current date, check Automatic Update. Click Insert to insert the date in your header.

- Click the Page Numbering button, and then choose Page Number to insert automatic page numbers at the insertion point.

- Click the Horizontal Line button to insert a horizontal graphics line that extends from margin to margin at the baseline of text on the current line.

- Click the Header/Footer Placement button on the Property Bar to specify whether the header or footer should be on odd pages, even pages, or all pages.

- Click the Header/Footer Distance button on the Property Bar to adjust the distance between text in the header and text on the page.
- Click the Header/Footer Prev button on the Property Bar to edit the previous header or footer, if one exists.
- Click the Header/Footer Next button on the Property Bar to edit the next header or footer if one exists.

4. Use the WordPerfect menu bar, the toolbar, and the Property Bar as needed to format and edit your header.
5. When you finish working in the header editing screen, click the Close button on the feature bar.

Tip #43 from
Trudi Reisner

To edit a header or footer, switch to Page view by choosing View, Page. You will be able to see the header or footer at the top or bottom of the page. Click in the header or footer to edit it, or delete the text in it to delete it.

Numbering Pages

Although you can insert page numbers in headers or footers, you also have the capability to number pages with the Page Numbering feature. The page number prints in the top or bottom line of the text area. WordPerfect inserts a blank line to separate the number from other text on the page. In Page view, page numbering is visible onscreen. To suppress page numbering, see the later section "Suppressing Headers, Footers, and Page Numbering."

Choosing a Page Number Format

To use the Page Numbering feature, you must specify a format for the numbering. Choose Format, Page, Numbering. The Select Page Numbering Format dialog box appears. Figure 7.2 illustrates the Select Page Numbering Format dialog box with Bottom Center as the selected position. Dashes can be added on each side of the number by selecting the appropriate format in the Page Numbering Format box. Choose OK to close the dialog box.

Figure 7.2
Add page numbers to your document with the Page Numbering Format feature.

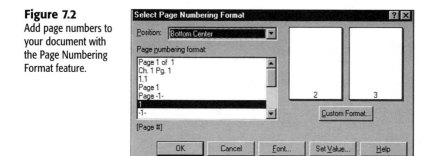

CHANGING THE PAGE NUMBER VALUE

By default, WordPerfect uses the physical page number as the page number value. The page number value is the number that will print, whether you ask for page numbering in a header or footer or whether you ask for it with the Page Numbering feature. When you have a title page at the beginning of your document, you need to change the page number value on the first page of body text so that WordPerfect thinks of that page as page 1.

This feature is useful for documents that will be interleaved with other documents—such as charts and maps—to create a presentation, annual report, and more. The pages of the WordPerfect document may end up being numbered 1, 5–12, 27–38, 74, for example, and the user can specify where to start numbering each time.

To change the page number value, position the insertion point on the page to be renumbered, and then choose Format, Page, Numbering to display the Select Page Numbering Format dialog box. Click Set Value to display the Values dialog box (see Figure 7.3). In the Page tab, set the page number, and then click OK to close the Values dialog box. Click OK again to return to the main editing window.

Figure 7.3
You can change the initial page number in the Values dialog box to account for title pages and tables of contents.

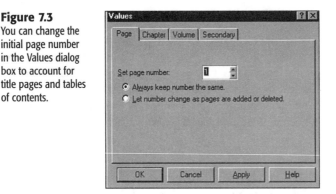

Tip #44 from
Trudi Reisner

You can also set the number of your chapter, volume, or secondary pages using this dialog box. This can be useful when creating large manuscripts or books. You can insert your chapter, volume, or secondary page number from the Select Page Numbering Format dialog box by choosing Format, Page, Numbering.

If you specified Page Numbering on the first page, and the number that prints is not 1, see "Changing the Page Number Value" in the Troubleshooting section at the end of this chapter.

SUPPRESSING HEADERS, FOOTERS, AND PAGE NUMBERING

To keep a header, footer, or page number from printing on a specific page, use WordPerfect's Suppress feature. A header or footer typically is created on the first page of body text, although it may be suppressed on that page. Headers and footers are usually suppressed on title pages at the beginning of new sections in a long document.

To suppress headers, footers, and page numbering, perform the following steps:

1. Position the insertion point on the page where you want to suppress the header/footer page numbering.

2. Choose Format, Page, Suppress. The Suppress dialog box shown in Figure 7.4 is displayed.

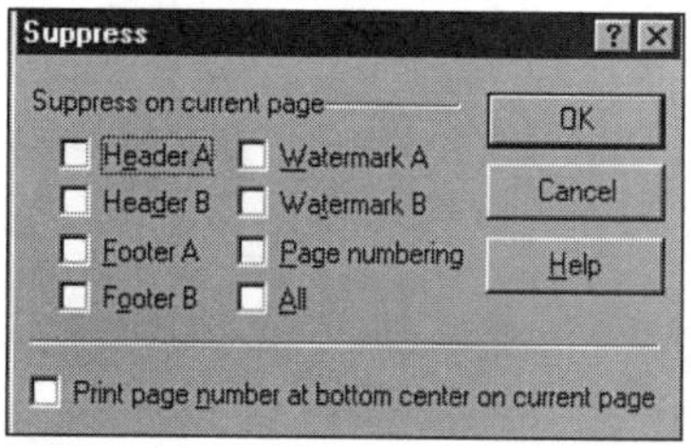

Figure 7.4
Suppress headers, footers, or page numbering on the current page in the Suppress dialog box.

3. Click beside the features that you want to suppress on the current page.

4. Choose OK.

> **Note**
>
> WordPerfect's Delay Codes feature provides you with a method for delaying the effects of headers and footers (and other types of formatting) for a specified number of pages. Use Delay Codes by choosing Format, Page, Delay Codes. Specify the number of pages to delay in the Delay Codes dialog box, and then choose OK. Insert codes such as headers and footers, and then click Close on the Delay Codes Feature Bar.

CHANGING THE PAGE SIZE

Whenever you start a new, empty document with the Standard template, you're using the Letter page size 8 1/2- by 11-inch paper in a portrait orientation. To use a different physical size or a different orientation, specify another page size with WordPerfect's Page Size feature. For example, if you need a lot of page width for a table with many columns, you could choose Letter Landscape as your page size.

> **Caution**
>
> Your printer must be able to use the size paper you select and print that size paper in the orientation you select, or you may get unpredictable results.

To change the Page Size, follow these steps:

1. Position the insertion point on the first page where you want to specify a page size.

2. Choose Format, Page, Page Setup. Ensure that the Size tab is selected. The Page Setup dialog box appears (see Figure 7.5).

PART
II

CH
7

Figure 7.5
Select your page defin-
ition in the Page Setup
dialog box.

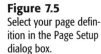

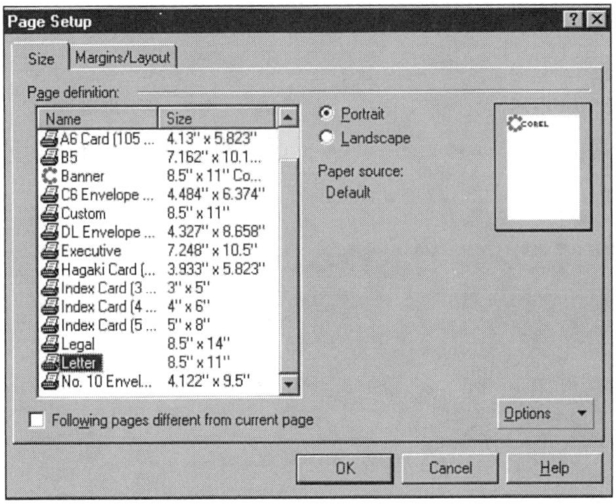

3. Select the paper size that you want from a list of predefined page definitions.

4. Choose OK. The selected page size takes effect on the current page.

Tip #45 from
Trudi Reisner

Sometimes WordPerfect doesn't have the predefined paper size that will accommodate the paper you're using. In that case, you can create your own paper size for printing on odd-size paper. You define the page width and length to add a new paper size to the list of pre-defined paper sizes. After you create the new paper size, you can use it anytime with any document.

To create a new paper size, choose File, Page Setup. On the Size tab, click the Options button and choose New. The New Page Definition dialog box opens. From here, you can give the new paper size a name, choose a type, and then choose User Defined Size for the Size. Enter the width and height in inches. Click OK to close the New Page Definition dialog box and click OK again to close the Page Setup dialog box. The invitation in Figure 7.6 can be printed on 5"×4" cardstock.

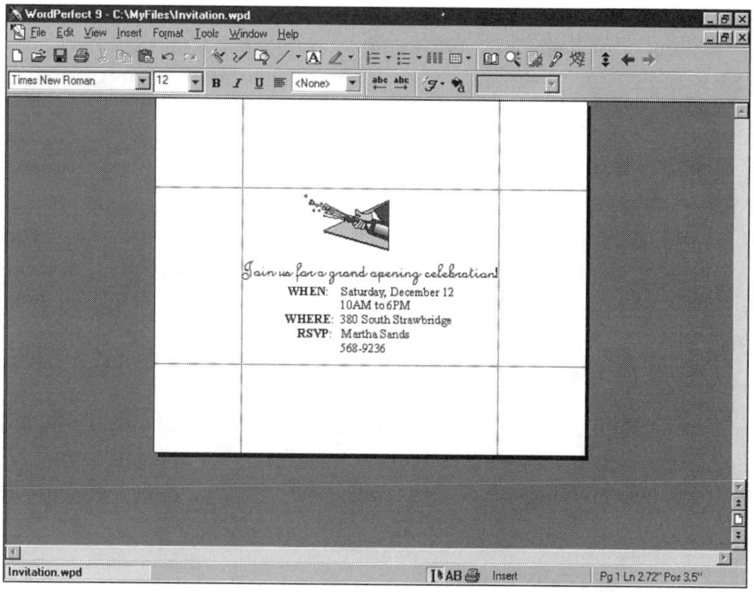

Figure 7.6
The invitation created can be matched with the paper stock you use in your printer(s).

USING MAKE IT FIT

It's easy to make a document fit on the page when you use the Make It Fit feature. Instead of making endless trial-and-error adjustments to margins, font size, and line spacing, let Make It Fit do it all for you. You get a perfect fit every time. You tell WordPerfect what kind of adjustments to make; if you don't like the results, Undo them and try Make It Fit with another set of specifications.

To use Make It Fit, take the following steps:

1. Select a block of text or position the insertion point anywhere in the document, and choose Format, Make It Fit. The Make It Fit dialog box is displayed (see Figure 7.7). In the Area to Adjust section, you should see Selected Area or Full Document.

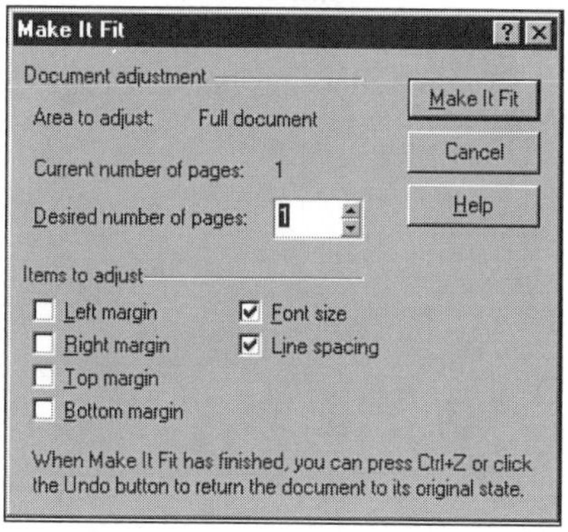

Figure 7.7
The Make It Fit feature contracts or expands a document to a specified number of pages.

2. Specify the number of pages you want the finished document to be in the Desired Number of Pages box. For example, to make a document that is just barely too long for a single page fit on one page, specify 1 as the number of pages to fill.

3. Check the options that you want adjusted in the Items to Adjust area.

4. Choose Make It Fit.

5. Check the results to see whether they are satisfactory. Remember that you can zoom back and forth from a Full Page view with the Zoom button. If you don't like the results, click Undo and repeat these steps with different adjustments.

PRACTICAL PROJECT

Generally, long documents require page numbering. Add your page numbers with Format, Page, Numbering and choose a position and page numbering format. Then, if you decide to add headers and footers, you can replace the page numbers with any text you want.

TROUBLESHOOTING

TOO MANY PAGE BREAKS

I created a hard page break, but now I have too many page breaks.

Be sure you're working in Draft view so that you can see which page breaks are hard page breaks (you can't remove a soft page break). Position the insertion point just in front of a hard page break and press Delete to remove it. Alternatively, turn on Reveal Codes so that you can delete the code (see the previous section, "Working with the Reveal Codes Window," in this chapter).

CHANGING THE PAGE NUMBER VALUE

I asked for Page Numbering on the first page where I wanted it, and the number that prints is not 1.

Unless you change the page number value, the number that prints is the same as the physical page number. Position the insertion point on the page that you want numbered with a 1, and change the page number value to 1 (after choosing Format, Page, Numbering, Set Value).

CHAPTER **8**

USING TEMPLATES AND PERFECTEXPERTS

In this chapter

INTRODUCING TEMPLATES AND PROJECTS

Every new document that you create is based on a template. A template is a master document that contains formatting codes that your new document will be based on. It can also contain standard text for the document, macros, styles, keyboard definitions, and anything else that any other WordPerfect document can.

When you create a new document by choosing File, New, you see a list of common documents. Projects you have recently used appear at the top of the project list.

These documents are based on different WordPerfect templates. Many of them also contain further PerfectScript programming commands that provide help in building the document and remember your preferences for previous documents.

Because these templates are often augmented with additional features, Corel has given them a special name. They are called PerfectExpert projects.

In fact, no matter what WordPerfect Office Suite application you are in, you see the same list of projects when you choose File, New from Project. In WordPerfect, the WordPerfect projects are initially selected, although in Quattro Pro, at first you see the Quattro Pro projects. However, you can select projects from any suite application, or see the entire list.

You can also access the project list by clicking the Corel New Project button on the Windows taskbar.

Note

Projects consist of a combination of templates with what were termed experts and coaches in previous versions of WordPerfect.

LEARNING ABOUT PERFECTEXPERT PROJECTS

At the heart of Corel WordPerfect Office 2000 is the concept that a suite is more than just a box full of otherwise unrelated products. Suite products need to be integrated. In the past, integration meant more work for you. Integrated products could *talk* together, but it was up to you to start the conversation.

Moderating the conversation required you to learn the nitty-gritty details of cross-application communication, such as DDE, OLE 2.0, or in-place editing. Just the terminology is enough to cause a headache.

Although most of us enjoy technology, we use software to get our work done, not simply for technology's sake. PerfectExpert projects reflect your need to do work rather than merely play with technology.

So what is a PerfectExpert project? It is an automated routine that does work for you. It takes you through the task, step-by-step, from start to finish. Some projects involve two or more applications—but to you it is application-independent. You don't need to know which applications are required. You need not start the applications at all. You simply choose a project, click its button, and the PerfectExpert does the work for you.

ACCESSING PERFECTEXPERT PROJECTS

You access the PerfectExpert in three different ways:

- You can click the Corel New Project button on the Desktop Application Director (DAD). When you do, you see a dialog box that contains all the available QuickTasks, shown in Figure 8.1.

Figure 8.1
The Corel PerfectExpert dialog box, which you can access from DAD, contains over 135 predefined tasks.

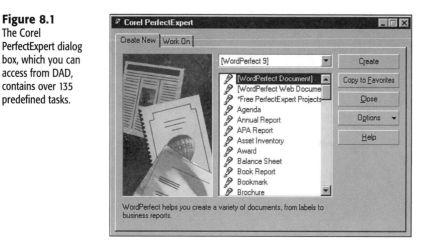

- You also can access the PerfectExpert from the Windows Start menu. Choose Start, Corel WordPerfect Office 2000, and select Corel New Project.
- Any time you choose File, New from Project in any WordPerfect Office 2000 application (for example, WordPerfect, Quattro Pro, or Presentations), the Corel PerfectExpert dialog box appears to help you start a new project.

Note

Unless you performed a complete installation of all WordPerfect Office 2000 components, some PerfectExpert projects may not reside on your hard disk. When you attempt to use such projects, you must insert your Corel WordPerfect Office 2000 CD into your CD-ROM drive, or you will not be able to use such projects.

If you try to use a particular project and it's not available, see "Installing Projects" in the Troubleshooting section at the end of this chapter.

UNDERSTANDING THE PERFECTEXPERT APPROACH

As you can see, the PerfectExpert dialog box contains two tabs: Create New and Work On. Click the Work On tab and the PerfectExpert displays all recent projects you have worked on, including WordPerfect, Quattro Pro, or Presentations projects (see Figure 8.2). Double-click any of these to resume work already in progress. You need not start up the application first; the PerfectExpert takes care of that for you. If you're not sure you want to open a work in progress, you can check the Preview Document box to see what the project is all about. You can even check the Work In Progress boxes next to the project names to remind yourself which projects you currently are working on.

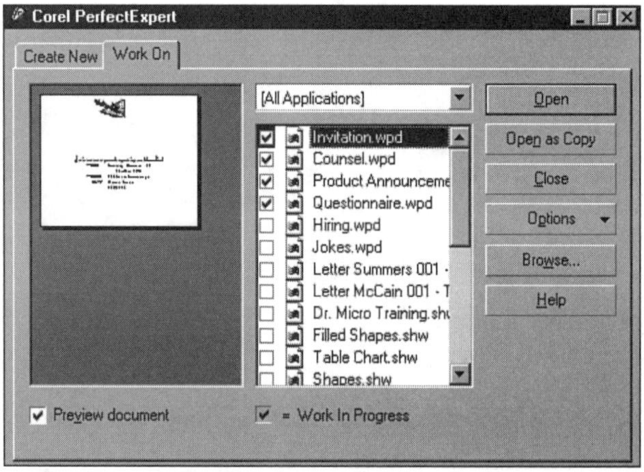

Figure 8.2
The PerfectExpert offers a quick and convenient way to resume work on projects in progress.

Note

The gray Work In Progress check box at the bottom of the dialog box does not serve any function other than to remind you to check a box if you want to indicate that it's a work in progress.

 If you want to pick up where you left off working on a project, see "Checking Work In Progress" in the Troubleshooting section at the end of this chapter.

REVIEWING PREDEFINED PERFECTEXPERT PROJECTS

A number of different projects are supplied with WordPerfect: projects related to business, education, legal documents, personal documents, publishing, and Web documents.

Some projects are further automated with dialog boxes that ask you a series of questions before constructing your document. That way, you can customize the document to your tastes and needs.

Click the Create New tab in the PerfectExpert dialog box to display the PerfectExpert's projects again. These are grouped by Category, such as Auto, Education, or Mortgage.

To display all the projects in a category, click the drop-down list (see Figure 8.3), click the category you want to see, and click the project you want to work on.

Figure 8.3
The PerfectExpert helps you with over 135 projects, grouped in task-oriented categories.

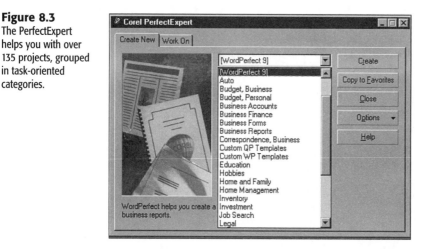

Tip #46 from
Trudi Reisner

Click a project and the PerfectExpert displays a brief description at the bottom of the dialog box.

The list of available projects is extensive—over 135 business and personal projects in all. Projects are grouped by category, as listed in Table 8.1. Some projects appear in more than one category to make it easier for you to find just the right one. In addition, you can create your own categories and group your projects as you please (see "Managing PerfectExpert Projects" later in this chapter.)

TABLE 8.1   PERFECTEXPERT PROJECTS IN WORDPERFECT OFFICE 2000

Category	Project Name	Application
Auto	Auto expense report	QP
	Auto expense report, monthly	QP
	Buy vs. Lease a Car	QP
Budget, Business	Ad Media Expenditures	WP QP
	Balance Sheet	WP
	Budget, Cash	QP
	Budget, Trade Show	QP
	Estimating Startup Capital	QP
	Income Statement	WP
	Statement of Cash Flows	QP

continues

TABLE 8.1   CONTINUED

Category	Project Name	Application
Budget, Personal	Personal	QP
	Retirement	QP
	School	QP
	Vacation	QP
	Wedding	QP
	Credit Card Log	QP
	Gain on the sale of home	QP
	Kiddie Tax Analysis	QP
	Life Insurance Needs	QP
	Maximum Loan Amount	QP
	Year End Tax Plan	QP
Business Forms	Agenda	WP
	Award	WP
	Balance Sheet	WP
	Company Equipment Receipt	WP
	Conference Room Scheduling	WP
	Daily Time Sheet	QP
	Employee Evaluation	WP
	Employee Vacation Schedule	WP
	Expense Report	QP
	Expense Report	WP
	Fax Cover Sheet	WP
	Fax Cover Sheet, Legal	WP
	Fax Log	WP
	Interview Summary	WP
	Invoice, Sales	WP
	Invoice, Service and Sales	WP
	Invoice, Service	QP
	Invoice, Service	WP
	Job Estimate	QP
	Legal Time Sheet	WP
	Purchase Order	WP
	Report	WP
	Seminar Evaluation	WP
	Telephone Message Form	WP
	Work Schedule	WP
	Correspondence, Business	
	Business Card	WP
	Fax Cover Sheet	WP
	Labels	WP
	Letter, Business	WP
	Memo	WP
	Newsletter	WP
	Press Release	WP
Custom	(Standard WP Document)	WP

Category	Project Name	Application
Education	APA Report	WP
	Award	WP
	Book Report	WP
	Bookmark	WP
	Exam Builder	WP
	Grade Schedule	WP
	Grading Sheet	QP
	Graph Paper	WP
	List	WP
	MLA Report	WP
	Multiplication Table	WP
	Report	WP
	Seminar Evaluation	WP
	Speech	WP
	Teaching a Concept Slideshow	PR
	Teaching a Skill Slideshow	PR
	Teaching and Training Slideshow	PR
	Turabian Report	WP
Hobbies	Bookmark	WP
	CD Cover	WP
	Exercise Chart	WP
	Gift Box, Tubular	WP
	Music Sheet	WP
	Recipe Card	WP
	Video Tape Log	WP
Home and Family	Award	WP
	Bookmark	WP
	Calendar, Monthly	WP
	Gift Box, Tubular	WP
	Gift Tags	WP
	Graph Paper	WP
	Hangman Game Sheet	WP
	Labels	WP
	Letter, Personal	WP
	List	WP
	Multiplication Table	WP
	Newsletter	WP
	Recipe Card	WP
	Sign	WP
	Tic Tac Toe Game Card	WP
Home Management	Asset Inventory	WP
	Home Improvements	WP
	Household Inventory	WP
	Menu Plan and Grocery List	WP
	Telephone Message Form	WP
	Vacation Check List	WP
	Video Tape Log	WP
	Vital Documents Inventory	WP

continues

TABLE 8.1 CONTINUED

Category	Project Name	Application
Investment	401K Planner	QP
	Asset Inventory	WP
	Basic Bond Valuation	QP
	Capital Gains and Losses	QP
	CD Switch Analysis	QP
	Deposits to a Sum	QP
	Mutual Fund Analyzer	QP
	Present Value Annuity	QP
	Present Value of a Lump Sum	QP
	Property and Estate	QP
	Real Rate Calculator	QP
	Real Rate of ROI	QP
	Statement of Net Worth	QP
Job Search	Business Card	WP
	Letter, Personal	WP
	List	WP
	Résumé	WP
Legal	Fax Cover Sheet, Legal	WP
	Legal Time Sheet	WP
	Pleading Paper	WP
Mortgage	7 Year Balloon Loan	QP
	Balloon Payment Loan	QP
	Closing Costs	QP
	Home Equity Comparison	QP
	Home Equity Qualification	QP
	Mortgage Amortization	QP
	Mortgage Qualification	QP
	Mortgage Refinancing	QP
	Mortgage, Added Payment	QP
	Mortgage, Biweekly	QP
Publish	Bookmark	WP
	Brochure	WP
	Business Card	WP
	CD Cover	WP
	Gift Tags	WP
	Labels	WP
	Newsletter	WP
	Recipe Card	WP
Retirement Planning	Budget, Retirement	QP
	Retirement Income Plan	QP
	Retirement Plan Contributions	QP
Slideshows	Annual Report	PR
	Award or Tribute	PR
	Budget Report	PR
	Business Plan	PR
	Company Meeting	PR
	Describing Alternatives	PR

Category	Project Name	Application
	Interactive	PR
	Market Research	PR
	Market Segmentation	PR
	Marketing Plan	PR
	Marketing Strategy	PR
	Multimedia	PR
	Persuasive	PR
	Product Launch	PR
	Project Proposal	PR
	Recommending a Strategy	PR
	Teaching a Concept	PR
	Teaching a Skill	PR
	Teaching and Training	PR
	Team Meeting	PR
	Welcome	PR
	Year-End Report	PR
Time Management	Agenda	WP
	Calendar, Monthly	WP
	Calendar, Year	QP
	List	WP
	Vacation Checklist	WP
Web Publishing	WordPerfect Web Document	WP

Tip #47 from
Trudi Reisner

Projects are listed alphabetically. However, recently used projects appear at the top of the category list so that you can access them more quickly.

TAKING A GUIDED TOUR OF A PERFECTEXPERT PROJECT

Enough about how PerfectExpert projects work—or do your work for you. Now it's time to experiment with a few projects. We'll take a guided tour through two specific tasks that automate common things you have to do.

USING THE MEMO PROJECT

Using projects can be an easy and even fun way to create great-looking documents, after you start using them. To demonstrate how easy they are, the following steps show you how to use a common project—preparing a memo:

1. Choose File, New from Project. The New dialog box appears as shown in Figure 8.4.

Figure 8.4
WordPerfect comes with projects to help you create many different types of documents.

When you select File, New from Project for the first time, WordPerfect installs the templates automatically.

2. Ensure that the [Corel WordPerfect 9] group is selected, and then select Memo in the list box.

Tip #48 from
Trudi Reisner

The first time you use a template, the Personalize Your Templates dialog box appears that enables you to enter personal information about yourself and your organization. This is discussed in Chapter 37, "Using Corel Address Book 9."

3. Assuming you have entered your personal information, after a few seconds, the formatted memo appears in the background, the PerfectExpert window pane appears at the left, and the Memo Heading dialog box appears, as shown in Figure 8.5.

4. Choose Fill in Heading Info, and Fill out the To, From, Date, and Subject boxes.

5. Choose Choose a Look, and select a style for your memo in the menu. The memo is created as shown in Figure 8.6, and you can add text to it and edit it as needed.

Tip #49 from
Trudi Reisner

You can also use the Address Book for this information in some projects, as discussed in Chapter 37.

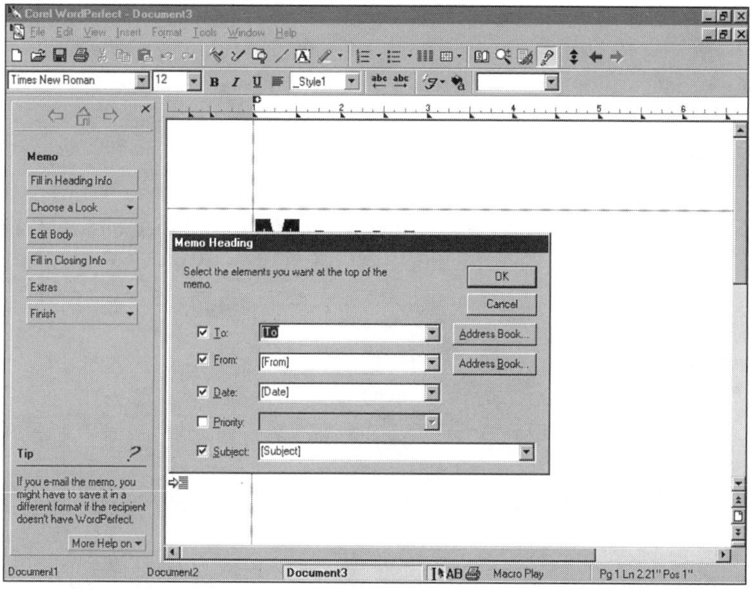

Figure 8.5
The Memo project allows you to modify various elements of the memo you are creating, such as the memo heading information in the Memo Heading dialog box.

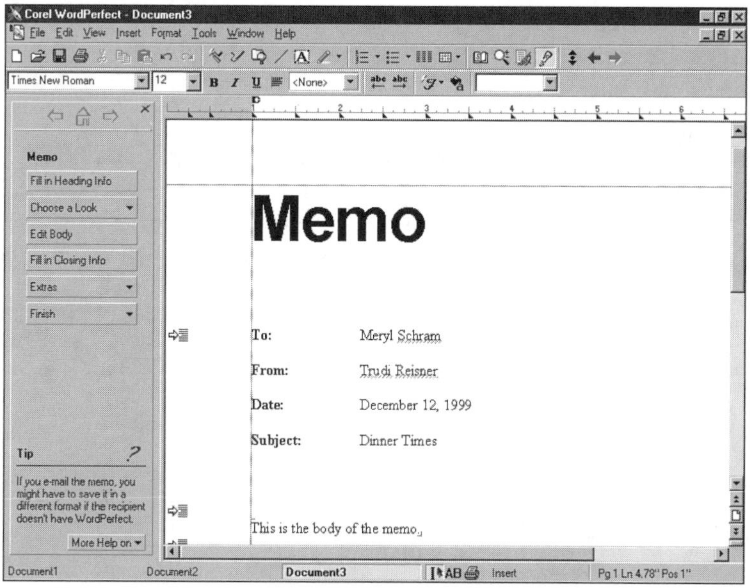

Figure 8.6
Your memo is created using the information you have provided.

6. Use the buttons in the PerfectExpert pane to complete additional tasks, such as editing the body; filling in the closing info; adding extras, such as a watermark, and header and footer; and changing the margins. Or finish it by spell checking, printing, faxing, converting it to an HTML document, or emailing it.

After you've used the Memo project, using other projects is simple. Choose File, New from Project, pick the category of your project, and then select the project you want to use. You are prompted for certain information, and then your document is created. It's that simple.

USING THE CALENDAR PROJECT

For example, creating a calendar is easy with a PerfectExpert project. To do so, choose File, New from Project. Select the WordPerfect group, and then choose Calendar. The Calendar Information PerfectExpert dialog box appears as shown in Figure 8.7.

Figure 8.7
Many projects use a template information dialog box, which enables you to enter information that will be placed in the document you create.

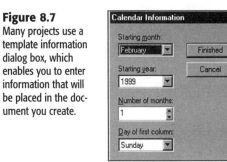

After you enter the information and choose Finished, you see the calendar, similar to the one shown in Figure 8.8.

Figure 8.8
You can create a calendar with a project.

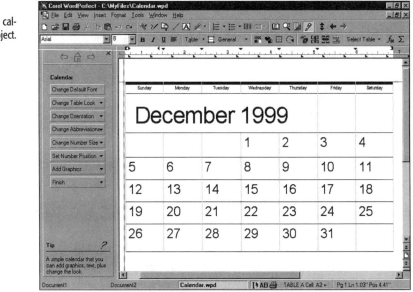

USING THE PERSONAL LETTER PROJECT

The Personal Letter project guides you through writing a letter from start to finish.

1. Start up the PerfectExpert by clicking the PerfectExpert button on the Desktop Application Director.

2. Click the Home and Family category, and then double-click Letter, Personal. Because this is a WordPerfect project, the PerfectExpert starts up WordPerfect for you.

Tip #50 from
Trudi Reisner

If you don't remember what category a project falls under, but you remember what type of application it is (for example, WordPerfect), you can choose the Corel WordPerfect 9 category, and choose the project from the lengthy master list of WordPerfect projects.

---

3. The PerfectExpert accompanies you through the task, appearing at the left side of the screen to coach, guide, and offer options (see Figure 8.9).

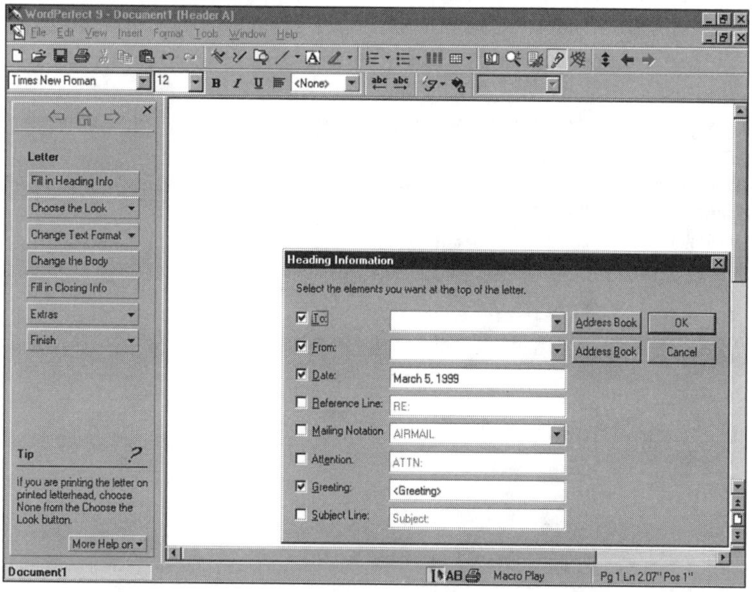

Figure 8.9
The PerfectExpert assistant appears to help guide you through your projects.

Note

Some projects automatically use personal information such as your name, your address, or your phone number. The first time you use a project that requires such information, you are prompted to enter your personal information. Fill in the requested information as carefully as possible because, after the first time, the PerfectExpert won't ask you again.

4. The Personal Letter project begins by asking you to whom the letter should be addressed. Fill in the name and address of the recipient, as well as the salutation you desire (for example, "Dear Prof. Steurer"). You also can choose such information from your address book, if you have one. Choose Finished, and the PerfectExpert inserts this information in your letter.

> **Note**
>
> When starting up a project, be patient. Even on fast computers, it often takes a while before projects are ready for your use.

5. Choose the type of letter you are writing. Of course, you can write your own letter, but the PerfectExpert can help you if you want. For example, from the drop-down list, choose Letters of Recommendation, and then choose Someone Attend School. Double-click or click Apply to insert the predefined paragraphs of information.

6. Some letters include special *fields* or areas needing custom information. For example, in the recommendation letter, you need to provide personalized information about the candidate you are recommending (see Figure 8.10). Click Fill In Entry Fields and the PerfectExpert prompts you to type the required information.

Figure 8.10
Click the Fill In Entry Fields button to automate the process of filling in form letters.

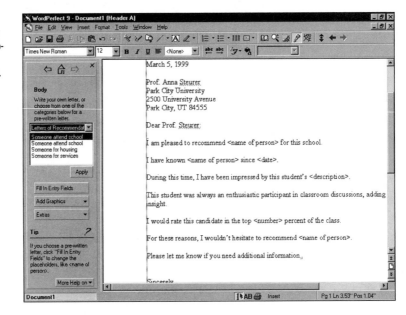

7. Add to or edit the information provided by the PerfectExpert. For example, in the case of the recommendation, only the outline of what needs to be said is provided. You add the rest.

Tip #51 from
Trudi Reisner

While editing the content or format of the letter, you can hide the PerfectExpert by clicking the Close (X) button at the upper-right corner of the expert. When you want to resume using the PerfectExpert, click the PerfectExpert button on the toolbar.

---

8. You also can change or add any formatting you want, such as font, graphic lines, margins, and so on.

9. Check the Tip section at the bottom of the PerfectExpert screen for suggestions on how to use the project, or click the More Help On button for specific ideas for creating a better document (for example, Punctuation of Letters). You may have to scroll down in the PerfectExpert to see the More Help On button.

10. Click the Finish button on the PerfectExpert to choose any or all of the following finishing activities:

   - Check Spelling
   - Print/Fax (print the document, or fax it to someone)
   - Make an ASCII Version
   - Make an HTML Copy
   - E-Mail (send the document as an email attachment)
   - Save

11. Close the document as you normally would (for example, File, Close). Note that the PerfectExpert reverts to a general WordPerfect document expert. Unless you want to use the expert, click the Close (X) button at the upper-right corner of the PerfectExpert to close it.

→ For more information on spell check, **see** "Checking Spelling," **p. 158**
→ For detailed information on saving files, **see** "Saving Files," **p. 37**

For example, you can make a thank-you note that includes the front cover with a graphic and a greeting, the inside cover message, and the back cover (see Figure 8.11).

Figure 8.11
Add graphics, greet-
ings, and messages to
a thank-you note.

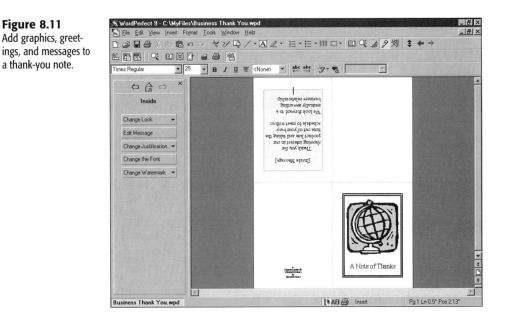

MANAGING PERFECTEXPERT PROJECTS

With over 135 available projects, keeping track of them is important if they are to be useful
to you. The PerfectExpert enables you to move projects from one category to another, to
create your own project categories, and even to create custom projects for your own specific
needs.

COPYING AND MOVING

To copy or move a project, first locate the project by opening the category where it is
found. Then click the project to select it.

Next, click the Options button on the PerfectExpert dialog box. A pop-up menu appears.
When you click or point at the Copy Project or Move Project button, another pop-up
menu appears with all the current category names. Click the category name where you want
the project to go, and the PerfectExpert copies or moves it to that category.

REMOVING AND RENAMING PROJECTS

If you mistakenly place a project in the wrong category, you can remove the project by
clicking it and then choosing Options, Remove Project. Choose OK to remove the project.

> **Caution**
>
> After you remove a project, you cannot restore it unless you have a copy in another
> category, or unless you install the project again from the installation CD.

⚡ *If you accidentally remove a project, see "Removing Projects" in the Troubleshooting section at the end of this chapter.*

To rename a project, select the project and choose Options, Project Properties. In the Modify a Project dialog box, change the Display Name or the Description as you please. Choose OK to save the changes.

CREATING NEW PROJECTS

Suppose that you want to create a custom business card and add it to your PerfectExpert gallery of fine custom documents. Follow these steps:

1. Locate and select the business card you want to use as a model (for example, Publish, Business Card).

2. In the Corel PerfectExpert dialog box, choose Options, Edit WP Template. WordPerfect opens up with the project in the WordPerfect template editor (see Figure 8.12).

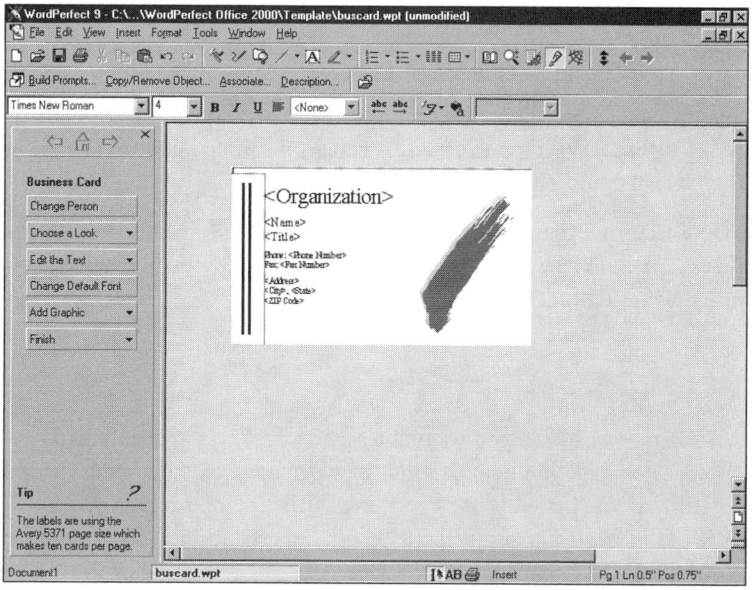

Figure 8.12
PerfectExpert projects are based on templates, and the WordPerfect Template Editor is a powerful tool for editing existing templates or creating new ones.

3. Make any changes you want to the business card, and click the Close button on the Property Bar. Answer Yes when asked whether you want to save the changes.

Note

If you are using a template from your CD drive, WordPerfect tells you that access is denied because you can't modify the CD. However, WordPerfect does offer to let you save it under a different name.

4. In the Save As dialog box, provide a new description for the project template, give it a different filename (for example, BUSCARD2.WPT), and choose a category for it to go into (for example, Custom WP Templates). Choose OK.

Now when you return to the PerfectExpert, you find the new Business Card project you just created in your Custom WP Templates category.

> **Note**
>
> You cannot create new Quattro Pro or Presentations projects, nor can you edit those that appear in the PerfectExpert categories. You only can edit or add WordPerfect-based projects.

CREATING NEW CUSTOM PROJECTS

You can create new custom projects by choosing Options, Create WP Template in the Corel PerfectExpert dialog box. The PerfectExpert takes you to the WordPerfect Template editing screen (refer to Figure 8.12).

There you can create an entirely new document, complete with all the formatting and text you want. When you are finished, choose File, Close and choose Yes. In the Save As dialog box, provide a description for the project template, give it a filename (for example, MYPROJECT.WPT), and choose a category for it to go into (for example, Custom WP Templates). Choose OK to save the project.

You also can use the Build Prompts option to create prompts for information when you use the template. For more information on advanced template features, refer to WordPerfect's online help (Templates, Prompts).

PRACTICAL PROJECT

How many times have you wanted to send a business greeting card to a customer or employee, and all you had on hand were personal greeting cards? WordPerfect makes it easy for you to create business greeting cards for appointments, follow-ups, thank-yous, and more. You can also create personal greeting cards for any occasion. Choose the WordPerfect 9, Greeting Card project to create a business or personal greeting card.

TROUBLESHOOTING

INSTALLING PROJECTS

You try to use a particular project and it's not available.

If you didn't perform a complete WordPerfect Office 2000 installation, all the projects are not installed. Insert your WordPerfect Office 2000 CD into your CD-ROM drive and install all the PerfectExpert projects.

CHECKING WORK IN PROGRESS

You want to pick up where you left off working on a project.

You can do two things to determine how to pick up where you left off working on a project. First, check the Preview Document box to see what the project is all about. Second, check the Work In Progress box next to the project name to remind yourself which projects you currently are working on.

REMOVING PROJECTS

You accidentally removed a project that you need to use.

Unfortunately, you cannot restore a project. If you have a copy of the project in another category, you can use that. Otherwise, you need to install the project again from the installation CD.

CHAPTER **9**

PROOFREADING

In this chapter

CHECKING SPELLING

The Spell Checker is the single most important proofreading tool you can use. No matter how long or short a document is, using the Spell Checker is well worth the time. Just think how you feel about the person who sends you a letter with a typo or a spelling error. Don't let this happen when someone else receives your letter.

The Spell Checker looks for misspelled words, duplicate words, and irregular capitalization. When it finds a word with one of these problems, it stops and offers suggestions. You can choose to replace the problem word, skip to the next problem, or select one of several other options for each word in which the WordPerfect dictionary finds an inconsistency.

You can also spell check your documents using one of WordPerfect's foreign language dictionaries (from Afrikaans to Zulu). From the Spell Checker dialog box tab, choose Options, Language and select a language from the Select Language dialog box.

WordPerfect includes two additional features that help you with your spelling. Spell-As-You-Go shows your spelling errors as you type; QuickCorrect corrects spelling mistakes as you make them.

USING SPELL-AS-YOU-GO

If Spell-As-You-Go is selected, spelling errors are shown to you as you type. As soon as you press the spacebar after misspelling a word, the misspelled word appears with a red wavy underline.

To activate the Spell-As-You-Go feature, choose Tools, Proofread, Spell-As-You-Go.

You can easily correct the word immediately by right-clicking it. You see a pop-up menu that provides alternative spelling choices, as shown in Figure 9.1.

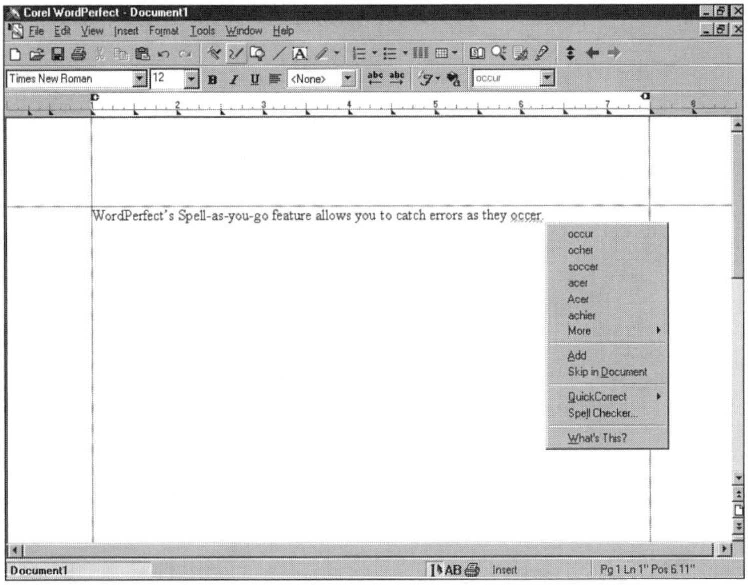

Figure 9.1
When you right-click a misspelled word, you see alternative spellings and other correction option choices.

You can use the following options for the misspelled word:

- Click any alternative word choice to replace the misspelled word with a correctly spelled one.

- Choose <u>A</u>dd to add the word to your spelling dictionary. It will never be marked as misspelled again.

Be careful in adding words to your dictionary. Don't add acronyms that would prevent the dictionary from finding a commonly misspelled word, and try not to add hundreds of words (such as names you'll use only infrequently) that can slow down your spell checking.

PART

II

CH

9

- Choose Skip in <u>D</u>ocument to ignore future occurrences of the misspelled word in the current document.

- Choose Spe<u>ll</u> Checker to start the spell checker (see the upcoming section "Using the Spell Checker").

If you want to remove a word from the dictionary, see "Removing a Word from the Dictionary" in the Troubleshooting section at the end of this chapter.

USING THE SPELL CHECKER

To start the Spell Checker, click the Spell Check button, press Ctrl+F1, or choose <u>T</u>ools, Spell Checker and confirm that the Spell Checker tab is selected. The Spell Checker dialog box tab shown in Figure 9.2 appears. The first problem found is both selected in the text and displayed in the dialog box, with a list of suggestions for replacement. Table 9.1 describes options in the Spell Checker dialog box.

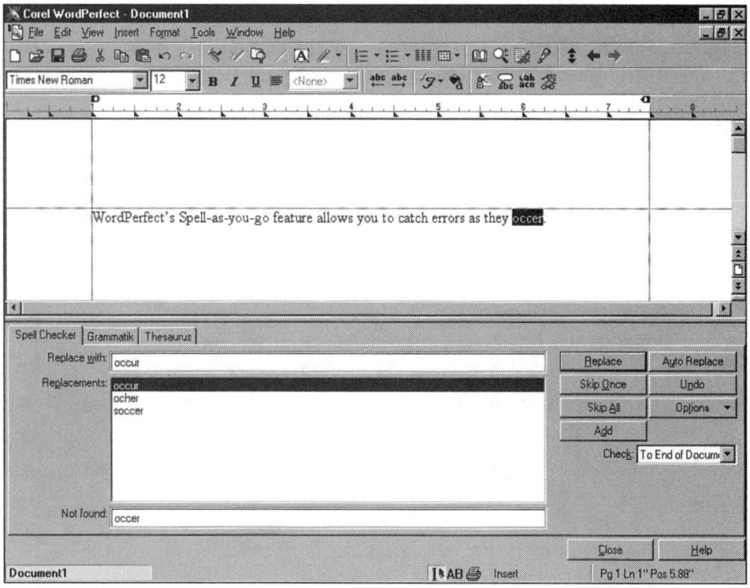

Figure 9.2
Select a word in the Replacements list, or enter the correct word in the Replace <u>W</u>ith box to correct the mistake in the text.

TABLE 9.1 SPELL CHECKER OPTIONS

Option	Description
Not Found	Displays the word in question.
Replace With	Displays the selected suggested spelling. If this is incorrect, enter correct spelling in this text box.
Replacements	Selects a word to replace the misspelled word. After clicking the correct word, it appears in the Replace With box.
Replace	Replaces the word in the Not Found box with the text specified in the Replace With box.
Skip Once	Skips this occurrence and moves to the next problem.
Skip All	Skips all occurrences of this word in this spell check session.
AutoReplace	Replaces the word with the word in the Replace With box, and adds the error and the replacement word to the QuickCorrect list. (See the following section "Using QuickCorrect" for more information.)
Undo	Undoes the last correction.
Add	Adds the word to the default supplemental dictionary. Use this option to add frequently used proper nouns (such as your name or street address) so the Spell Checker won't stop on them again.
Options	Customizes spell-checking options.
Check	Specifies the portion of the document to be spell checked.
Close	Closes the Spell Checker.

If the problem word contains a capitalization error, WordPerfect displays a Capitalization box instead of the Not Found box. Select the correct suggestion, or type it into the Replace With box, and then choose Replace.

If the problem word is a duplicate word, WordPerfect displays a Duplicate Words box instead of a Not Found box, and suggests that you replace the duplicate word with a single word. You can replace or skip to the next problem.

Tip #52 from
Trudi Reisner

If you select text before starting the Spell Checker, only the selected text is spell-checked.

Tip #53 from
Trudi Reisner

WordPerfect automatically replaces all occurrences of a word throughout the document unless you specify otherwise. If you want to selectively replace occurrences of a word, choose Options, Prompt Before Auto Replacement in the Spell Checker dialog box tab. Then you can choose Auto Replace, and WordPerfect prompts you for each replacement.

⚠ *If you have words with numbers in your document and you don't want to spell check them, see "Skip Spell Checking Words with Numbers" in the Troubleshooting section at the end of this chapter.*

USING QUICKCORRECT

QuickCorrect saves time and effort by correcting common spelling errors as you make them. QuickCorrect replaces the error with the correct spelling (or the correct capitalization) as soon as you move past the misspelled word. If, for example, you often type *teh* instead of *the*, QuickCorrect corrects the word as soon as you press the spacebar, or as soon as you press another punctuation key (such as a comma, period, or semicolon). In addition to correcting spelling errors, QuickCorrect can automatically correct other problems, such as double spacing between words. You can also program QuickCorrect to replace open and close quotes with typesetter-style quotes called SmartQuotes.

QuickCorrect has a built-in list of common misspellings and their correct spellings. You can add your own common misspellings to the list. QuickCorrect is just one of WordPerfect's many features that can be customized for the way you work.

To add items to the list of common misspellings and their corrections, or to change QuickCorrect options, choose Tools, QuickCorrect. The QuickCorrect dialog box is shown in Figure 9.3.

Figure 9.3
The QuickCorrect dialog box is used to identify the common spelling errors that will be automatically corrected and their replacements.

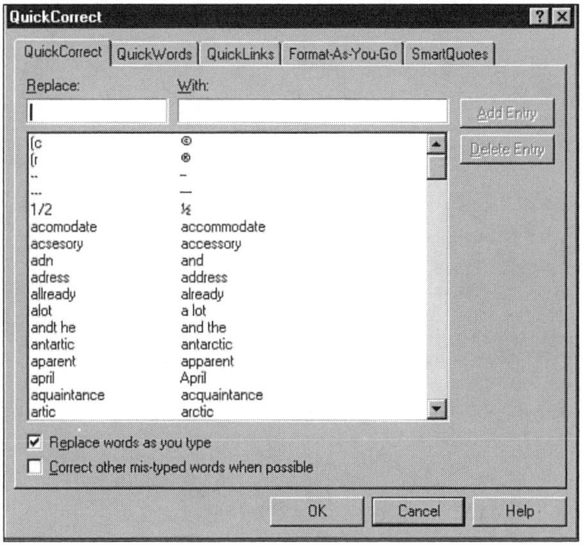

Add an entry by typing what you want to correct in the Replace box, typing what you want the correction to be in the With box, and then choosing Add Entry.

USING QUICKWORDS ABBREVIATIONS

If you like to do work efficiently, QuickWords abbreviations are for you. With QuickWords, you can define an abbreviation for words or phrases that you type often. As you type the abbreviation, it expands automatically—saving you time and keystrokes.

To create a QuickWord, do the following:

1. Type the expanded text for the abbreviation in your document.
2. Select the expanded text.
3. Choose Tools, QuickWords. You see the QuickWords tab of the QuickCorrect dialog box shown in Figure 9.4.

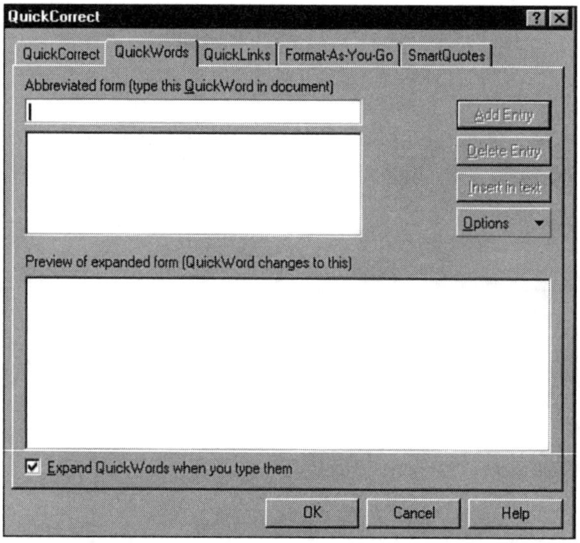

Figure 9.4
Add abbreviations for frequently typed words with QuickWords.

4. Type the abbreviation in the Abbreviated Form (Type This QuickWord in Document) list box.
5. Choose Add Entry. You return to your document, and the abbreviation is added to the QuickWords list.

To use your new abbreviation, just type it in the document.

Tip #54 from
Trudi Reisner

Sometimes, short abbreviations, such as b, expand when you don't want them to. To avoid this, precede them with a period—such as .b—because this letter combination doesn't usually occur in documents.

You can easily delete or rename a QuickWord. To do so, access the QuickWords tab of the QuickCorrect dialog box by choosing Tools, QuickWords. Then do the following:

- To delete a QuickWord abbreviation, highlight it, and then click Delete Entry.
- To rename it, choose Options, Rename Entry, and then type the new name in the Rename QuickWord dialog box and click OK.

USING THE THESAURUS

WordPerfect's Thesaurus can help you improve your composition skills. When you can't think of the word that means exactly what you want to say, or you think that you've used the same word too often, let the Thesaurus help you. The Thesaurus supplies a variety of alternatives (synonyms and antonyms) for the word you're looking up. You can choose the word you want from the list of alternatives and ask the Thesaurus to provide a replacement.

If you want to look up a word in a foreign language, WordPerfect provides many foreign language dictionaries (from Afrikaans to Zulu) for use with Thesaurus. From the Thesaurus dialog box tab, choose Options, Language and select a language from the Select Language dialog box.

To find a synonym for a word:

1. Place the insertion point in the word.
2. Choose Tools, Thesaurus or press Alt+F1. The Thesaurus dialog box tab appears, as shown in Figure 9.5.

Figure 9.5
Find alternative words or definitions with the Thesaurus.

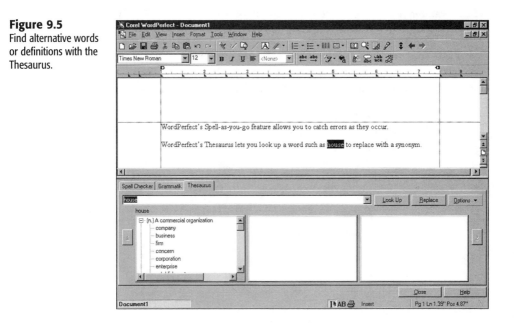

If available, synonyms and antonyms for the word appear in the leftmost column. The alternatives are divided into categories, such as Synonym, Related Words, and Antonym. (Use the scrollbars along each side of the box to see alternatives that are not visible.) Scroll through this box to view alternative definitions.

3. To look up synonyms for the displayed alternatives, double-click them.

4. Select the replacement you want to use, and then choose Replace. If you decide not to make a replacement, choose Close.

If you want to go back to the original word you looked up in the Thesaurus, see "Returning to the Original Word You Looked Up" in the Troubleshooting section at the end of this chapter.

If you're already using the Thesaurus and want to look up a different word from dialog box, see "Looking Up a Different Word from the Thesaurus Dialog Box" in the Troubleshooting section at the end of this chapter.

CHECKING GRAMMAR

Grammatik is yet another proofreading feature that WordPerfect provides for you. Grammatik is a built-in grammar checker that checks your document for correct grammar, style, punctuation, and word usage, and thus catches many errors that are bypassed by the Spell Checker. Grammatik checks both grammar and spelling; so you actually take care of grammar problems and spelling problems all at once.

Even if you don't think you have problems with your writing style, Grammatik may help you. When Grammatik points out a potential problem and explains the logic behind the problem, you may realize that its suggestions offer real improvement.

When Grammatik reports a potential grammar problem, you can review the error and suggestion, and then decide whether to change the text.

Grammatik lets you check for grammar errors in a foreign language with any of WordPerfect's foreign language dictionaries. From the Grammatik dialog box tab, choose Options, Language and select a language from the Select Language dialog box.

To proofread your document with Grammatik, choose Tools, Grammatik or press Alt+Shift+F1. Proofreading begins and the first item for review brings up the Grammatik dialog box tab, as shown in Figure 9.6.

Figure 9.6
Grammatik checks your word usage, punctuation, and sentence structure, as well as your spelling.

Tip #55 from
Trudi Reisner

If Grammar-As-You-Go is selected, grammar errors are shown to you as you type. As soon as you press the spacebar after making a grammar error, the error in the sentence appears with a blue wavy underline.

To activate the Grammar-As-You-Go feature, choose Tools, Proofread, Grammar-As-You-Go.

You can easily correct the grammar error immediately by right-clicking it. You see a pop-up menu that provides a suggestion, and the Skip option to ignore the grammar error.

CORRECTING ERRORS

When Grammatik stops on a problem, you see information in the four boxes shown previously in Figure 9.6. The dialog box is dynamic, so the boxes and buttons change slightly depending on the error that is found:

- The Replacements box shows choices for a new suggested word or phrase.
- The New Sentence box shows the new sentence as it will look.
- The bottom box shows information on the grammatical rule that is being applied. This box changes depending on the error found.
- The Check box shows you the area of the document that is being checked.

When Grammatik finds an error, you can respond with the options described in Table 9.2.

TABLE 9.2	GRAMMATIK OPTIONS
Option	**Description**
Resume	This option appears after you pause Grammatik to edit the document. Click Resume to resume proofreading.
Replace	Replace the problem word or phrase with the suggested replacement that is listed in the New Sentence box.
Skip Once	Ignore the highlighted problem and move on to the next problem.
Skip All	Ignore the highlighted problem for the rest of this proofreading session.

continues

PART

II

CH

9

TABLE 9.2   CONTINUED

Option	Description
Turn Off	Turn off the current rule.
Add	Add the word to the selected dictionary.
Auto Replace	Add the misspelled word and its replacement to the QuickCorrect list.
Undo	Undo your last replacement.
Options	Change Grammatik options, including the checking style.
Close	End the proofreading session.

In some cases, the grammatical problem might require manual editing. When this occurs, click in the document window and, using the scrollbar if necessary, edit the problem in the document window. When you finish your manual editing, choose Resume on the Grammatik tab.

Tip #56 from	If you want to ignore spelling errors while checking grammar, choose Options, Suggest
Trudi Reisner	Spelling Replacements to turn off the option in the Grammatik dialog box.

CHANGING THE CHECKING STYLE

The Grammatik checking style determines what is identified as a potential problem. For example, in a formal checking style, a contraction (such as won't) is identified as a potential problem. You can change the checking style to one that's best for your work.

To change the checking style for this session and future sessions:

1. Choose Options from the Grammatik dialog box.

2. Choose Checking Styles. You see the Checking Styles dialog box in Figure 9.7.

Figure 9.7
Choose the checking style most appropriate for your writing style and the style of the document being checked.

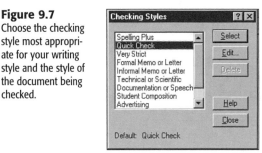

3. To examine the rules for any style or to edit the style, select the checking style and choose Edit. You see the Edit Checking Styles dialog box shown in Figure 9.8.

Figure 9.8
Each editing style has different rules that are applied to the text being checked.

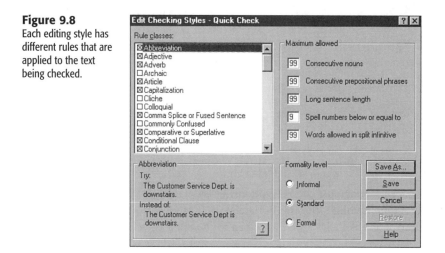

4. In the Edit Checking Styles dialog box, you can see which rule classes are selected for the style and other rules that apply to the style. To edit the style:
   • Check or uncheck the rule classes you want to use.
   • You may also select the numbers in any of the boxes in the Maximum Allowed section and type in new numbers.
   • Click the button of the Formality Level based on the type of document being checked and your writing style.

5. Save your changes with Save (to keep the same style name) or with Save As (to give the edited style a new name). You return to the Checking Styles dialog box.

6. Choose Close to return to the Grammatik tab.

If you get frustrated when Grammatik stops on contractions (won't, doesn't), see "Turning Off the Contractions Grammar Rule" in the Troubleshooting section at the end of this chapter.

ANALYZING YOUR WRITING

Grammatik can analyze your writing in a number of ways. If you choose Options, Analysis from the Grammatik tab, you can choose to parse the selected sentence, show which part of speech each word in the selected sentence is, or show how many words, sentences, and so on are in your document. You can show the flagged rules in your document, which identify potential errors. You can even compare the readability of your document to an IRS form, a Hemingway short story, or the Gettysburg Address.

Tip #57 from
Trudi Reisner

To view another set of statistics about your document, use File, Properties, and choose the Information tab. The document information tells you the number of characters, words, sentences, lines, paragraphs, and pages, average word length, average words per sentence, and maximum words per sentence in your document.

→ For more information on customizing a document summary, **see** "Customizing Document Summaries," **p. 312**

TROUBLESHOOTING

REMOVING A WORD FROM THE DICTIONARY

I want to remove a word that I inadvertently added to my dictionary.

From the Spell Checker dialog box, choose Options, User Word Lists. Highlight the appropriate word list, and then highlight the appropriate entry in the Word List Contents group. Choose Delete Entry, and then click Close to return to the Spell Checker dialog box.

SKIP SPELL CHECKING WORDS WITH NUMBERS

I have a lot of words that contain numbers, such as measurements, in my document. I want the Spell Checker to skip these words.

Choose Options from the Spell Checker dialog box, and then deselect Check Words with Numbers.

RETURNING TO THE ORIGINAL WORD YOU LOOKED UP

I looked up several meanings, and now I want to go back to the original word I looked up in the Thesaurus.

Use the Replace With drop-down list to see the previous words you have looked up, and then select the original word.

LOOKING UP A DIFFERENT WORD FROM THE THESAURUS DIALOG BOX

While I was using the Thesaurus, I thought of a different word that I wanted to look up. Can I do it without closing the Thesaurus and typing the word into the document?

Type the word that you want to look up in the Replace With box, and then choose Look Up.

TURNING OFF THE CONTRACTIONS GRAMMAR RULE

Grammatik keeps stopping on contractions (won't, you're, and so on) and I want it to skip them.

You can either change the checking style to a less formal style, or you can turn off the rule with the Turn Off button located on the Grammatik tab.

PRINTING

In this chapter

PRINTING YOUR WORK

Whether you use WordPerfect to create simple documents or desktop publishing masterpieces, printing is a task that you perform often. Because you are working in a WYSIWYG environment, what you print is not the mystery it was a few short years ago. If you're working in Draft view, you can see almost everything just as it will print. You can click the Page/Zoom Full button to get a quick look at a full page in Page view. Alternatively, you can use the View menu to switch to Page view.

Print Preview is like looking through the lens of a camera to see what you're going to photograph. With Print Preview, you see document pages onscreen as they will appear printed on paper, including page numbers, headers, footers, fonts, font sizes and styles, orientation, vertical alignment, and margins. Previewing your document is an excellent way to catch formatting problems, such as awkward margins and spacing inconsistencies.

PREVIEWING A DOCUMENT

To preview a document, choose File, Print Preview. The Print Preview window is displayed, as shown in Figure 10.1.

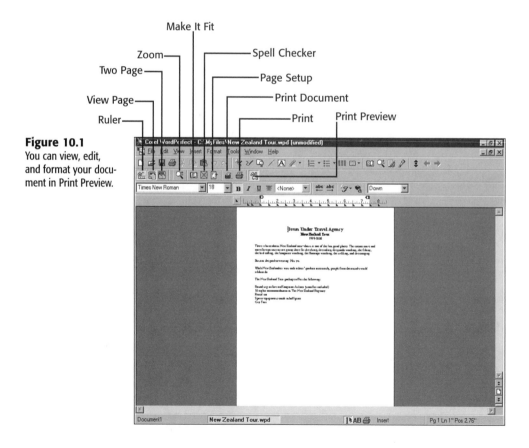

Figure 10.1
You can view, edit, and format your document in Print Preview.

You can edit your document in Print Preview as you would in any other view. Type in the document to insert text, use Typeover, or select text and use any WordPerfect editing command. You can also change the tabs, indents, column markers, and margins on the ruler.

The Print Preview toolbar gives you tools for viewing and formatting your documents. With the default Page view, you see headers, footers, footnotes, and watermarks. If you want to display two pages side by side, click the Two Page button on the Print Preview toolbar. The Zoom button enables you to specify how large or small a document appears onscreen, which is similar to the View, Zoom feature you use to zoom in and out of your document.

→ For more information on altering the magnification of your document, **see** "Changing the View Magnification," **p. 104**

→ To find out how to make your documents fit, **see** "Using Make It Fit," **p. 135**

To spell check your document in Print Preview, click the Spell Checker button. You can shrink or expand your document to a specified number of pages by clicking the Make It Fit button. The Page Setup button allows you to change the paper size, orientation (portrait or landscape), and margins.

PART

II

CH

10

You can print the document with its default print settings directly from Print Preview by clicking the Print Document button. If you want to change any print settings before you print, click the Print button. To close Print Preview, click the Print Preview button.

PRINTING A DOCUMENT

To print the document in the active window, click the Print button, press Ctrl+P, or choose File, Print. The Print dialog box is displayed, as shown in Figure 10.2.

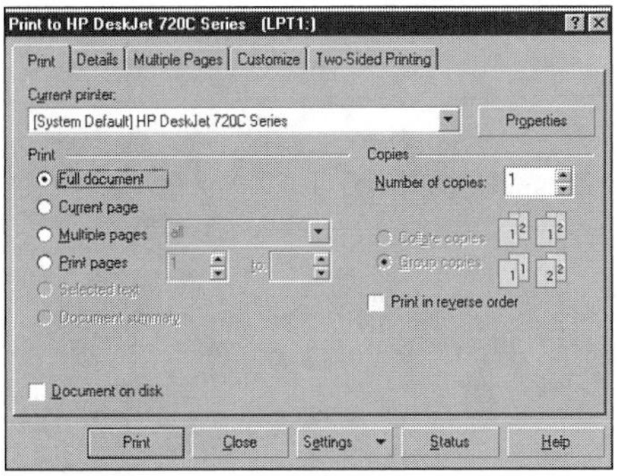

Figure 10.2
You can set all the print options in the Print dialog box.

When you print a document, most often you will print using the default options in the Print dialog box, which prints one copy of all the pages in the document. Switch between the Print, Details, Multiple Pages, Customize (was Enlarge/Reduce in previous versions), and Two-Sided Printing tabs of the dialog box to see all the print options. Table 10.1 describes options in the Print dialog box.

Note

The exact tabs in this dialog box will vary according to the type of printer you have. Similarly, the options in Table 10.1 will vary.

TABLE 10.1   IMPORTANT PRINT OPTIONS IN THE PRINT DIALOG BOX

Option	Description
Print	Select which parts of the document to print (Full Document, Current Page, Multiple Pages, Print Pages) on the Print tab.
Resolution	Choose from available resolutions for your printer on the Details tab.
Print in Color	Use the color printing capability of your printer (if available) on the Details tab.
Include Summary	Print the document summary as well as the document, which you'll find on the Print tab.
Document on Disk	Print a document on the disk rather than the document on the screen, which you'll see on the Print tab.
Number of Copies	Specify the number of copies on the Print tab.
Collate or Group	Print all pages of one copy together (versus printing all copies of each page together), which is on the Print tab.
Print in Reverse Order	This option is useful for some printers that cannot collate copies or that print "face up" output, which is on the Print tab.
Print Text Only	Speed up printing by not printing graphics, which is on the Details tab.

Tip #58 from
Trudi Reisner

You can print several files directly from the disk. Select all the files to be printed in the Open dialog box. Right-click them, and then choose Print.

Note

If you have more than one printer on your system, you can choose which printer to use in the Print tab of the Print dialog box.

The Multiple Pages tab enables you to specify exactly which pages will be printed. You can also use this tab to indicate that certain chapters or volumes of the document will be printed.

The new Customize tab offers PerfectPrint features, allowing you to enlarge or reduce a document to fit any paper size without changing the format of the page. You can specify a poster size and the Poster text box shows how many pieces of paper will be used when you print. You can enlarge or reduce your document by specifying a percentage. You can scale your printed document to fit the page size. Click the Output Page button to view and modify the page size. Finally, you can print miniature pictures of the pages on one piece of paper (a maximum of 64 pictures on a page).

The Two-Sided Printing tab allows you to set two-sided printing options, if your printer supports two-sided (duplex) printing. If it doesn't, you can still manually print two-sided documents by specifying that the printer print the odd, and then the even pages. Also use this tab to set options for binding offsets (the whitespace on the inside margin of the document).

The Settings button allows you to name and save printer settings, and to specify one set of printer settings as the default for this application. This can be useful if you prefer to have Quattro Pro or Presentations print landscape by default, or if you want to have a named setting for printing on both sides of the paper.

Tip #59 from
Trudi Reisner

If you want to fax a document, choose a fax option from the Current Printer list on the Print tab in the Print dialog box, select any options, and click the Fax button.

PRINTING AN ENVELOPE

WordPerfect's Envelope feature automatically formats and addresses your envelope for you. If you have already typed the inside address into a letter and you want an envelope for the letter, just choose Format, Envelope.

To address an envelope after typing a letter, follow these steps:

1. Choose Format, Envelope to display the Envelope area and Property Bar shown in Figure 10.3.

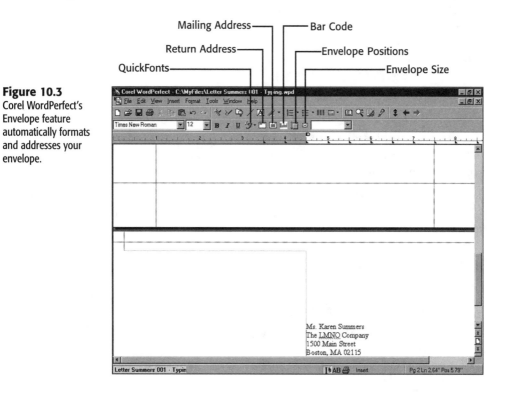

Figure 10.3
Corel WordPerfect's Envelope feature automatically formats and addresses your envelope.

2. Type the mailing address in the mailing address position, where the insertion point appears in the Envelope area.

3. Click in the upper-left corner of the Envelope area and type your return address.

4. To change the font face or size used in the return address, choose the QuickFonts button on the Property Bar.

> **Note**
>
> The font on an envelope is automatically taken from the document default font (File, Document, Default Font). To save yourself the work of changing fonts twice—once in the document text and once in the envelope window—make sure that the document default font is what you want, both for the letter and the envelope.

> **Tip #60 from**
> *Trudi Reisner*
>
> You can also click the Return Address or Mailing Address button and Address Book to choose the return or mailing address from Corel Address Book. Using Corel Address Book is discussed further in Chapter 37, "Using Corel Address Book 9."

5. As with the return address, you can change the font face or font size used in the mailing address.

6. Select the envelope size by clicking the Envelope Size button on the Property Bar.

7. If you want a USPS bar code printed on the envelope, click the Bar Code button. To change the vertical or horizontal position of the mailing address and/or return address, click the Envelope Positions button and drag the guidelines in the Envelope area.

8. To print the envelope, click the Print button on the WordPerfect 9 toolbar.

 When creating an envelope, if the inside address doesn't appear in the mailing address area, see "Inside Address Is Missing in Envelope Mailing Address Area" in the Troubleshooting section at the end of this chapter.

PRINTING LABELS

WordPerfect makes it easy to print labels by showing you each label onscreen exactly as it will appear on the printed sheet. All you have to do is find and select the brand name and item number on WordPerfect's list of label types and then enter the names and addresses.

If you're printing three-across labels, you probably want to select a font that is smaller than the font you usually use for your documents; otherwise, long names and addresses may not fit on your labels.

CHOOSING A LABEL DEFINITION

To choose a label definition, take the following steps:

1. Place the insertion point at the beginning of an empty document or on a blank page.

2. Choose Format, Labels to open the Labels dialog box shown in Figure 10.4.

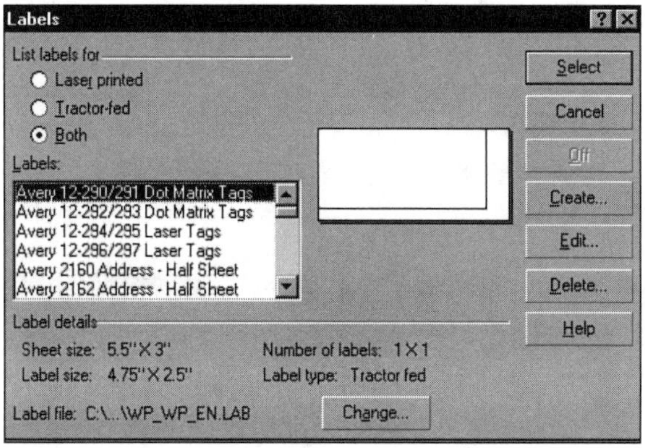

Figure 10.4
Select the labels you want to print from WordPerfect's list of label types.

3. In the Labels list, choose the definition you want to use, and then choose Select. An empty label is displayed onscreen.

CENTERING TEXT ON LABELS

To center the name and address information vertically on each label so that it doesn't start at the top edge of the label, use Corel WordPerfect's Center Page feature.

To center all names and addresses between the top and bottom of each label, follow these steps:

1. Position the insertion point at the beginning of an empty document, or on the first label.

2. Choose Format, Page, Center.

3. In the Center Page(s) dialog box, choose Current and Subsequent Pages.

4. Choose OK.

If you're having trouble centering your labels vertically, see "Centering Labels Vertically" in the Troubleshooting section at the end of this chapter.

ENTERING TEXT ON LABELS

To understand how the Labels feature works, imagine that each separate label is a page, although there may be many labels on a single sheet of paper. Each label is treated as a logical page, although it may not be a physical page. This means that you can print page headers on each label, you can apply the Center Page(s) feature to all labels, and you can (and need to) create hard page breaks between labels. After choosing a label definition and determining whether you want the labels centered:

1. Type the name and address as you want them to appear on the printed label.

2. At the end of each line, press Enter to move to the next line, but only if there are more lines to be typed for this label. If the line you just typed is the last line for this label, press Ctrl+Enter to create a hard page break.

3. Continue typing names and addresses (or other label text) and inserting hard page breaks after each label, until you have typed all the labels that you want to print. As you add each label, it appears onscreen exactly as it will print. Be careful not to press Enter after you type the last line of each label; this adds an unnecessary blank line and distorts the vertical centering. After you add several names and addresses, your screen may look like Figure 10.5.

Figure 10.5
See your labels onscreen just as they will print. End lines by pressing the Enter key; separate labels with hard page breaks.

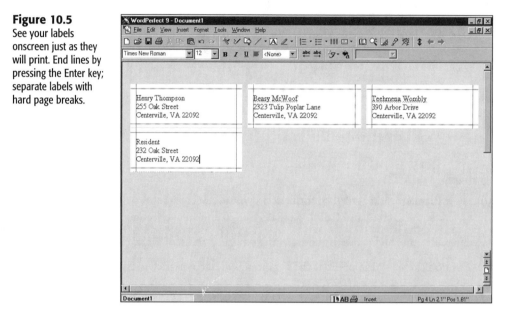

PRACTICAL PROJECT

When you print envelopes on an HP DeskJet printer, you may have noticed that the return addresses do not print near the edge of the envelope. There's a remedy for this. You can now print return addresses closer to the edge of the envelope on an HP DeskJet printer by using the new Print Upside Down feature. To accomplish this, check the Print Upside Down check box on the Details tab in the Print dialog box. Figure 10.6 shows an envelope in Print Preview where the Print Upside Down option has been selected.

Figure 10.6
Use the Print Upside Down feature to print return addresses closer to the envelope's edge.

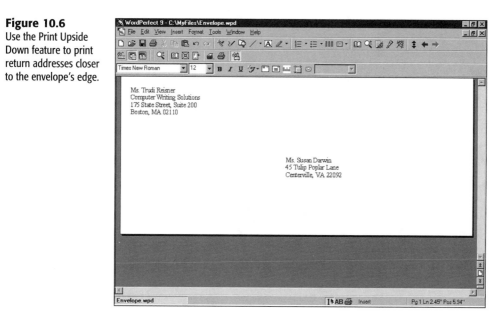

TROUBLESHOOTING

INSIDE ADDRESS IS MISSING IN ENVELOPE MAILING ADDRESS AREA

After I typed a letter, I told WordPerfect to create an envelope, but the inside address didn't appear in the mailing address area.

If your letter isn't in a standard business format, WordPerfect may not be able to find the address inside and copy it to the mailing address. If this happens, close the Envelope dialog box, select the inside address, and access the Envelope dialog box again. When you select a name and address before using the Envelope feature, the selected information appears automatically in the mailing address on the envelope.

CENTERING LABELS VERTICALLY

Some of my labels aren't centered vertically, even though I used the Center on Page feature.

If you press Enter too many times at the bottom of your labels, you may distort the vertical centering. Look in Reveal Codes for extra hard returns and eliminate them.

CHAPTER **11**

ORGANIZING AND FORMATTING LARGE DOCUMENTS

In this chapter

USING BULLETS AND NUMBERS

Corel WordPerfect's Bullets & Numbers feature gives you a quick and easy way to create an outline in a simplified format. Use the Bullets & Numbers feature to create lists such as the ones shown in Figure 11.1. A bullet or number appears at the left margin, followed by an indent. Numbers increase automatically with each item in the list.

Figure 11.1
Create bulleted and numbered lists easily with the Bullets & Numbers feature.

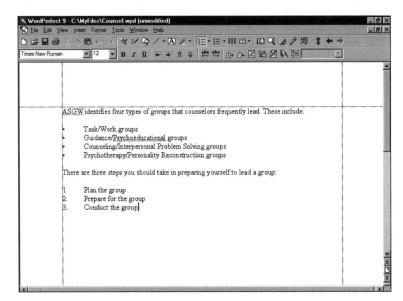

Follow these steps to create a simple list:

1. Position the insertion point at the left margin of the first line in the list.
2. Choose Insert, Outline/Bullets & Numbering. You see the Bullets and Numbering dialog box shown in Figure 11.2.
3. Select the style that you want for your list.
4. Click OK. WordPerfect inserts the first bullet (or number) followed by an indent into your document.
5. Type your text and press Enter.
6. You see the next bullet or number. Continue typing text and pressing Enter until you finish typing the list. To enter a blank line, press the Enter key twice. Use the Backspace key to remove the extra bullet or number at the end of the list and to stop the sequence.

Tip #61 from
Trudi Reisner

Use the Bullets or Numbering buttons to quickly create another bullet or number.

Figure 11.2
Making a selection at the Bullets and Numbering dialog box produces a number with an indent.

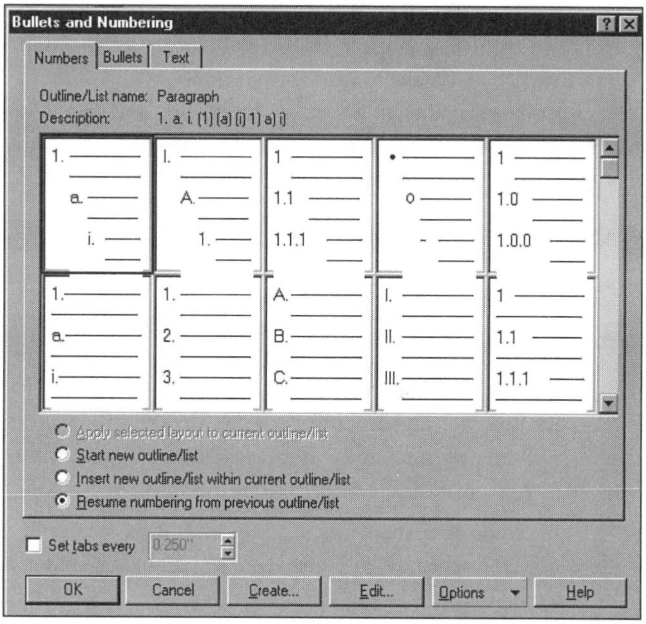

PART
II
CH
11

> **Note**
>
> WordPerfect gives you a choice of 10 types of bullet styles and 11 types of number styles with its Bullets & Numbers feature. There also are three predefined Text styles on the Text tab that insert predefined text at the beginning of each paragraph. You can customize any of the predefined styles. You can, for example, use a different WordPerfect character as a bullet by editing one of the predefined styles and replacing the bullet character with the character of your choice.

If you created a numbered list and you would rather have a bulleted list, see "Converting a Numbered List to a Bulleted List" in the Troubleshooting section at the end of this chapter.

If you need to add another item to your numbered list, see "Adding Items to a Numbered List" in the Troubleshooting section at the end of this chapter.

If you typed a list and want to add bullets to it, see "Adding Bullets After You Type a List" in the Troubleshooting section at the end of this chapter.

If you want to add items without bullets within a bulleted list, see "Adding Bullets After You Type a List" in the Troubleshooting section at the end of this chapter.

OUTLINING A DOCUMENT

Whenever you create a numbered list, you are creating an outline as well.

A WordPerfect outline is more than numbers that are typed in at the beginning of each new topic. After you start an outline, the numerals, if there are any, are created and sequenced automatically.

When you change your mind about the order of topics in your outline, you can easily rearrange topics. The rest of the topics resequence automatically when you rearrange topics—or when you add or delete topics. If you change your mind about the style of the outline, place the insertion point anywhere in the outline and choose a different style. To see only the most important topics in your outline, collapse the outline down to the first level.

Before you work with outlines, it helps to familiarize yourself with outline concepts and terminology and with the Outline Property Bar.

UNDERSTANDING OUTLINE CONCEPTS AND TERMINOLOGY

The following concepts and terminology will help you work with outlines:

- An outline is a series of paragraphs, called outline items, in which each paragraph has an optional number or letter and a hierarchical level. The level number or letter type generally corresponds to the number of tabs or indents that separate the beginning of the topic from the left margin.

- An outline can include body text. Body text does not have a number, and may not have the same level of indentation as the portions of the outline that surround it.

- An outline family is a group of related material consisting of all the numbered paragraphs and body text that are subitems of the first item in the group.

- An outline style is a formatting style that uniquely defines the appearance of the number and text for each level of an outline.

UNDERSTANDING THE OUTLINE PROPERTY BAR

The Outline Property Bar shown in Figure 11.3 is your gateway to the commands that you use when you work with outlines. This section introduces you to the Outline Property Bar. Table 11.1 describes individual buttons on the Property Bar.

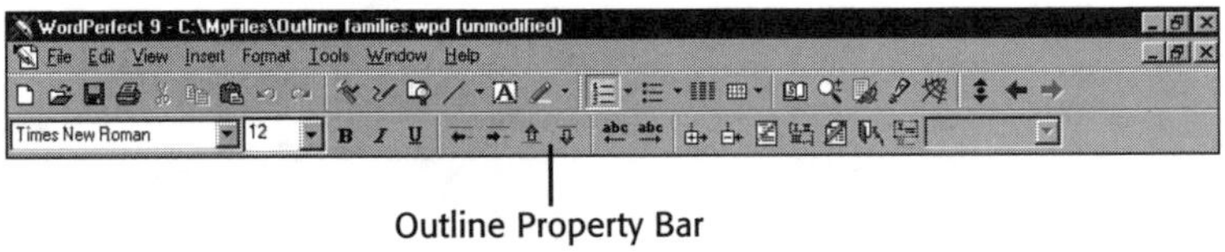

Figure 11.3
The Outline Property Bar provides one-button access to Outline's capabilities.

Outline Property Bar

TABLE 11.1 BUTTONS ON THE OUTLINE PROPERTY BAR

Button	Name	Function
←	Promote	Changes the current outline item to the previous level. Decreases an outline item's level number or letter by 1 (same as Shift+Tab).
→	Demote	Changes the current outline level to the next level. Increases an outline item's level number or letter by one (same as pressing Tab).

Button	Name	Function
⬆	Move Up	Moves the current or selected family or item up; keeps the same level. Moves the outline item or selection text up one item without changing its level letter or number.
⬇	Move Down	Moves the current or selected family or item down; keeps the same level. Moves the outline item or selection text down one item without changing its level letter or number.
⊞→	QuickFind Previous	Finds the previously selected element of the document. You can also press Alt+Ctrl+P.
⊟→	QuickFind Next	Finds the next selected element of the document. You can also use Alt+Ctrl+N.
abc←	Show Family	Shows all levels of the outline family. Shows/redisplays the collapsed family that is below the current outline item.
abc→	Hide Family	Hides all but the current level of the outline family. Hides/collapses the family that is below the current outline item.
🗐	Show/Hide Body Text	Toggles the display of nonoutline items.
🗐	Set Paragraph Number	Allows you to manually set the paragraph number of the current paragraph.
🗐	Modify	Selects an outline format. You see the Create Format dialog box that allows you to create or edit your outline style.
🗐	Show Icons	Lets you display and hide Outline icons in the left margin.
🗐	Show Levels	Specifies how many levels of the outline should display. You can display up to nine outline levels. Choosing None will display only body text.

CREATING AN OUTLINE

The general steps for creating an outline are as follows:

1. Position the insertion point at the left margin of the line that will be the first line in the outline.

2. Click the Numbering button on the toolbar, or type 1 and press the Tab key. The Outline Property Bar appears.

3. If the style of the inserted outline number is not the one you want, use the down arrow on the right side of the Numbering button to select another style, or choose Insert, Outline/Bullets & Numbering and select a different style from the Bullets and Numbering dialog box.

4. Type the text, and then press Enter. The insertion point is automatically positioned at the same level to enter the text for the next item.

5. To change the level of an outline item, click anywhere in the item, and then click the Promote or the Demote button, or press Tab or Shift+Tab. Note that the Property Bar displays the outline level of the current paragraph.

6. To add body text to the outline, press the Backspace key to delete the paragraph number. You see the Outline Property Bar change to the Text Property Bar. To resume the outline numbering, click the Numbering button at the beginning of a paragraph. You see the next consecutive number.

7. To complete the outline and start typing text again, press the Backspace key at the beginning of a new paragraph to delete the outline number. You see the Outline Property Bar change to the Text Property Bar.

Note

If you accidentally delete an outline number, either Undo the action, or Backspace to the end of the previous item and press Enter.

COLLAPSING AND EXPANDING PORTIONS OF AN OUTLINE

WordPerfect makes it easy to work with a portion of your outline by letting you display only the portion in which you're currently interested.

When you're displaying just the portion that you want to work with, it's easy to edit (or reorganize) outline items. Because outline items are just normal text with automatic numbering applied to them, you edit text in outline items just as you do any other text.

Figure 11.4 is an example for the hiding and showing techniques that follow.

Figure 11.4
The complete outline used in the hiding and showing examples.

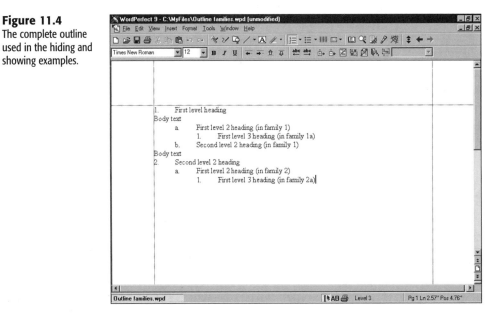

Using the Outline Property Bar, you have the following methods to control what portion of an outline is displayed:

- To hide an outline family—that is, to collapse the family so only its first-level item is visible—click in the first level of the family and click the Hide Family button.

- To show a collapsed outline family, place the insertion point in the visible outline item and click the Show Family button.

- To hide the body text and leave only the outline, click the Show/Hide Body Text button. The body text is hidden. To redisplay body text, click the Show/Hide Body Text button again.

Figure 11.5 shows the result of hiding elements of the outline.

Figure 11.5
The same outline is shown with body text hidden.

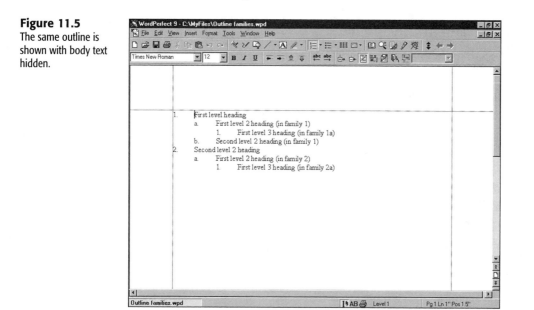

MODIFYING AN OUTLINE'S STRUCTURE

You can modify an outline's structure by rearranging items and families, inserting new families, or deleting families. You can also switch an outline item to body text or vice versa. WordPerfect automatically adjusts the numbering of the outline.

ADJUSTING LEVELS

Levels of the outline can be adjusted according to the following options:

- To increase the level of an outline item, position the insertion point anywhere in the item and choose the Promote button.

- To decrease the level of an outline item, position the insertion point anywhere in the item and click the Demote button.

To increase or decrease several items at once, select the desired items; then click the Promote or Demote button.

CHANGING TO AND FROM BODY TEXT

To change an outline item to body text, click at the beginning of the item and press the Backspace key to delete the outline number. The text is placed at the left margin. You may want to adjust its indentation with Tab or Indent (F7).

 To change body text back to an outline item, place the insertion point anywhere in the body text and click the Numbering button.

CHANGING AN OUTLINE'S STYLE

You can select from among several different predefined outline numbering styles. To change an outline's style, take the following steps:

1. Position the insertion point anywhere in the outline.
2. Click the down arrow at the right of the Numbering button. You see several choices for numbering styles.
3. Select your preferred numbering style. The outline numbering changes accordingly.

USING STYLES

Use styles to format your documents and templates easily and quickly, and to give them a consistent and professional look. Styles are an extraordinarily powerful formatting tool. Instead of applying several separate formatting changes to a subtitle in a long document, you can apply them all at once with a style. You can apply the same style over and over again to every subtitle in the document. If you change your mind about any of the formatting, you have only one change to make—to the style itself. Styles are readily available for use in other documents; see the section "Sharing Styles Between Documents" later in this chapter for more information.

Because styles can incorporate nearly any WordPerfect formatting feature—as well as text, graphics, and even other styles—their potential is nearly unlimited. You can save a great deal of time and work by learning to use styles, especially when you work with long documents.

Tip #62 from *Trudi Reisner*	Chapter 15, "Creating Graphics," also covers working with graphics lines and creating paragraph and page borders, drop caps, graphics boxes for figures and text, special text effects with text art, and watermarks.

CONSIDERING TYPES OF STYLES

Styles are classified in three ways: by who creates them, by their location, and by their type.

Styles that are part of the WordPerfect program are called system styles. When you first access the style list in a new document, immediately after installation of the program (see Figure 11.6), you see a style list that displays the built-in system styles. When you create a new style, it is added to the style list. The styles that you create are called user styles.

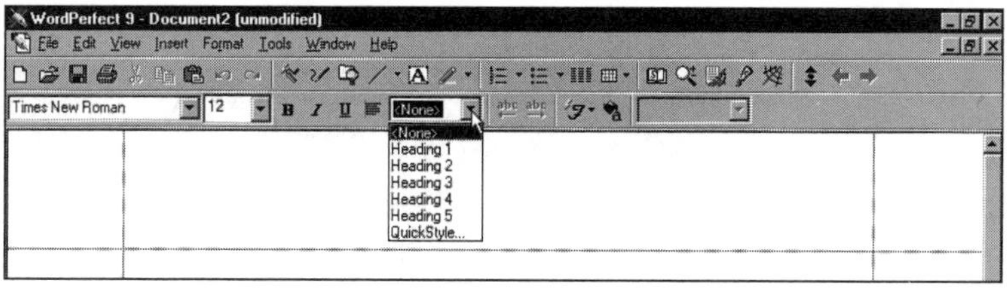

Figure 11.6
WordPerfect comes with styles for five levels of headings.

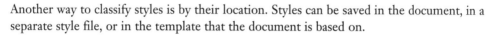

Another way to classify styles is by their location. Styles can be saved in the document, in a separate style file, or in the template that the document is based on.

In addition, there are five types of styles:

- Character Style—The formatting in a Character style takes effect at a specified character, and it ends at another character. Characters following the character style revert to their previous formatting. Character styles are especially good for applying multiple character formatting attributes to individual words or letters. For instance, if you need to print certain words in bold small caps, a character style would be useful.

- Automatic Character Style—This type of style is like the Character style, except that formatting in the style is automatically updated when you change any paragraph that is formatted with the style. Therefore, if you change the character formatting style of one paragraph, all other paragraphs in the document with that style will change as well.

- Paragraph Style—The formatting in a Paragraph style affects the current paragraph (or a series of selected paragraphs). A Paragraph style is ideal for formatting one-line titles and headings.

- Automatic Paragraph Style—This type of style is like the Paragraph style, except that formatting in the style is automatically updated when you change any paragraph that is formatted with the style. Thus, if you change the style of one paragraph, all other paragraphs in the document with that style will change as well.

- Document (open)—A Document style applies a formatting command from the insertion point until the end of the document, unless overridden by another formatting command. This can be useful when you want to change margins, the base font, or a paper orientation for the remainder of the document.

WordPerfect's styles are much more powerful than those of competing word processing programs that can only include formatting codes in styles. With WordPerfect, you can also include text and graphics in your styles. Thus, you could have a style that inserts your company logo, or a style that even inserts text for you.

USING SYSTEM STYLES

The easiest way to learn about styles is to start using the built-in System Styles to format headings in your document. To do so, create or click a document heading, then click in the Styles list box, and choose Heading 1 through Heading 5 for the paragraph, as shown in Figure 11.7.

Figure 11.7
This document is using several heading styles; the Styles list box is open.

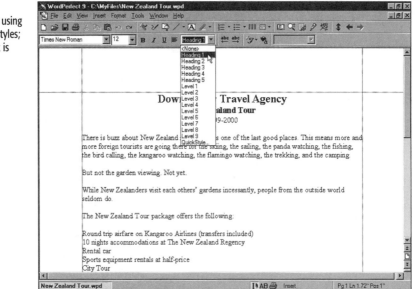

To understand styles a little bit more, it's helpful to open the Styles dialog box shown in Figure 11.8. Do so by choosing Format, Styles or by pressing Alt+F8.

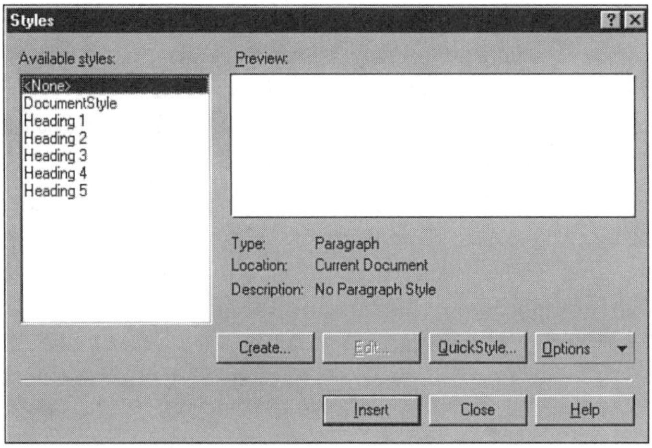

Figure 11.8
The Styles dialog box shows the styles saved in the standard template.

In the Styles dialog box, you can highlight each style name on the list and see the description and other information about that style below the list.

The DocumentStyle sets formatting defaults that affect the entire document. The Heading styles are designed to format the title and various levels of headings in a document; these styles contain font changes, centering, and Table of Contents markings. The number and bullet styles (if present) contain formatting for Bullets & Numbers styles.

CREATING AND USING YOUR OWN STYLES

When you see and feel the power of styles, you'll be willing to put in some extra time and work learning how to create your own styles. Although the use of styles adds a level of complexity to your work, the results are well worth it. You'll save time formatting; your documents will have a professional, consistent appearance; and you'll be able to make global formatting adjustments quickly and easily.

Tip #63 from
Trudi Reisner

To learn more about styles, explore WordPerfect's templates. Create a document based on a template as discussed in Chapter 6, "Formatting Text," and then access the Styles dialog box, select a style, and choose Edit to see what codes it contains.

CREATING A STYLE WITH QUICKSTYLE

An easy way to create a style is to format some text as you want it to look, and then use the QuickStyle feature to copy the formatting into a style. With QuickStyle, you can create a Paragraph style that contains all the formatting codes and font attributes in an existing paragraph; or, you can create a Character style that contains all the font attributes on an existing character.

To create a style with QuickStyle, complete the following steps:

1. Format a section of text or a paragraph with the features that you want included in the style.
2. Click anywhere in the paragraph to create a Paragraph style, or select the formatted text to create a Character style.
3. Click the Select Style button, and then choose QuickStyle; or, choose Format, Styles, QuickStyle. Another alternative is to press Alt+F8. The QuickStyle dialog box appears as shown in Figure 11.9.
4. Enter a name for the style.
5. Enter a description for the style.
6. Select the Paragraph or Character Style type.
7. Click OK. The style is created, and you are returned to the document window or the Styles dialog box.

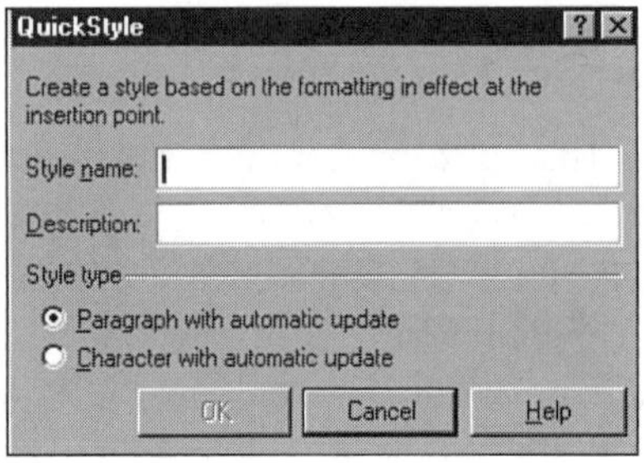

Figure 11.9
Format text as you
want it to look,
and then use the
QuickStyle dialog box
to copy the formatting
into a style.

If you prefer to create your own styles from scratch, take a look at the next section for directions.

CREATING A STYLE FROM SCRATCH

Maximize the power of styles by creating your own styles with exactly the formatting, text, graphics, and even other styles that suit your work.

To create a style from scratch, you need to enter formatting codes (and any other contents for the style) in the Styles Editor window. Follow these steps to create a style from scratch:

1. Choose Format, Styles. The Styles dialog box appears.
2. Choose Create. The Styles Editor window is displayed such as the one shown in Figure 11.10.

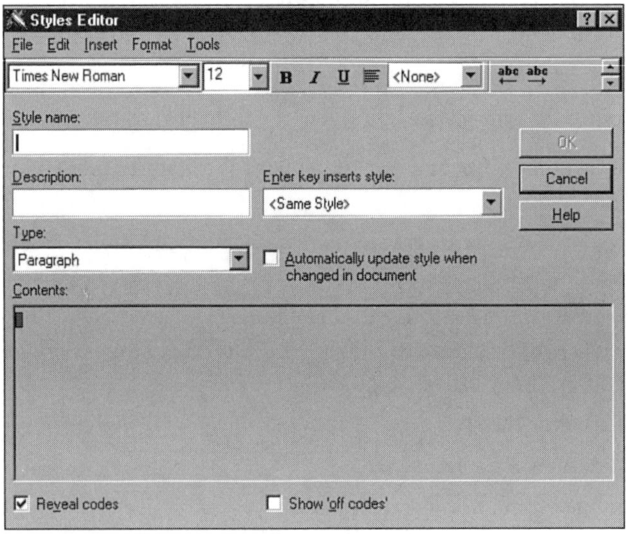

Figure 11.10
A paragraph style
named Body, used to
format the body text
for a report, is shown
in the Styles Editor
dialog box.

3. Enter a name for the style in the Style Name box.
4. Enter a description for the style in the Description box. It's helpful to describe the formatting used in the style or the purpose for which it will be used.

5. Change the style type, if desired, from the Type drop-down list.

6. For a Paragraph or Character style, program the Enter key, if desired. In the Enter Key Inserts Style list box, choose an option. The Enter key can be programmed to make the next paragraph the same style, another style that you specify, or no style at all.

7. Click in the Contents area and enter formatting codes, text, or graphics that should be included in the style. (Inserting graphics is discussed further in Chapter 15, "Creating Graphics.")

8. If the style type is Paragraph or Character, you can specify formatting and text that takes effect after the text that is included in the style. For example, you might want to insert a graphics line after a heading that is formatted with the style. To do so, check Show 'Off Codes'. You see a comment in the Contents box that reads Codes to the left are ON - Codes to the right are OFF. Click to the right of this comment, and then put the text or formatting you want to have take effect after the style, such as the paragraph border code in Figure 11.11.

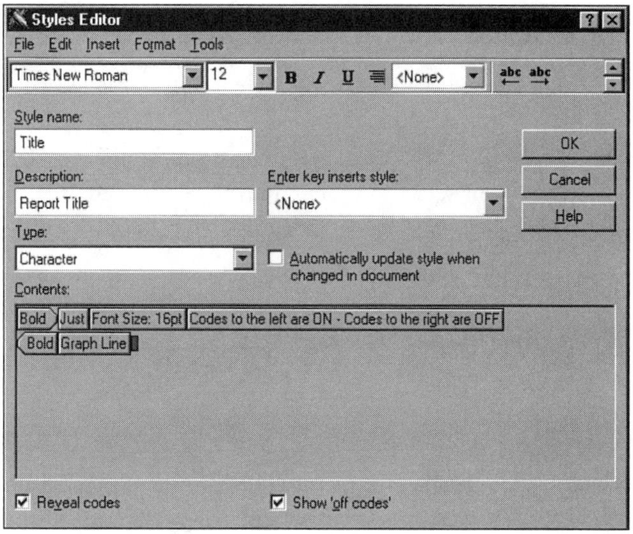

Figure 11.11
You can include elements such as graphics lines that should be inserted after the style is turned off.

9. Click OK, and then click Close to return to the document window.

If you want to add Table of Contents markings to a style, see "Adding Table of Contents Markings to a Style" in the Troubleshooting section at the end of this chapter.

→ For more information on creating a table of contents, **see** "Creating a Table of Contents, **p. 198**

APPLYING A STYLE

You can apply a style either to existing text or to new text.

Tip #64 from
Trudi Reisner

> If the style type is Character or Paragraph (Automatic), you don't have to edit a style with the Styles Editor. When you change any paragraph that is formatted with the style, the changes are automatically reflected in the style.

To apply a style to new text, complete the following steps:

1. Click at the end of the document.
2. Click the Styles button on the Power Bar to display the style list.
3. Select the style that you want to apply.
4. If the style being applied is a Document type or a Paragraph type, you have finished applying the style.

    If the new text is at the end of the document and the style being applied is a Character style, type the text that is to be affected by the style, pull down the style list again, and select None or another style from the list. This turns off the first style.

To apply a style to existing text, complete the following steps:

1. If the style being applied is a Document style, position the insertion point where you want its effects to begin.

    If the style being applied is a Paragraph style, position the insertion point in the paragraph to be affected, or select the paragraphs to be affected.

    If the style being applied is a Character style, select the text to be affected.
2. Click the Styles button and select the style.

After you create and apply a style, you may change your mind about the formatting in the style.

EDITING A STYLE

Styles are flexible; as soon as you change the style, the changes take effect wherever that style is applied. To make any changes that should apply to the document as a whole, edit the Document Style. Every document contains the Document Style code at the beginning of its text (you can't remove the code). When you edit the Document Style, therefore, your formatting takes effect at the beginning of the document. Because the Document Style is a Document (open) style, its formatting stays in effect for the rest of the document, or until it is overridden by other formatting of the same type. You might, for example, insert justification and margin codes in the Document Style.

Note

> Formatting codes that appear in the body of a document, or in other styles that are applied in the document, override similar formatting in the Document Style.

To edit a Character (auto) or Paragraph (auto) style, merely edit text in your document that has that style applied to it. The changes are automatically reflected in the style and in other text that has that style applied to it.

To edit other types of styles:

1. Choose Format, Style to open the Styles dialog box.
2. Select the style you want to edit and choose Edit. The Styles Editor window appears.
3. Make any desired changes, click OK, and then click Close.

If you created a style to format the company name, but when you apply it, it formats the entire paragraph, see "Character and Paragraph Styles" in the Troubleshooting section at the end of this chapter.

SHARING STYLES BETWEEN DOCUMENTS

When you create a new document, it contains all the styles that the template upon which it is based has. Additionally, you can specify an Additional Objects template that contains other styles that you use frequently.

Tip #65 from
Trudi Reisner

Often, the Additional Objects template is used for your office or workgroup templates, such as a letterhead. Specify the Additional Objects Template in the File Settings dialog box by choosing Tools, Settings, Files, Template.

Styles are automatically saved with the document containing them. They are not, however, saved in the template unless you specify this as described in this section.

When you work on an existing document, your style list may thus contain system styles (saved in the Default template), styles from the template upon which the document was based, styles from the Additional Objects template, and styles previously created and saved in the document.

When you want to use your styles in a new document, the easiest way to do it is by saving the current document's style list in a separate file that contains only the style list. Then you can retrieve the style file into the style list of another document.

If you want customized styles to be available in all new documents based on a particular template, copy the styles to the template, or create the styles while you edit the template.

You can save and retrieve styles in the following ways:

- To save styles in the current document to a separate style file, access the Styles dialog box. Choose Options, Save As. Type a name for the style file in the resulting Save Styles To dialog box. Choose whether to save the User Styles, the System Styles, or Both; then click OK, and click Close to close the Styles dialog box.

- To save a style in the current document to the current template, display the Styles dialog box; select the style name; choose Options, Copy. Click Default Template in the Styles Copy dialog box; and then click OK and click Close to close the Styles dialog box.

- To retrieve styles from a style file (or from another document), display the Styles dialog box; choose <u>O</u>ptions, <u>R</u>etrieve; enter a filename (and path); and choose OK. You are asked whether you want to overwrite current styles (with incoming styles that have the same names). Answer <u>Y</u>es or <u>N</u>o to complete the retrieve operation. Click Close to close the Styles dialog box. You can also click the folder icon to the right of the block for path to the styles. This will show a browse dialog box from which you can choose a template by clicking the filename and clicking Select.

If you want to use the styles you created in your document in a new document, see "Using Styles You Created in a New Document" in the Troubleshooting section at the end of this chapter.

PRACTICAL PROJECT

Not only can you apply styles to text, but you can apply graphics styles to text, too. WordPerfect offers a variety of graphics styles such as text box, figure, table, watermark, sticky note text, and so on. The sticky note text is one of the more interesting graphics styles, which is useful when you want to draw attention to certain text in a document. For example, Figure 11.12 shows how you can use the Sticky Note Text graphics style to insert reminders when giving a presentation or teaching a class.

Figure 11.12
Use the Sticky Note Text graphics style to draw attention to certain text in your document.

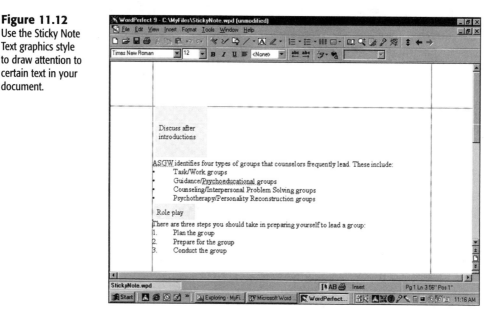

First you apply the Sticky Note Text graphics style, and then you type your text in the yellow sticky note text box. To apply the style, choose Format, Graphics Styles, and choose Sticky Note Text in the Style list. Then type the text in the yellow sticky note text box. Click anywhere outside the box to deselect it. You can move and size the text box by selecting it and using the selection handles surrounding the box.

TROUBLESHOOTING

CONVERTING A NUMBERED LIST TO A BULLETED LIST

You created a numbered list and now you would rather have a bulleted list.

Select the entire list, click the Numbering button to remove the numbering, and then click the Bullets button to insert bullets.

ADDING ITEMS TO A NUMBERED LIST

You created a numbered list, and you want to add another item to the list.

Insert the item using the Numbering button to create a number at the beginning of the item. Numbers will resequence automatically.

ADDING BULLETS AFTER YOU TYPE A LIST

You typed a list of items without bullets, and now you want to add bullets at the beginning of each item.

Select the entire list and click the Bullet button.

ADDING ITEMS WITHOUT BULLETS

When you're typing a bulleted list, you may want to add a line without bullets.

Press Shift+Enter and the new line will not have a bullet. When you press Enter again, the next line will have a bullet.

ADDING TABLE OF CONTENTS MARKINGS TO A STYLE

You want to add Table of Contents markings to a style, but you can't figure out how to do it.

You can add Table of Contents markings to any paired style. At the Styles Editor window, select the Show 'Off Codes' check box option. Select only the comment code [Codes to the left...]. Choose Tools, Reference, Table of Contents. Choose the level you want by choosing one of the Mark buttons on the Table of Contents dialog box that appears at the bottom of the screen. [Mrk Txt ToC] codes now surround the comment, and will surround any text that is formatted with the style.

CHARACTER AND PARAGRAPH STYLES

You created a style to format the company name, but when you apply it, it formats the entire paragraph.

Change the style type from Paragraph to Character.

USING STYLES YOU CREATED IN A NEW DOCUMENT

You want to use the styles you created in a Report file in a new document.

With the new document onscreen, access the Styles dialog box. Choose Options, Retrieve, and then enter the filename (and path) of your Report file and choose OK. When asked whether you want to overwrite current styles, answer Yes. The retrieve operation will then be completed.

CHAPTER **12**

USING DOCUMENTATION TOOLS

In this chapter

CREATING A TABLE OF CONTENTS

One of WordPerfect's automated documentation tools automates the process of creating a table of contents for a document. This feature saves you time and improves your accuracy when creating a table of contents.

There are three major steps in creating a table of contents:

- Mark the text to be included
- Define the table of contents format
- Generate the table of contents

A table of contents contains a listing of headings and corresponding page number references, as shown in Figure 12.1. You can assign a level to headings or subheadings in your document to designate a table of contents entry. WordPerfect gives you the choice of five numbering formats for table of contents entries.

Figure 12.1
A table of contents with headings and corresponding page number references.

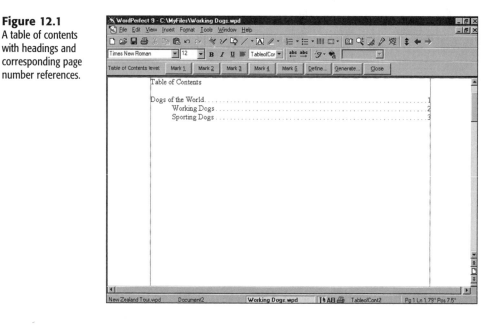

MARKING TABLE OF CONTENTS ENTRIES

The first step toward creating a table of contents is marking the text you want to include in the table. Marking text means to select the text and choose a level number for the table. You can choose up to five levels. A level defines how far the table item is indented from the left margin. For example, you might want to use chapter headings for level 1 and subheadings for level 2.

Follow these instructions to mark table of contents items:

1. Choose Tools, Reference, Table of Contents. The Table of Contents toolbar appears, as shown in Figure 12.2.

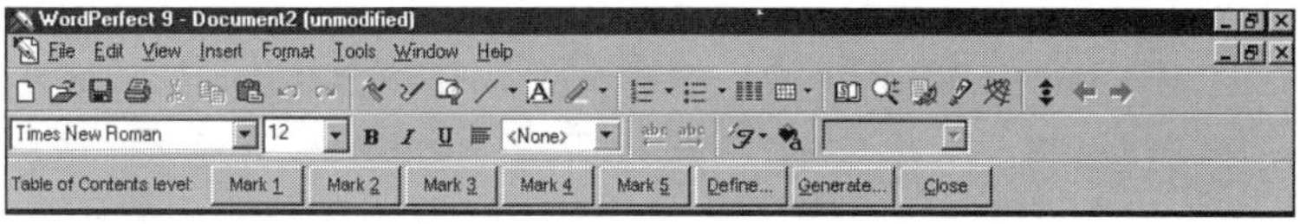

Figure 12.2
The Table of Contents toolbar is used to mark text, define the table of contents format, and generate the table.

2. Select the text for the first item.

3. Click the Mark <u>1</u> button on the Table of Contents toolbar.

4. Continue marking until you include all text for the table of contents.

After you mark the text for the items in the table, you'll need to tell WordPerfect where you want to place the table and its format.

DEFINING THE TABLE OF CONTENTS FORMAT

Generally, a table of contents is located at the beginning of a document. To place the table of contents at the beginning of the document, position the insertion point there. Insert a page break, and move to the page above the page break. Type a title and press Enter several times to separate the title from the list.

You can select the number of levels, and design how the item numbering and page numbers will look in the table of contents.

The following steps show you how to define the table of contents format:

1. Click the <u>D</u>efine button on the Table of Contents toolbar. The Define Table of Contents dialog box opens, as shown in Figure 12.3. A sample table of contents appears in the box at the bottom of the dialog box.

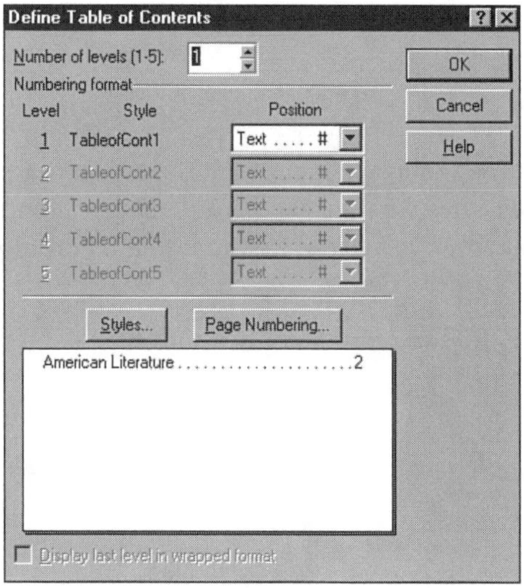

PART

II

CH

12

Figure 12.3
The Define Table of Contents dialog box is used to specify the number of levels, numbering format, and page-numbering format.

2. Choose the number of levels.

3. If the position of the numbering format of a level is not the one you want, choose a numbering format for the level from the Position drop-down list in the Numbering Format group.

4. Click OK. You will see `<<Table of Contents will generate here>>` on the line where your insertion point is located.

> **Caution**
>
> If you choose a flush-right style for the last level and specify that the line will word wrap (Display Last Level in Wrapped Format), you will have trouble aligning the last level. The text for the entry and the page number will not align properly. Choose a different position (Numbering Format option) for the page number.

 If you don't like the appearance of your table of contents, see "Redefining the Table of Contents" in the Troubleshooting section at the end of this chapter.

GENERATING A TABLE OF CONTENTS

After you mark text and define the table of contents format, the final step is to generate the table. WordPerfect generates the table of contents with the page numbers where those headings can be found. When you add or make changes to table of contents entries, you need to regenerate the table. WordPerfect automatically updates the headings and page numbers to reflect the changes.

To generate a table of contents, click the <u>G</u>enerate button on the Table of Contents toolbar. The Generate dialog box appears. Click OK. WordPerfect inserts the table of contents with headings and page numbers.

 If you accidentally place the table of contents in the wrong location in your document, see "Placing the Table of Contents Where You Want" in the Troubleshooting section at the end of this chapter.

If you modified or deleted table of contents items, and your table of contents did not reflect the changes, see "Updating a Table of Contents" in the Troubleshooting section at the end of this chapter.

CREATING AN INDEX

Another valuable documentation tool is the Index feature that lets you compile an index for a document. WordPerfect generates the page number references automatically and makes the process of creating an index quick and easy. Essentially, index creation is a three-step process, just like table of contents creation:

- Mark the text for index entries or create a concordance file
- Define the index format
- Generate the index

The index gives you an alphabetic listing of key topics and corresponding page number references, as shown in Figure 12.4. You can designate an index entry as a heading (an entry with a separate alphabetic listing in the index) or a subheading (an entry beneath a heading). You can mark text to be indexed or you can create a concordance file. The concordance file automatically searches your document for each occurrence of the word or phrase, and then inserts the correct page numbers in the index.

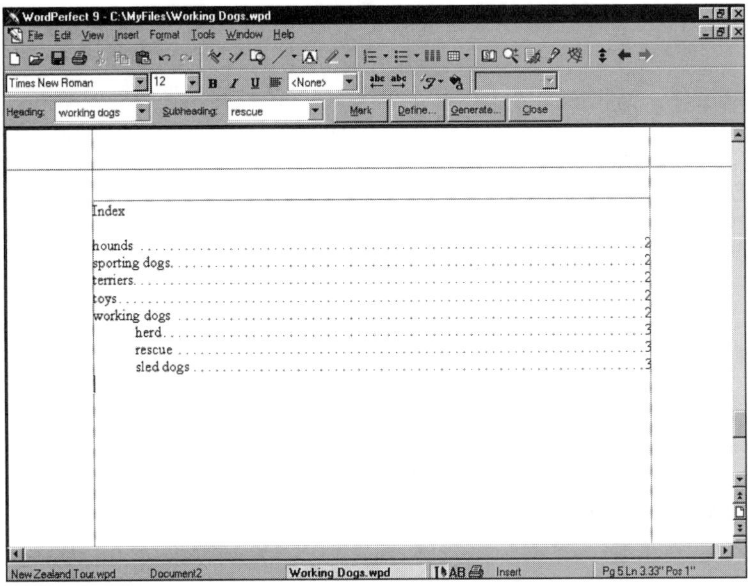

Figure 12.4
An index with a list of alphabetic key topics and corresponding page number references.

MARKING INDEX ENTRIES

If you want to create an index with marked text, perform these steps:

1. Choose Tools, Reference, Index. The Index toolbar appears, as shown in Figure 12.5.

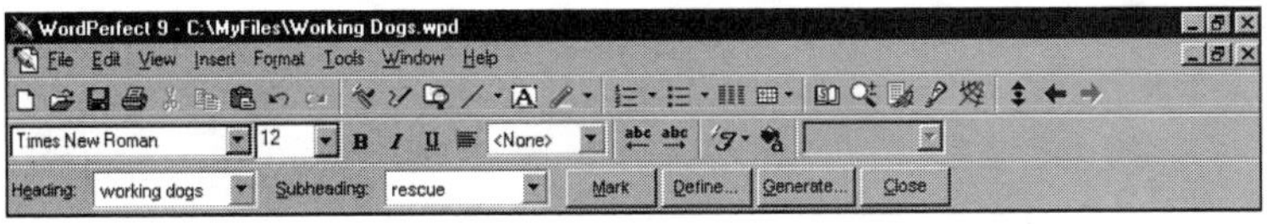

Figure 12.5
The Index toolbar is used to mark text for index entries, define the index format, and generate the index.

2. Type the word or phrase for a heading in the Heading box.

3. Click the Mark button on the Index toolbar.

4. Click the down arrow in the Heading box and choose a heading entry for which you want to create a subheading.

5. Type the word or phrase for a subheading in the Sub<u>h</u>eading box.

6. Click the <u>M</u>ark button on the Index toolbar.

7. Continue marking entries until you include all text for the index.

Tip #66 from
Trudi Reisner

> For faster marking, select the word or phrase, click the Copy button on the WordPerfect 9 toolbar, and click in the <u>H</u>eading or <u>S</u>ubheading box on the Index toolbar. Then click the <u>M</u>ark button on the Index toolbar.

CREATING A CONCORDANCE FILE

You might find it easier and faster to type your index entries in a concordance file than to mark entries in the existing document. To create an index with a concordance file, perform these steps:

1. Create a new document.

2. Type a word or phrase for a heading or subheading entry for the index and press Enter. Place only one item on each line.

3. Repeat step 2 until all items are entered.

4. Save the file.

DEFINING THE INDEX FORMAT

After you mark text or create a concordance file for index entries, the next step is to designate where you want the index to appear in the document. Often, an index is located at the end of a document. To insert an index at the end of your document, position the insertion point there. Insert a page break, and move to the page below the page break. Type a title and press Enter several times to separate the title from the index list.

When you format the index, you can decide whether a page number should appear with the entry.

Here are the steps for defining the index format:

1. Click the <u>D</u>efine button on the Index toolbar. The Define Index dialog box opens, such as the one in Figure 12.6. A sample table of contents appears in the box at the bottom of the dialog box.

2. If the numbering format is not the one you want, choose a numbering format in the <u>P</u>osition list in the Numbering Format group.

3. If you are using a concordance file, enter that filename in the Filename box in the Concordance File area at the bottom of the dialog box.

4. Click OK. You will see `<<Index will generate here>>` on the line where your insertion point is located.

⚡ *If you don't like the appearance of your index, see "Redefining the Index" in the Troubleshooting section at the end of this chapter.*

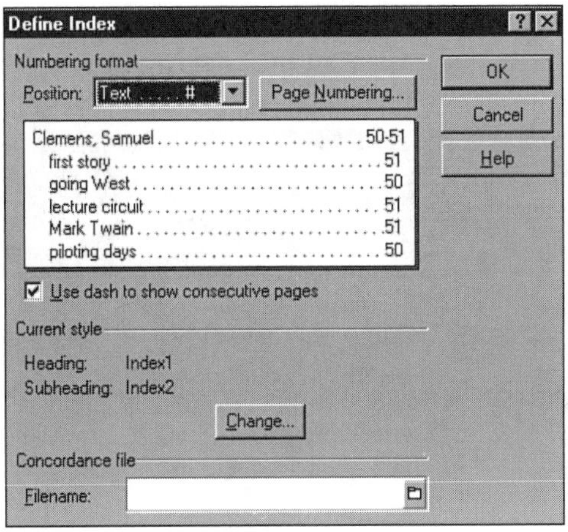

Figure 12.6
The Define Index dialog box is used to define the numbering format and page numbering format, and where you can enter the name of the concordance file.

GENERATING AN INDEX

WordPerfect generates an index with the page numbers where those headings and subheadings can be found. When you add or make changes to index entries, you need to regenerate the index. WordPerfect automatically updates the entries and page numbers to reflect the changes.

To generate an index, click the Generate button on the Index toolbar. The Generate dialog box comes into view. Click OK. WordPerfect inserts the index with headings, subheadings, and page numbers.

⚡ *If you accidentally place the index in the wrong location in your document, see "Placing the Index Where You Want" in the Troubleshooting section at the end of this chapter.*

If you modified or deleted index items, and your index did not reflect the changes, see "Updating an Index" in the Troubleshooting section at the end of this chapter.

CREATING CROSS-REFERENCES

WordPerfect's Cross-Reference tool lets you guide your readers to related information in the document to reference page numbers, footnote numbers, section numbers, endnote numbers, and graphics box numbers. Cross-references point to a related topic in another part of a book or other lengthy document. These are the main steps for creating cross-references:

- Mark the reference entries
- Mark the target entries
- Generate the cross-references

There are two kinds of cross-reference entries: reference and target. The reference is where you direct the reader to look in another part of the document for information. The target is the information to which you are directing the reader. For example, on page 5, if you refer to related information on page 10, place the reference entry on page 5 (such as "Refer to page 10") and the target entry on page 10. Figure 12.7 shows a cross-reference.

Figure 12.7
A cross-reference for directing the reader to look in another part of the document for information.

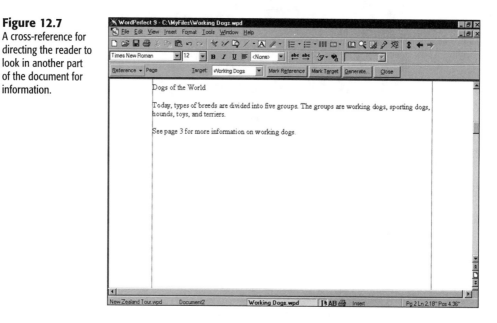

When you add or make changes to references, you need to regenerate the cross-references. WordPerfect automatically renumbers the references.

MARKING REFERENCE AND TARGET ENTRIES

To mark reference and target entries:

1. Choose Tools, Reference, Cross-Reference. The Cross-Reference toolbar appears, as shown in Figure 12.8.

2. Position the insertion point where you want to create a reference.

3. Type introductory text for the cross reference, such as See page #.

4. Press the spacebar to add a space between the introductory text and the page number or other reference-type number.

5. Click the Mark Reference button on the Cross-Reference toolbar.

6. Click the Reference drop-down arrow on the Cross-Reference toolbar and choose a reference type.

7. Type a unique name in the Target box on the Cross-Reference toolbar. WordPerfect uses this name to tie the reference to the target when you generate the cross-reference.

8. Click the Mark Target button on the Cross-Reference toolbar. The reference and target codes are inserted and the page number or other tie-reference type appears at the reference marker.

9. Repeat steps 2–8 for each reference and target in your document.

Figure 12.8
The Cross-Reference toolbar is used to mark references and targets and generate the index.

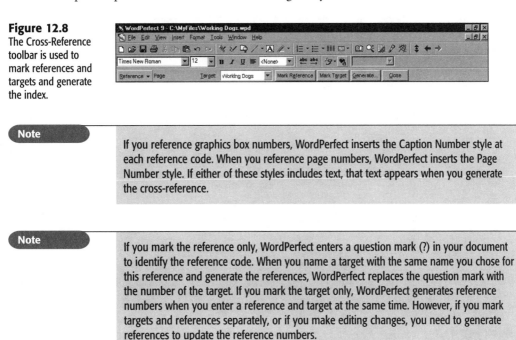

> **Note**
>
> If you reference graphics box numbers, WordPerfect inserts the Caption Number style at each reference code. When you reference page numbers, WordPerfect inserts the Page Number style. If either of these styles includes text, that text appears when you generate the cross-reference.

> **Note**
>
> If you mark the reference only, WordPerfect enters a question mark (?) in your document to identify the reference code. When you name a target with the same name you chose for this reference and generate the references, WordPerfect replaces the question mark with the number of the target. If you mark the target only, WordPerfect generates reference numbers when you enter a reference and target at the same time. However, if you mark targets and references separately, or if you make editing changes, you need to generate references to update the reference numbers.

GENERATING CROSS-REFERENCES

WordPerfect generates cross-references with the page numbers where those targets can be found.

To generate cross-references, click the Generate button on the Cross-Reference toolbar. The Generate dialog box appears. Click OK. WordPerfect inserts the cross-references with page numbers.

WORKING WITH FOOTNOTES AND ENDNOTES

The footnotes and endnotes feature lets you add footnotes and endnotes to your document to refer the reader to a source of information or to provide additional information.

Footnotes appear at the bottom of the page, and endnotes are grouped together at a location you specify. Endnotes usually appear at the end of your document or end of each chapter or section. You can mark both types of notes in the text with a number or special character, such as an asterisk (*). WordPerfect prints a two-inch line to separate the text from the footnotes on the page with the text it references.

The default list style for footnotes or endnotes is numbers. The format for footnotes or endnotes is normally set to the Open Style: left tab, superscript in 6-point Courier half-height; footnote display is level one. By default, WordPerfect prints footnotes at the bottom of the page, as shown in Figure 12.9.

Figure 12.9
Footnotes appear at the bottom of the page.

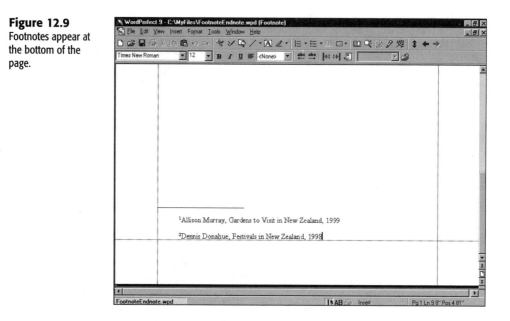

> **Note**
>
> WordPerfect doesn't allow footnotes in tables. If you create a footnote in a table header row, WordPerfect changes the footnote to an endnote when you close the Footnote window.

ADDING FOOTNOTES OR ENDNOTES

To add footnotes or endnotes:

1. Position the insertion point where you want to insert a footnote or endnote.
2. Choose Insert, Footnote/Endnote. The Footnote/Endnote dialog box appears, as shown in Figure 12.10.

Figure 12.10
The Footnote/Endnote dialog box is used for adding footnotes or endnotes to your document.

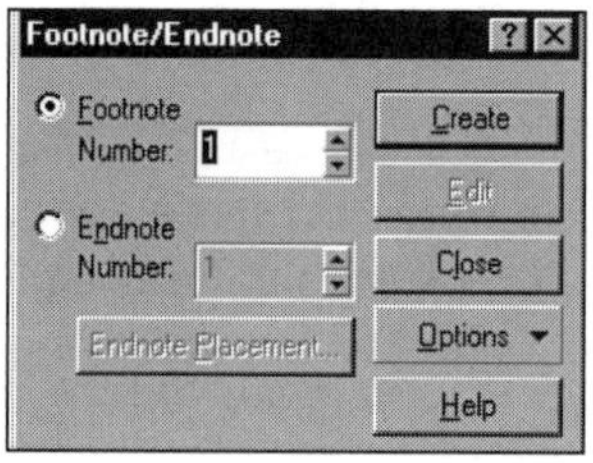

3. Choose Footnote Number or Endnote Number.

4. If you're adding endnotes, click Endnote Placement and choose a location for the endnotes.

> **Note**
> If you want to mark a footnote or endnote with an asterisk (*) instead of a number, click the Options button in the Footnote/Endnote dialog box. Choose Advanced to display the Advanced Footnote Options dialog box. Use the Characters Numbering Method and enter an * in the Characters box.

5. Click Create.

6. Type the text for the footnote or endnote.

> **Tip #67 from**
> *Trudi Reisner*
> For faster footnote/endnote text entry, copy or cut text from your document and paste it into the Footnote or Endnote area.

7. Click anywhere in the document to exit the Footnote/Endnote area.

When you create a footnote or endnote, WordPerfect inserts a footnote or endnote code that contains a maximum of 50 characters in the note. You can view the code and partial text in the Reveal Codes window.

In Draft view, WordPerfect displays the footnote or endnote reference as a superscripted number and doesn't show footnotes on the page. In Page view, you should see the footnote or endnote reference as a superscripted number and the footnotes appear at the bottom of the page. The endnotes appear at the end of a section.

If you want to view the footnotes and endnotes as they will appear when printed, use Print Preview. Figure 12.11 shows endnotes at the end of a section in Print Preview.

PART

II

CH

12

> **Note**
> When a long footnote needs to be continued to the following page, WordPerfect leaves a half-inch of the note of text on the first page. If not enough room is available to print a half-inch of the footnote and the lines of text in which the footnote number occurs, WordPerfect moves both the text and footnote to the next page.

Figure 12.11
Endnotes at the end of
a section in Print
Preview.

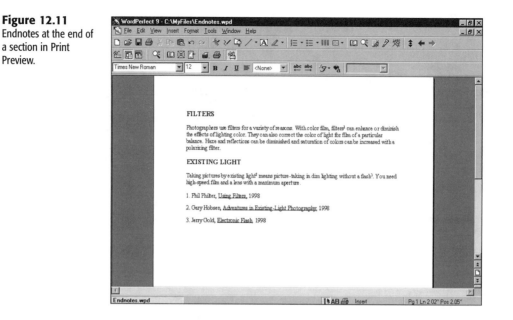

EDITING FOOTNOTES OR ENDNOTES

To make changes to the footnote or endnote text, you should work in Page view. On the Property Bar, you'll see the Footnote/Endnote Next and Footnote/Endnote Previous for moving back and forth among footnotes or endnotes. An easy way to edit footnotes or endnotes is to click the text and make your changes.

If you want to delete a footnote or endnote, just move the insertion point under the footnote or endnote reference and press Delete.

If you mistakenly delete a footnote or endnote number while you are creating or editing a note in the Footnote/Endnote window, just click the Note Number button on the Property Bar. WordPerfect restores the footnote or endnote number in the Footnote or Endnote window. You can also click the Undo button on the WordPerfect toolbar.

PRACTICAL PROJECT

If you work with legal briefs or scholarly manuscripts, you will find that WordPerfect's Table of Authorities feature will help you create a well-organized table of authorities that is easy to read. The Table of Authorities feature enables you to create a list of court cases, rules of court, statutes, agency opinions, and miscellaneous authorities referenced in a document. Each type of authority is usually assigned its own section in the table. Each section is alphabetized separately. You can set up lists for case citations, constitutional citations, and legal citations. You must define each section separately.

Within each section, the citations are listed alphabetically. You can set up to two types of entries in the Table of Authorities full form and short form. The full form entry contains the case name and where the case can be referenced. The short form entry contains only the case name or a unique identifier so that WordPerfect can collect these subsequent references and compile them in a table with their page references. After you mark the authorities, you define the format for the table.

A table of authorities can have up to 16 sections. You can mark authorities in footnotes, endnotes, graphics boxes, and in the body text.

To create a table of authorities, select the text for the full form entry you want to include in the table. Choose Tools, Reference, Table of Authorities. Click Create Full Form on the Property Bar, assign the section name, and edit the Short Form text, if necessary. Select and mark the text for each entry (see Figure 12.12).

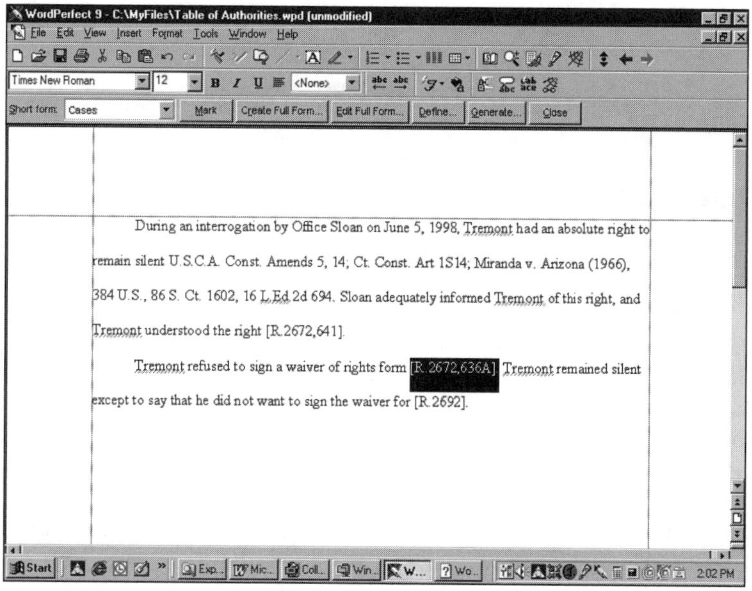

Figure 12.12
Mark the text for each entry.

Define the table and then generate the table. Figure 12.13 shows a table of authorities.

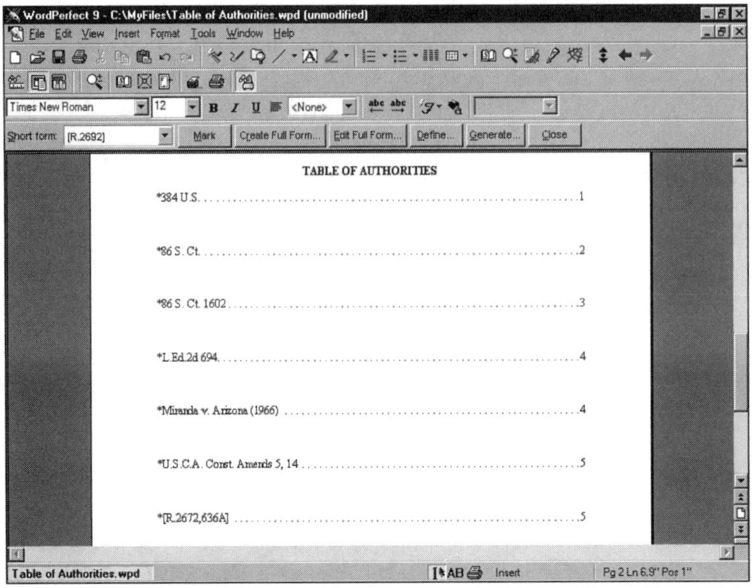

Figure 12.13
This shows a table of authorities.

TROUBLESHOOTING

REDEFINING THE TABLE OF CONTENTS

You don't like the appearance of your table of contents.

Change the definition by moving the insertion point to the [Def Mark: TOC] code in the Reveal Codes window, and then redefine and regenerate the table of contents.

PLACING THE TABLE OF CONTENTS WHERE YOU WANT

You accidentally placed the table of contents in the wrong location in your document.

Wherever your insertion point is located when you generate the table is where the table will appear. Delete the table of contents and delete the [Def Mark: TOC] code in the Reveal Codes window. Then move the insertion point where you want the table of contents to appear, and generate the table in the new location.

UPDATING A TABLE OF CONTENTS

You modified or deleted table of contents items or made changes and additions in your document, and the items and page numbers in your table of contents didn't reflect those changes.

When you make changes to your table of contents entries, WordPerfect doesn't automatically update the table of contents to reflect the changes. You should regenerate the table of contents so that it contains the updated, accurate page numbers.

REDEFINING THE INDEX

You don't like the looks of your index.

Change the index definition by moving the insertion point to the [Def Mark: Index] code in the Reveal Codes window, and then redefine and regenerate the index.

PLACING THE INDEX WHERE YOU WANT

You unintentionally inserted the index in the wrong location in your document.

Wherever your insertion point is located when you generate the index is where the list will appear. Delete the index and delete the [Def Mark: Index] code in the Reveal Codes window. Then move the insertion point where you want the index to appear, and generate the index in the new location.

UPDATING AN INDEX

You modified or deleted index items or made changes and additions in your document, and the items and page numbers in your index didn't reflect those changes.

When you make changes to your index entries, WordPerfect doesn't automatically update the index to reflect those changes. You should regenerate the index so that it contains the updated, accurate page numbers.

CHAPTER 13

USING REVISION TOOLS

In this chapter

PASSWORD-PROTECTING A DOCUMENT

To keep your documents confidential and secure, you can assign a password to them by using the Password feature. This locks your document so that no one can open or print it without the password. Other files associated with the document, such as backup or temporary files, are also locked. Every time you open or look at the password-protected document, WordPerfect asks you to enter the password.

To password-protect a document, first save the document by choosing File, Save or File Save As. Then name the file, put a check mark in the Password Protect check box, and click Save. The Password Protection dialog box appears, as shown in Figure 13.1.

Figure 13.1
Password protect your document in the Password Protection dialog box.

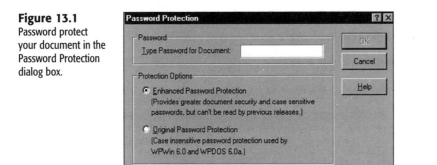

A password can have up to eight characters, and can be case sensitive or not case sensitive, depending on the type of password protection you want. You have a choice between two protection options:

- Enhanced Password Protection (default) offers high document security and case-sensitive passwords, but cannot be read by previous releases of WordPerfect.

- Original Password Protection allows passwords that are not case sensitive and can be read by WordPerfect for Windows 6.0 and WordPerfect for DOS 6.0a.

Choose a protection option, and enter your password in the Type Password for Document box. The characters you type appear as asterisks onscreen. Click OK, type the password again, and click OK again.

When you open the file, WordPerfect displays the Password dialog box. Enter the password and click OK.

Caution

Use passwords with caution. WordPerfect will not open a password-protected file unless you enter the correct password. If you forget a password, unfortunately Corel's technical support staff can do nothing to help. The document is unavailable forever. So, jot down your passwords and put them in a safe place. Otherwise, you'll have to delete the password-protected file.

To change a password or a password-protection option, choose File, Save As, and click Save. WordPerfect prompts you to replace the existing file. Choose Yes. Pick a protection option, and enter the new password twice. This replaces the old password information with the new.

To remove a password, choose File Save As, remove the check from the Password Protect check box, and click Save. When WordPerfect tells you that the file exists, choose Yes.

Tip #68 from	An alternative way to remove password protection is by saving the file in another file
Trudi Reisner	format. Keep in mind that the original file keeps the password.

 If you want to change the password for your document, see "Changing the Password" in the Troubleshooting section at the end of this chapter.

REDLINING WITH DOCUMENT REVISION MARKS

Redlining is a method of indicating changes to a document by displaying marks in the margins and using formatted characters for inserted text and strikeout (dashes superimposed over other characters) for deleted text. These revision marks are useful when several people work on a document and you need a way to let everyone know what changes are proposed.

The Redlining method is used in combination with the Document Compare feature to show how one document differs from the other by displaying inserted and deleted text with distinctive markings.

You can specify how redlining appears on the printed page, which you need to do before you use the Redline feature. To change the redline method and character, choose Document, Redline Method. The options available in the Redline Method dialog box are

- Printer Default Format marks the redline according to your printer's definition of redlining. On most printers, redline appears as a mark in the margin next to the redlined text. On other printers, redlined text appears shaded or highlighted. On a color printer, redlined text appears in red.
- Mark Left Margin displays the redline character in the left margin to indicate redlined text.
- Mark Alternating Margin displays the redline character for redlined text in the left margin for even-numbered pages and in the right margin for odd-numbered pages.
- Mark Right Margin displays the redline character in the right margin to indicate redlined text.

By default, the Redline feature is set to printer dependent, and the Redline character is a vertical bar (|). WordPerfect does not insert text marked with redline and delete text marked for strikeout until you use the Compare and Review Documents feature.

→ For more information on comparing documents, **see** the section "Comparing a Document" later in this chapter on **p. 218**

PART

II

CH

13

USING REDLINE TO SHOW INSERTED TEXT

The Redline feature shows inserted text in red onscreen. If you want to remove redline from your document, delete the [REDLN] codes from the Reveal Codes window.

Note

Before you insert any redline characters in your document, it's wise to save your file with a different name. That way, you can perform redlining in the copy of the file, leaving your original file intact.

Take the following steps to redline inserted text:

1. Select the text you inserted.
2. Choose Format, Font. You see the Font Properties dialog box.
3. In the Appearance group, choose Redline.
4. Click OK. WordPerfect shows the inserted text in red in your document, as shown in Figure 13.2.

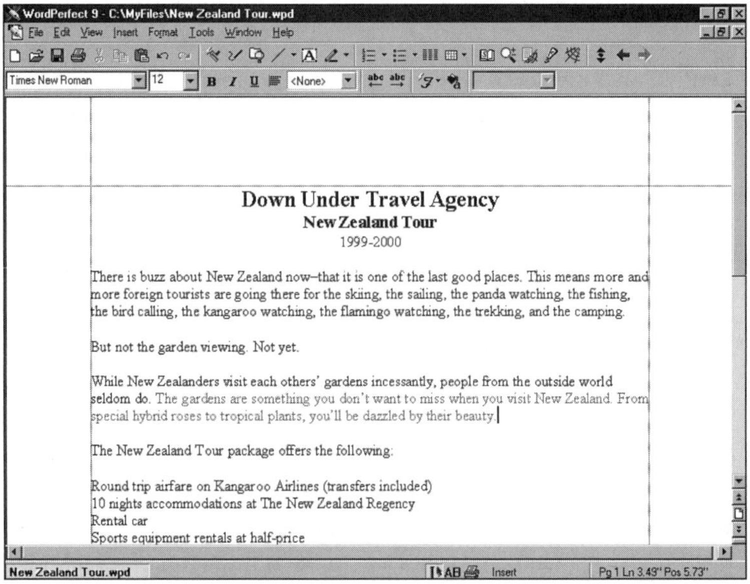

Figure 13.2
Inserted text marked with Redline.

If you want to remove redline from your document, see "Removing Redline" in the Troubleshooting section at the end of this chapter.

USING STRIKEOUT TO SHOW DELETED TEXT

The Strikeout feature shows deleted text with dashes superimposed over other characters onscreen. If you want to remove strikeout from your document, delete the [STKOUT] codes from the Reveal Codes window.

These steps show you how to strike out deleted text:

1. Select the text you want to delete.

2. Choose Format, Font. The Font Properties dialog box opens.

3. In the Appearance group, choose Strikeout.

4. Click OK. WordPerfect shows the deleted text with dashes superimposed over the characters in your document, as shown in Figure 13.3.

Figure 13.3
Deleted text marked with Strikeout.

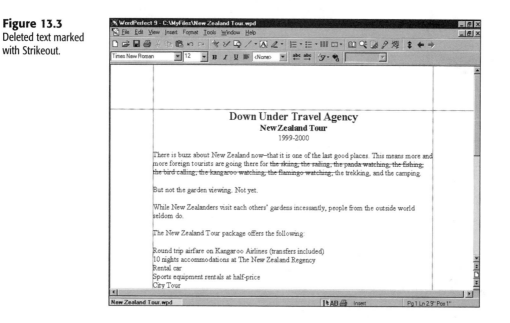

If you want to remove strikeout from your document, see "Removing Strikeout" in the Troubleshooting section at the end of this chapter.

USING DOCUMENT COMPARE

WordPerfect lets you compare an edited document to the original document with the Document Compare feature. The text in the edited document that doesn't exist in the original document is redlined. The text that exists in the original document but not in the edited document is copied to the edited document and marked with strikeout.

By default, WordPerfect compares differences by phrase. The program uses phrase indicators such as punctuation marks and codes, and compares the text between those indicators. The comparison involves all text, including footnotes, endnotes, and tables. It does not compare text in headers, footers, or graphics boxes.

PART

II

CH

13

There are several ways to use the Document Compare feature: Compare Only and Compare/Review as a reviewer or author. With the Compare Only feature, WordPerfect inserts or removes Redline and Strikeout codes. Compare/Review as a reviewer lets you edit the document and insert Redline and Strikeout codes in a color. Compare/Review as an author lets you annotate the document with comments and remove the annotations.

COMPARING A DOCUMENT

The Document Compare feature lets you compare documents and show the markings in either a new document or the current document (original document).

> **Caution**
>
> Save a backup copy of the current document with a distinctive filename before you begin making comparisons. That way, you have the original file just in case you decide against the editing changes.

The steps for comparing documents are as follows:

1. Open the first document that you want to compare, which is called the current document.

2. Choose File, Document, Compare. The Compare Documents dialog box appears, as shown in Figure 13.4. The current document name appears in the With box.

Figure 13.4
The Compare Documents dialog box is used to compare documents and show markings in either the new document or the current document.

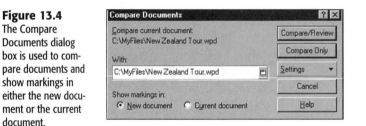

3. Specify the name of the file you are comparing in the With box.

4. Choose an option to show markings in a new document or the current document.

5. Choose Compare Only. The current document appears with inserted text marked as redline text and deleted text marked as strikeout text.

> **Note**
>
> If you want to delete redline and strikeout markings, choose File, Document, Remove Markings. Pick any one of the four choices: Remove Redline Markings and Strikeout Text, Remove Strikeout Text Only, Remove Document Compare Deletions Only, or Remove All Document Compare Markings.

Tip #69 from	If you want to compare documents by word, sentence, or paragraph instead of by phrase, choose Settings in the Compare Documents dialog box and change any of the options for the Compare Only feature.
Trudi Reisner	

 If you want to keep your original document intact before you compare documents, see "Keeping the Original Comparison Document Intact" in the Troubleshooting section at the end of this chapter.

REVIEWING A DOCUMENT AS A REVIEWER

The Compare/Review feature lets you decide whether to insert or remove Redline and Strikeout codes by editing the document in the Review window in a specific color.

The steps for reviewing a document as a reviewer are as follows:

1. Open the first document that you want to compare, which is called the current document.
2. Choose File, Document, Compare. The Compare Documents dialog box appears.
3. Specify the name of the file you are comparing in the With box.
4. Choose an option to show markings in a new document or the current document.
5. Choose Compare/Review.

Tip #70 from	You can also choose File, Document, Review, and click the Reviewer button to review a document.
Trudi Reisner	

6. Type your username and initials, and click OK. The Review window and its Review Property Bar appear, as shown in Figure 13.5.
7. To select a color for your changes, click the Set Color button on the Review Property Bar, and choose a color.
8. Insert, delete, copy, and move text to edit the document.
9. Click the Close button on the Review Property Bar to close the Review window.
10. Save the document.

PART
II

CH

13

Insert the Current
Annotation into
the Document.

Insert All the
Annotations into
the Document.

Delete the Current
Annotation from
the Document.

Delete All the
Annotations from
the Document.

Figure 13.5
The Review window
and Property Bar are
used to set a color for
your markings and
show redline and
strikeout as you edit
the document as a
reviewer.

Display
Annotations in
Normal Text Color.

Go to the Previous
Annotation.

Go to the Next
Annotation.

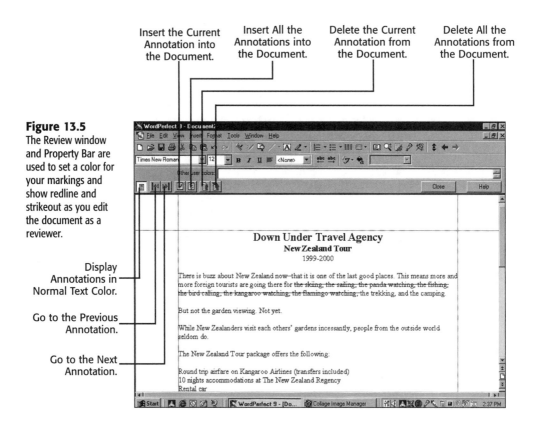

REVIEWING A DOCUMENT AS AN AUTHOR

With the Compare/Review feature, you can decide whether to accept or reject Redline and Strikeout codes and annotate the document with your comments.

To review a document as an author:

1. Open the first document that you want to compare, which is called the current document.

2. Choose File, Document, Compare. The Compare Documents dialog box appears.

3. Specify the name of the file you are comparing in the With box.

4. Choose an option to show markings in a new document or the current document.

5. Choose Compare/Review.

Tip #71 from
Trudi Reisner

You can also choose File, Document, Review, and click the Reviewer button to review a document.

6. Type your username and initials, if prompted, and click OK. If the username and initials have already been entered, the dialog box doesn't come up. The Review window and its Review Property Bar appear.

7. Click the Author button.

8. Click the Previous or Next button on the Property Bar to move from change to change.

9. Choose one of the following buttons to review the document as an author:

   - Show/Hide—To see the edited text in the document without color markings.
   - Insert Current Annotation—Accepts the current annotation.
   - Insert All Annotations—Accepts all the annotations.
   - Delete Current Annotation—Rejects the current annotation.
   - Delete All Annotations—Rejects all the annotations.

10. Save the document.

11. Click the Close button on the Property Bar to close the Review window.

> **Note**
>
> If you accidentally removed all markings, close the document and don't save the changes. This restores the current document to its precomparison state.

If you accidentally removed all markings, see "Restoring the Comparison Document" in the Troubleshooting section at the end of this chapter.

HIGHLIGHTING TEXT

The Highlighting feature is the electronic version of that transparent yellow (or any color) pen you may have used in school. You can highlight important parts of a document with a transparent highlighting color.

To turn on the Highlighting feature, choose Tools, Highlight, On. You can also click the Highlight button on the WordPerfect toolbar to turn on the Highlighting feature. The mouse looks like a highlighting pen. Select the text you want to highlight and like magic, you should see highlighted text in your document.

WordPerfect can highlight in any of the numerous colors available. If you prefer some color other than the default yellow color, choose Tools, Highlight, Color or click the down arrow next to the Highlight button and choose a color, as demonstrated in Figure 13.6.

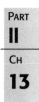

PART

II

CH

13

Figure 13.6
Choosing a color with
the Highlight tool, and
a sample of highlighted
text in a document.

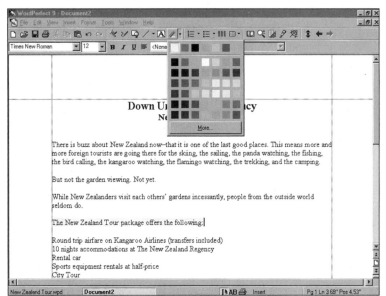

Another way to use highlighting is to first select your highlight color, and then drag across the text you want highlighted. You can highlight several separate blocks of text this way, before clicking the Highlight button again to turn highlighting off.

By default, WordPerfect doesn't show highlighting in the document and doesn't print highlighting. The Print/Show command on the Highlight menu should have a check mark next to it. To show highlighting and print it, choose Tools, Highlight, Print/Show. WordPerfect shows the highlighting in the document and will print it, too.

To remove highlighting, select all the text that contains the highlighting that you want to remove. Choose Tools, Highlight, Remove or click the Highlight button on the WordPerfect toolbar. If you want to remove highlighting in a single section from your document, click anywhere in the section, and click the Highlight button on the WordPerfect toolbar.

If you got carried away with highlighting and highlighted too much text, see "Dehighlighting Text" in the Troubleshooting section at the end of this chapter.

USING DOCUMENT COMMENTS

The Document Comments feature is useful for including personal notes, comments, or special instructions in your WordPerfect documents. Comments are especially helpful for reminding you or others to follow up on certain details of the text. You can also use comments to leave messages about the document to someone else working on the same document.

The document comment appears where you inserted it in your text, enclosed in a double-ruled box. You can edit and delete comments, display and hide comments, as well as convert comments to text and print them.

INSERTING A COMMENT

Follow these instructions to insert a comment:

1. Choose Insert, Comment, Create. A Comment window with a Comment Property Bar appears onscreen.

2. Type the text of your comment in the Comment window, as shown in the comment example in Figure 13.7.

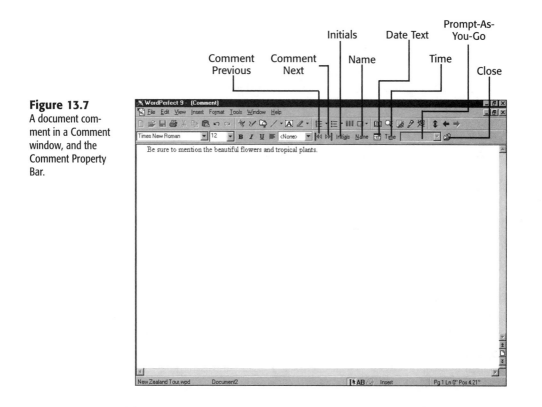

Figure 13.7
A document comment in a Comment window, and the Comment Property Bar.

3. Use the buttons on the Comment Property Bar to specify the text to be bold, italicized, or underlined.

4. You can assign user information to a comment such as initials, author name, and the creation date and time of comments, by using the buttons on the Comment Property Bar.

5. Click Close on the Comment Property Bar to close the Comment window.

PART

II

CH

13

To delete a comment, right-click the Comment icon, and choose Delete from the QuickMenu. If you delete text that includes a comment, you also delete the comment. Always look for comment boxes in the left margin when deleting text.

Tip #72 from	If more than one person is creating comments, specify a different color font for the text for
Trudi Reisner	each person to distinguish his or her comments from the comments of other users. Use the Format, Font command and pick a color.

 If you inadvertently delete text that includes a comment, see "Accidentally Deleting Comments" in the Troubleshooting section at the end of this chapter.

EDITING A COMMENT

You can make changes to a comment and navigate to other comments in a document to change them one at one time.

To edit a comment, choose Insert, Comment, Edit or double-click the Comment icon in the left margin. The comment appears in its Comment window. Make any changes to the text of your comment. Use the Comment Next button or Comment Previous button on the Comment Property Bar to edit other comments in the document. Click the Close button to return to the main document text.

Tip #73 from	You can quickly edit a comment by right-clicking it, and choosing Edit.
Trudi Reisner	

If you want to cut or copy a comment, right-click the Comment icon, and choose Cut or Copy. Click in the document where you want the comment to appear, and click the Paste button on the WordPerfect toolbar. You should see the comment in the new location.

SHOWING AND HIDING COMMENTS

By default, the comments are hidden unless you decide to display them or convert them to text. In Draft view, comments appear as shaded text in the body of a document. In Page view and Two Pages view, comments appear as balloon icons in the left margin. To view a comment in Page or Two Pages view, click the Comment icon. The comment appears in a gray balloon in the document, as shown in Figure 13.8.

To display a comment, click the Comment icon in the left margin. To open the Comment window, double-click a Comment icon. Click the Comment Next or Comment Previous button on the Comment Property Bar to navigate to other comments in the document.

 If you created a comment and you don't see it in your document, see "Viewing Comments" in the Troubleshooting section at the end of this chapter.

Figure 13.8
A Comment icon and
comment.

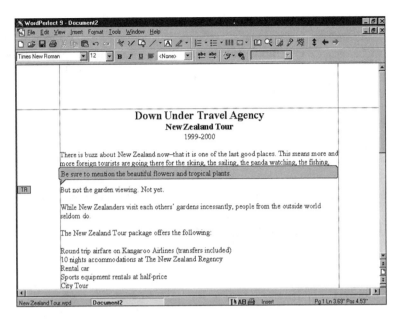

CONVERTING A COMMENT TO TEXT

You can convert a comment to text and print it. When you convert comments to text, WordPerfect searches backward from the insertion point and converts the first comment found. The comment is converted whether or not it is displayed.

If you want to convert a comment to text, click the comment that you want to convert to text, and choose Insert, Comment, Convert to Text. The comment now appears in your document as normal text.

PRINTING COMMENTS

Before you can print a comment, you must convert a comment to text. Then you can print your document that contains the comment as you normally would.

WORKING WITH BOOKMARKS

The Bookmark command lets you create invisible bookmarks. A WordPerfect bookmark is just like a bookmark that you insert between the pages of a book so that you can find your place again. With a document bookmark, you can mark a specific location in your document and return quickly to that location. This is useful for keeping track of specific locations throughout a document to insert text, make changes, and so on.

After you create a bookmark, you can move it to a new location in your document, and rename the bookmark, if desired.

PART

II

CH

13

QuickMarks is another bookmark feature that lets you set a temporary bookmark in your document. A QuickMark marks one location at a time. When you insert the next QuickMark, the previous location is replaced with the new QuickMark location.

INSERTING A BOOKMARK

Bookmarks appear in the Bookmark dialog box in the order in which you create them. You can insert up to 10,920 bookmarks in one document.

To insert a bookmark, follow these steps:

1. Position the insertion point where you want to insert a bookmark.

2. Choose Tools, Bookmark. The Bookmark dialog box opens, as shown in Figure 13.9.

Figure 13.9
The Bookmark dialog box is used to create, go to, delete, move, and rename book-marks.

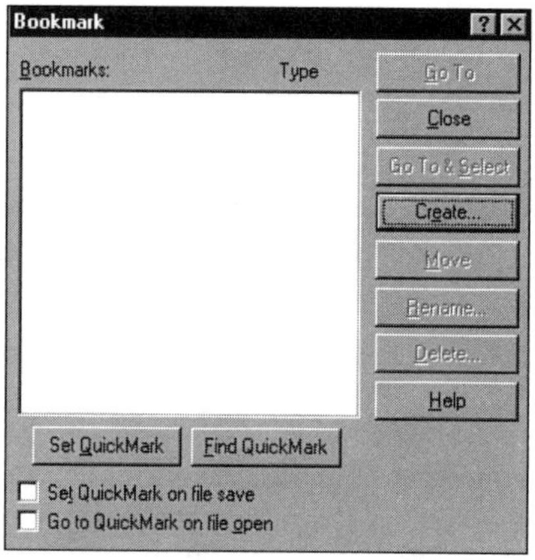

3. Click Create. The Create Bookmark dialog box opens, as shown in Figure 13.10.

Figure 13.10
The Create Bookmark dialog box is for nam-ing and creating a new bookmark.

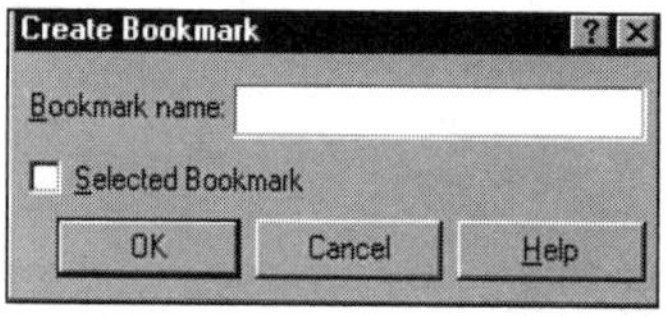

4. Type a bookmark name in the Bookmark Name text box.

Tip #74 from
Trudi Reisner

If you prefer to associate a bookmark with selected text, select the text, and then check the Selected Bookmark check box. That way, you can go to that bookmark and the text will be automatically selected for you.

---

5. Click OK.

If you no longer need a bookmark, you can delete it. Choose <u>T</u>ools, <u>B</u>ookmark. In the Bookmark dialog box, select the bookmark you want to delete, and click <u>D</u>elete. Then choose <u>Y</u>es to confirm the deletion.

GOING TO A BOOKMARK

To go to a bookmark, choose <u>T</u>ools, <u>B</u>ookmark. From the Bookmark dialog box, select the bookmark to which you want to go, and click Go To. If you created a Selected Bookmark, choose the selected bookmark, and click Go To & Select. WordPerfect takes you to the bookmark location and positions the insertion point there, or selects the text (see Figure 13.11), depending on which type of bookmark you created.

Figure 13.11
A bookmark chosen in the Bookmarks list and the selected bookmark in the document.

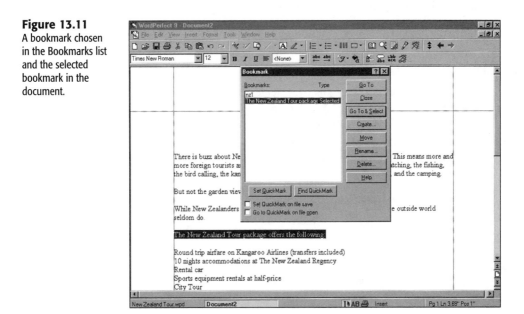

MOVING A BOOKMARK

If you want to change the location of an existing bookmark, you can use the Bookmark Move command. First move the insertion point to the new location in the document. Then use <u>T</u>ools, <u>B</u>ookmark, select the bookmark you want to move, and click <u>M</u>ove. When you next use this bookmark, WordPerfect finds it in the new location.

RENAMING A BOOKMARK

If you want to change the bookmark name, choose <u>T</u>ools, <u>B</u>ookmark. Select the bookmark you want to rename, and click Rename. Type the new bookmark name and click OK. The new bookmark name appears in the Bookmarks list. Now you can find the bookmark using the new name.

PART
II

CH
13

USING QUICKMARKS

To set a QuickMark, start by positioning the insertion point where you want the QuickMark. Choose Tools, Bookmark. At the bottom of the Bookmark dialog box, click Set QuickMark. WordPerfect sets the QuickMark location. To find the QuickMark, click Find QuickMark in the Bookmark dialog box.

You can also set a QuickMark at the insertion point whenever you save a document so that you can return to that location quickly. To do so, check the Set QuickMark on File Save check box in the Bookmark dialog box.

Additionally, you can set a QuickMark to move the insertion point directly to the QuickMark each time you open the current file. Just check the Go To QuickMark on File Open check box.

PRACTICAL PROJECT

If you had created a press release that was suggested in the Practical Project section at the end of Chapter 5, "Getting Started with Corel WordPerfect 9," go in and edit the document. Make changes to the text using Redline and Strikeout, add comments, bookmarks, and QuickMarks, and highlight any text to which you want to bring attention. Then, review the document and accept or reject the changes.

TROUBLESHOOTING

CHANGING THE PASSWORD

You want to change the password for your document.

Use File, Save As, click Save, and choose Yes to replace the existing file. Choose a protection option, and enter a different password for the document twice.

REMOVING REDLINE

You want to remove redline from your document.

One way to remove redline from your document is to delete the [REDLN] codes from the Reveal Codes window. Another way is to use File, Document, Remove Markings, and choose Remove Redline Markings and Strikeout Text.

REMOVING STRIKEOUT

You want to remove strikeout from your document.

To remove strikeout from your document, delete the [STKOUT] codes from the Reveal Codes window. Another way is to use File, Document, Remove Markings, and choose Remove Redline Markings and Strikeout Text or Remove Strikeout Text Only.

KEEPING THE ORIGINAL COMPARISON DOCUMENT INTACT

You want to leave your original document intact when comparing documents.

Save a backup copy of the current document with a distinctive filename before you begin making comparisons. That way, you have the original file just in case you decide against the editing changes.

RESTORING THE COMPARISON DOCUMENT

You accidentally removed all markings, which was not your intention.

Close the document and don't save the changes. This restores the current document to its precomparison state.

DEHIGHLIGHTING TEXT

You highlighted more text that you wanted to.

Select the highlighted text, and click the Highlight button on the WordPerfect toolbar.

ACCIDENTALLY DELETING COMMENTS

You deleted text that includes a comment.

When you delete text that includes a comment, you also delete the comment. Always look for comment boxes when deleting text. To bring back the comment, click the Undo button on the WordPerfect toolbar.

VIEWING COMMENTS

You created a comment and you don't see it in the document.

In Draft view, you will see comments as shaded text in the body of a document. In Page view and Two Pages view, you should see comments as balloon icons in the left margin. To display a comment in Page Mode view, click the Comment icon in the left margin. A gray balloon with a comment appears in the document.

CHAPTER **14**

CREATING COLUMNS AND TABLES

In this chapter

WORKING WITH PARALLEL COLUMNS

You can create parallel text columns in WordPerfect that are read from left to right across the page. Parallel columns are useful for entering tables, scripts, exhibits, side-by-side translations, video scripts, inventory lists, personnel rosters, duty schedules, and instructions. For example, in a set of instructions, you can type tips in the first column and basic instructions in the second column.

You can create standard parallel columns or you can set up parallel columns with block protect. You can view your parallel columns in any view. Setting up parallel columns involves three tasks:

- Define parallel columns.
- Enter column headings.
- Enter text into parallel columns.

Figure 14.1 shows an example of parallel columns.

Figure 14.1
Create parallel columns of text by defining the parallel columns, entering the column headings, and entering text into the columns.

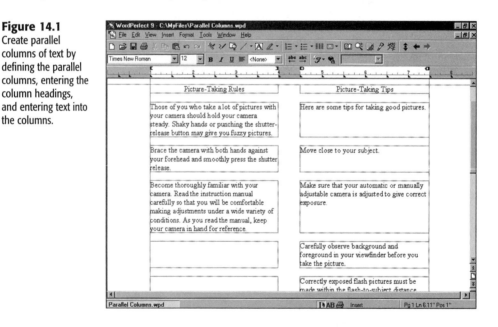

DEFINING PARALLEL COLUMNS

To define parallel columns, choose Format, Columns to display the Columns dialog box (see Figure 14.2). In the Type of Columns section, choose Parallel. Specify the number of columns you want.

Figure 14.2
The Columns dialog box is used to define parallel columns.

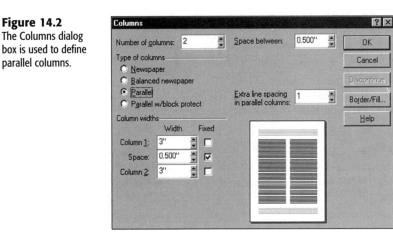

By default, the distance between two or more columns is one-half inch; however, you can specify the new space between columns in the Space Between box. You can also specify the amount of line spacing between rows in the Extra Line Spacing in Parallel Columns box.

Check the sample box to see the results after you specify an option. When the parallel columns appear the way you want, click OK to turn the columns on.

> **Note**
>
> If you didn't set up your distance between columns properly, your columns are probably misaligned. Change the distance between columns in the Space Between box to realign your columns.

 If the distance between parallel columns look misaligned, see "Aligning Parallel Columns" in the Troubleshooting section at the end of this chapter.

Tip #75 from
Trudi Reisner

To quickly create parallel columns, click the Columns button on the WordPerfect toolbar, and choose the number of columns you want. Click the Columns button on the WordPerfect toolbar again or choose Format, Columns to open the Columns dialog box. Then change the column type from Newspaper-Style to Parallel in the Type of Columns group.

Parallel with Block Protect columns prevent a horizontal block of text from being divided by a soft page break. When a column (except for the last column) reaches the bottom margin, the entire block of columns is moved to the next page. To turn on Block Protect for your parallel columns, in the Columns dialog box, choose the Parallel with Block Protect option in the Type of Columns section.

PART
II

CH
14

Note

If a block of columns is longer than a page, and Block Protect is turned off, the text continues in the same column on the next page without starting a new page to keep the blocks together.

If your column items are splitting at the end of a page, see "Grouping Column Items" in the Troubleshooting section at the end of this chapter.

If you change your mind about the definition of your parallel columns, you can make adjustments at any time. Create the new definition without moving the insertion point from the location where you defined the original columns. WordPerfect replaces the previous definition code with the new one, and the new column definition settings will be preserved in the Columns dialog box.

If you find that your text in columns is misaligned, there is an excellent way to align the text. You separate the columns with borders, especially when the text is aligned flush with the vertical lines in the border. You can insert borders before or after you type text in columns. Just use the Border/Fill button in the Columns dialog box and choose a border style. You can also add shading to the columns by choosing a fill style.

Caution

If you change the font for text in parallel columns, the tops or bottoms of the columns will be misaligned. Use the Advanced feature to reposition the text at the top or bottom of each column. To align the tops of the columns, use Format, Typesetting, Advance. Next, in the Vertical Position section, select Up from Insertion Point or Down from Insertion Point, and then enter a value in the Vertical Distance box. To specify a fine increment, enter a value in points, Remember, a point is equal to 1/72 of an inch. For example, enter 2p to specify two points. Repeat these steps to adjust the bottoms of the columns by adding or subtracting 1 or 2 points of leading between the last lines of sections and subsequent headings.

If you changed the font for text in columns, and the columns are misaligned, see "Aligning Tops or Bottoms of Columns" in the Troubleshooting section at the end of this chapter.

ENTERING COLUMN HEADINGS FOR PARALLEL COLUMNS

After you define your parallel columns, the next step is to enter the column headings. Start by positioning the insertion point in the left margin where you want to enter the first column heading. Type the column heading and center it. Press Ctrl+Enter to enter a hard column break and move to the next column. Type the second column heading (see Figure 14.3). Repeat these steps until you finish entering all the column headings.

Figure 14.3
The column headings for parallel columns.

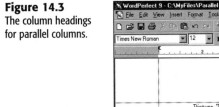

> **Caution**
>
> Be sure to use a hard column break (Ctrl+Enter) to end each column. WordPerfect uses the hard column break to determine where a column begins and ends. Without hard column breaks, you will have a problem creating and editing your columns.

If you pressed Enter instead of Ctrl+Enter to end a column, and the insertion point moved to the next line, see "Using a Hard Column Break" in the Troubleshooting section at the end of this chapter.

If you accidentally pressed Ctrl+Enter twice to end a column, and WordPerfect moved the column heading to the previous column, see "Ending a Column" in the Troubleshooting section at the end of this chapter.

ENTERING TEXT INTO PARALLEL COLUMNS

After you define the parallel columns and enter the column headings, the final step is to enter the text for your parallel columns. Begin by positioning the insertion point in the left margin below the first column heading. If you had centered the column headings, change the alignment back to Left justification. Then type the text for the first column. Press Ctrl+Enter to move to the next column. Repeat these steps until you finish entering all the columns.

After you type the text in the last column, press Ctrl+Enter to move the insertion point to the left margin. Type the next group of columns. Then, choose Format, Columns, and click the Discontinue button to turn Columns off, as shown in Figure 14.4.

PART

II

CH

14

Tip #76 from
Trudi Reisner

A quick way to turn Columns off is to click the Columns button on the WordPerfect toolbar and choose Discontinue.

Figure 14.4
Discontinue parallel columns.

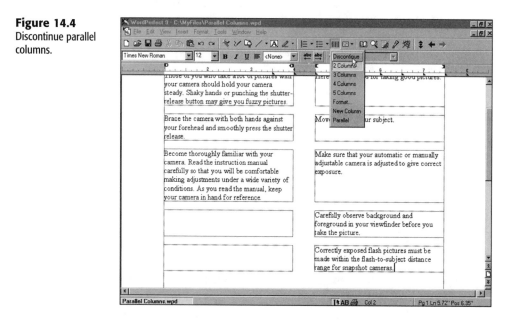

Tip #77 from
Trudi Reisner

If you want to create a blank column, press Ctrl+Enter (Hard Column Break) twice.

 If you accidentally forgot to turn columns off, see "Discontinuing Columns" in the Troubleshooting section at the end of this chapter.

WORKING WITH NEWSPAPER-STYLE COLUMNS

Newspaper-style columns are sometimes referred to as snaking columns. Snaking columns contain text that wraps from the bottom of one column to the top of the next column. Newspaper columns are best suited for magazine articles, lists, indexes, bulletins, and newsletters. As you type the text, WordPerfect wraps the text within the column until you reach the bottom of the page and then wraps to the top of the next column, as shown in Figure 14.5.

Figure 14.5
Create newspaper columns when you want text to wrap from the bottom of one column to the top of the next column.

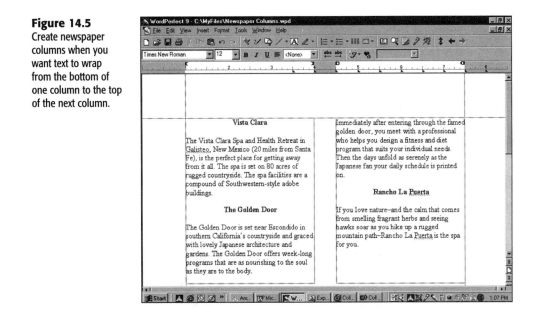

WordPerfect's default column setting for columns is Newspaper with two columns and a half-inch gutter between the columns. You can enter a maximum of 24 newspaper columns per page.

You can create standard newspaper columns or balanced newspaper columns. You can view newspaper columns in any view.

CREATING NEWSPAPER-STYLE COLUMNS

To set up newspaper columns, choose Format, Columns to display the Columns dialog box (see Figure 14.6). In the Type of Columns section, choose Newspaper. Specify the number of columns you want.

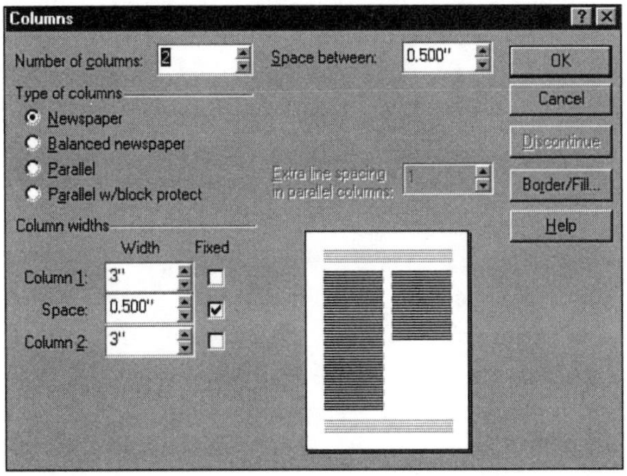

Figure 14.6
The Columns dialog box is used to set up newspaper columns.

By default, the distance between two or more columns is one-half inch; however, you can specify the new space between columns in the Space Between box. Look at the sample box to see the results after you specify an option. When the newspaper columns appear the way you want, click OK to turn the columns on.

Type the text for the columns. Then, the last thing you need to do is turn columns off by clicking the Columns button on the WordPerfect toolbar and choosing Discontinue.

Note

If you didn't set up your distance between columns properly, your columns are probably misaligned. Change the distance between columns in the Space Between box to realign your columns.

Tip #78 from
Trudi Reisner

You can quickly create newspaper columns by clicking the Columns button on the WordPerfect toolbar, and choosing the number of columns you want.

If you want to make all the newspaper columns the same length, use the Balanced Newspaper columns feature. To turn on Balanced Newspaper columns, in the Columns dialog box, choose Balanced Newspaper in the Type of Columns section.

Tip #79 from
Trudi Reisner

You can convert text to newspaper columns instantly by selecting the text, clicking the Columns button on the WordPerfect toolbar, and choosing the number of columns you want. If the last newspaper column is shorter than the rest of the columns, use the Balanced Newspaper columns to make all the columns the same length.

You can change newspaper column definition whenever you want. Create a new definition without moving the insertion point from the location where you set up the original columns. WordPerfect replaces the previous definition code with the new one, and the new column definition settings are preserved in the Columns dialog box.

If the text in your columns is misaligned, you can separate the columns with borders. That way, the text will be aligned flush with the vertical lines in the border. You can insert borders before or after you type text in columns. Just use the Border/Fill button in the Columns dialog box and choose a border style. You can also add shading to the columns by choosing a fill style.

Caution

> If you change the font for text in newspaper columns, the tops or bottoms of the columns will be misaligned. Use the Advanced feature to reposition the text at the top or bottom of each column. To align the tops of the columns, use Format, Typesetting, Advance. Next, in the Vertical Position section, select Up from Insertion Point or Down from Insertion Point, and then enter a value in the Vertical Distance box. To specify a fine increment, enter a value in points, Remember, a point is equal to 1/72 of an inch. For example, enter 2p to specify two points. Repeat these steps to adjust the bottoms of the columns by adding or subtracting 1 or 2 points of leading between the last lines of sections and subsequent headings.

Editing Newspaper-Style Columns

WordPerfect's Columns feature enables you to move columns around with cursor movement keys. You can also copy and delete columns.

To edit a column, start by positioning the insertion point in the column you want to change. If you want to copy, cut, or delete text within a column, be sure to select a block of text before you perform any editing commands. See Table 14.1 for the editing keys that you can use to edit columns.

TABLE 14.1   COLUMN-EDITING KEYS

Editing Key(s)	Effect
Ctrl+C (Copy)	Copies selected text within a column
Ctrl+X (Cut)	Moves selected text within a column
Ctrl+V (Paste)	Pastes selected text within a column
Delete	Deletes selected text within a column
→	Moves the insertion point to the right within the current column
←	Moves the insertion point to the left within the current column
↑	Scrolls up through all columns
↓	Scrolls down through all columns
Ctrl+Home	Moves the insertion point to the top of the first column
Ctrl+End	Moves the insertion point to the bottom of the last column
Ctrl+→	Moves the insertion point to the column on the right
Ctrl+←	Moves the insertion point to the column on the left

You can also use the mouse to drag the borders between columns. Point to a vertical border and the mouse pointer changes into a double arrow. Drag the border left or right to adjust column width.

PART

II

CH

14

WORKING WITH TABLES

Corel WordPerfect's Tables feature offers many practical uses. Tables can illustrate, define, and explain text; they can enhance your documents and make them more effective.

A table also gives you a convenient way to organize text. Use a table to organize columns of numbers, produce forms, or add spreadsheets to your documents. There are many formatting options you can apply to a table to make it visually appealing. WordPerfect even provides a Table SpeedFormat to let you preview and apply a table style (a set of formats) to your table all at once.

A table consists of columns and rows that form a grid of cells. You can fill cells with text or graphics. When you type text into a cell, the text wraps automatically from one line to the next, and the cell expands vertically to accommodate your text.

Tip #80 from	Several PerfectExpert Projects, including the calendar and the Balance Sheet, are based on
Trudi Reisner	tables.

An example of a WordPerfect table is shown in Figure 14.7.

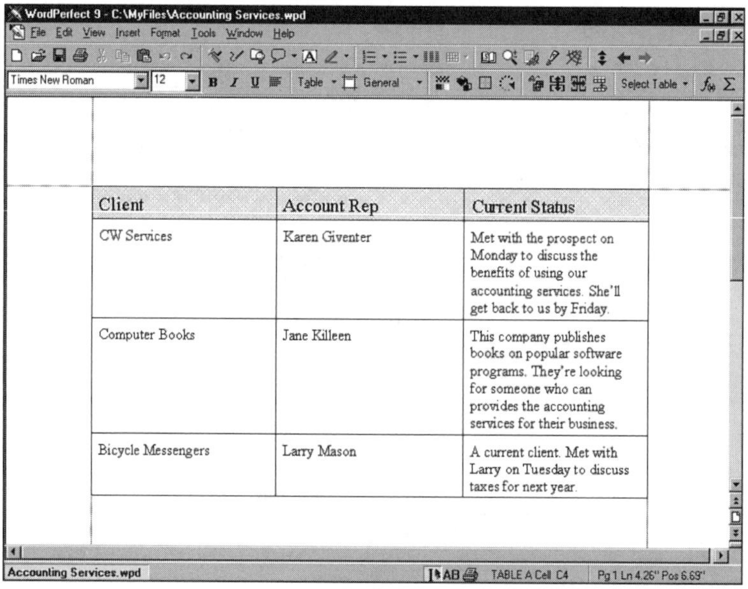

Figure 14.7
Enter columns of text with automatic word wrap by placing the text in a WordPerfect table.

CREATING A TABLE

A table can be inserted at any point in a document. You can create a table either by choosing Insert, Table or with the Table QuickCreate button on the toolbar.

> **Note**
>
> The quickest way to create a table is by pulling down a grid from the Table QuickCreate button on the toolbar, and dragging through the number of columns and rows that you want for your table. The size of the grid doesn't limit the size of your table; the grid expands as you drag past its edge.

To create a table from the menu, take the following steps:

> **Tip #81 from**
> *Trudi Reisner*
>
> It's a good idea to already have your margins set before creating a table. When you change margins after you've created the table, it tends to mess up the column widths.

1. Position the insertion point where you want the table to begin.
2. Choose Insert, Table or click the Table QuickCreate button on the toolbar. The Create Table dialog box is displayed, as shown in Figure 14.8.

Figure 14.8
Specify the number of columns and rows when you create a table.

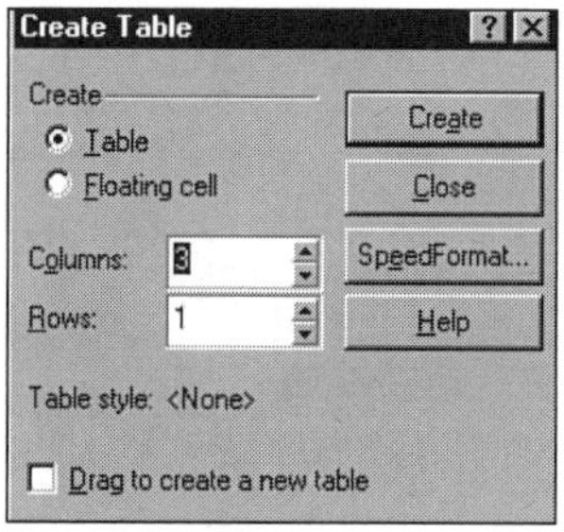

> **Tip #82 from**
> *Trudi Reisner*
>
> You can also create a floating cell with this dialog box, which is a 1×1 table. Floating cells are useful because they can be linked to Quattro Pro notebooks to present dynamically changing information in the middle of a paragraph.

3. Enter the number of Columns and Rows that you want.
4. Choose a style for your table, if desired, with the SpeedFormat button. For information on using this feature, see the section "Using Table SpeedFormat to Enhance a Table," later in this chapter.

PART
II

CH
14

Note

It's easy to add rows to a table after you create it. See the section "Inserting and Deleting Columns and Rows," later in this chapter.

5. Click Create. A table with the specified number of columns and rows (and predefined style, if any) is inserted in your document. The table spans the width between the left and right margins. All columns have the same width.

MOVING WITHIN A TABLE

The easiest way to move within a table is to use the scrollbars until the part of the table you want is visible onscreen, and then click with the mouse in the desired cell.

Tip #83 from
Trudi Reisner

When the insertion point is positioned in a table, WordPerfect automatically displays the Tables Property Bar for you.

You can also move within a table by using the keyboard, as shown in Table 14.2.

TABLE 14.2 KEYBOARD COMMANDS FOR MOVING IN A TABLE

Command	Result
Tab or →	Next cell
Shift+Tab or ←	Previous cell
↑	Up one row
↓	Down one row

ENTERING TEXT WITHIN A TABLE

As you enter text into your table, consider each cell a miniature document with its own margins and formatting. As you enter text, words wrap automatically to a new line and the row increases in depth. Press Enter only when you need to force words to wrap to the next line.

→ For more information on typing text, **see** "Typing Text," **p. 82**

When you have completed entering text for a cell, press Tab to move to the next cell. When you reach the last cell of the table, pressing Tab creates a new row so that you can continue entering data.

EDITING TABLE DESIGN

Tables have flexible structures. When you first create a table, it has a specified number of columns and rows, and every column has the same width. While you work with the table, you can adjust the column width to suit your taste, and you can add or delete columns and rows. You can even join cells to create a single cell, or you can split a cell into rows or columns.

When your insertion point is in a table, you see the Tables Property Bar. If you have one or more cells selected, you see the Table Cell Selected Property Bar instead. These toolbars have a number of buttons that make editing your table design a snap.

Tip #84 from
Trudi Reisner

You can also access most table formatting commands by right-clicking in the table to display the QuickMenu.

SELECTING TABLE CELLS

Many editing operations can be performed more quickly if you select the group of rows, columns, or cells that you want them to apply to. Follow these guidelines for selecting table elements:

- Turn on row/column indicators by clicking the Table button on the Property Bar, and then choosing Row/Col Indicators on the drop-down menu.

- To select a single cell, position the mouse pointer against any edge of the cell so that it becomes a white arrow as shown in Figure 14.9, and then click the mouse button. The entire cell should be highlighted.

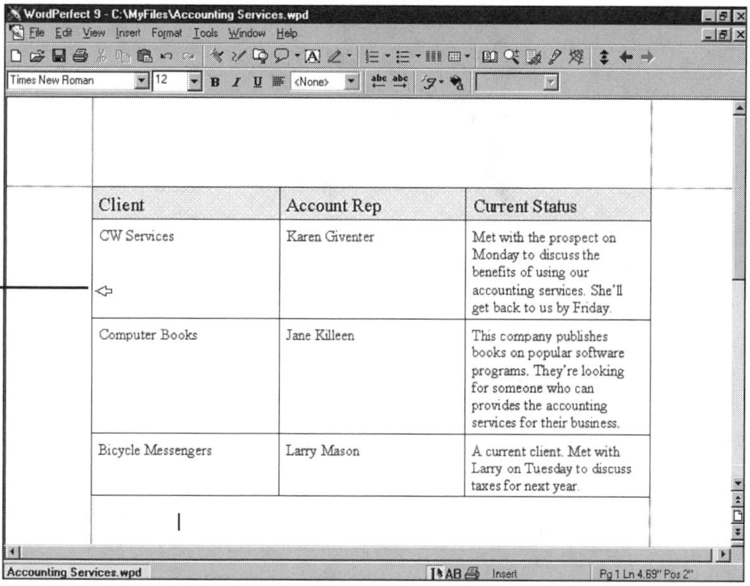

Figure 14.9
You can select a cell to change the formatting of all the text in that cell at once.

White arrow pointer

- To select several cells, position the mouse pointer in the cell that is in the upper-left corner of all the cells that you want to select. Drag through the cells that you want to select. The cells should be entirely highlighted.

■ To select columns or rows if the row and column indicators are displayed, click or drag in the row/column indicators. The columns or rows in your selection should be entirely highlighted.

■ To select columns or rows if the indicators are not displayed, position the mouse pointer against the top edge of the top cell in a column, or the left edge of the left cell in a row so that it becomes a white arrow. Double-click to select the entire column or row.

Figure 14.10 illustrates a table after column A has been selected. Row/column indicators have been turned on (from the Tables toolbar) to make selection easier.

Figure 14.10
You should select table cells before formatting those cells.

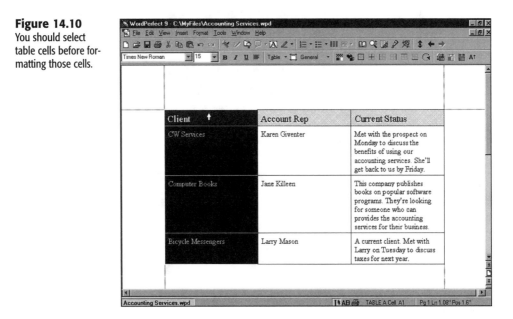

CHANGING COLUMN WIDTH

To change the column width in a table, you can use the Size Column to Fit button or drag the column border. To use the Size Column to Fit button, select one or more cells in the column(s) to be resized. Click the Table button on the Property Bar, and then choose Size Column to Fit.

To adjust column width by dragging a column border, take the following steps:

1. Position the mouse pointer against the right edge of the column you want to adjust, so the pointer becomes a cross with horizontal arrowheads.

Tip #85 from
Trudi Reisner

It's a good idea to start with the leftmost column that you're going to adjust and work your way to the right.

2. Drag the border to a new position. As you drag, a dotted vertical line appears and the exact position is indicated in a small pop-up window (see Figure 14.11).

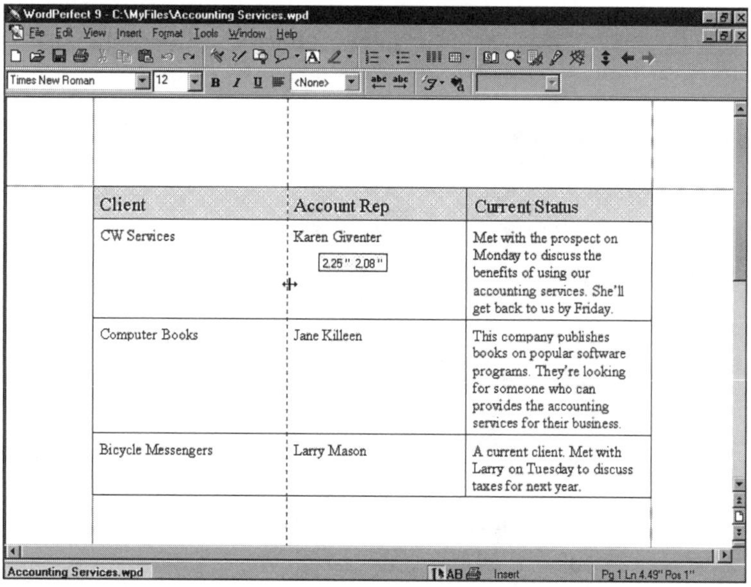

Figure 14.11
Drag a column border to adjust the column's width.

Tip #86 from
Trudi Reisner

Alternatively, you can drag a Column Break icon on the Ruler to adjust the width of a table column.

Note

You can also set a number of columns to have an equal width. Select one or more cells in each column to be resized, click the Table button, and then choose Equal Column Widths.

INSERTING AND DELETING COLUMNS AND ROWS

What if you enter several rows of information in your table and you realize that you need a new row in the middle of the table? No problem. You can insert a row anywhere in the table without disturbing what's already there.

To do so, click in the row below the row to be inserted, and then click the Insert Row button on the Table Property Bar. You can add a new row at the bottom of a table with the Tab key. Position the insertion point in the last cell of the table and press Tab to create a new row. If you're entering a list of names and addresses into your table, you can press Tab to add a new row just before you add the next name and address.

You can also insert new rows or columns by using the Table menu and following these steps:

1. Position the insertion point in the row or column next to where you want a new row or column.

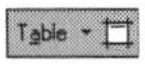

 2. Click the T**a**ble button on the Table Property Bar, and then choose **I**nsert. You see the Insert Columns/Rows dialog box (see Figure 14.12).

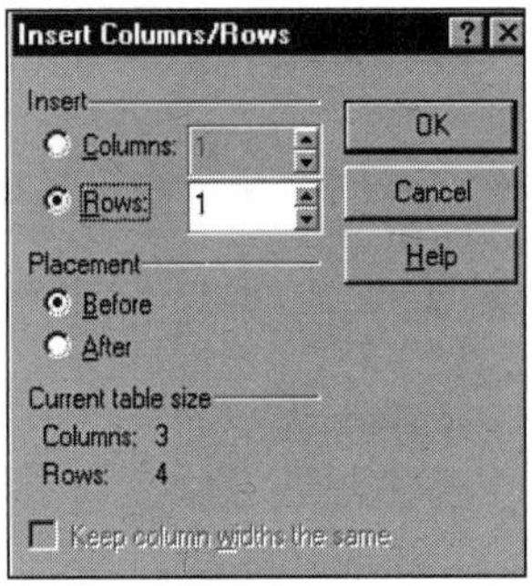

Figure 14.12
Use the Insert Columns/Rows dialog box to indicate how many rows or columns to insert before the current column or row.

3. Choose **C**olumns or **R**ows, and then specify how many to insert.

4. If desired, adjust the Placement from **B**efore to **A**fter.

5. Click OK.

> **Note**
>
> New rows and columns will contain the same formatting as the current row (or column).

Tip #87 from
Trudi Reisner

Insert a row just above the current row by pressing Alt+Insert. Delete the current row by pressing Alt+Delete.

⚠ *If you inserted some rows in the wrong place, see "Placement of Rows" in the Troubleshooting section at the end of this chapter.*

You can delete rows and columns just as you can easily insert them by following these steps:

1. Position the insertion point in the row or column that you want to delete, or select the rows or columns that you want to delete (see the section "Selecting Table Cells," earlier in this chapter).

2. Click the T**a**ble button on the Table Property Bar, and then choose **D**elete. The Delete Structure/Contents dialog box is displayed, as shown in Figure 14.13.

Figure 14.13
Delete selected rows
or columns with the
Delete Structure/
Contents dialog box.

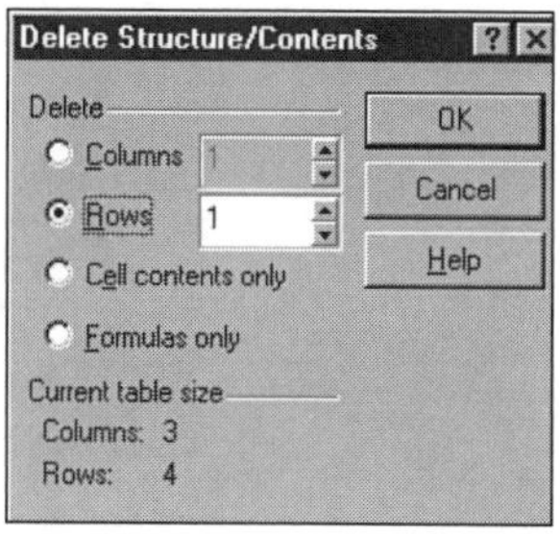

3. Choose Columns or Rows. If you selected rows or columns before accessing the Delete Structure/Contents dialog box, click OK. If you positioned the insertion point before accessing the Delete Structure/Contents dialog box, you can specify how many rows or columns to delete, and then click OK.

Tip #88 from
Trudi Reisner

You can also delete cell contents or cell formulas by using the Delete Structure/Contents dialog box.

If your table has cells with paragraphs of text and one row has an extra blank line, see "Removing Extra Table Rows" in the Troubleshooting section at the end of this chapter.

JOINING AND SPLITTING CELLS

What do you do when you want a title centered between the left and right edges of your table? You join table cells. When you first create a table, it has the same number of cells in every row and in every column. It doesn't have to stay that way; you can select the cells that you want to join and tell WordPerfect to join them. The top row of the table shown in Figure 14.14 has a single cell that was created by joining adjacent cells.

To join table cells, click the QuickJoin button on the Table Property Bar. Drag across the appropriate cells to join them. Click the QuickJoin button again to deselect it.

Tip #89 from
Trudi Reisner

A quick way to join cells is to select the cells you want to join, right-click in the table, and then select Join Cells from the QuickMenu.

On occasion, you may find it useful to split cells. You can split a cell into two or more cells either vertically or horizontally. The second row of the table shown in Figure 14.15 has a single cell that was split into three cells.

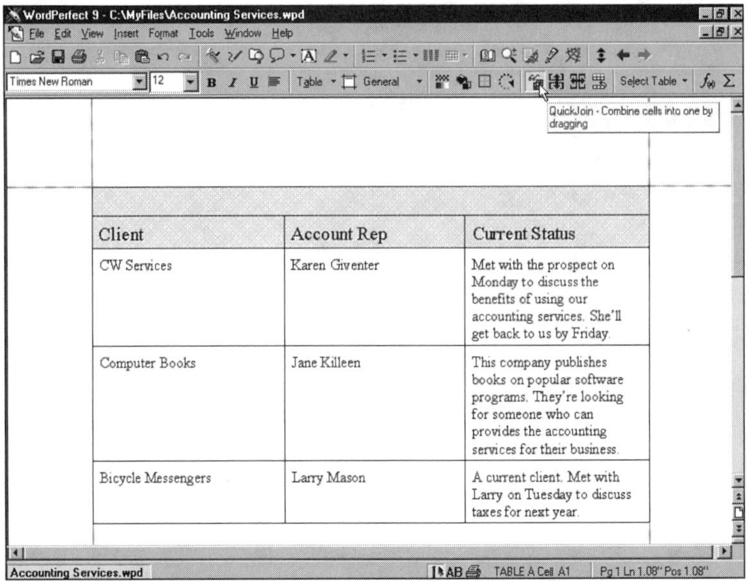

Figure 14.14
Join cells in the top row to create an attractive title row.

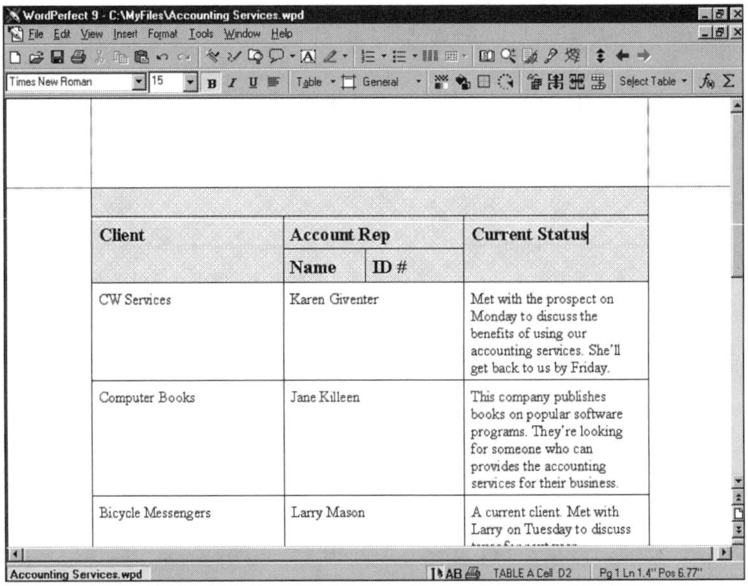

Figure 14.15
Split cells with QuickSplit Row and QuickSplit Column to create multiple cells where needed.

To split table cells, follow these steps:

1. Select the cells that you want to split.

2. Click the T<u>a</u>ble button, and then choose <u>S</u>plit, <u>C</u>ell.

3. Select whether you want to split the cell into <u>R</u>ows or <u>C</u>olumns and the number of cells that should be created.

4. Click OK to split the cells.

Rather than having WordPerfect create evenly sized columns or rows with the T<u>a</u>ble, <u>S</u>plit, <u>C</u>ell feature, you can use T<u>a</u>ble, <u>S</u>plit, QuickSplit Row or Quick<u>S</u>plit Column. The QuickSplit feature requires you to mark where the borders of the row or column are to be placed. Then you need to turn off the QuickSplit option by deselecting it on the T<u>a</u>ble, <u>S</u>plit menu.

Alternatively, if no cells are selected, click the QuickSplit Row or QuickSplit Column button. When the QuickSplit feature is active, the pointer becomes a dotted line in the direction of the split, with arrows pointing out at 90-degree angles to the dotted line. Click in the cell to be split, and then click the button again to deselect it.

FORMATTING A TABLE

Use Table Format options to specify justification, text attributes, column margins, and so on for table cells. You can specify formatting either before or after you enter text in cells; in either case, the text is formatted according to the cell format.

> **Note**
>
> A table format is overridden by a column format; a column format is overridden by a cell format. You could, for example, format an entire column for decimal alignment and the cell at the top of the column for center alignment.

Formatting cells could be a matter of changing the alignment in the cells, applying attributes such as bold or underline to text in cells, or specifying header rows within the table. In this section, formatting table cells is used to mean formatting that is applied to any table element, whether that element is a cell, column, row, or the entire table.

Many common cell-formatting tasks can be done quickly and easily by using the toolbar and Property Bar. Select the appropriate cell(s), and then click the Font Face, Font Size, Bold, Italic, Underline, or Justification buttons to change the cell format. There are other specialized buttons that you can use as well, as listed in Table 14.3.

TABLE 14.3 SPECIALIZED BUTTONS FOR CELL FORMATTING

Button	Button Name	Description
General ▾	Numeric	Shows a list of numeric formats you can apply to numbers in your table
	Cell Fill	Sets the background color for cells
	Table Cell Foreground Fill Color	Sets the color for the foreground when you are using patterns that have two colors
	Change Outside Line	Allows you to specify type of line that goes around the outside of your table
	Rotate Cell	Rotates the text 90 degrees each time you click it; this works only if there is text in a cell

You can also format cells from the Properties for Table Format dialog box. To do so, follow these steps:

1. Select the cell(s) or column(s) that you want to format; or to format the entire table, click anywhere in the table.

2. Open the Properties for Table Format dialog box by clicking the T<u>a</u>ble button and choosing F<u>o</u>rmat; or click the Table Format button if cells are selected. Figure 14.16 illustrates the Format dialog box with Table format options displayed as tabs (types of format options are Cell, Column, Row, and Table).

Figure 14.16
The Properties for Table Format dialog box with Table format options displayed.

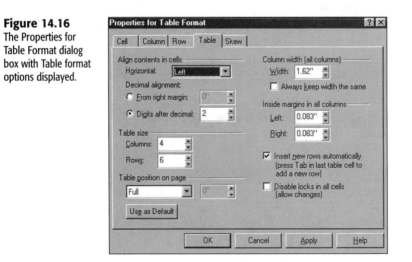

3. Choose the tab for the option type that you want to format: Cell, Column, Row, Table, or Skew.

4. Make the desired formatting changes. Your changes might include items in the following list:

   - When you format cells or columns, you can adjust the alignment with the Horizontal option. Cells containing numbers should be decimal-aligned.

   - When you format cells, you can lock cells to keep the insertion point from moving into the cells. You can also set vertical alignment and rotation, and place diagonal lines in cells. When a cell is locked, the mouse pointer becomes a circle with a diagonal line through it when the pointer is over the locked cell.

   - When you format cells, you can specify that cell contents should be ignored in calculations (you might have to do this if you're adding a column that has a number in its column header).

   - When you format the table, you can adjust the Table Position relative to the page margins.

   - When you format rows, you can designate the selected row to be a header row if desired. When a table spans a page break, header rows print at the top of each page.

   - When you format rows, you can specify a fixed row height. This feature is useful when you create a table with "boxes" (cells) that should have a fixed height, regardless of any text they contain—for example, when you create a calendar. Unless you specify a fixed row height, the row height is a function of the number of text lines in the row. You can add more text to a fixed row and while you're adding the text, it appears that the row size is not fixed. When the insertion point is in another row, the text that went beyond the fixed row size doesn't show.

   - You can slant (skew) table cells on the top row or the left or right column of a table, giving the cells a three-dimensional look. On the Skew tab, choose the part of the table you want skewed from the Skew Settings list. To change the skew angle, click More on the Skew tab, and enter the skew angle in the Angle box. The text you type in skewed cells is also skewed. To prevent this from happening, click More on the Skew tab, and remove the check mark from the Skew Text check box. If you want to remove the skew in a table, choose None in the Skew Settings list.

5. Click OK to exit the Format dialog box and apply the specified changes to your table.

If you skewed the top row of a table and the text in that row looks strange, see "Adjusting Row Height for Skewed Text" in the Troubleshooting section at the end of this chapter.

CHANGING BORDERS, LINES, AND SHADING IN A TABLE

Give your tables visual appeal by changing table borders and lines and adding shading to cells. Your "desktop publishing" efforts can make the table more attractive and easier to read. For example, when you shade every other row in a table, it's easier to read across a row.

The lines around a table are called its border. Lines around cells are called lines. By default, tables have no border and single lines around each cell. Borders and lines are created and formatted separately, and borders mask lines. Thus, if you have single lines around each cell but a double-lined border, you will see the double line, not the single line, around the table.

In addition to formatting table borders and lines, you can apply a fill style to table cells. Fill styles range all the way from standard gray shading to gradient patterns with blended colors.

You can use Table SpeedFormat to apply a set of changes for you, or you can make your own changes to table borders, lines, and shading.

USING TABLE SPEEDFORMAT TO ENHANCE A TABLE

The fastest and easiest way to make changes to borders, lines, and shading in a table is to apply a table style (a set of changes) all at once with Table SpeedFormat.

Tip #90 from
Trudi Reisner

You can Undo the effects after you apply a table style with Table SpeedFormat by choosing Edit, Undo, or by clicking the Undo button.

To use Table SpeedFormat, take the following steps:

1. Position the insertion point anywhere in the table.
2. Click the Table button, and then choose SpeedFormat. The Table SpeedFormat dialog box appears (see Figure 14.17).

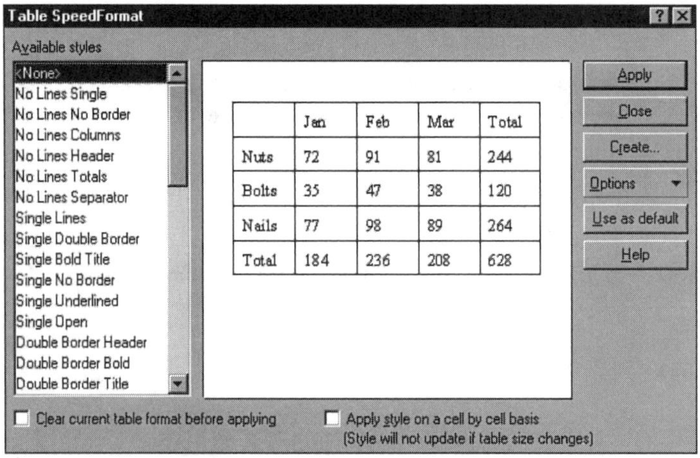

Figure 14.17
Apply a set of formats to your table in the Table SpeedFormat dialog box.

3. Examine the available styles, if desired, by selecting a style and looking at the preview area.

4. Select the style you want to apply.

Tip #91 from *Trudi Reisner*	To set the current table style as a default style for all new tables, access the Table SpeedFormat dialog box, choose Use As Default, and then choose Yes.

5. If you have already applied changes to borders, lines, or shading, you may want to check the Clear Current Table Format Before Applying check box.

6. When you finish making selections in the Table SpeedFormat dialog box, choose Apply.

7. Click Close to close the Table SpeedFormat dialog box.

MAKING YOUR OWN TABLE ENHANCEMENTS

You can make many changes to table borders, lines, or shading from the Property Bar. To do so, select the cells to be formatted, and then click the Change Left Line, Change Right Line, Change Top Line, Change Bottom Line, Change Inside Line, or Change Outside Line button on the Cell Selected Table Property Bar.

Alternatively, you can use the Table Lines/Fill dialog box to make formatting changes as follows:

1. Select the cells for which you want to change borders or lines or add shading.

2. Click the Table button, and then select Borders/Fill. The Table Borders/Fill dialog box is displayed.

3. If you want changes to affect the entire table, select the Table tab at the top of the dialog box. Figure 14.18 illustrates the Properties for Table Borders/Fill dialog box with the Table options displayed.

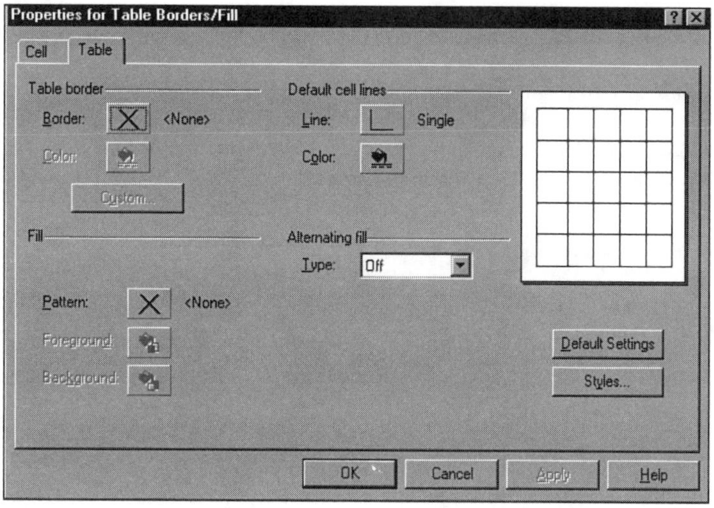

Figure 14.18
The Properties for Table Borders/Fill dialog box with Table options displayed.

II

14

4. Select the border for the table by displaying the Border palette of border styles. To add a table border, choose any border style other than <None>. Change the default cell lines in the Table tab as well by changing the Line and Color options in the Default Cell Lines group.

5. To format lines or shading for selected cells, choose the Cell tab. Options in the dialog box now apply to the current selection, as shown in Figure 14.19.

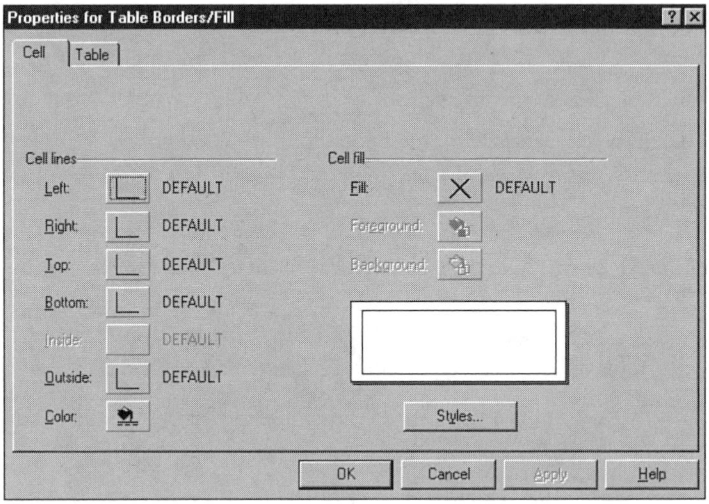

Figure 14.19
The Properties for Table Borders/Fill dialog box with the Cell tab displayed.

6. Change the line style for the sides you want to change (left, right, top, bottom, or outside) by clicking the Styles button and choosing a line from the Styles list box in the Graphics Styles dialog box. Click Close to close the dialog box.

7. With either the Table or Cell tab displayed, you can display a palette of fill styles and select a style. If the selected fill style has only one color, select a Foreground color, if desired. If the selected fill style has two colors, you can choose Foreground and Background colors.

8. Click OK to return to the table.

If your table doesn't have any lines and is difficult to read, see "Adding Table Gridlines" in the Troubleshooting section at the end of this chapter.

PRACTICAL PROJECT 1

You might want to align columns of word and numbers. To do so, use the Decimal Tab to align the numbers on the decimal point; if you have whole numbers, they will be aligned where the decimal point is understood to be. You can even use the Decimal Tab to align single words on the right.

To create aligned columns of numbers, display the ruler with <u>V</u>iew, Ruler, and set decimal tabs for the numbers and words to be right aligned in each column.

→ For more information on setting decimal tabs, **see** "Setting and Using Tabs," **p. 116**

In each column, press Tab and type the number. As you type, WordPerfect moves the number to the left, and when you type a decimal point, subsequent numbers move to the right. If you want to right-align a column of single words, press Tab and type the word. To adjust the spacing between the column, just change the decimal tab stops on the ruler; WordPerfect adjusts the text accordingly (see Figure 14.20).

Figure 14.20
WordPerfect will adjust the text when you adjust spacing between columns.

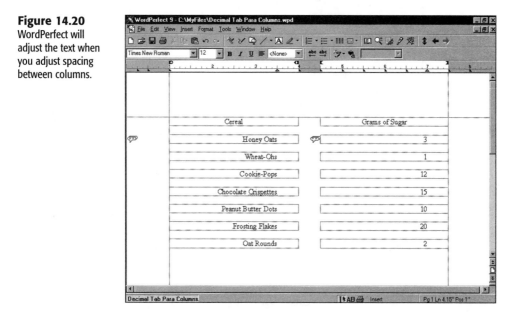

PRACTICAL PROJECT 2

Suppose you have a three-column page that contains body text in the first two columns, and you want to add sidebar text in the third column. Sidebar text is a brief addendum to the main text. You can create a shaded sidebar using a column border.

Start by creating newspaper columns as you normally would. Type the sidebar text and then select the text in the third column. Use For<u>m</u>at, <u>P</u>aragraph, <u>B</u>orders/Fill and choose None for the border style to create no border. Then choose a Fill option for the fill style. Figure 14.21 shows three columns with a sidebar in the last column and shaded with 10% fill. To make a coupon from the sidebar, add a dashed line border.

If you are planning to make a photocopy of the document, make a test copy before you decide on the percentage of shading. Keep in mind that photocopying can darken or lighten shading.

Figure 14.21
Create a shaded side-bar using a column border.

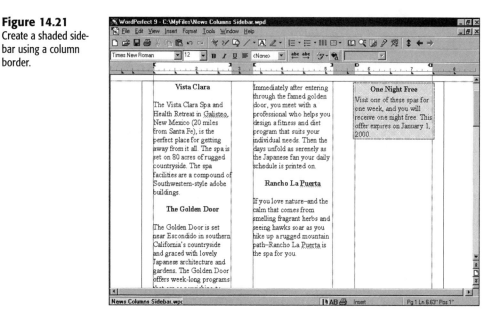

PRACTICAL PROJECT 3

If you want to make a table more interesting with a skewed 3D look, use the SpeedFormat feature and choose one of the skewed styles at the bottom of the styles list in the Table SpeedFormat dialog box. Figure 14.22 shows a table with the Skewed Left Up SpeedFormat style.

Figure 14.22
Skewed Left Up SpeedFormat style.

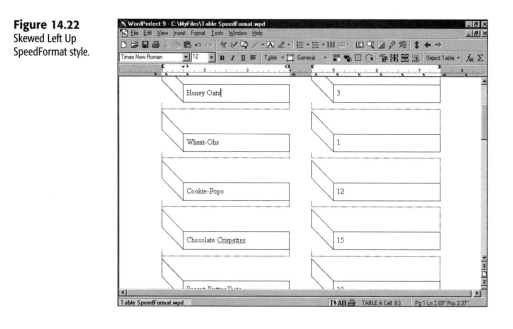

TROUBLESHOOTING

ALIGNING PARALLEL COLUMNS

The distance between your parallel columns looks misaligned.

You need to change the distance between columns. In the Columns dialog box, specify the distance in the Space Between box to realign your columns.

GROUPING COLUMN ITEMS

Your column items are splitting at the end of a page.

To prevent column items from splitting at the end of a page, choose Parallel with Block Protect from the Type of Columns options in the Columns dialog box. This option groups column items together.

ALIGNING TOPS OR BOTTOMS OF COLUMNS

You changed the font for text in columns and the columns are misaligned.

You need to reposition the text at the top or bottom of each column. To align the tops of the columns, choose Format, Typesetting, Advance. In the Vertical Position section, select Up from Insertion Point or Down from Insertion Point, and enter a value in the Vertical Distance box. To specify a fine increment, enter a value in points, Remember, a point is equal to 1/72 of an inch. For example, enter 2p to specify two points. Repeat these steps to adjust the bottoms of the columns by adding or subtracting 1 or 2 points of leading between the last lines of sections and subsequent headings.

USING A HARD COLUMN BREAK

You pressed Enter instead of Ctrl+Enter to end a column, and the insertion point moved to the next line.

This is a common mistake. When you press Enter instead of Ctrl+Enter to end a column, WordPerfect inserts a hard return and moves the insertion point to the next line. To fix this, remove the HRt code in the Reveal Codes window. Then press Ctrl+Enter (Hard Column Break) to end the column without moving the insertion point. WordPerfect inserts the HCol hard column break code.

ENDING A COLUMN

You accidentally pressed Ctrl+Enter twice to end a column, and WordPerfect moved the column heading to the previous column.

Pressing Ctrl+Enter twice to end a column causes WordPerfect to insert an extra HCol hard column break code and moves the column heading to the previous column. To correct this, just remove the extra HCol hard column break code in the Reveal Codes window. WordPerfect then adjusts the column heading above the column.

DISCONTINUING COLUMNS

You accidentally forgot to turn columns off.

Forgetting to discontinue columns is a common error. Any text you type is formatted as columns. To remedy this, move the insertion point to the location where you want to discontinue columns. Click the Columns button on the WordPerfect toolbar, and choose Discontinue. WordPerfect adjusts any text following the insertion point as a normal document, and the column number disappears from the Status Bar.

PLACEMENT OF ROWS

You inserted several rows in the wrong place.

Click the Undo button to remove the unwanted rows. Then position the insertion point in a row right next to where you want a new row or rows. Choose Table, Insert. Specify how many rows you want and make sure that you choose the correct placement (before or after the current row).

REMOVING EXTRA TABLE ROWS

Your table has cells with paragraphs of text in them. One row has an extra blank line at the bottom and you don't know how to get rid of it.

Turn on the display of nonprinting characters by choosing View, Show ¶. Look for a ¶ somewhere in the row and delete it.

ADJUSTING ROW HEIGHT FOR SKEWED TEXT

You skewed the top row of your table and the text in that row doesn't look right.

You may need to increase the row height of the skewed row to accommodate the height of the text. Drag the row border up to make the row taller.

ADDING TABLE GRIDLINES

You removed all the lines in your table and now it's hard to tell which part of the table you're working in.

Choose View, Table Gridlines to display gridlines at the edges of cells. When table gridlines are displayed, you see gridlines at the edges of cells, regardless whether any lines are defined for the cells. To view the table again as it will print (without the gridlines but with any defined lines or shading), choose View, Table Gridlines again.

CHAPTER 15

CREATING GRAPHICS

In this chapter

WORKING WITH GRAPHICS

Take advantage of WordPerfect's graphics features to add visual pizzazz to your documents. You can add lines, borders, shading, and pictures. Use graphics to call attention to your document, break the monotony of straight text, emphasize text, and pique the reader's interest.

You can add a line above (or below) headings to make them stand out or to help divide information on the page. Create a box with a border and enter text in the box, or add clip art to make a document more interesting. Use the Drop Cap feature to enlarge and emphasize the first letter in a paragraph. Use the Watermark feature to add a logo or clip-art image or text behind the printed document text.

WORKING WITH GRAPHICS LINES

The easiest way to insert horizontal or vertical graphics lines is through buttons on the Graphics toolbar. To display the Graphics toolbar, right-click the toolbar and select Graphics.

The default graphics lines are thin lines that extend from margin to margin (left to right, or top to bottom). You can tell WordPerfect how thick to make the line, what the color should be, how long it should be, or exactly where it should be on the page. Alternatively, you can use the mouse to adjust the thickness, length, and position of the line.

Note

You can also insert lines and shapes by choosing Insert, Shape.

Figure 15.1 illustrates the use of a default horizontal graphics line to separate headings in a memo from the body of the memo.

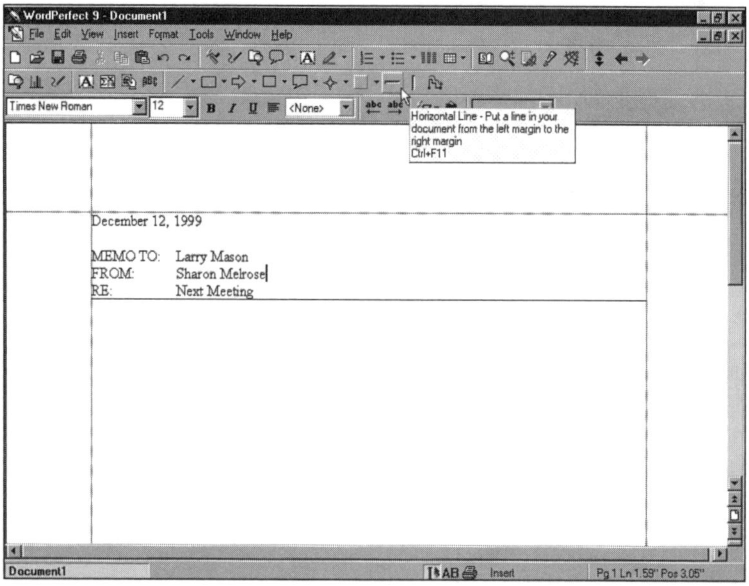

Figure 15.1
Click the Horizontal Line button to create a horizontal graphics line that effectively separates the headings in a memo from the body of the memo.

CREATING INSTANT LINES

You can instantly create a horizontal graphics line by clicking the Horizontal Line button on the Graphics toolbar. The result is a thin line that extends from margin to margin at the baseline of text on the current line.

Correspondingly, you can instantly create a vertical graphics line by clicking the Vertical Line button on the Graphics toolbar. The result is a thin vertical line that is placed at the insertion point and extends from the top margin to the bottom margin.

Note

WordPerfect won't insert a vertical line in the middle of centered text. It puts the line to the left of the text instead.

CREATING A CUSTOM LINE

To create a custom line, follow these steps:

1. If the line is to be a horizontal line, position the insertion point where you want the horizontal line. If you want the line to be placed slightly below a line of text, insert a hard return between the text and the horizontal line.

2. Click the Custom Line button. The Create Graphics Line dialog box is displayed, as shown in Figure 15.2.

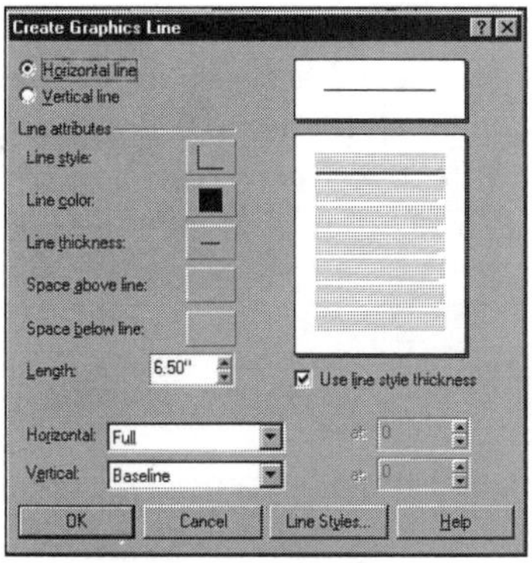

Figure 15.2
Customize a graphics line in the Create Graphics Line dialog box (or in the Edit Graphics Line dialog box).

3. Adjust settings for the line as desired. For example, use the Position Horizontal option to adjust the length of the line. When you finish adjusting settings, click OK.

4. If the line you created is a horizontal line, you probably want to insert a hard return after the line.

Note

The Create Graphics Line dialog box becomes the Edit Graphics Line dialog box when you edit a line.

EDITING A GRAPHICS LINE

Edit a graphics line either with the mouse or through the Edit Graphics Line dialog box. The mouse is quick and easy to use, but not as precise as the dialog box.

To edit a graphics line with the Edit Graphics Line dialog box, take the following steps:

1. Click the line to select it. You see small square dots called handles around the selected line, and you see the Horizontal/Vertical Line Property Bar.

2. Click the Line Graphic Edit button. The Edit Graphics Line dialog box appears (it looks like the Create Graphics Line dialog box shown earlier).

Tip #92 from	You can also access the Edit Graphics Line dialog box by double-clicking the selected line or
Trudi Reisner	right-clicking the line and choosing Edit Horizontal (or Vertical) Line from the QuickMenu.

3. Change any settings as desired and click OK.

To edit a line with the mouse, select the line first. To move the line, place the mouse pointer against the line so that the pointer becomes a four-headed arrow. Then drag the line to a new position. To adjust the thickness or length of the line, position the mouse pointer against a selection handle so that the mouse pointer becomes a two-headed arrow. Then drag the handle to adjust the thickness or length.

CREATING BORDERS

A graphics border is a box that surrounds text, emphasizes your message, separates text, or adds pizzazz to the page. You can use a paragraph border to call attention to one particular paragraph of text in a letter, for example; or you can add a page border to each page of a report to guide the reader and to create consistency within the report.

Tip #93 from	You can use a variety of line styles and thicknesses with page and paragraph borders.
Trudi Reisner	

Figure 15.3 illustrates a newsletter with a paragraph border, a page border, and a column border.

CREATING PARAGRAPH BORDERS

A paragraph border is a frame that surrounds an individual paragraph or selected paragraphs. The border can include a fill style. WordPerfect gives you a choice of many border styles and fill styles.

To add a paragraph border to your document, follow these steps:

1. Place the insertion point in the paragraph to which you want to apply a border, or select the paragraphs to which you want to apply a border.

2. Choose Format, Paragraph, Border/Fill. The Paragraph Border/Fill dialog box appears, as shown in Figure 15.4.

Figure 15.3
The page border
dresses up the page.
The paragraph border
emphasizes the
announcement about
what's new.

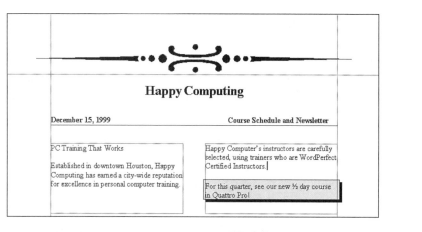

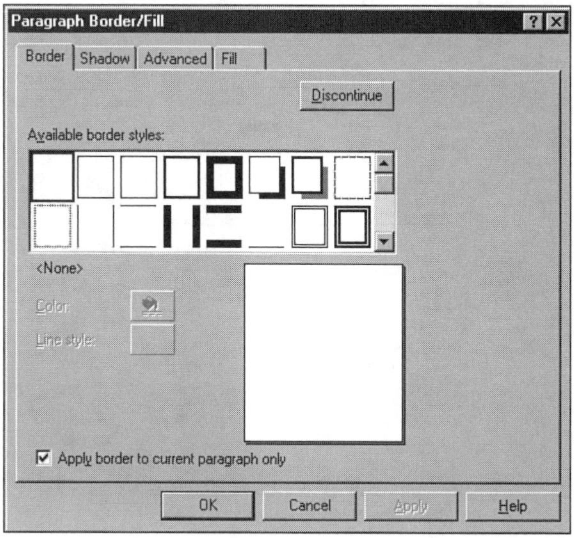

Figure 15.4
Use the Paragraph
Border/Fill dialog
box to add a
paragraph border
(and a fill, if desired)
that calls attention
to specific text.

3. In the Border tab, choose an available Border Style to put a border around the selection, and select a Color, Line Style, and Drop Shadow if desired. Click the Shadow tab in the Border/Fill dialog box to get the Drop Shadow option.

4. To frame the current paragraph and not all subsequent paragraphs, ensure that the Apply Border to Current Paragraph Only check box is not selected.

5. To add a fill to your border, choose the Fill tab, and then pick a style from the Available Fill Styles. Choose a Foreground color, a Background color, and a Pattern if desired.

6. Click OK.

CREATING PAGE BORDERS

A page border can add style to any document. Usually, you repeat the page border on all pages of a document, but you can choose to apply it to the current page only.

Tip #94 from
Trudi Reisner

Use Page view to see page borders onscreen; you can't see them in Draft view.

To add a page border to your document, do the following:

1. Position the insertion point on the first page where you want to apply a page border.
2. Choose Format, Page, Border/Fill. The Page Border/Fill dialog box is displayed, as shown in Figure 15.5.

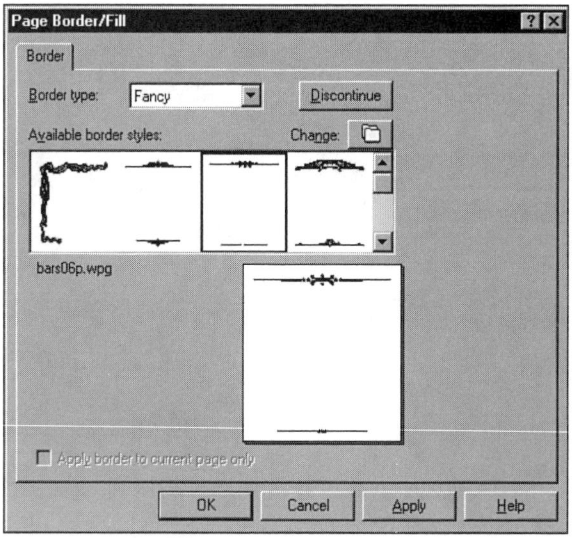

Figure 15.5
Select the available border styles and you can see what the actual page will look like in the accompanying page border preview.

3. Select Fancy or Line as the Border Type.
4. In the Available Border Styles area, select a border style.
5. Click OK.

Note

To remove a page border, place the insertion point on the page where the page border begins. Open the Page Border dialog box and choose Discontinue.

⚡ *If you add a page border and can't see it onscreen, see "Viewing a Page Border" in the Troubleshooting section at the end of this chapter.*

If your page border prints only on the first page and not on every subsequent page, see "Repeating a Page Border on Every Page" in the Troubleshooting section at the end of this chapter.

INSERTING GRAPHIC OBJECTS

You can insert a number of different types of graphic objects into your WordPerfect documents. These objects are contained in graphics boxes.

A graphics box is a box that holds an image—for example, clip-art images, drawings, charts, equations, tables, or text sections—such as the pull quotes you see in newsletters. The contents of the document are adjusted to make room for the box. The box can be selected and moved or resized. A graphics box has its own contents and its own border; a paragraph or page border, on the other hand, is simply an ornamental frame surrounding text that is already in your document.

Adding graphics boxes to your documents illustrates the text, draws attention to the message, and adds interest to the document. Images, for example, help the reader understand the text, whereas text callouts attract the reader's attention to the text and break up "gray space" on the page. WordPerfect enables you to add several types of graphics boxes to your documents, each with a style and purpose of its own.

UNDERSTANDING GRAPHICS BOX STYLES

Each of WordPerfect's graphics box styles is designed to work best with one particular type of image or text. For example, the Image, Figure, and User styles work well with graphics images; the Text Box and User styles work well with text. Any box, however, can hold any type of image, text, table, equation, and so on. The box style is simply a suggestion for the box's use. Each type of graphics box has a default line style (width and type of border line). Other aspects of the box style include its placement (how it is attached or anchored to the document), its caption style, and the amount of space allowed both outside and inside the box. When you choose a box style, you choose the default settings for that box style. The style of an individual box, however, can be customized.

An example of a graphics box containing an image is shown in Figure 15.6.

Graphics boxes are attached to the document in three ways: paragraph, character, or page. The way the box is attached to the document determines whether and how it will move when the document is edited. Table 15.3 describes how each type of placement works and for what it is suited.

Figure 15.6
Add graphics boxes to your document for visual interest.

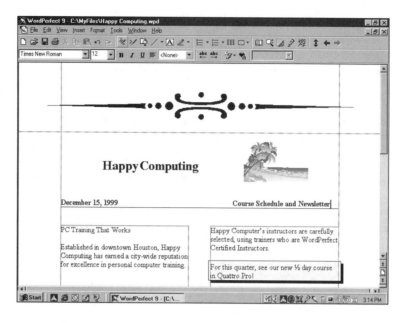

TABLE 15.3 GRAPHICS PLACEMENT

Attach Box To	How It Works	Suitable For
Paragraph	The box stays with the paragraph that contains it.	Boxes that are associated with text in the same area.
Character	The box is treated like a single character on a particular line of text.	Very small boxes that areassociated with a line of text.
Page	The box stays in a fixed position on the page, regardless266 of editing changes to the text.	Boxes that are meant to stay in the same place on the page, such as a masthead at the top of a newsletter page.

UNDERSTANDING GRAPHICS OBJECTS

You can insert a number of different types of graphics objects into your WordPerfect document. Some of these are files on your disk. You create others as charts using applications that are common throughout the WordPerfect Suite. Graphics objects include

- Clipart—Artwork that ships with WordPerfect.
- TextArt—Fancy-shaped text, used for logos and titles.
- Pictures—Artwork that you create with Suite drawing tools.
- Charts—Pie charts, histograms, and so on.
- Acquired Images—Images that you scan in.

→ For more information about graphics, **see** "Adding Images," **p. 275**

CREATING A GRAPHICS BOX

By default, WordPerfect inserts the graphics box close to where the insertion point is. After it is inserted, you can move or size the box.

Tip #95 from *Trudi Reisner*	If you prefer to be able to click and drag with the mouse to position and size your box when it is created, choose Tools, Settings, Environment, click the Graphics tab, and check the Drag to Create New Graphic Boxes check box.

To create a graphics box, follow these steps:

1. Click in the document where you want the graphic box to appear.
2. Choose Insert, Graphics, and then select the type of box you want: Clipart, From File, TextArt, Draw Picture, Acquire Image, Select Image Source, or Custom Box.
3. What you see next depends on the type of box you selected.

Tip #96 from *Trudi Reisner*	If you want to insert clip art or a text box into your WordPerfect document, you can do so quickly by clicking the Clipart or Text Box buttons.

- If you choose Clipart, you see the Scrapbook dialog box shown in Figure 15.7. Double-click the image you want to insert in your document. WordPerfect's Scrapbook contains a myriad of professionally prepared images. You can search and preview the images, drag and drop, and copy and paste them. Scrapbook organizes the images by category. You can even create your own category; view automatic updates of thumbnails; as well as preview sounds, movies, and bitmap images.

Tip #97 from
Trudi Reisner

If you want more clip art to choose from, you can buy packages of clip art (in black and white or color) from software stores, mail-order catalogs, and the Web. Some clip art on the Web is free. These clip-art "libraries" are packaged by topics such as animals, business, holidays, music, people, and so on. If you want more professional artwork, look for photo collections, which are usually sold on CDs.

Figure 15.7
WordPerfect comes with clip-art images that you can include in your document.

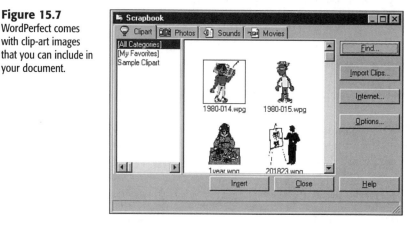

- If you choose TextArt, you see the Corel TextArt 9 dialog box. Create the text art as described in "Adding TextArt Images" later in this chapter, and then click OK to insert it into your document.

- If you choose Draw Picture, you see the Presentation toolbars and menu. You can use Presentation's drawing tools to create the image as discussed later in this chapter. Click outside the selected object to return to WordPerfect.

- If you choose Acquire Image, what you see depends on the type of scanner and scanning software you have installed. Follow your usual steps for scanning an image.

- If you choose Select Image Source, you see the Select Source dialog box, which lets you draw a graphic from a scanner. You select a TWAIN source and adjust the properties of your scanner.

- If you choose Custom Box, you can create a graphics box from any of the 14 pre-defined graphics box styles, such as a box that looks like a raised button, a sticky note with a yellow background, or a text box.

4. Adjust the size or position of the box by ensuring that the graphics box is still selected (has handles around it). Then use the two-headed sizing pointer or the four-headed moving pointer to size or move it.

To edit a graphics box, ensure that it is selected, and then click the Image Tools button on the Property Bar. You see the Image Tools floating dialog box (see Figure 15.8), which contains a variety of tools to edit the graphics box. When you finish working with the graphics box, deselect it by clicking outside the box.

Figure 15.8
The floating Image Tools dialog box allows you to change how the graphics box appears in the document.

You can do a number of things to enhance the appearance of the image in your document:

- To contour text around the image in a box, click the Wrap button on the Property Bar.
- To quickly edit the text or the actual image in a graphics box, double-click the box.
- To remove a graphics box, select it and then press the Delete key.
- To select a style for a box before you create the box, choose Insert, Graphics, Custom Box. The box is created using default formatting options for your selected style.
- To edit the graphic image using Corel Presentations, double-click a graphic.

⚠ *If you created a box and placed an image in it, and want to change the border lines, see "Changing the Border Lines" in the Troubleshooting section at the end of this chapter.*

CREATING DRAWINGS

You can include drawings in your WordPerfect document to illustrate points, or use drawing objects to call attention to important points. You can use all of Presentations' tools to draw your picture, or you can add simple drawing shapes directly from WordPerfect.

To use Presentations' tools to draw a picture, do the following:

1. Click where you want the picture to appear.
2. Choose Insert, Graphics, Draw Picture or click the Draw Picture button. Your menu and toolbar change to Presentations, and the title bar indicates that you are in the Presentations Drawing mode, as shown in Figure 15.9.

Figure 15.9
When inserting a complex drawing, you can use all the power of Presentations' drawing tools.

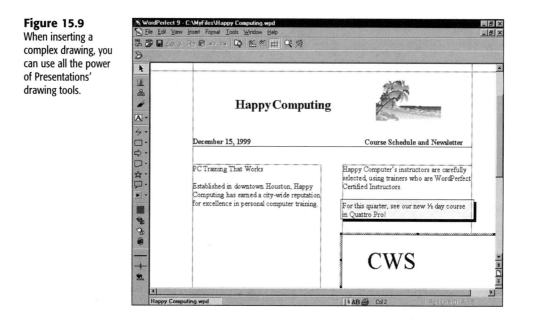

3. Draw the picture using Presentations drawing tools, as described in the section "Using Drawing Tools" in Chapter 20, "Getting Started with Corel Quattro Pro 9."

4. Click outside the object to return to WordPerfect.

5. Adjust the size or position of the graphics box by ensuring that the graphics box is still selected (has handles around it). Then use the two-headed sizing pointer or the four-headed moving pointer to size or move it.

Alternatively, if you want to place a simple object such as a rectangle or circle in your document, it may be easier to do this directly within WordPerfect, as follows:

1. Click the down arrow to the right of the Draw Object button, and then click the shape you want to draw.

2. Move your mouse pointer into the document and notice that the pointer is now a crosshair.

3. Click and drag over the area where the object should appear. The object appears with handles around it.

4. Move or size the object using the fill handles as needed.

5. Click outside the object to deselect it.

Note

WordPerfect 9 gives you over 100 new shapes to choose from, including Text in Shapes that enable you to add text to a shape.

USING DRAWING LAYERS

When you insert graphic objects in your WordPerfect document, they are layered. In other words, they appear one over the top of another and can thus obscure one another. You can specify which object goes in front of another very easily, however.

To do so, click the desired graphic object. You see selection handles and the Graphics Property Bar. Click the Object(s) Back One button to move the object one level back and the Object(s) Forward One button to move it toward the front of the stack of objects.

EDITING GRAPHICS OBJECTS

Moving graphics objects lets you change the location of the object in your document. You can move a graphic object wherever you want. Just click the graphic object, point to the object and drag it to the new location.

Sizing a graphics object allows you to change the dimensions of the object. To size an object, click the object to select it, point to a selection handle, and drag the object's border to expand or shrink the object.

You can also edit graphics objects no matter which view you're currently in, either Draft or Page view. Click the object, and QuickSpot provides a Property Bar that displays buttons for graphics editing tools, as shown in Figure 15.10.

Figure 15.10
When editing a graphics object, the graphics editing tools on the Property Bar make the job easy.

Graphics editing tasks can be done in a snap using the Property Bar. Table 15.4 shows the graphics editing buttons and their use:

TABLE 15.4   GRAPHICS EDITING BUTTONS

Button	Button Name	Description
 Graphics ▾	Graphics	Shows a list of graphics editing commands you can use to layer, flip, group, size, and move graphics objects
⏮	Previous Box	Selects the previous graphics box according to the order in which you created graphics objects in your document
⏭	Next Box	Selects the next graphics box according to the order in which you created graphics objects in your document

continues

TABLE 15.4 CONTINUED

Button	Button Name	Description
	Shadow	Adds shading to an object
	Shadow Color	Changes the color for the shadow
	Fill Style	Changes the fill style for the object, such as a dotted or lattice pattern
	Foreground Color	Changes the foreground color of the object
	Background Color	Changes the background color of the object
	Line Pattern	Changes the line style of the object's border
	Line Width	Changes the width of the object's border line
	Outline Color	Changes the color of the object's border line
	Object(s) Forward One	Moves the selected object forward one layer
	Object(s) Back One	Moves the selected object back one layer
	Wrap	Changes how text wraps around a box

CREATING DROP CAPS

WordPerfect's Drop Caps feature puts desktop publishing within everyone's reach. Now it's easy to add visual interest to your text by creating an oversized character at the beginning of a paragraph, such as the one in Figure 15.11.

Figure 15.11
Drop Caps add interest and visual appeal to text.

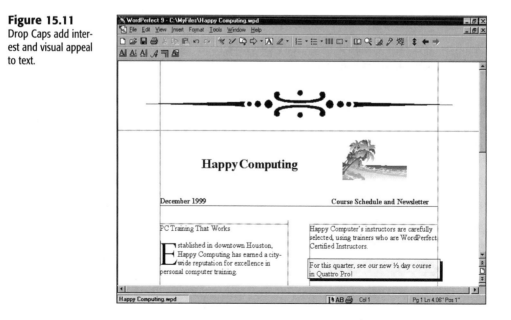

To create a drop cap, take the following steps:

1. Position the insertion point in the paragraph in which you want a drop cap.

2. Choose Format, Paragraph, Drop Cap. WordPerfect creates a drop cap three lines deep using the first character in the paragraph and displays the Drop Cap Property Bar.

3. Adjust the drop cap, if desired, by using buttons on the Property Bar. For example, if you want the drop cap to drop down through four lines of text instead of three, click the Size button, and then select 4 Lines High.

4. Begin to type your paragraph. The first letter you type is put into the drop cap format you selected.

CREATING WATERMARKS

A watermark is a special type of graphics box that contains either text or graphics but prints in the background. The watermark prints lightly so that the text you enter in the foreground is readable.

There are many uses for watermarks. You can dress up a letter to a client with your company logo, you can add text ("Draft") to the background of reports, and so on. You can use any of WordPerfect's watermark files, create your own images or text to use as watermarks, or use images and text from other applications.

USING A TEXT WATERMARK

Most of WordPerfect's watermark files consist of text that has been saved as a graphics image. You can use WordPerfect's watermark text, or you can create your own text (it doesn't have to be saved as a graphics image). Figure 15.12 illustrates using your own text (Draft) as a watermark in a draft copy of a newsletter.

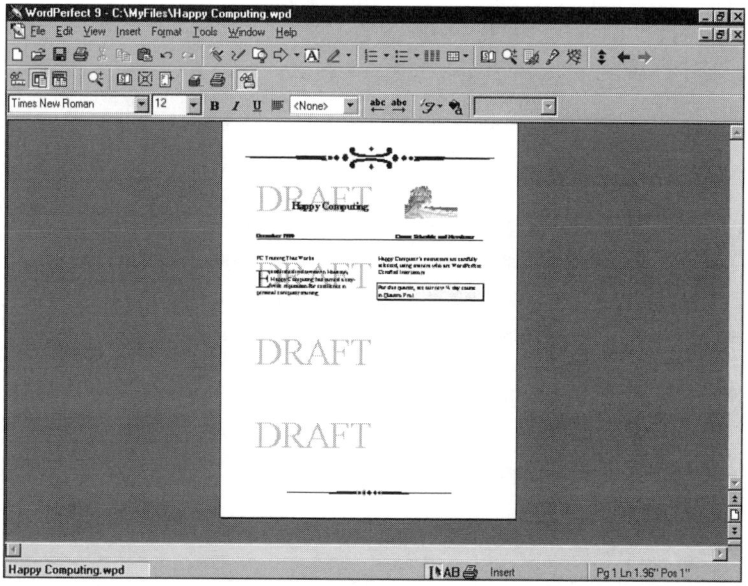

Figure 15.12
You can place a watermark with text to indicate the nature of your document.

USING IMAGES AS WATERMARKS

You can use images created in other applications, or you can use any of the images in WordPerfect's Graphics folder as a watermark image. The image you use doesn't have to be designed specifically as a watermark image. Figure 15.13 illustrates one of WordPerfect's image files (Rose.wpg) used as a watermark in a newsletter.

Figure 15.13
You can also use an image, such as a rose, for your watermark.

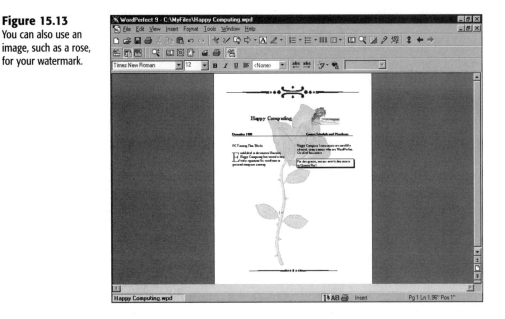

CREATING A WATERMARK

Before creating a watermark, enter and format all document text. When the watermark appears onscreen, text editing slows considerably. To add a watermark to a document, follow these steps:

1. Position the insertion point on the first page that is to have a watermark (the watermark will appear on that page and on every subsequent page).

2. Choose Insert, Watermark. In the Watermark dialog box, choose Create. You are placed in the Watermark A editing screen shown in Figure 15.14. The Watermark Property Bar appears above the text area at the top of the screen.

3. If you're going to create a watermark from text, you can type the text directly on the screen. You'll probably want an extremely large font size, however. Type (and format) the text that you want as a watermark. Then click the Close button on the Watermark Property Bar to return to your document.

4. To create a watermark that contains an image, click the Insert File button on the Watermark Property Bar and choose an image. The image you choose is automatically sized to fill the entire page. If you want to edit the image, right-click the image, and then choose **E**dit Image from the QuickMenu. Click the Close button on the Watermark Property Bar to return to your document.

Figure 15.14
You can create watermarks that appear behind the text on each page.

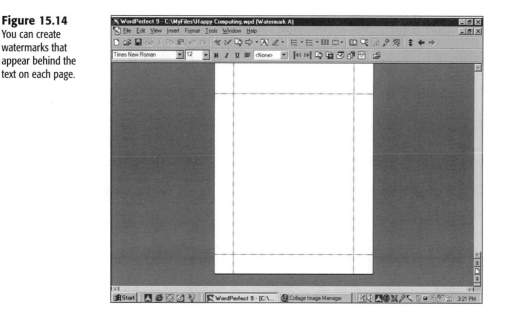

 If your watermark is too dark, see "Adjusting the Shading for a Watermark" in the Troubleshooting section at the end of this chapter.

ADDING IMAGES

If you don't want to create your own drawing using WordPerfect's drawing tools, you can add images to your documents in other ways—add TextArt, download images from the Web, and insert images from earlier versions WordPerfect Suite (7 and 8).

TextArt enables you to choose from many preset special text effects to add designs and shapes to plain text. TextArt manipulates fonts in any way, shape, or form—it squeezes them, bends them into shapes, stretches them, and adds shadows, borders, and a host of other text effects. TextArt is wonderful for creating desktop publishing effects, especially logos (see Figure 15.15).

Figure 15.15
A fancy TextArt logo.

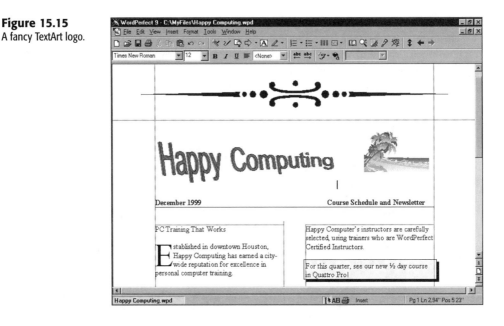

ADDING TEXTART IMAGES

You can insert a TextArt image at any point in a document by using the Insert, Graphics, TextArt command.

To create a TextArt image, use the following steps:

1. Position the insertion point where you want the TextArt to appear.

2. Choose Insert, Graphics, TextArt. The Corel TextArt 9.0 dialog box opens, as shown in Figure 15.16.

Figure 15.16
The Corel TextArt 9.0 dialog box is used for creating fancy text such as logos and desktop publishing text effects.

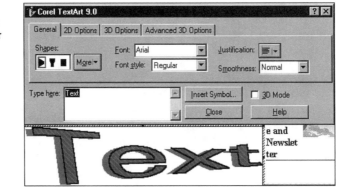

3. Type the text for the TextArt image in the Type H<u>e</u>re box, replacing the word Text.

4. Choose a shape for the text in the S<u>h</u>apes palette. If you want to see more shapes, click the M<u>o</u>re button and choose a shape from there.

5. Choose a font, font style, and justification to format the text.

6. Change any of the following TextArt options on the 2D Options, 3D Options, or Advanced 3D Options tabs to custom tailor the TextArt image:

   • The 2D Options tab lets you change the pattern, shadow, outline, rotation, and text color for the TextArt image.

   • The 3D Options tab gives you options for changing the lighting, bevel, depth of the bevel, and rotation for the TextArt.

   • The 3D Advanced Options tab offers options for specifying the texture for the face and bevel of the image, texture size, texture lighting, and color quality.

7. Click Close. The TextArt appears where you positioned the insertion point in its default position and size.

Note

If you no longer want the TextArt in your document, select the image by clicking it and press the Delete key.

ADDING IMAGES FROM THE WEB

You can download clip art and photos directly from the Internet (if you're online) by using the <u>I</u>nternet button on the right side of the Scrapbook dialog box, and then supplying the URL for the clip-art Web site.

Some quality clip-art and photograph Web sites you can check out are

■ www.desktoppublishing.com/cliplist.html

■ www.clipart.com

■ www.clipartnow.com

■ www.banner.arttoday.com/PD-0025041/full.click

■ www.expectation.com/photo

IMPORTING IMAGES FROM EARLIER VERSIONS OF WORDPERFECT

You can import images that were created in earlier versions of WordPerfect, WordPerfect 7 and 8. To do so, click the <u>I</u>mport Clips button on the right side of the Scrapbook dialog box. In the Insert File - Programs dialog box, display the folder that contains the images from WordPerfect 7 or 8. Then select the clips you want to import, and click Open. WordPerfect adds the images to the Clipart tab, and then you can pick any one of these images to insert into your WordPerfect document.

PRACTICAL PROJECT

You can add spice to a newsletter by inserting a graphic to illustrate the text, as shown in Figure 15.17.

Figure 15.17
Add a graphic to spice up your document.

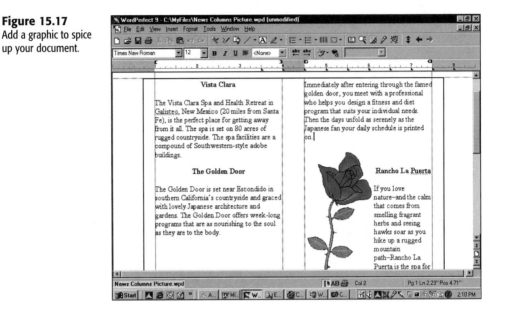

TROUBLESHOOTING

VIEWING A PAGE BORDER

I keep creating a page border, but no matter what I do I can't see it onscreen.

Change the view from Draft view to Page view by choosing View, Page.

REPEATING A PAGE BORDER ON EVERY PAGE

My page border prints only on the first page, and I have to specify it again and again on every page.

When you create the page border on the first page, be sure that the Apply Border to Current Page Only check box is not selected. This option is available for the Line border type, not the Fancy border type.

CHANGING THE BORDER LINES

I created a box and placed an image in it, and now I want to change the border lines.

Right-click your graphic and choose Border/Fill from the QuickMenu. Make whatever changes you want in the Box Border/Fill Styles dialog box, and click OK. Click outside of the box to deselect it.

ADJUSTING THE SHADING FOR A WATERMARK

My watermark is too dark.

Edit your watermark by choosing Insert, Watermark, Edit. Click the Shading button to display the Watermark Shading dialog box. Adjust the percent of the text or image shading as needed and choose OK. Click the Close button on the Watermark Property Bar to return to your document.

CHAPTER 16

PRODUCING MERGE DOCUMENTS

In this chapter

USING MERGE

Using WordPerfect's Merge feature, you can mass-produce letters, envelopes, mailing labels, and other documents. When you merge a form letter with a list of names and addresses, each resulting document contains a different name, address, and company name. The process of merging a form letter with names and addresses is sometimes referred to as a mail merge. Because the names and addresses are saved in a separate file (the data file), you have to enter them only once—when you create the data file. You can use that same data file over and over again when you perform a merge.

Not only can you perform a merge in WordPerfect using a data file, but you can also perform a keyboard merge. A keyboard merge merges a form file with input from the keyboard rather than from a data file. The result of a keyboard merge is a single, filled-in form document.

WHAT IS A MERGE?

A merge is the process of combining fixed information and variable information. The fixed information—a form letter, for example—is in a file referred to as a form file. Every merge has a form file. The variable information can come from another file (referred to as a data file) or it can come from user input at the keyboard. A data file could be a WordPerfect data file or it could be a file from a database program such as Paradox, dBASE, or Access.

To create a merge data file or form file, or to perform a merge, access the Merge dialog box. Choose Tools, Merge or press Shift+F9. You see the Merge dialog box shown in Figure 16.1.

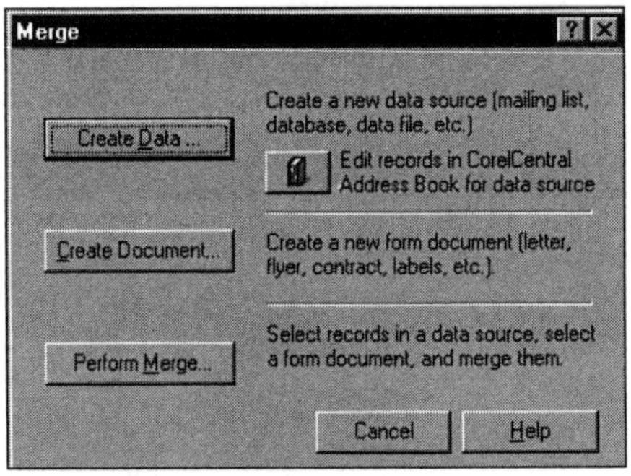

Figure 16.1
Create a merge file or
perform a merge in
the Merge dialog box.

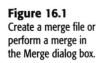

Performing a simple merge is a matter of creating a data file with variable information, creating a form file that asks for information from the data file, and performing the merge.

In the following sections, you learn to create the data file and form file that are used to perform a merge. You also learn to create the form file for a keyboard merge and to perform a keyboard merge.

CREATING A DATA FILE

When you create a data file through the Merge dialog box, WordPerfect guides you through the process of creating the file.

A WordPerfect data file can be either a text file or a table. In either form, the data file is organized into fields and records. A field is one category of information; for example, a field might be a name or a phone number. A record contains all the information about one person and is composed of a complete set of fields.

To create a data file, take the following steps:

1. In an empty document window, choose Tools, Merge. The Merge dialog box appears (refer to Figure 16.1).

PART

II

CH

16

Tip #98 from
Trudi Reisner

If you already have a table that is formatted as a list, you can use the table as a data file. You can also click the Address Book icon to use your Address Book as the data file for the merge.

Note

If you have text in the active document window when you choose Create Data, WordPerfect displays a Create Merge File dialog box that asks whether you want to use the file in the active window or open a new document window to create the data file. Choose New Document Window if you want to create the data file from scratch.

2. Choose Create Data. After WordPerfect knows that you want to create a data file, the Create Data File dialog box appears.

3. In the Create Data File dialog box, create a field name list by typing each field name and pressing Enter to add the name to the list. Figure 16.2 illustrates the Create Data File dialog box after field names have been defined.

4. After you finish creating the field name list, click OK to close the Create Data File dialog box and open the Quick Data Entry dialog box.

5. In the Quick Data Entry dialog box, enter the data for each record, pressing Enter between each field and record. Figure 16.3 illustrates the Quick Data Entry dialog box with a filled-in record.

Note

A field can have more than one line. An address field, for example, could have one or more lines for the street address and a line for the city, state, and zip code. In general, however, it's easier to sort and select records when fields are broken down into small categories. If you do want to enter more than one line of data in a field, press Ctrl+Enter before each subsequent line. Scroll arrows at the right end of the field box let you see different lines in the field.

Figure 16.2
Define field names in the Create Data File dialog box.

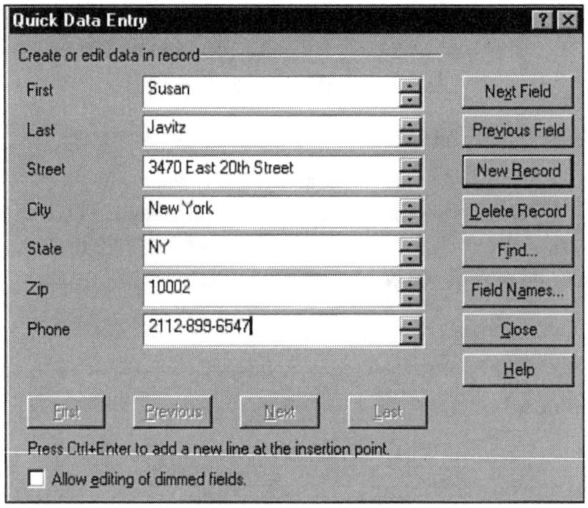

Figure 16.3
Enter data records in the Quick Data Entry dialog box.

6. Choose Close after you finish entering records. WordPerfect then prompts you to save the data file. You don't have to type an extension for the filename unless you want to. WordPerfect automatically supplies a .dat extension.

7. Choose Yes to save the data file. Then specify a filename and click Save. If your data file is in a text format (rather than a table format), you see something like the illustration shown in Figure 16.4. At the top of the data file are the field names, followed by a page break. The end of each field is marked with an ENDFIELD code, even if the field is empty (the phone field in the second record is empty). The end of each record is marked with an ENDRECORD code and a hard page break. The Merge Property Bar is displayed at the top of the screen.

Figure 16.4
A text data file with records created in the Quick Entry dialog box.

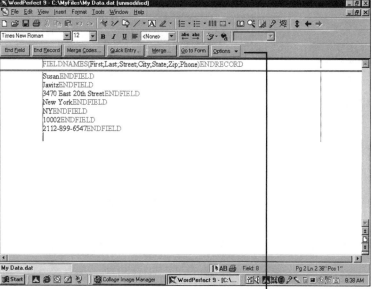

FIELDNAMES(First;Last;Street;City;State;Zip;Phone)ENDRECORD

SusanENDFIELD
JavitzENDFIELD
3470 East 20th StreetENDFIELD
New YorkENDFIELD
NYENDFIELD
10002ENDFIELD
212-899-6547ENDFIELD

PART

II

CH

16

Merge Property Bar

EDITING AND PRINTING A DATA FILE

You can edit your data file after creating it to add more records or to change existing data. You may want to print the data for verification. To edit a data file if it's not already in the active window, open it like any other file. When WordPerfect opens the file, it recognizes it as a data file and displays the Merge Property Bar at the top of the screen.

ADDING RECORDS

When you don't have time to enter all your data file records at once, or you don't have all the information when you create the data file, you'll want to reopen the file later and add records.

To add more records to the data file in the active window, follow these steps:

1. Choose Quick Entry on the Property Bar.

2. In the Quick Entry dialog box, choose New Record if one is not already displayed. An empty record form appears.

3. Enter new records until you're finished, and then choose Close.

4. When WordPerfect prompts you to save your file, answer Yes to save it to its existing name.

| Tip #99 from | It's easier to read the data onscreen if you choose Options on the Property Bar, and then |
| *Trudi Reisner* | select Hide Codes. |

EDITING RECORDS

When you need to update the information in your data file—for example, when someone's address changes—reopen the data file and take the following steps:

1. Position the insertion point anywhere in the first record that you want to change, and then choose Quick Entry; or position the insertion point at the beginning of the document and choose Quick Entry.

2. If the record that you want to change isn't displayed in the Quick Entry dialog box, choose Find. A Find Text dialog box appears. Enter the text that you want to find and choose Find Next. The first record that contains matching text is displayed in the Quick Entry data form (you may have to perform more than one find operation).

3. When the record you want to edit appears in the data form, make the desired changes and choose Close.

PRINTING THE DATA FILE

It's often helpful to have a printout of your data file. WordPerfect makes it easy to print your data in a readable format. To print your data, follow these steps:

1. With the data file that you want to print onscreen, choose Options. To suppress the display of codes in the printout, be sure that Hide Codes is selected.

2. From the Options menu, choose Print. WordPerfect asks you to confirm that you want to print with no page breaks between records.

3. Click OK; the data file is printed.

CREATING A FORM FILE

Every merge has to have a form file; the form file controls the merge. The form file contains merge codes that ask for information from another source. It should also contain any text, formatting, and graphics that you want in the final merged documents. When the merge is executed, the text, formatting, and graphics, if any, in the form file appear in every merged document. Merge codes in the form file are replaced by information from the data file or from the keyboard.

To create a form file, take the following steps:

1. If you already have a document with the fixed information for your form file, open the document.

2. Choose Tools, Merge. The Merge dialog box appears (refer to Figure 16.1).

3. Choose Create Document. WordPerfect asks whether you want to use the current document window for your form file, or whether you want to create the form file in a new, empty window. Make the appropriate choice.

4. WordPerfect then prompts you for the name of the data file to associate with your form file, as shown in Figure 16.5. The associated data file is the file that is merged with the form file. Enter a name for the data file, or select it after clicking the list button to the right of the text box.

Figure 16.5
Associate a data file with your form file in the Associate Form and Data dialog box.

5. Alternatively, if you are in your Data Source file, to create a form file click the Go to Form button on the Property Bar. You see the Associate dialog box shown in Figure 16.6. Choose Create to create a form file.

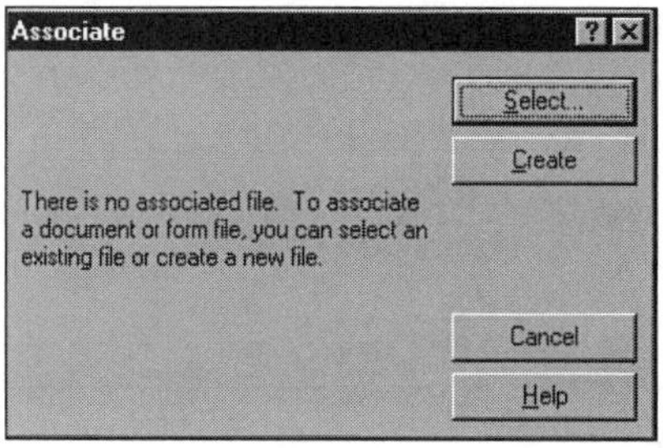

Figure 16.6
The Associate dialog box allows you to create or open a form file to associate with the data file.

6. Type, edit, and format any text that should appear in your form file. Formatting text is described further in Chapter 6, "Formatting Text."

7. Position the insertion point where you want to insert the first merge code. If the form file is a form letter, for example, you might want to merge in the computer date at the top of the letter.

8. To insert a Date merge code, choose the Date button.

9. To insert a Field merge code, choose the Insert Field button. The Insert Field Name or Number dialog box appears, displaying a list of field names from the associated data file. Select the desired field name and choose Insert. The field merge code is inserted in the document and the dialog box is still onscreen. Figure 16.7 shows a form file just after inserting a date merge code and the first field merge code.

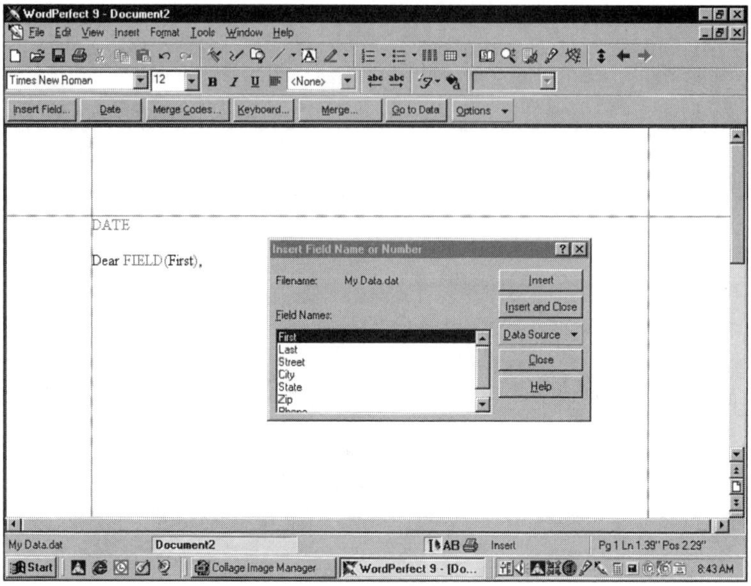

Figure 16.7
The merge code is
inserted in a form file.

10. Position the insertion point where you want another merge code; or type, edit, and for-mat text until the insertion point is where you want to insert the next merge code. Place commas and spaces between merge codes on the same line as appropriate. For example, if you have just inserted a Field code for the City in the inside address of a form letter, press the comma key and then the spacebar.

Tip #100 from
Trudi Reisner

If the Insert Field Name or Number dialog box obscures your view of the form file, drag it to a new position.

11. When the insertion point is positioned where you want another merge code, select it from the list and choose Insert.

12. Repeat steps 10 and 11 until you have entered all the merge codes that you want to enter. When you finish, close the Insert Field Name or Number dialog box. You can insert the last field and close the dialog box at the same time by clicking Insert and Close. The finished result may appear as illustrated in Figure 16.8.

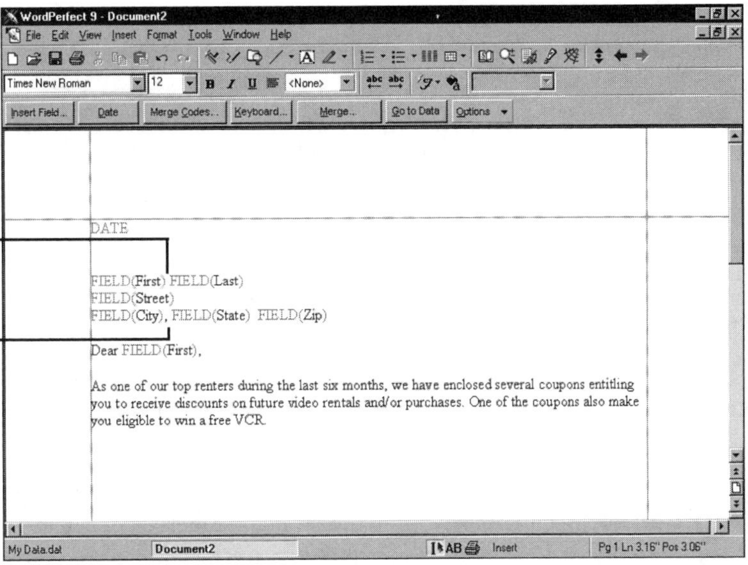

Figure 16.8
A sample form file includes the form letter and the inserted fields.

A space separates fields on this line.

A comma and a space separate the City and State fields.

13. Save and close the form file as you would any document. You don't have to type a filename extension; WordPerfect automatically adds an .frm extension to the filename.

⚠ *If the inside address in your mail merge letter looks jammed together, see "Spacing in the Inside Address" in the Troubleshooting section at the end of this chapter.*

PERFORMING THE MERGE

When you have a form file and a data file, you have the ingredients for a merge. To perform a merge, follow these steps:

1. If you are not in the Form or Data file, choose Tools, Merge, and then choose Perform Merge from the Merge dialog box. If you are in the Form or Data file, select Merge from the Property Bar. The Perform Merge dialog box appears (see Figure 16.9).

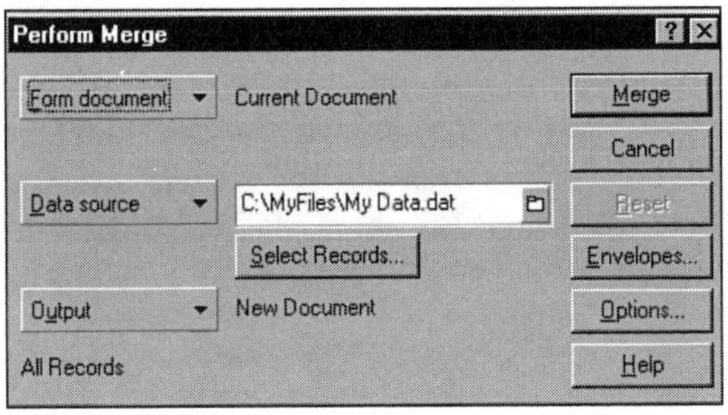

Figure 16.9
The Perform Merge dialog box allows you to specify options for the merge.

2. If they do not already appear, enter the names of your form file and data file, or use the list button for each option to select the name from a list.

> **Note**
>
> To create merged envelopes at the same time that you create merged form letters, see the next section, "Creating Envelopes."

> **Tip #101 from**
> *Trudi Reisner*
>
> You can select specific records from your data file or address book for your merge. See Records (merge), Select in the WordPerfect Help Index.

3. Choose Merge to perform the merge. When the merge has been completed, the insertion point is positioned at the end of the last merged document. Page breaks separate each document.

4. Scroll through the merged documents to verify the success of the merge. If there are any problems, close the window containing the merged documents (don't save), edit the file that is causing the problem (either the form file or the data file), resave the corrected file, and perform the merge again.

5. When the merge has completed without problems, you can save the results, if desired, and print the merged documents all at once.

CREATING ENVELOPES

WordPerfect simplifies a merge by making it possible to create merged letters and envelopes all at once. When the merge is completed, both the form letters and the envelopes are in the active document window, ready to print.

To create merged envelopes and form letters in a single merge operation, perform the following steps:

1. Enter the names of the form file and data file in the Perform Merge dialog box (see the previous section).

2. Choose Envelopes. The Envelope Property Bar is displayed.

3. Leave your insertion point in the Mailing Address area, then click the Insert Field button. Select the field you want to insert and choose Insert and Close. Position the insertion point for the next field, and then repeat this step until you have added all fields for your envelope. A completed Envelope Mailing Address area is shown in Figure 16.10.

Figure 16.10
To create merged envelopes, enter field merge codes in the Mailing Addresses area.

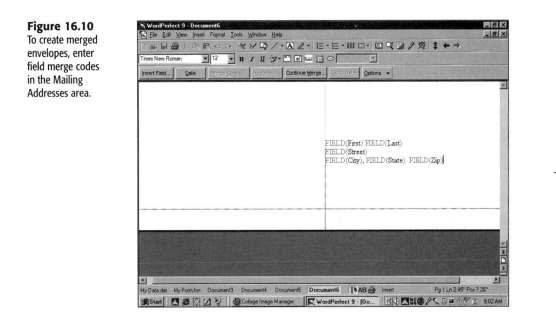

4. Add a bar code, if desired, through the Bar Code button on the Envelope Property Bar.

> **Note**
>
> Adding a bar code speeds the delivery of your mail.

5. Specify a return address, if desired. You can pick your return address from the Address Book by clicking the Return Address Book button on the Envelope Property Bar.

6. When you finish working in the Envelope window, click Continue Merge on the Merge Property Bar to return to the Perform Merge dialog box.

7. Choose Merge to perform the merge. Merged letters and envelopes are created in the designated output file (usually a new document). The insertion point is positioned at the end of the last letter; the envelopes are below the letters.

8. As with any merge, check the results before printing or saving. If there are problems, close the current window (don't save), edit and resave the problem file (it could be either the form file or the data file), and perform the merge again.

9. When the results are successful, you can save the output file, if desired, and print it all at once.

If you merged envelopes and cannot find them in your document, see "Viewing the Merge Envelopes" in the Troubleshooting section at the end of this chapter.

FILLING IN A FORM WITH A KEYBOARD MERGE

You can pause the merge operation to fill in information that is unique to each record. You can even create a form file that has no references to data file fields, but only has pauses for you to enter information. Creating and merging such a file is called a keyboard merge.

Tip #102 from *Trudi Reisner*	Many of WordPerfect's templates are automated merge forms. The fax expert, for example, prompts you for keyboard input and then places your input in appropriate places on the fax form.

You can use this technique to quickly create forms that require you to enter text in specific areas. All you have to do is start a merge and enter information as prompted. You don't have to move the insertion point to the next place that needs input; WordPerfect does it for you. You even get help on what to input (from the prompt that is associated with each keyboard merge code).

CREATING A FORM FILE FOR A KEYBOARD MERGE

When you create a form file for a keyboard merge, it's usually easier to create the document text first and add the merge codes later. You can, however, add the merge codes while you create the text.

To create a form file for a keyboard merge, do the following:

1. Create a boilerplate document containing all the fixed information and formatting that should appear in every merged document.

Tip #103 from *Trudi Reisner*	Boilerplate is the term for unchanging text in a document. For example, a collections letter may use the same text every time it's sent out, with only the recipient's name and the amount owed changing.

2. Choose Tools, Merge. In the Merge dialog box, choose Create Document. In the Create Merge File dialog box, choose Use File in Active Window. Click OK.

3. At the Associate Form and Data dialog box, choose No Association (to indicate that there is no associated data file), and then click OK.

4. In your form file, position the insertion point where you want input from the keyboard. Choose Keyboard. The Insert Merge Code dialog box appears (this dialog box appears whenever you insert a merge code that requires additional information, such as a prompt).

5. Enter a prompt for the user to see when he inputs information at this specific place on the form. An example of the Insert Merge Code dialog box with a filled-in prompt is shown in Figure 16.11. When you finish entering the prompt, click OK.

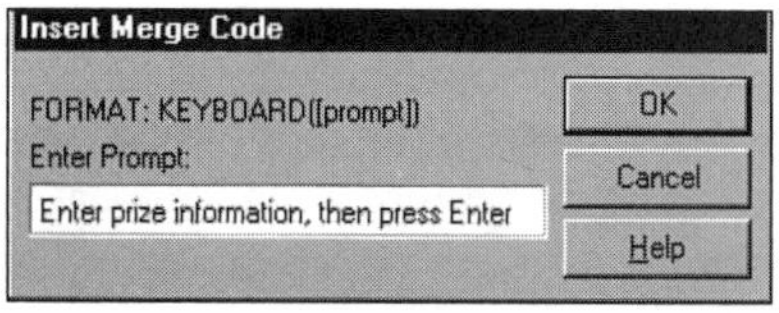

Figure 16.11
Remind the user
what he should
do while filling in
variable information
from the keyboard.

> **Note**
>
> It's helpful to tell the user which keystrokes to press to continue the merge after filling in data at the current location. For example, include the prompt `Type recipient's name, then press Alt+Enter to continue`.

6. Continue to enter keyboard merge codes wherever you want input from the keyboard. A completed form might look like the illustration shown in Figure 16.12.

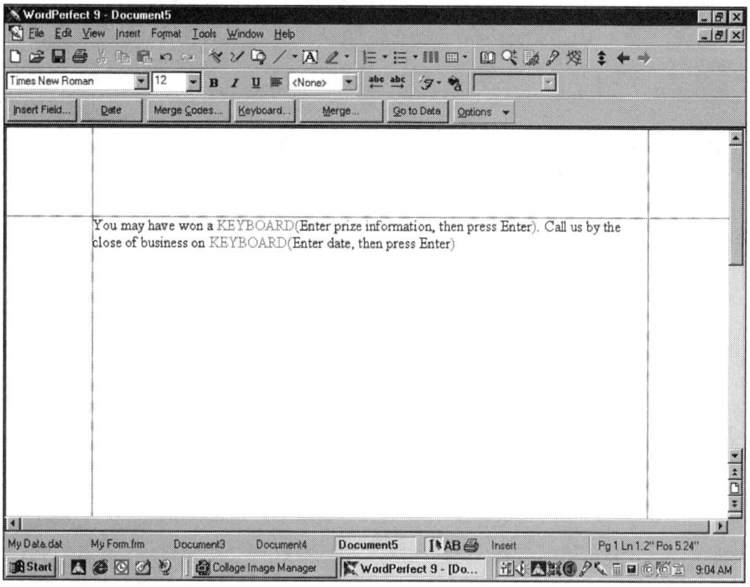

Figure 16.12
This is a completed
form file for a key-
board merge.

7. Save and replace the completed form file.

PERFORMING A KEYBOARD MERGE

When you perform a keyboard merge, you fill in the blanks in your form file from the keyboard while the merge occurs. The result is a single merged document. After the form is filled in, you can print the results and save them.

To perform a keyboard merge, take the following steps:

1. In an empty document window, choose Tools, Merge. In the Merge dialog box, choose Perform Merge. In the Perform Merge dialog box, specify a form file, and then be sure that the Data Source text box is empty. Choose Merge to begin the merge.

2. A merge Property Bar appears at the top of the screen. When the merge pauses at the first keyboard merge code (see Figure 16.13), the prompt that is associated with that particular keyboard code appears in the center of the screen. Type the appropriate information. When you finish typing, press Alt+Enter or choose Continue from the Property Bar. This tells WordPerfect that you have finished entering information here and that you are ready for the merge to move on.

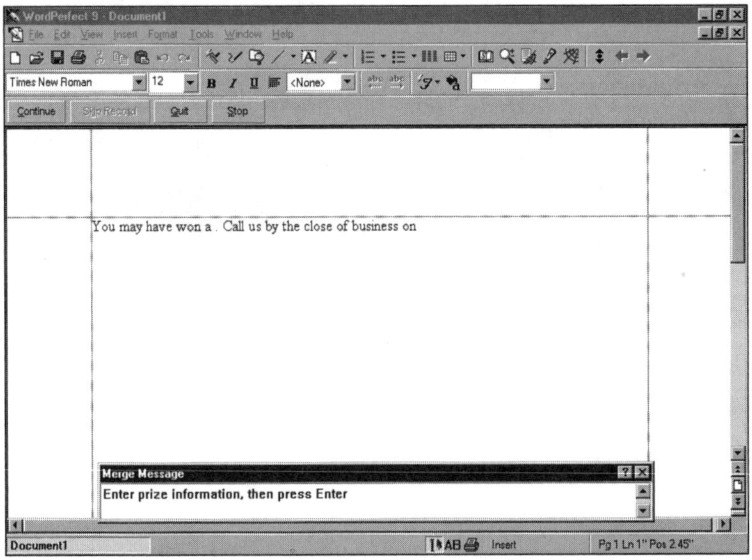

Figure 16.13
A merge paused for input at a Keyboard merge code. What you type is entered at the insertion point.

3. The merge moves to the next keyboard code, if there is one, and prompts you for input. As long as you are being prompted for input, the merge is in process. You must tell WordPerfect to move on from each Keyboard merge code, whether or not you type input at that code.

Tip #104 from
Trudi Reisner

You can type as many lines as necessary at a keyboard prompt. You can also add or correct any formatting on previous entries.

4. When the merge is complete, you can print the document onscreen and save it, if desired.

⚠ *If you performed a keyboard merge and couldn't move on to the next keyboard merge code, see "Moving On to the Next Keyboard Merge Code" in the Troubleshooting section at the end of this chapter.*

PRACTICAL PROJECT

Create a form file that contains a letter requesting a recycling service in your neighborhood. Create a data file that contains the names and addresses of your neighbors, the mayor, and other town or city officials. Merge the two files and print your form letters, and then print envelopes using the data file and the envelope feature.

TROUBLESHOOTING

SPACING IN THE INSIDE ADDRESS

I created a data file and a form file and then I performed a mail merge, but the city, state, and zip code are all jammed together in the inside address.

In a normal letter, you have a comma and a space separating the city and the state in an inside address. In a form file, you need the same text (a comma and a space) between the Field code for the city and the Field code for the state. Correspondingly, you need spaces between the state and zip code fields.

VIEWING THE MERGE ENVELOPES

I performed a merge and asked for envelopes, but they're not there.

When a merge completes, the insertion point is beneath the last form letter but above the envelopes. Scroll downward to see the envelopes after you perform the merge.

MOVING ON TO THE NEXT KEYBOARD MERGE CODE

I created a keyboard merge form file but when I performed a merge, I pressed Enter and the merge didn't move on to the next place that needed keyboard input. Then I didn't know what to do.

When you get into a mess like this, the best solution is to cancel the merge (click Stop), close the document window without saving, and start again. The only way you will move on from the current Keyboard merge code during a merge is by choosing Continue or by pressing Alt+Enter. You must repeat this action for every Keyboard merge code in the form file for the merge operation to come to a normal termination.

CHAPTER 17

AUTOMATING WITH MACROS

In this chapter

USING MACROS

Macros can save you time by performing repetitive tasks automatically. You can, for example, record a macro that types a closure to a letter. You can use macros to speed everyday formatting and editing, to automate an elaborate set of tasks, or to combine several commands into one (the one that plays the macro).

In addition to using macros you create yourself, you can use macros that WordPerfect provides for you. Macros that WordPerfect provides include CLOSEALL.WCM, which closes all open documents; PLEADING.WCM, which creates a sample pleading for legal offices; and WATERMRK.WCM, which prompts you for text or a graphic and creates a watermark out of it.

Tip #105 from
Trudi Reisner
To see a description of the macros included with WordPerfect, choose Help, then look up Macro in the index, and select Macros Included with WordPerfect.

This section introduces you to playing macros, recording macros, and making simple editing changes to macros.

Note
WordPerfect enables you to save macros inside templates, or as files on the disk. In the former case, they are saved as part of the template file, and are available only when you are using the appropriate template. In the latter case, they are saved as standalone files and are always accessible.

Template macros are accessed by choosing Tools, Template Macro; the other macros are accessed by choosing Tools, Macro. Other than the location in which they are saved, they work the same way. The remainder of this chapter discusses macros saved as files, but the discussion applies to template macros as well.

PLAYING A MACRO

When you play a macro, you execute the keystrokes and commands that are saved in the macro. The macro may type in text. It may perform formatting functions. It may even ask for your input and then perform certain steps depending upon your input.

Tip #106 from
Trudi Reisner
After you have played macros, you can play recently played macros again easily. Choose Tools, Macro, and then choose a recently played macro listed at the bottom of the Macro menu.

To play a macro, take the following steps:

1. Choose Tools, Macro, Play. The Play Macro dialog box appears (see Figure 17.1).

Figure 17.1
Select a macro to play in the Play Macro dialog box.

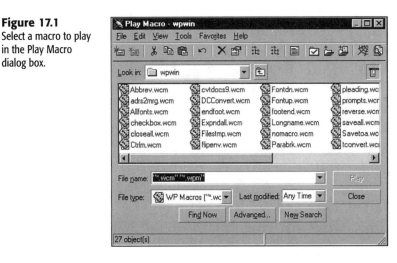

Note

WordPerfect automatically lists macros in the default directory specified for macros through File Preferences. To change this directory, choose Tools, Settings, Files, Merge/Macro, Default Macro Folder.

2. Select the desired macro.

3. Choose Play. If this is the first time that you have played the macro, it compiles before it plays, and it takes a little extra time to get going.

STOPPING A MACRO

When you're testing a macro, it's a good idea to save any open documents before you play the macro. If something goes wrong during playback (for instance, if the macro adds text to the wrong part of your document), you'll want to cancel macro execution. You can usually stop a macro during playback by pressing the Esc key; however, the Esc key could be disabled or assigned to a specific function by the macro. After you cancel macro execution, you can always close all open documents without saving and then reopen them.

CREATING A MACRO

Creating a macro is simply a matter of starting the macro recorder, performing the actions that you want recorded, and ending the recording session.

To record a macro, follow these steps:

1. Choose Tools, Macro, Record. The Record Macro dialog box appears (see Figure 17.2).

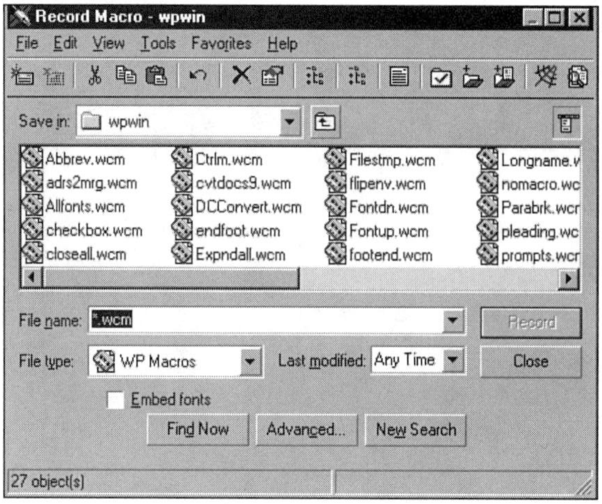

Figure 17.2
Enter a name for your macro in the Record Macro dialog box.

2. Enter a name for your macro. WordPerfect assigns a .wcm extension to the name.

3. Choose Record. The macro recorder is activated and the Macro Property Bar is displayed at the top of the screen (see Figure 17.3). `Macro Record` is also displayed on the Application Bar.

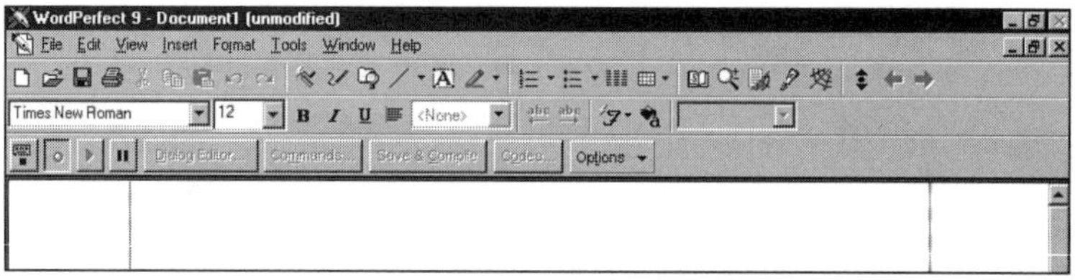

Figure 17.3
The Macro Property Bar displays while a macro is being recorded.

4. Perform the actions that you want the macro to record. You can enter text from the keyboard, and you can choose commands from menus (with the keyboard or the mouse). Use Shift+arrow key to select items because you cannot use the mouse to move the insertion point or to select text while the macro recorder is active.

5. To finish recording, click the Stop Record button on the Macro Property Bar; or choose Tools, Macro, Record. The Macro Record message disappears from the Application Bar and the macro is saved to disk. You can close the document window without saving changes after you end recording, because the macro was saved when you ended recording.

⚠ *If you couldn't use the mouse to move the insertion point when you were recording a macro, see "Moving the Insertion Point While Recording a Macro" in the Troubleshooting section at the end of this chapter.*

MAKING SIMPLE EDITING CHANGES TO A MACRO

Don't be afraid to make simple editing changes to a macro. If you decide that you want to add a middle initial to a closure that is typed by a macro, for example, you can add the text without having to learn macro syntax and commands.

To make simple editing changes to a macro, do the following:

1. Choose Tools, Macro, Edit. The Edit Macro dialog box appears (it looks similar to the Record Macro dialog box).

2. Select the macro that you want to edit, and then choose Edit. The macro file is opened into an editing window and the Macro Property Bar appears just above the text window, like the macro being edited in Figure 17.4.

Figure 17.4
You can edit macros as you would edit any other WordPerfect document.

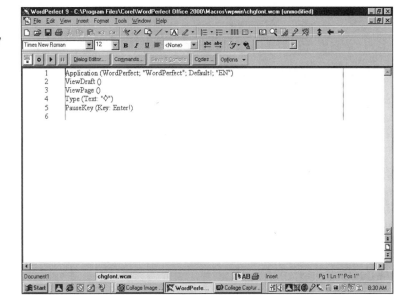

3. Use normal editing techniques to make simple editing changes.

    For example, to add a middle initial to the signature in the First_Macro.wcm macro, insert the middle initial in the appropriate place in the Type command. To remove one of the blank lines before the signature line, select a HardReturn() command and press Delete. To add a blank line above the signature line, type the command HardReturn(), or copy and paste a HardReturn() command.

    While you're editing the macro, you can press Enter (or Tab or the spacebar) to separate commands. This formats the macro so that it's easier to read, but it doesn't affect what happens when you play the macro.

Caution

Be careful, however, not to press Enter when the insertion point is positioned in the middle of a command; the Enter key signals the end of a macro command.

4. When you finish editing the macro, click the Save & Compile button on the Macro Property Bar. The save and compile process begins. If there are no errors, the process is completed and the macro remains onscreen. If WordPerfect detects errors during compilation, a dialog box appears describing the error and its location. You can then cancel compilation, correct the error, and try the save and compile operation again.

5. After the macro successfully saves and compiles, choose Options, Close Macro to close the document window.

Note

WordPerfect provides extensive onscreen help information about macros. For help with a specific macro command, choose Help, Help Topics. In the Contents tab, choose Macros, Writing and Editing Macros Using PerfectScript or Customizing WordPerfect Macros. You can also refer to the Reference Center if you installed it from your CD.

Tip #107 from
Trudi Reisner

Make your macros easy to use by adding them to the toolbar.

→ To add your macros to the toolbar, **see** "Adding Toolbar Buttons and Menu Items," **p. 68**

 If you're editing a macro and want to add more macro commands to it, and don't know the macro syntax, see "Recording While Editing a Macro" in the Troubleshooting section at the end of this chapter.

PRACTICAL PROJECT

Create a macro for reviewing a document. Have the macro compare the edited version of the document with the original document, review the edited document, and add a comment to the reviewed document that reminds you to highlight differences between the reviewed and original documents, as well as add comments to the text.

TROUBLESHOOTING

MOVING THE INSERTION POINT WHILE RECORDING A MACRO

I'm recording a macro to move the insertion point and select text; however, I can't use the mouse to move the cursor within the text.

The macro recorder cannot record mouse actions, such as selecting text, within document text. Use the keyboard to record these actions.

RECORDING WHILE EDITING A MACRO

I want to type some commands into my macro when I'm editing it, but I don't know the syntax.

While you're editing a macro, you can click the Begin Record button on the Macro Property Bar and record commands (this is easier than looking up the syntax and typing in the command). When you turn on the macro recorder, you access a new document window where you can choose the commands you want to record in the macro, either through the menu, the toolbar, or the Property Bar. When you finish recording, click the Stop Record button on the Macro Property Bar to return to the editing window for the macro. The steps you performed while recording are added to the macro at the insertion point. You can also press Ctrl+M while you are editing your macro to see a dialog box of macro commands.

CHAPTER 18

CUSTOMIZING COREL WORDPERFECT 9

In this chapter

USING THE SETTINGS DIALOG BOX

Because many of the features you will learn to customize are accessed from one starting point—the Settings dialog box—let's begin by looking at this dialog box. Choose Tools, Settings. You see the Settings dialog box (see Figure 18.1).

Figure 18.1
Customize
WordPerfect to suit
your taste by using the
Settings dialog box.

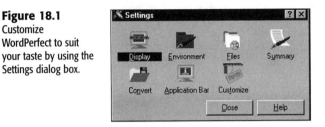

Tip #108 from
Trudi Reisner

Right-click the toolbar, Property Bar, Application Bar, or either scrollbar and choose Settings from the QuickMenu; you'll go directly to the Settings dialog box for that screen element.

Starting from the Settings dialog box, you can customize Display Settings, Environment Settings, File Settings, and Summary Settings. These subjects are covered in detail in the following sections. Customizing toolbars, the Property Bar, the Application Bar, the keyboard, the menu bar, and file conversions are summarized under "Customizing Other Settings," later in this chapter.

CUSTOMIZING DISPLAY SETTINGS

Use Display Settings to customize the way various screen elements are displayed onscreen. Choose Tools, Settings, Display to open the Display Settings dialog box. Figure 18.2 illustrates the Document tab of the Display Settings dialog box.

The selected tab (Document, Symbols, Reveal Codes, and so on) determines the options that are available in the lower portion of the dialog box. When you select Reveal Codes, for example, the available options involve the Color, Format, and Font. Figure 18.3 illustrates the Display Settings dialog box with the Reveal Codes tab selected. Set the Text and Background colors to any colors you want instead of using the system colors.

Figure 18.2
Document options are displayed in the Display Settings dialog box.

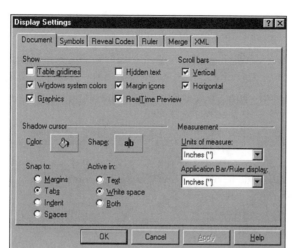

Figure 18.3
Color and Format options are displayed in the Display Settings dialog box.

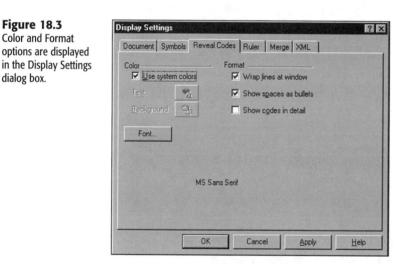

PART

II

Cʜ

18

→ For more information on how to use view modes, **see** "Using View Modes," **p. 102**

Most users never need to change most of these settings. However, some of the options that you can change through Display Settings will speed up your work. As you increase the graphics display onscreen, you slow down the screen refresh rate; whatever you do to reduce graphical display makes your work go faster.

Display settings you can select to speed up your work include

■ Deselect Graphics to suppress the display of graphics in the editing window (in the Show section of the Document tab); when Graphics is deselected, an empty box is used as a placeholder.

- Deselect the RealTime Preview check box in the Show section of the Document tab if you don't want to see how text looks in the document before applying font changes.

- Deselect the Horizontal check box in the Scroll Bars section of the Document tab if you don't want to display the horizontal scrollbar onscreen.

- Deselect the Vertical check box in the Scroll Bars section of the Document tab if you don't want to display the vertical scrollbar onscreen.

You can also temporarily change many display settings from the View menu. Page View is the default view, but you can always use the View, Draft menu selection to switch to Draft view when you want to hide headers, footers, and page borders. If you've told WordPerfect to show table gridlines in your Display Settings, you can use the View, Table Gridlines menu selection to see lines and fill styles in a table. When speed is not a priority, you can use the View, Graphics menu selection to display graphics.

View, Show (¶) options can help by showing you what keys you've pressed (you won't have to look in Reveal Codes). Although showing nonprinting characters as symbols (spaces, hard returns, tabs, and so on) add clutter to the screen, many of us can benefit from seeing these symbols. For example, if you can't tell by looking whether you pressed the spacebar once or twice, you would know for sure by the number of dot symbols that represent spaces. Then, you can easily position the insertion point in the correct location and delete an unneeded symbol. By default, these symbols show all the time on new and current documents. The Symbols tab of the Display Settings dialog box (see Figure 18.4) shows the symbols to display.

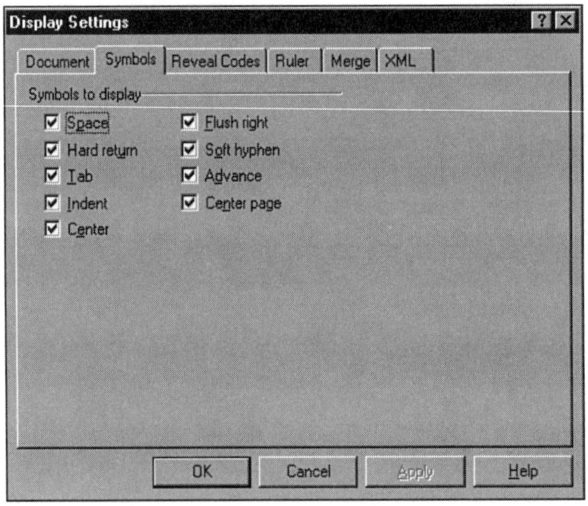

Figure 18.4
You can tell WordPerfect which characters you want to display as symbols from the Symbols tab of the Display Settings dialog box.

You can determine what suits you best only when you know what options are available. After you know what your options are, you can think about how the various choices affect your work.

Tip #109 from
Trudi Reisner

See the online Help system for the functions of infrequently used Display Settings options.

If you don't see any table gridlines after you change the settings to display table gridlines and format your table with table lines, see "Displaying Table Gridlines" in the Troubleshooting section at the end of this chapter.

If you want to display your ruler all the time without having to ask for it, see "Displaying the Ruler" in the Troubleshooting section at the end of this chapter.

CUSTOMIZING ENVIRONMENT SETTINGS

The first time you access Environment Settings by choosing Tools, Settings, Environment, you should see the name you entered during installation in the Name text box (see Figure 18.5). Enter your correct name (if it's not already entered correctly), your initials, and select a personal color. What you enter in the User Information area will be applied in document comments or summaries.

Figure 18.5
Customize User Information, Language options, Beep On options, and other environment options through the Environment Settings dialog box.

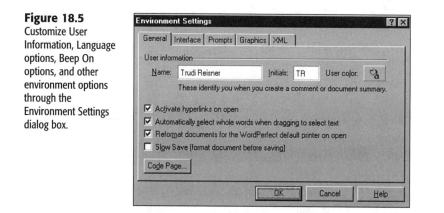

PART

II

CH

18

Tip #110 from
Trudi Reisner

All comments you make display in your personal color. If several reviewers make comments on a document, it is helpful if they have different personal colors.

Commonly used options in this dialog box include the following:

- General Tab—Hypertext links allow you to jump to another location in the same document or a different document, or to execute a macro. When Activate Hypertext Links on Open is enabled, all hypertext links in your documents are automatically activated (although Hypertext still can be activated on an as-needed basis).

  When Automatically Select Whole Words When Dragging to Select Text is selected, entire words are selected automatically as you drag through text with the mouse (you can still hold down the Shift key and press an arrow key to adjust the selection on a character-by-character basis). By default, this option is turned on.

→ For more information on hypertext Web links, **see** "Using Hypertext Web Links," **p. 593**

■ Interface Tab—Menu options are listed in the Interface tab. You may want to check Display Shortcut Keys so that these keys display on the menu. This makes it easier to learn them.

The Save Workspace options can be especially handy if you frequently want to work on the same document(s) that you were working on during your last work session in WordPerfect. You can, for example, exit WordPerfect while a particular document is still open, and then start WordPerfect and automatically open the same document all at once. To accomplish this, choose the Always option in the Save Workspace (documents and window layout) group.

If you have purchased another language version of WordPerfect and you want to use that language's formatting conventions, select the appropriate language from the Interface Language drop-down list.

■ Prompts—In the Prompts tab, you can tell WordPerfect whether you want to confirm the deletion of formatting codes and to note the position of these codes. Leave Confirm Deletion of Table Formulas selected to help you guard against the accidental deletion of table formulas.

You can specify conditions under which WordPerfect beeps at you. For example, if you want to be beeped when a find operation is unsuccessful, select the On Find Failure option in the Prompts tab.

→ To learn how to apply page formatting, **see** "Formatting the Page," **p. 128**

■ Graphics—When you create or import a graphic, WordPerfect puts it on the current page near the insertion point by default. Instead, you may prefer to check Drag to Create New Graphic Boxes. If you do so, you can drag with the mouse to size and position your graphic.

■ XML—If you import HTML documents that were prepared for use on the Web, and want WordPerfect Office to recognize them as XML documents, turn on the option called Import HTML Documents Using the XML Component.

When you import XML/SGML documents, and you want WordPerfect Office to prompt you to choose a format for the documents, use the option called Prompt for File Type When Importing XML/SGML Documents.

When you import SGML documents, and you want WordPerfect Office to generate paired tags where they weren't created and insert tags that were omitted (for the WordPerfect template), check the option called Insert Omitted Tags Required by DTD During SGML Import.

CUSTOMIZING FILE SETTINGS

The Files Settings dialog box, accessed by choosing Tools, Settings, Files, includes options about where and how you save or access various types of files. Figure 18.6 shows the Document tab of the Files Settings dialog box. Important settings in this tab include Default Save File Format. If you are sharing many files with users of earlier versions of WordPerfect, you may want to save your document as a WordPerfect 6/7/8/9 or WordPerfect 5.1/5.2 file. The Default Document Folder option allows you to specify where your documents will be saved by default.

Figure 18.6
Tell WordPerfect where you want to save and access files using the Files Settings dialog box.

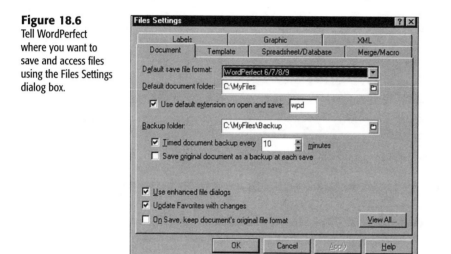

PART

II

CH

18

The Use Default Extension on Open and Save box has been selected, and the default extension is specified as wpd. Files Settings also includes choices on the default extension for new documents and on automatic backup options.

WordPerfect expects to back up any open documents every 10 minutes; you can adjust the interval, but it's not a good idea to deselect the Timed Document Backup option. If your system freezes and you haven't saved changes, the timed backup can spare you a lot of grief.

When you install WordPerfect on your computer, the location of files is defined for you by default (you can, however, specify your own locations during installation by using Custom Install rather than Traditional Install). Documents are stored in one location, templates in another location, and graphics in another location. This normally works exactly the way you want, so you probably wouldn't want to change these settings, although you can change them if desired. When you're working with Files Settings, you can see where a particular type of file is stored by selecting that file type (Document, Template, Spreadsheet/Database, and so on), or you can see all the default storage locations at once by clicking the View All button. The Update Favorites with Changes option tells WordPerfect whether to update the Favorites list of folder names in directory dialog boxes, such as the Open dialog box.

➔ For more information on how to save files, **see** "Saving Files," **p. 37**

> **Caution**
>
> Even though WordPerfect backs up open documents for you, don't wait until you finish working on a document to save it. Save your work at regular intervals—every 10 minutes, for example. Automatic backup is a disaster recovery feature; it is not a substitute for regular file save operations.

Just as with Display Settings and Environment Settings, you can easily customize your Files Settings to suit the way you work. Through Files Settings, you can specify whether to use automatic filename extensions for documents (and for merge files); you can also change default storage locations and customize backup options.

CUSTOMIZING DOCUMENT SUMMARIES

Would you like to include a general overview of a document with the document, or other reference information such as keywords that are used in the file? If the answer to either one of these questions is yes, then customize WordPerfect's document summary Settings.

➔ For more information on how to use the QuickFinder, **see** "Using QuickFinder," **p. 52**

INCLUDING SUMMARY INFORMATION WITH INDIVIDUAL DOCUMENTS

Even if you don't customize summary Settings, you can include summary information with individual documents through the File menu. Choose File, Properties to enter or change summary information for an individual document. The Properties dialog box appears (see Figure 18.7). Any summary information that you enter is saved with the document when you save the document.

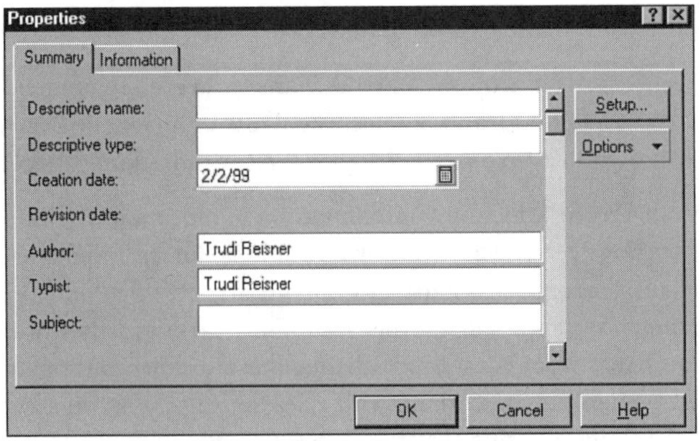

Figure 18.7
Enter or change summary information for a document, or change the configuration for summaries, in the Properties dialog box. Use the scrollbar to see other summary fields.

Tip #111 from
Trudi Reisner

Click the Setup button in the Properties dialog box to specify which fields to use in summaries and the order in which the fields appear.

To customize your Summary Settings for all documents, choose Tools, Settings, Summary. The Document Summary Settings dialog box appears (see Figure 18.8). By default, all three check box options are deselected; in this example, summary Settings have already been customized so that options are selected. You can use the Subject Search Text option to tell WordPerfect how to identify a document subject. For example, when RE: is the specified subject search text, any text that appears in the document, following RE: is automatically inserted in the Subject field in the document summary.

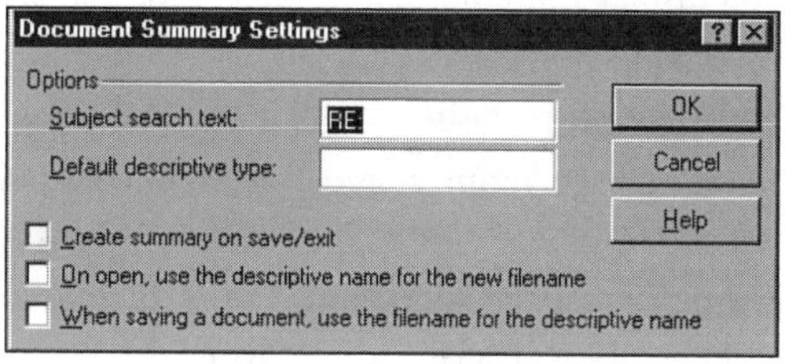

Figure 18.8
Create summary information by default by customizing your Document Summary Settings.

Document Summary Settings

Options
Subject search text: RE:
Default descriptive type:

OK
Cancel
Help

☐ Create summary on save/exit
☐ On open, use the descriptive name for the new filename
☐ When saving a document, use the filename for the descriptive name

CREATING SUMMARIES ON SAVE/EXIT

When you specify that you want to Create Summary on Save/Exit in the Document Summary Settings dialog box, WordPerfect automatically asks for summary information when you save a document for the first time. Although this might seem like a nuisance when you don't want to enter summary information, it takes only a single click (OK) or keystroke (Enter) to get past the request. This feature can be helpful when you are in a workgroup environment, and people use keywords when saving their documents.

If you want to include a document number for your document summaries, see "Including a Document Number in Summaries" in the Troubleshooting section at the end of this chapter.

If you want to print your document summary, see "Printing Document Summaries" in the Troubleshooting section at the end of this chapter.

CUSTOMIZING OTHER SETTINGS

You can customize Display Settings, Environment Settings, Files Settings, and Summary Settings; you can also customize Settings for toolbars, the Property Bar, the Application Bar, the keyboard, the menu bar, writing tools, printing, and file conversions.

This section summarizes some of the changes you can make for each of these other types of Settings. See Chapter 4, "Customizing Toolbars, Property Bars, and Menus," for more information.

PART

II

CH

18

Tip #112 from *Trudi Reisner*	Double-click any Application Bar item to either toggle the action or open its related dialog box. Clicking the date or time item adds the date or time text to your document.

The following list summarizes some of the changes you can make for settings that are not covered previously in this chapter. Customize settings for toolbars, Property Bars, menus, and keyboards by choosing Tools, Settings, Customize. The Customize dialog box appears with the following tabs:

- Toolbars—Use Options to customize the appearance or location of toolbars; you can display text on toolbar buttons, a picture, or both. You can also specify the maximum number of rows to be used for displaying a toolbar (displaying two rows takes more screen space but lets you display more buttons at once). You can also edit the toolbar to add, remove, or rearrange buttons.

- Property Bars—Edit and reset property bars to their original defaults.

- Menu—Display, create, or manage another predefined menu bar, including any that you have created.

- Keyboard—Display, create, or manage another keyboard, including any customized keyboard that you have created for special-purpose work.

⚡ *If you made some changes to your Application Bar and didn't like the results, see "Restoring the Application Bar" in the Troubleshooting section at the end of this chapter.*

If you want to remove the quotation marks in a database file you imported, see "Stripping Quotation Marks in Imported Database Files" in the Troubleshooting section at the end of this chapter.

You can also specify default delimiters, encapsulation characters, and characters to strip for ASCII text files (options that are most commonly used or referenced when merging with database data files). Choose Tools, Settings, Convert, and select options from the Convert tab in the Convert Settings dialog box shown in Figure 18.9.

Figure 18.9
Specify which characters define delimited text files in the Convert Settings dialog box.

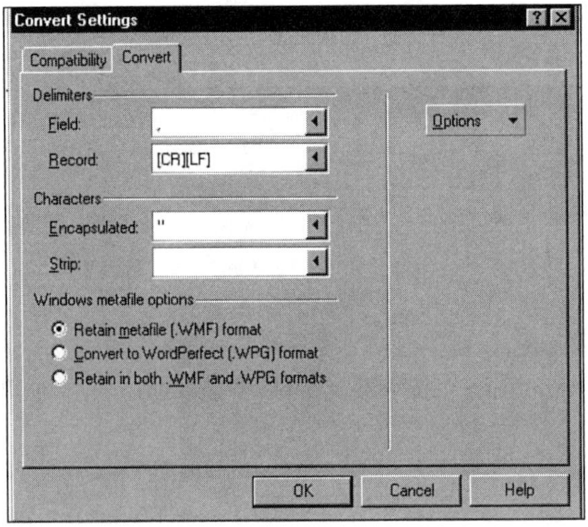

CUSTOMIZING THE DEFAULT SETTINGS FOR NEW DOCUMENTS

Whenever you open a new, empty document, you accept default settings that are associated with the standard template. Many other formatting defaults are included in these settings, including margin settings, the justification setting, and tab settings. If you prefer to work with settings that are not the same as these defaults, you can change the defaults for these other settings for new documents through the Current Document Style. This section shows you how to change the default settings for new documents that are based on the standard template. The Settings dialog box is just one way to customize WordPerfect. Other customization methods follow.

→ For more information on how to use styles, **see** "Using Styles," **p. 186**

To change the default settings for new documents that are based on the standard template, follow these steps:

1. Choose File, Document, Current Document Style. The Styles Editor dialog box appears (see Figure 18.10).

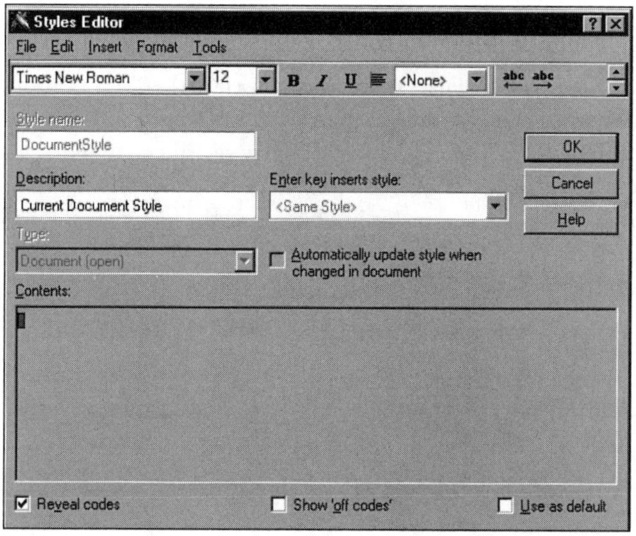

Figure 18.10
Customize formatting for new documents in the Styles Editor dialog box.

2. In the style Contents area, insert any format settings that you want as defaults for all new documents based on the standard template. For example, if you prefer to work with full justification rather than left justification, insert a formatting code for Full justification by selecting Format, Justification, Full in the menu bar of the Styles Editor dialog box.

3. Check Use As Default.

4. Click OK.

After you customize the Current Document Style and specify that the formatting should be used as a default, all new documents based on the standard template will use the customized settings. An illustration of the Current Document Style with customized settings is shown in Figure 18.11. The Use As Default check box option has been selected.

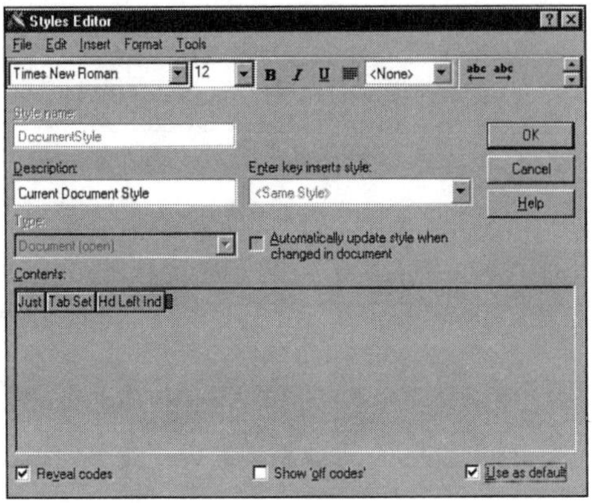

Figure 18.11
When you customize formatting for new documents in the Styles Editor dialog box, make sure to select the Use As Default check box.

PRACTICAL PROJECT

If you import XML documents, you'll need to specify the XML settings in the Display Settings dialog box. These settings include how you display XML codes in your WordPerfect document; font size; how to display reveal codes and colors for elements, entity references, marked sections, and WP data. Next, specify the XML settings in the Environment Settings dialog box for importing XML documents. Finally, specify the XML settings in the Files Settings dialog box, such as the template folder, project base template, document type, and catalog files.

TROUBLESHOOTING

DISPLAYING TABLE GRIDLINES

I changed my settings to display table gridlines and now when I format my table with table lines, they're not there.

Your table lines are there; you'll see them when you choose View, Table Gridlines (to turn off the gridlines and display any defined table lines), or when you preview or print the document.

DISPLAYING THE RULER

I want to have my Ruler onscreen all the time without having to ask for it.

Just choose View, Ruler to display the ruler.

Including a Document Number in Summaries

I want to include a document number in my summaries, but there isn't a place to do it.

Choose File, Properties, Setup. You see the Document Summary Setup dialog box. Check Document number in the Select Fields list, and then choose OK twice.

Printing Document Summaries

I want to print the document summary for my document.

Choose File, Print, and then select Document Summary in the Print dialog box.

Restoring the Application Bar

Help! I experimented with customizing the Application Bar, and now I want to put it back the way it was.

Choose Tools, Settings to display the Settings dialog box. Select Application Bar, and choose Reset.

Stripping Quotation Marks in Imported Database Files

I frequently import database files in an ASCII-delimited format, and I want to have quotation marks stripped when the file is imported.

Choose Tools, Settings to see the Settings dialog box. Choose Convert to see the Convert Settings dialog box. Specify Quotation marks as characters to be stripped.

CHAPTER **19**

TRANSFERRING DATA BETWEEN APPLICATIONS

In this chapter

UNDERSTANDING THE TYPES OF DATA TRANSFER

Data can be transferred between documents in three basic ways:

- Moving/copying
- Linking
- Embedding

Before you learn the different commands and methods used to transfer data, it's a good idea to get a conceptual understanding of what is happening with the different processes.

→ For more information on copying and moving text, **see** "Copying and Moving Text," **p. 86**

UNDERSTANDING MOVING AND COPYING

Most people are familiar with cut-and-paste, which refers to the moving and copying of data. When you move a sentence from one WordPerfect paragraph to another, or when you move a Quattro Pro cell to another location, you do two operations. First, you cut the data, which removes it from the original location. Then, you paste the data to its new location. Copying works the same way, except that a copy of the data is left in the original location as well. You move data by copying it to the Clipboard, and then you paste it where you want to move it.

Note

When you cut or copy data, it goes to the Windows Clipboard. This is a temporary storage area that holds the last item that you cut or copied. The data stays in the Clipboard until you either exit Windows or copy something else into the Clipboard.

There are a few important implications:

- The same Clipboard is used in all Windows applications, enabling you to move data from one application to another.
- Because the Clipboard holds only one item, if you put something else in the Clipboard, the first item is erased.
- You can paste the same copy of the data from the Clipboard multiple times—until you copy something else into the Clipboard.

Moving and copying data between applications works the same way as it does within applications. The data is moved or copied to the Windows Clipboard, from which it is retrieved when you paste the data in the destination application.

Note

When you move or copy data using the drag-and-drop method discussed in previous chapters, the data is not put into the Clipboard, nor are the contents of the Clipboard affected. Because the data is not in the Clipboard, you cannot repetitively paste multiple copies of it.

UNDERSTANDING LINKING

Linking data adds another dimension to the copying process. For example, when you link a range of spreadsheet cells in Quattro Pro to a WordPerfect word processing document, the spreadsheet information is displayed in the word processing document. This means the word processing document maintains information that specifies where the linked data is to be obtained: the application that created it, the path and filename, and the selected information in that file. When you link data, you create a pointer from the file where you want the data to appear to the file in which the data exists.

> **Note**
>
> You might want to become familiar with the technical terminology used for linked and embedded data (see the following table).
>
> In this chapter, the terms *source application* and *destination application* are used, rather than server and client, for clarity.

Term	Refers To
Object	The data that is linked or embedded
Source file	The file from which the object comes
Source application	The application in which the source file is created
Server	Another term for source application
Destination application	The application in which the object appears
Client	Another term for the destination application
Destination file	The file in which the object appears

Because a link consists of a pointer to a source file, when the option for data updating is set to automatic, the object that appears in the destination file is always the latest version. When you or someone else changes the source file containing the object, the object in the destination file is updated with the new information. For example, if someone changes the Quattro Pro file, which affects the cells that are linked to WordPerfect, the spreadsheet cells appearing in your word processing document immediately reflect this change.

Alternatively, you can specify that the link be updated manually. In this case, the object remains static (it retains the old information) unless you manually update it.

PART
II

CH
19

Tip #113 from
Trudi Reisner

When creating a link, first ensure that your source document has been saved so that information about the link can be stored. If the document has not yet been saved, you won't be able to create the link.

Windows applications use different technologies to create links. Three of the most common are DDE, OLE 1.0, and OLE 2.0. DDE, the oldest, stands for Dynamic Data Exchange. It allows for linking, but not embedding. DDE was later subsumed under OLE, Object Linking and Embedding.

The major differences between OLE 1.0 and 2.0 are that OLE 2.0 allows for dragging and dropping data between applications, and it enables you to edit the source data from within the destination application. Corel WordPerfect Office 2000 applications support OLE 2.0 where possible. However, you may have links to other applications that support only OLE 1.0. If you stay in the destination application and the menus change to those of the source application when you double-click a linked object, then the link is an OLE 2.0 link. If, on the other hand, you double-click and the original application opens up, then the link may be OLE 1.0 or 2.0.

Note

> OLE and DDE are complex. Usually, the method being used for linking and embedding is immaterial to the user. However, if you are interested in the details, Corel WordPerfect 9 is an OLE 2.0 server, meaning that you can link WordPerfect information to Quattro Pro 9 or Corel Presentations 9, for example. It is not, however, an OLE 2.0 in-place server. Thus, when you double-click WordPerfect objects that are embedded in Quattro Pro, you will not be able to use in-place editing.

UNDERSTANDING EMBEDDING

Embedding data is like copying it, with one difference: When you embed an object, a copy of it is stored in the destination file, just as it is when you copy it. Because OLE is used to transfer the data, however, you can edit the embedded data using the source application by double-clicking the embedded data. For example, if you have a Quattro Pro spreadsheet embedded into a WordPerfect document, you can double-click the spreadsheet inside WordPerfect, and then use Quattro Pro to edit it.

Depending on the specific applications involved, when you double-click an embedded object to edit it, a window may open enabling you to edit the object using its source application. Alternatively, the title bar, toolbar, and menus may change to those of the source application, enabling you to edit the object in-place from within the destination document.

For instance, when you double-click an embedded Quattro Pro object within WordPerfect, the title bar, menu bar, and toolbar change to those of Quattro Pro, enabling in-place editing. However, when you double-click an embedded WordPerfect object within Quattro Pro, WordPerfect is launched in a separate window, enabling you to edit the WordPerfect object. Because WordPerfect is an OLE 2.0 server, it is not an "OLE 2.0 in-place server" that allows for in-place editing.

COMPARING THE METHODS OF TRANSFERRING DATA

In summary, the differences between the three methods of transferring data can be seen in the following table:

Method	Copies Data to Destination	Allows Editing Using Source Application	Updates When Source Changes
Copying/Moving	Yes	No	No
Linking	No	Yes	Yes
Embedding	Yes	Yes	No

Having looked at the principles behind the three methods of transferring data, let's see how to actually do it.

LEARNING THE TECHNIQUES FOR MOVING AND COPYING

You can use several methods to move or copy data between applications. These include using menus and toolbars, keyboard shortcuts, and drag and drop.

Moving and copying data using the menus, toolbars, and keyboard shortcuts is the same whether you are transferring the data within or between applications:

1. Open the source application, and select the data to be moved or copied.

2. Choose Edit, Cut or Edit, Copy; or click the Cut or Copy button on the toolbar, if they are visible. Alternatively, right-click the data to be moved, and then choose Cut or Copy from the QuickMenu that pops up.

PART

II

CH

19

Tip #114 from *Trudi Reisner*	You can also use shortcuts for cutting and pasting: Ctrl+X for cut; Ctrl+C for copy; and Ctrl+V for paste.

3. Open the destination application, and place the insertion point where the data should go.

4. Choose Edit, Paste, or click the Paste button on the toolbar, if it is visible. Alternatively, right-click at the insertion point, and then choose Paste from the QuickMenu.

LEARNING TECHNIQUES FOR LINKING AND EMBEDDING

To effectively work with linked and embedded data, you need to be able to

- Create links and embed data
- Edit a linked object
- Edit the link itself

CREATING LINKS AND EMBEDDING DATA

Creating links and embedding data takes an extra step than merely copying data, but you'll soon find that you can accomplish them efficiently by following these steps:

1. Open the source application and select the data to be linked or embedded. (If you are going to link the data, the file must be saved before you cut or copy the data.)

2. Cut or copy the data as described previously.

3. Open the destination application, and place the insertion point where the data should go.

> **Caution**
>
> In Quattro Pro, you need to clear a space for the information, or the new information could overwrite the old information in the destination cells.

4. Choose Edit, Paste Special. You see the Paste Special dialog box in Figure 19.1.

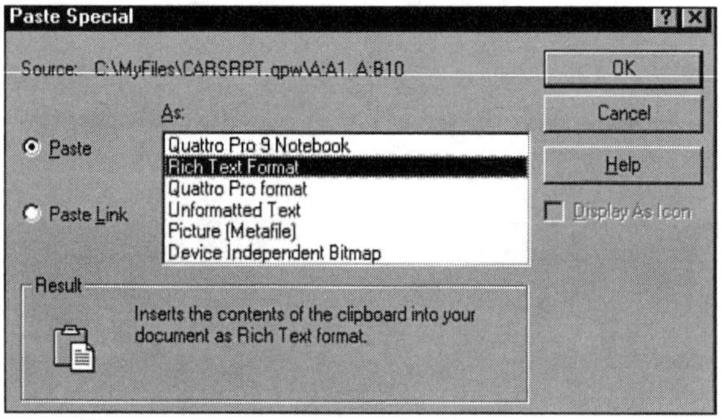

Figure 19.1
The Paste Special dialog box enables you to embed and link objects, as well as specify the object type.

5. To embed the data, choose Paste; to link it, choose Paste Link.

6. Select a data type as discussed in the later section "Choosing Data Types," and then click OK. The data appears in your destination application.

Alternatively, if the windows for both applications are simultaneously visible on the Windows desktop, you can drag selected text or objects from one application to another. An easy way to embed an object while keeping it in the source application is to open both application windows, select the data, and then hold down the Ctrl key while dragging the data from one window to another. Just follow these steps:

1. Be sure that both the source application and the destination application are open.

2. Right-click a blank area of the taskbar, and then choose Tile Vertically or Tile Horizontally. Alternatively, move and size the application windows until you can see both the data to be moved in the first application and the destination for that data in the other application.

3. Select the text or object in the source application, and position your mouse pointer inside it.

4. Embed the object and remove it from the source application by dragging it to the appropriate position in the destination application. Or, embed the object and keep it in the source application by holding down the Ctrl key and dragging it to the appropriate position in the destination application.

> **Note**
>
> **Drag doesn't move objects from Presentations.**
>
> *If you find that sometimes you can drag text from a non-Corel WordPerfect Office 2000 application into WordPerfect, and sometimes you can't, see "Transferring Data from Non-Corel Applications" in the Troubleshooting section at the end of this chapter.*

CHOOSING DATA

When you are linking or embedding an object in the Paste Special dialog box, you see a number of different object types from which you can choose. The list you see depends on the characteristics of both the source and destination application.

In general, the first data type on this list is the file type of the source application. Therefore, when you link or embed a Quattro Pro file into Presentations, the first data type on the list is Quattro Pro 9 Notebook, as you see in Figure 19.2. Similarly, when you link or embed a Presentations drawing into WordPerfect, the first entry on the list is Corel Presentations 9 Drawing. Choosing this option is often advantageous, because it offers full OLE 2.0 functionality.

Figure 19.2
The first data type listed usually provides the best way of linking data. If the Display As Icon option is active, it indicates that the data type provides an OLE 2.0 link.

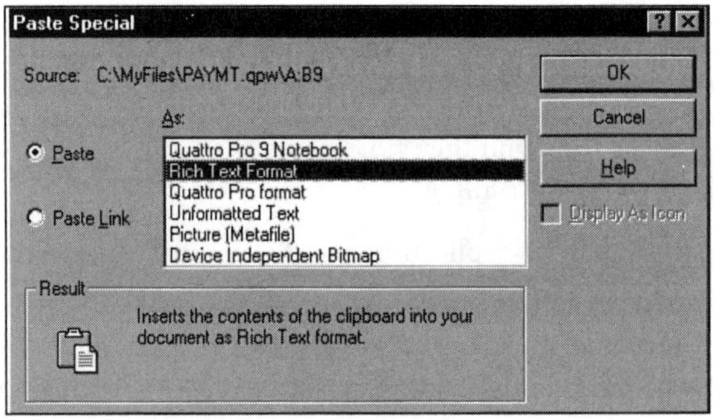

Tip #115 from *Trudi Reisner*

When you choose OLE 2.0 data types, the Display As Icon option becomes active. This can be particularly useful when you attach sound files or background text files to a document.

Other data types that you can choose may include

- Rich Text Format—This data type is useful in transferring data from one word processor to another, when you want to retain the maximum formatting information possible.
- Unformatted Text—This data type is useful in opposite situations, when you want to merely transfer text and no formatting.
- Picture, Metafile, or Device Independent Bitmap—These options convert the object into different graphic formats.

When embedding an object, you'll often see options such as Quattro Pro 9 Notebook, Rich Text Format, QB1, or WordPerfect 9 Document. These options enable you to paste the object into your document in a slightly different, often earlier, format than that of the current version of the source application.

Note

You often have more options when embedding a file with the Paste option than when linking it with Paste Link. This makes sense, because a link usually must be established with the file in its original format.

INSERTING OBJECTS

You can also embed an object by choosing Insert, Object from the menu of Corel WordPerfect Office 2000 applications such as WordPerfect, Presentations, and Quattro Pro. You see the Insert Object dialog box shown in Figure 19.3.

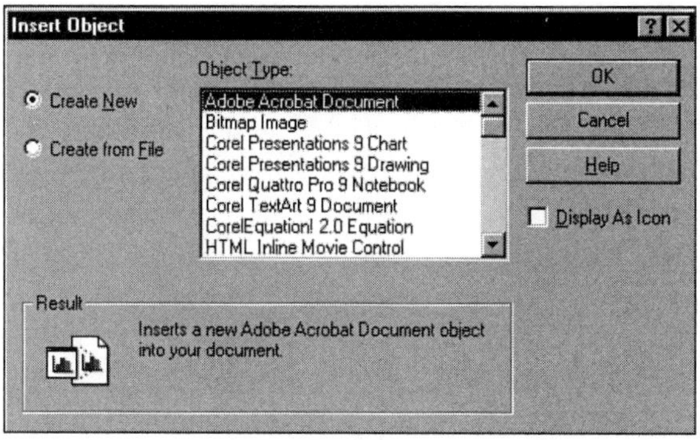

Figure 19.3
The Insert Object dialog box enables you to create new embedded objects in your file using a variety of OLE-compliant applications.

This dialog box provides two choices for embedding an object. If you choose Create New, you see a list of OLE object types that are supported on your system.

Tip #116 from
Trudi Reisner

If you have installed applications from other vendors that are OLE-compliant, they may also appear on this list.

This option enables you to create a new object using one of the listed types of objects. When you choose an Object Type, the appropriate application opens. If the source application is an OLE 2.0 in-place service, you use in-place editing. Otherwise, it opens in its own window, and you can create the new object there. See the next section for details on editing linked objects.

Alternatively, you may want to embed an object that already exists as a file on the disk. In this case, choose Create from File while you are in the Insert Object dialog box. The dialog box changes to the one shown in Figure 19.4. You can type the name of the desired file, or use the Browse button to see a Corel Office Open dialog box, and then choose the file from there.

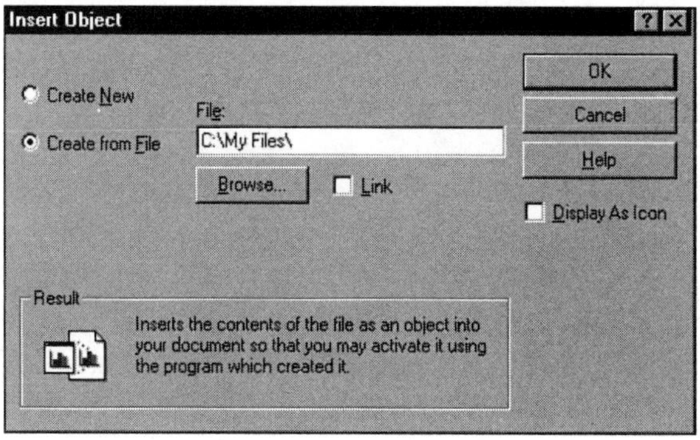

PART

II

CH

19

Figure 19.4
You can embed or link an entire file into your document by choosing Create from File in the Insert Object dialog box.

Tip #117 from
Trudi Reisner

When you create an object from a file, you have the option of creating it as a link rather than embedding the object or displaying it as an icon.

EDITING A LINKED OBJECT

One of the nicest things about linking objects is that you can go back through the link to edit the source file in the source application that created it.

When you double-click a linked object, another application window opens onscreen. This is the source application that created the object, and you see the source file in that window. Edit the object within the application window and save it as you normally would. When you're finished, choose File. There is an option that enables you to exit and return to the destination application, which is called Exit and Return to Document X, where X is the document name.

EDITING A LINK

When you have linked one or more objects into your documents, you can edit information about the link. You may want to edit the links in your document for a number of reasons:

- To redefine the link if the source file is renamed or moved.
- To break the link so that the object no longer changes in your document.
- To change the link from automatically updated (whenever the source file changes) to manually updated (when you specify).
- To update a manual link.

To edit a link in WordPerfect or Presentations, choose Edit, Links. The Links dialog box appears (see Figure 19.5). All the links in your document are listed.

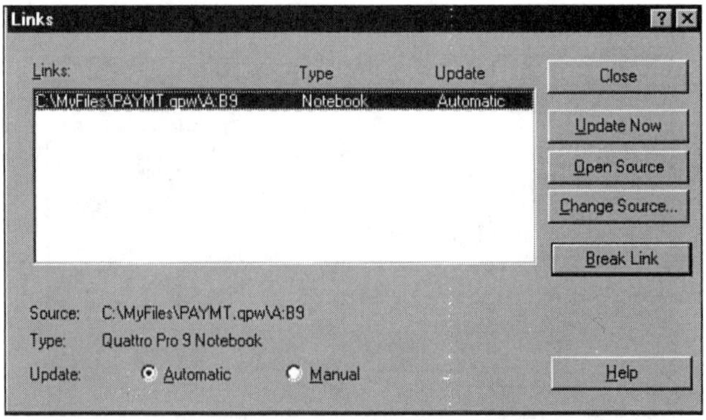

Figure 19.5
The Links dialog box lists all links in your document and enables you to edit them, break them, or specify their update as manual or automatic.

The Links dialog box provides the following options that affect links you have selected:

- Update Automatic or Manual—Choosing Automatic causes objects to be updated as soon as they are changed. Choosing Manual causes objects not to be updated until an Update command is given.

- Update Now—This option causes all selected manual links to be updated—that is, the objects are refreshed from the latest versions of the source files. Be sure to save the source file for the Update Now option to update the destination file.

- Open Source—This option opens the source file in the source application.

- Change Source—When you choose this option, the Change Source dialog box appears. You can then change the filename and (in the case of spreadsheets) the cell range.

- Break Link—This option breaks the link between the object and its source file.

If the Links option is grayed out on the Edit menu, see "Embedded Versus Linked Objects" in the Troubleshooting section at the end of this chapter.

If changes in your source document aren't reflected in your destination document, see "Linking the Source Document" in the Troubleshooting section at the end of this chapter.

PRACTICAL PROJECT

What if you create a memo every quarter and attach a spreadsheet that contains the quarterly budget? You can streamline the process by creating a memo in WordPerfect using the PerfectExpert Memo project, and then add a Quattro Pro spreadsheet to the memo to help illustrate and explain the text. You can insert the spreadsheet into the WordPerfect document with the linking feature. Figure 19.6 shows a WordPerfect memo that was created with the PerfectExpert Memo project with a linked budget spreadsheet that was created in Quattro Pro.

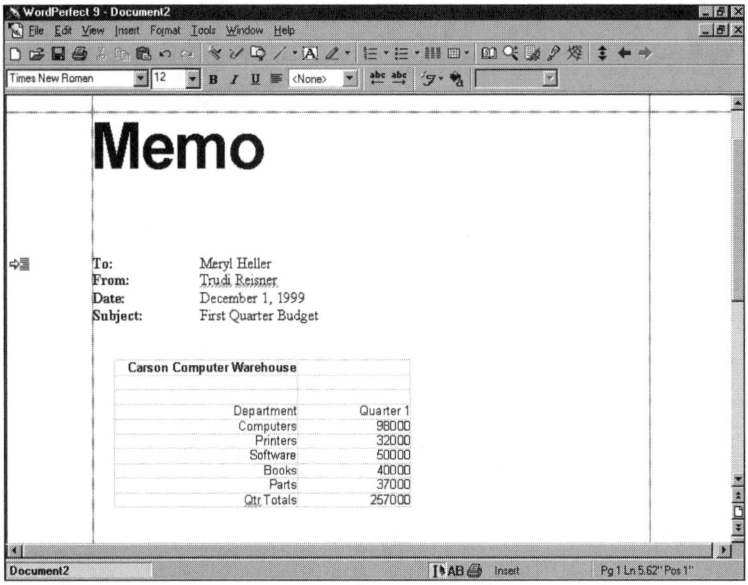

Figure 19.6
Add a Quattro Pro spreadsheet to your memo.

TROUBLESHOOTING

TRANSFERRING DATA FROM NON-COREL APPLICATIONS

Sometimes you can drag text from a non-Corel WordPerfect Office 2000 application into WordPerfect, and sometimes you can't.

If the other application is OLE 2.0-compliant, you can drag and drop objects into WordPerfect (which is also OLE 2.0-compliant). If the other application is not compliant, you still may be able to cut and paste data using the Edit menu. However, some Windows applications do not use the Windows Clipboard in a standard way. You won't be able to move or copy data from these applications at all.

EMBEDDED VERSUS LINKED OBJECTS

The Links option is grayed out on the Edit menu.

The Links option is active only if you have links in your document. If you have embedded objects rather than linked objects, the option is not active. If the linked object is selected, the Links option will be grayed out, too. Clicking beside the linked object may activate the Links option.

LINKING THE SOURCE DOCUMENT

Sometimes changes in your source document aren't reflected in your destination document.

The source document may not be available, either because it no longer exists, it has been moved, or you cannot establish a connection to it on the network. In this case, the last copy of the object will display in your destination document.

Alternatively, the link may be one that is manually updated, rather than one that is updated automatically. In either case, you can examine the link information and make necessary changes.

USING COREL QUATTRO PRO

CHAPTER 20

GETTING STARTED WITH COREL QUATTRO PRO 9

In this chapter

UNDERSTANDING COREL QUATTRO PRO

Corel Quattro Pro is a spreadsheet program. You might like to think of a spreadsheet program as an electronic notebook that can quickly calculate the results of any entered formulas. Quattro Pro is a very capable electronic notebook, with hundreds of built-in features designed to make creating your spreadsheets as easy as possible.

WHAT CAN YOU DO WITH COREL QUATTRO PRO?

Even the most powerful tool is useless if you don't know what it can do and how to use it. Quattro Pro is one of the most advanced spreadsheet programs available, but it is also very easy to understand and use. You don't have to be an accountant or a computer whiz to use it. In only a short time, you'll be able to create Quattro Pro notebooks that solve some of your problems with ease.

Preparing reports that summarize data is a typical, traditional use for a spreadsheet. By automatically performing a report's calculations with complete accuracy, a spreadsheet makes quick work of the task. If you run a small business, you probably perform many different calculations on a daily basis. You might, for example, want to keep track of the receipts for a video rental business you recently began. To know whether the new business is worthwhile, you want to know whether you're making a profit after paying for the new movies, the utilities, and other expenses, and maybe even the cost of hiring someone for evenings.

You also may want to calculate the cost of refinancing your mortgage and determine how long it will take to make up for the fees your lender charges. In addition, it is useful to know which products you sell bring the highest profits, and when those products are most likely to be sold. Finally, suppose you need to calculate the cost of building permits, which are based on many combinations of features for each property. Wouldn't it be nice to just enter the proposed building's size, type, and quantity of fixtures, and have a totally accurate bill printed instantly?

These are but a small sample of the things you can do with Quattro Pro.

STARTING COREL QUATTRO PRO

When you start Quattro Pro, a new, blank notebook named NOTEBK1.QPW appears (see Figure 20.1). This new notebook is your starting point for creating your own applications. You can use a more descriptive name when you save your notebook in a file on disk.

Figure 20.1
Quattro Pro displays a new, blank notebook when you start the program.

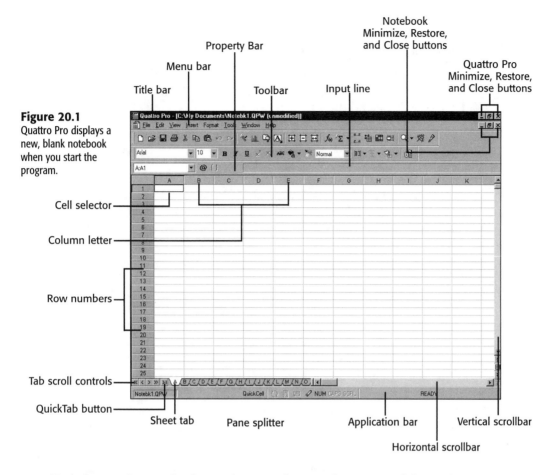

Title bar
Menu bar
Property Bar
Toolbar
Input line
Notebook Minimize, Restore, and Close buttons
Quattro Pro Minimize, Restore, and Close buttons

Cell selector
Column letter
Row numbers
Tab scroll controls
QuickTab button
Sheet tab
Pane splitter
Application bar
Vertical scrollbar
Horizontal scrollbar

Each Quattro Pro notebook provides a very large workspace—much larger than you can see onscreen. Each notebook has 256 sheets, and each sheet includes 256 columns and 8,192 rows. The intersection of each row and column on each sheet is a *cell*, which is where you store data, formulas, or labels. A Quattro Pro notebook has an incredible 536,870,912 cells—many more than you will ever need, no matter how complex a report you produce.

Cells are identified by the sheet letter, followed by a colon, the column letter, and row number. The cell in the first row of the first column on the first sheet of a notebook is designated by the cell address A:A1. If you're referring to a cell on the current sheet, you don't have to include the sheet letter or colon, but can instead refer to this same cell address as simply A1.

The location of the current, or *active*, cell is indicated by the *cell selector*—a darker outline around the cell. The cell selector in Figure 20.1 is in cell A:A1, making this the active cell. You can place only data, formulas, or labels in the active cell. To place anything in a different cell, you first must make the new cell the active cell by clicking it with the mouse or

PART

III

CH

20

using the arrow keys on the keyboard. The address of the active cell appears in the cell indicator box at the left end of the input line. The column letter and row number in the notebook frame also indicate which cell is active; they appear depressed, or selected.

 If you tried to use a shortcut key and it didn't perform the proper procedure, see "Understanding the Notebook Numbering System" in the Troubleshooting section at the end of this chapter.

MOVING AROUND IN A NOTEBOOK

When you want to enter data, formulas, or labels in a cell, you first must move to that cell. There are several methods you can use to move around in a notebook, and the best method often depends on your destination.

You can use the arrow keys, as well as the PgUp, PgDn, Home, and End keys to move the cell selector between cells. Table 20.1 describes the functioning of these navigational keys.

TABLE 20.1 THE NAVIGATION KEYS

Key(s)	Action(s)
→ or ←	Moves right or left one cell
↑ or ↓	Moves up or down one cell
Ctrl+←	Moves left one screen
Ctrl+→	Moves right one screen
Ctrl+F6	Makes the next open notebook window active, if multiple notebooks are open; acts as a toggle between open notebooks
Ctrl+Home	Moves to cell A1 on the first sheet of the current notebook
Ctrl+PgDn	Moves to the notebook sheet immediately below the current sheet (from sheet A to sheet B)
Ctrl+PgUp	Moves to the notebook sheet immediately above the current sheet (from sheet B to sheet A)
End+→ or End+←	Moves right or left to a cell that contains data and is next to a blank cell
End+↑ or End+↓	Moves up or down to a cell that contains data and is next to a blank cell
End+Ctrl+Home	Moves to the lower-right corner of the active area on the last active sheet
End+Home	Moves to the lower-right corner of the active area on the current sheet
F5 (Go to)	Moves to the cell, formula, value, named cell, or comment you specify
Home	Moves to cell A1 of the active sheet
PgUp or PgDn	Moves up or down one screen on the current notebook sheet

It is often quicker and easier to perform tasks such as moving the cell selector via the mouse instead of the navigation keys. For example, to move from cell A1 to cell C4, you could press the right-arrow key twice and the down-arrow key three times, or you could simply point to cell C4 and click the left mouse button. Of course, if you hold down an arrow key instead of quickly pressing and releasing it, the cell selector will move several rows or columns instead of just one. Even so, a single mouse click is often much faster than the equivalent keystrokes. Moving between sheets with the mouse is even faster—just click the appropriate sheet tab. Use the tab scroll controls to display different sheet tabs if necessary.

You can also use the scrollbars at the right edge or bottom edge of a notebook to view other parts of the current notebook sheet. Click the scrollbar or drag the scroll box to bring a different part of the sheet into view.

Quattro Pro's new Browse By button appears at the bottom of the vertical scrollbar and is used to select the type of data you want to browse through, such as values, blanks, labels, formulas, precedents, dependents, the current region, locked and unlocked cells, or the current array. Right-click on the Browse By button to display a QuickMenu, and choose the type of data you want to browse through.

The Previous and Next buttons on each side of the Browse By button change, depending on what you selected with the Browse button. For example, if you choose Browse by Values, you will see Previous Value and Next Value buttons.

⚠ *If you use the scrollbars and the cell selector disappears, see "Using the Cell Selector" in the Troubleshooting section at the end of this chapter.*

USING THE MENUS

Many tasks you perform in Quattro Pro require use of a command. Commands help you analyze and organize data effectively, copy and move data, chart and format data, sort and manipulate databases, open and close notebooks, and use colors and fonts to customize notebooks.

The Quattro Pro menu appears on the menu bar near the top of the screen. If you use the mouse to select commands, just click the command you want to use. To access a command on the menu bar with the keyboard, you first must activate the menu by pressing the Alt key. A reverse video highlight, the menu pointer, appears in the menu bar when you choose a menu command by highlighting it with the arrow keys. You can also simply press the Alt key and the underlined letter of the command name.

PART
III

CH
20

Tip #118 from
Trudi Reisner

Learn Quattro Pro's commands by moving the menu pointer through the menus. A description of the command appears in a yellow tip box next to the menu. This box is called a *QuickTip*; it also appears when you point to other parts of the screen, such as toolbar buttons.

In addition, dimmed commands are currently unavailable.

Quattro Pro has several different menus. The menus change depending upon the type of task you're performing. For example, the main menu appears when you work with normal data in a notebook. If you create or modify a chart, the menu changes to include commands appropriate to charts. Most of the time, however, you see the main menu.

Note

If you have used earlier versions of Quattro Pro, you'll notice that the menu structure and dialog boxes have been streamlined in Quattro Pro 9. These interface improvements will make your work easier because related commands and options are now more closely grouped.

If you prefer to use the familiar menus and dialog boxes from Quattro Pro 7 (until you have time to learn the new Quattro Pro 9 commands), you can easily switch to the Quattro Pro 7 menu. Right-click the menu bar and then click QP7 Menu. If you are switching from Microsoft Excel to Quattro Pro 9, you can use the same method to switch to the Microsoft Excel menu. Just right-click the menu bar and choose the Excel Menu option.

LEARNING THE SHORTCUTS

The most productive people in any field are usually those who know the fastest way to get things done—the shortcuts. Quattro Pro provides many different shortcuts. You don't have to learn all of them, but you will find that you'll use some quite often.

USING TOOLBAR BUTTONS

The Quattro Pro toolbar contains many buttons you'll find very helpful as you build your notebooks (see Figure 20.2). Table 20.2 describes the buttons on the main Notebook toolbar, which are used later in this and several following chapters. For more information on the complete range of toolbar buttons, choose Help, Help Topics and see the "toolbars" topic on the Index tab of Quattro Pro's online help.

Figure 20.2
Toolbar and Property Bar buttons are another way to access the tools you need to create powerful notebook sheets.

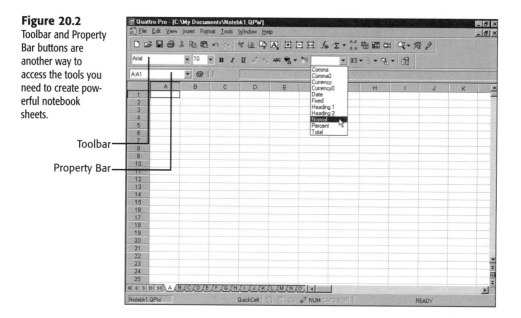

Toolbar

Property Bar

TABLE 20.2   NOTEBOOK TOOLBAR BUTTONS AND THEIR FUNCTIONS

Button	Function
	Opens a new notebook
	Opens an existing notebook into a new window
	Saves the current notebook
	Prints a notebook or chart
	Moves the selection to the Clipboard
	Copies the selection to the Clipboard
	Inserts the Clipboard contents into the notebook
	Reverses the last change made
	Reverses the last change undone
	Copies and pastes the format from the current selection to all subsequent selections (until QuickFormat is turned off)
	Creates a floating chart on the notebook sheet
	Imports clip art and other graphics files
	Inserts a text box
	Inserts cells, rows, columns, or sheets
	Deletes cells, rows, columns, or sheets
	Adjusts a column's width to its widest cell entry

PART

III

Cн

20

continues

TABLE 20.2 CONTINUED

Button	Function
$f_{(x)}$	Builds complex formulas with @functions
Σ	Totals values in the selection and performs other calculations with the most common functions
A..Z	Sorts data in ascending order
Z..A	Sorts data in descending order
	Fills blank cells in the selection
	Applies a predefined format to the selection
	Joins and centers cells
	Zooms the sheet by a specified percentage
	Brings you to the Corel site on the Web
	Displays the PerfectExpert

USING QUICKMENUS AND DIALOG BOXES

Almost everything in Quattro Pro is an *object*—something that has properties you can change. However, you're not required to search through Quattro Pro's menus to find the commands necessary to change an object's properties. You have another choice: When you right-click an object, you will see either a dialog box or a QuickMenu associated with the object. The dialog boxes contain all the property settings for the object. *QuickMenus* are short command menus containing commands most appropriate for the selected object. QuickMenus always include a Properties selection at the bottom of the menu, which displays the dialog box for the selected object.

If you have not used them before, QuickMenus and dialog boxes may be a little confusing at first. After you begin using them, however, you'll find them very helpful. Figure 20.3 shows the QuickMenu that appears when you right-click a notebook cell. The commands on this menu are also available if you search through several of Quattro Pro's standard menus, but the QuickMenu has gathered several of the most frequently used commands that you might want to apply to a cell in one convenient place.

Notice Cell Properties, the last item on the QuickMenu. The Active Cells dialog box appears if you select this item (see Figure 20.4). You can also use the F12 shortcut key to display the Active Cells dialog box. This dialog box contains six tabs that have every possible setting for a cell (or block of cells). The Cell Font tab is selected in Figure 20.4, so the dialog box displays all possible font settings. As you select different options or a different tab (such as Numeric Format), the dialog box changes and displays the available options.

Figure 20.3
QuickMenus gather commands from several menus into one convenient menu.

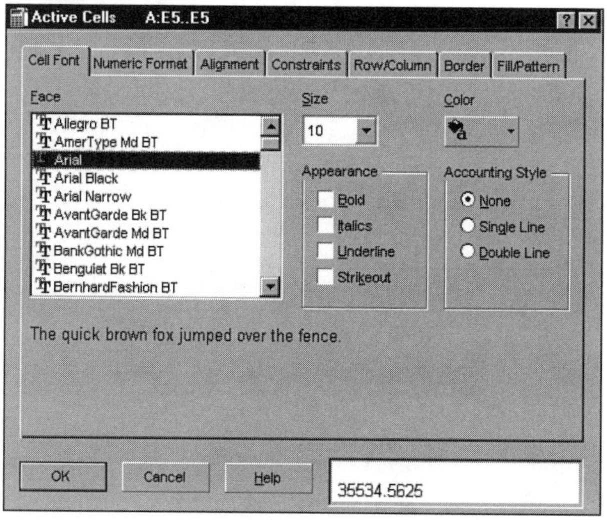

Figure 20.4
Dialog boxes enable you to adjust object properties.

If you change a property setting, such as switching the font from Arial to Times New Roman, the name of the changed property tab is displayed in blue letters rather than black—as long as the dialog box is open—so that you can tell what changes you have made. You can adjust more than one property while the dialog box is active. Click OK when you've made all of your changes; click Cancel if you decide you don't want to apply the changes. All the tabs will be black, regardless of whether the change was accepted or canceled, when you re-enter the dialog box.

Table 20.3 shows some of the Quattro Pro objects (other than individual cells) that you can adjust by right-clicking.

TABLE 20.3 COREL QUATTRO PRO OBJECTS

Object	Action
Blocks of cells	Right-click in the selected area.
Notebook sheets	Right-click the sheet tab.
Notebook	Right-click the Notebook title bar if the notebook is in a window and not maximized.
Toolbar	Right-click the toolbar.
Chart objects	Right-click the object, including drawn objects, titles, data series, and the chart background objects.
Quattro Pro	Right-click the Quattro Pro title bar.

IMPORTANT SHORTCUT KEYS

Table 20.4 describes many of the more useful Quattro Pro shortcut keys. To learn about even more shortcut keys, see the topic "key shortcuts" in the Quattro Pro online help system.

TABLE 20.4 IMPORTANT QUATTRO PRO SHORTCUT KEYS

Key(s)	Action(s)
F1	Displays a Help topic
F2	Places Quattro Pro in edit mode so that you can edit an entry
Alt+F2	Displays the Play Macro dialog box
F3	Displays the Save File dialog box
Alt+F3	Displays a list of functions
Ctrl+F3	Displays the Cell Names dialog box if pressed while a group of cells is selected
F4	Toggles formulas from relative to absolute and vice versa as you are entering formulas or when you edit formulas in the Input line
Alt+F4	Closes Quattro Pro 9 for Windows or a dialog box
F5	Displays the Go To dialog box
Ctrl+F6	Displays the next open window
F9	In ready mode, recalculates formulas; in edit or value mode, converts a formula to its current value
F10	Activates the menu bar by pressing the File menu command
F11	Displays the current chart
F12	Displays dialog box for the selected object
Alt+F12	Displays the Settings dialog box

Key(s)	Action(s)
Shift+F12	Displays the Active Notebook dialog box
Alt+Tab	Switches from one Windows application to another
Ctrl+letter	Same as choosing Tools, Macro, Play; executes a macro in Quattro Pro
Ctrl+Break	Exits from a macro and returns to ready mode
Ctrl+Esc	Activates the Start menu on the taskbar for Windows

⚡ *If you tried to use a shortcut key and it didn't perform the proper shortcut procedure, see "Using Macro and Quattro Pro Shortcut Keys" in the Troubleshooting section at the end of this chapter.*

Using Experts

Quattro Pro includes some specialized tools—*Experts*—that can ease your way through learning Quattro Pro and executing difficult tasks. This section takes a quick look at the Experts.

Using an Expert Approach

Computer-based training isn't new; programs have included tutorials for years. Quattro Pro's Experts, however, use a different approach to completing tasks. Instead of using a carefully preselected data set unrelated to the data you want to enter (as many tutorials do), the Experts allow you to use your own data. Not only that, the Experts also allow you to save your work in a Quattro Pro notebook. When you complete a task, the notebook contains your data.

Experts provide the expertise to solve complex problems while you provide the data. These Experts cover a broad range of topics. Table 20.5 provides a brief description of Quattro Pro's Experts.

TABLE 20.5 COREL QUATTRO PRO'S EXPERTS

Expert	Description
Analysis	Helps you use the Analysis tools (choose Tools, Numeric Tools, Analysis)
Budget	Helps you create and manage home and small business budgets (choose Tools, Numeric Tools, Budget)
Chart	Helps you create charts (choose Insert, Chart)
Map	Helps you create maps of your data (choose Insert, Graphics, Map)
Slide Show	Helps you create professional-looking slide shows (choose Tools, Slide Show, New)
Consolidate	Helps you combine data from different sources, such as different stores or company divisions (choose Tools, Consolidate, New)

PART
III
CH
20

continues

TABLE 20.5   CONTINUED

Expert	Description
Scenario	Helps you create and manage *scenarios*, which are multiple groups of related data that enable easy what-if analyses (choose Tools, Scenario, New)
What-If	Helps you generate what-if scenarios (choose Tools, Numeric Tools, What-If, Expert)

For example, the Chart Expert leads you through the steps necessary to create powerful business graphics that will present your data in a highly effective visual manner. You don't have to be a graphics expert; you need only answer some questions and make a few selections along the way. The Budget Expert shown in Figure 20.5 is another tool you'll probably find quite useful. Everyone knows the importance of a budget, especially in running a small business. The Budget Expert helps you prepare a Quattro Pro notebook that contains a budget specific to your needs. You can access the Budget Expert by choosing Tools, Numeric Tools, Budget.

Figure 20.5
Use the Budget Expert to simplify creating a budget for your home or small business.

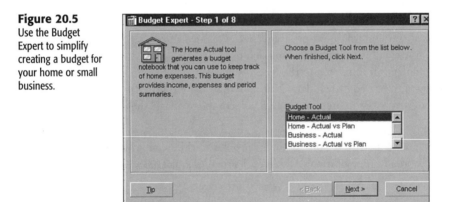

USING THE ADDED MORTGAGE PAYMENT PROJECT

Your forté is word processing and you don't need an expert telling you how to do it? What about financial projects? You've heard, for example, that you can save a great deal of money and pay off your loan much sooner if you simply add a little extra to your monthly mortgage payment. How much extra, and what effect will it really have? How do you calculate the savings?

Enter the PerfectExpert with the Added Payment Mortgage project. Follow these steps to use this project:

1. Open the PerfectExpert by choosing File, New from Project; select the Mortgage, Added Payment project. The PerfectExpert opens the Quattro Pro spreadsheet program and inserts the worksheet shown in Figure 20.6. As you can easily see, each PerfectExpert is different and tailored to the specific task at hand.

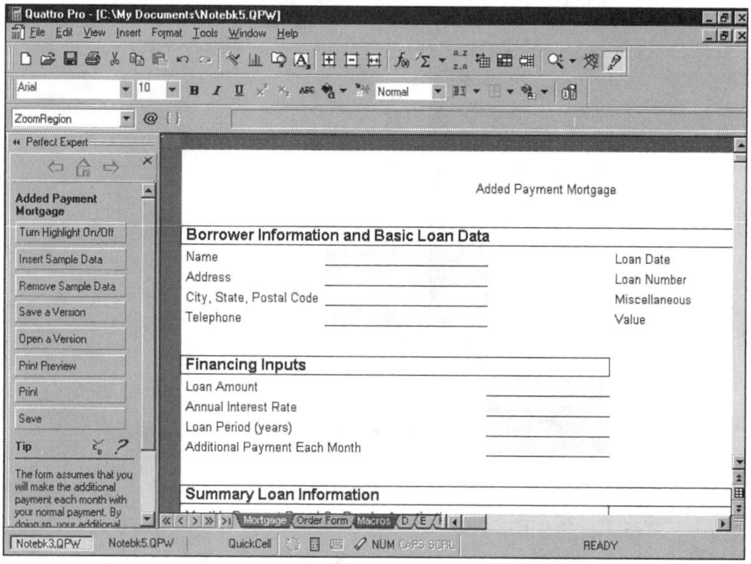

Figure 20.6
Even if spreadsheets are intimidating to you, the PerfectExpert can make it easy to calculate mortgage payments and more.

2. If you're not sure exactly where you're headed with this project, click the Insert Sample Data button. The PerfectExpert inserts sample information from a fictitious loan. Study the results to understand what kind of information you need to provide. Click Remove Sample Data to clear the worksheet.

3. Enter your data in the appropriate highlighted areas, including the remaining loan amount, the number of years remaining on the loan, the interest rate (for example, enter 9.25% as .0925), and finally, the extra amount you intend to add each month.

4. Finish the document by saving it, previewing it, or printing it.

Tip #119 from
Trudi Reisner

With this project, and with many other financial projects, you don't have to save the file because you may be interested only in the results. However, you still can save different versions or scenarios for comparison. Simply click the Save a Version button and provide a name. Click Open a Version to retrieve saved versions. You still must save the spreadsheet if you want to keep the results.

The PerfectExpert 401K Planner project is excellent for planning your retirement and investments, as shown in Figure 20.7. The 401K Planner project can be found under the Investment category in Quattro Pro.

Figure 20.7
PerfectExpert's 401K Planner project.

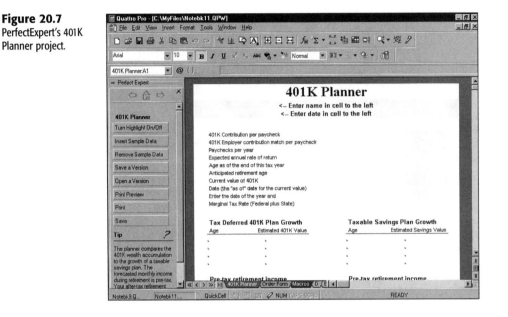

Another way to keep track of your investments is to use PerfectExpert's Capital Gains and Losses project, which is shown in Figure 20.8. This project helps you determine whether you have any investment losses that you can use to offset capital gains at tax time.

Figure 20.8
PerfectExpert's Capital Gains and Losses project.

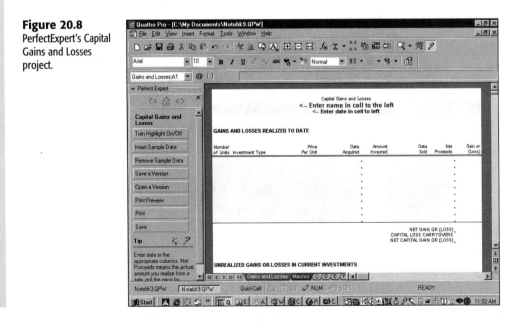

TROUBLESHOOTING

UNDERSTANDING THE NOTEBOOK NUMBERING SYSTEM

Your screen shows NOTEBK2.QPW instead of NOTEBK1.QPW.

Quattro Pro starts new notebooks using sequential numbers. If you create a new notebook, it is automatically named NOTEBK*xx*.QPW, with *xx* replaced by the next higher number. When you save the notebook, you are prompted for a new name.

USING THE CELL SELECTOR

The cell selector disappears when I use the scrollbars.

The scrollbars change only the portion of the sheet that is visible. To move the cell selector, first use the scrollbars to display the destination cell, and then click the destination cell to make it the current cell.

USING MACRO AND QUATTRO PRO SHORTCUT KEYS

Some Ctrl+letter shortcut keys don't perform the proper shortcut procedure.

If you create macros that use the Ctrl+letter naming convention, Quattro Pro runs the macro instead of using the key combination to run the shortcut. If the shortcut is one you use often, consider renaming the macro to restore the default shortcut.

CHAPTER 21

LEARNING SPREADSHEET BASICS

In this chapter

UNDERSTANDING NOTEBOOKS AND FILES

In Corel Quattro Pro, a single spreadsheet is called a *sheet*—a two-dimensional grid of columns and rows. A file that contains 18,278 sheets and an Objects sheet in a three-dimensional arrangement is called a *notebook*. Besides working with a single notebook, you also can work with several notebooks at the same time, as well as link notebooks by writing formulas that refer to cells in another notebook.

> **Note**
>
> The Quattro Pro 9 notebook size has increased and has more sheets than ever before: 18,278. Its predecessors contained 256. Now a sheet can contain approximately 1,000,000 rows and 18,278 columns—a big jump from previous versions that supported 8,192 rows and 256 columns. A larger notebook capacity allows for greater flexibility when it comes to converting Microsoft Excel workbooks to Quattro Pro notebooks.

To convert an Excel workbook to a Quattro Pro notebook, all you have to do is open the Excel workbook in Quattro Pro, just as you would any Quattro Pro notebook. Quattro Pro automatically opens the Excel workbook, converts the data in the workbook, and displays the data in a Quattro Pro notebook.

USING 3D NOTEBOOKS

You will often need only a single sheet to analyze and store data. You can organize simple reports effectively on a single sheet without the added complication of sheet references in your formulas. Sheet references are necessary, though, for accessing data that spreads across several sheets.

Some situations, however, are well suited to multiple notebook sheets. Reports that consolidate data from several departments often work well as multiple-sheet reports. You also can use multiple sheets to separate different kinds of data effectively. You might place data input areas on one sheet, macros on another, constants on another, and the finished report on yet another sheet. This technique can provide some assurance that a spreadsheet isn't damaged by an inadvertent error. For example, a data-entry error can write over formulas, or the insertion or deletion of a row or column can destroy macros or data tables contained on the same sheet. Building your notebook by using several sheets provides some protection against these all-too-common problems.

Quattro Pro notebooks are automatically three-dimensional, whether you have data on one sheet or multiple sheets. You don't have to manually add sheets to a Quattro Pro notebook as you do with most other spreadsheet programs.

NAMING NOTEBOOK SHEETS

One good way to use multiple notebook sheets is to place each month's data on a separate sheet and use a 13th sheet for the yearly totals. Because Quattro Pro enables you to name individual notebook sheets, you can name each sheet for one month so that you can locate the correct sheet easily. Figure 21.1 shows a notebook that uses named sheets to hold each month's sales data separately.

Figure 21.1
Named notebook sheets indicate purpose.

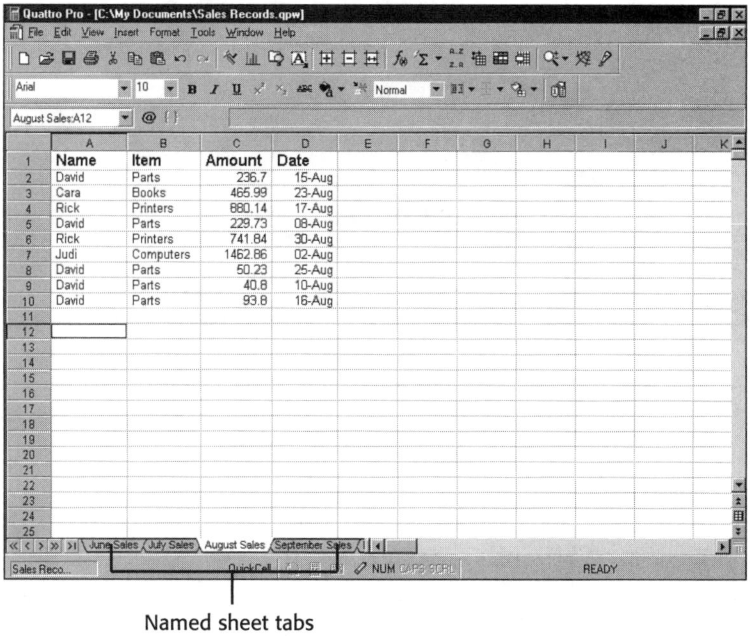

Named sheet tabs

You can name a notebook sheet by pointing to the sheet tab and double-clicking. Simply type the new name directly on the tab after you double-click. Alternatively, you can display the Active Sheet dialog box and select the Name tab. To display the Active Sheet dialog box, right-click the sheet tab and choose Sheet Properties. Click the Name tab (see Figure 21.2). Either type the new name for the sheet in the Sheet Name text box, or click Reset to restore the original sheet letter.

Sheet names can be up to 63 characters in length, but longer sheet names allow fewer sheet tabs to appear onscreen. You can use both letters and numbers in sheet names, as well as spaces and several special characters. If you have grouped notebook sheets, you cannot use the same name for a notebook sheet and a group.

PART

III

CH

21

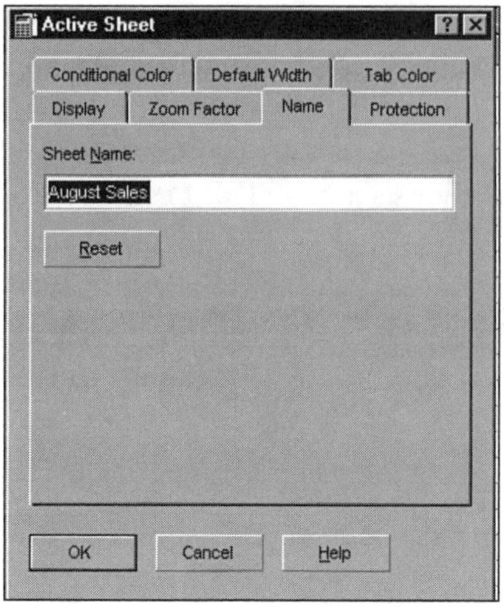

Figure 21.2
You can use the Active Sheet dialog box to name a notebook sheet.

> **Note**
>
> Group notebook sheets so that any changes you make to one sheet, such as applying formatting, affect all sheets in the group. To group sheets, hold down the Shift key while you click the sheet tabs for the first and last sheets you want to group. A line appears under the sheet tabs of grouped sheets. To ungroup the sheets, click any sheet tab except the current sheet tab.

Tip #120 from
Trudi Reisner

You can also name blocks of data. Learn more about this in the "Naming Blocks" section of this chapter.

MOVING BETWEEN SHEETS

Multiple notebook sheets wouldn't be of much value if there weren't a quick way to move between sheets. You have already learned that the key combinations Ctrl+Page Down and Ctrl+Page Up enable you to move through the notebook one sheet at a time. In addition, you can click a sheet tab to move to that sheet.

Sometimes, though, you may want to move to a sheet that has a tab not currently visible, such as a sheet far removed from the current sheet. The best method for moving to a distant notebook sheet is to use the Edit, Go To command (or press F5 or Ctrl+G) to display the Go To dialog box (see Figure 21.3). Select the sheet in the Sheets list box and click OK.

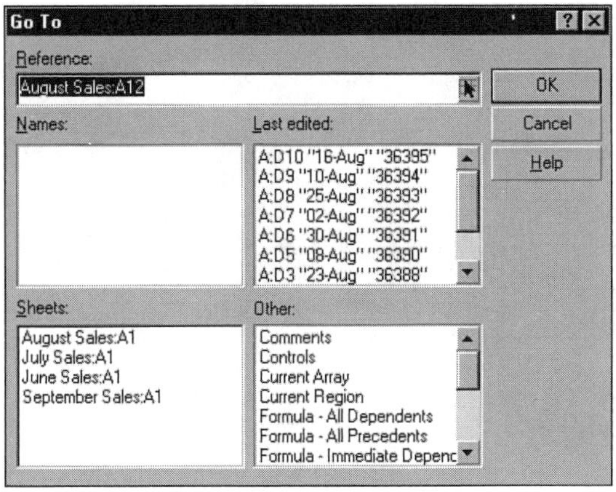

Figure 21.3
Use the Go To dialog box to move to a distant notebook sheet.

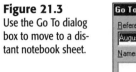

If you're frustrated that the cell selector always moves to cell A1 when you use the Edit, Go To command, see "Selecting a Sheet and a Specific Block" in the Troubleshooting section at the end of this chapter.

LINKING NOTEBOOKS

A single notebook, whether it uses multiple sheets or is contained on a single sheet, is not always the best solution for storing data. Linking multiple notebook files with formulas is often a better solution than using a single notebook. Consolidating data from several departments or company locations may be easier when using multiple notebooks, especially if several people are producing the individual reports. The person producing the consolidated report can create a notebook that uses formula links to consolidate the data from each notebook.

Tip #121 from
Trudi Reisner

Link notebooks with formulas rather than combining all the data into a single notebook.

When you work with data from several notebook files, you enter a formula in one notebook cell that refers to cells in another notebook. This technique is called *linking*. With this capability, you can easily consolidate data from separate notebook files. A consolidation notebook can use formulas to combine the data from each notebook.

Figure 21.4 shows the notebook CONSRPT.qpw, which is used to consolidate data from three other notebooks: CARSRPT.qpw, RENORPT.qpw, and SPARRPT.qpw. Formulas link the notebooks. For example, the formula in cell A:B5 of CONSRPT.qpw is as follows:

```
+[CARSRPT]A:B5+[RENORPT]A:B5+[SPARRPT]A:B5
```

PART

III

CH

21

Figure 21.4
You can use formulas to link to data in other notebooks.

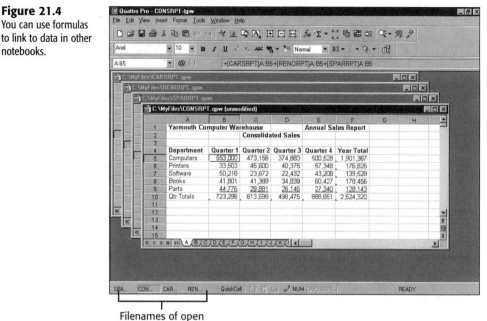

Filenames of open
notebooks

This formula, as shown in the input line of Figure 21.4, tells Quattro Pro to add the values in cell A:B5 of CARSRPT.qpw, cell A:B5 of RENORPT.qpw, and cell A:B5 of SPARRPT.qpw. In this case, the same cell in each notebook supplies the data for the formula, but that is not a requirement. You could, for example, create a linking formula, which adds values from cell A:A1 in one notebook and cell D: AA216 in another notebook. In most cases, it is less confusing if each linked notebook uses a similar structure. However, when taking data from different departments or companies, you may not always have control over their spreadsheet structure development.

Linking formulas can refer to notebooks that are open or closed. Quattro Pro maintains the formula links even after the supporting notebooks are closed, but must be able to locate the supporting notebooks when the notebook containing the formula links is opened. If the supporting notebooks are unavailable, Quattro Pro will not be able to determine a value for the linking formulas and will display NA (not available) instead of a value in the open notebook.

Tip #122 from
Trudi Reisner

Use full path names to make certain Quattro Pro can find the linked notebook.

When you open a notebook containing formula links to closed notebooks, Quattro Pro displays a Hotlinks dialog box that offers three options: Open Supporting, Update References, and None. If you select None, Quattro Pro changes the linking formula values to NA, but you can use the Edit, Links, Open Links or Edit, Links, Refresh Links commands to later update your linking formulas. See "Entering Formulas" later in this chapter for more information on creating formulas to link notebooks.

Tip #123 from	If you don't need to see the values of linking formulas, select None when you open notebooks containing linking formulas. The linked notebook will open much faster.
Trudi Reisner	

USING WORKSPACES

Figure 21.4 shows four different Quattro Pro notebooks open at the same time. If you are using linked notebooks, it may be convenient to open all of the linked notebooks, especially if you need to create additional formula links or enter data in more than one of the notebooks. When you work with multiple notebooks, it is often handy to create a standard window arrangement, such as the cascaded windows in Figure 21.4; that lets you always know where to find each notebook.

Quattro Pro has two commands—File, Workspace, Save and File, Workspace, Restore—that enable you to save the current notebook layout and to restore that same layout at a later time. Quattro Pro saves the current screen layout in a file with a WBS extension when you use File, Workspace, Save. You use File, Workspace, Restore to open the same group of notebook files and restore their screen layout in a single command. When restoring a workspace that has linked files, select Update References when the Hotlinks dialog box appears. If you select Open Supporting, the files will be opened full screen.

Caution	The File, Workspace, Save command does not save the notebook files, only their current screen layout. You must also save the individual notebook files to save any changes they contain.

ENTERING DATA FOR THE FIRST TIME

You can enter data only in the currently active cell; so to begin entering data, you first must move the cell selector to the target cell. From there, you type the data and press Enter. As you type, the data appears in the Input line and also in the current cell. If you enter data in a cell that already contains an entry, the new data replaces the existing entry.

Tip #124 from
Trudi Reisner

Always be certain the cell selector is in the correct cell before you begin entering data.

If you are entering a column of data, the cell selector automatically moves down one row in the same column when you press Enter. If the cell selector does not move when you press Enter, you need to select this option. Right-click the Quattro Pro title bar and select Application Properties; alternatively, you can press Alt+F12. Click the General tab and select Move Cell Selector on Enter Key. This setting makes entering columnar data much faster and easier.

Editing Cell Entries

You can edit cell entries several ways. If you want to completely replace a cell entry, just retype the entire entry. (First be certain the cell selector is in the correct cell.) When you press Enter or move the cell selector to another cell, your new entry replaces the existing entry. To cancel the new entry, press Esc before you press Enter or move the cell selector.

To replace part of a cell's current contents, select the cell and press F2 (Edit), or double-click the cell. You can then use the mouse pointer or the arrow keys to place the insertion point where you want to insert or delete characters. You can also select the characters you want to replace by dragging over them and typing the new characters. Press Enter or click another cell to confirm your edits. To cancel any edits before you press Enter, press Esc. To reverse the edits already entered, immediately choose Edit, Undo Entry.

Note

Now when you edit data, you'll see an enhancement: Quattro Pro 9 displays the numeric formatting, making it easier to edit and format your data. For instance, if a cell contains 12/12/99 and the input line contains the date's Julian value 36506, when you press F2 or double-click that cell to edit it, you see a date value (12/12/99) instead of a Julian value in the Input line.

Understanding the Kinds of Data You Can Enter

If you plan to enter labels or values in more than one cell, you do not need to press Enter after each entry. Instead, you can enter the data and then move the cell selector to the new cell with an arrow key to complete the entry and move the cell selector in a single step. This technique does not work if you are entering formulas.

You can create two kinds of cell entries: labels or values. A *label* (or *string*) is a text entry, and a *value* is a number or formula. Quattro Pro usually determines the entry type from the first character you type. The program always treats the entry as a value (a number or a formula) if you begin with one of the following characters:

    + – (@ # . $

If you begin an entry with a number, Quattro Pro assumes you are entering a value unless you include any nonnumeric character other than a single period. If you begin by typing any other character, Quattro Pro treats the entry as a label.

ENTERING LABELS

Labels make the numbers and formulas in a notebook understandable. In Figure 21.4, shown earlier, labels identify the departments and the time periods that generated the displayed results. The numbers are meaningless without labels.

In Quattro Pro, you can place up to 1,022 characters in a single cell. Although this allows you to create very long labels, remember that you will probably not be able to display nearly that many characters onscreen or in a single line of a report.

As mentioned in the previous section, Quattro Pro determines the kind of entry from the first character you type in a cell. You can override this, however, by adding a *label prefix*—a punctuation mark that controls the label's alignment in the cell—to the cell entry. The label prefix is not displayed in the spreadsheet. You can change the way a label is aligned by using one of the following label prefixes:

'	Left-aligned (default)
"	Right-aligned
^	Centered
\	Repeating (a character repeats as many times as necessary to fill the column width)
|	Nonprinting (if the label is in the leftmost column of the print block)

Note

Quattro Pro allows you to enter labels that begin with numbers. You need to use a label prefix only if you want to make a number by itself into a label, such as a zip code.

Regardless of the label prefix you enter, any label longer than the column width is displayed as a left-aligned label. If a label is longer than the cell width, the label appears across empty cells to the right. A label that is too long to display onscreen appears in its entirety in the Input line when you edit the cell.

If the cells to the right of a cell that contains a long label are not blank, Quattro Pro cuts off the entry display at the nonblank cell border. The complete entry is still stored in the cell, however. To display more of the label in the spreadsheet, you can insert new columns to the right of the cell that contains the long label. Alternatively, you can widen the column by moving the cell selector to the cell that contains the long label and clicking the Adjust Column's Width to Its Widest Cell Entry button on the toolbar.

You can also use the Wrap Text option on the Active Cells dialog box's Alignment tab to make text fit within the column width. (Press F12 or right-click the cell and select Cell Properties to display the Active Cells dialog box.) If you select this option, however, the row height may automatically increase when the text wraps in the cell.

→ For more information on inserting columns, rows, and sheets, **see** "Inserting Columns, Rows, or Sheets," **p. 413**

Tip #125 from *Trudi Reisner*	You can also adjust column width by dragging the right border between the column letters when the mouse pointer changes into a double-headed arrow. To automatically fit the column to the widest entry in that column, double-click the border between the column letters.

ENTERING NUMBERS

Spreadsheets were designed to make calculation less time-consuming and easier to do. Most calculations involve numbers, so numbers will represent a large portion of the data you enter in your Quattro Pro notebooks. When you enter a number, type the number and certain other characters according to the following rules:

- A number can start with a plus sign (+), but the plus sign is not stored when you press Enter. For example, +302 is stored and displayed as 302.

- If you start a number with a minus sign (–), the number is stored as a negative number. Negative numbers are usually displayed with the minus sign, but some numeric formats display negative numbers in parentheses. Therefore, –302 may be displayed as –302 or (302).

- Numbers can include only one decimal point and no spaces. Multiple decimal points and spaces in an entry are recognized as labels.

- If you enter a number with commas, you must include the correct number of digits following the comma if you want Quattro Pro to recognize the entry as a number. That is, the entry 12,000 is recognized as a number, but 12,00 is recognized as a label.

- If you include a currency symbol, such as a dollar sign ($), Quattro Pro displays the currency symbol in the cell.

- If you end a number with a percent sign (%), the number is divided by 100, and the number appears as a percent.

- Numbers are stored with up to 15 significant digits. If you enter a number with more significant digits, the number is rounded and stored in scientific notation; only 15 digits are retained, and any extra digits are dropped. Scientific notation uses powers of 10 to display very large or small numbers.

The appearance of a number in the notebook depends on the cell's format, font, and column width. If the number is too long to fit in the cell, Quattro Pro tries to show as much of the number as possible. If the cell uses the default General format and the integer portion of the number does not fit in the cell, Quattro Pro displays the number in scientific notation.

⚠ If Quattro Pro displays asterisks instead of numbers, see "Displaying Numbers Instead of Asterisks" in the Troubleshooting section at the end of this chapter.

ENTERING FORMULAS

Formulas are the real power of a spreadsheet program such as Quattro Pro. Formulas enable the program to calculate results and analyze data. As you change or add data to a spreadsheet, Quattro Pro recalculates the results. With little effort, you can quickly see the effects of changing information on the end results.

Formulas can operate on numbers, labels, or the results of other formulas. A formula can contain up to 1,022 characters and can include numbers, text, operators, cell and block addresses, block names, and functions. A formula cannot contain spaces except in a block name, a quoted text string, or a note (see "Adding Reference Notes" later in this chapter).

Note

Operators are symbols that represent mathematical operations, such as the plus sign (+) to indicate addition, the asterisk (*) to indicate multiplication, or the forward slash (/) to indicate division.

You can use Quattro Pro as a calculator by typing numbers directly into a formula, as in 123+456, but doing so ignores the real power of Quattro Pro formulas. A more useful formula uses cell references or block names in the calculation. Figure 21.5 demonstrates this capability.

Figure 21.5
Use cell references instead of the numbers in formulas.

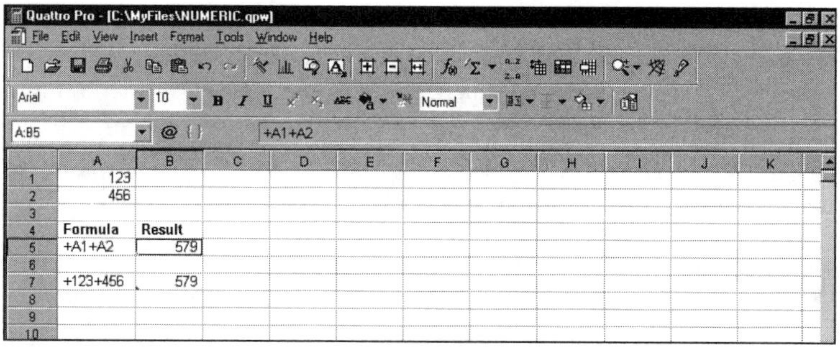

In this figure, the values 123 and 456 are placed in cells A1 and A2, respectively. In cell A5, the listed formula +A1+A2, which refers to these two cells, produces the same result as the formula 123+456 listed in cell A7—the value 579. (Notice that the formula in cell B5 begins with a plus sign. If the formula begins with a letter, not a plus sign, Quattro Pro assumes that you are entering a label and performs no calculations.) Suppose, however, that the data changes and you discover the first value should be 124, not 123. If you used the cell reference formula, just type 124 in cell A1; the formula recalculates the new value of 580. If you used the formula with numeric values rather than the cell reference formula, you must edit or retype the formula to change the data and obtain the new result.

There are two new features for quickly identifying formulas on the worksheet: formula markers and QuickTips. A *formula marker* is a blue triangle that appears in the lower-left corner of a cell that contains a formula. This marker helps you immediately identify which cells have formulas on the worksheet. To see the formula that was entered in the cell, point to that cell. Quattro Pro instantly displays the formula in a QuickTip box next to the cell. Figure 21.6 shows a formula marker and QuickTip.

Figure 21.6
A formula marker and QuickTip for quickly identifying a formula.

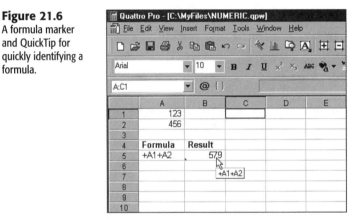

Quattro Pro uses four kinds of formulas: numeric, string, logical, and function. The following sections briefly describe each type of formula.

Using Numeric Formulas

Numeric formulas are instructions to perform mathematical calculations. Use operators to specify the mathematical operations and the order in which they should be performed. Operators are used for addition, subtraction, multiplication, division, and *exponentiation* (raising a number to a power).

> **Note**
>
> Because Quattro Pro attempts to evaluate simple numeric formulas that use division, such as 6/26, as a date entry, you must begin such formulas with a plus sign (+6/26). This tells Quattro Pro you want to perform a calculation rather than try to use the entry as a date.

Quattro Pro evaluates formulas according to a set of defined operator preferences. Exponentiation is performed before multiplication or division, and all three are performed before any addition or subtraction. If the formula includes two operators of the same precedence, this portion of the equation is evaluated left to right. You can control a formula's evaluation order by placing portions of a formula within parentheses; Quattro Pro always first evaluates items within a set of parentheses.

For example, the formula 5+3*2 results in a value of 11, while the formula (5+3)*2 results in a value of 16. In the first formula, Quattro Pro multiplies 3 times 2 and adds the result (6) to 5. In the second formula, Quattro Pro adds 5 and 3, and multiplies the result (8) by 2. As you can see, a very small change in the formula produces quite different results.

USING STRING FORMULAS

A string is a label or the result of a string formula; it is text rather than numbers. Only two string formula operators exist: the plus sign (+), which repeats a string, and the ampersand (&), which concatenates two or more strings. String formulas use different rules than numeric formulas. String formulas always begin with the plus sign but cannot include more than one plus sign. You concatenate two strings by using the ampersand.

Figure 21.7 shows several examples of string formulas. In the figure, cell C10 shows the results when the plus sign is used to repeat a string value. The formula to repeat a string or a numeric value is the same. C11 shows the result of concatenating two strings. Notice that no spaces exist between the two concatenated values. C12 and C13 demonstrate how to include spaces and commas in quoted strings to produce better-looking results.

Figure 21.7
Use string formulas to join text, such as first and last names.

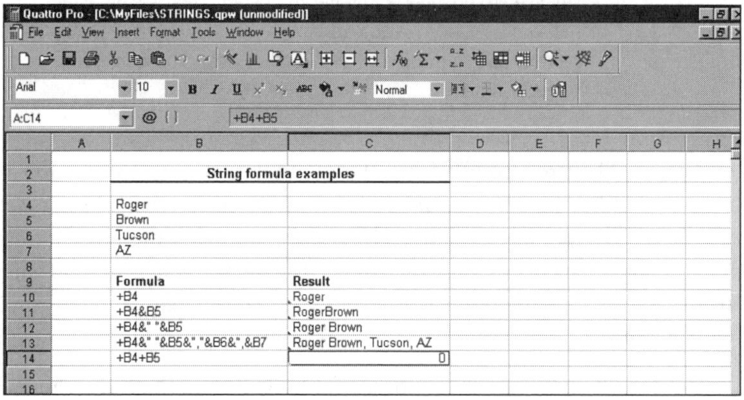

If you attempt to add two strings using the plus sign rather than the ampersand, Quattro Pro treats the formula as a numeric formula rather than a string formula. A cell that contains a label has a numeric value of 0, so the formula +B4+B5 in C14 returns a value of 0. You can use the ampersand only in string formulas. In addition, if you use any numeric operators after the plus sign at the beginning of a formula that contains an ampersand, the formula results in ERR.

PART

III

CH

21

USING LOGICAL FORMULAS

Logical formulas are true/false tests. A logical formula returns a value of 1 if the test is true and a value of 0 if the test is false. Logical formulas often are used in database criteria tables as well as to construct the tests used with the @IF function, discussed in the next section, "Using Function Formulas."

Tip #126 from *Trudi Reisner*	Logical formulas are also called *Boolean formulas*.

Logical formulas provide a shortcut method of performing conditional calculations. Suppose that you want to include the value contained in cell A1 only if this value is greater than 100. The logical formula +A1*(A1>100) returns the result you want. In this formula, the logical test, A1>100, evaluates as 0 unless the value in A1 is greater than 100. If A1 contains a value over 100, the logical test evaluates to 1. Because any value multiplied by 0 equals 0, and any value multiplied by 1 is the original value, the logical formula returns the result you want.

USING FUNCTION FORMULAS

Although you can build many formulas by using the numeric, string, or logical operators, some calculations are simply too complex to create with these simple operators. For example, if you want to calculate the interest due on a loan payment, you can simply multiply the beginning balance by the periodic interest rate. It's much more difficult, however, to calculate the actual payment amount necessary to pay off a loan in a series of equal payments.

Tip #127 from *Trudi Reisner*	Quattro Pro provides a number of built-in projects (sometimes referred to as templates) that can help when setting up notebooks that calculate loan payments, budgets, expense reports, and so on. To access these projects, choose File, New from Project; then select a project from the list and click Create.

Fortunately, Quattro Pro provides a large number of built-in functions—preconstructed formulas that handle a broad range of complex calculations. These functions enable you to perform many types of calculations by simply supplying the raw data. For example, to determine the payments on a loan, you can use the @PAYMT function. You supply the necessary data—the interest rate, number of payments, and the loan amount—and Quattro Pro solves the problem.

Quattro Pro includes nearly 500 powerful built-in functions you can use in your formulas. Figure 21.8 shows an example of how the @PAYMT function calculates the loan payment on a slightly more complex loan—one with a balloon payment due at the end of the loan. In this case, a borrower wants to know the monthly payments on a loan with the following terms:

Principal	$100,000
Annual interest rate	9%
Term	15 years
Balance due at end of loan (balloon)	$10,000

Figure 21.8
Function formulas quickly perform complex calculations by using your data.

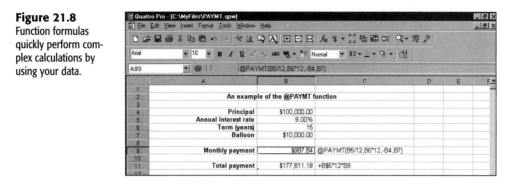

The term must be multiplied by 12 because the payments in this case are made monthly, but the interest rate and term are stated in yearly amounts. The rate must be divided by 12 to obtain the term in months and the monthly interest rate. The monthly loan payment, $987.84, is automatically adjusted if any of the raw data in cells B4 through B7 is changed.

Tip #128 from
Trudi Reisner

See the @Function Reference item on the Contents tab of the Quattro Pro online help system for a complete listing of all built-in functions.

When you create formulas in a Quattro Pro notebook, you can often combine functions with numeric, logical, and string formulas to produce the results you need. The next chapter provides much more information on functions.

→ For more information on using functions, **see** "Using Functions," **p. 393**

CREATING FORMULAS BY POINTING TO CELLS

Most formulas you create will contain operators and cell references. One way to enter a cell reference in a formula is to type the cell address itself. However, you can also point to the cell by clicking the cell, or moving the cell selector to the cell with the navigation keys. When you move the cell selector as you are entering a formula, the mode indicator at the right edge of the Application bar changes from VALUE to POINT, and the address of the cell selector appears in the Input line (see Figure 21.9).

If the formula requires additional entries, type the next operator and continue entering *arguments*—the information you must supply to complete the formula—until you finish. Press Enter or click the Confirm button, which is indicated by the blue check mark at the left of the input line, to place the formula in the notebook (see Figure 21.9). You can combine pointing and typing cell addresses; the result is the same.

To refer to a cell on another notebook sheet, include the sheet letter or name, followed by a colon and the cell address. To include the value of cell A14 from a sheet named EXPENSES, for example, type +EXPENSES:A14. To point to a cell on another sheet, click the sheet tab with the mouse and then point to the cell. You also can type + and then use the navigation keys, including Ctrl+Page Down and Ctrl+Page Up, to move the cell selector to other sheets.

PART
III

CH
21

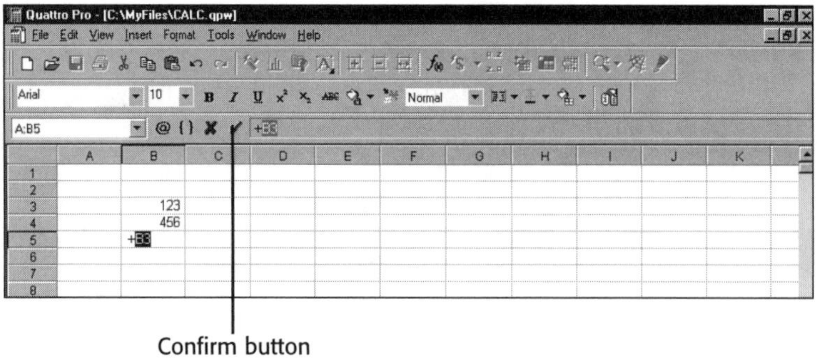

Figure 21.9
The mode indicator changes from VALUE to POINT when a formula is entered into the cell.

Confirm button

FINDING FORMULA ERRORS

Sometimes you may find your formulas display ERR or NA instead of the value you expected. ERR means the formula contains an erroneous calculation, such as dividing by 0. This can result from missing data or even from an error in entering a cell address. NA means some of the necessary information is currently unavailable, and can result from including a reference to a cell containing the @NA function or from linking formulas that were not updated when the notebook was opened. Finding the source of such errors can prove difficult, especially in a complex formula. Quattro Pro enables you to track down such errors using two methods.

Tip #129 from
Trudi Reisner

Use the F5 (Go To) key to quickly move the cell selector.

To quickly find the source of an ERR or NA value, use the Go To feature. First, move the cell selector to the cell displaying ERR or NA; second, press F5 (Go To) or choose Edit, Go To. Do not change the destination in the Reference text box; instead, choose Formula Values - Error in the Other List box. The cell selector will move to the cell that is the source of the error. If the cell selector is already on the cell that is the source of the error, it remains in the current cell.

To understand how this works, imagine that cell A5 contains the formula +1/A1, cell A10 contains the formula +A5, and cell A1 is empty. ERR is displayed in both A5 and A10. If you select cell A10, press F5 (Go To), and choose Formula Values - Error in the Other List box, the cell selector will move to A5. This is because cell A5 contains the original formula that generated the error. If you select cell A5, press F5 (Go To), and press Enter, the cell selector will move to A10. This tells you that there is another formula contributing to the error.

ADDING REFERENCE NOTES

Documentation is always important, and it is even more important when you create complex formulas that may be difficult to understand. It's pretty easy to forget why you built a formula exactly as you did, but even a brief note is often all you need to remind yourself. Quattro Pro makes documenting formulas and values easy by allowing you to add notes to cell entries.

These reference notes don't appear when you print a report, but as Figure 21.10 shows, the notes appear onscreen in the Input line when you move the cell selector to a cell that contains a note. You can press F2 (Edit) or double-click the cell to see the note in the current cell (see Figure 21.10). Use this option if the note is too long to appear in the Input line when you select the cell.

Figure 21.10
Add notes to formulas to provide valuable documentation.

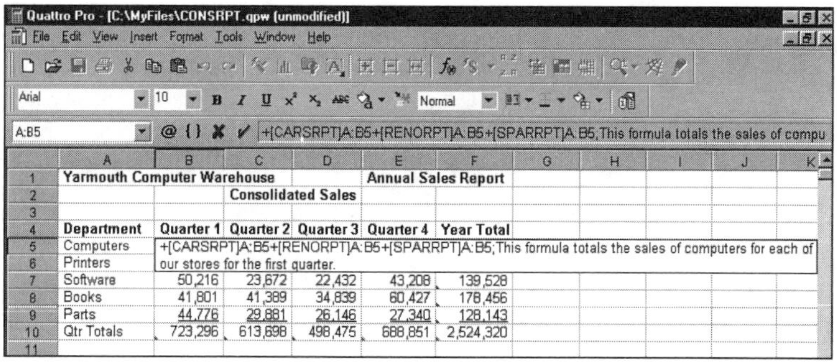

The note attached to the formula in B5 in Figure 21.10 clearly states the purpose of the formula: to show the combined total of sales of computers in each store during the first quarter.

To attach a note to a cell containing data, type a semicolon immediately following the formula or value—don't leave any spaces before the semicolon—and then type the note. You can include up to 1,022 characters in a cell, including the length of the formula or value and the note. Because these notes won't have any effect on your printed reports, they are a good method of creating internal documentation that will remain with the notebook.

Tip #130 from
Trudi Reisner

To print the notes attached to formulas, choose File, Page Setup; click the Options tab, select Cell Formulas, and click Print.

CORRECTING ERRORS WITH UNDO

You make changes in the notebook when you type an entry, edit a cell, or issue a command (such as Edit, Delete). If you make a change in error, you can usually choose the Edit, Undo command (or press Ctrl+Z) to reverse the previous change. You can also use the Undo button on the toolbar. If you type over an entry in error, you can undo the new entry to restore the previous entry. The Undo feature undoes only the last action performed, whether you were entering data, using a command, running a macro, or using Undo.

The Undo feature is powerful, and using it can be a little tricky. To use Undo properly, you first must understand what Quattro Pro considers to be a change that can be undone. A change occurs between the time Quattro Pro leaves ready mode and the time it returns to ready mode. If you press F2 (Edit), Quattro Pro enters edit mode. After you press Enter to

PART
III

CH
21

confirm the edits, Quattro Pro returns to ready mode. If you choose Edit, Undo or click the Undo button, Quattro Pro restores the cell contents that existed before you pressed F2 (Edit). To restore the last change that was undone, choose Edit, Redo (which replaces Edit, Undo until you make another change that can be undone); alternatively, you can click the Undo button again. If a single command makes the change, the Undo feature can undo changes (such as Edit, Delete) made to an entire block of cells or even an entire notebook.

> **Note**
>
> The Edit, Undo and Edit, Redo commands inform you of the action that can be undone or redone by including a one-word description. That description changes with each type of action that follows the command. If you make an entry in a cell, for example, the command appears as `Edit, Undo Entry`. If you use the Edit, Undo Entry command, the command changes to `Edit, Redo Entry`.

Quattro Pro cannot undo some commands. Moving the cell selector, saving a notebook, and the effects of recalculating formulas are examples of commands that cannot be undone. Before you make a serious change to an important file, always save the work to protect against errors that Undo may not reverse.

Quattro Pro has two levels of Undo command functionality. To ensure that the full Undo feature is available, make sure that the Enable Undo check box in the Settings dialog box's General tab is checked (see Figure 21.11). To access this dialog box, right-click the Quattro Pro title bar and choose Application Properties (or press Alt+F12). Click the General tab. Even if you don't enable the full Undo command, you will still be able to undo certain actions, such as entering data into a cell or changing a chart type or a chart title.

Figure 21.11
Select Enable Undo to ensure that the full Undo feature is available.

SAVING YOUR WORK

When you create a Quattro Pro notebook, it first exists only in your computer's volatile memory—RAM. To make the notebook available for future use, you must also save the notebook in a file on disk. You lose your work if you don't save new notebooks or changes before you quit Quattro Pro. You must also save a notebook in a disk file if you want to share the notebook with other people. The notebook file remains on disk after you quit Quattro Pro or turn off the computer.

SAVING NOTEBOOK FILES

To save your work, choose File, Save or File, Save As. Click the Save button on the toolbar as an alternative. If you have not yet saved the notebook, Quattro Pro suggests a default name, such as NOTEBK1.QPW. When you use File, New to open blank notebooks, Quattro Pro increases the numerical portion of the filename. The second new notebook is NOTEBK2.QPW, and so on.

If you already have saved the active notebook and assigned a name, File, Save saves the active notebook to disk using the assigned name. If you choose File, Save As, Quattro Pro saves the active notebook using a name you specify in the Save File dialog box (see Figure 21.12).

Figure 21.12
Use the Save File dialog box to name your notebook files.

The standard extension for Quattro Pro notebooks is QPW, but you can open or save notebook files in many different formats by selecting the appropriate type in the File Type list box shown in Figure 21.11. The standard extensions for Quattro Pro notebooks created in earlier versions of the application are WB3, WB2, and WB1. When you type a notebook name to save, type only the descriptive part of the name. Quattro Pro adds the appropriate file extension for you.

PART

III

CH

21

PROTECTING FILES WITH PASSWORDS

When you save a Quattro Pro notebook in a disk file, anyone with access to your computer can open the file. Although this isn't a problem in most instances, you may have some files that should remain confidential and restricted. To prevent unauthorized access to certain notebook files, you can apply a password to them when you save them. When a notebook is protected by a password, you must know the correct password before Quattro Pro permits you to retrieve or open the notebook.

To apply a password to a notebook file you are saving, select the Password Protect check box in the Save File dialog box, type a filename, and select Save. In the Password text box, type a password of up to 15 characters. As you enter characters, Quattro Pro displays number signs (#) rather than the password. After you click OK to confirm the dialog box, Quattro Pro displays a dialog box with a Verify Password text box. Retype the password using the same combination of uppercase and lowercase characters. Passwords are case sensitive. Click OK to confirm the dialog box.

If you're trying to open a password-protected file and Quattro Pro says you're using the wrong password, see "Using Case-Sensitive Passwords" in the Troubleshooting section at the end of this chapter.

SAVING FILES IN OTHER FORMATS

Quattro Pro can read and save files in many popular formats, including Lotus 1-2-3 for DOS, Lotus 1-2-3 for Windows, Quattro Pro for DOS, Excel, Paradox, dBASE, ASCII text, and HTML. If you want to save a Quattro Pro notebook in another format, select the correct file extension in the File Type drop-down list box in the Save File dialog box (refer to Figure 21.12). To save a notebook as a Lotus 1-2-3 for Windows file, for example, select 1-2-3 v4/v5.

Tip #131 from
Trudi Reisner

Unless you need to share a notebook file with someone who does not have Quattro Pro, always save notebooks using the QPW v9 file format.

If you save a notebook in any type other than the default QPW v9 format, any features unique to the newest version of Quattro Pro will be lost. For example, because Lotus 1-2-3 release 2.x spreadsheets cannot have multiple sheets, only the first notebook sheet is retained if you save the file by using the 1-2-3 v2.x file type.

MAKING SPACE ON YOUR DISK

When you save a notebook file, Quattro Pro automatically compresses the file to a smaller size. This new feature conserves disk space, especially for large notebook files.

Each time you create a file, you use space on a disk—usually your hard disk. You'll eventually run out of disk space if you don't occasionally erase old, unneeded files from the disk. Even if you have disk space left, too many files make it difficult to search through the list for a specific file.

Before you delete old files, consider saving them to a floppy disk in case you need them again. Quattro Pro notebook files are quite space efficient, and you can store a large number of files on a single floppy disk. Quattro Pro has no command for deleting files. You can use the Windows Explorer to delete old, unneeded files.

USING AUTOMATIC BACKUPS

Many problems can cause you to lose the results of your work. If there is a power failure, for example, any changes to a Quattro Pro notebook that haven't been saved to disk will be lost. If a program crashes and locks up your system, the same thing may occur. There's always the problem of the over-confident user, too. Have you ever lost work because you thought you already saved it, but then realized you hadn't because you were distracted? These are only a few of the many problems that present a danger to your notebooks and your data.

Saving your work frequently is the best insurance against losing a notebook or data to any of these problems. Unfortunately, it's pretty easy to forget to save your work often enough. Who remembers to select File, Save when they're under deadline pressure?

Fortunately, Quattro Pro can automatically and quickly save your notebooks at intervals you specify. By default, the automatic backup feature is set to back up your files every 10 minutes. To change the automatic backup feature, right-click the Quattro Pro title bar and select Application Properties or press Alt+F12 to display the Settings dialog box. Select the File Options tab (see Figure 21.13). Use the Timed Backup Every option to specify how often you want Quattro Pro to automatically back up your notebook files. Select the Timed Backup Every check box to disable the automatic backup feature. Click OK to save the change and close the dialog box.

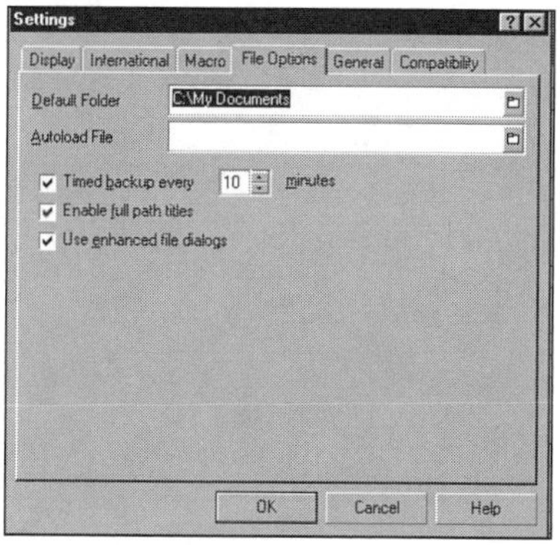

Figure 21.13
Use the automatic backup feature to automatically save your notebook files at specified intervals.

How often should you have Quattro Pro save your files? The best answer to that question is another question: How much work are you willing to do over? Most notebook files can be saved quite quickly, so there isn't much of a delay as they're saved. A setting of 10 minutes between backups is probably a good compromise, but you can adjust the setting to one that suits your work style.

PART

III

CH

21

PRACTICAL PROJECT

The Expense Budget PerfectExpert project can assist you in creating a budget for expenses. All you need to do is enter the budget and actual figures in the Budget and Actual columns for each category in the Personnel and Operating sections. You can either type the numbers from scratch or link the Expense Budget notebook to existing budget notebooks by using linking formulas in the Budget and Actual columns. The PerfectExpert provides formulas for the difference between budget and actual in dollars and percentages, as shown in the sample expense budget in Figure 21.14.

Figure 21.14
Expense Budget
PerfectExpert project.

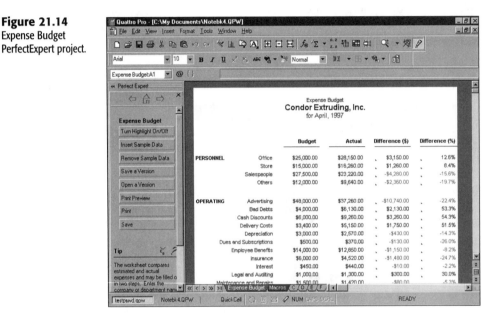

TROUBLESHOOTING

SELECTING A SHEET AND A SPECIFIC BLOCK

Selecting a sheet by using the Edit, Go To command always moves the cell selector to cell A1 on the selected sheet.

Create a block name (see "Naming Blocks" in the next chapter) and select the named block in the Cell Names list box as the destination. The cell selector moves to the upper-left corner of the named block.

DISPLAYING NUMBERS INSTEAD OF ASTERISKS

Quattro Pro displays asterisks instead of the number entered in a cell.

If the cell uses a format other than General, Currency, or Scientific, or if the cell width is too narrow to display in scientific notation and the number cannot fit in the cell width, Quattro Pro displays asterisks instead of the number. Use the Adjust column's width to its widest cell entry button on the toolbar to change the column width, select a different numeric format, or change the font to a smaller size.

USING CASE-SENSITIVE PASSWORDS

Quattro Pro reports that I used the wrong password when I attempted to open a password-protected notebook file.

Passwords are case sensitive and can be very tricky to use. BRIAN is not the same as brian or Brian. Try entering the password again with the case reversed (press the Caps Lock key before entering the password) or with only the first letter of the word capitalized.

CHAPTER 22

BUILDING A SPREADSHEET

In this chapter

CHOOSING COMMANDS FROM MENUS

You use commands for almost everything in Corel Quattro Pro. Commands tell Quattro Pro to perform a task, change its basic operation, or operate on a notebook, a notebook sheet, a block of cells, or individual cells. Some commands are general enough to apply to all notebooks; still others are specialized and apply to individual objects such as blocks or cells.

The Quattro Pro main menu includes eight options. Each option leads to a drop-down menu.

Each drop-down menu provides a series of commands you can use to accomplish specific types of tasks. You'll save quite a bit of time if you understand the basic purpose of each main menu selection. Take a quick look at the main menu options:

- The File commands enable you to save and open notebooks; print reports; set up your printer; send reports directly from Quattro Pro to others via email; and quit Quattro Pro.

- The Edit commands enable you to undo commands; use the Windows Clipboard to copy, cut, and paste information; convert formulas to unchanging values; create links to other Windows applications; delete cells, rows, columns, and sheets; fill blocks with data and define customized fill series; and search and replace.

- The View commands enable you to zoom in or out; control the display of screen elements; group sheets; split the notebook into horizontal or vertical panes; lock rows or columns onscreen; and switch between the notebook draft view, notebook page view, and the Objects sheet.

- The Insert commands enable you to insert cells, rows, columns, and sheets; name blocks of cells; add a QuickButton onto a sheet; query, link to, or import external databases; use the Database Desktop utility; add functions to cells; add charts, images, or other objects to a notebook; and insert comments and page breaks.

- The Format commands enable you to create and modify styles; modify styles of blocks, sheets, and notebooks; reformat text; apply SpeedFormats; use QuickFit; and adjust the position of objects added to a sheet.

- The Tools commands enable you to check spelling and use QuickCorrect; create, run, and debug macros; use QuickFilter and sort to organize data; use Scenario Manager; perform what-if analyses, data regression, and matrix manipulation; use the Consolidator, Optimizer, and Solve For utilities; create your own dialog boxes and toolbars; customize Quattro Pro's default settings; create geographical maps; and create onscreen slide shows.

- The Window commands enable you to cascade or tile windows; create additional views of your notebooks; control the display of open windows; and select a window.

- The Help commands enable you to access the Quattro Pro Help system; use the PerfectExpert; access help on the Internet; and display product and license information.

> **Note**
>
> The Quattro Pro menus have been reorganized for easy access to the most frequently used features. For a detailed list of the differences between Quattro Pro 9 and Quattro Pro 8 menus, see Appendix B, "Index of New and Enhanced Features."

For more detailed information on Quattro Pro's menus, you can use the Help, Help Topics command. You can also press F1 (Help) when a command is selected for context-sensitive help that explains how to perform the selected task.

Tip #132 from
Trudi Reisner

> Right-click a menu to choose a menu similar to the one used in a previous version of Quattro Pro, Microsoft Excel, or Lotus 1-2-3.

⚠ *If it's difficult to determine where to find the command necessary to perform a task, see "Asking the PerfectExpert for Help" in the Troubleshooting section at the end of this chapter.*

USING BLOCKS

A block is usually a rectangular group of cells in a notebook. In Quattro Pro, a *block* also can contain several groups of cells defined by collections of rectangular blocks. In other words, a single named block does not have to be rectangular, but can contain several smaller rectangular blocks. Figure 22.1, for example, shows one rectangular block in cells A1..B3; a nonrectangular block including B5..B6, B7..D9, and E7..F7; and a noncontiguous block that includes C22..D15 and E17..F18. (The blocks are shaded gray to make them easier to see.)

Figure 22.1
You can create several kinds of Quattro Pro blocks on one page.

Rectangular block ⎯

Nonrectangular block consists of several rectangular blocks.

Noncontiguous block consists of two rectangular blocks.

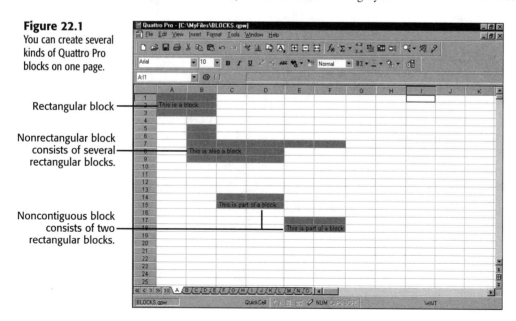

Tip #133 from	Blocks are called *ranges* in Excel and Lotus 1-2-3.
Trudi Reisner	

You specify a block address (usually in a text box of a dialog box) by using cell addresses of any two diagonally opposite corners of the block. You separate the cell addresses with one or two periods and separate each rectangular block with commas. You can specify the nonrectangular block shown in Figure 22.1 by typing B5–B6,B7–D9,E7–F7, for example. You also can specify this block in several other ways, as long as you separate each rectangular block with commas.

A block can also span two or more notebook sheets. This three-dimensional block includes the same cells on each sheet. When you use a three-dimensional block, you must include the sheet letter or sheet name with the cell addresses. For example, to extend the rectangular block in Figure 22.1 to a three-dimensional block, type A:A1..C:B3.

SELECTING BLOCKS

Many commands act on blocks. The Edit, Copy Cells command, for example, displays a dialog box asking for a From and a To block. To enter a block, you can type the address of the block, select the block with the mouse or the keyboard before or after you choose the command, or type the block name. (To learn about creating a name, see "Naming Blocks" later in this chapter.)

Tip #134 from	You can specify a rectangular block address using any two diagonally opposite cells.
Trudi Reisner	

TYPING THE BLOCK ADDRESSES

If you want to type a block address, type the addresses of cells diagonally opposite in a rectangular block, separating each cell with one or two periods. If the block is nonrectangular, you must specify each rectangular block and separate each block with a comma. To specify the block A1..C4, for example, you type either A1..C4, A1.C4, A4..C1, or A4.C1. Quattro Pro regards each of these addresses the same as A1..C4.

SELECTING BLOCKS

The easiest method of specifying a block's cell addresses is usually selecting the block by pointing with the mouse or the keyboard. You can select a block before or after you issue a command. In a formula, however, you must select the block after you begin typing the formula. A block remains selected if you select it before issuing a command. This allows you to use the same block with more than one command without reselecting the block. In the case of a Copy, Paste operation, the selected block doesn't remain highlighted. To use the mouse to select a block, simply hold down the left mouse button as you drag the mouse across the block.

Tip #135 from	If you use the keyboard to select a block, you can use Shift+F7 as a method of anchoring a
Trudi Reisner	block selection. To *anchor* means to retain the location of the active cell as you extend the highlight to include other cells in the block. You can also anchor a block selection by pressing and holding down the Shift key while moving the cell selector.

When you preselect a block, the address automatically appears in the text boxes of any command dialog boxes. Some dialog boxes, however, require you to specify more than one block. For example, if you use the Edit, Copy Cells command, you must specify both a From (source) and a To (destination) block. If you have selected a block before you issue the command, the From text box will show the selected block. You can use the mouse or Shift+Tab to move the highlight between the text boxes. Enter the second block either by typing its address or block name or by pointing.

In some dialog boxes, a button with an arrow appears beside text boxes. This means that you can click the arrow button to select a cell or block directly in the sheet; the dialog box changes to show only the title bar, enabling you to see more of the sheet. After you've finished selecting the cell or block, click the Maximize button in the dialog box title bar to return to the dialog box. The address of the cell or block you selected in the sheet now appears in the text box of the dialog box.

SPECIFYING A BLOCK WITH A NAME

You also can specify a block in a dialog box by using a name you assign to the block (see "Naming Blocks" later in this chapter). You can specify a block name whenever Quattro Pro expects the address of a cell or a block. You can enter a block name in the Go To dialog box, for example; Quattro Pro moves the cell selector to the upper-left corner of the named block.

You gain a number of advantages by using block names:

- Block names are easier to remember than block addresses—especially if a block is non-contiguous.

- Typing a block name usually is easier than pointing to a block in another part of the notebook.

- Macros that use block names rather than cell addresses automatically adjust after you move a block.

- Block names also make formulas easier to understand. The formula +QTR_1_TOTAL (using the block name QTR_1_TOTAL) is easier to understand than the formula +B10.

EXTENDING BLOCK SELECTIONS

Extending a block selection to include a three-dimensional block or a group of blocks allows you to include more than a single two-dimensional block in a command or a block name. These extended blocks make some operations easier and faster because one command can replace a series of commands, such as applying numeric formats, adding shading, and choosing a text font.

Selecting noncontiguous blocks (when you want to change the formatting of multiple blocks in a sheet, for example) using the mouse is much easier than selecting noncontiguous blocks using the keyboard. You can select noncontiguous blocks using the mouse before or after you choose a command; to select noncontiguous blocks using the keyboard, you must select the block after choosing a command.

If you use the mouse to extend a block selection that includes noncontiguous blocks, you can select the blocks before or after you choose a command. Use the following procedure:

1. Select the first rectangular block.

2. Press and hold down the Ctrl key.

3. Select each additional rectangular block.

4. Release the Ctrl key.

Tip #136 from
Trudi Reisner

To work on noncontiguous blocks using the keyboard, choose the command first and then select the block.

To use the keyboard to extend a block selection that includes noncontiguous blocks, perform the following steps:

1. Choose the command in which you want to use the noncontiguous blocks.

2. Select the appropriate block text box by pressing the Tab key. If the text box has an underlined letter, press Alt plus the underlined letter.

3. Enter the block addresses by typing the addresses of rectangular blocks and separating each block with a comma. You also can point to the first cell of each rectangular block, press the period key to anchor the selection, and use the navigation keys to select the block. Before you point to the first cell in the subsequent blocks of cells, be sure to press Ctrl to prevent the cells between the first block and the subsequent cells from being selected. Enter a comma and continue selecting rectangular blocks until you have selected each block.

NAMING BLOCKS

Block addresses can be difficult to remember, and it's easy to type the wrong set of cell addresses when specifying a block. Quattro Pro provides a very good solution to this problem: block names. If you name blocks, you can always substitute the block name for the block's cell addresses in commands and formulas, ensuring that the correct block will be affected by the command or formula. Block names also make formulas much easier to read and understand because Quattro Pro will always substitute block names where appropriate in formulas—even if you didn't use block names when you created the formula.

Tip #137 from
Trudi Reisner

Quattro Pro does not distinguish between uppercase and lowercase letters: Block_1, block_1, and BLOCK_1 are equivalent block names.

You should follow certain rules and cautions when creating block names:

- You can use up to 63 characters to name a block.

- You can use block names in formulas, functions, commands, and macros.

- Don't use the following characters in block names:

  + - * / & > < @ # ^ $ ( )

- Although block names that start with numbers are valid, try to avoid starting block names with numbers. They may cause problems in formulas.

- Don't create block names that also are cell addresses, column letters, or row numbers (such as A1, AA, or 199), names of keys (such as Edit), function names (such as @AVG), or macro commands (such as WRITE).

- Use descriptive block names.

- Join parts of block names together with the underscore (such as QTR_1_TOTALS) rather than spaces.

- If you share spreadsheet files with users of other spreadsheet programs (such as Microsoft Excel, Lotus 1-2-3, or even earlier versions of Quattro Pro), limit block names to 15 characters to ensure compatibility.

Quattro Pro provides several methods of creating block names. Each method uses the Insert, Name, Cells command (Ctrl+F3) to first display the Cell Names dialog box (see Figure 22.2). The following sections describe the block naming options available through this dialog box.

Figure 22.2
The Cell Names dialog box provides several block-naming options.

Caution

Don't confuse the Insert, Cells and Insert, Name, Cells commands. The Insert, Cells command adds a rectangular block of cells to a notebook sheet, thus moving other cells down or to the right. The Insert, Name, Cells command creates block names.

If some formulas don't show the correct results even though they appear to contain correct block names, see "Naming Blocks" in the Troubleshooting section at the end of this chapter.

CREATING BLOCK NAMES WITH INSERT, NAME, CELLS, ADD

You can use the Insert, Name, Cells, Add command to assign a name to a cell or a block. To create a block name using this command, follow these steps:

1. Select the cell or block you want to name.
2. Choose Insert, Name, Cells (or press Ctrl+F3). The Cell Names dialog box shown in Figure 22.2 appears.
3. Type the block name in the Name text box and then click Add.
4. Click Close.

If you want to add more than one block name, repeat step 3 as necessary.

CREATING BLOCK NAMES WITH INSERT, NAME, CELLS, GENERATE

You can also create block names automatically by using the Insert, Name, Cells, Generate command. This command can generate block names for a row, a column, or for every cell in a selected block, using labels in the block. To create block names using this command, follow these steps:

1. Select the cell or block you want to name.

> **Caution**
>
> The cell or block for which you want to generate a name must contain labels. If the cells contain values, no name will be generated.

2. Choose Insert, Name, Cells (or press Ctrl+F3).
3. Click Generate to display the Generate Cell Names dialog box (see Figure 22.3).

Figure 22.3
You can create block names automatically by using the Generate Cell Names dialog box.

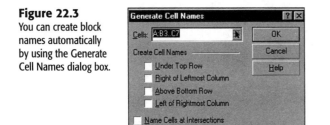

4. The check boxes in this dialog box determine which cells (in the selected block) the labels identify. Choose Under Top Row, Right of Leftmost Column, Above Bottom Row, or Left of Rightmost Column. For example, you might use labels to identify product lines and time periods.

5. To name all cells in the block using the label cells in combination, select Name Cells at Intersections.

6. Click OK to return to the Cell Names dialog box.

The Name Cells at Intersections option creates block names by *concatenating* (joining, but not adding) the column label, an underscore, and the row label. For example, if the column label is Year Total and the row label is Software, the name generated for the intersecting cell is Year Total_Software.

CREATING BLOCK NAMES WITH INSERT, NAME, CELLS, LABELS

You also can use the Insert, Name, Cells, Labels command to create block names. With this command, you use labels already typed on a notebook sheet as block names for adjacent cells, such as to identify cells where users will input data. To create block names using this command, follow these steps:

1. Select the cell or block you want to name.

2. Choose Insert, Name, Cells (or press Ctrl+F3).

3. Click Labels to display the Name Cell from Labels dialog box (see Figure 22.4).

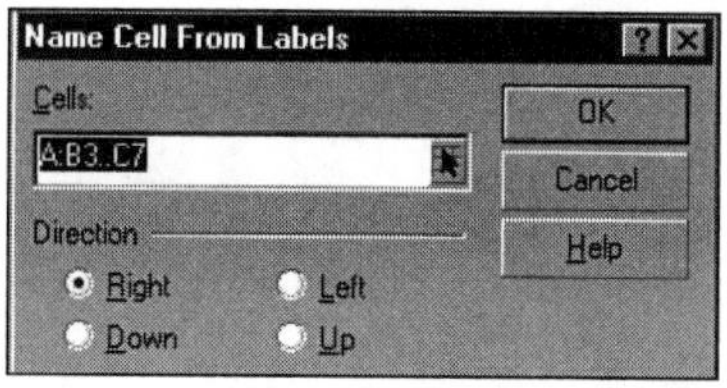

Figure 22.4
The Name Cell from Labels dialog box is useful for creating block names.

4. The Directions option buttons determine which cells are named using the labels. Select the appropriate direction: Right, Left, Up, or Down.

5. Click OK to return to the Cell Names dialog box.

The Insert, Name, Cells, Labels command ignores blank cells in the label block as it creates single-cell blocks. If you need to create multiple-cell blocks, you must use the Insert, Name, Cells, Add command.

LISTING BLOCK NAMES

A table of block names serves as important notebook documentation. Quattro Pro creates a two-column table of block names and addresses using the Insert, Name, Cells, Output command. When you choose this command, select an area with enough room for the block name table. The table overwrites any existing data without warning.

If the block name table doesn't show the correct addresses for some blocks, see "Updating the Block Name Table" in the Troubleshooting section at the end of this chapter.

DELETING BLOCK NAMES

There's usually little reason to remove block names from a Quattro Pro notebook. Block names don't use much memory, and the documentation they provide can be invaluable. Still, if you want to delete existing block names, Quattro Pro has two commands that delete block names from the notebook. Use the Insert, Name, Cells, Delete command to delete a single block name or several block names. You can delete all block names at one time by using the Insert, Name, Cells, Delete All command.

COPYING AND MOVING INFORMATION

Few Quattro Pro notebooks are masterpieces when first created. Most often, it's useful to copy or move data from one place to another. You might, for example, want to duplicate the appearance of an existing report, or you might simply find it's awkward to enter data correctly in the notebook's initial layout. Whatever your reason, you'll discover that Quattro Pro offers several methods of copying and moving data.

Tip #138 from
Trudi Reisner

Chapter 23, "Changing the Display and Appearance of Data," shows you how to make your Quattro Pro notebooks look as good as they should.

The three primary methods of moving and copying data in Quattro Pro are

- The Edit, Cut; Edit, Copy; Edit, Paste; and Edit, Paste Special commands, which all use the Windows Clipboard
- The Edit, Copy Cells command, which does not use the Clipboard
- The mouse

Note

The Edit, Move Block command that appeared in earlier versions of Quattro Pro is no longer available in Quattro Pro 9; you must use the Windows Clipboard method or the mouse to move data.

In the following sections, you'll learn the advantages and disadvantages of each method, and why each method is important to you. You'll also learn the different ways to copy formulas.

COPYING AND MOVING USING THE CLIPBOARD

The Windows Clipboard is a feature shared by most Windows applications. Data stored on the Clipboard is available to any Windows program that knows how to use the data. When you place data on the Clipboard, it remains there until new data replaces it, or until you exit from Windows. This permits you to make multiple copies of the same data without having to copy the data to the Clipboard each time (as long as you don't use another command that places new data on the Clipboard).

USING EDIT, CUT

The Edit, Cut command removes—*cuts*—data from the notebook and places the data on the Clipboard. Any existing Clipboard data is lost unless it has been saved elsewhere. When you place data on the Clipboard, you can make as many copies of the data as you want by using Edit, Paste.

> **Caution**
>
> The Edit, Cut command replaces any existing Clipboard data with new data. You cannot recover the old data, so be sure to use Edit, Paste to save the old data before you use the Edit, Cut command on the new data.

You can place any selectable object on the Clipboard. If you select a single cell, the Edit, Cut command removes the data from the selected cell and places the data on the Clipboard. If you select a block of cells, the entire block is removed from the notebook and placed on the Clipboard. You can also use Edit, Cut to place other types of objects, such as charts or drawn objects, on the Clipboard. Any object placed on the Clipboard using Quattro Pro's Edit, Cut command can later be returned to the notebook using Edit, Paste, but other Windows applications may not be able to accept all types of Quattro Pro objects.

To use Edit, Cut, select the object you want to cut. Choose Edit, Cut (Ctrl+X) or click the Cut button on the toolbar. The selected object will disappear from the Quattro Pro notebook. If you cut an object in error, immediately choose Edit, Undo before selecting any other commands.

Edit, Cut places any numeric formatting, alignment, or other object properties on the Clipboard along with the data. If you've used the dialog boxes to modify any of the properties for the selected object, these properties are removed from the notebook, along with the object and placed on the Clipboard for later possible use.

USING EDIT, COPY

The Edit, Copy command works very much like the Edit, Cut command, but there is one very important difference. When you use Edit, Copy, the selected object remains in your Quattro Pro notebook, and an exact duplicate is created on the Clipboard. This duplicate shares all of the original object's properties, including any numeric formatting, alignment, and so on. After the duplicate is placed on the Clipboard, however, the two objects—the original and the duplicate—are totally independent of each other. In other words, any changes you make to the original object in your notebook are not reflected in the duplicate on the Clipboard. If you want the duplicate to match the changed original, choose Edit, Copy again to create an updated duplicate.

Tip #139 from
Trudi Reisner

Edit, Copy adds a copy of the object to the Clipboard. You need to use Edit, Paste to add the copy to your notebook.

It's easy to become confused by the title of the Edit, Copy command. Although you might expect this command to make a copy of an object, the copy it produces isn't visible to you. The copy of the selected object exists only on the Windows Clipboard, ready to be pasted into another location in your Quattro Pro notebook or into another document created in another Windows application.

To use Edit, Copy, select the object you want to copy. Choose Edit, Copy (Ctrl+C) or click the Copy button on the toolbar. You won't see any change in the notebook, but the Clipboard will contain an exact duplicate of the selected object.

Note

Objects placed on the Windows Clipboard are stored in your computer's memory until you choose Edit, Cut or Edit, Copy to replace them with another object, or until you exit from Windows. Very large objects, such as bitmaps or sound files, can use a large portion of your system's memory, making your system operate at an unusually slow pace (especially if your notebook has lots of complex calculations). If you have copied a very large object to the Clipboard, but no longer need to store the object there, copy a single notebook cell to the Clipboard to free the memory for other uses.

USING EDIT, PASTE

The Edit, Paste command places a copy of data contained on the Clipboard into your Quattro Pro notebook. The object on the Clipboard is unaffected by this command and can be pasted into more than one location by using additional Edit, Paste commands. Quattro Pro notebooks can contain most types of objects that can be placed on the Clipboard.

To use the Edit, Paste command, choose Edit, Copy or Edit, Cut to place the object on the Clipboard. Position the cell selector in the location you want to place a copy of the data; select Edit, Paste (Ctrl+V) or click the Paste button on the toolbar.

The following guidelines enable you to determine the number and type of copies that will be created:

- If the data placed in the Clipboard with the Edit, Copy or Edit, Cut command is from a single cell, one copy of the data is added to each selected cell after you choose Edit, Paste.

- If the data moved to the Clipboard with the Edit, Copy or Edit, Cut command is from several rows in a single column, one copy of the data is added to each selected column after you choose Edit, Paste.

- If the data moved to the Clipboard with the Edit, Copy or Edit, Cut command is from several columns in a single row, one copy of the data is added to each selected row after you choose Edit, Paste.

- If the data moved to the Clipboard with the Edit, Copy or Edit, Cut command is from several rows and several columns, one copy of the data is added to the sheet starting at the selected cell after you choose Edit, Paste.

Three-dimensional data always creates a three-dimensional copy. If the source or destination data block includes more than one sheet, the same rules that apply to rows and columns also apply to the sheet dimension.

If you want additional copies of the same data, reposition the cell selector and select Edit, Paste. Don't use any additional Edit, Copy or Edit, Cut commands if you want additional copies of the same data; the Clipboard holds the most recent Edit, Copy or Edit, Cut contents.

Caution

If you paste data to a block that already contains data, Quattro Pro replaces the existing data with the new data. Use care with Edit, Paste to avoid pasting data into cells that contain formulas or other data you don't want to lose.

COPYING DATA USING THE EDIT, COPY CELLS COMMAND

Quattro Pro includes another command you can use to copy data from one place in the notebook to another. Edit, Copy Cells copies data directly within the notebook without using the Clipboard. Quattro Pro 9 doesn't include a comparable command to move cells; you must use the Clipboard method or the mouse to move cell data.

Because this command doesn't use the Clipboard, any objects you've already placed on the Clipboard aren't affected by the Edit, Copy Cells command. You can still use Edit, Paste to make copies of the unchanged Clipboard contents even after you use Edit, Copy Cells.

When you copy data, the copy contains the same labels, values, formatting, and style properties as the original data. The data in the original location remains unchanged.

You can copy a single cell or a block to another part of the same notebook sheet, to another notebook sheet, or to another open notebook. You can make a single copy or multiple copies at the same time. To copy data with the Edit, Copy Cells command, follow these steps:

1. Select the cell or block you want to copy. Preselected blocks appears in the From text box.
2. Choose Edit, Copy Cells. The Copy Cells dialog box shown in Figure 22.5 appears.
3. Press Tab to select the To text box.
4. Type the destination address or use the mouse or navigation keys to select the destination block.
5. Click OK to confirm the dialog box and copy the block.

Quattro Pro copies the data, overwriting any existing data in the destination block.

You can use the Model Copy option to make a copy that uses the From block as a model for the To block. If you check Model Copy, formula references—even absolute references—adjust to fit the To block. (See "Copying Formulas" later in this chapter for more information on formula references.) In addition, if you check Model Copy, you can specify whether to copy formula cells, label cells, number cells, properties, objects, row/column sizes, or cell comments.

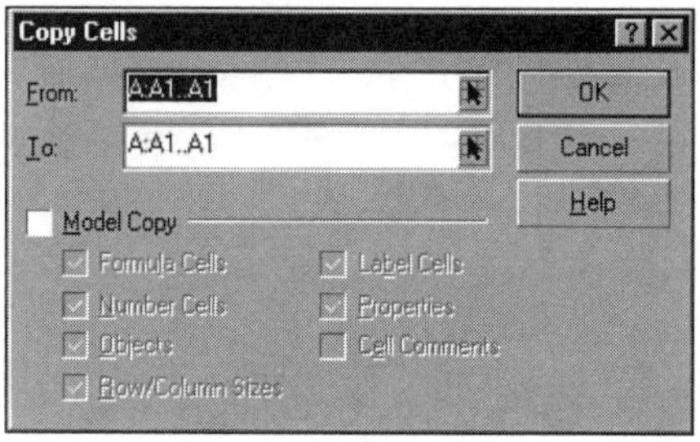

Figure 22.5
You can use the Copy Cells dialog box to copy a single cell or a block of cells.

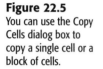

COPYING AND MOVING DATA USING THE MOUSE

Quattro Pro offers yet another method of moving or copying data—one that takes advantage of the graphical nature of the Windows environment. This method, called *drag and drop*, uses the mouse and is by far the easiest way to move data short distances within a Quattro Pro notebook.

To move data using the drag-and-drop method, perform the following steps:

1. Make sure the *destination block* (where the data is to be moved) does not contain any information of value, as it will be deleted by the block move.

2. Select the block of data you want to move. The block can be any size, including a single cell.

3. Point to a border of the selected block until the mouse pointer changes into a four-headed arrow.

4. Hold down the left mouse button and drag the selected block to the new location. As you move the mouse pointer, Quattro Pro displays an outline the size of the selected block. Any existing data within this outline will be overwritten.

5. Release the mouse button to drop the block of data into the new location.

To copy rather than move the selected block of data, hold down the Ctrl key when you point to the block while performing step 3. When you hold down the left mouse button, a plus sign appears next to a hand-shaped mouse pointer when you are copying data.

If the mouse pointer changes too quickly when you are selecting a block, you can adjust the delay time. Either right-click the Quattro Pro title bar and choose Application Properties or press Alt+F12 to display the Settings dialog box. Select the General tab (see Figure 22.6). To increase the delay time, type a higher number in the Cell Drag and Drop Delay Time text box. Delay time is measured in milliseconds and 5,000 milliseconds is the default delay time.

Figure 22.6
The General tab in the Settings dialog box is where the cell drag-and-drop delay time may be changed.

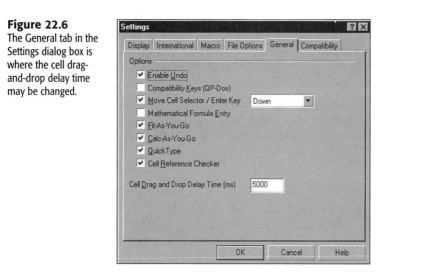

COPYING FORMULAS

Copying formulas in Quattro Pro is more complex than copying data because of the way the program stores addresses in formulas. Addresses may be

- Relative. Refers to column, row, and sheet *offsets*—distances measured in columns, rows, or sheets—from the formula cell.
- Absolute. Always referring to a specific cell.
- Mixed. A combination of relative and absolute.

RELATIVE ADDRESSING

If you enter the formula +B2 in cell C5, Quattro Pro does not store the formula quite the way you might expect. The formula tells Quattro Pro to add the value of the cell one column to the left and three rows above C5. When you copy this formula from C5 to D6, Quattro Pro uses the same relative formula but displays the formula as +C3. This method of storing cell references is called *relative addressing*. After you copy a formula that uses relative addressing, Quattro Pro automatically adjusts the new formula so that its cell references are in the same relative location as they were in the original location.

ABSOLUTE ADDRESSING

Sometimes you do not want a formula to address new locations after you copy the formula. You may, for example, create a formula that refers to data in a single cell, such as an interest rate or a growth factor percentage. Formulas that always refer to the same cell address, regardless of where you place the copy of the formula, use absolute addressing.

Tip #140 from
Trudi Reisner
You can use the F4 key to toggle cell addresses in a formula between relative and absolute modes. When you press F4, Quattro Pro will insert a dollar sign ($) in the formula before each part of the address you want to have stay the same.

To specify an absolute address, type a dollar sign ($) in the formula before each part of the address you want to have remain the same. The formula +$B:$C$10, for example, always refers to cell C10 on notebook sheet B regardless of where you place the copy of the formula.

MIXED ADDRESSING

You also can create formulas that use mixed addressing, in which some elements of the cell addresses are absolute and other elements are relative. You can create a formula, for example, that always refers to the same row but adjusts its column reference as you copy the formula to another column. To create a mixed address, use a dollar sign to indicate the absolute address portions of the formula, leaving off the dollar sign for relative addresses. The formula +$B1, for example, always refers to column B on the current notebook sheet, but adjusts the row reference relative to the current row.

FILLING BLOCKS

Creating Quattro Pro notebooks can seem like quite a task, especially if the model you want to build requires you to enter a series of information in a large number of consecutive cells. For example, a notebook based on an incrementing time series, such as a loan amortization schedule, may require you to include dates in monthly intervals. A notebook tracking results from each of your company's locations may require you to enter the location names, possibly in several different places. Entering the same data numerous times seems like a lot of work, doesn't it? Wouldn't it be nice if you could get someone else to do that sort of thing for you?

Fortunately, there is one thing computers are very good at: repetitive work. Quattro Pro takes this concept a step further by providing easy-to-use methods of filling blocks automatically with either a number series or groups of related labels. In the following sections, you'll learn how to use two types of block-filling options.

USING EDIT, FILL

You use the Edit, Fill, Fill Series command to fill a block with numeric values. This command offers a large range of options, as shown in Figure 22.7. These commands are suitable for almost any instance needing an incrementing number series, such as a series of interest rates or budget percentages.

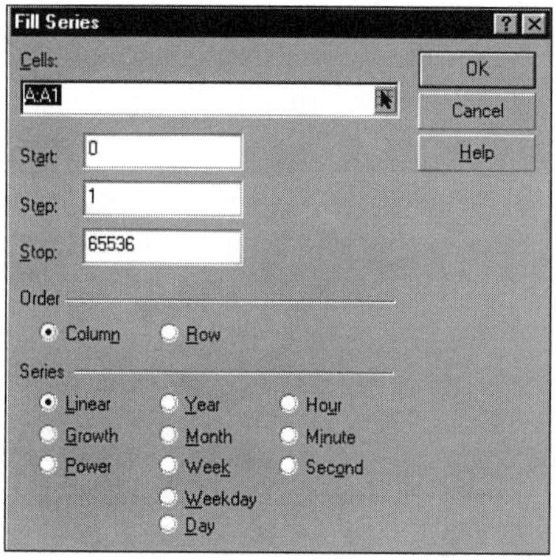

Figure 22.7
The Fill Series dialog box is used to fill blocks with numeric values.

To use the Edit, Fill, Fill Series command, follow these steps:

1. Select the block you want to fill.

2. Choose Edit, Fill, Fill Series. The Fill Series dialog box appears (refer to Figure 22.7).

3. Enter the Start, Step, and Stop values in the appropriate text boxes.

4. If the block spans multiple rows and multiple columns, choose Column to begin filling the block in the first column, then the second column, and so on; choose Row to fill the first row, then the second row, and so on.

5. In the Series field, choose the type of fill. Table 22.1 summarizes the fill options.

6. Click OK to confirm the dialog box and fill the block.

TABLE 22.1   DATA FILL TYPES

Series	Type of Fill
Linear	Step value is added to start value.
Growth	Step value is used as a multiplier.
Power	Step value is used as an exponent.
Year	Step value is in years and is added to start value.
Month	Step value is in months and is added to start value.
Week	Step value is in weeks and is added to start value.
Weekday	Step value is in days with weekend days skipped and is added to start value.
Day	Step value is in days and is added to start value.
Hour	Step value is in hours and is added to start value.
Minute	Step value is in minutes and is added to start value.
Second	Step value is in seconds and is added to start value.

By default, Quattro Pro uses 0 for the start number, 1 for the step (or increment), and 65536 for the stop number. Be sure to adjust these values to fit your needs. When filling a block, Quattro Pro stops entering additional values when the specified block is filled or the stop number is reached.

Tip #141 from
Trudi Reisner

If you specify a start value larger than the stop value, no values enter the block.

If you want to fill a block with a sequence of dates, it's important to understand how Quattro Pro enters date values. Quattro Pro uses date serial numbers to determine dates. Date serial numbers increment by 1 for each day, starting with 1 for December 31, 1899.

Note

For compatibility with Lotus 1-2-3 and Microsoft Excel, Quattro Pro uses the value 61 for March 1, 1900, even though the year 1900 was not a leap year. Dates prior to March 1, 1900 are incorrect in Lotus 1-2-3 and Microsoft Excel. Dates prior to January 1, 1900, and dates after December 31, 2099, are not allowed in Lotus 1-2-3. Dates prior to January 1, 1900, and dates after December 31, 2078 are not allowed in Excel. Quattro Pro correctly determines dates in the entire range of January 1, 1600, through December 31, 3199, using negative date serial numbers for dates prior to December 30, 1899. You can obtain the serial number for a starting date by entering the date into a cell and then getting the serial number as shown on the input line.

Because date serial numbers increment by 1 each day, the default stop value is too small for most useful dates. For example, you cannot use Edit, Fill, Fill Series to enter a date such as June 26, 1997, which has a serial number of 35607, unless you remember to increase the stop value to a number at least as high as the serial number of the ending date you want.

USING QUICKFILL

Another Quattro Pro option for filling blocks is QuickFill. Unlike Edit, Fill, Fill Series, QuickFill can fill a selected block with a set of labels, such as month names or store locations. You activate the QuickFill feature either by clicking the QuickFill button on the toolbar, or by choosing Edit, Fill, QuickFill.

The QuickFill option functions two ways, depending on whether the block you select already has sample values. If the block has sample values, these values are used as a pattern for filling the block. If the block is empty, QuickFill presents a list of predefined fill series for selection.

FILLING A BLOCK USING SAMPLE VALUES

Follow these steps to fill a block based on sample values enter in the block (such as Jan, Feb, Mar, or Qtr 1, Qtr 2, Qtr 3):

1. First enter some sample values in the top-left corner of the block that you want to fill. If the first sample value is enough to define the series, you have to enter only one value. If you want to use an increment other than 1, you must enter at least two sample values.

2. Select the block you want to fill. (Remember to include the cells containing the sample values you entered in step 1.)

3. Click the QuickFill button.

FILLING A BLOCK USING A QUICKFILL

You can also use a predefined series to fill a block. To fill a block based on a predefined series, follow these steps:

1. Select the block you want to fill. The block should not contain any sample values.

2. Click the QuickFill button to display the QuickFill dialog box (see Figure 22.8).

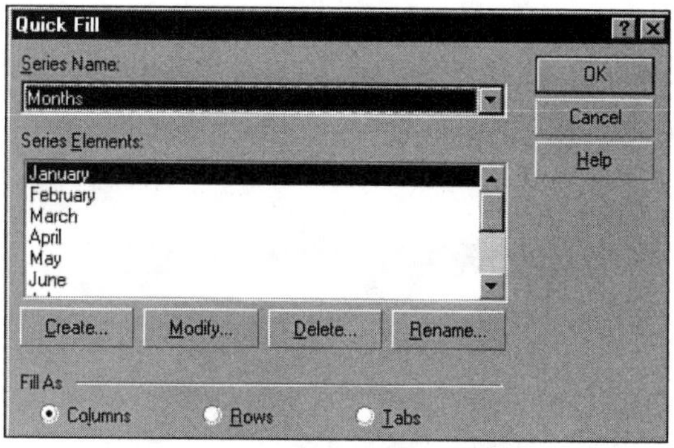

Figure 22.8
The QuickFill dialog box is used to fill a block based on a predefined series.

3. Select the series you want in the Series Name list box.

4. If necessary, select Columns, Rows, or Tabs; then click OK.

If you can't use QuickFill to name sheet tabs because the Tabs option doesn't appear in the QuickFill dialog box, see "Using QuickFill to Name Sheet Tabs" in the Troubleshooting section at the end of this chapter.

CREATING A CUSTOM QUICKFILL SERIES

Quattro Pro includes several predefined QuickFill series for entering months, quarters, and days, but this limited set of options is really only a sampling of what you can do with QuickFill. This tool can really make the task of creating a Quattro Pro notebook much easier by automatically entering any series of labels you want.

Imagine, for example, that you work for a company with 20 stores, and that you're often asked to create new analyses of sales data, advertising costs, or any other factors that affect your business' bottom line. Each time you create a notebook, you have to enter each of the stores' names, the sales representatives' names, or even the region names associated with store groupings. Sounds like quite a job, doesn't it? Fortunately, you can do the job just once by creating a custom QuickFill series.

Creating a custom QuickFill series is rather easy. You can enter the series as a set of labels in a dialog box, or you can even use a series of labels you've already entered in a notebook block. Modifying or deleting an existing series is just as easy. To create or modify a custom series, follow these steps:

1. Choose Edit, Fill, Define QuickFill to display the Define QuickFill Series dialog box (see Figure 22.9).

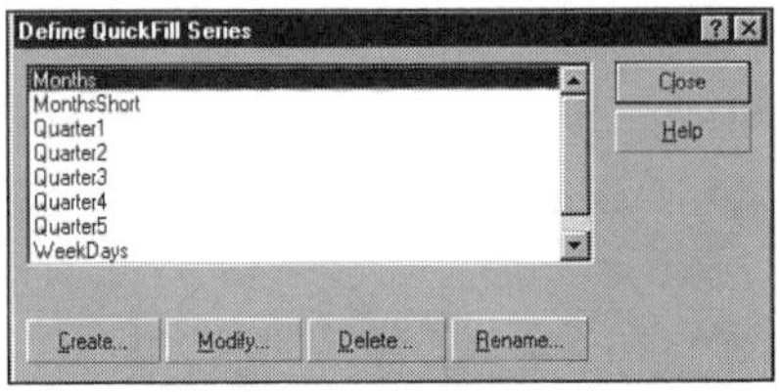

Figure 22.9
Using existing series to fill blocks is easy in the Define QuickFill Series dialog box.

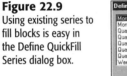

2. Select the Create or Modify button to display the Create Series or Modify Series dialog box. Figure 22.10 shows the Create/Modify Series dialog box.

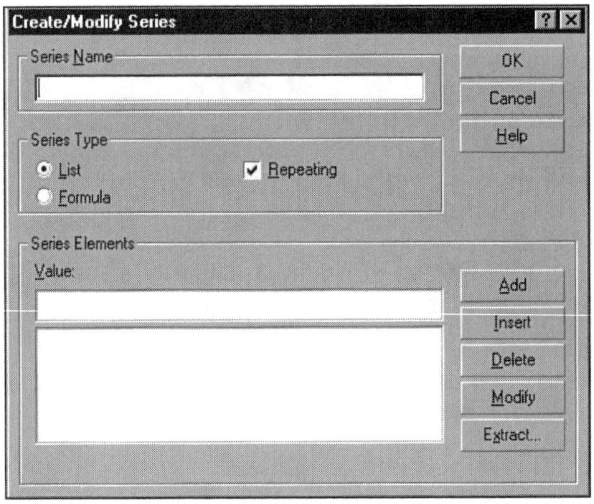

Figure 22.10
Use the Create/Modify Series dialog box to easily create a customized series for filling blocks.

3. Use the options in the Create Series or Modify Series dialog boxes to customize the fill series to suit your needs. For example, to create a custom series that automatically fills in your company's store locations, enter each location in the Series Elements text box and click Add. Continue until you have completed the series. Be sure to use a descriptive series name in the Create Series dialog box.

4. Click OK to confirm the dialog box.

> **Note**
>
> If the selected block is empty, you can also access the Create Series or Modify Series dialog boxes using the Create or Modify buttons in the QuickFill dialog box. If you use this method to access the Create Series or Modify Series dialog boxes, you can immediately use the new or modified series when you return to the QuickFill dialog box following step 4.

To use an existing series of labels in the Create Series or Modify Series dialog boxes, select Extract in step 3 and specify the notebook block containing the labels you want to save as a custom QuickFill series. For example, if you already have the set of store names in cells A1..A20, select Edit, Fill, Define QuickFill, Create, Extract and specify A1..A20 as the block to use.

Use custom QuickFill series to make repetitive notebook entries, even if the fill series is not an incrementing series. When you create a custom QuickFill series, it will be available for use in all your Quattro Pro notebooks. You don't have to save the custom QuickFill series; it is automatically saved for you.

VIEWING AND PRINTING FORMULAS

There are a couple of simple ways to catch errors in your formulas: View your formulas and print your formulas. If you want to look at the formulas in their cells in the spreadsheet, choose View, Formulas. To turn off showing the formulas, choose View, Formulas again.

To print your formulas, choose File, Page Setup. In the Spreadsheet Page Setup dialog box, click the Options tab. In the Print Options group, check the Cell Formulas check box and click OK. When you print the spreadsheet, Quattro Pro will print a list of all the cells that contain data. You will see the cell addresses and their content—numbers, labels, and formulas.

USING FUNCTIONS

As you learned in the previous chapter, the real power of a Quattro Pro notebook is its capability to perform calculations. You can create many different types of formulas and perform many different types of calculations quickly and easily in Quattro Pro. The built-in functions can make your formulas even more powerful, permitting you to perform calculations far too complex to build using simple arithmetic operators.

UNDERSTANDING FUNCTIONS

When electronic spreadsheets were introduced in the late 1970s, the programs included a few limited built-in functions. The calculations you could perform using these functions were fairly simple. When Lotus 1-2-3 made spreadsheets a standard business tool in the early 1980s, the program offered nearly 100 different functions, covering a wide range of calculations. Despite that, there were gaps in what the built-in functions offered, and PC users with specialized needs often had to resort to complex contortions, or had to turn to third-party developers to solve demanding equations.

Quattro Pro sets a new standard in spreadsheets by offering nearly 500 built-in functions, covering the bases with specialized functions for many unique types of calculations. Some of these functions perform sophisticated financial calculations; others conduct engineering calculations, execute various statistical analyses, or analyze database records. The following sections briefly summarize the function categories included in Quattro Pro.

Tip #142 from
Trudi Reisner

See the @Function Reference on the Contents tab of online help for a complete listing of the functions. You can view the function information by category or as a comprehensive alphabetical listing.

UNDERSTANDING DATABASE FUNCTIONS

You use database functions to perform statistical calculations and queries on a database. Each database function has an equivalent statistical function. Database functions differ from statistical functions in a very important way: Database functions calculate values that meet criteria you specify, whereas statistical functions calculate all values in a block.

For example, @DAVG finds the average value in a database's field, but only for records that meet specified criteria; @AVG finds the average value of all cells in a block.

UNDERSTANDING DATE AND TIME FUNCTIONS

You use the date and time functions to perform date and time arithmetic. These functions enable you to easily calculate differences between dates or times, sort by dates or times, and compare a range of dates or times. Date and time arithmetic uses date/time serial numbers.

For example, to convert a date into a date/time serial number, you can use the @DATE function to convert a date given as a year, month, and day into a date/time serial number. You can then use this serial number in additional calculations. You can use the @BDAYS function to find the number of business days between two dates.

UNDERSTANDING ENGINEERING FUNCTIONS

You use the engineering functions to perform calculations for solving complex engineering problems; perform binary, octal, decimal, and hexadecimal number manipulations; work with imaginary numbers; convert between numbering systems; and test results. The engineering functions return modified Bessel functions; join, compare, and shift values at the bit level; convert or modify a *complex number* (a number whose square is a negative real number); and return error functions or test the relationship of two numeric values.

For example, you use the @BASE function to convert a decimal number to another numbering system. You can use the @CONVERT function to convert between different systems of measurement, such as miles to kilometers.

UNDERSTANDING FINANCIAL FUNCTIONS

You use the financial functions to discount cash flow, calculate depreciation, and analyze the return on an investment. These functions greatly ease the burden of complex financial and accounting calculations. They also provide tools that allow the average user to perform less complex, everyday financial computations.

PART

III

CH

22

For example, you can use the @AMPMTI function to calculate the interest portion of the *n*th periodic payment of an amortized loan. You can use the @PRICEDISC function to calculate the price per $100 face value of a security that pays periodic interest.

Chapter 24, "Analyzing Data," provides a look at some additional Quattro Pro analysis tools.

UNDERSTANDING LOGICAL FUNCTIONS

You use the logical functions to add standard true/false logic to the spreadsheet. The logical functions evaluate Boolean expressions, which are either true (returning a value of 1) or false (returning a value of 0). These functions can help prevent errors that may occur if a cell used in a formula contains the wrong data, to test for the values ERR (error) or NA (not available), or to determine whether a specified file exists. These functions are important for decision making when conditions elsewhere in the spreadsheet lead to different answers in the function results. Logical functions also control the operations of advanced macro programs.

For example, you can use the @IF function to select between different results based upon evaluation of an expression, such as including a value only if it is positive.

UNDERSTANDING MATHEMATICAL FUNCTIONS

You use the mathematical functions to perform a variety of standard arithmetic operations, such as adding and rounding values or calculating square roots.

For example, you can use the @CEILING function to round a number up to the nearest integer, @RANDBETWEEN to generate a random number between two values, and @LN to calculate a number's natural logarithm.

UNDERSTANDING MISCELLANEOUS FUNCTIONS

You use the miscellaneous functions to determine information about notebooks and cell attributes, current command settings, system memory, object properties, and Quattro Pro's version number. You also use the miscellaneous functions to perform table lookups.

For example, you can use @CELL to determine whether a given cell is blank, contains a label, or contains a numeric value. You can determine the value contained in a given cell in a block using @INDEX. A single @ARRAY function can perform a series of calculations, producing many different results from a single formula.

UNDERSTANDING STATISTICAL FUNCTIONS

You use the statistical functions to perform all standard statistical calculations on your notebook data, such as aggregation, counting, and analysis operations on a group of values.

For example, you can use the @AVG function to determine the average of all numeric values in a list and @COUNT to determine the number of occupied cells in the list. You can use @CONFIDENCE to compute the confidence interval around the mean for a given sample size, using the normal distribution function.

UNDERSTANDING STRING FUNCTIONS

You use the string functions to manipulate text. You can use string functions to repeat text characters, convert letters in a string to upper- or lowercase, change strings to numbers, and change numbers to strings. You also can use string functions to locate, extract, or replace characters. String functions can be important when you need to convert data for use by other programs. They are invaluable when you need to read or write directly to ASCII text files.

@PROPER, for example, converts to uppercase the first letter of each word in a string; it converts the rest to lowercase. @REPLACE changes specified characters in a string to different characters. @STRING changes a numeric value into a string, making it possible to use the value in a string formula.

USING THE FORMULA COMPOSER

If these short descriptions of Quattro Pro's function categories have whetted your interest in using functions, you're probably wondering how you can ever build your own function formulas, especially with nearly 500 functions to select from. After all, a comprehensive description of each function, especially one with examples, would fill a complete book. How can you possibly get started, and how can you use the functions effectively in your formulas?

One answer to learning and using Quattro Pro's many functions is to turn to the Formula Composer, which is a calculator-like tool that helps you include functions in your formulas. Using this tool, you build formulas one step at a time, adding functions and supplying arguments as necessary. You can even see an outline of the formula as you build it, so you can be certain you're creating exactly what you need.

To use the Formula Composer, click the Formula Composer button on the toolbar. This displays the Formula Composer dialog box (see Figure 22.11). You use this dialog box to build your formula.

Figure 22.11
Use the Formula
Composer dialog box
to more easily create
formulas.

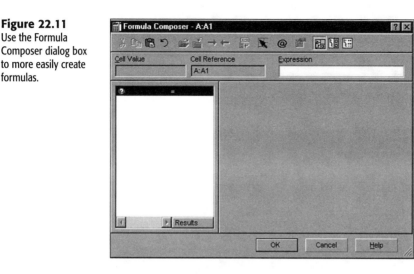

The Formula Composer functions like a sophisticated scientific calculator but has capabilities far beyond any calculator you can buy. If you want to use one of the Quattro Pro built-in functions, simply click the @ button in the Formula Composer dialog box toolbar. The Formula Composer adds the function you want to use to the formula. When you select a function, the right pane of the Formula Composer dialog box describes the selected function as well as any arguments.

For example, suppose you want to enter a formula in cell A1 that calculates the number of business days between June 26, 1997 and December 25, 1997. To make your formula flexible—to allow you to use the same formula to determine the number of business days between any other two dates—place the two dates in cells A2 and A3. This enables you to replace the dates in these two cells and instantly calculate new formula results. To begin building your formula, follow these steps:

1. Select cell A1 and then click the Formula Composer button on the toolbar (or press Ctrl+F2).

2. Click the @ button in the Formula Composer dialog box toolbar.

3. The Functions dialog box appears. Select Date in the Function Category list box and select BDAYS in the Function list box. As you select a function, the description pane at the bottom of the dialog box describes the selected function (see Figure 22.12).

4. Press Enter or click OK to return to the Formula Composer dialog box. The dialog box changes to display the function pane and describes the selected function, as well as its arguments (see Figure 22.13).

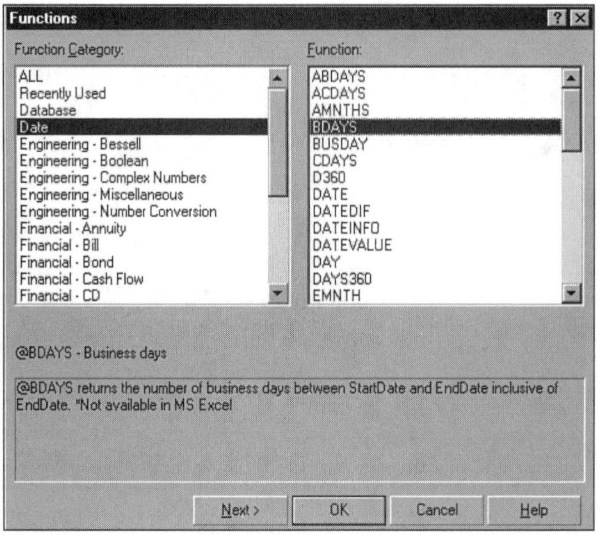

Figure 22.12
Use the Functions dialog box to select the function you want to use in the formula.

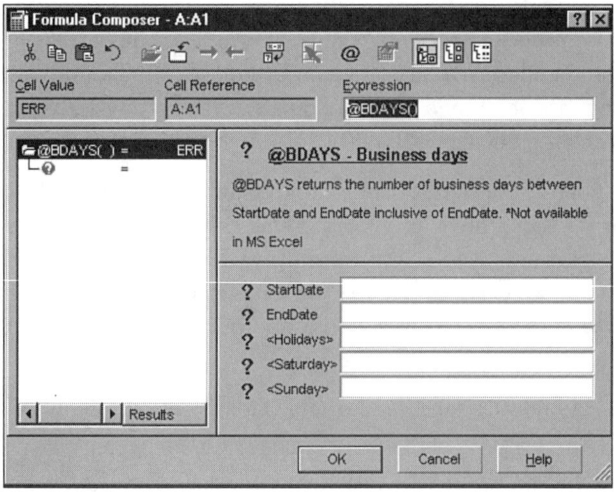

Figure 22.13
After you select a function, the Formula Composer dialog box displays the function pane into which you enter the required arguments.

5. Fill in each argument by selecting the argument's text box and then pointing to the notebook cell containing the argument. Click the Pointer button on the Formula Composer toolbar to shrink the Formula Composer dialog box. Select the notebook cells and click the Maximize button on the Formula Computer title bar to enlarge the dialog box. When you have entered the minimum required set of arguments, the dialog box displays the results of the calculation (see Figure 22.14). In this case, Holidays, Saturday, and Sunday are optional arguments and do not require an entry.

6. Click the OK button to return to the notebook and enter the formula in the cell.

Figure 22.14
After you specify all required arguments, the Formula Composer dialog box displays the result in the Cell Value box.

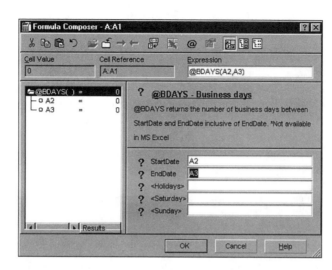

To enter any of the required or optional arguments in step 5, point to the cell containing the argument or type an address or block name. If you want to use another function to specify the value for an argument, click the @ button.

USING AUTO TOTAL

When you insert a total label above or next to a column or row of data, Quattro Pro automatically inserts a total for you. For example, if you have a column of numbers, type the word Total or Totals next to the cell where you want the total to appear and then press Enter. You'll see the formula and the result in the cell next to the word Total, as shown in Figure 22.15.

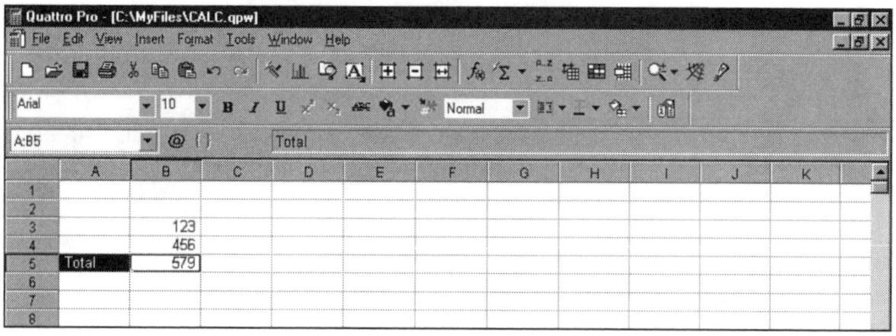

Figure 22.15
After you type the word *Total* next to a column (or row) of numbers and press Enter, AutoTotal automatically enters the formula and result for you.

USING SPEEDFUNCTIONS

The SpeedFunctions feature gives you a fast way to enter a function. SpeedFunctions provides 14 of the most commonly used functions, so that you don't have to remember how to spell the function name or enter the arguments for the function.

To use SpeedFunctions, select the cell where you want the result to appear and then click the small down arrow beside the Perform Calculations Using Common Functions button on the toolbar. A list of the common functions appears in a menu, as shown in Figure 22.16. Choose the function you want to use; Quattro Pro automatically inserts the function and shows the result in the selected cell.

Figure 22.16
Commonly used functions on the SpeedFunctions menu.

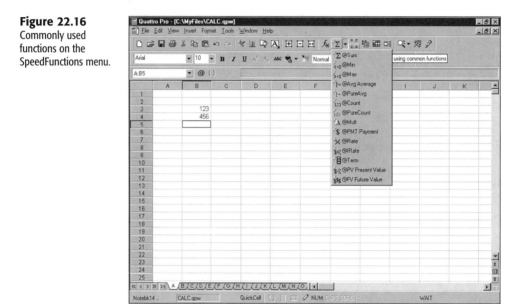

Tip #143 from
Trudi Reisner

The Perform Calculations Using Common Functions button on the Quattro Pro 9 toolbar has replaced the Quick Total button on the Quattro Pro 8 toolbar.

USING FORMULA TIPS TO CREATE FUNCTIONS

Complex functions or functions that you don't use often are difficult to create. When this is the case, you probably need to access Help to read up on what values, arguments, and order the function requires. With Quattro Pro's new Function Tip-As-You-Type features, you are guided through the process of building a function with QuickTips. Each value requested by the function displays a QuickTip with help information (see Figure 22.17), saving you time and hard work.

Figure 22.17
The Function Tip-As-You-Type feature guides you through the process of building a function with QuickTips.

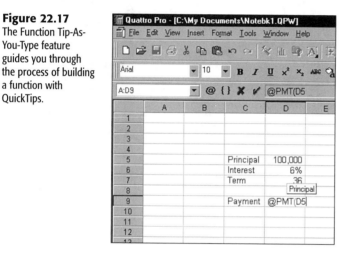

If you often have difficulty remembering which cells hold each of the function arguments, see "Labeling Function Arguments" in the Troubleshooting section at the end of this chapter.

Functions really unlock the power of Quattro Pro. The brief descriptions provided in these sections on using functions have only touched the surface of how powerful Quattro Pro's built-in functions really are.

PRACTICAL PROJECT

PerfectExpert has a project that is perfect for tracking weekly cash flow. Use the Weekly Cash Flow project in the Business Finance category to create the cash flow spreadsheet. Change the dates and then fill in the numbers for cash received, cash disbursed, and cash position. Enter the SUM function to total each column in the Cash Received and Cash Disbursed sections for each week. Use the SUM function to total the cash position for the end-of-month balance, as shown in Figure 22.18.

Figure 22.18
PerfectExpert's Weekly Cash Flow project.

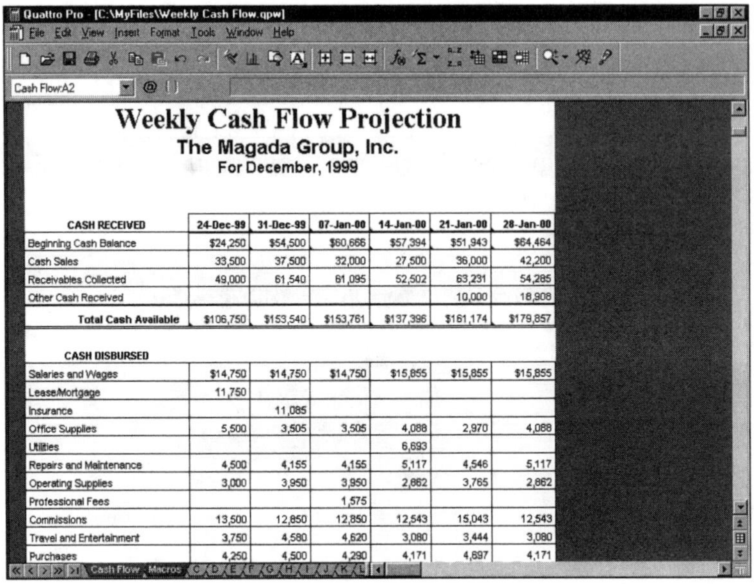

CASH RECEIVED	24-Dec-99	31-Dec-99	07-Jan-00	14-Jan-00	21-Jan-00	28-Jan-00
Beginning Cash Balance	$24,250	$54,500	$60,666	$57,394	$51,943	$64,464
Cash Sales	33,500	37,500	32,000	27,500	36,000	42,200
Receivables Collected	49,000	61,540	61,095	52,502	63,231	54,285
Other Cash Received					10,000	18,908
Total Cash Available	$106,750	$153,540	$153,761	$137,396	$161,174	$179,857
CASH DISBURSED						
Salaries and Wages	$14,750	$14,750	$14,750	$15,855	$15,855	$15,855
Lease/Mortgage	11,750					
Insurance		11,085				
Office Supplies	5,500	3,505	3,505	4,088	2,970	4,088
Utilities				6,693		
Repairs and Maintenance	4,500	4,155	4,155	5,117	4,546	5,117
Operating Supplies	3,000	3,950	3,950	2,862	3,765	2,862
Professional Fees			1,575			
Commissions	13,500	12,850	12,850	12,543	15,043	12,543
Travel and Entertainment	3,750	4,580	4,620	3,080	3,444	3,080
Purchases	4,250	4,500	4,290	4,171	4,697	4,171

TROUBLESHOOTING

ASKING THE PERFECTEXPERT FOR HELP

Sometimes it's difficult to determine where to find the command necessary to perform a task.

Try choosing Help, Ask the PerfectExpert for help on how to perform a task. The PerfectExpert will show you a number of topics relating to the task, and you can select the topic you want.

NAMING BLOCKS

Some formulas don't show the correct results even though they appear to contain correct block names.

Be certain your block names don't contain any mathematical operators, such as a plus or minus sign. Quattro Pro may be confused if you include these operators in block names that appear in formulas.

UPDATING THE BLOCK NAME TABLE

The block name table doesn't seem to show the correct addresses for some blocks.

If you change the definition of a block name, or add or delete block names, the block name table is not updated automatically. You must issue the Insert, Name, Cells, Output command again to update the table.

USING QUICKFILL TO NAME SHEET TABS

The Tabs option doesn't appear in the QuickFill dialog box, so I can't use QuickFill to name sheet tabs.

The Tabs option will appear only if an empty, single-cell block is selected when you click the QuickFill button. The same also applies to the Columns and Rows options. If the selected block consists of multiple cells in a single row or a single column, none of these options is available. Also, if the selected cell contains data, QuickFill will not display the QuickFill dialog box.

LABELING FUNCTION ARGUMENTS

It's often difficult to remember which cells hold each of the function arguments.

Enter labels in the notebook to identify the arguments; then use the Insert, Name, Cells, Labels command to name the cells. You can then use the block names instead of cell addresses in your formulas, making the formulas much easier to understand.

CHAPTER 23

CHANGING THE DISPLAY AND APPEARANCE OF DATA

In this chapter

CHANGING THE DISPLAY

The Quattro Pro display is extremely flexible, and allows you to select screen preferences. For example, you can zoom in to enlarge the onscreen appearance of a notebook on small screens. You can also control whether screen elements such as the toolbar, the property bar, or the application bar is displayed. These options exist for your convenience, but they don't really have much effect on the display of data or reports.

Some other options, such as adjusting the width of each column, or locking rows or columns onscreen as you scroll, directly affect your Quattro Pro notebooks. Column widths, for example, determine whether numbers are displayed properly. Locked titles enable you to scroll the display to different locations in the notebook without losing track of which type of data should be entered in the individual cells. These options are covered in the following sections.

ADJUSTING COLUMN WIDTHS AND ROW HEIGHTS

When you start a new notebook, all the columns on each sheet are set to the default column width of approximately nine characters. All the row heights are set to a default height of 12 points (one-sixth of an inch).

> **Note**
>
> Column widths are stated in characters, but are valid only for nonproportional (or fixed-pitch) fonts. Most Windows fonts are proportional fonts, allowing each character to have a different width, which is based on the actual space necessary to display a character. For example, the letter *m* requires more space than the letter *i*. In a proportional font, several *i*'s will fit in the space required for a single *m*.

If columns are too narrow to display numeric data, asterisks may appear rather than the numbers. If columns are too narrow for the length of labels and the cell to the right contains data, the labels are truncated. If columns are too wide, you might not see all the columns necessary to view the complete data, and you might not be able to print reports on the number of pages you want.

By default, Quattro Pro columns automatically widen to fit the numbers you enter in cells. If this doesn't happen when you enter numbers, the Fit-As-You-Go feature might not be enabled. To enable this feature, choose Tools, Settings; click the General tab, select Fit-As-You-Go, and then click OK (see Figure 23.1).

Quattro Pro automatically adjusts row heights to fit different fonts and point sizes, vertical orientation, or word wrap, but you can override the default to create special effects or to add emphasis. You can also adjust row heights in Quattro Pro to make notebook entries easier to understand and more attractive.

This number is too long to fit the default column width, so asterisks are displayed in place of the number.

When the column width is adjusted, the number displays correctly.

Figure 23.1
Sometimes you must adjust column widths or row heights.

Quattro Pro automatically adjusts row heights so larger font sizes are displayed correctly instead of being cut off.

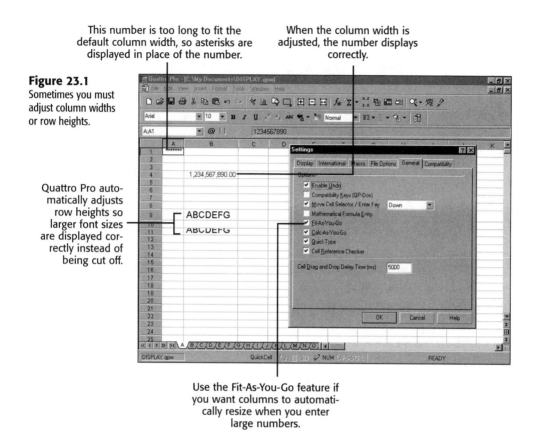

Use the Fit-As-You-Go feature if you want columns to automatically resize when you enter large numbers.

Figure 23.1 shows why you must sometimes adjust column widths or row heights. Cells A1 and B4 contain the same number: 1,234,567,890. Both cells are formatted to display the number using the comma numeric format with two decimals. Because column A is set to the default width, asterisks appear in place of the number in cell A1. The width of column B was adjusted to correctly display the number. Even though Quattro Pro automatically adjusts row heights to fit different fonts and point sizes, as shown in row 9 of Figure 23.1, you can make manual adjustments, too. In the figure, the height of row 11 was adjusted to show how Quattro Pro cuts off the tops of characters if a row is too short.

SETTING COLUMN WIDTHS

Whether a number fits in a cell depends on the column width, the numeric format, the font type, and the font size. If a number appears as a series of asterisks, you need to enable the Fit-As-You-Go feature (as described in the preceding section), or change the column width, numeric format, font type, font size, or some combination of these factors.

Tip #144 from
Trudi Reisner

Column widths you set manually do not change if you later change the default column width for the sheet.

You can change the width of a single column or a group of columns. When you are adjusting the column width, Quattro Pro displays a dashed line to indicate the position of the new column border. If you move the right column border to the left of the left border, you hide the column.

 There are several methods you can use to set column widths. You can select the Active Cells dialog box; either click the QuickFit button or drag a column width using the mouse. Each method may be useful, depending on your needs.

To change column widths by dragging with the mouse, follow these steps:

1. If you want to adjust more than one column at a time, select the columns you want to adjust by pointing to the column letter in the spreadsheet frame and clicking. (Drag the mouse pointer to select adjacent columns.) If the columns are not adjacent, hold down the Ctrl key as you select the columns.

2. Point to the column border to the right of the column letter (in the spreadsheet frame). The mouse pointer changes into a horizontal double arrow.

3. Press and hold the left mouse button.

4. Drag the column border left or right until the column is the width you want. Notice that the application bar lists the current column width as you drag the column border. Release the mouse button.

Note

If the columns aren't adjacent, you need to drag the rightmost column edge to widen and drag the right side of the leftmost column to make the columns narrower.

Tip #145 from
Trudi Reisner

To reveal columns after they have been hidden, select the columns that surround the hidden columns, right-click, select Column Properties, select the Row/Column tab, select Reveal in the Column Options area, and click OK. To hide columns, refer to the explanation at the beginning of this section.

To change column widths using the Active Cells dialog box, perform the following steps:

1. Select a block of cells containing each column whose width you want to adjust. You can use the keyboard or the mouse to select adjacent columns, but you can select only nonadjacent columns when using the mouse.

2. Right-click inside the selection to activate the QuickMenu, and then select Cell Properties to display the Active Cells dialog box (see Figure 23.2).

Figure 23.2
You can use the Active Cells dialog box to change column width settings.

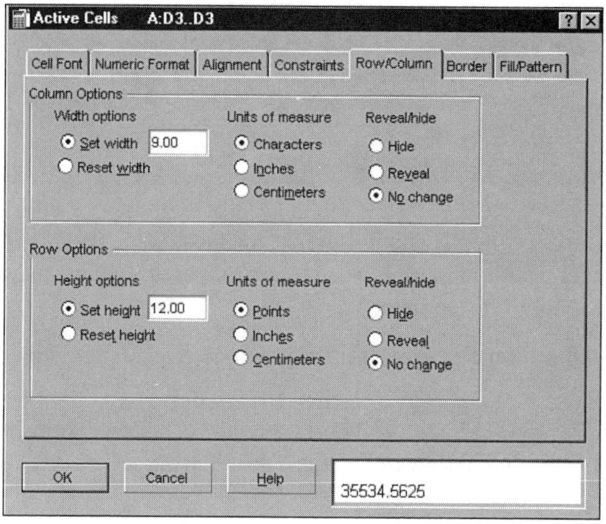

PART

III

CH

23

Tip #146 from
Trudi Reisner

You can press F12 to activate the Active Cells dialog box.

3. Select the Row/Column tab, if necessary.

4. If you want to enter the column width in inches or centimeters rather than characters, choose the appropriate option button under Units of Measure in the Column Options area.

5. If you want to reset the column width, select Reset Width to return the selected columns to the sheet default column width.

6. If you want to specify the column width, type the value in the Set Width text box.

7. Click OK to confirm the dialog box.

You also can click the QuickFit button on the toolbar to adjust the widths of columns automatically. The width of columns set using the QuickFit button depends on the number of rows selected when you adjust the width. If you select a single row, the column width adjusts to fit the longest data below the cell selector in the entire column. If you select more than one row, the column width adjusts to fit the cell with the longest data below the cell selector in the same column.

Tip #147 from
Trudi Reisner

The QuickFit button can be used only on contiguous blocks.

Tip #148 from
Trudi Reisner

If you prefer to use the mouse instead of the QuickFit button, move the mouse pointer to the column border on the right side of the column you want to change. The mouse pointer changes into a horizontal double arrow; double-click the column border.

SETTING THE DEFAULT COLUMN WIDTH FOR A SHEET

If you find yourself setting the column widths for most columns on a sheet, you can change the default column width for the entire notebook sheet. To select a new default column width for a sheet, follow these steps:

1. Right-click the sheet tab and select Sheet Properties to display the Active Sheet dialog box.

2. Select the Default Width tab and enter the new default width in characters, inches, or centimeters, depending on which Unit option button you choose.

3. Click OK to confirm the dialog box.

Each sheet in a notebook has its own default column width setting. You change the default column width setting for each sheet individually.

 If some columns don't adjust when a new default column width is set for a notebook sheet, see "Setting the Default Column Width for a Sheet" in the Troubleshooting section at the end of this chapter.

SETTING ROW HEIGHTS

You can adjust row heights in Quattro Pro to make notebook entries easier to understand and more attractive. As you change fonts and point sizes or apply vertical orientation or word wrap, Quattro Pro automatically adjusts row heights to fit the data. However, you can override the default to create special effects or to add emphasis.

You can set the row height for an individual row or a group of rows at one time. You also can hide rows by setting their height to 0. You can set row heights by using the Active Cells dialog box and by dragging the row height using the mouse. By default, Quattro Pro automatically adjusts row heights to fit cell data. The new Auto Row Height feature lets you adjust row heights automatically.

To adjust the height of rows by dragging with the mouse, follow these steps:

1. Select the rows you want to adjust. If the rows are not adjacent, hold down the Ctrl key as you select them.

2. Point to the row border just below the row number (in the spreadsheet frame). The mouse pointer changes into a vertical double arrow.

3. Press and hold down the left mouse button.

4. Drag the row border up or down until the row is the height you want. Notice that the application bar lists the current row height as you drag the row border. Release the mouse button. When you are adjusting the row height, Quattro Pro displays a dashed

line to indicate the position of the new row border. If you move the lower row border above the top border, you hide the row.

Tip #149 from
Trudi Reisner

To reveal rows after they have been hidden, select the rows that surround the hidden rows, right-click, select Row Properties, and select the Row/Column tab. Select Reveal in the Row Options area and click OK.

To change the height of rows by using the Active Cells dialog box, follow these steps:

1. Select the rows you want to adjust. If the rows are not adjacent, hold down the Ctrl key as you select the rows by using the mouse. If you want to adjust the height of adjacent rows, place the cell selector in the first row you want to adjust, hold down the Shift key, and move the cell selector to select each of the rows you want to adjust.

2. Right-click inside the selection to activate the QuickMenu, and select Cell Properties to display the Active Cells dialog box (refer to Figure 23.2).

3. Select the Row/Column tab.

4. If you want to enter the row height in inches or centimeters rather than points, select the appropriate option button under Units of Measure in the Row Options area.

5. If you want to reset the row height, choose Reset Height to return the selected rows to automatic.

6. If you want to specify the row height, type the value in the Set Height text box.

7. Click OK to confirm the dialog box.

Quattro Pro's new Auto Row Height feature lets you automatically adjust the heights of rows. Auto Row Height is similar to QuickFit, except there is no QuickFit button for adjusting row height; you must use the mouse.

To adjust row height automatically, first point to a row border below the row number in the spreadsheet frame. The mouse pointer changes into a vertical double arrow. Double-click the row border. The row height is automatically adjusted to fit the tallest entry in that row.

REMOVING COLUMNS, ROWS, OR SHEETS

Sometimes you might want to delete sections from a notebook. Perhaps you made extra copies of some data while you were creating the notebook, or you simply rearranged a notebook and have some unsightly gaps you'd like to eliminate.

Tip #150 from
Trudi Reisner

Don't forget to use Edit, Undo immediately if you delete the wrong data in error.

You can remove part or all of a notebook in several ways. Any data that you remove is cleared from the notebook in memory but does not affect the notebook file on disk until you save the notebook file. Edit, Undo can restore the data if you use the command before making any other changes.

Some Quattro Pro commands (such as Edit, Cut; Edit, Clear, Cells; or Edit, Clear, Values) erase cell contents, but leave behind blank cells. In contrast, after you delete a row, column, or sheet, Quattro Pro deletes the row, column, or notebook sheet and moves remaining data to fill the gap created by the deletion. Cell addresses in formulas are also updated when you delete a row, column, or sheet.

To delete a row, column, or sheet, follow these steps:

1. Choose Edit, Delete. Quattro Pro displays the Delete dialog box (see Figure 23.3).

Figure 23.3
Use the Delete dialog box to select the cells you want to eliminate.

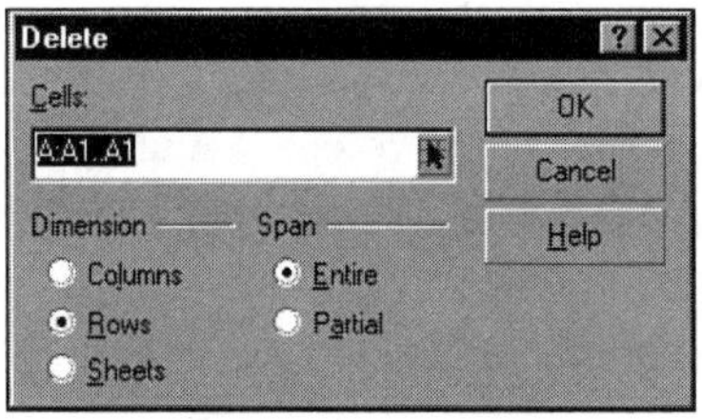

2. In the Cells text box, specify the cells you want to delete. You can type the address, select cells, or preselect the cells.

3. Select the Columns, Rows, or Sheets option button.

4. Select the Entire or Partial option button.

5. Click OK to confirm the dialog box and delete the block.

Note

Deleting a column, row, or sheet does not reduce the number of columns, rows, or sheets in the notebook. Quattro Pro replaces the deleted columns, rows, or sheets at the end of the sheet or the notebook, so each sheet continues to have 256 columns and 8,192 rows; each notebook continues to have 256 sheets.

When you delete an area, Quattro Pro moves data to fill the gap created by the deletion. If you delete a row, data below the deletion moves up on the current sheet. If you delete a column, data to the right of the deleted column moves to the left. If you delete a sheet, data on following sheets moves forward in the notebook.

Formula references adjust to reflect the new addresses of the data. If you delete rows 5 and 6, for example, the formula @SUM(A1..A10) becomes @SUM(A1..A8). If a formula refers specifically to a deleted cell, however, the formula returns ERR.

If you delete rows, columns, or sheets that are part of a named block, the block becomes smaller. If you delete a row, column, or sheet that contains one of the block borders, the block becomes undefined and any references to the block return ERR.

You don't have to delete an entire row, column, or sheet. You may want to delete only part of a row, column, or sheet, and move remaining data to fill the gap. To accomplish this task, choose the Partial option button. When you specify Partial as the span, Quattro Pro does not remove data from surrounding rows, columns, or sheets.

INSERTING COLUMNS, ROWS, OR SHEETS

You also can insert rows, columns, or sheets anywhere in the notebook. After you insert a row, column, or sheet, all existing data below, to the right, or on subsequent notebook sheets moves to create room for the new data. Cell references in formulas and block names adjust automatically, but explicit cell addresses in macros do not adjust. If you make an insertion in the middle of a block, the block expands to include the new rows, columns, or sheets. Formulas referring to that block automatically include the added cells.

PART

III

CH

23

> **Note**
>
> Inserting a column, row, or sheet does not increase the number of columns, rows, or sheets in the notebook. Each sheet continues to have 256 columns and 8,192 rows. If Quattro Pro cannot delete the columns, rows, or sheets at the end of the sheet or the notebook because data would be lost, an error message is displayed and the insertion fails.

To insert a row, column, or sheet, perform the following steps:

1. Move the cell selector to the cell where you want to begin inserting.
2. Choose Insert, Cells. In the Insert Cells dialog box, select Columns, Rows, or Sheets.
3. Select the number of rows, columns, or sheets you want to insert.

> **Note**
>
> If you selected entire rows, columns, or sheets in step 2, Quattro Pro automatically performs the insertion without displaying the Insert Cells dialog box.

4. To insert a partial row, column, or sheet, select the Partial option button.
5. Click OK to confirm the dialog box and make the insertion.

LOCKING DATA ONSCREEN

Notebook sheets often are too large to display all the data at one time. As you move the cell selector to display different areas of the sheet, data scrolls off the opposite edge of the display. This can make it difficult to understand data because you can't see the labels describing the data. To prevent titles from scrolling off the screen, you can lock a number of rows and columns so they remain onscreen as you move the cell selector.

Before you lock rows or columns to keep them onscreen, you need to position the cell selector to tell Quattro Pro which rows or columns you want to remain visible. If you are locking horizontal titles, place the cell selector in the row below the last row you want locked. If you are locking vertical titles, place the cell selector in the column to the right of the last column you want locked. If you are locking both horizontal and vertical titles, place the cell selector in the row just below and the column just right of the intersection of the rows and columns you want to lock.

After you position the cell selector properly, choose View, Locked Titles. Quattro Pro displays blue lines to indicate the position of the locked titles. As you scroll the worksheet, data above and to the left of the blue lines remains onscreen.

Figure 23.4 shows a Quattro Pro notebook with an address database. In this figure, the cell selector was placed in cell B2 before issuing the View, Locked Titles command. The cell selector was then moved to cell H46, the last cell in the database. Column A and row 1 remain visible, enabling you to more easily understand the data because you can see both the field names (row 1) and the value contained in the LAST_NAME field (column A).

Figure 23.4
Titles locked onscreen can make data easier to understand.

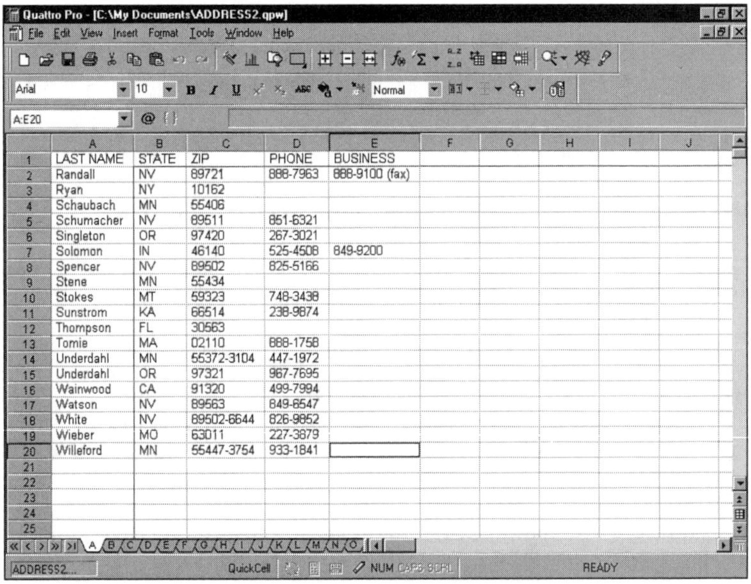

When rows or columns are locked onscreen, pressing the Home key moves the cell selector to the position below and to the right of the titles rather than to cell A1. You can use the mouse or the navigational keys to move the cell selector into the locked titles, however.

CHANGING THE APPEARANCE OF DATA

How your data appears in a notebook or in a report really doesn't affect the data, but it can have a major effect on how well people understand the data. Appearance can also make quite a difference in how people perceive your business. A well-prepared financial statement, for example, might not guarantee that small business loan, but you'd probably feel more comfortable presenting your banker something that looked professional and polished.

A few simple steps can greatly improve the appearance of data. Simply applying the proper numeric format can change 1234567 into $1,234,567.00, changing raw data into a value anyone can quickly understand. In addition to numeric formats, you can use alignment, different fonts, borders, and shading to turn an ordinary report into something that is much more. The following sections show you some of the options that can improve the appearance of your Quattro Pro notebooks.

USING NUMERIC FORMATS

You can display data in a cell in a variety of different numeric formats. Quattro Pro offers a wide choice of numeric formats, which you access through the Active Cells dialog box. Most formats apply only to numeric data, although Text format can apply to string formulas, and Hidden format can apply to any type of data.

Formatting changes the appearance but not the value of data. The number 7892, for example, can be displayed as 7,892, $7,892.00, or 789200.0%, as well as many other formats. No matter how Quattro Pro displays the number in a cell, the actual value remains the same.

To change the numeric format of a cell or block, follow these steps:

1. Select the cell or block.
2. Choose Format, Selection or right-click the cell or block and select Cell Properties from the QuickMenu.
3. Select the Numeric Format tab. The default General format is selected, as shown in Figure 23.5, if no numeric format has been assigned. Select the desired numeric format.

Figure 23.5
Select a numeric format from the Active Cells dialog box.

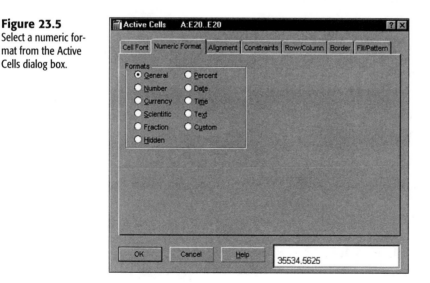

4. If you chose Number, Currency, Scientific, or Percent, enter the number of decimal places in the spin control that appears after you choose one of these formats. Quattro Pro suggests a default of two decimal places, but you can type another number between 0 and 15.

5. Click OK to confirm the dialog box and apply the format to the selected cell or block.

The following sections briefly describe Quattro Pro's numeric format options.

If you format a block and some cells display asterisks instead of values, see "Displaying Values Rather Than Asterisks" in the Troubleshooting section at the end of this chapter.

GENERAL FORMAT

General format is the default format for all new notebooks. Numbers in General format have no thousands separators and no zeros to the right of the decimal point. A minus sign precedes negative numbers. If a number contains decimal digits, it contains a decimal point. If a number contains too many digits to the right of the decimal point to display in the current column width, the decimals are rounded in the display. If a number is too large or too small, it appears in Scientific format.

NUMBER FORMAT

You use the Number format when you want to display values with a specified, fixed number of decimal points. Quattro Pro displays values up to 15 decimal places. Negative numbers follow a minus sign, and decimal values have a leading zero. No punctuation is used to denote thousands.

The comma is available when you select the Number format and select the Use 1000 Separator check box. This option displays data with a fixed number of decimal places and thousands punctuation. The thousands separator and the decimal point depend on the current international settings. Negative numbers appear with a minus sign in front of them or with parentheses, and positive numbers less than 1,000 appear the same as Number format.

If a value has more decimal digits than the cell can display using the specified number of decimal places, the displayed value is rounded but the stored value is used in calculations.

CURRENCY FORMAT

Currency format displays values with a currency symbol, such as a dollar sign ($), or the British pound sign (£), and punctuation, depending on the current international settings. When you select the Currency option in the Active Cells dialog box, a list box appears from which you can select the name of the country. When you click the name of a country, the Preview box displays how the number will appear. If you specify a currency symbol, the column width needs an extra position to display each character in the currency symbol. Values formatted as Currency can have from 0 to 15 decimal places. Thousands are separated by commas, periods, or spaces according to the current international settings. Negative numbers appear with a minus sign in front of them or with parentheses. Click the option in the Negative Numbers preview box.

The Accounting option is nearly identical to the Currency format discussed earlier in this section. The primary difference is the location of the currency symbol. In the Accounting format (depending on which country you choose), the symbol might appear left-justified in the cell rather than immediately preceding the number. This format is easier to read if you are working with multiple columns of currency data.

Choose the Currency format and check the Use Accounting Alignment check box to format numbers with the Accounting option.

> **Note**
>
> The Euro currency symbol is available in Quattro Pro 9. To format your data with the Euro, choose Currency in the Formats section, and choose Euro from the box where you select a country.

SCIENTIFIC FORMAT

You use the Scientific format to display very large or very small numbers. Such numbers usually have a few significant digits and many zeros.

A number in scientific notation has two parts: a mantissa and an exponent. The *mantissa* is a number from 1 to 10 that contains the significant digits. The *exponent* tells you how many places to move the decimal point to get the number's actual value.

If a number has more significant digits than the cell can display using the specified number of decimal places, the displayed value is rounded, but the stored value is used in calculations.

FRACTION FORMAT

You use the Fraction format when you want to display a value as a fraction, such as $3/4$. If the number can be confused as a date, however, you should format the cell before you enter the number. The Fraction format also enables you to choose whether Quattro Pro should reduce the fraction for you; in addition, you can specify a set denominator for the fraction.

HIDDEN FORMAT

A cell or block formatted as Hidden always appears blank. You use Hidden format for intermediate calculations that you don't want to appear in a final report, or for sensitive formulas you don't want displayed. The contents of a Hidden cell appear in the input line when you select the cell, so keep in mind that Hidden format offers little security.

PERCENT FORMAT

Percent format is used to display values as percentages with 0 to 15 decimal places. The number appears with its value multiplied by 100, followed by a percent sign (%). The number of decimal places you specify is for the number displayed with the percentage sign in the cell, not the number of decimal places in the value that appears on the input line.

If a value has more decimal digits than the cell can display using the specified number of decimal places, the displayed value is rounded but the stored value is used in calculations.

DATE FORMAT

Date formats display date serial numbers as dates rather than as numbers. Quattro Pro stores dates as serial numbers starting with January 1, 1600 (which is –109571) and increases the number by 1 for each whole day. December 31, 1899 is counted as 1. The latest date Quattro Pro can display is December 31, 3199, with a serial number of 474816.

If the number is less than –109571 or greater than 474816, a date format appears as asterisks. Date formats ignore decimal fractions; 34876.55 with a short international date format appears as 6/26. The decimal portion of a date serial number represents the time as a fraction of a 24-hour clock.

Quattro Pro gives you a choice of five different Date display formats, plus the Long Data Intl. and Short Date Intl. Date formats. Both Long Date Intl. and Short Date Intl. depend on the current international date format set using the Settings dialog box, with the International tab and the Date Format option.

TIME FORMAT

You use the time formats to display date serial numbers as times. The decimal portion of a date serial number is a time fraction. The time fraction represents a fraction of a 24-hour day. For example, the time fraction for 8 a.m. is .3333, the time fraction for noon is .5, and the time fraction for 3 p.m. is .675. When you use a Time format, Quattro Pro displays the fraction as a time.

If a date serial number is greater than 1, the time formats ignore the integer portion. Both .5 and 33781.5 display 12:00:00 P.M.

Quattro Pro gives you a choice of two time-display formats. Both Long Time Intl. and Short Time Intl. depend on the current international time format set using the Application dialog box.

TEXT FORMAT

You use Text format to display the text of formulas rather than their results. Numbers in cells formatted as text appear in General format. Unlike long labels that appear in blank cells to the right, formulas formatted as text are truncated if they are too long to display in the column width. Quattro Pro continues to use the value of formulas when you format them as text.

CUSTOM FORMAT

Quattro Pro enables you to define and apply your own numeric formats. Custom formats can include many different elements. For example, you can include text, the names of days or months, or leading zeros.

There are more custom numeric formats available in Quattro Pro, including font attributes, cell attributes, and conditional formatting (explained later in this chapter). To use a predefined custom format, choose Custom and then select any one of the formats listed in the Custom Formats list box. Click Edit to modify a custom format; click Add to create your own format. When you create a custom numeric format, give the custom format a name and define the format.

→ For more information on creating your own numeric formats, **see** "Working with Custom Formats" in the Quattro Pro Help system.

→ For detailed information on conditional formatting, **see** "Using Conditional Formatting," **p. 426**

AVOIDING APPARENT ERRORS WITH FORMATTING

Some formats display a number in rounded form. Even when the displayed number appears rounded, however, Quattro Pro stores and uses the exact value in calculations. If you format the value 1.5 as Number with zero decimal places, Quattro Pro displays the number as 2 in a cell, but uses the actual value of 1.5 in calculations. This can make it seem as though Quattro Pro is making arithmetic errors, such as 2+2=3. In fact, Quattro Pro is correct because the two values it is adding are 1.5 and 1.5; the formula is therefore actually 1.5+1.5=3. Rounding the display but not rounding the values causes this apparent error.

> **Caution**
>
> You easily can create apparent rounding errors—especially when you produce cross-tabulated reports. To avoid apparent rounding errors, you need to round the actual value of the numbers used in formulas, not just their appearance or format. To round the values used in a formula, use the @ROUND function to round each value before the value is used in the formula.

ALIGNING DATA

Just as Quattro Pro offers a very broad range of numeric format options, it also provides quite a few choices for aligning labels and values. By default, labels are aligned to the left side of cells and values are aligned to the right side of cells. These default alignments are easily changed. You can change alignment for both labels and values.

You can align labels and values to the left or right side of cells, or center them in a cell or across a block. You can also align them to the top, center, or bottom of the cell, and indent them from the edge of the cell. You can orient labels and values horizontally or vertically. Finally, you can wrap text on multiple lines in a single cell and join multiple cells to form a single cell.

Tip #151 from
Trudi Reisner

You can also change horizontal alignment using the Alignment button on the property bar.

To change the label alignment for existing labels or values, follow these steps:

1. Select the cell or block.

2. Right-click the selection and choose Cell Properties from the QuickMenu.

3. Select the Alignment tab in the Active Cells dialog box (see Figure 23.6).

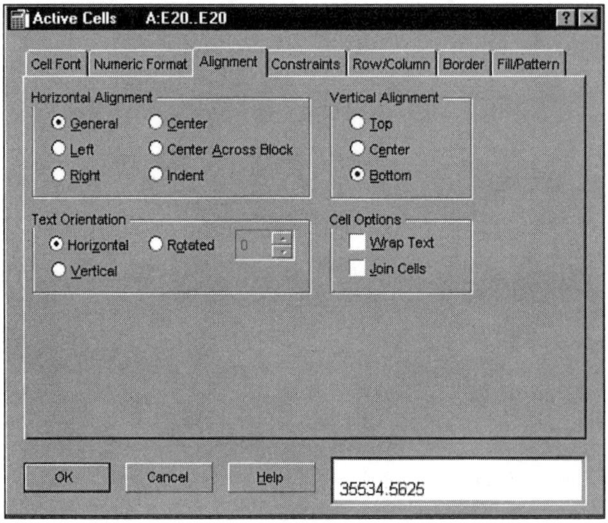

Figure 23.6
Use the Alignment section of the Active Cells dialog box to specify data alignment.

4. In the Horizontal Alignment area, choose General to reset the alignment to the sheet default; alternatively, choose Left, Right, Center, Center Across Block, or Indent.

5. In the Vertical Alignment area, choose Top, Center, or Bottom.

6. In the Text Orientation area, decide whether you want horizontal, vertical, or rotated text. If you choose Rotated, specify the degrees to rotate the text in the spin box that appears when you choose this option.

7. In the Cell Options area, select the Wrap Text check box to wrap labels on multiple lines within a single cell; select Join Cells if you want to merge the selected cells into a single cell.

8. Click OK to confirm the dialog box and apply the selected alignment options.

Figure 23.7 demonstrates the various horizontal and vertical alignment and orientation options.

Figure 23.7
Quattro Pro offers many horizontal and vertical alignment and orientation options.

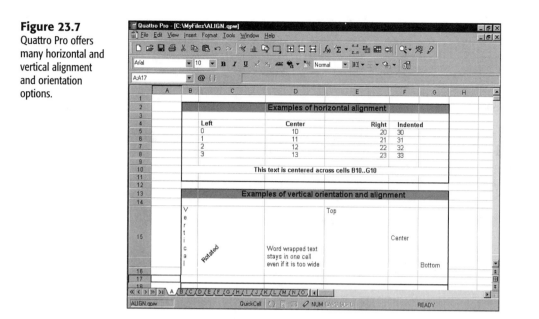

CHANGING FONTS

Quattro Pro applies the term *font* to the combination of typeface, point size, and attributes used for the characters displayed in your notebooks. A *typeface* is a type style, such as Arial, Courier New, or Times New Roman. Typefaces are available in a number of point sizes that represent character height. A standard 10 character-per-inch (cpi) size usually is considered equivalent to a 12-point type size. Typefaces also have different attributes, such as weight (normal or bold) and italic.

You can use the Cell Font tab in the Active Cells dialog box to choose different fonts. You can also use the Font and Font Size buttons on the property bar to make these two selections, and the Bold, Italic, and Underline buttons to apply any of these attributes.

Several factors determine which font options are available. If you have installed additional fonts on your system, you can select from a larger list of options. Scalable fonts, such as TrueType fonts, greatly improve the quality of your reports. Corel includes more than 1,000 additional fonts on the Corel WordPerfect Office 2000 CD-ROM, which you can install using custom install and selecting TrueType Fonts under the Corel WordPerfect Suite Setup install option.

If you increase font size, Quattro Pro enlarges the row height to fit the selected fonts. Column widths do not adjust automatically, however, so numeric data may not fit in a cell after you change the font, and the data may display as asterisks. Adjust the column widths as needed to display the data correctly. Figure 23.8 shows how several typefaces, point sizes, and attributes change your data's appearance. (You probably will have a different selection of fonts installed on your system.)

Figure 23.8
Different fonts change the appearance of data in your notebooks.

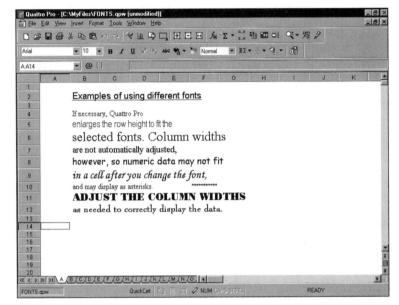

With Quattro Pro's new Real Time Preview feature, you can experiment with formatting and preview formatting before you apply it to your spreadsheet data.

When you point to a font face or font size in a drop-down menu on the property bar, Quattro Pro shows a preview of your font selection in two locations. You see a Preview window beneath the property bar with all or a portion of the selected text.

Each time you select a font face or size, Quattro Pro displays the font change for the text in the Preview window. You also see a preview of the font change on the spreadsheet before you apply it.

INSERTING SYMBOLS

Sometimes you might need to insert a special symbol into your spreadsheet. Quattro Pro offers a wide range of symbols such as typographic symbols, mathematical and technical operators for complex formulas, Greek letters, trademark and copyright marks, and other special characters and symbols.

To insert symbols, carry out these steps:

1. Select the cell that will contain the symbol.

2. Choose Insert, Symbol or click the WP Characters button on the toolbar. The Symbols dialog box appears (see Figure 23.9).

Figure 23.9
The Symbols dialog box is used for inserting symbols into your spreadsheets.

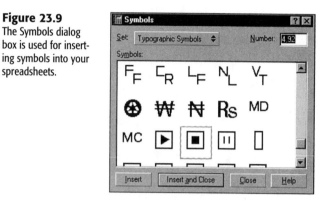

3. The symbol sets menu appears when you click the Set button.

4. Choose a symbol set.

5. Select a symbol from the Symbols section.

6. Click Insert and continue selecting symbols if necessary. Click Insert and Close when you're finished selecting symbols.

ADDING BORDERS AND SHADING

If you really want to add a professional touch to your notebooks, borders and shading can do the trick. *Borders* are lines around a cell or block. *Shading* is a background tint within a cell or block.

You can use borders to effectively isolate groups of data, making it easy to see all related data. You can also use borders as separators between report sections. Shading is most often used for emphasis, or to make certain report data cannot be altered without the alterations being immediately apparent.

ADDING BORDERS TO CELLS OR BLOCKS

You can use the Border tab in the Active Cells dialog box to draw lines above, below, on the sides, and around cells and blocks. You can also use the Line Drawing button on the Property Bar to draw lines at the bottom of cells or blocks. Borders can be single lines, double lines, or thick lines.

To draw borders within or around a cell or block, follow these steps:

1. Select the cell or block.
2. Right-click inside the selection and choose Cell Properties from the QuickMenu.
3. Select the Border tab (see Figure 23.10).

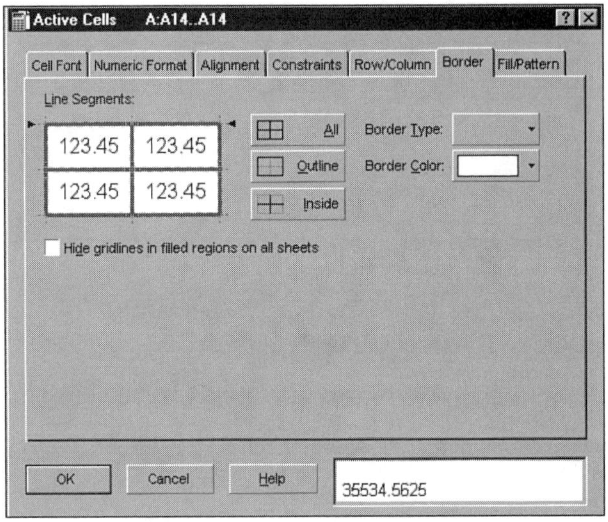

Figure 23.10
Use the Border options in the Active Cells dialog box to add borders to cells or blocks.

4. Select the placement options you want using the Line Segments, All, Outline, and Inside options.
5. Select the border type you want.
6. Select the border color you want.
7. Click OK to confirm the dialog box and add the selected borders.

ADDING SHADING TO CELLS OR BLOCKS

You can draw attention to cells or blocks by adding *shading*, a special effect that changes the background from white to a color. When you select shading, you also can select the blend of two colors.

To add shading, follow these steps:

1. Select the cell or block.
2. Right-click inside the selection and choose Cell Properties from the QuickMenu.
3. Select the Fill/Pattern tab and then select the Pattern Color option.
4. In the Pattern Color palette, select a background and pattern color.
5. Select a shading pattern from the Shading palette (see Figure 23.11). Quattro Pro enables you to select from 25 shading patterns.

Note

Quattro Pro applies a shading pattern only to cells that contain data, not blank cells.

Figure 23.11
Use the options in the Shading palette to add shading to cells or blocks.

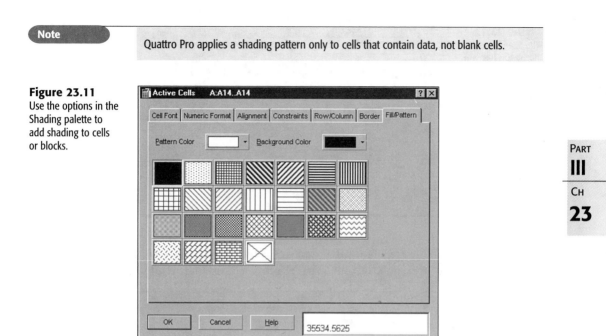

6. Click OK on the Fill/Pattern tab to apply the shading.

Caution

Not all printers can properly print text on a shaded background. Test printing shades on your printer.

Any borders or shading you add to cells or blocks print with the labels and values in a report. It's generally best to use light shading in cells or blocks containing values that must be visible in a printed report, or one that must be photocopied.

Using SpeedFormat

Quattro Pro also has several predefined formats called *SpeedFormats*, which enable you to quickly set combinations of numeric and text formatting, lines, and shading. SpeedFormats take some of the pain out of formatting your spreadsheets.

These steps show you how to use SpeedFormats:

1. Select the block you want to format.

2. Choose Format, SpeedFormat or click the SpeedFormat button on the toolbar. Alternatively, press Ctrl+Shift+F. The SpeedFormat dialog box comes up, as shown in Figure 23.12.

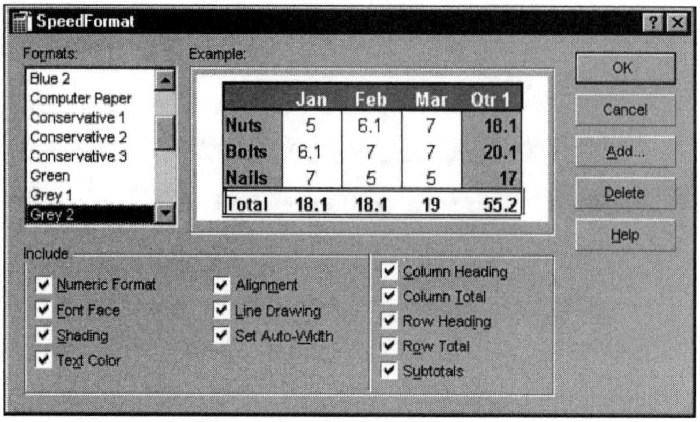

Figure 23.12
The SpeedFormat dialog box lets you format your spreadsheet with predefined formats.

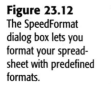

3. Select from the available SpeedFormat options in the Formats list. The Example box shows you an example of a spreadsheet formatted with the SpeedFormat you chose.

> **Note**
>
> If you want to exclude certain elements from a SpeedFormat, choose the elements in the Include section that you want to turn off.

4. Click OK to apply the SpeedFormat.

To create your own SpeedFormat, select the cell or block that contains the format you want to create. Click the Add button in the SpeedFormat dialog box, give the format a name, and click OK. Quattro Pro will add the SpeedFormat to the Formats list in the SpeedFormat dialog box.

To remove a SpeedFormat style, use the Delete button in the SpeedFormat dialog box.

USING CONDITIONAL FORMATTING

With Quattro Pro's Conditional Formatting feature, you can easily apply special formatting settings that take effect when the contents of a cell meet specified conditions. For example, if the values fall below a specific number, you can show those values in bold blue, and, if the values are greater than a specific number, you can display those values in bold green.

To use conditional formatting, perform these steps:

1. Choose Format, Sheet. The Active Sheet dialog box opens.
2. Click the Conditional Color tab, as shown in Figure 23.13.

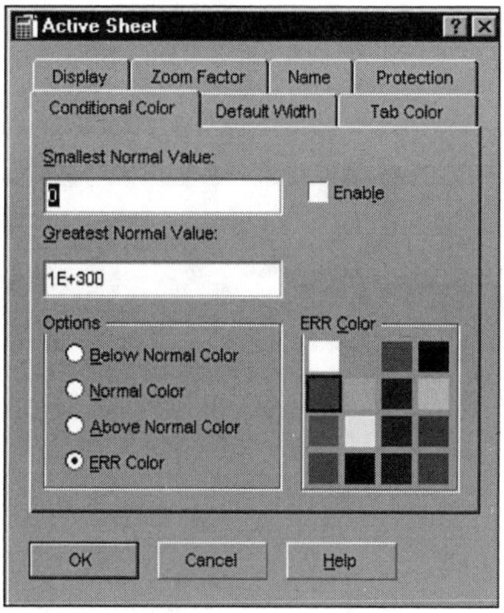

Figure 23.13
The Conditional Color tab in the Active Sheet dialog box lets you set up conditional formatting for values to appear in different colors on the spreadsheet.

3. In the Smallest Normal Value box, enter the minimum value of the range of values you want to format.

4. In the Greatest Normal Value box, enter the maximum value of the range of values you want to format. The default greatest normal value is 1E+300.

5. Put a check mark in the Enable check box. This tells Quattro Pro to use the default conditional colors set for below normal (red), normal (black), above normal (green), and ERR (red).

> **Note**
>
> If you want to change the default conditional colors, choose an option in the Options section and click a color in the Color palette.

6. Click OK. Quattro Pro shows the cells with values within the range you specified in black, values below the smallest value in red, values above the greatest value in green, and ERR in red.

To remove unconditional formatting, remove the check mark in the Enable check box.

INSERTING ART

You can add artwork to your documents in several ways: Draw shapes, create TextArt, download images from the Web, and insert images from earlier versions of WordPerfect suite (7 and 8).

Drawing a shape in Quattro Pro doesn't take any artistic skill. You can quickly and easily draw any of these shapes: text box, arrow, line, rectangle, rounded rectangle, ellipse, and polyline/polygon (see Figure 23.14).

Figure 23.14
The shapes you can draw on a spreadsheet.

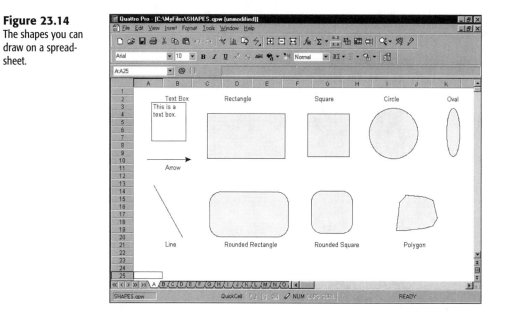

With TextArt, you can select preset special text effects to add designs and shapes to plain text. TextArt changes fonts in various ways by squeezing them, bending them into shapes, stretching them, and adding shadows, borders, and a host of other text effects. Using TextArt is an excellent way to create desktop publishing effects, especially for making logos (see Figure 23.15).

Quattro Pro's new and improved Scrapbook contains numerous professionally prepared images. You can search and preview the images, drag and drop, and copy and paste them. Scrapbook organizes the images by category. You can even create your own category and view automatic updates of thumbnails, as well as preview sounds, movies, and bitmap images.

DRAWING SHAPES

Follow these steps to draw shapes in your spreadsheets:

1. Choose Insert, Shape, and pick the shape you want.

2. Click where you want to start drawing the shape on the spreadsheet and drag the mouse pointer to where you want to stop drawing the shape. The shape appears on the spreadsheet with squares surrounding it. These squares are called selection handles and allow you to move and size the shape.

3. To move the shape, make sure it's selected and point to it. The mouse pointer changes into a four-headed arrow. Drag the shape to the new location.

4. To size the shape, make sure it's selected and point to a selection handle. The mouse pointer changes into a double arrow. Drag the shape's border to enlarge or shrink the shape.

Figure 23.15
A logo created with TextArt.

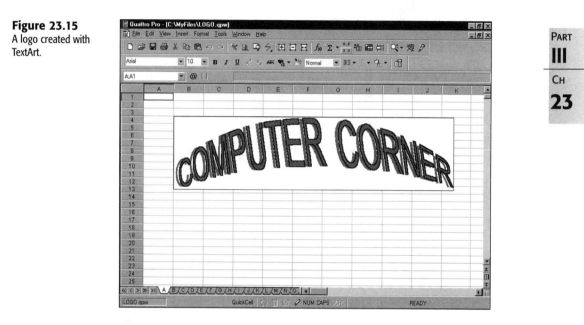

ADDING TEXTART IMAGES

To create a TextArt image, perform these steps:

1. Click in the cell where you want the upper-left corner of the TextArt graphic to appear.

2. Choose Insert, Graphics, TextArt. The Corel TextArt 9.0 dialog box opens, as shown in Figure 23.16.

3. Type the text for the TextArt image in the Type Here box, replacing the word Text.

4. Choose a shape for the text in the Shapes palette. If you would like to see more shapes, click the More button and choose a shape from there.

5. Choose a font, font style, and justification to format the text.

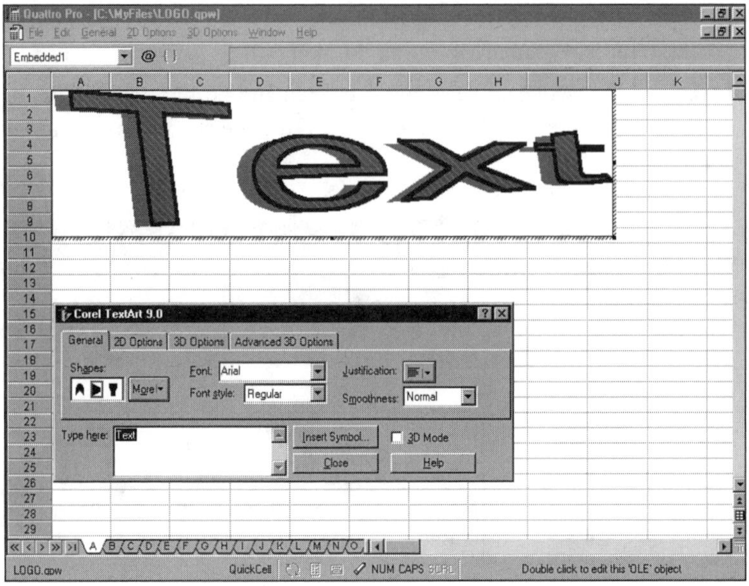

Figure 23.16
You can create fancy text and desktop publishing text effects by using the Corel TextArt 9.0 dialog box.

6. Change any of the following TextArt options on the 2D Options, 3D Options, or Advanced 3D Options tab to customize the TextArt image:

- The 2D Options tab lets you change the pattern, shadow, outline, rotation, and text color for the TextArt image. If you want to insert a symbol in your TextArt artwork, click the 2D Options tab and then click the Insert Symbol button. In the Symbols dialog box, choose a symbol and click the Insert and Close button.

- The 3D Options tab gives you options for changing the lighting, bevel, depth of the bevel, and rotation for the TextArt. Be sure to check the 3D Mode check box on the General tab before you change any 3D options. Otherwise, the 2D options are used.

- The 3D Advanced Options tab offers options for specifying the texture for the face and bevel of the image, texture size, texture lighting, and color quality. Be sure to check the 3D Mode check box on the General tab before you change any Advanced 3D options. Otherwise, Quattro Pro uses 2D options for your TextArt image.

7. Click Close. The TextArt appears where you positioned the insertion point in the default position and size.

If you no longer want the TextArt image in your document, select the image by clicking it and pressing the Delete key.

INSERTING CLIP ART

To insert clip art, choose Insert, Graphics, Clipart. The Scrapbook dialog box appears, as shown in Figure 23.17. Choose a category, click the image you inserted in your document, and click the Insert button. The mouse pointer changes into a bar graph symbol with a plus sign. Click in the notebook to place the clip art—in its default size and shape—where you want it. Alternatively, you can click and drag diagonally in the notebook to size the image and insert it. Click Close to close the Scrapbook dialog box.

PART

III

CH

23

> **Note**
>
> To add to your clip-art collection, you can buy packages of clip art (in black and white or color) from software stores and mail-order catalogs. These clip-art "libraries" are packaged by topics such as animals, business, holidays, music, people, and so on. If you want more professional artwork, look for photo collections, which are usually sold on CD-ROMs.

Figure 23.17
The Scrapbook dialog box contains clip-art images that you can add to your spread-sheet.

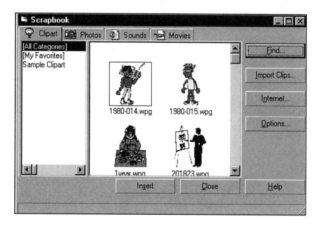

ADDING IMAGES FROM THE WEB

You can download clip art and photos directly from the Internet (if you're online) by using the Internet button on the right side of the Scrapbook dialog box and then supplying the URL for the Clipart Web site.

> **Caution**
>
> Some computer setups interfere with the process of getting clip art from the Internet because Microsoft Internet Explorer overrides any connections to your chosen ISP. If so, connect to your ISP, open Netscape Navigator, and then enter the URL for the Clipart Web site.

IMPORTING IMAGES FROM EARLIER VERSIONS OF QUATTRO PRO

You can import images that were created in earlier versions of the WordPerfect suite, Quattro Pro 7 and 8. To do so, click the Import Clips button on the right side of the Scrapbook dialog box. In the Insert File - Programs dialog box, display the folder that contains the images from Quattro Pro 7 or 8. Select the clips you want to import and then click Open. Quattro Pro adds the images to the Clipart tab. You can pick any one of these images for insertion into your spreadsheet.

PRACTICAL PROJECT

You can use the Computer Paper SpeedFormat style to make your spreadsheet have that green-bar computer-paper effect, as shown in Figure 23.18.

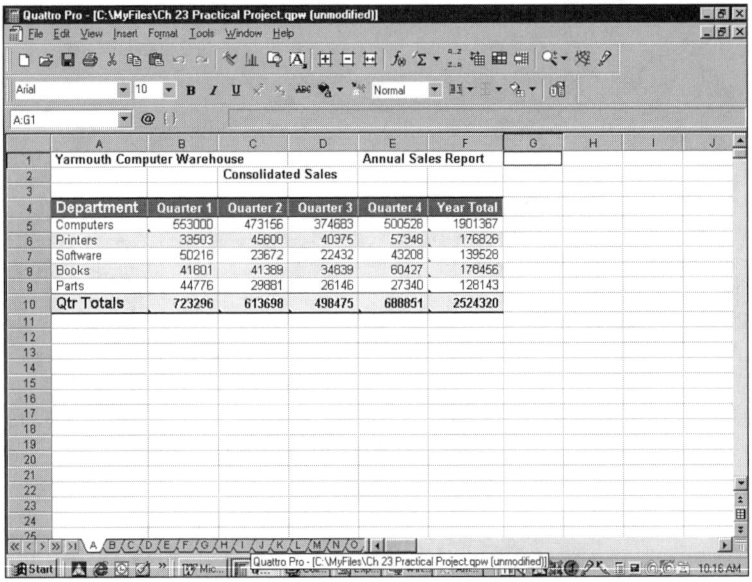

Figure 23.18
Using the Computer Paper SpeedFormat style.

TROUBLESHOOTING

SETTING A DEFAULT COLUMN WIDTH FOR A SHEET

Some columns don't adjust when a new default column width is set for a notebook sheet.

Column widths you set using the QuickFit button remain at the current setting even when the length of data in the column changes. If you want the column width adjusted to fit new data, you must click the QuickFit button again.

DISPLAYING VALUES RATHER THAN ASTERISKS

After formatting a block, some cells display asterisks instead of the values.

If you apply a numeric format to a cell, the column width must be wide enough to display the cell's data in the format. Asterisks rather than the formatted value display in the cell otherwise. You might need to adjust the column width to fit the new format.

CHAPTER **24**

ANALYZING DATA

In this chapter

USING THE OPTIMIZER AND SOLVE FOR TOOLS

The Optimizer and Solve For tools are powerful utilities that help you create what-if scenarios with notebook data. What-if scenarios are a common way to analyze problems, using many different values for a set of variables to find optimal answers. What-if scenarios can be time-consuming, especially if done manually, because even problems with a limited number of variables have many possible solutions.

Tip #152 from	Use Solve For when you want to find an answer by changing one variable.
Trudi Reisner	

The Optimizer tool can analyze problems with up to 200 variables and 100 constraints to determine the best answer. The Solve For tool modifies a single variable to find a specified answer to a problem.

SOLVING COMPLEX PROBLEMS USING THE OPTIMIZER

You use the Optimizer to determine a series of possible answers to a specific problem, and to select the answer that best fits your criteria. You can use the Optimizer, for example, to find the production mix that produces the highest profit, to analyze investment portfolios, to determine the least costly shipping routes, and to schedule your staff.

Each Optimizer problem must have one or more adjustable cells. Adjustable cells contain the variables that the Optimizer changes while searching for the optimal answer—and can contain numbers only. Adjustable cells might include production quantities, numbers of employees, or capital invested in a project.

Constraints are conditions that serve as problem limits, such as the range of acceptable values. Constraints are expressed as logical formulas that evaluate to true or false, and all constraints must be met before an answer is considered acceptable. Constraints might include limits on production levels, a requirement to produce a profit, or an obligation that at least one employee be on duty.

A solution cell contains the formula that defines the problem, and is optional. If you do not include a solution cell, the Optimizer finds answers that meet all the defined constraints. Solution cells might include formulas that calculate profits, overall costs, or the amount earned from different activities.

USING A PRODUCTION SCHEDULING NOTEBOOK

Figure 24.1 shows a sample notebook that represents the costs involved in producing three different products. In this example, it is assumed that the factory can produce 50,000 total parts per month and that the production can be divided among the three parts in the most profitable manner.

Figure 24.1
We'll use this note-book to compute an optimal product mix.

	A	B	C	D	E
1	Part:	A	B	C	
2	Material	$0.45	$0.48	$0.51	
3	Labor	$0.31	$0.46	$0.32	Constants
4	Unit Price	$1.09	$1.11	$1.15	
5	Fixed Costs		$12,500.00		
6					
7	Minimum	5,000	5,000	5,000	
8	Maximum	25,000	25,000	25,000	Constraints
9	Capacity		50,000		
10					
11	Quantity	15,000	15,000	20,000	Variables
12	Total Production	50,000			
13					
14	Extended Cost	$11,400.00	$14,100.00	$16,600.00	
15	Extended Price	$16,350.00	$16,650.00	$23,000.00	
16					
17	Total Cost	$54,600.00			
18	Total Price	$56,000.00			
19	Net Profit	$1,400.00			

Tip #153 from
Trudi Reisner

Optimizer will find a solution more quickly if the initial values in the adjustable cells are a reasonable solution to the problem.

Several factors affect the final profit. As shown in row 11 of Figure 24.1, the production manager has scheduled the production run at 15,000 each for parts A and B, and 20,000 for part C. The net profit with this mix is $1,400. Of course, it would be possible to try other sets of values for each product's production quantity. Because each of the three values can vary between 5,000 and 25,000, however, the number of possibilities would be enormous.

Caution

Don't use logical (or Boolean) functions in Optimizer problems; they can make a solution difficult or impossible to find.

To use the Optimizer to find a better solution, follow these steps:

1. Choose Tools, Numeric Tools, Optimizer to display the Optimizer dialog box.
2. To make the production quantities of the three parts adjustable in the notebook, enter the cell addresses in the Variable Cell(s) text box. In this example, you enter B11..D11.

   Next, define the constraints that the Optimizer must satisfy in solving the problem.
3. Select Add to display the Add Constraints dialog box.

   The quantities of the parts (cells B11..D11) must be equal to or greater than the minimum quantity shown in cells B7..D7.
4. Enter B11..D11 in the Cell text box, select the >= (greater than or equal to) option button in the Operator area, and enter B7..D7 in the Constant text box.

5. Select <u>A</u>dd Another Constraint to enter additional constraints.

The quantities of the parts (cells B11..D11) must be less than or equal to the maximum quantity shown in cells B8..D8.

6. Enter B11..D11 in the <u>C</u>ell text box, select the <= (less than or equal to) option button in the <u>O</u>perator area, and enter B8..D8 in the Co<u>n</u>stant text box.

7. Select <u>A</u>dd Another Constraint to enter the last constraint.

Cell B12 (total production) must be less than or equal to the value in C9 (capacity).

8. Enter B12 in the <u>C</u>ell text box, select the <= (less than or equal to) option button in the <u>O</u>perator area, and enter C9 in the Co<u>n</u>stant text box.

9. Choose OK when all constraints have been entered.

10. Select the <u>S</u>olution Cell text box in the Optimizer dialog box and enter B19, the formula.

11. Choose <u>T</u>arget Value and type 3000 in the Target Value box. The dialog box should now look like Figure 24.2.

Figure 24.2
The Optimizer dialog box shows the completed entries.

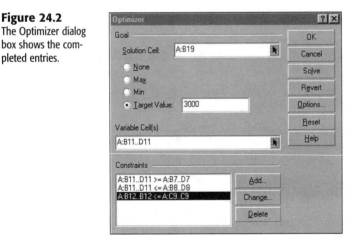

12. Click So<u>l</u>ve to instruct the Optimizer to calculate the solution, and then click <u>C</u>lose to close the Optimizer dialog box. Figure 24.3 shows the result in the production mix example. The numbers used in the cells for Extended Cost, Extended Price, Total Cost, Total Price, and Net Profit are the result of a formula.

The Optimizer found a much different solution than the one proposed by the production manager. After redistributing the production quantities shown in row 11, the total monthly profit jumped from $1,400 to $3,000. Although this example did not take all possible factors into account, it clearly demonstrates the value of applying the Optimizer to a what-if scenario.

Figure 24.3
The notebook shows the optimal solution for the product mix example, as determined by the Optimizer.

	Part:	A	B	C	
2	Material	$0.45	$0.48	$0.51	
3	Labor	$0.31	$0.46	$0.32	Constants
4	Unit Price	$1.09	$1.11	$1.15	
5	Fixed Costs		$12,500.00		
6					
7	Minimum	5,000	5,000	5,000	
8	Maximum	25,000	25,000	25,000	Constraints
9	Capacity		50,000		
10					
11	Quantity	17,198	16,132	22,132	Variables
12	Total Production	50,000			
13					
14	Extended Cost	$13,070.61	$15,164.45	$18,369.19	
15	Extended Price	$18,746.00	$17,906.95	$25,451.29	
16					
17	Total Cost	$59,104.25			
18	Total Price	$62,104.25			
19	Net Profit	$3,000.00			

> *If Optimizer is unable to find an optimal solution to a complex problem, or it sometimes produces different results when solving the same problem a second time, see "Getting Good Results with Optimizer" in the Troubleshooting section at the end of this chapter.*
>
> *If you can't tell whether the Optimizer's solution is the best solution to your problem, see "Creating an Optimizer Answer Report" in the Troubleshooting section at the end of this chapter.*

SOLVING FOR A KNOWN ANSWER USING SOLVE FOR

Sometimes you know the answer you want, but don't quite know how to get there. The Solve For tool is a Quattro Pro analysis utility that you use to find the value of a variable when you are seeking a specific goal. Rather than calculating an optimal answer by adjusting a block of variables, the Solve For tool adjusts a single variable to produce an answer you specify.

For example, suppose that you know you can afford $325 as a monthly payment on an automobile, but you don't know how large a loan you can receive for such a payment. The Solve For tool makes it easy to make this type of reverse calculation, where you already know the answer, but don't know the key to finding the answer.

To use Solve For to find the loan amount, follow these steps:

1. Create a Quattro Pro notebook that uses the @PMT *function* to calculate the loan payment on a loan. For this example, enter a loan amount of $10,000 in cell C2, 9% interest in cell C3, a term of 60 months in cell C4, and the formula @PMT(C2,C3/12,C4) in cell C6.

2. Choose Tools, Numeric Tools, Solve For.

3. Specify C6 in the Formula Cell text box. This is the cell that contains the formula whose value you want to specify.

4. Specify 325 in the Target Value text box. This is the value you want to achieve in the goal cell.

5. Specify C2 as the Variable Cell, the cell whose value Solve For will adjust. Your screen should now appear similar to Figure 24.4 (in this figure, cells were formatted to display numbers correctly).

Figure 24.4
The Solve For dialog box is completed and ready to find the solution.

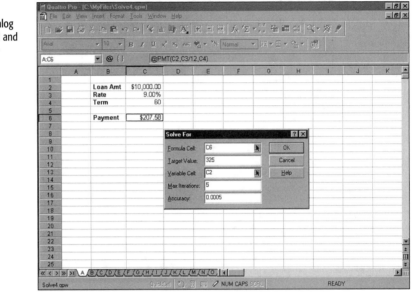

6. Click OK to execute the command and return to the notebook. Figure 24.5 shows the notebook with the solution.

Your $325 monthly budget allows for payments on a loan of $15,656.35. Although you could probably find an answer close to this by trying several different values in cell C2, using Solve For makes the process both simple and fast.

Tip #154 from
Trudi Reisner

Save the notebook before you use Solve For so that you can easily revert to the original values if necessary.

When you use Solve For, the adjustable value is permanently changed in the notebook. You can return to the previous value if you immediately choose Edit, Undo.

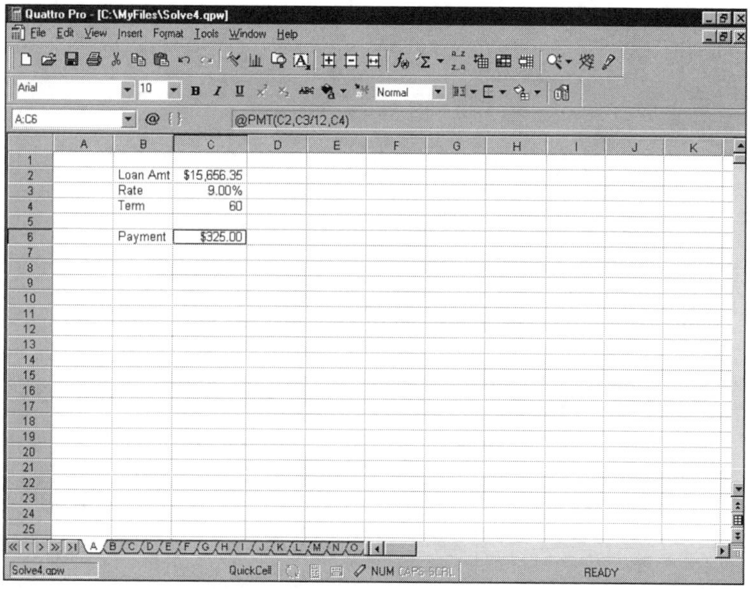

Figure 24.5
The solved problem shows the answer you seek, in cell C2.

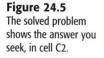

USING WHAT-IF TABLES

In most *notebook (page 350)* models, the variables your formulas use are known quantities. What-if tables enable you to work with variables whose values are unknown. Models for financial projections often fall into this category. For example, next year's cash flow projection may depend on prevailing interest rates or other variable costs you cannot predict exactly.

With the Tools, Numeric Tools, What-If command, you can create tables that show the results of changing one variable in a problem or the combined effect of changing two variables simultaneously. Another function of the Tools, Numeric Tools, What-If command is to create cross-tabulation tables. A cross-tabulation table provides summary information categorized by unique information in two fields, such as the total amount of sales each sales representative makes to each customer.

CREATING A WHAT-IF TABLE

A what-if table is an onscreen view of information in a *column* format with the field names at the top. A variable is a formula component whose value can change. An input cell is a notebook cell used by Quattro Pro for temporary storage during calculation of a what-if table. One input cell is required for each variable in the what-if table formula. The cell addresses of the formula variables are the same as the input cells. The formulas used in what-if tables can contain values, strings, cell addresses, and functions, but you should not use logical formulas because this type of formula always evaluates to 0 or 1, which is usually meaningless in a what-if table.

PART

III

CH

24

Tip #155 from *Trudi Reisner*

Use One Free Variable What-If tables when you need to see the results from more than one formula.

You can build two types of what-if tables in Quattro Pro. They differ in the number of variables and the number of formulas that can be included. A One Free Variable What-If table can contain one variable and can have one or more formulas. A Two Free Variables What-If table can contain two variables, but only one formula. In a One Free Variable What-If table, you place the formulas in the top row of the table. In a Two Free Variables What-If table, you place the formula at the intersection of the top row and the left column of the table.

A common use for a One Free Variable What-If table would be to calculate both the interest and principal portions of each payment on a loan. A Two Free Variables What-If table might be used to calculate monthly payments on a given loan amount at different combinations of interest rates and terms.

Figure 24.6 shows a typical Two Free Variables What-If table. This table calculates monthly payments on a given loan amount at different combinations of interest rates and terms.

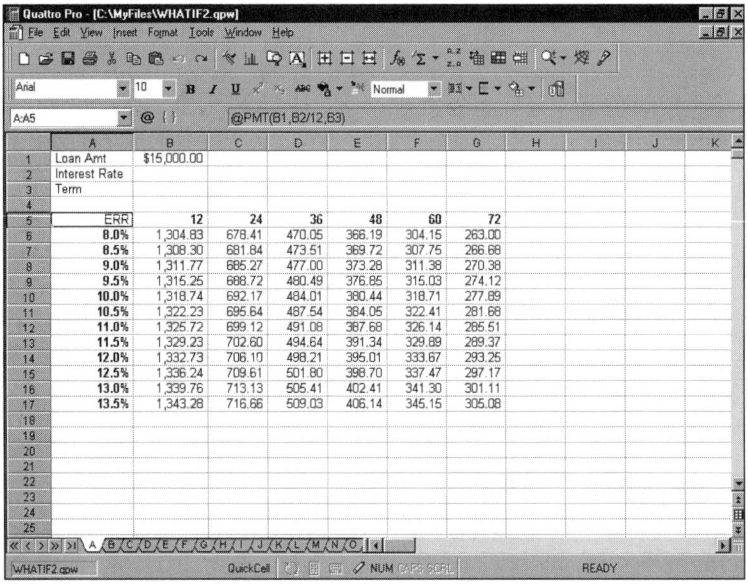

	A	B	C	D	E	F	G
1	Loan Amt	$15,000.00					
2	Interest Rate						
3	Term						
4							
5	ERR	12	24	36	48	60	72
6	8.0%	1,304.83	678.41	470.05	366.19	304.15	263.00
7	8.5%	1,308.30	681.84	473.51	369.72	307.75	266.68
8	9.0%	1,311.77	685.27	477.00	373.28	311.38	270.38
9	9.5%	1,315.25	688.72	480.49	376.85	315.03	274.12
10	10.0%	1,318.74	692.17	484.01	380.44	318.71	277.89
11	10.5%	1,322.23	695.64	487.54	384.05	322.41	281.68
12	11.0%	1,325.72	699.12	491.08	387.68	326.14	285.51
13	11.5%	1,329.23	702.60	494.64	391.34	329.89	289.37
14	12.0%	1,332.73	706.10	498.21	395.01	333.67	293.25
15	12.5%	1,336.24	709.61	501.80	398.70	337.47	297.17
16	13.0%	1,339.76	713.13	505.41	402.41	341.30	301.11
17	13.5%	1,343.28	716.66	509.03	406.14	345.15	305.08

Figure 24.6
This completed What-If table of loan payment amounts uses Two Free Variables.

To create a similar what-if table, follow these steps:

1. Enter the loan amount of `$15,000.00` in cell B1.
2. For documentation purposes, place identifying labels in column A. In this case, enter `Loan Amt` in A1, `Interest rate` in A2, and `Term` in A3.
3. Enter the formula `@PMT(B1,B2/12,B3)` in cell A5. The formula will show `ERR` because it refers to blank cells, but Quattro Pro will correctly calculate the what-if table.

4. Enter the interest rates in A6..A17. The fastest method of entering these rates is to enter 8% in A6, 8.5% in A7, select A6..A17, and click the QuickFill button. (To improve the appearance of the table, format A6..A17 as Percent, 1 decimal.)

5. Enter the loan terms in B5..G5. Once again, you can use QuickFill.

6. Select the table block A5..G17.

7. Choose Tools, Numeric Tools, What-If.

8. Select Two Free Variables.

9. Type B2 in the Column Input Cell text box, and then type B3 in the Row Input Cell text box.

10. Click Generate to calculate the what-if table values.

11. Click Close to confirm the dialog box and return to the notebook.

Tip #156 from
Trudi Reisner

You can also use PerfectExpert to automate several types of analysis in your Quattro Pro notebooks. See the section "Using Experts" in Chapter 20 for more information.

If what-if tables don't display new values when the formula variables are changed, see "Recalculating to Update What-If Tables" in the Troubleshooting section at the end of this chapter.

CREATING A SIMPLE CROSS-TABULATION TABLE

Cross tabs (or cross-tabulation tables) are tables that summarize the values in a database. For example, an address list showing customers in many different states might include information you could use to determine where you get most of your business, and therefore, where you should plan to spend your advertising dollars. You might also use a cross tab to see a sales summary by salesperson for each product line. Quattro Pro can even generate a chart to quickly display the results of the analysis.

→ For more information on creating a chart, **see** "Creating a Simple Chart," **p. 454**

The structure of a what-if table block for a cross-tabulation analysis is similar to the structure for a what-if analysis. If you are analyzing the effects of one variable, the upper-left cell might be empty, the top row contains the formula(s) that are to be evaluated, and the left column contains the sample values. If you are analyzing the effects of two variables, you place the formula in the upper-left cell of the table, and the two sets of sample values in the top row and left column of the table. In most cases, the formulas contain one or more database functions.

In addition, you must create one or two input cells, depending on the number of variables in the cross tab. For a cross-tab analysis, you must place the input cells directly below cells that contain the corresponding database field names.

You also use the Tools, Numeric Tools, What-If command to create a cross-tabulation table. The sample values in the left column, or in the left column and top row, are used to select the values displayed in the cross tab. The sample values for a cross-tabulation analysis are the values or labels that you can use as criteria for the analysis.

Tip #157 from *Trudi Reisner*	If your data changes, remember to use the <u>T</u>ools, <u>N</u>umeric Tools, <u>W</u>hat-if, <u>G</u>enerate command to recalculate the results.

After the what-if table has been calculated, each cell in the results block contains the result of the formulas. The formulas have been applied to those database records that meet the cross tab criteria.

USING THE CROSS TABS FEATURE

By now you can see that the cross tabs feature can be an effective data-analysis tool. A cross tab can often display data relationships you might not otherwise be able to grasp quickly. Unfortunately, creating a cross tab takes some planning and a lot of work. Not only that, but cross tabs created with the <u>T</u>ools, <u>N</u>umeric Tools, <u>W</u>hat-If command aren't too flexible—after you create a cross tab, it's difficult to change so that you can see different data relationships.

Quattro Pro includes a new integrated tool, the Cross Tabs feature, which enables you to manipulate data easily and create detailed cross-tab reports. This tool is flexible, and it's fun to use, too.

Note	In addition to the Cross Tabs feature, Quattro Pro 9 also includes the Data Modeling Desktop, a separate application that provided the only method of creating cross tabs in Quattro Pro 7 and 8. You might still want to use the Data Modeling Desktop in certain instances, such as when you need to summarize data from an external database file.

UNDERSTANDING THE CROSS TABS FEATURE

Until now, whenever you've created a cross tab, the finished cross tab was static and unchanging. You determined the data relationships you wanted to view and created a cross tab displaying that view. If you wanted to see a different view, you had to go back to the beginning and start over.

The Cross Tabs feature provides a much different approach to cross-tab generation. Instead of a static and unchanging cross tab, the Cross Tabs feature creates a cross tab you can quickly modify to display additional data relationships.

The Cross Tabs feature analyzes data by using certain data sets as row or column labels, and a single numerical data set as the data being analyzed. The labels are used as selection criteria to determine which values to include at the intersections of the labels. For example, if your database contains sales information, you might place the names of the salespeople as labels along the left side of the workspace and items along the top. The intersection of the labels "John" and "Computers" would show the total of all computers sold by John.

Simple cross tabs, such as the preceding example, really don't show the true power of the Cross Tabs feature. Adding even one additional piece of data to the picture, however, really complicates matters. Suppose that you decide to add time-period data to the cross tab. You track sales by date, so you want to analyze how well each salesperson did each month, but you want to know how well they did in each product line, too. Now your cross tab is considerably more complicated, and you've only scratched the surface. Imagine that you want to change the focus and see how well each product line did each month rather than each salesperson. The Cross Tabs feature enables you to quickly make such changes in focus so that you can find the hidden relationships in your data.

SUMMARIZING DATA IN A CROSS TABS REPORT

To analyze data using the Cross Tabs feature, you must organize the data—using a layout identical to a typical Quattro Pro notebook database. Data must be in tabular format, with each record in a single row and field names in the top row.

To summarize data in a Cross Tabs report, follow these steps:

1. Select the notebook database block—the block containing the data you want to analyze (see Figure 24.7).

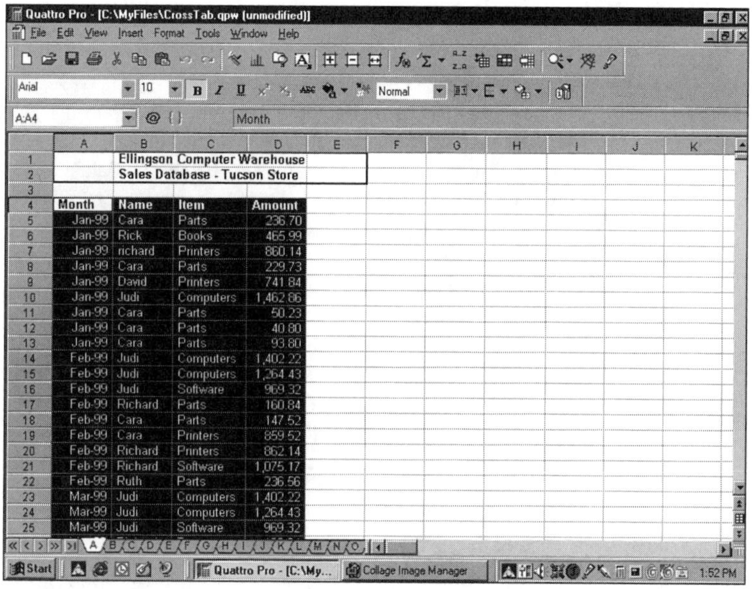

PART

III

CH

24

Figure 24.7
This Sales database includes fields for Month, Name, Item, and Amount.

2. Choose Tools, Data Tools, Cross Tabs, Report to display the Cross Tabs Report dialog box (see Figure 24.8).

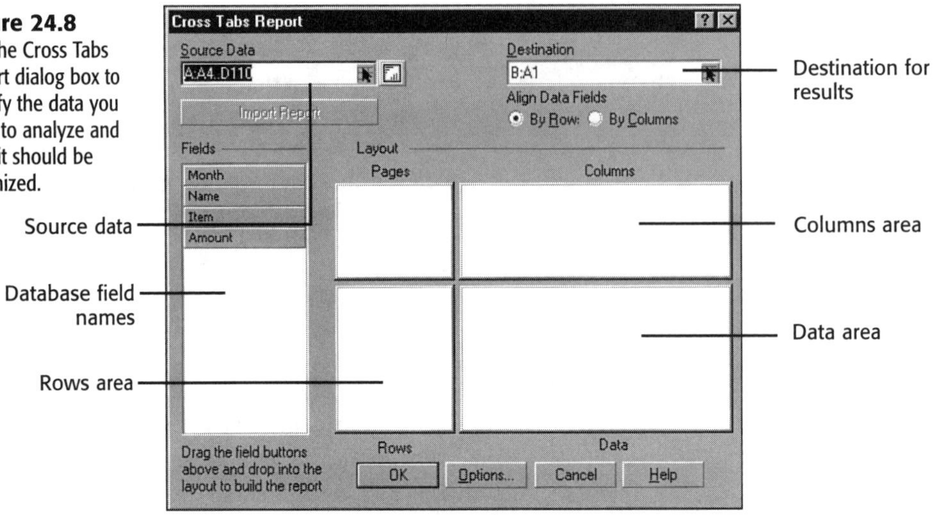

Figure 24.8
Use the Cross Tabs Report dialog box to specify the data you want to analyze and how it should be organized.

Source data

Database field names

Rows area

Destination for results

Columns area

Data area

3. If necessary, edit the block address that appears in the Source Data box. Then, in the Destination box, type the address of the top left cell where you want the cross tab results to appear. (In this example, the default entries for these two text boxes are acceptable.)

> **Note**
>
> Use the Rows and Columns areas in the Cross Tabs Report dialog box to specify the database fields you want to analyze. Usually, these data categories include labels or dates, such as a month, item, or sales representative's name. The Data area in the Layout section in the Cross Tabs Report dialog box includes the summary data. In this example, you want to summarize the sales for each month, showing which sales representatives sold which items. The data categories you add to the Data area should contain numeric data that can be summarized mathematically, such as the sales totals.

4. In the Fields list box, select the field you want to use for the row labels; then drag the button to the Rows area in the Layout section. (This area is in the lower-left quadrant of the Layout section, just to the right of the Fields list box.)

In this example, select Month in the Fields list box, and then drag the button to the Rows area in the Layout section. Notice that Month is copied from the Fields list box and now appears as a large button in the Rows area.

5. In the Fields list box, select the field you want to use for the column labels; then drag the button to the Columns area in the Layout section.

In this example, select Item in the Fields list box, and then drag the button. Notice that Item is copied from the Fields list box and now appears as a large button in the Columns area.

6. Select any other remaining fields you want to add to the Row or Column areas, and drag the appropriate button to an area in the Layout section beside the Fields list box.

   In this example, select Name in the Fields list box, and then drag the button to the Rows area. The Rows area now contains two field labels, with the Name field displayed beneath the Month field.

Tip #158 from *Trudi Reisner*

Always add text data to the Columns or Rows areas and numeric data to the Data area.

---

7. In the Fields list box, select the field containing the values you want to summarize in the main body of the report; then click the button on the left and drag it to the Data area in the Layout section.

   In this example, select Amount in the Fields list box, and then drag the button to the Data area in the Layout section. The Sum of Amount button now appears as a large button in the Data area. The dialog box is now completed and looks like Figure 24.9.

Figure 24.9
The completed Cross Tabs Report dialog box shows how the Cross Tab report will be organized.

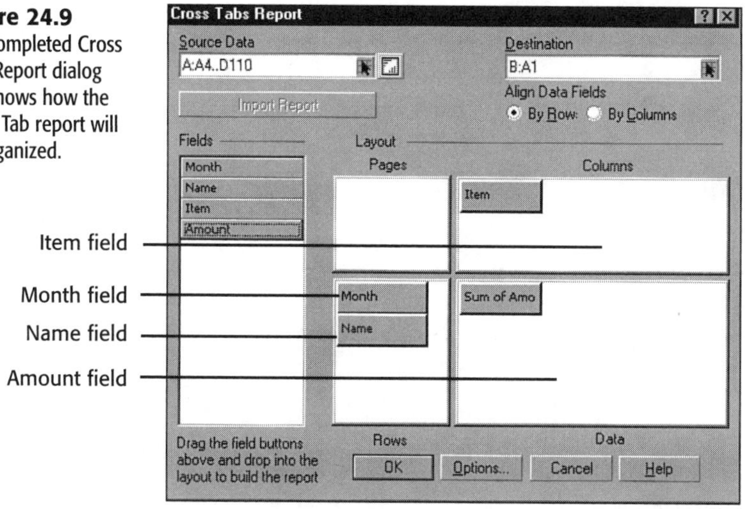

Tip #159 from *Trudi Reisner*

At this point, you can click one of the bars in the Rows, Columns, or Report Data area in the Cross Tabs dialog box if you want to change the type of value that Quattro Pro reports for the specified field (such as sum, average, count, percent, or string).

---

8. Click OK to close the Cross Tabs dialog box and create the cross-tab report.

   The initial cross-tab report appears as shown in Figure 24.10. For this example, line borders and other basic formatting has been applied manually to the report, to make the data easier to read.

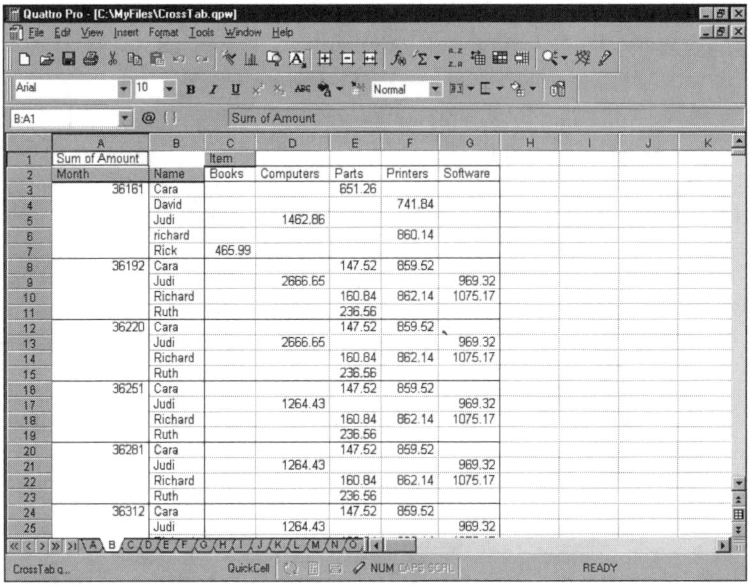

Figure 24.10
The completed cross-tab report now has basic formatting applied to the data.

⚠ If numbers appear in one of the label areas instead of being shown in the Report Data area, see "Adding Numeric Data to a Report" in the Troubleshooting section at the end of this chapter.

REARRANGING DATA IN A CROSS-TAB REPORT

To rearrange the data that appears in a cross-tab report, repeat the previous steps, but choose a different arrangement of field items for the Row, Column, and Report Data areas in the Cross Tabs dialog box. Remember to select a different destination cell if you want to keep previous cross-tab results and avoid overwriting existing data.

Tip #160 from
Trudi Reisner

A quick way to rearrange data in a cross-tab report is to drag the fields in the report. To do so, point the field button you want to move, and hold down the left mouse button, which puts a thick black border around the button. Continue to hold down the mouse button and drag the field to a new location.

Caution

Quattro Pro doesn't let you drag fields to certain locations in a Cross Tabs report. A warning message appears if you try to change a field's position that is restricted.

SHOWING TOTALS IN A CROSS-TAB REPORT

The detail information in a cross-tab report are the column and row data. The totals and grand totals for columns and rows can also be displayed, which is helpful because the totals clearly show how each field relates to the total.

To show column and row totals, click a cell in the report, and click the Options button on the Cross Tabs Report toolbar. Put a check mark in either or both the Show Column Summaries or Show Row Summaries check box.

To hide column and row totals, repeat the previous steps to remove the check mark in either or both the Show Column Summaries or Show Row Summaries check box.

DRILLING DOWN AND ROLLING UP DATA IN A CROSS-TAB REPORT

A cross-tab report can get quite large and complex, containing two or three layers of information. Two-dimensional data in cross-tab reports show rows and columns; three-dimensional data shows rows and columns, stacked in pages. Quattro Pro lets you drill down through layers to see the details of a particular field in two ways: to the bottom of an element or one level at a time.

To drill down through the data elements, first click the Drill Down button on the Cross Tabs Report toolbar. Then click the Plus button next to the element in a report. Quattro Pro moves down through a layer each time you click the Plus button.

After you drill down, you can roll up through the data to hide the detailed information within an element. To roll up through the data elements, click the Rollup button on the Cross Tabs Report toolbar. Then click the Minus button next to the element in a report. Quattro Pro moves up through a layer each time you click the Minus button.

EXPANDING AND COLLAPSING PAGES IN A CROSS-TAB REPORT

If you want to display cross-tab report data on several spreadsheets or pages in a notebook, you can expand the report. You must have a Pages field in your report to expand pages. For instance, you create a cross-tab report on spreadsheet A with a Pages field called "Year" and two field items, 1998 and 1999. When you expand the report, Quattro Pro places the data for 1998 on spreadsheet B, and the data for 1999 on spreadsheet C.

To expand a cross-tab report, click any cell in the report, and click the Expand button on the Cross Tabs Report toolbar. To collapse the pages, click the Remove button on the Cross Tabs Report toolbar.

USING THE DATABASE DESKTOP

By now you've learned that Quattro Pro provides many options for analyzing your notebook data. Sometimes, however, you might want to use Quattro Pro to analyze data that isn't already in a notebook file. For example, you might want to use data contained in a dBASE or Paradox database file. In this case, you should use the Database Desktop feature in Quattro Pro to access the external data.

UNDERSTANDING THE DATABASE DESKTOP

Quattro Pro can open many database file types directly, treating them as though they were actually Quattro Pro notebook files. This isn't always the best option, however, and if the database file is very large, it might not be possible. To use a Quattro Pro notebook, it must be loaded completely into your computer's memory. Database managers, such as Paradox, access database files differently. Instead of loading an entire database into memory, Paradox loads a few records into memory, leaving the rest of the records in the database file on disk. Because only a small portion of the database must fit into memory, disk-based databases can be much larger than databases in a Quattro Pro notebook.

The Database Desktop is a companion program to Quattro Pro that enables you to access information in dBASE and Paradox database files. Through the Database Desktop, you can query a database, add new records to a database, modify existing records in a database, create a new dBASE or Paradox database, modify the structure of an existing database file, or delete records from a database.

USING DATABASE FILES

To load the Database Desktop into memory, choose Insert, External Data, Database Desktop. Your system briefly displays a message informing you of its progress loading the program, and then displays the Corel Database Desktop (see Figure 24.11). If only the Corel Database Desktop title bar appears, or if the Corel Database Desktop does not fill the screen, click the Maximize button or select Maximize from the Corel Database Desktop Control menu to provide the largest possible work area.

Tip #161 from
Trudi Reisner

Queries enable you to select the database records you want to see.

Rather than opening a database table and viewing the complete set of records, you often might want to view a subset of those records that you select by using specified criteria. For example, you might want to search for records for a single customer, for records applying to sales over a specified amount, or for customers in a certain group of states. You use the Query commands in the Database Desktop to select specified records. You can then save the query and use the saved query from Quattro Pro to add the selected records into a Quattro Pro notebook.

Figure 24.11
Use the Corel Database Desktop to access disk-based database tables.

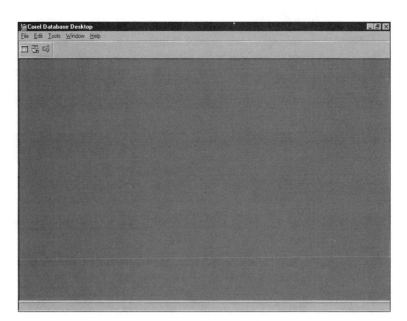

To create a new query, choose File, New, QBE Query and choose the database table whose records you want to view. After you select a database table, the Database Desktop Query Editor appears. The Query Editor uses Query by Example (QBE) to build a database query; you place example values in the fields displayed in the Query Editor, and records are selected based on these values.

To build a query, you use symbols, operators, and reserved words. Query Editor symbols indicate the fields you want included in the answer table, whether to include duplicate values, and the default sort order. Operators select field values based on criteria you specify. The >= operator, for example, selects records that contain a value in the selected field greater than or equal to a specified value. Reserved words perform special database operations, such as inserting and deleting records. To run the query, choose Query, Run Query or press F8.

Figure 24.12 shows an example of a query that selects customers from a database. In this example, the query specifies that only those customers living in California should be selected. The results of running the query appear in the answer table.

In this case, the answer table shows that the database contains six customers living in California. By changing the comparison value and rerunning the query, you can produce different sets of answers. To reuse the same query in the future, use the File, Save or File, Save As command before you close the query or the Database Desktop. Queries you create in the Database Desktop are saved in text files that use the extension .qbe. You can use such saved queries in the Database Desktop, Paradox, or through the Quattro Pro Insert, External Data, Table Query command.

Figure 24.12
A query selects specific database records.

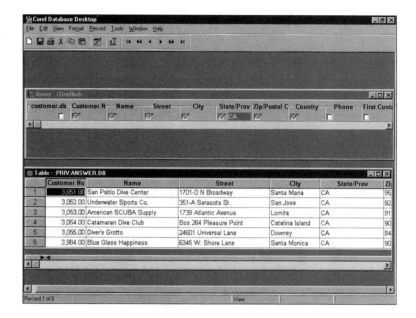

Tip #162 from
Trudi Reisner

If you want to save the results of a query, use the Query, Properties, Table Name command and save the results in a table other than ANSWER.DB.

SHARING RESULTS WITH QUATTRO PRO

The Database Desktop stores the current answer in a temporary file called ANSWER.DB in your working directory. You can import this file into a Quattro Pro notebook, but when you do, the imported information is static and is not updated when the database changes.

A better way to share database information between the Database Desktop and Quattro Pro is to use the Database Desktop QBE file along with the Quattro Pro Insert, External Data, Table Query command. In this way, the information in your notebook is updated to reflect changes in the database. You can, for example, create and refine a database query, and then execute your fully developed query from within a notebook application.

To run a saved query from within a Quattro Pro notebook, follow these steps:

1. Choose Insert, External Data, Table Query to display the Table Query dialog box.

2. Select Query in File to execute a query in a QBE file, or Query in Selection to execute a query that you previously imported into a notebook block (remember, QBE files are text files).

3. If you select Query in File, specify the name of the QBE File. If you select Query in Selection, specify the QBE Block that contains the query, which is a block in the Quattro Pro notebook.

4. Specify the <u>D</u>estination—the upper-left corner of the notebook block—where you want to place the database records.

5. Click OK to confirm the dialog box and execute the query.

The Database Desktop serves as a tool for creating more powerful Quattro Pro applications that feature easy access to dBASE and Paradox database files. You could use a saved query to automatically update the information in a Quattro Pro notebook to include the latest data—especially if you use shared database files on a network and need to be certain your notebooks are up-to-date.

PRACTICAL PROJECT

If you want to refinance your home, you can use the Solve For feature to experiment with different interest rates and determine the payments for each interest rate.

TROUBLESHOOTING

GETTING GOOD RESULTS WITH OPTIMIZER

Optimizer is unable to find an optimal solution to a complex problem, or it sometimes produces different results when solving the same problem a second time.

Try to supply initial values for the variables that you feel will be somewhat close to their final values. Optimizer usually has better success when it can start with a reasonable solution.

CREATING AN OPTIMIZER ANSWER REPORT

I can't tell whether the Optimizer's solution is the best solution to my problem.

Use the <u>T</u>ools, <u>N</u>umeric Tools, <u>O</u>ptimizer, <u>O</u>ptions, <u>R</u>eporting command to create an answer report. This report shows the values Optimizer used to find its solution.

RECALCULATING TO UPDATE WHAT-IF TABLES

What-if tables don't display new values when the formula variables are changed.

What-if tables don't recalculate when values change because the tables don't contain formulas. Choose <u>T</u>ools, <u>N</u>umeric Tools, <u>W</u>hat-If, <u>G</u>enerate to recalculate the what-if table values.

ADDING NUMERIC DATA TO A REPORT

Numbers appear in one of the label areas instead of being shown in the Report Data area.

Always add numeric data to the Report Data area and the identifying data labels to the Row and Column areas. If you add numeric data to the Row or Column area, or labels to the Report Data area, your report will be meaningless.

CHAPTER **25**

Using Charts

In this chapter

CREATING A SIMPLE CHART

You can create sophisticated, complex, and stunning charts with Quattro Pro. You can even create onscreen slideshows that automatically change from one chart to the next at specified intervals using fancy effects such as dissolves, fades, wipes, or spirals. For most of us, a relatively simple chart that effectively displays our data is a much more reasonable goal, so that's where you start—by learning how to create a simple chart.

Although most of your work in Quattro Pro is done in the spreadsheet, Quattro Pro also provides a Chart window that gives you much more power and control over charting. The Chart window provides you with specialized commands and toolbars that are designed to help you enhance a chart. Before you can access the Chart window, however, you first must create a chart.

STARTING A BASIC CHART

The data you want to chart must be in a tabular format, similar to a typical Quattro Pro notebook database. The requirements for data you want to chart aren't as strict as they are for a database, however, because you can use either rows or columns for similar data. A crosstab table is often a good choice for the layout of data you want to chart, because a crosstab has labels identifying the groups and the elements in your data.

→ For more information on creating Cross Tab reports, **see** "Using the Cross Tabs Feature," **p. 442**

Figure 25.1 shows a notebook containing the annual sales report for a fictitious company. You use this notebook to demonstrate the steps in creating a Quattro Pro chart.

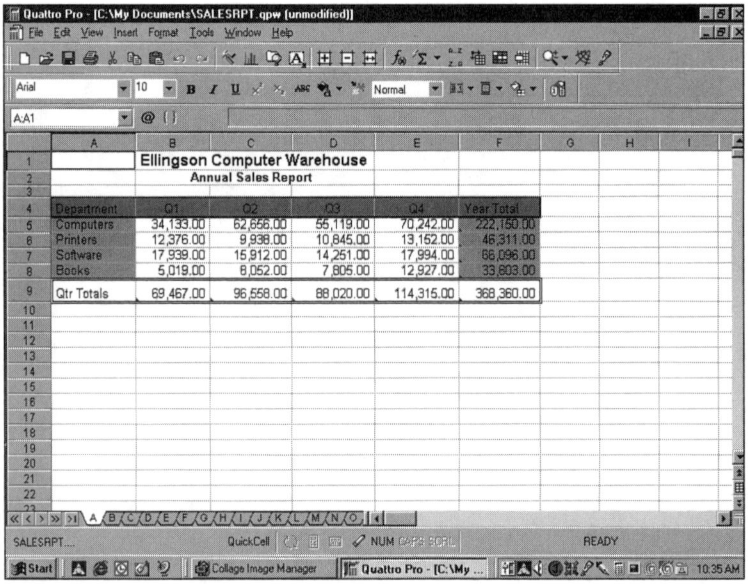

Figure 25.1
A sample sales data notebook can be used for creating charts.

Choose Insert, Chart to create a chart. By default, Quattro Pro names the first chart Chart1, the second Chart2, and so on. After you create a chart, you have access to several commands on the Chart menu for enhancing the chart. The Chart menu appears only when you have activated a chart. In addition, the Property Bar changes to include buttons that help you to modify the chart. You'll learn more about this later in the section, "Enhancing a Chart."

Quattro Pro uses the currently selected spreadsheet block as the block to be charted. If you don't select a block, but the cell selector is located within a block of data, Quattro Pro uses the entire block. If the block you want to chart is contained within a larger block of data, select the block of data to chart before choosing Insert, Chart. You can also click the QuickChart button on the Quattro Pro toolbar to insert a chart directly onto the notebook.

To chart information from the sales data notebook, you need to know which data you want to plot and which data you want to use in labeling the chart. In Figure 25.1, time-period labels are listed across row 4. Category identifiers are located in column A. The numeric entries in rows 5 through 9, as well as the formula results in row 9 and column F, are suitable for charting as data points. For this example, however, the totals in row 9 and column F are not included in the charted data, because including these totals would make the other data difficult to see by comparison. In this example, you should select the block A4..E8 before choosing Insert, Chart. The column and row labels can be used to label the points on the chart.

PART
III
CH
25

To create a chart using the Chart Expert, follow these steps:

1. Select the block you want to chart, and then choose Insert, Chart. The Chart Expert - Step 1 of 5 dialog box displays (see Figure 25.2).

Figure 25.2
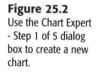
Use the Chart Expert - Step 1 of 5 dialog box to create a new chart.

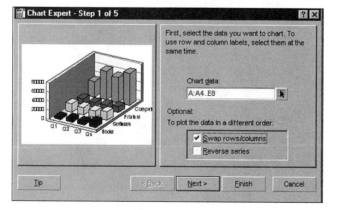

2. If necessary, adjust the block shown in the Chart Data text box. A preview of the chart appears on the left side of the dialog box. If you want to plot your chart data in a different order, you can select one or both of the Swap Rows/Columns and Reverse Series check boxes. The chart preview automatically updates to reflect your selections.

In this example, Swap Rows/Columns is selected because it improves the appearance of this chart.

3. Click Next to display Step 2 of the Chart Expert (see Figure 25.3). Click the button representing the general chart type you want to create, such as Bar or Pie; or, if you want Quattro Pro to make this choice for you (based on the data you've selected), click the Expert's Choice button.

Figure 25.3
Use the Chart Expert - Step 2 of 5 dialog box to choose the general chart type.

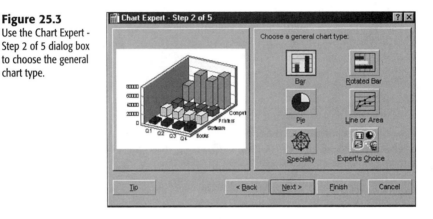

4. Click Next to display Step 3 of the Chart Expert (see Figure 25.4). Click the button representing the specific chart type you want to use. The buttons that appear vary depending on the general chart type you chose in the previous step.

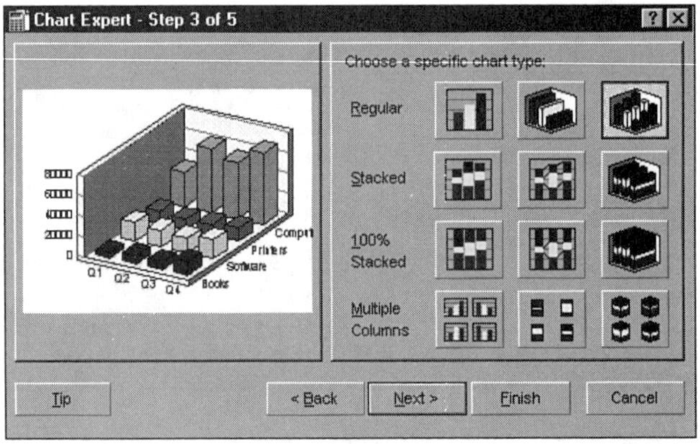

Figure 25.4
Use the Chart Expert - Step 3 of 5 dialog box to choose the specific chart type.

5. Click Next to display Step 4 of the Chart Expert. If you want to include titles with your chart, type the title(s) in the appropriate text boxes (see Figure 25.5). Then choose the destination for your chart—the Current Sheet or the Chart Window.

Figure 25.5
Use the Chart Expert -
Step 4 of 5 dialog box
to type the chart titles
and select the desti-
nation for the chart.

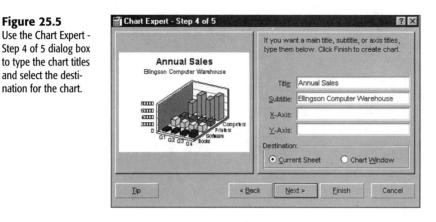

Tip #163 from
Trudi Reisner

To place your chart on a separate sheet, select Chart Window; otherwise, select Current
Sheet to place it on the current sheet with your data.

6. Click Next to display Step 5 of the Chart Expert. In the Choose a Color Scheme list
   box, select the color scheme you want to use in your chart. The chart preview on the
   left side of the dialog box shows what the selected color scheme will look like. In most
   cases, you might prefer to use the default colors that Quattro Pro has chosen for you.

7. Click Finish. Quattro Pro displays a mouse pointer in the shape of a mini-chart. Click
   in the worksheet where you want the upper-left corner of the chart to appear.

   Quattro Pro places the chart in the current sheet as shown in Figure 25.6 (or in the
   Chart window, depending on your selection in the previous step). You learn how to
   modify the basic chart to improve its appearance in "Enhancing a Chart" later in this
   chapter.

Note

You can easily move or resize the chart in the current sheet. To do so, click a border of the
chart to select it (if it isn't already selected—black handles surround a selected chart). To
resize the chart, position the mouse pointer on a black handle and drag to the desired size.
To move the chart, position the mouse pointer on a border of the chart (but not on a black
handle); a four-headed arrow pointer appears. Drag the chart to the desired position.

*If a new chart includes data you don't want to chart, see "Selecting a Block for Charting" in the
Troubleshooting section at the end of this chapter.*

*If most of the data values on a chart can't be determined because the Y-axis goes too high, see
"Charting Large Values" in the Troubleshooting section at the end of this chapter.*

Figure 25.6
The completed chart appears in the notebook.

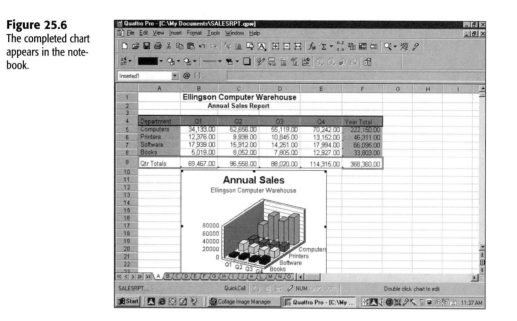

UNDERSTANDING COMMON CHART TERMS

Most charts (except for bullet charts, text charts, pie charts, and doughnut charts) have a Y-axis (a vertical left edge), and an X-axis (a horizontal bottom edge). In rotated charts, the Y-axis is the bottom edge, and the X-axis is the left edge. Quattro Pro automatically divides each axis with tick marks and scales the numbers on the Y-axis, based on the minimum and maximum numbers in the associated data block. The intersection of the Y-axis and the X-axis is called the origin. The origin is zero unless you specify otherwise.

A chart is made up of one or more data series, each of which reflects a category of data. The first category of data is always series 1, the second is series 2, and so on. Some chart types use a limited number of data series; for example, pie and doughnut charts use one data series, and XY charts use two or more. Other chart types, such as line charts, can chart multiple data series.

Legends are text blocks that are placed beside or below a chart to explain the symbols, colors, or fill used to denote each data series. Titles are text blocks placed above the chart and along the horizontal and vertical axes that provide information about the overall chart. Labels are text entries used to explain specific data items or entries in a chart.

UNDERSTANDING CHART TYPES

Several types of charts are available in Quattro Pro: Area/Line, Bar, Stacked Bar, Pie, Specialty, and Text. Each of the chart types also offers several variations.

SELECTING A DIFFERENT TYPE OF CHART

You can change a chart to a different type in several ways, but you can change a chart's type only if the chart is displayed in the Chart window, or if you first select the chart if it is displayed in a notebook.

To select a new chart type for a chart that is displayed in the Chart window or which has been selected in the notebook, point to an area in the chart outside any chart objects, and click the right mouse button. Choose Type/Layout from the QuickMenu to display the Chart Types dialog box (see Figure 25.7). You can also display this dialog box by activating the chart and choosing Chart, Type/Layout.

Figure 25.7
Use the Chart Types dialog box to select the type of chart to display.

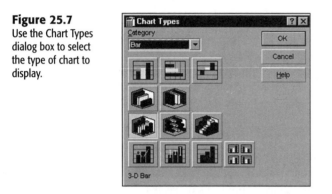

> **Note**
>
> If your chart is displayed in the worksheet, you need to activate the chart before you can access the Chart main menu. To activate a chart, click an area in the chart that is outside any chart objects (but inside the chart border). An activated chart displays a thick border with diagonal lines. Click outside the activated chart to return to the default Quattro Pro main menu.

As you select each basic type of chart from the Category drop-down list box—Area/Line, Bar, Stacked Bar, Pie, Specialty, or Text—small samples of each of the optional variations are shown in the dialog box. Clicking once on any sample chart in the dialog box shows the name of the chart type at the bottom of the dialog box. As soon as you select a new chart type and click OK, your chart is changed to the selected type. The following sections briefly describe the basic chart types.

You can also click the down arrow next to the Change the Chart Type button on the Chart Property Bar. A palette of chart samples appears. As you point to a chart sample on the palette, Quattro Pro instantly changes the chart in the spreadsheet, displaying the chart type to which you're pointing. Click a chart sample on the Chart Type palette to change the chart type.

UNDERSTANDING VARIATIONS WITHIN CHART CATEGORIES

Quattro Pro offers many different variations within the different chart categories. These include 2D (two-dimensional) charts, 3D (three-dimensional) charts, rotated charts, and combination charts. To make the best choice of a chart for your needs, you should understand these variations.

UNDERSTANDING 2D CHARTS

Two-dimensional (2D) charts are the most common type of business charts. In this chart, data is plotted using an X-axis and a Y-axis or, in the case of column and pie charts, using no axis at all. If you want to chart some data using the second Y-axis, you must use a 2D chart.

UNDERSTANDING 3D CHARTS

A 3D chart plots data in a three-dimensional perspective. Instead of just using an X-axis and a Y-axis, a 3D chart adds a Z-axis. In some cases, 3D charts do a better job than 2D charts of showing the complex relationships between groups of data items. You might want to experiment with the Chart, Perspective settings to change the view of 3D charts.

UNDERSTANDING ROTATED CHARTS

Sometimes you can create a more stunning visual effect by rotating a chart. Rotated charts place the X-data series along the left vertical axis and the Y-data series along the horizontal axis. Values are plotted as horizontal distances from the left axis instead of vertical distances from the lower axis. Don't overdo the use of rotated charts. Most people find rotated charts harder to interpret.

UNDERSTANDING COMBO CHARTS

Quattro Pro enables you to mix chart types so that you can compare different sets of data. You can combine a bar chart and a line, area, or a high-low chart. You also can display multiple columns, 3D columns, pies, 3D pies, or bar charts. Charts that combine a bar chart and a line, area, or a high-low chart, are used to display data that is related, but that requires different types of plotting to best show different data series.

Charts that show multiple columns, pies, or bars show several different data series plotted as individual charts, but include each individual chart within a single-named chart in the notebook. When you use multiple columns or pies, each column or pie is the same size. You can compare how the data items within each data series relate as a percentage of the total of the data series, but you cannot determine the relative values of data items between series.

UNDERSTANDING AREA/LINE CHARTS

Quattro Pro offers several variations on the theme of area and line charts. These include the following types.

LINE CHARTS

Line charts are the most common type of chart and one of the easiest to understand. Line charts plot values using individual lines to connect the data points for each data series.

Standard line charts plot data values using the height of the line above the bottom of the chart to indicate differences. Rotated line charts plot data value variations as distances from the left side of the chart.

Tip #164 from	If one data set in a line chart has much higher values than the remaining data sets, consider plotting the out-of-proportion data set against the secondary Y-axis. Right-click the line plotting the data set, select Line Series Properties, and Secondary.
Trudi Reisner	

AREA CHARTS

Area charts emphasize broad trends. Area charts plot the first data series closest to the X-axis and stack additional data series one above another. Each data series line represents the total of the data series being plotted plus all lower data series. Area charts are filled between the origin and the plotted lines.

Area charts can also be displayed using either standard or rotated orientation, depending on your needs.

3D AREA CHARTS

3D area charts are similar to 2D area charts, except that 3D area charts appear to have depth. This third dimension is not used to plot data, but rather to provide a more substantial appearance. 3D area charts plot the first data series closest to the X-axis, and stack additional data series one above another. Each data series line represents the total of the data series being plotted plus all lower data series. 3D area charts are filled between the origin and the plotted lines. Figure 25.8 shows a 3D area chart of the sales data in the Chart window, after the Row/Column Swap check box in the Chart Series dialog box was selected.

PART

III

CH

25

Figure 25.8
Use 3D area charts to emphasize trends in your data.

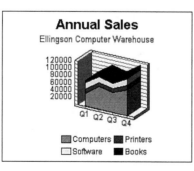

Tip #165 from
Trudi Reisner

To change the emphasis of your chart, select the Row/Column Swap check box in the Chart Series dialog box. Right-click an empty area in your chart and select Series from the QuickMenu to display this dialog box.

3D UNSTACKED AREA CHARTS

3D unstacked area charts plot values using lines (which are stretched to add depth) to connect the data points for each data series, while filling the area between the lines and the origin. Because larger values in a 3D unstacked area chart can hide lower values plotted behind them, this type of chart is best suited to displaying sorted data.

RIBBON CHARTS

Ribbon charts are similar to 3D unstacked area charts; they plot values using lines (which are stretched to add depth) to connect the data points for each data series. Ribbon charts, however, do not fill the area between the lines and the origin. Ribbon charts are better than 3D unstacked area charts at displaying unsorted data because larger values are less likely to hide lower values plotted behind them in a ribbon chart.

3D FLOATING MARKER CHARTS

3D floating marker charts are also similar to 3D unstacked area charts. Instead of using lines to connect the data points for each data series, however, small floating blocks are used to represent the data points. 3D floating marker charts are good at displaying unsorted data because the floating blocks are unlikely to hide lower values plotted behind them. Figure 25.9 shows a 3D floating marker chart of the sales data.

Figure 25.9
The floating blocks in 3D floating marker charts are unlikely to hide lower values plotted behind them.

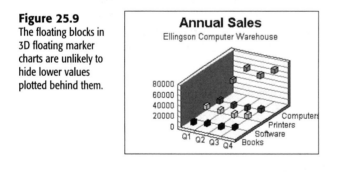

Caution

It might be difficult to see small differences in data values in 3D floating marker charts.

UNDERSTANDING BAR CHARTS

Quattro Pro offers several variations of bar charts. These include 2D, 2.5D, 3D, and several combo chart types.

BAR AND ROTATED 2D BAR CHARTS

A bar chart shows data as a series of bars drawn next to one another. This type of chart is useful for showing how data categories compare over time. In addition to standard bar charts that plot data values as height above the X-axis, rotated 2D bar charts plot data values as the distance from the left axis.

Tip #166 from
Trudi Reisner

In rotated charts, the left axis is the X-axis and the bottom axis is the Y-axis.

VARIANCE CHARTS

A variance chart is similar to a bar chart, except that the origin is adjustable to show how data varies from a specified value. Initially, a variance chart has the origin set to 0, so the chart appears identical to a standard 2D bar chart. After you create the basic variance chart, adjust the origin by pointing to the chart Y-axis values, clicking the right mouse button, and choosing Y-Axis Properties, or by choosing Chart, Axes, Primary Y-Axis. Select the Low text box in the Scale tab of the Y-Axis dialog box, and enter a new value for the origin. Figure 25.10 shows the sales data plotted on a variance chart with the origin adjusted to 30,000.

Figure 25.10
Use a variance chart to plot data with a nonzero origin.

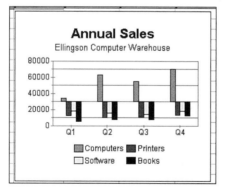

Tip #167 from
Trudi Reisner

Use variance charts to emphasize data that falls below targeted values.

2.5D BAR CHARTS

2.5D bar charts show data as a series of deep bars drawn next to one another. A 2.5D bar chart is not a true 3D chart, because it does not use depth to portray a Z-axis value, but instead to add a third dimension to the bars. This type of chart is useful for showing how data categories compare over time.

Rotated 2.5D bar charts are similar to standard 2.5D bar charts with the data plotted as distances from the left chart axis.

3D BAR CHARTS

3D bar charts show data as groups of bars plotted on a three-dimensional grid. Often a 3D bar chart provides an easier-to-understand display of the relationship between the plotted data series than a 2D bar chart can.

3D bar charts can also be plotted using either standard or rotated orientation. Rotated 3D bar charts might be more difficult to understand.

Tip #168 from
Trudi Reisner

A 3D bar chart might hide smaller values behind large values. Arrange the data series with the largest values first and the smallest values last. If this is not possible, consider using a 2D chart to prevent data from being hidden.

3D STEP CHARTS

3D step charts are nearly identical to 3D bar charts, except that the bars in a step chart touch. Step charts are most useful for displaying data that changes in regular increments, rather than data that might change abruptly in either direction. Figure 25.11 shows the sales data plotted as a 3D step chart.

Figure 25.11
3D step charts use bars that touch one another to plot data.

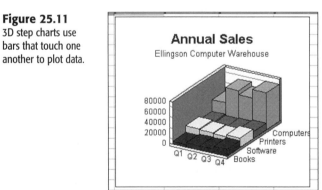

COMBO BAR CHARTS

Quattro Pro provides several types of charts that combine bars and other types of data markers:

- Line-Bar—Plot some data as lines and the rest as bars. This type of chart can be handy for showing trends such as temperature variations over a period of time.

- High Low-Bar—Plot some data using High-Low markers (see the section "Understanding Specialty Charts" later in this chapter) and some as bars. This chart variation is often used to plot stock market data.

- Area-Bar—Combine area charts and bar charts. These charts can be used to display data that exceeds predictions, such as sales that are higher than expected. Because the area chart typically hides bars that fall below the level of the area chart, this type of combo chart can be more difficult to use than line-bar charts.

- Multiple-Bar—Display each data series in a separate bar chart. Each chart uses the same scale, so large values in one data series might reduce the size of the bars in the remaining charts.

| **Tip #169 from** | All data series in multiple-bar charts are plotted against the primary Y-axis so that each |
| *Trudi Reisner* | individual bar chart uses the same scale. |

UNDERSTANDING STACKED BAR CHARTS

Stacked bar charts are similar to area charts because all data is plotted together in a bar, which represents the sum of the data values. There are several variations of stacked bar charts.

STACKED BAR CHARTS

A stacked bar chart shows data as a series of bars stacked one on top of another. This type of chart is useful for showing the portion that data categories contribute to a whole, as well as comparing changes in those contributions over time. Stacked bar charts not only show how each data item varies over time, but also how the total of all data items varies over the same time period.

Comparison charts are variations of stacked bar charts. For these chart types, the boundaries between the data segments in each bar are connected to the corresponding boundaries between the data segments in the next bar. These connecting lines can help you to spot trends more easily, but they might be difficult to understand if the bars contain too many data segments.

Both stacked bar charts and comparison charts can be displayed in standard or rotated format. Figure 25.12 shows the sales data plotted on a rotated 2D comparison chart.

Figure 25.12
Rotated 2D compari-
son charts use lines
to connect the data
segments on each of
the bars.

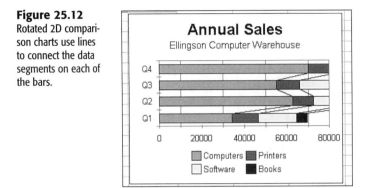

100% STACKED BAR CHARTS

A 100% stacked bar chart is a variation of the stacked bar chart; in this type of chart, the bar is always full height, and the individual data items are shown as their percentage of 100 percent. In addition, 100% stacked bar charts quickly show percentage comparisons between the different data series.

100% stacked bar comparison charts are also a variation of stacked bar charts. For these chart types, the bar is always full height, the individual data items are shown as their percentage of 100 percent, and the boundaries between the data segments in each bar are connected to the corresponding boundaries between the data segments in the next bar.

3D STACKED BAR CHARTS

Similar to regular stacked bar charts, 3D stacked bar charts work best with small amounts of data in comparing sets of data over time. A 3D stacked bar chart shows data as a series of 3D bars stacked one on top of another. This type of chart is useful for showing the portion that data categories contribute to a whole, as well as comparing changes in those contributions over time. 3D stacked bar charts not only show how each data item varies over time, but also how the total of all data items varies over the same time period.

3D 100% stacked bar charts show the data as a percentage. Both 3D stacked bar charts and 3D 100% stacked bar charts can use either standard or rotated orientation. Neither 3D stacked bar charts nor 3D 100% stacked bar charts are truly 3D charts because neither uses the Z-axis to plot data.

UNDERSTANDING PIE CHARTS

All pie chart variations compare values in a single set of data that contains only positive numbers. Each value appears as a slice of the pie, column, or doughnut and represents a percentage of the total. You can plot only one row or one column of numeric data in a pie chart unless you use the multiple pie or column chart options.

Each of the pie chart types can be displayed in 2D or 3D variations. Pie and column charts can also be plotted as multiple 2D or 3D charts if you need to display more than one data series.

PIE CHARTS

Pie charts plot data as wedges or pie slices in a circular chart, with each section representing one data value. You can explode a pie chart section to make it stand out from the pie by right-clicking the section you want to explode, choosing Pie Chart Properties, and typing the Explode Distance as a percentage of the radius in the text box.

Tip #170 from *Trudi Reisner*	If you attempt to plot too many data items, the wedges of the pie chart become too small to understand easily. Use column charts to plot data series with large numbers of individual items.

DOUGHNUT CHARTS

A doughnut chart is a variation of a pie chart; unlike a pie chart, however, a doughnut chart has a center ring cut out. You use a doughnut chart exactly as you use pie charts.

COLUMN CHARTS

A column chart compares values in a single set of data that contains only positive numbers. Each value appears as a section of the column and represents a percentage of the total. You can plot only one row or one column of numeric data in a single column chart. Column charts are similar in function to pie charts, but column charts are more effective when you want to plot a large number of data items.

A 3D column chart compares values in a single set of data that contains only positive numbers. Each value appears as a section of the column and represents a percentage of the total. You can plot only one row or one column of numeric data in a 3D column chart. 3D column charts are similar to 2D column charts, except that the column is displayed with a third dimension: depth.

PART

III

CH

25

Tip #171 from *Trudi Reisner*	Use multiple column or pie charts to plot more than one data series.

UNDERSTANDING SPECIALTY CHARTS

Specialty charts provide you with several chart types that can plot certain types of data more effectively than any of the other types of charts.

UNDERSTANDING XY CHARTS

The XY chart, often called a scatter chart, is a variation of a line chart. Like a line chart, an XY chart has values plotted as points in the chart. Unlike a line chart, an XY chart has its X-axis labeled with numeric values instead of labels.

Quattro Pro always plots the independent variable (data you can change or control) on the X-axis, and the dependent variables (data you cannot control or change, and which is dependent on the independent variable) on the Y-axis; thus, the independent data should be in the first row or column, and the dependent data should be in the second and succeeding rows or columns. Figure 25.13 shows an XY chart of the sine function for X-axis values from 0 to 360 degrees.

Figure 25.13
XY charts plot the independent variable on the X-axis and the dependent variables on the Y-axis.

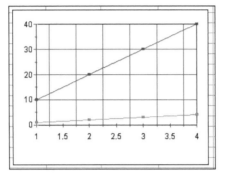

HIGH-LOW CHARTS

High-low charts are sometimes called HLCO charts, which stands for high-low-close-open. A high-low chart is especially useful for charting data about the price of a stock over time. The HLCO figures represent the stock's highest and lowest price in the given time period, the stock's price at the end of the time period, and the stock's price at the start of the time period.

Each set of data normally consists of four figures representing high, low, close, and open values. The set of data is typically represented on the chart as a vertical line with tick marks. The line extends from the low value to the high value. The close value is represented by a tick mark extending to the right of the line, and the open value is represented by a tick mark extending to the left. The total number of lines on the chart depends on the number of time periods included. If you have a fifth data series, it is plotted as a volume series against the second Y-axis.

RADAR CHARTS

A radar chart plots data radiating from a single center point. X-axis values appear as spokes in a wheel, and Y-axis data is plotted on each spoke. Radar charts might make spotting trends easier, depending on the type of data being charted.

3D SURFACE

3D surface charts display data as lines connecting the data items for each series. The line for each data series is connected to the line for the next data series, and the area between the lines is filled in with different colors.

3D CONTOUR CHARTS

3D contour charts are similar to surface charts, except in the method used to color the surface plot. Instead of coloring the segments between each set of lines with a distinct color, contour charts apply color to show how far the surface lies above the origin. Contour charts can be used to show elevations, as in contour maps.

3D SHADED SURFACE CHARTS

3D shaded surface charts are another variation on surface and contour charts. The shaded surface chart uses a single color to create the surface, but applies different shading to show the slope of the surface between data points. Shaded surface charts might reproduce better than surface and contour charts on black-and-white printers.

UNDERSTANDING TEXT CHARTS

Text charts are unlike the other types of Quattro Pro charts because they are not used to display numerical data. There are two types of text charts: bullet charts and blank charts.

BULLET CHARTS

Bullet charts are a special type of chart often used in presentations. Instead of charting numerical data, bullet charts display notebook text in a special format. In a bullet chart, a title line is followed by one or more levels of bulleted text, usually presenting information in an outline-style format.

To create a bullet chart, you use a block of text either two or three columns wide in the notebook as the source of chart data. The first column contains the chart title, the second contains the first level of bulleted text, and the third contains an optional second level of bulleted text.

BLANK CHARTS

Blank charts are another special type of Quattro Pro chart. Instead of plotting notebook data, blank charts enable you to create graphics objects that you can place anywhere you like in a notebook. Blank charts can contain text, objects you create using the drawing tools available in the Chart window, and imported graphics.

PART
III
CH
25

Tip #172 from	Use the Chart and Drawing Tools toolbar to draw floating objects directly on a notebook
Trudi Reisner	page rather than using a blank chart. That way, the chart pane won't cover your data.

You can also use the tools on the notebook window Chart and Drawing Tools toolbar to draw floating objects directly on a notebook page. Floating objects drawn on the notebook page are similar to the objects you draw in a blank chart, except that floating objects drawn on the notebook page do not have an opaque chart pane to obscure other objects on the page. For example, if you draw an arrow directly on a notebook page, objects under the arrow's path are not covered by a rectangular box as they would be by an arrow drawn in a floating chart and then added to the page.

ENHANCING A CHART

Quattro Pro offers several options for improving the appearance of your charts and producing final-quality output suitable for business presentations. After you have created the basic chart, you use the Chart menu commands to change the selection of chart blocks, types and orientation; data labels and legends; X-, Y-, and optional second Y-axes; borders and grids; colors; hatch patterns; fonts; and lines.

CHANGING THE CHART ORIENTATION

The initial orientation Quattro Pro selects for the rows and columns of data might not always be the optimal choice. A different chart layout might be more effective in representing your data.

By default, Quattro Pro assumes that the first row or column of your data with labels contains the X-axis labels (the labels along the bottom of the chart that group the data series in comparable sets). To change the orientation of the data series, choose Chart, Series; and then select the Row/Column Swap check box in the Chart Series dialog box.

ADDING TITLES

When you chart data from a notebook, you can specify the titles with the Chart Expert, or after you create and view the chart. With the Chart, Titles command, you can create a Main Title, a Subtitle, an X-axis Title, a Y1-Axis Title, and a Y2-Axis Title (see Figure 25.14).

Figure 25.14
Use the Chart Titles dialog box to add titles to your charts.

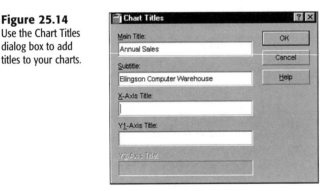

You use the Main Title and Subtitle text boxes to create the first and second titles; they appear centered above the chart, with the first title in larger type above the second title. You use the X-Axis Title, Y1-Axis Title, and Y2-Axis Title text boxes to add titles for the chart axes. You can move the main and subtitles, but you cannot move the X- or Y-Axis titles.

You can edit the titles and notes by choosing Chart, Titles and changing or editing the contents of the text boxes. When you have finished entering or editing the titles, click OK. You also can change the color, font, and text attributes of any title by right-clicking the title you want to change, and choosing the Title Properties option.

Right-click any chart object to see the many properties you can change in your charts.

Quattro Pro offers many different options for enhancing charts. These sections have shown only a few of the possibilities. You'll also want to explore some other options such as changing the viewpoint for a 3D chart, changing the fonts used to display text objects in a chart, and even using bitmaps (pictures) as backgrounds in your charts. To see the many possibilities, right-click an object, such as a data series, the chart background, or a title, and choose the object's Properties selection. You'll find that the resulting dialog boxes provide hundreds of options you can use to fully customize your Quattro Pro charts.

PRINTING CHARTS IN THE NOTEBOOK

Quattro Pro can print a chart from the Chart window or as part of a notebook sheet. In many cases, however, you'll find that adding a chart directly into a notebook sheet will be much more effective.

Whenever you plan to print a chart, you should first preview it by choosing File, Print Preview. You might, for example, find that you need to adjust the size of charts added to the notebook. Figure 25.15 shows a print preview of a notebook with a chart added to the notebook. To print the notebook and chart, click the Print button.

PART

III

CH

25

Figure 25.15
A print preview of a chart added to a notebook block shows how your report will print.

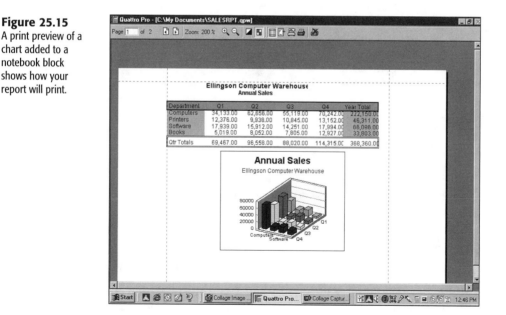

PRACTICAL PROJECT

If you're a stock market investor, you will find the High Low chart helpful for tracking daily stock market prices. The High Low chart is a specialty line chart. This format is used to show two values for each Y-axis category. To create a High Low chart, select two rows of data (and as many columns as you like). The first row represents the high value, and the second represents the low value. The High-Low chart is an Y-axis-oriented chart, causing the data series to have little bearing on the data, as shown in Figure 25.16.

Figure 25.16
You can use the High Low chart to track stock market prices.

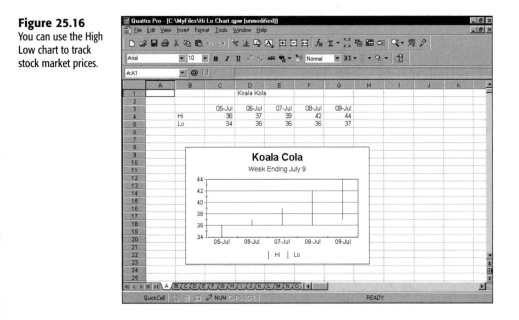

TROUBLESHOOTING

SELECTING A BLOCK FOR CHARTING

The new chart includes data you don't want to chart.

Select the block you want to chart before you choose Insert, Chart. Otherwise, Quattro Pro includes the entire current block of data in the chart.

CHARTING LARGE VALUES

Most of the data values on a chart can't be determined because the Y-axis goes too high.

Quattro Pro automatically scales the Y-axis to show the largest values in the chart. You might need to select a smaller data block that doesn't include the largest values, or change the chart to a 2D chart and chart the largest values on the second Y-axis.

CHAPTER **26**

PRINTING REPORTS

In this chapter

SETTING UP A REPORT

Setting up a report in Quattro Pro can be simple. A basic report, for example, requires only a few mouse clicks or commands to print. Usually, however, an effective report is a little more thought out. Quattro Pro has many options that enable you to customize your printed reports so that they look professional and convey the information properly.

The following sections show you how to print reports quickly and efficiently. Whether your report is a short report of a page or less or a longer multiple-page report, you'll find the process is quite similar.

SELECTING THE PRINT BLOCK

If you don't specify a block to print, Quattro Pro automatically sets the entire active area of the current notebook sheet as the print block, so it's important to understand how Quattro Pro determines the active area of a notebook sheet. The active area of a sheet is defined as the rectangular area between cell A1 and the intersection of the last column and the last row that contain entries. Figure 26.1 demonstrates how this works. In this figure, the active area extends from A1 to E14. Cell E14 does not contain any data, but is at the intersection of the last column and the last row used in the notebook. If you print the notebook shown in Figure 26.1, but don't specify a print block, Quattro Pro will print the block A1..E14.

Figure 26.1
Quattro Pro automatically prints the active area of the current sheet if you don't specify a block.

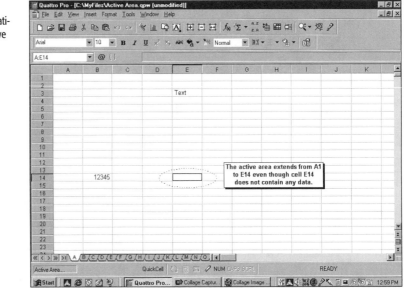

PRINTING A SINGLE BLOCK

If you preselect a block, the selected block becomes the print block. When a print block has been specified, Quattro Pro remembers the specified block and uses the same block as the print block unless you specify a different block. If you forget to preselect the block to print, you can specify the block in the Selection text box of the Spreadsheet Print dialog box. You can select the block with the mouse or the keyboard, or you can type the block addresses.

Tip #174 from	If you don't want to print the entire active area of the notebook, be sure to preselect the
Trudi Reisner	desired print block.

To print a specified print block, follow these steps:

1. Select the block you want to print.

2. Choose File, Print or click the Print a Notebook or Chart button to display the Spreadsheet Print dialog box (see Figure 26.2).

Figure 26.2
Use the Spreadsheet Print dialog box to specify what you want to print.

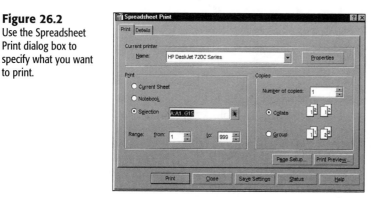

3. Select the Print tab if necessary, and then click Print.

Tip #175 from	If your printer doesn't print in color, be sure the Adjust Image to Print Black and White
Trudi Reisner	check box on the Details tab is selected before you print. Keep in mind that this check box
	might be grayed out for some black-and-white printers.

PART

III

CH

26

If you selected the correct print block, and text is cut off when a report prints, see "Extending the Print Block" in the Troubleshooting section at the end of this chapter.

If the printed report includes blank pages, see "Specifying Exactly What to Print" in the Troubleshooting section at the end of this chapter.

PRINTING MULTIPLE BLOCKS

For many reports, a two-dimensional block—a single rectangular area on one notebook sheet—is all you need to print. Sometimes, however, you might need to print three-dimensional blocks or multiple 2D blocks contained on one or more notebook sheets.

A 3D print block includes the same block on two or more notebook sheets. You specify a 3D print block by preselecting the block or by entering the block address or name in the Selection text box of the Spreadsheet Print dialog box—the same way you specify a 2D block. After you have selected the block on the first sheet, hold down the Shift key and click the notebook sheet tabs to move to the final sheet of the block. When you have selected a 3D block, Quattro Pro draws a thick line under the sheet tabs to show the sheets that are included in the block.

→ For more information on blocks, **see** "Using Blocks," **p. 375**

Multiple print blocks are two or more blocks that might be on the same or different notebook sheets. You can use multiple print blocks when you want to print part of the information on a sheet, but you don't want to include certain information that might be between the blocks you do want to print. To specify multiple print blocks, select the first block, and then press and hold down the Ctrl key while you select additional blocks. To type the names or addresses of multiple print blocks, enter the first block name or address in the Selection text box of the Spreadsheet Print dialog box, type a comma, and then type the next block.

Tip #176 from
Trudi Reisner

When you specify multiple print blocks, previewing the printed output is always a good idea, so you might want to choose File, Print Preview; or File, Print, and click the Print Preview button to open Print Preview. Press Esc or click the Close the Print Preview Window button to close Print Preview.

Figure 26.3 shows a notebook with two print blocks selected, and Figure 26.4 shows the result of selecting File, Print Preview to preview the printed output. Press Esc to return to the notebook display.

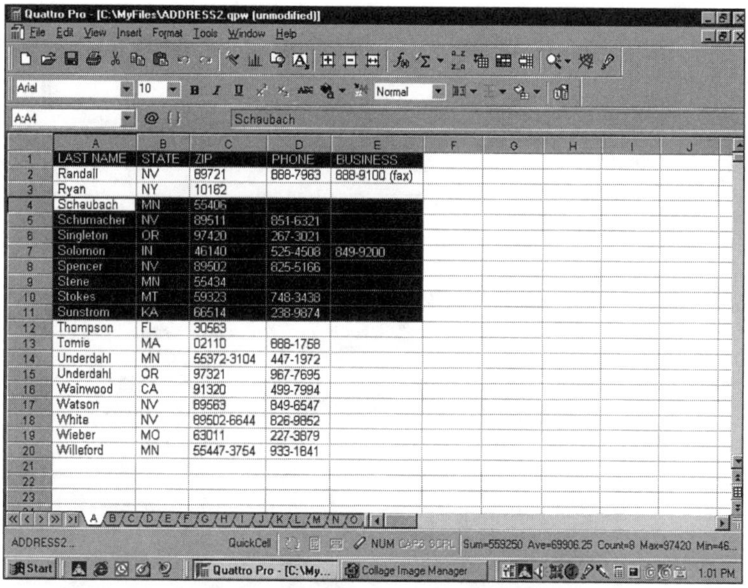

Figure 26.3
If you want to print only selected areas of your notebook, pre-select the print blocks before printing.

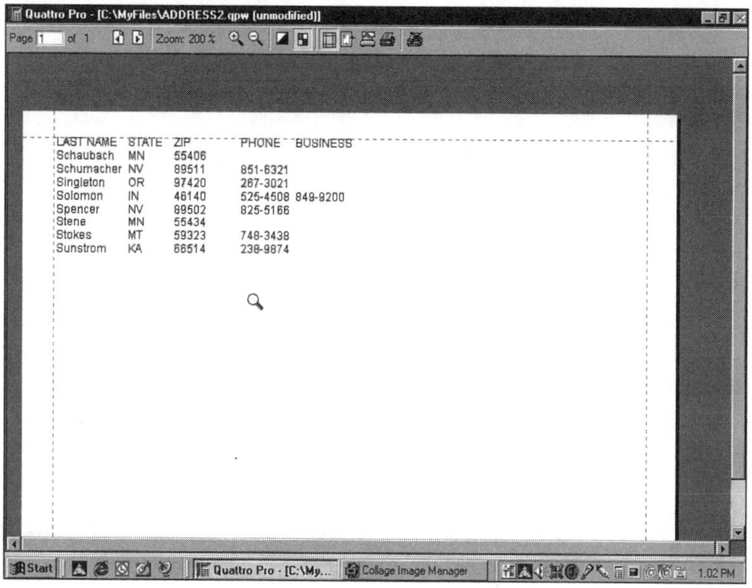

Figure 26.4
Print Preview shows that the printed report will contain only the preselected print blocks.

You can specify any combination of 2D and 3D print blocks. Quattro Pro prints the blocks in the order in which you select the blocks or enter the block names or addresses.

ADDING ENHANCEMENTS TO THE REPORT

You can use Quattro Pro's options to enhance your reports in many different ways. You select many printing options through the Spreadsheet Page Setup dialog box, which displays when you choose File, Page Setup or File, Print or click the Print tool on the toolbar, and choose Page Setup from the Print dialog box. The Spreadsheet Page Setup dialog box includes tabs for specifying paper type, a header and footer, margins, print scaling, named print settings, and other options (see Figure 26.5).

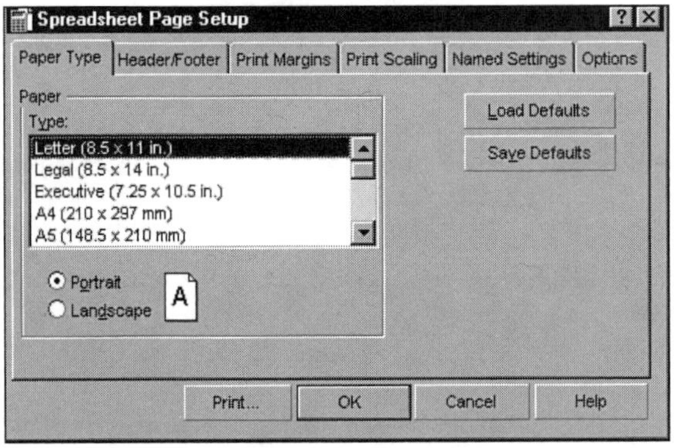

Figure 26.5
Use the Spreadsheet Page Setup dialog box Paper Type tab to specify the size and orientation of your paper.

Note

Use the Save Defaults button to save your settings so that Quattro Pro will automatically use them in the future. Use the Load Defaults button to return all settings to their default settings.

SELECTING THE TYPE OF PAPER

The Paper Type tab of the Spreadsheet Page Setup dialog box shown earlier in Figure 26.5 enables you to select the type of paper and whether the report will print in Portrait or Landscape orientation. The Portrait selection prints with the paper tall and narrow; the Landscape selection prints with the paper short and wide. The Type list box displays the paper sizes available for the selected printer.

Note

You might have to change the paper in your printer if you select a different paper size. The Type list shows the paper sizes your printer can use, not the sizes loaded into your printer.

PRINTING A HEADER OR FOOTER

A header is information printed in one or two lines at the top of each page of a report. A footer is information printed in one or two lines at the bottom of each page of a report. You specify a header or footer in the Spreadsheet Page Setup dialog box Header/Footer tab (see Figure 26.6).

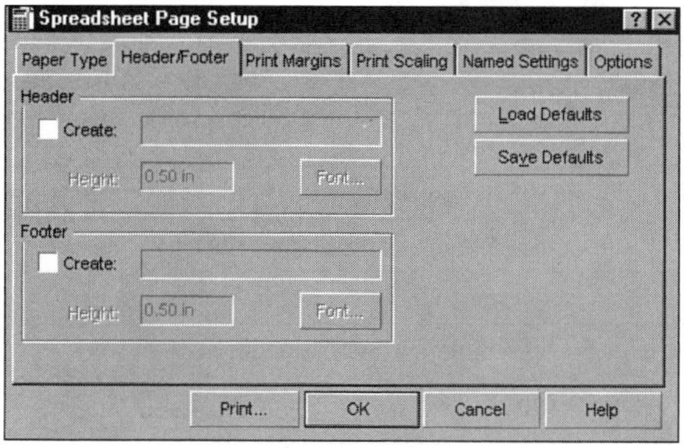

Figure 26.6
Use the Spreadsheet Page Setup dialog box Header/Footer tab to specify report headers and footers.

Tip #177 from
Trudi Reisner

Include the name of your Quattro Pro notebook in the header or footer to make it easy to remember which notebook produced the report.

Each line of a header or footer can have up to three parts: a left-aligned, a centered, and a right-aligned section. When you enter header or footer text, separate the segments with a vertical bar (|). Segments that precede the first vertical bar are left-aligned; segments following the first vertical bar but preceding the second vertical bar are centered; and segments following the second vertical bar are right-aligned. To place the remaining segments of the header or footer on a second line, use (pound signs)Quattro Proprinting headers/footers#n in the header or footer at the point where you want to create the line break.

Table 26.1 describes the symbols you use to display information in headers and footers. You also can instruct Quattro Pro to include the contents of a cell by entering a backslash (\), followed by the cell address or block name.

PART

III

CH

26

TABLE 26.1   HEADER AND FOOTER FORMATTING SYMBOLS

Symbol	Description
#	Current page number
#d	Current date in Short International format
#D	Current date in Long International format
#ds	Current date in standard Short format
#Ds	Current date in standard Long format
#f	Notebook name
#F	Notebook name with path
#n	Prints balance of text on new line

continues

TABLE 26.1   CONTINUED

Symbol	Description
#p	Current page number
#P	Total number of pages in printout
#p+n	Current page number plus the number
#P+n	Total number of pages in printout plus the number
#t	Current time in Short International format
#T	Current time in Long International format
#ts	Current time in standard Short format
#Ts	Current time in standard Long format
@	Current date
|	Left-, center-, or right-aligned text

SETTING PRINT MARGINS

Print margins are the distance between the edges of the paper and the beginning of the area where Quattro Pro can print. The Spreadsheet Page Setup dialog box Print Margins tab enables you to change margins (see Figure 26.7).

Figure 26.7
Use the Spreadsheet Page Setup dialog box Print Margins tab to specify the size of margins.

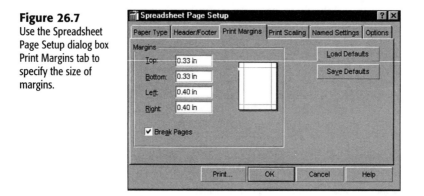

Tip #178 from
Trudi Reisner

Most laser and inkjet printers cannot print to the edge of a sheet of paper. See your printer manual to determine the minimum acceptable margins. If you are outside the printable margin, you will usually get a message box alerting you.

By default, Quattro Pro reserves a margin that cannot be used for any printing: 0.33 inch at the top and at the bottom of each page, and 0.4 inch at each side of the page. In addition, another 0.5 inch is reserved between the top and bottom margins and any data for headers or footers.

The Spreadsheet Page Setup dialog box Print Margins tab contains four different text boxes you can use to set the page margins: Top, Bottom, Left, and Right.

Use the Break Pages check box to specify whether Quattro Pro should print continuously, regardless of margin settings, or start new pages on a new sheet observing the margin settings. This option applies only to printers using continuous forms that can print to the edge of the paper. If the Break Pages check box is not checked, any header will print only on the first page, and any footer will print only on the final page.

Tip #179 from
Trudi Reisner

Quattro Pro 9 includes a new Page view that displays your notebook sheets the way they will look when printed. To access this view, choose View, Page. While in Page view, you can change margins onscreen by dragging the dotted blue lines to the desired location. In addition, you can move hard page breaks by dragging the solid blue lines that separate each page.

You also can access the Page Setup dialog box while in Page view by double-clicking in the margin area. To return to the normal view when you are finished, choose View, Draft.

SETTING PRINT SCALING

You can reduce or enlarge the size of a printed report by using print scaling. This option enables you to specify an exact percentage, or to have Quattro Pro automatically reduce the size of the printout enough to fit the entire report on the number of pages you specify. You use the Print Scaling tab of the Spreadsheet Page Setup dialog box to specify print scaling (see Figure 26.8).

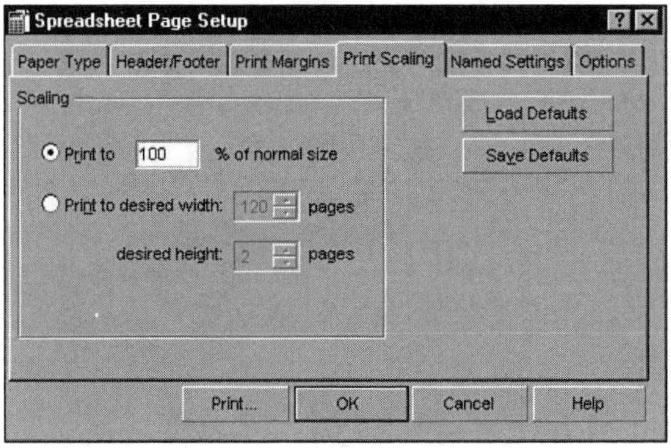

Figure 26.8
Use the Spreadsheet Page Setup dialog box Print Scaling tab to reduce or enlarge the scale of the printed report.

Tip #180 from
Trudi Reisner

> If you use Print to Desired Width and Desired Height, choose File, Print Preview before printing to preview the printed report. This enables you to verify that the report will not be reduced to an unreadable size.

To fit all the printed output on a specified number of pages, select the Print to Desired Width and Desired Height option. Then type the number of pages for the width and height, or use the spin boxes to select the number of pages you want. Quattro Pro attempts to reduce the size of the print enough to fit the entire report on a single page. If the report still doesn't fit on a single page, Quattro Pro uses the maximum compression on all pages.

To control the exact level of compression, select the Print to % of Normal Size option and enter a percentage in the text box. To reduce the size of print area by one-half, for example, type 50 in the text box. You can expand the print area also by entering a number larger than 100. To print the report three times the normal size, type 300 in the text box.

⚠️ *If you used Print to Desired Width and Desired Height and your reports printed much too small and left large blank spaces at the right or the bottom of the page, see "Specifying the Print Block" in the Troubleshooting section at the end of this chapter.*

If the correct print area is specified, and the printed report is still too small to read, see "Printing a Percentage of the Normal Size" in the Troubleshooting section at the end of this chapter.

USING NAMED PRINT SETTINGS

You can save current print settings under a unique name, recall the settings with this name, and reuse the settings without specifying each setting individually. You use the Named Settings tab in the Spreadsheet Page Setup dialog box to create or use named print settings (see Figure 26.9).

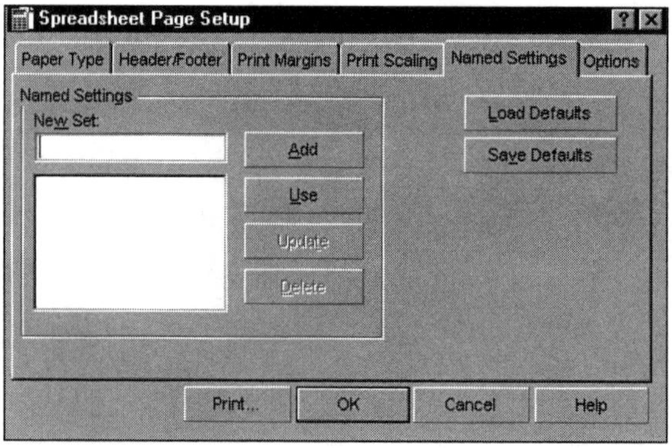

Figure 26.9
Use the Spreadsheet Page Setup dialog box Named Settings tab to save or reuse groups of print settings.

To assign a name to the current print settings, enter the name in the New Set text box and select Add. This enables you to reuse the same group of print settings without going through all the steps to select each option. To change an existing named print setting, highlight the setting you want to change, and select Update. To remove a named setting, select the setting you want to remove, and select Delete. To use an existing named setting, highlight the setting you want to use, and select Use.

PRINTING ROW AND COLUMN HEADINGS

Multiple-page reports can be difficult to understand. This is especially true when you cannot easily determine the correct column or row for data on pages after the first page. One improvement that can make multiple-page reports easier to understand is to include row or column headings, so each printed page includes the descriptive text that explains the data being presented. Setting headings in a printout has an effect similar to freezing titles on a notebook sheet.

Caution

Don't include any rows you designate as a Top Heading and any columns you designate as a Left Heading in the print block—they'll be printed twice.

You use the Options tab in the Spreadsheet Page Setup dialog box to include row or column headings (see Figure 26.10). For the Top Heading, select one or more rows of labels to print above each page of data. For the Left Heading, select one or more columns of data to print at the left of each page of data.

Figure 26.10
Use the Options tab of the Spreadsheet Page Setup dialog box to specify row or column headings and several other print options.

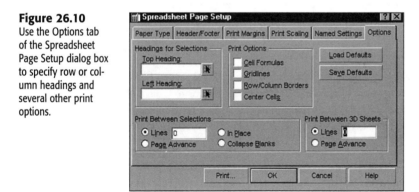

PART

III

CH

26

USING ADDITIONAL PRINT OPTIONS

The Spreadsheet Print Options dialog box has several additional settings you can use to enhance your printed reports. These include

- Cell Formulas—Prints cell formulas instead of the calculated results. This option is primarily for notebook documentation purposes.
- Gridlines—Prints the spreadsheet gridlines. This makes your report look more like the onscreen notebook sheet.
- Row/Column Borders—Includes the spreadsheet frame in your printed report. This is useful when you are developing a notebook, because the printouts show the location of data on the notebook sheet.
- Center Cells—Prints the report centered between the page margins.

You use the Print Between Selections and Print Between 3D Sheets options to specify the separation you want between multiple or 3D blocks.

WORKING WITH PAGE BREAKS

Quattro Pro automatically inserts soft page breaks in your spreadsheet(s). However, you can insert hard page breaks where you want a new page to begin.

You can delete one or all hard page breaks in a spreadsheet.

Page Breaks view shows you where the page breaks are on a sheet, and allows you to change the page breaks to include or exclude columns and rows. You can adjust soft and hard page breaks. Information on how to adjust soft page breaks are covered later in this chapter.

INSERTING AND DELETING PAGE BREAKS

To manually insert page breaks into your spreadsheets, click in the far-left column of the block and the row you want to begin on the next page. Choose Insert, Page Break, Create. Quattro Pro displays a page break marker, a solid black line in the row above the cell you selected for the hard page break.

> **Caution**
>
> Don't make entries in the row containing the page break marker. Entries in this row do not print.

To delete a single page break, choose Insert, Page Break, Delete. To delete all page breaks, choose Insert, Page Break, Delete All.

USING PAGE BREAKS VIEW

To use Page Break view, choose View, Page Breaks. Quattro Pro displays your sheet in the Page Breaks view, as shown in Figure 26.11. A border surrounds the page. You can drag a border to include and exclude columns and rows on the sheet.

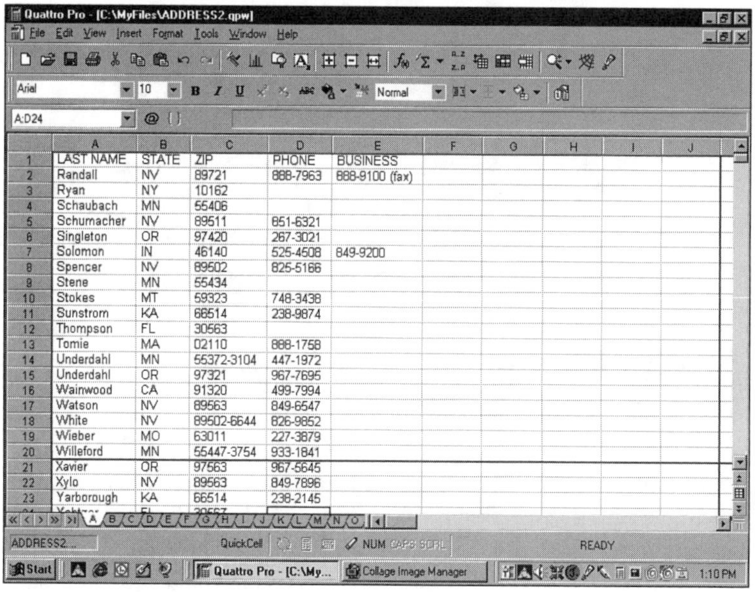

Figure 26.11
Use Page Breaks view to see where page breaks are and to change the page breaks.

If you want to exclude a column, drag the right border to the left one column. To include a column, drag the right border to the right one column. If you want to change the page breaks for a row, drag the bottom border of the sheet.

To exit Page Breaks view, choose a different view from the View menu.

SELECTING YOUR PRINTER

To select or configure a printer, or to redirect print output to a file, choose File, Print, and then click the Details tab (see Figure 26.12). The available choices that appear in the Name drop-down list depend on your system configuration.

To configure your printer, select the printer and click Properties. When you make this selection, Windows displays a dialog box specific to your printer. Click OK to return to the Details tab of the Spreadsheet Print dialog box.

If you want to delay printing, perhaps because you want to create a report you'll print on a printer that is temporarily unavailable, select the Print to File option and specify a name for the print file. The print file contains instructions specific to the selected printer and will probably not print correctly on any other type of printer.

PART
III

CH
26

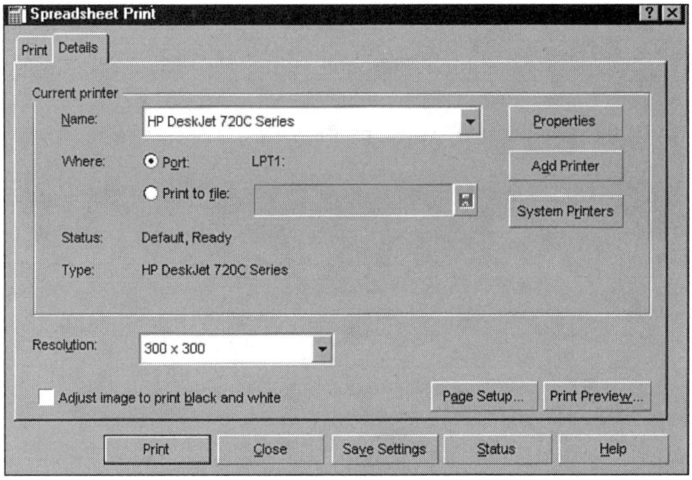

Figure 26.12
Use the Details tab of the Spreadsheet Print dialog box to select your printer.

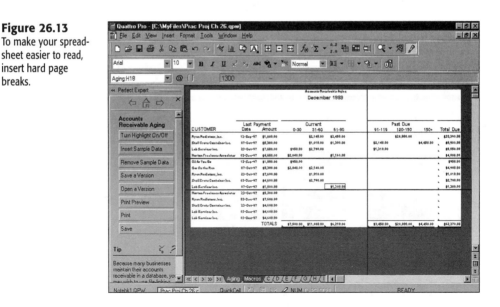

PRACTICAL PROJECT

In many cases, you will be working with a huge spreadsheet that needs to be broken into pages. You can easily insert hard page breaks wherever you need them for better readability. For example, you can set up an accounts receivable spreadsheet using the Accounts Receivable Aging PerfectExpert project. Keep adding data to the spreadsheet, and break the data into sections by inserting hard page breaks, as shown in Figure 26.13. Examine the location of the page breaks in Page Breaks view, and adjust them if necessary. Drag the right and bottom borders to include and exclude columns and rows, perfecting just how you want the spreadsheet to print on individual pages.

Figure 26.13
To make your spreadsheet easier to read, insert hard page breaks.

TROUBLESHOOTING

EXTENDING THE PRINT BLOCK

Even though the correct print block is selected, text is cut off when a report prints.

Long labels can spill over into empty cells to the right. If a label spills over to a cell outside the print block, only the text within the block is printed. Extend the print block to the right to include all the text, or adjust the width of the rightmost column of the print area to include the entire label.

SPECIFYING EXACTLY WHAT TO PRINT

The printed report includes blank pages.

If the print area selection is Notebook, all pages will print even if some pages are blank. Use the Selection text box to specify the exact areas to print.

SPECIFYING THE PRINT BLOCK

Reports printed using Print to Desired Width and Desired Height print much too small, and leave large blank spaces at the right or the bottom of the page.

Be sure to specify the print block. Quattro Pro is probably printing the entire active area of the current notebook page.

PRINTING A PERCENTAGE OF THE NORMAL SIZE

Even though the correct print area is specified, the printed report is still too small to read.

You might need to specify an exact percentage in the Print to % of Normal Size check box rather than using the Print to Desired Width and Desired Height option. Your report might require more pages, but at least you'll be able to read it without a magnifying glass.

CHAPTER **27**

SHARING NOTEBOOKS

In this chapter

PROTECTING A NOTEBOOK WITH A PASSWORD

You can keep your notebooks confidential and secure by assigning a password to them with Quattro Pro's Password feature. This feature enables you to lock your notebook so that no one can open or print it without the password. Other files associated with the document, such as backup or temporary files, are also locked. Every time you open or look at the password-protected notebook, Quattro Pro prompts you to enter the password.

To password-protect a notebook, first save the notebook with File, Save or File Save As. Then name the file, put a check mark in the Password Protect check box, and click Save. The Password Protection dialog box appears (see Figure 27.1).

Figure 27.1
Password-protect your notebook in the Password Protection dialog box.

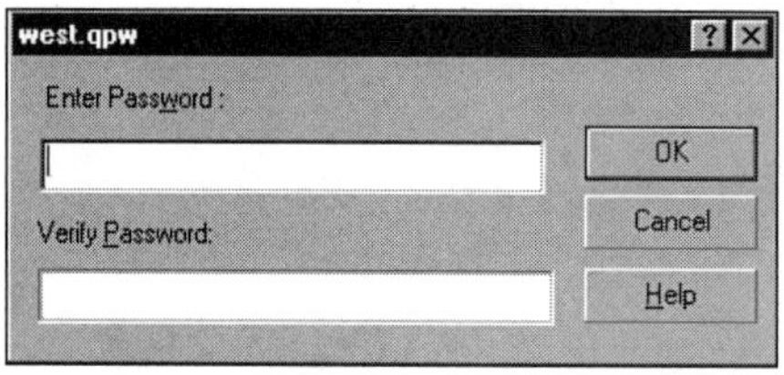

A password can have up to eight characters, and is case sensitive. Enter your password in the Enter Password box. The characters you type appear as pound signs (#) onscreen. Press Tab, type the password again in the Verify Password box, and click OK.

When you open the file, Quattro Pro displays the Password dialog box. Enter the password and press Enter or click OK.

> **Caution**
>
> Use passwords with caution. Quattro Pro will not open a password-protected file unless you enter the correct password. If you forget a password, unfortunately Corel's technical support staff can do nothing to help. The notebook is unavailable forever. So, jot down your passwords and put them in a safe place. Otherwise, you'll have to delete the password-protected file.

To change a password, use File, Save As, and click Save. Quattro Pro prompts you to replace the existing file. Choose Yes. Enter the new password twice. This replaces the old password information with the new.

To remove a password, choose File, Save As, remove the check from the Password Protect check box, and click Save. When Quattro Pro tells you that the file exists, choose Yes.

Tip #181 from
Trudi Reisner

An alternative way to remove password protection is saving the file in another file format.

If you want to change the password for your notebook, see "Changing the Password" in the Troubleshooting section at the end of this chapter.

UNDERSTANDING SHARED WORKBOOKS

Sometimes you might need to interact with associates who also use Quattro Pro. Quattro Pro users can easily work collaboratively and manage shared notebooks effectively.

The Workgroup Sharing feature allows you to share notebooks with colleagues, track and display changes in notebooks, review the notebook to accept and reject changes, resolve conflicts, and use comments.

Quattro Pro's Workgroup Sharing feature allows multiple users to modify a single notebook simultaneously. The shared notebook resides on a network so the users can make changes at the same time. Then, the shared notebook is updated to incorporate the changes. Each user can format the workbooks and make other choices, such as viewing and printing choices, which are used for their own filtered version of the notebook. Changes from multiple users are consolidated automatically at specified intervals, which is called merging workbooks.

In the Notebook Sharing dialog box, you can tell Quattro Pro that you want to allow simultaneous access to a notebook. After doing so, you can set further options. Here are the options you'll need to set up:

- Updating Changes enables you to control how changes made by multiple users are consolidated into the main notebook. You can choose to see the changes whenever the file is saved or in minute-based intervals.

- Tracking Changes lets you control how long to track notebook changes. You need to enable the Keep Change History For option to see merged changes from other users.

- Resolving Conflicts controls how conflicting changes are resolved (for example, when two users change the same cell to different values). Usually, this should always be set to the Ask Me Which Changes to Keep option.

When you share notebooks, you can track changes made by users over a number of days. Quattro Pro uses the History sheet to show a complete list of changes to the notebook. The History list includes the names of the users who made the changes, data that was deleted or replaced, and information about conflicting changes.

PART
III
CH
27

SETTING UP A SHARED NOTEBOOK

To set up a shared notebook, follow these steps:

1. Choose Tools, Workgroup, Sharing to display the Notebook Sharing dialog box.
2. Click the Enable Notebook Sharing check box to turn on the Notebook Sharing feature (see Figure 27.2).

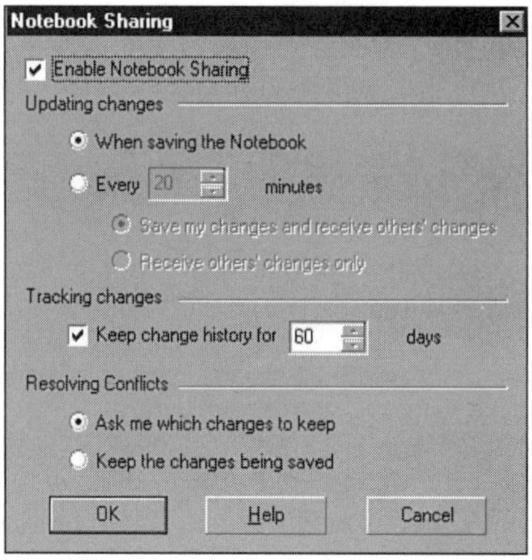

Figure 27.2
Use the Notebook
Sharing dialog box to
enable notebook
sharing and specify
sharing options.

Notebook Sharing ☒

☑ Enable Notebook Sharing

Updating changes

  ⦿ When saving the Notebook

  ○ Every [20] ⬆ minutes

    ⦿ Save my changes and receive others' changes

    ○ Receive others' changes only

Tracking changes

  ☑ Keep change history for [60] ⬆ days

Resolving Conflicts

  ⦿ Ask me which changes to keep

  ○ Keep the changes being saved

[OK] [Help] [Cancel]

3. In the Updating Changes section, choose the When Saving the Notebook option, if it's not already chosen.

4. In the Tracking Changes section, enter the number of days for which you want to keep the change history. Sixty days is the default number of days.

5. In the Resolving Conflicts section, choose the Ask Me Which Changes to Keep option.

6. Click OK. Quattro Pro asks you to save the notebook.

7. Choose Yes to save the notebook.

REVIEWING CHANGES IN A SHARED NOTEBOOK

You can review changes in a shared notebook by all the users. You can view a list of user-names to see who is sharing the notebook with you. The Reviewing feature lets you review changes to the entire workbook, a specific cell, or a block. Each change is identified with a red triangle in the upper-right corner of the cell that contains the changed information.

When you point to a cell that contains a change, Quattro Pro displays a comment in a box near the cell. The comment contains the user's name, date, time, and a description of the change.

You have four choices when reviewing changes: Accept, Accept All, Reject, or Reject All. You must accept or reject a change before you can advance to the next change.

MAKING CHANGES TO A SHARED NOTEBOOK

After the notebook is set up to be shared, Quattro Pro saves the notebook on a network drive so that others can gain access to the shared notebook.

You and other users can make changes to the data in the shared notebook as you normally would edit any notebook. When you make a change to data in a shared notebook, Quattro Pro automatically inserts a comment near the cell that contains the change. This comment contains the user's name, date, time, and a description of the change.

After the changes are made, the next step is to review the notebook. The Review toolbar contains all the tools you need for reviewing a shared notebook. Setting up how to review a shared notebook is described in the next section.

SETTING UP THE REVIEW

Follow these steps to set up the review:

1. Choose Tools, Workgroup, Review Notebook, Review Start/Stop. The Review toolbar appears. The cells that contain changes are surrounded by a thick black border and display a red triangle in the upper-right corner of the cell (see Figure 27.3).

Figure 27.3
The Review toolbar lets you review changes in a shared notebook; a thick black border and a red triangle indicate a cell change.

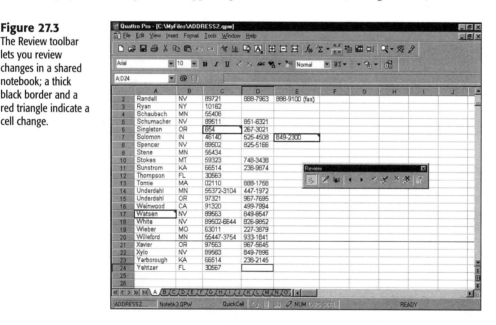

2. To display a list of the users that made changes to the notebook, click the User List button on the Review toolbar. Quattro Pro displays the Select User dialog box.

3. If you want to review only the changes you made to the notebook, check the Mine check box. The All option (default) means that you can review changes made by all the users.

PART

III

CH

27

4. Click OK to close the Select User dialog box.

5. If you want to choose colors for the users, click the Select Color button on the Review toolbar. The Select Color dialog box opens.

6. Select each username and assign it a color. Click the User Color button and choose a color from the palette.

7. Click OK to close the Select Color dialog box.

After you set up how you want to review the notebook, you can use the review tools to accept and reject changes.

SHOWING/HIDING COMMENTS

You can see all the comments in the notebook by choosing Tools, Workgroup, Review Notebook, Show/Hide Comments or clicking the Cell Comments button on the Review toolbar. To hide the comments, repeat the step.

ACCEPTING OR REJECTING CHANGES

Here's how you accept or reject changes:

1. Use the Previous and Next buttons on the Review toolbar to move to the previous and next change in the notebook.

2. Point to a cell that contains a change. You see a comment near the cell that tells you the username, date, time, and description of the change (see Figure 27.4).

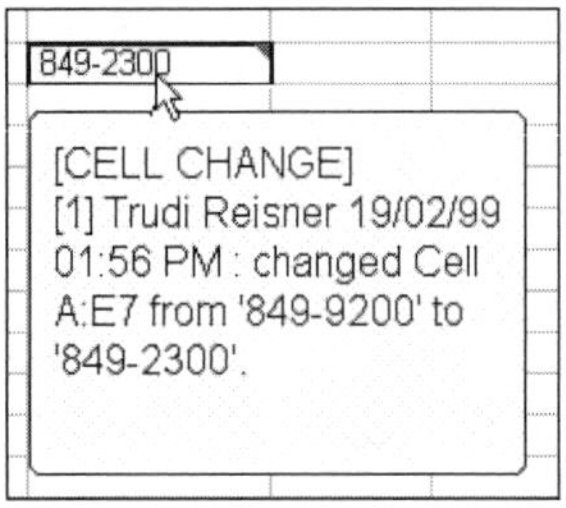

Figure 27.4
A comment contains a username, date, time, and a description of the change.

849-2300

[CELL CHANGE]
[1] Trudi Reisner 19/02/99
01:56 PM : changed Cell
A:E7 from '849-9200' to
'849-2300'.

3. For each change, you have the following choices for accepting and rejecting changes:

- To accept the change and clear its border and red triangle, click the Accept button on the Review toolbar.

- To reject the change and clear its border and red triangle, click the Reject button on the Review toolbar. If Quattro Pro prompts you to select a value for a cell, click the value you want, and then click the Accept button.

- To accept all the changes in the notebook, click the Accept All button on the Review toolbar.

- To reject all the changes in the notebook, click the Reject All button on the Review toolbar.

> **Caution**
>
> Be careful when you choose Accept, Reject, Accept All, or Reject All. Quattro Pro discards the change history when you click these buttons on the Review toolbar.

When two people work on a shared notebook, if User 1 makes a change to a cell and saves the notebook, and then User 2 also saves his or her copy of the notebook, User 2 will see any changes that User 1 has made. The changes will be highlighted with a comment in the notebook that show User 2 the changes that User 1 made, and the changes will be accepted as a matter of course.

If a conflict among changes occurs, you will see a Conflict Resolutions dialog box similar to the one in Figure 27.5. In this dialog box, you choose which version of the change you want to accept.

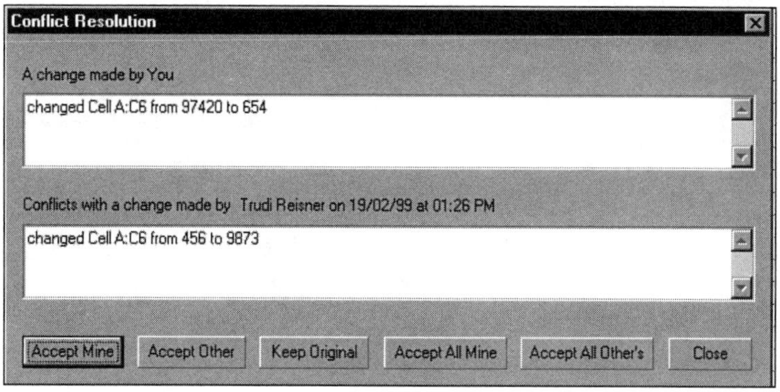

Figure 27.5
The Conflict Resolution dialog box lets you decide which version of the change to keep.

DISABLING NOTEBOOK SHARING

When you're finished sharing and reviewing a notebook, you need to disable the notebook-sharing feature. To do so, choose Tools, Workgroup, Sharing to display the Notebook Sharing dialog box. Click the Enable Notebook Sharing check box to remove the check mark and click OK. Quattro Pro prompts you to save the file. Choose Yes. The notebook is no longer in a shared mode.

PRACTICAL PROJECT

If you created the spreadsheet that was suggested earlier in this book or have a spreadsheet on hand, go in and edit the spreadsheet. Make changes to the data and add comments. Then, review the spreadsheet and accept or reject the changes.

TROUBLESHOOTING

CHANGING THE PASSWORD

You want to change the password for your notebook.

Use File, Save As, click Save, and choose Yes to replace the existing file. Choose a protection option, and enter a different password for the document twice.

USING COREL PRESENTATIONS

CHAPTER 28

GETTING STARTED WITH COREL PRESENTATIONS 9

In this chapter

STARTING COREL PRESENTATIONS 9

You start Corel Presentations 9 like you start any of the applications in Corel WordPerfect Office 2000—by clicking the Start button, and then choosing WordPerfect Office 2000, Corel Presentations 9 from the menu. Additionally, you can start Corel Presentations 9 from the Corel WordPerfect Office 2000 DAD (Desktop Application Director) by clicking the Corel Presentations 9 button on the taskbar.

The Corel Presentations 9 screen displays the Corel PerfectExpert dialog box that puts you to work immediately. You can create a new presentation drawing, a slideshow master, or a slideshow; build one based on a template; or work on another existing document or project.

If you choose to create a new slideshow, Presentations helps you by letting you choose a master slide format made up of various colors, patterns, and graphic lines that make your slides attractive and professional-looking. The master slide style also defines the contents of each slide—bullets, charts, or text, for example—and how each element is to be displayed.

Note

If you want to create a drawing such as a poster, a graphic image, or a sign, choose Presentations Drawing from the list. In fact, when you choose Insert, Graphics, Draw Picture in WordPerfect, Presentations becomes the tool you use to draw the picture. For information on how to use Presentations for drawing, see Chapter 30, "Adding and Enhancing Objects."

SELECTING A PRESENTATION

When you start Corel Presentations 9, the Corel PerfectExpert dialog box appears, as shown in Figure 28.1. From this dialog box, choose to Create New Project or to Work on an Existing Document or Project.

Figure 28.1
You can choose to open or create a file, set preferences, or exit the program in the Corel PerfectExpert dialog box.

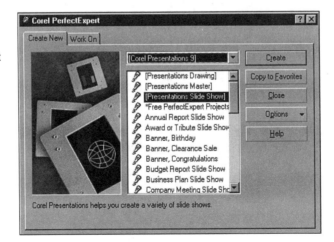

Among the options available to you for creating a new project are

- Presentations Drawing—You can create posters, signs, banners, flyers, and even your own clip-art images.

- Presentations Master—This option lets you create a master slide format made up of various colors, patterns, and graphic lines. A slideshow master also defines the contents of each slide—whether it will contain bullets, charts, or text, and how each element is to be displayed.

- Presentations Slide Show—This option enables you to combine text, graphics, and charts with attractive backgrounds and color schemes to produce professional slides, electronic presentations, or printed handouts.

- PerfectExpert Projects—You can choose from several predefined PerfectExpert projects, each of which helps you through the process of creating a specific type of presentation document.

To begin a new project, click the project type that you want to create and choose Create.

USING THE MASTER GALLERY

If you choose to create a new slideshow, Presentations first takes you to the Startup Master Gallery dialog box where you can choose the background for all the slides in your slideshow (see Figure 28.2).

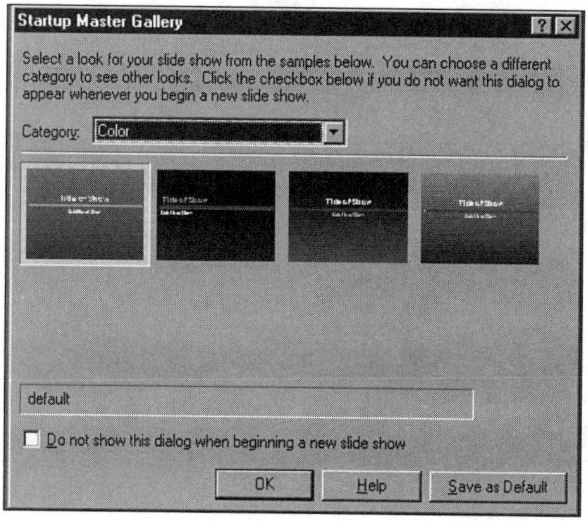

Figure 28.2
In the Startup Master Gallery dialog box, you choose the master that Corel Presentation will use consistently throughout all your slides.

A master is a background for the slideshow that you can apply to one or all slides. Normally, you apply the same master to all slides in the show to create consistency in the presentation. Although you can create your entire show using the default background and change that background later, you might prefer to choose a different background before you begin.

While in the Startup Master Gallery, you can

1. Choose one of the master styles you see displayed on the screen.

2. In the Category drop-down list, choose to see the set of masters appropriate to your presentation mode: Color, Design, Nature, Theme, or Business (for color printers and electronic presentations), Printout (for printing with black-and-white printers), and 35mm (for sending to a slide service).

3. Choose a master from the Master Gallery and click OK. The Master Gallery dialog box closes and takes you to the main Presentations editing screen where you can begin work on your slideshow (see Figure 28.3). If you change your mind later, you can always change the master while working on a slideshow by choosing Format, Master Gallery, and then by using this same simple process.

Figure 28.3
Presentations starts your slideshow with a default background and layout style, including title, subtitle, and so on.

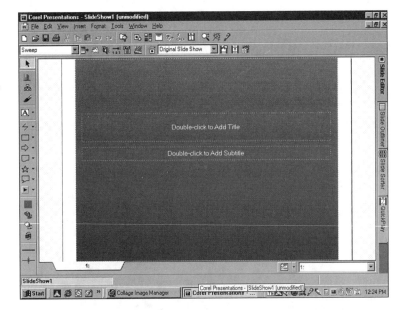

Note

In this and other chapters on Presentations, keep in mind that we are talking about artistic creativity—something that is up to you, the creator. Although we can make suggestions, you should always feel free to experiment with shapes, colors, or layouts, and to ultimately decide what looks and works best for you.

SELECTING A SLIDE LAYOUT

You next choose the slide layout or template you want to use for the first slide. When you click the Select Layout button on the Slide Show Property Bar, a pop-up list appears, as shown in Figure 28.4.

Figure 28.4
You can choose from
among seven slide lay-
outs or templates for
your first slide from
the Select Layout pop-
up list.

Select a slide type. Table 28.1 describes the slide types.

TABLE 28.1   SLIDE TYPES

Type	Description
Title	Background with formatted area for a title and subtitle.
Bulleted List	Background with formatted area for a title, subtitle, and a list of bulleted text.
Text	Background with formatted area for a title and paragraph text.
Org Chart	Background with formatted area for a title and an organizational chart.
Data Chart	Background with formatted area for a title and a data chart.
Combination	Background with formatted area for a bulleted list and a data chart.
None	Background colors and lines only, no text boxes.

Click the type of slide you want to use, and Presentations applies the layout to the slide
onscreen.

Note

When you first create a drawing, the screen that is brought up automatically is blank, like a
white sheet of paper ready for you to fill with your ideas. When you create a slideshow,
you normally work with a background of some sort. To choose to have no background at
all, similar to the draw screen, you must choose Format, Slide Properties, Appearance; click
the blank background; and choose OK. You still have to choose a slide layout, even when
you have no background.

Tip #182 from
Trudi Reisner

The slide layout you choose applies only to the first slide; you select each additional slide's
layout each time you add a slide. The background, on the other hand, remains the same
for all slides.

PART

IV

CH

28

VIEWING THE COREL PRESENTATIONS 9 SCREEN

The Corel Presentations 9 screen includes many screen elements to help you complete your work. In addition to the common Windows features—title bar, menu bar, minimize/ maximize buttons, and so on—Corel Presentations 9 offers a toolbar and a Property Bar to help you perform commands quickly, format your presentation, add elements, and move around your presentation with ease.

In addition to screen elements that help you in your work, Presentations offers a variety of views, or zooms, that enable you to look at your work in the best view for you. Although the default view is Full Page or Slide view, you can, for example, zoom into a specific part of the slide for a closer look. Figure 28.5 shows the Corel Presentations 9 screen in Full Page view, with the screen elements labeled, including the Tool palette.

Figure 28.5
Initially, you see the first slide in Slide view, which is valuable for selecting and editing specific elements on a slide.

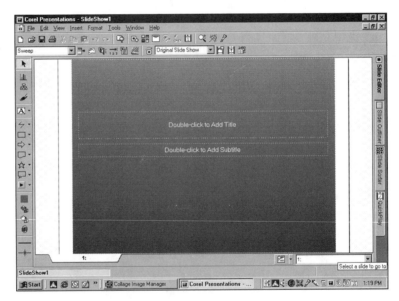

USING THE TOOLBAR, PROPERTY BAR, AND TOOL PALETTE

The various icon bars and tabs on the Corel Presentations 9 screen help you complete your work by providing formatting, command, and navigating shortcuts you use every day in your work. By using the Slide Tabs, for example, you can move quickly to any slide in the presentation; the Property Bar can be used to change the slide layout type; and so on.

TOOLBAR

Table 28.2 identifies the toolbar icons, or buttons, specific to Corel Presentations 9, and describes their uses.

TABLE 28.2   TOOLBAR BUTTONS

Button	Name	Function
	ClipArt	Inserts a clip-art image.
	New Slide	Inserts one or more slides into a slideshow.
	Master Gallery	Displays and retrieves slideshow masters.
	Slide Layout	Chooses the type of slide layout from seven slide layouts or templates.
	Object Animation	Chooses a transition or animation effect for objects and bulleted lists.
	SpeedLink	Creates buttons for playing a sound, launching a file, or performing other actions for slides.
	Play Show	Displays the Play Slide Show dialog box; chooses Show Options and plays the show.
	Zoom Options	Choose how much of your screen you want to see.
	Corel Web Site	Launches your Web browser to access the Corel Web Site on the Internet.
	PerfectExpert	Help feature that displays on the left side of the screen and assists you through the slideshow creation process.

PROPERTY BAR

The Property Bar, located directly below the toolbar, also enables you to format text and other objects, and edit slides. However, it is different from the toolbar in that it changes automatically to offer you tools that match whatever you happen to be working on. There are 20 different Property Bars, and more than 100 different icons. Figure 28.6, shown in the next section, illustrates the basic slideshow Property Bar.

Note

In Presentations 9, the Property Bars have been redesigned, giving you quick and easy access to the features you use most frequently. Many features that you could access only through menus in previous versions of Corel Presentations, you can now access through the Property Bars.

Tip #183 from
Trudi Reisner

If you're not sure what a button on the Property Bar actually does, point at the button with the mouse, and after a second or so, a QuickTip box appears describing the name and purpose of the button.

PART

IV

CH

28

TOOL PALETTE

The Tool palette (see Figure 28.6) is another set of tools you can use while creating your slideshow. By default, the Tool palette displays along the left side of the screen. If you need to activate the Tool palette, choose View, Toolbars and from the Toolbars dialog box, choose Tool palette. The buttons on the Tool palette have text tools, and buttons to insert various shapes, fill objects with color and patterns, create bulleted lists, TextArt, charts, organizational charts, bitmap images, or spreadsheets.

Figure 28.6
Some Tool palette buttons offer a palette of choices when you click the drop-down arrow next to them. Others enable you to select an object type and drag the area on the screen where you want to place them.

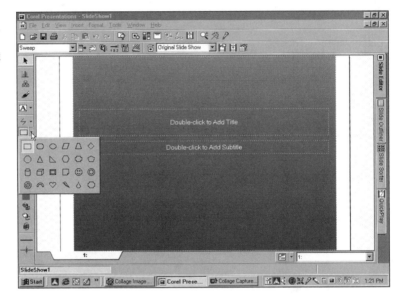

The Selection tool enables you to click graphic objects on the screen to select and manipulate them.

The next four buttons—Chart, Organization Chart, Bitmap, and Text Object Tools— actually start up other programs that create special objects to add to your slideshow.

To use the next six tools—Line Shapes, Basic Shapes, Arrow Shapes, Flowchart Shapes, Star Shapes, Callout Shapes, or Action Shapes—click the button, and then use the mouse to drag an area where you want to insert the type of object you have chosen.

The Fill Pattern, Foreground Fill Color, Background Fill Color, and Reverse Colors tools enable you to fill the selected object(s) with colors and patterns.

Finally, the Line Style and Line Width tools let you change the line style and line thickness for an object's lines and borders.

VIEWING THE PRESENTATION

The default view in Presentations Slide Editor is Margin Size view. You also can change the view to various magnifications. When you zoom or change views, the actual size of the objects, pages, text, and so on does not change; only the view of what you see onscreen changes.

To change the view, choose the Zoom Options button on the toolbar. A submenu appears. Table 28.3 describes each of the available views (except specific percentage views) and lists the shortcuts you can use to switch views.

TABLE 28.3   CHANGING SCREEN VIEWS

Screen Views	Shortcut	Description
Zoom to Area	Ctrl+Shift+F5	Magnifies the view of a selected area; drag the magnifying glass, thus drawing a rectangle across the area you want to enlarge.
Margin Size	Alt+F5	Displays the margins in the drawing window.
Full Page	Shift+F5	Displays the entire document.
Screen Size		Displays the page as it will look when you play the slideshow.
Selected Objects		Magnifies the view of the selected objects.
Previous View	Ctrl+F5	Displays the last view before you used Zoom. This can be handy to toggle between a close-up view and a full-screen view.

Figure 28.7 shows the screen at Margin Size view with the Zoom Area tool preparing to zoom to a specific part of the screen.

Figure 28.7
You can define an area to zoom with the magnifying glass Zoom Area tool in a Presentation slide.

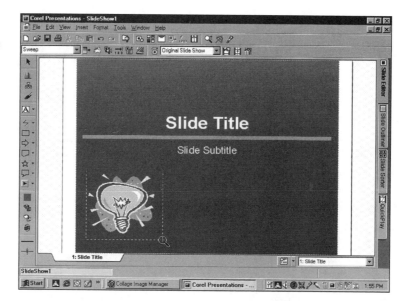

Tip #184 from
Trudi Reisner

You can quickly zoom in or out a little bit at a time by pressing Shift+Page Up (zoom in, or magnify 20 percent each time), or Shift+Page Down (zoom out, or reduce 20 percent each time).

USING OUTLINER

Slide Outliner view is useful for entering text into your slideshow. You can add slides and create titles, text, bullets, and so on in Slide Outliner view. Using Slide Outliner view enables you to plan and organize the slideshow, rearrange slides, and perfect the show before transferring it to slides, especially if your slideshow contains many bullet or text slides.

To change to Slide Outliner view, click the Slide Outliner tab at the right side of the Presentations screen, or choose View, Slide Outliner. Figure 28.8 shows Slide Outliner view.

Figure 28.8
Slide Outliner view looks like a ruled sheet of paper on which you can organize your presentation.

Tip #185 from
Trudi Reisner

In addition to entering your Presentations outline in Slide Outliner view, you also can prepare an outline in WordPerfect and insert it into the Presentations Slide Outliner. Choose Insert, File and select the document that contains an outline.

ENTERING TEXT AND ASSIGNING LEVELS

Enter the text for your slides in Slide Outliner so that you can easily view, edit, and rearrange the slides before viewing them in Slide Editor view. As you enter the text, or even after entering it, you can assign various levels to the text such as title, subtitle, bullets, and so on.

To enter text in Slide Outliner:

1. Position the insertion point and type the text.
2. The first line of any slide type is a Title. Press Enter to create a subtitle.
3. Press Enter again to create bullets. Each time you press Enter after creating the first bullet line, Slide Outliner adds more bullets on the same level.

To change a level:

- Press Tab to move down one level (to the right); or click the Next Level button on the Property Bar. You can create up to six levels of bullets by pressing the Tab key five times.

- Press Shift+Tab to move up one level (to the left); or click the Previous level button on the Property Bar. For example, to change a bullet to a subtitle, press Shift+Tab. To change the subtitle to a title, press Shift+Tab again.

Figure 28.9 shows a sample outline with titles, subtitles, and two levels of bullets.

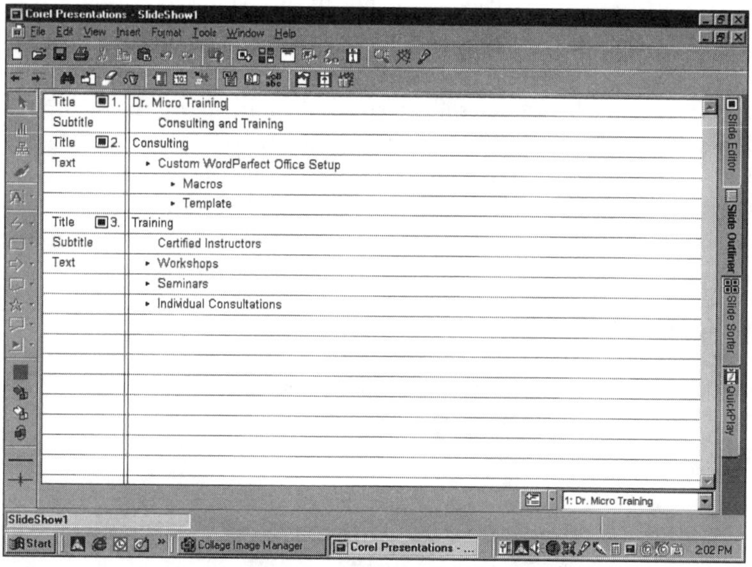

Figure 28.9
You can create an outline of your slides with titles, subtitles, and bullets in Slide Outliner, and easily arrange and rearrange the levels of the slide contents.

Note

You can use many customary word processing editing tools while editing an outline, including cut, copy, and paste, and even the spell checker.

ADDING SLIDES

You can add slides while in Slide Outliner view by using the menu, Insert Slide button, or keyboard. Additionally, you can delete slides if you choose. When you add a slide in Presentations 9, you choose the slide type; alternatively, you can choose to add more than one slide at a time and choose the slide type as you enter the text for each slide.

To add a slide to a presentation, follow these steps:

1. In Slide Outliner view, choose Insert, New Slide. The New Slide dialog box appears, as shown in Figure 28.10.

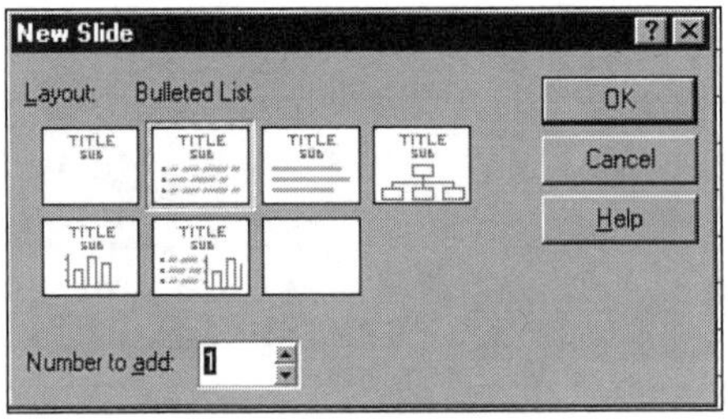

Figure 28.10
Add a slide to the
slideshow in Slide
Outliner view through
the New Slide dialog
box.

2. In Number to Add, enter or select the number of slides you want to add.

3. In the Layout area, choose the type of slide you want to add.

4. Click OK to close the dialog box and add the slide(s).

If you want to add just one slide, you can click the Insert Slide button next to the Slide List box at the lower-right of the screen, or you can press Ctrl+Enter. If you click the drop-down list at the right side of the button, you can choose the type of slide you want, while pressing Ctrl+Enter or clicking the button automatically assigns the current slide layout to the new slide. Alternatively, you can click the New Slide button on the toolbar and select the slide type.

Note

If you add two or more slides, they will all be the same type—Title, for example. You can change the type by clicking the slide number in the Slide Outline and then clicking the Select Layout button on the toolbar and choosing a layout type.

Caution

If you add too many slides or change your mind after adding, you can click the line in Slide Outliner for the slide you want to delete, and choose Edit, Delete Slides. Or you can select the slide(s) and press Delete. You can also delete slides in Slide Sorter by selecting a slide and pressing Delete. Presentations displays a message asking whether you are sure you want to delete it permanently; click Yes to delete or No to cancel. When you delete a slide, you delete the entire outline family, including all sublevels.

REARRANGING SLIDES

As you create your outline, you can rearrange the slide order of the presentation in Slide Outliner view. Change the slide order by dragging the slide to a new position. All the slide's text follows the title when you move it.

To move a slide:

1. Position the mouse pointer over the slide icon until the pointer changes into an arrow.

2. Drag the slide up or down to the new position. As you drag, the mouse pointer changes into a drag icon. Additionally, the screen scrolls up or down if you drag the icon past the window borders.

3. Drag the slide icon pointer to a line that holds another slide title. A short, horizontal line appears above the slide title to indicate the new slide will position ahead of it.

4. When you release the mouse button, the slide and the entire outline family slips into its new location.

Figure 28.11 illustrates a slide in the process of being moved to a new location.

Figure 28.11
Move a slide and its contents by dragging it to a new position.

Line indicates placement.

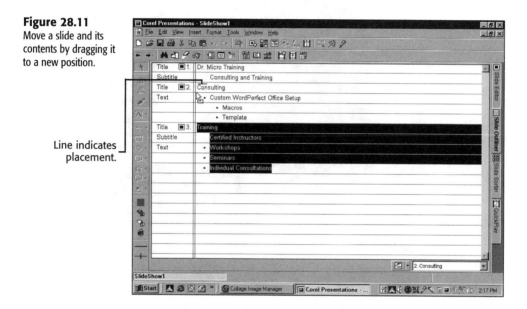

Using the Slide Editor

You use the Slide Editor to view each individual slide as it will look in the slideshow or when printed. You can switch to the Slide Editor after using Slide Outliner to enter your text, or you can create the text and other objects for the presentation directly in Slide Editor view.

To switch to Slide Editor view, choose View, Slide Editor, or click the Slide Editor tab at the right side of the screen to quickly switch views.

Tip #186 from
Trudi Reisner

Click the numbered Slide tabs at the bottom of the editing screen to quickly move to other slides as you work with the presentation. You also can click the Slide List pop-up list and jump directly to another slide.

PART

IV

CH

28

Adding Text

In Slide Editor view, text box outlines appear which enable you to enter titles, subtitles, bullets, and so on. You can enter, edit, and format the text in a text box. Additionally, you can move the text box or resize it.

To enter text into a text box:

1. Double-click the box. The box changes into a text box with a blinking vertical cursor and a grayed outline (see Figure 28.12).

Figure 28.12
You enter and edit all kinds of text–titles, subtitles, bulleted items, and body text– in the text box.

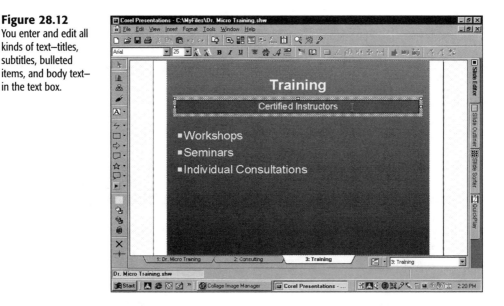

2. Type the text.
3. When you are finished entering text, click outside the text box.

To edit the text in a text box, double-click the box, and the cursor appears in the text box.

Tip #187 from
Trudi Reisner

When you are finished typing in a text box, press the Esc key to indicate you are finished typing. The box remains selected for moving or resizing.

To move or resize a text box, follow these steps:

■ Click the box once to select it; small handles appear on the corners of the text box. Drag the box to a new position to move it.

■ To resize the box, position the mouse pointer over any handle; the pointer changes into a double-headed arrow (see Figure 28.13). Drag the handle toward the center to make the text box smaller, or away from the center of the box to make the box larger.

Figure 28.13
When you resize or move a selected text box with its handles, the pointer changes into a double-headed arrow.

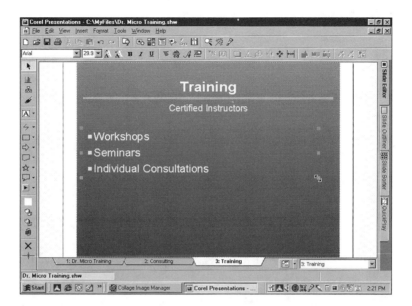

Changing the size of some text boxes (for example, a title box) also changes its font size, thus making the text box inconsistent with other similar boxes. To change the size of the box without changing its content, double-click the box and use the corner and side sizing handles to change the shape of the box.

To create a new text box:

1. Click the Text Objects tool and the Create a Text Box or the Create a Text Line tool and position the tool in the work area of the slide. The tool for the text box looks like a hand holding a rectangle, and the tool for the text line looks like large crosshairs.

2. Drag the hand to create the width of the multiline text block you want to create, or click at the location in which you want to begin a single line of text.

   When you release the mouse button, the new text box appears with a blinking cursor, ready to receive text.

3. To close either type of box, press Esc.

Note

QuickFonts have been removed since Corel Presentations 8.

FORMATTING TEXT

You format the text in a text box similar to formatting any text in other Corel WordPerfect Office 2000 applications, with one exception. In Corel Presentations 9, you must first double-click the text box. If necessary, drag the mouse to select specific text. Choose a font, size, or attribute.

PART
IV

CH
28

After selecting the text:

- Use the various buttons on the Property Bar to change font and size.
- Choose Format, Font to format text in text boxes.

Figure 28.14 shows the Font Properties dialog box where you can choose which options to apply to your selected text.

Figure 28.14
Choose the font, size, and attributes all at one time in the Font Properties dialog box.

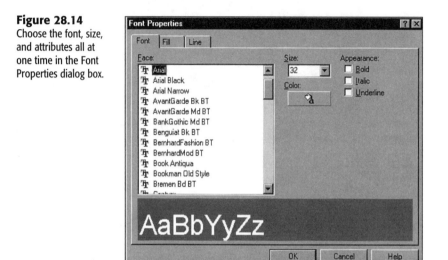

If you switched from Slide Outliner view to Slide Editor view, and the text in your titles is too long, thus overlapping other text, see "Fixing Overlapped Text for Slide Titles" in the Troubleshooting section at the end of this chapter.

If you can't move to another slide in Slide Editor view, see "Creating a Drawing or a Presentation" in the Troubleshooting section at the end of this chapter.

SORTING SLIDES

Presentations includes another view—Slide Sorter—for you to use when creating and organizing your presentation. You will most likely use this view when you are preparing to play a slideshow.

Slide Sorter shows a minigallery of each slide so that you can visually organize them.

USING SLIDE SORTER TO REARRANGE SLIDES

Slide Sorter view displays the slides in your presentation as small slides so that you can see the visual impact of the overall presentation. In addition, you can change the order of the slides in Slide Sorter view. To change the view to Slide Sorter, choose View, Slide Sorter, or click the Slide Sorter tab at the right side of the screen. Figure 28.15 shows the Slide Sorter view.

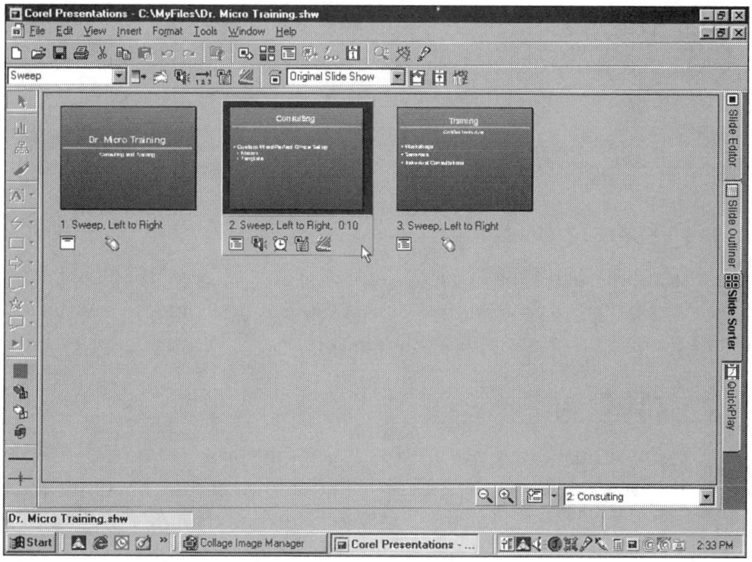

Figure 28.15
Slide Sorter view is handy for preparing your slideshow. You can easily change the order of your slides, and see what kinds of special effects you have added to them.

In Slide Sorter view, you can click and drag a slide to a new position. Additionally, you can select more than one slide to move:

- To select consecutive slides, click the first slide, hold the Shift key, and click the last slide in the consecutive set of slides.
- To select nonconsecutive slides, click the first slide, press the Ctrl key, and click the other slides you want to move.

Drag the selected slides to a new position to complete the move.

Tip #188 from
Trudi Reisner

To edit a slide from Slide Sorter view, you can double-click the slide, and the slide appears in Slide Editor view.

UNDERSTANDING SLIDE SORTER INFORMATION

Beneath each slide, Presentations lists any transition effects you added, and also displays icons that represent special properties that you add. These include

- An icon showing the type of slide (such as a bullet or title).
- A mouse or a clock, to indicate whether the slide is advanced by a mouse click or after a specified amount of time.
- A speaker, if you added sound.
- A notepad, if speaker notes were added.
- A keyboard, if you assigned QuickKeys.

→ For more information on how to create an electronic slideshow, **see** "Creating an Electronic Slideshow," **p. 575**

PART

IV

CH

28

SAVING, IMPORTING, AND EXPORTING PRESENTATIONS

You can save, import, and export presentations in Presentation 9. Saving a presentation works the same way as in other Corel applications. You can import data that was created in another application and place that data on slides in your presentation. You can export a presentation to Microsoft PowerPoint or graphics file for use on the Internet.

SAVING A PRESENTATION

You save a presentation as you would any WordPerfect Office application file by using File, Save or clicking the Save button on the toolbar. You can also save an existing presentation with a different name and in a different drive or folder by using File, Save As.

IMPORTING A PRESENTATION

You can import data that was created in another program into a Corel presentation. For example, you can import data from a Quattro Pro spreadsheet into a Presentations table that will become a fully functional spreadsheet, feeding data to a chart for your slideshow. You can even import an entire Microsoft PowerPoint slideshow into a Presentations 9 slideshow.

To import data from a Quattro Pro spreadsheet, choose Insert, Object. The Insert Object dialog box lets you import data from spreadsheets and Microsoft PowerPoint slideshows. Choose the Create from File option to import data from an existing notebook file. Click the Browse button, select the notebook file from which you want to obtain the data, and click Insert. You can bring in data from an entire spreadsheet or from a range of cells.

To select only a range of data, enter the range in the space provided. You can overwrite the current data, depending on your situation.

To import a Microsoft PowerPoint slideshow, choose Insert, Object. Choose the Create from File option, click the Browse button, select the PowerPoint file from which you want to obtain the data, and click Insert.

EXPORTING A PRESENTATION

The Export feature can help you make your presentation viewable by those without Corel Presentations. Presentations 9 can now export a presentation in Microsoft PowerPoint file format.

You can run your Presentations slideshows in Microsoft PowerPoint. To do so, use File, Save or File, Save As. In the ? box, choose Microsoft PowerPoint to save the file in the Microsoft PowerPoint format. Then you can play the presentation in Microsoft PowerPoint.

Presentations also lets you export your slideshows to a number of different graphic file formats. These include JPEG (JPG), Windows MetaFile (WMF), Encapsulated PostScript (EPS), PICT, and CompuServe Bitmap (GIF). Use File, Save to save the presentation in a different file format.

→ For more information on how to export slides shows as graphics files, see "Saving Graphic Objects As Separate Files," p. 568

Using PerfectExperts in Presentations

Presentations offers templates to make it easy for you to design your own slideshows with predefined slides. In this section, we'll take a quick look at the PerfectExperts in Presentations.

PerfectExperts provide the template and allow you to use your own data. You can also save your work in a Presentations file. When you complete a task, the file contains your slide information.

Experts provide the expertise to create beautifully designed slides while you provide the data. These PerfectExperts cover a broad range of topics.

For example, the Persuasive Slideshow PerfectExpert leads you through the steps necessary to create slides that will present your information in a highly persuasive visual manner. You don't have to be a graphics expert; all you need to do is answer some questions and make a few selections along the way.

Creating a Persuasive Slideshow

You've decided that early mortgage payoff sounds like a good idea, but you don't have quite enough income each month. Perhaps it's time to persuade your company's management to accept your project idea and appoint you team leader, along with an appropriate raise, of course.

You've heard about computer-based slideshows, but you're not sure just where to begin. If you let the PerfectExpert help you, you'll find the perfect slideshow. Try these steps:

1. Choose File, New from Project to open the PerfectExpert, and go to the Slide Shows category. Choose the Persuasive Slide Show project. The PerfectExpert opens Presentations and displays the screen shown in Figure 28.16.

2. Each slide shows you what kind of information is needed. For example, to present the problem, click the Slide 3 tab. Double-click each item shown in Figure 28.17 and replace the information there with your own. Repeat this for each slide in the series.

3. Add Speaker Notes (notes to yourself that you'll refer to during the presentation) or other elements by clicking the appropriate PerfectExpert button.

4. You can return to the "home" PerfectExpert base by clicking the Home button at the top of the expert. There you can add special effects (sound, transitions, or animation), or you can get More Help on what it takes to make a persuasive presentation. You might even want to choose a different layout—one that more closely matches the content or purpose of your presentation.

5. Click the Finish button to save the slideshow, to play it or print it, to mail it to someone, or to publish it to the Web.

Figure 28.16
Creating perfect slideshows is a snap when you let the PerfectExpert help you.

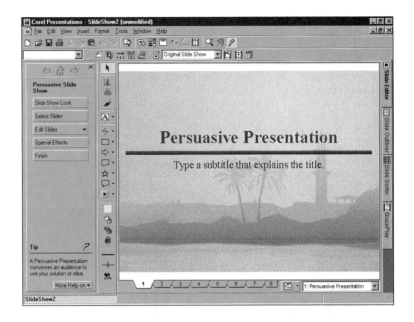

Figure 28.17
The PerfectExpert helps you build professional slideshows by showing you what to include on your slides.

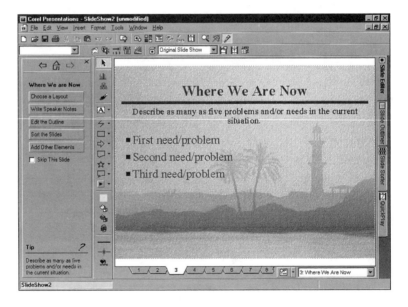

CUSTOMIZING THE PRESENTATIONS STARTUP SCREEN

If you don't want to see the PerfectExpert or the Startup Master Gallery dialog boxes each time you start up, you can turn them off. For example, choose File, New from Project, and while in the Corel PerfectExpert dialog box, choose Options, Show This Dialog at Startup. The next time you start up Presentations, the Slide Show option starts automatically. To turn off the Startup Master Gallery dialog box, while in that dialog box check Do Not Show This Dialog When Beginning a New Slide Show.

To make these dialog boxes appear again upon startup, you have to make a change to the settings in Presentations. First, of course, you have to get to the Presentations main editing screen to see the menus.

To change the settings in Presentations, choose Tools, Settings, and click the Environment icon. In the Startup tab of the Environment dialog box, you can choose various startup options. These include

- Display Document Selection (New...) Dialog Box, the default, but which you may have turned off from the Options button of the Corel PerfectExpert dialog box.
- Create New Slide Show, whereby no dialog box is displayed before starting a new slideshow.
- Create New Drawing, which takes you to the draw editing screen.

In addition to these three mutually exclusive options, you can also choose to display the Master Gallery each time you choose to create a new slideshow.

PRACTICAL PROJECT

If you have the honorable job of introducing a speaker or starting a meeting, and usually have a hard time getting started, Presentations has the solution. The PerfectExpert Welcome Slide Show leads the way to welcoming an audience and guests and introducing a speaker. The Welcome Slide Show supplies five predesigned slides and one blank slide with the welcome theme. The first slide welcomes or introduces the topic. Slide 2 is a bulleted text slide that reviews the occasion. Slide 3 is another bulleted text slide—it defines the audience. Slide 4 is a bulleted text slide that introduces the speaker. Slide 5 concludes your presentation and gives the floor to the speaker or lets the meeting begin. Slide 6 is blank so that you can add anything you want to introduce the speaker or the meeting. For example, you can add an animated graphic, making for smooth segues as the speaker walks up to the podium.

TROUBLESHOOTING

FIXING OVERLAPPED TEXT FOR SLIDE TITLES

You switched from Slide Outliner view to Slide Editor view, and the text in your titles is too long, thus overlapping other text.

You can do any of three things to solve the problem: Change the font size, edit the text, or move the text box on the page so that the text does not overlap other text. However, it's better not to crowd too much text into one slide; rather, divide your slides into smaller logical groups of information.

CREATING A DRAWING OR A PRESENTATION

You can't move to another slide in Slide Editor view.

You might be creating a drawing rather than a presentation. A drawing has only one "slide"; a presentation can have several. You need to create a new presentation rather than a new drawing.

CHAPTER 29

WORKING WITH DATA CHARTS

In this chapter

CREATING A DATA CHART

A data chart is a chart created using figures you enter in a datasheet—similar to a table or spreadsheet. The chart visually represents the figures, contained in the datasheet, using column bar, pie pieces, lines, and so on. The chart type you choose depends on the data and how you want to represent it; comparing data, for example, is a common use for pie and bar charts.

Note

Although we are adding a chart to a slideshow, you also can add a chart to a Presentations drawing using the procedures described in this chapter.

INSERTING A CHART

Before you create a chart, you must first choose a chart type. After you make your selection, you will enter the data. You can create a chart using the Data Chart slide layout type, the Insert menu, or the Chart button on the Tool Palette. Following is a summary of the three methods of inserting a chart into a presentation:

■ Define a slide as a data chart layout type, and then double-click in the Add Data Chart; the Data Chart Gallery dialog box appears (see Figure 29.1).

Figure 29.1
When you create an area for the chart, the Data Chart Gallery dialog box appears.

Data Chart slide type name

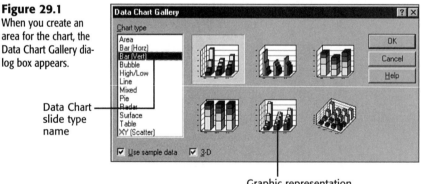

Graphic representation of Data Chart slide type

■ Choose Insert, Data Chart. The mouse pointer changes into a hand holding a frame. Drag the hand on the slide or drawing to indicate the area designated for the chart. When you release the mouse button, the Data Chart Gallery dialog box appears.

Tip #189 from
Trudi Reisner

To create a chart that fills the entire screen, just single-click the mouse in the slide area.

■ Click the Chart button on the Tool Palette. The mouse pointer changes into a hand. Drag the hand on the slide or drawing to create the area for the chart. When you release the mouse button, the Data Chart Gallery dialog box appears.

Tip #190 from
Trudi Reisner

You can change the chart type at any time by clicking the Data Chart Gallery button on the toolbar.

CHOOSING THE CHART TYPE

You choose the <u>C</u>hart Type in the Data Chart Gallery dialog box. The type of chart you choose depends on the type of data you are planning to use and how you want to present it. Table 29.1 describes the chart types available in Presentations and their common uses.

TABLE 29.1   DATA CHART TYPES

Chart Type	Description
Area	A chart that shows the height of all values with the area below the line filled with color or patterns. Use an area chart to compare several sets of data or trends over a period of time.
Bar	A chart that represents data by the height or length of the columns or bars; you can create horizontal or vertical bars. Use a bar chart to compare one item to another or to compare different items over a period of time.
Bubble	A chart that displays x, y, and z data on two axes with the bubble size representing the values. For example, you could plot units sold (x-axis data) versus gross profit (y-axis data) and you could make the bubble size represent net profit.
High/Low	A chart that shows the high and low values compared over time using lines and bars. Use High/Low charts to track fluctuating data (stocks, commodities, and so on) over a period of time.
Line	A chart consisting of a series of data elements at various points along the axis; the points are connected by a line that indicates a trend or rate of change over a period of time.
Mixed	A chart that combines parts from a line, bar, or area chart so that you can plot data in two forms on the same chart. Use a mixed chart to show a correlation between two or more data series.
Pie	A circular, pie-shaped chart with each piece (wedge) showing a data segment and its relationship to the whole. Use a pie chart to sort data and compare parts of the whole.
Radar	A chart that starts from the center using a grid to represent the various data. Use a radar chart to show data over a period of time and to show variations and trends.
Surface	A chart that represents values to look like peaks and valleys, or landscape. Solid areas contour to the data, which is useful in tracking profits or losses.
Table	Not a graphical chart, but a representation of the data in rows and columns, similar to the datasheet.
XY (Scatter)	A chart that plots two sets of data, placing a marker at each point where the data intersects. Use a scatter chart when there are extremely large amounts of data you want to plot along an interception course.

To choose a chart type in the Data Chart Gallery dialog box, first choose an option in the Chart Type list. When you do so, the appropriate graphic views of the chart is displayed. From the graphic views, select the view of the chart that will best represent your data to your audience (see Figure 29.2). Additionally, you can choose to make a chart three-dimensional by selecting the 3-D check box at the bottom of the dialog box. Click OK to accept the chart type and close the dialog box. When you close the dialog box, the datasheet appears.

Figure 29.2
Select chart type options from the Data Chart Gallery dialog box. Note the difference in the graphic representation between the Line type here and the Bar chart type in the previous figure.

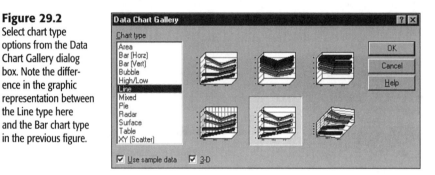

Tip #191 from
Trudi Reisner

Radar charts, Bubble charts, and Tables cannot be created in 3D.

Note

When you close the Data Chart Gallery dialog box, the datasheet appears with sample data already entered, by default. You can clear this data to enter your own, or you can deselect the Use Sample Data option in the Data Chart Gallery dialog box. If the option is not checked, a blank datasheet appears.

ENTERING DATA

After you choose the chart type, the datasheet appears with sample data (unless you chose to not display the sample data). Figure 29.3 illustrates the datasheet, sample data, and the chart created from the data. Additionally, the Data menu is added to the menu bar.

Tip #192 from
Trudi Reisner

If you cannot see all the data, you can enlarge the datasheet by positioning the mouse pointer over a corner of the sheet and dragging to enlarge the window.

Figure 29.3
The datasheet looks
and acts like a
spreadsheet.

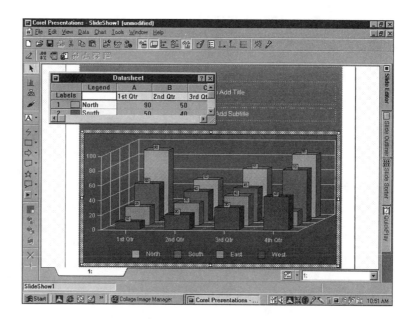

INPUTTING DATA

To enter data in the datasheet, follow these steps:

1. Select the cells containing sample data by clicking the Select All button (see Figure 29.4).
   Notice how the mouse pointer changed into a combination right and down arrow.

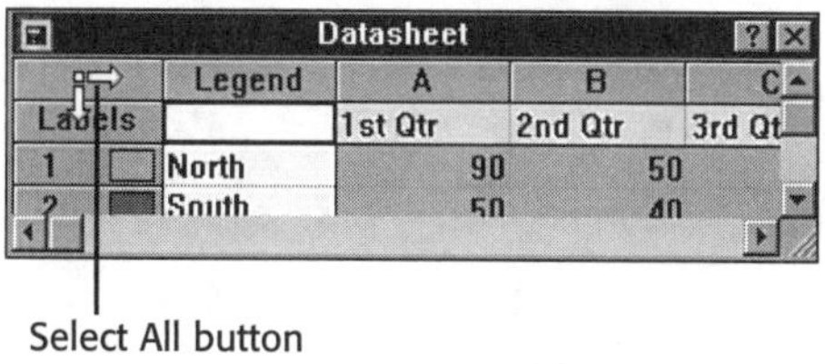

Figure 29.4
The Select All button
on the datasheet per-
mits you to quickly
select all information
in the datasheet to
apply new formatting
or for deletion.

Select All button

2. Choose Edit, Clear; or press the Delete key. The Clear dialog box appears with the
   Data option selected (see Figure 29.5).

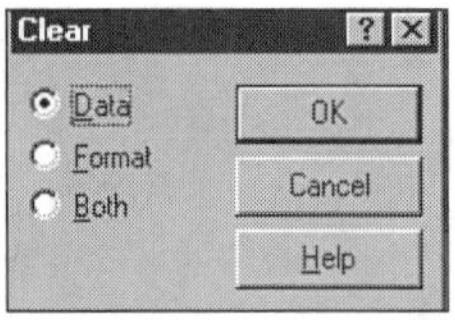

Figure 29.5
Clear the data from
the datasheet and fill
in your own.

3. Click OK. The data in the datasheet is deleted.

4. To enter the values, enter the legend text, the data labels, and then the values.

5. The legend text appears in a box near the chart and tell what each color or symbol in the chart's data series represents.

   The data series is a range of values in a worksheet and each data series is represented by a marker; for example, a column in a bar chart is a marker, as is a wedge in a pie chart. Data labels are names put along the vertical (Y-axis) or horizontal (X-axis) axis to describe the data, such as the year, quarter, dollar amounts, and so on.

   Figure 29.6 illustrates a sample datasheet and the resulting chart after the text and values are added.

Figure 29.6
The Bar chart displays
the text and values
after they have been
entered into the
datasheet.

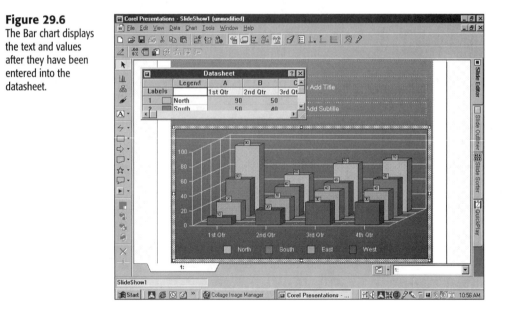

6. When you are finished entering the data, click outside the chart area to close the datasheet window and to leave the chart-editing mode. You see the finished chart in your slide, with handles around it indicating that it is selected.

| **Tip #193 from** *Trudi Reisner* | You can edit the data in the datasheet at any time by clicking the View Datasheet button in the toolbar. |

| **Note** | The first time you create a chart using your own data, it might be a good idea to take a few minutes and see what your data looks like displayed in different data chart types. Then compare each chart against its description in Table 29.1. Be sure to try each chart type in both 2D and 3D. This gives you a better understanding of how each chart type displays your data, and a better idea of which chart types most effectively present the concepts you want to convey to your particular presentation audience. To change the chart type easily, click the Data Chart Gallery button on the Property Bar. |

IMPORTING DATA

You can import data into the datasheet from a spreadsheet program, such as Corel Quattro Pro, by following these steps:

1. Select the cell in the datasheet where you want to import the data.

| **Caution** | Be sure any cells that will be filled with data do not contain important data that you want to keep. (If there is existing data in the destination cells of the datasheet, it will be written over.) |

2. Choose Data, Import. The Import Data dialog box appears (see Figure 29.7).

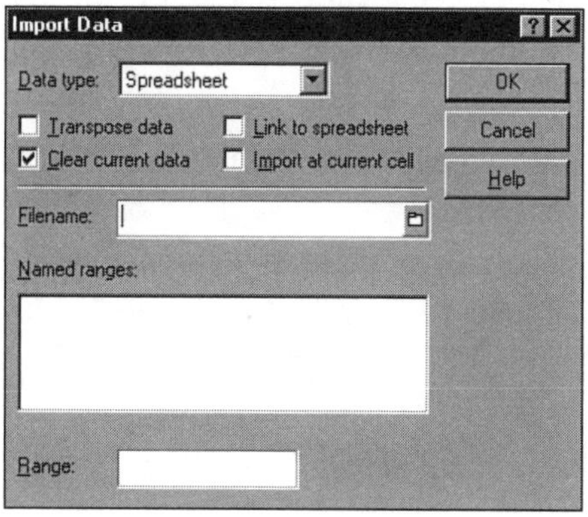

Figure 29.7
Use the Import Data dialog box to import part or all of a spreadsheet.

3. Choose the type of data you will import from the Data Type list.
4. Enter the path and filename in the Filename text box.
5. Specify a Range, or you can import the entire worksheet.
6. Select Import at Current Cell if you want the new data to begin where you currently are in the datasheet.

7. Choose any other options you need (refer to Figure 29.7). These include

- Transpose Data—Enables you to import row data to columns, and column data to rows.

- Clear Current Data—Clears current spreadsheet data.

- Link to Spreadsheet—Updates the resulting chart if the spreadsheet changes.

- Import at Current Cell—Does just that, instead of at the upper-left corner of the datasheet.

- Named Ranges—Brings in selected areas of the spreadsheet, based on named ranges specified in the spreadsheet itself.

- Range—Enables you to import just a specific area of the spreadsheet.

8. Click OK. The specified data imports to the selected cell in the Chart Datasheet.

EDITING A CHART

You can easily edit chart data or other chart options by double-clicking the chart. When you double-click the chart, the chart's border appears as a screened line to indicate it's selected. Additionally, the datasheet containing the charting data appears, the Data menu appears, new options appear on the menu bar, and several new buttons appear on the toolbars and Property Bar that pertain only to charts (refer to Figure 29.6).

EDITING DATA

To edit the data in a chart, double-click the chart. The datasheet appears, unless you closed the datasheet previously. If you did, click the View Datasheet button on the toolbar. Click the cell you want to edit and type the text or value. Press Enter and the chart changes to reflect the new data.

In addition to entering new text or editing text, you can format the values in the chart and sort the data in the cells of the datasheet.

FORMATTING VALUES

You can format a cell in a datasheet to contain specific data types, such as numeric, currency, or text. To format values, do the following:

1. Select the cells you want to format and choose Data, Format, or right-click the cells; then choose Format from the QuickMenu. Alternatively, you can press Ctrl+F12 or click the Format Data tool on the toolbar. The Format dialog box appears (see Figure 29.8).

Figure 29.8
Format the data in
selected cells using the
Format dialog box.

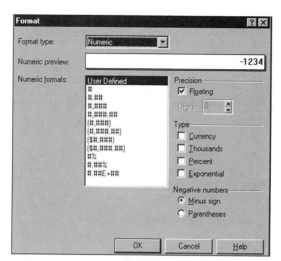

2. In Format Type, choose either General, Numeric, or Date. If you choose General, there are no options; otherwise, the options change depending on the Format Type.

3. Select the format you want to use and other options appear. The Numeric and Date options are described in Tables 29.2 and 29.3.

4. Click OK to close the dialog box.

TABLE 29.2 NUMERIC OPTIONS

Option	Description
Numeric Preview	Displays the selected numeric format.
Numeric Formats	Choose a format to display the numbers.
Precision	Choose only one option.
Floating	Decimal points and places appear only if needed.
Digits	Specify the number of decimal places; this option is available only if Floating is not selected.
Type	Choose any or all options.
Currency	Displays values with a dollar sign.
Thousands	Displays commas to indicate thousands.
Percent	Displays the percent sign with the number.
Exponential	Displays the exponent of the values.
Negative Numbers	Choose only one option.
Minus Sign	Displays a minus sign to indicate negative numbers.
Parentheses	Displays negative numbers in parentheses instead of with a minus sign.

TABLE 29.3 DATE OPTIONS

Option	Description
Date Preview	Displays the selected date format.
Date/Time Formats	Choose a format to display date and/or time.
Custom	Create your own date format.

Tip #194 from
Trudi Reisner

The numeric format you choose in the Format dialog box changes the axis labels in your chart to the format you select.

SORTING DATA

You can sort the data in a datasheet in a descending or ascending alphabetical or numerical order. Sorted data is more organized than data that is not sorted, and therefore, sorted data makes a chart easier to read.

To sort in a datasheet, follow these steps:

1. Select the text or values in the datasheet to be sorted.

2. Choose Data, Sort; or right-click the cells, and then choose Sort from the QuickMenu. You can also click the Sort button on the toolbar or press Alt+F9. The Sort dialog box appears (see Figure 29.9).

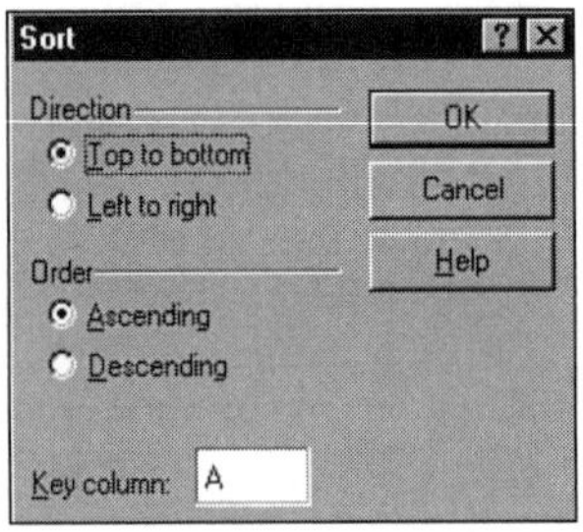

Figure 29.9
You can Sort data by rows or columns of the datasheet, and in ascending or descending order.

3. In the Sort dialog box, choose to sort the data Top to Bottom (Rows), or Left to Right (Columns) and in either Ascending or Descending order. The Key Column or Row (the column or row by which the data will be sorted) shows the letter or number of the selected column by default, so you should not need to change this.

4. Click OK to close the dialog box and sort the data. Changes are reflected in the data chart.

> **Caution**
>
> Undo is not available in the datasheet, so be careful before you perform a sort on datasheet data. If you click outside the chart area and then choose Undo from the Presentations menu, the chart and data do revert to their original order. However, any other formatting changes you made to the chart also are undone.

CHANGING CHART TYPES

After you create a chart, you might decide a different chart type would better represent the data. You can change the chart type to pie, line, area, or any other available chart. To change a chart type, double-click the chart to open the Chart Editor. Choose <u>C</u>hart, <u>G</u>allery to view the larger variety of chart types, or choose <u>C</u>hart, <u>L</u>ayout/Type to quickly select a type and edit the properties of the chart. Alternatively, click the Data Chart Gallery button on the toolbar (see Figure 29.10). Choose the chart type you want and the selected chart changes.

Figure 29.10
Choose a chart type from the palette displayed when you click the Data Chart Gallery button on the toolbar.

Data Chart Gallery button ⌐

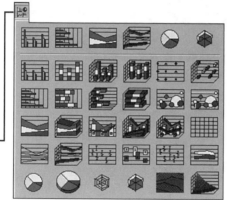

> **Tip #195 from**
> *Trudi Reisner*
>
> You can choose the Show Table button on the toolbar to add the data to your chart in table format.

MODIFYING LAYOUT AND SERIES OPTIONS

You can edit the layout and the series of a selected chart to further modify the way the data is represented. Layout refers to the style, width, size, and general appearance of the chart's markers. The Layout options change depending on what type of chart you are working on. The Series options refer to each individual data series. You can change the color, type, and even the shape of each series in the chart to further represent the chart's data.

CHANGING LAYOUT

To change the layout of the chart, perform these steps:

1. Open the chart in the Chart Editor by double-clicking it.

2. Choose Chart, Layout/Type, or click the Layout button on the toolbar. The Layout/Type Properties dialog box appears (see Figure 29.11). The specific options you see depend on the type of chart selected.

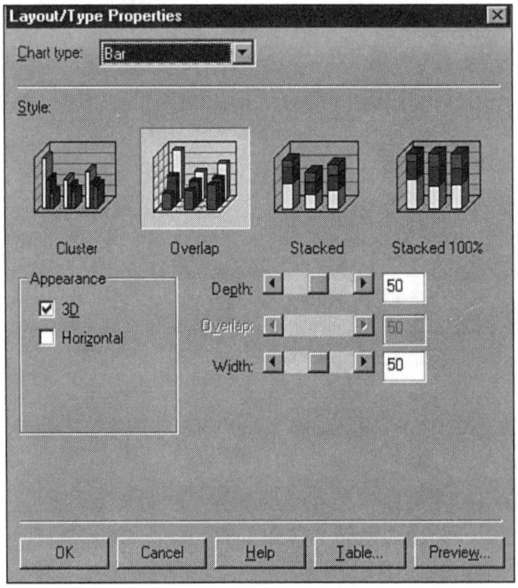

Figure 29.11

The Layout/Type Properties dialog box allows you to both select the type of chart you want and set properties for the chart.

3. Change any of the options in the dialog box as described in Table 29.4. (The options that are available depend on the chart type that is selected, and not all the options in the table will be available at once. Some options are available for more than one type of chart.) Click the Preview button to view the change before accepting it. Click OK to accept the changes.

4. Click OK to accept the changes and close the dialog box.

> **Caution**
>
> Save your presentation before you modify the layout of a chart in case you change your mind about the changes; you can always revert to the saved copy. Additionally, use the Preview button in the Layout/Type Properties dialog box before accepting the changes you make. If you make many changes, you might never be able to undo them all and the changes might not look good in your chart. If you use the Preview button first, you have the option of canceling the changes and trying again.

PART

IV

CH

29

Tip #196 from
Trudi Reisner

When using the Preview button in the Layout/Type Properties dialog box, click and drag the title bar of the dialog box to move it for a clearer preview.

TABLE 29.4 LAYOUT/TYPE PROPERTIES OPTIONS

Option	Description
Area Charts	
Overlap	Overlaps the markers.
Stacked	Stacks the markers one on top of another.
Stacked 100%	Stacks the markers so they are even along the top and bottom.
3-D	Applies a three-dimensional look to the markers in the chart.
Horizontal	Changes the direction of the markers from vertical to horizontal.
Depth	Sets depth percentages (only in 3D).
Bar Charts	
Cluster	Groups each section of markers together so that they can better be compared.
Overlap	Overlaps the markers.
Stacked	Stacks the markers one on top of another.
Stacked 100%	Stacks the markers so they are even along the top and bottom.
3-D	Applies a three-dimensional look to the markers in the chart.
Horizontal	Changes the direction of the markers from vertical to horizontal.
Depth	Sets depth percentages (only in 3D).
Overlap	Sets overlap percentages (only in 2D bar charts).
Width	Sets width percentages.
High/Low Charts	
Line	Changes markers to lines.
Bar/Error	Changes markers to bars with error indicators.
Error Bar	Changes markers to bars with top and bottom error markers.
Area	Changes markers to area markers.

continues

TABLE 29.4   CONTINUED

Option	Description
Pie/Exploded Pie Charts	
Pie	Displays data as pie slices.
Column	Changes pie slices to bar or column markers.
3-D	Applies a three-dimensional look to slices in the pie.
Proportional	If using two or more pies, the pie sizes are proportional to their total value.
Sort Slice	Changes the positioning of the exploded slice(s).
Explode Slice	Specifies which slice to explode and how much distance to place between pie and exploded slide.
Link Pie 2 to Slice	Indicates with lines how one pie two relates to a specific slice of pie one. This enables the user to show visually the details of one slice of pie.
Depth	Sets the thickness of a pie chart (3D only).
Size	Sets the size of the pie.
Angle	Rotate the slices.
Tilt	Sets orientation (3D only).
Radar Charts	
Overlap	Overlaps the markers.
Stacked	Stacks the markers one on top of another.
Stacked 100%	Stacks the markers so that they are even along the top and bottom.
Line	Displays lines instead of filled areas.
Area	Displays filled areas along with lines.
Radial	Displays on a radial grid (Stacked 100% only).
Linear	Displays on a linear grid (Stacked 100% only).
Separate Y axis	Both series of data are displayed on their own Y-axis.
Surface Charts	
3D	Applies a three-dimensional look to the surfaces of the chart.
Outline Contours	Draws an outline around each area.
Outline	Sets the color for the outline of the chart.
Starting to Ending Color Rows (%)	Sets the range colors for the data in the chart.
Blend Range Colors	Blends the range colors for the data in the chart.

> **Note**
>
> Each of the Layout/Type Properties chart types includes the Table button. The feature enables you to combine a data table along with the chart. See "Inserting and Formatting Tables" in Chapter 22, "Building a Spreadsheet," for more information on working with data tables.

CHANGING SERIES

A series is a row of data in a chart. A series is represented by a column, pie slice, line, or other chart element, also called a marker. You can change how the series looks by setting series options.

> **Tip #197 from**
> *Trudi Reisner*
>
> Not all series options are available for all chart types. However, you can mix series types in the same chart. For example, one row of data could be represented by Area markers, while another could be represented by Line markers.

To change the series options, follow these steps:

1. Choose Chart, Series, or click the Series button on the toolbar. You also can right-click the series marker (for example, the bar in a bar chart) on the chart itself and choose Series Properties from the QuickMenu. Alternatively, you can double-click the series marker or click the Series icon on the toolbar. The Series Properties dialog box appears, as in Figure 29.12.

Figure 29.12
Open the Series Properties dialog box to further enhance and modify a chart.

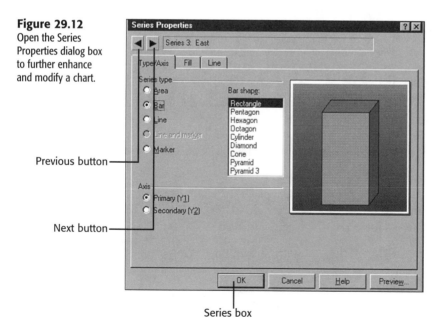

Previous button

Next button

Series box

Tip #198 from
Trudi Reisner

Nearly any element of a data chart can be modified by double-clicking that element. For example, to modify a series, double-click the data series marker for that series to display the Series Properties dialog box. For example, click a bar in a bar chart.

2. In the Series box at the top of the dialog box, choose the Next or Previous button to select the series you want to edit.

3. On the Type/Axis tab, choose your Series Type (Area, Bar, Line, Marker, and so on) and the style or Bar Shape of the Series Type (Rectangle, Cylinder, Pyramid, and so on). Also, choose whether to use the Primary (Y1) or Secondary (Y2) Y-axis.

Tip #199 from
Trudi Reisner

Click the Preview button at any time to see how the change looks.

4. On the Fill tab, choose Pattern, Gradient, Texture, or Picture to display a palette of fill choices. Select a new choice to apply to the current series. You also can reverse the colors in a two-color pattern or gradient fill, and also set which of the two colors is transparent, allowing what's behind the marker to show through.

5. In the Outline tab, choose the Color, Style, and Width as desired.

6. Use the Next or Previous buttons, if desired, to choose another series, and then repeat steps 3 through 6.

7. Click OK to accept the options and close the dialog box.

 If you made changes to the Series of the selected chart, and you don't like the changes, see "Canceling Changes to a Series" in the Troubleshooting section at the end of this chapter.

CHANGING THE GRID AND AXIS

The chart's grid is formed by the horizontal and vertical lines behind the chart's markers. The grid enables you to better see the markers in conjunction with the axes' labels and, therefore, the lines make the data easier to read. You can add two grids to a chart: the major grid and minor grid. The minor grid further divides the values so that you can better read the numbers.

A chart's axes are lines used as reference points for the chart data. The X-axis represents the horizontal line and the Y-axis represents the vertical. You can change axis options to help you define the data on the chart.

CHANGING THE AXIS

To change the axis options, follow these steps:

1. In the Chart Editor, select the axis you want to change. Handles appear at each end of a selected axis. Choose Chart, Axis, and then select X, Primary Y, or Secondary Y. The Axis Properties dialog box appears (see Figure 29.13).

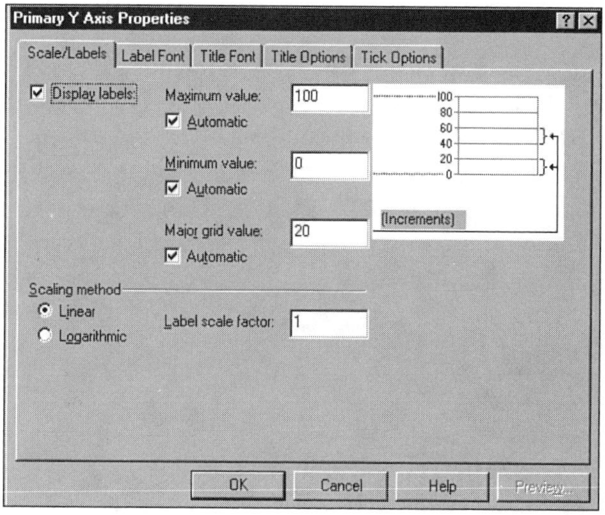

Figure 29.13
Double-click the
axis to display the
Scale/Labels tab of
the Primary Axis
Properties dialog
box for that axis.

Tip #200 from
Trudi Reisner

Alternatively, double-click the axis you want to modify to display the Axis Properties dialog box.

2. In the Labels tab (X-Axis), choose to display your labels in a variety of ways. This can make your chart readable if you have many labels, or if your labels are long.

   Alternatively, in the Scale/Labels tab (Y-Axis), choose the Maximum and Minimum values for the axis.

3. Click the Label Font tab to specify the font and size for your labels.

4. In the Title Options tab, enter the title for your axis, and the font for that title.

5. Ticks are short lines that are used to mark off values, such as dollars, distances, and so on. Major ticks are those lines that fall on a label and minor ticks are lines that fall between labels. Set options for the ticks in the Tick Options tab, then click OK.

6. Select the other axis in the Axis area and set options for that axis, if desired.

Tip #201 from
Trudi Reisner

If you change the font style on one axis, your chart will look more readable and professional if you change to the same style on the other axis.

CHANGING THE GRID

The grid in a data chart consists of horizontal and/or vertical lines that help to measure distance between the markers.

To change the grid options, do the following:

1. Select the chart, and then choose Chart, Grids or click the Grid Properties tool on the toolbar. You can also right-click the grid in the slide or double-click the grid in the slide. The Grid Properties dialog box appears (see Figure 29.14).

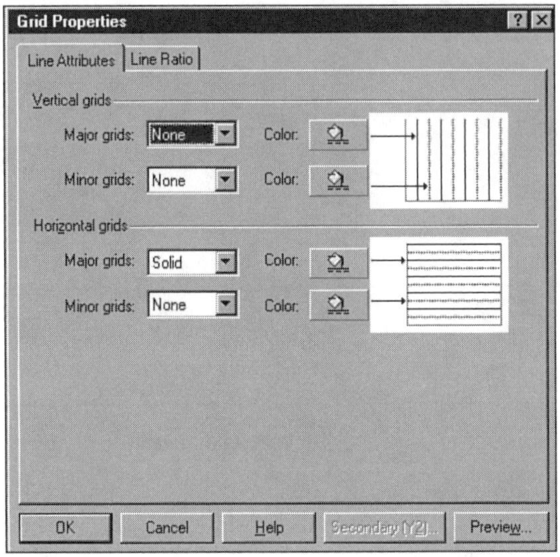

Figure 29.14
Open the Grid Properties dialog box to change the appearance of the chart's grids.

2. On the Line Attributes tab, choose appearance options for the vertical and horizontal grids.
3. On the Line Ratio tab, choose how many vertical and horizontal grids you want to display.
4. Click OK to accept the changes and close the dialog box.

If you cannot see whether you have made changes in the Axis Properties dialog box when you click the Preview button, see "Previewing Axis and Grid Properties" in the Troubleshooting section at the end of this chapter.

If you make changes in the Grid Properties dialog box, and the axis changes do not look right, see "Choosing the Primary Y Axis Properties" in the Troubleshooting section at the end of this chapter.

WORKING WITH TITLES AND LEGENDS

You can add and edit chart titles, a legend, and data labels to help identify the data in the chart. Titles name the subject of the chart; you also can add a subtitle and axis titles to your chart. The legend lists the colors, patterns, or symbols used for the chart markers and tells you what each represents. You can choose to show or hide the legend in a chart and if you choose to show the legend, you can set its placement, orientation, and various other attributes. Finally, you can edit the data labels in the chart. The labels show the numeric value, time period, or category of the markers.

ADDING AND EDITING TITLES

You can add titles to the chart and format the titles so that they are easy to read. Editing titles is also quick and easy.

To add or edit titles, follow these steps:

1. Double-click the chart to open the Chart Editor and choose Chart, Title or right-click the title and choose Title from the QuickMenu. The Title Properties dialog box appears (see Figure 29.15).

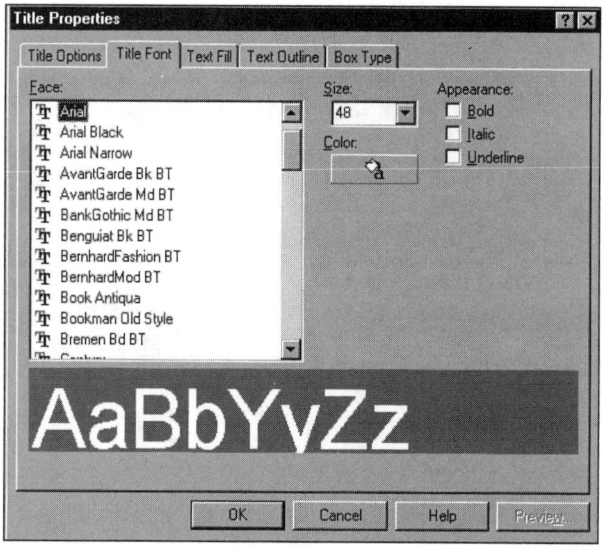

Figure 29.15
Use the Title Font tab of the Title Properties dialog box to enter the chart's title, and select its font style, size, and other attributes.

2. Check the Display Chart Title box, and type in the title for your chart.
3. Use the tabs of the dialog box to specify the title's font, text fill, text outline, box type (for a box around the title), box fill, and position of the title relative to the chart.
4. Click OK to close the Titles Properties dialog box.

> **Note**
> If you create a chart on a Data Chart slide in a slideshow, you may prefer to use the slide's title and subtitle. You need not create titles in both places.

EDITING LEGENDS

You can show or hide the legend for the chart. If you choose to show the legend (the default), you can change the position, orientation, box style, and font of the legend box to suit your chart and data.

To modify a legend, follow these steps:

 1. Select the chart and choose <u>C</u>hart, <u>L</u>egend or click the Legend tool on the toolbar. The Legend Properties dialog box appears (see Figure 29.16).

Figure 29.16
Use the Legend Properties dialog box to modify the legend for your chart.

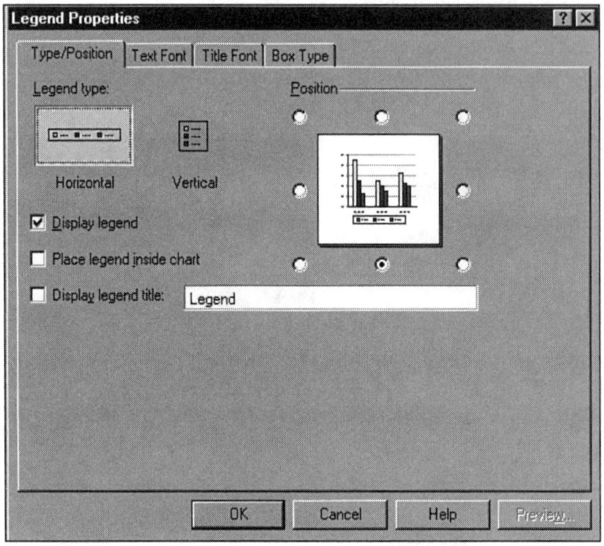

Legend Properties

Type/Position | Text Font | Title Font | Box Type

Legend type: Position

Horizontal   Vertical

☑ <u>D</u>isplay legend

☐ Place legend <u>i</u>nside chart

☐ Displa<u>y</u> legend title: Legend

OK   Cancel   Help   Preview...

Tip #202 from
Trudi Reisner

With the datasheet onscreen, double-click the chart's legend to open the Legend Properties dialog box.

---

2. Check the <u>D</u>isplay Legend check box to display the legend. If you prefer not to show the legend, deselect the <u>D</u>isplay Legend option in the Legend Properties dialog box so that no check mark displays in the check box.

3. Use the tabs of the dialog box to specify the legend's type and position, font for the legend text, font for the legend title, box type (for a box around the legend), and box fill.

4. Click OK to close the Legend Properties dialog box.

EDITING DATA LABELS

Data labels are tags that identify the tick marks or grid lines in a chart. You can show or hide the data label, plus change attributes, positions, and the fonts of the labels.

To edit the data labels, do the following:

1. Select the chart and choose <u>C</u>hart, Data La<u>b</u>els. The Data Labels dialog box appears as shown in Figure 29.17.

Figure 29.17
Choose how to display the data labels in the Data Labels dialog box.

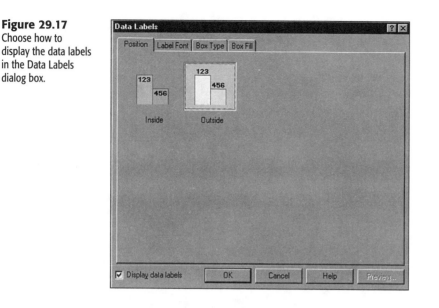

2. Check the Display Data Labels check box to display data labels.

3. Use the tabs of the dialog box to specify the data labels' position, font, box type, and box fill.

4. Click OK to close the Data Labels dialog box.

PRACTICAL PROJECT

Some PerfectExpert projects have wonderful data charts already made up for you. You just enter the data in the datasheet and the chart reflects your data. For example, the Annual Report Slideshow project has a slide that contains a 3D line graph representing stock prices and the number of shares, as well as a slide with a 3-D Overlap Bar chart illustrating revenues, income, gross and net profits, as shown in Figure 29.18.

Figure 29.18
Some data charts are already made for you.

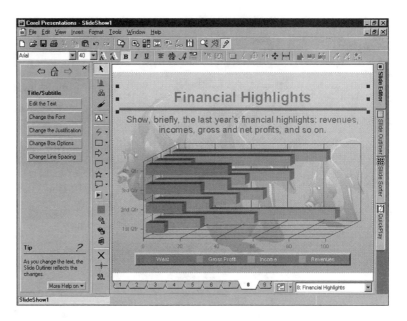

TROUBLESHOOTING

CANCELING CHANGES TO A SERIES

You made changes to the Series of the selected chart, and you don't like the changes.

Click the Cancel button before closing the Series Properties dialog box. Alternatively, you can deselect the data chart and click the Undo button on the toolbar to reverse the changes. Don't depend on this method, however, because you might undo more than you expected.

PREVIEWING AXIS AND GRID PROPERTIES

You cannot see whether you have made changes in the Axis Properties dialog box when you click the Preview button.

Some options in the Axis Properties dialog box are codependent on options you set in the Grid Properties dialog box. Set grid and tick options and then come back to the Axis Properties dialog box.

CHOOSING THE PRIMARY Y AXIS PROPERTIES

After you make changes in the Grid Properties dialog box, the axis changes do not look right.

Switch back to the Primary Y Axis Properties dialog box and change some of the options back to automatic by clicking the check box in front of the Minimum Value, Maximum Value, and Major Grid Value options.

CHAPTER 30

ADDING AND ENHANCING OBJECTS

In this chapter

ADDING LINES AND SHAPES

You can add a variety of lines and shapes to any slide in your presentation to enhance text or other graphics, such as a logo or clip-art picture. After adding the lines or shapes, you can choose from a variety of line styles, colors, and thicknesses.

CREATING LINES

To draw a line in Presentations, use the Line Shapes button on the Tool Palette. You can draw a curved, arced, straight, or freehand line using the tools, and you can select the line, move the line, or change its attributes.

> **Note**
>
> You can draw objects in the drawing screen or while working with a slideshow. The procedures are identical. You might want to try the examples in this chapter using the drawing screen because it is easier to see what you're doing without being distracted by the slide background.

DRAWING LINES

To create a line, click the Line Shapes button. You see the pop-up palette shown in Figure 30.1. Move the mouse pointer over the type of line you want to choose and click. Click and drag the tool in the work area to create a line. Each line tool looks like the line type that it creates. Experiment with the tools to get a clear idea of how each works. Table 30.1 describes the Line Shapes Tools.

Figure 30.1
Create a variety of lines to enhance text or graphics using the Line Shapes button on the Tool Palette.

Line Shapes Palette

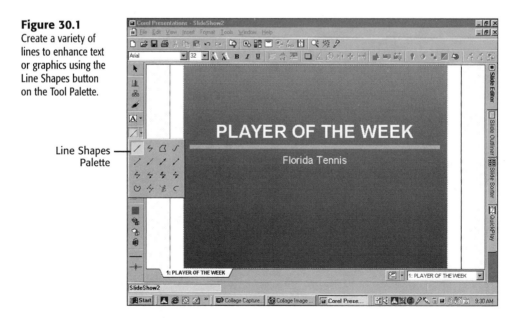

TABLE 30.1   THE LINE SHAPES TOOLS

Tool	Tool Name	Description
	Draw a line	Create a straight horizontal, vertical, or diagonal line. Click and drag from the beginning to the end of the line.
	Draw a polyline	Draw a line with several straight line segments. Click to begin the line, and then at each point you want the line to change directions, click again. Double-click to end the line.
	Draw a polygon	Draw several straight line segments that create a polygon shape. Click to begin the line, and then at each point you want the line to change directions, click again. Double-click to end the shape.
	Draw a curved line	Draw soft curves. Click to begin the curve, and then at each point you want the curve to change directions click again. Double-click to end the line.
	Draw a line with a dot on each end	Create a straight horizontal, vertical, or diagonal line with a dot on each end. Click and drag from the beginning to the end of the line.
	Draw a line with an arrow on the end	Create a straight horizontal, vertical, or diagonal line with an arrow on one end. Click and drag from the beginning to the end of the line.
	Draw a line with an arrow on each end	Create a straight horizontal, vertical, or diagonal line with an arrow on both ends. Click and drag from the beginning to the end of the line.
	Draw a line with a dot on one end and an arrow on the other end	Create a straight horizontal, vertical, or diagonal line with a dot on one end and an arrow on the other end. Click and drag from the beginning to the end of the line.
	Draw a polyline with a dot on each end	Draw a line with several straight line segments with a dot on each end. Click to begin the line, and then at each point you want the line to change directions, click again. Double-click to end the line.
	Draw a polyline with an arrow on the end	Draw a line with several straight line segments with an arrow on one end. Click to begin the line, and then at each point you want the line to change directions, click again. Double-click to end the line.
	Draw a polyline with an arrow on each end	Draw a line with several straight line segments with an arrow on both ends. Click to begin the line, and then at each point you want the line to change directions, click again. Double-click to end the line.

continues

TABLE 30.1 CONTINUED

Tool	Tool Name	Description
	Draw a polyline with a dot on one end and an arrow on the other end	Draw a line with several straight line segments with a dot on one end and an arrow on the other end. Click to begin the line, and then at each point you want the line to change directions, click again. Double-click to end the line.
	Draw a closed curve	Draw a closed curve. Click to begin the curve, and then at each point you want the curve to change directions, click again. Double-click to end the curve.
	Bézier Curves	Create Bézier curves, or curves with sectors you can edit and move independently. Click to begin the curve, then move the pointer to where the curve changes directions, and drag the pointer to display the two handles. Move the handle to change the shape of the curve. Double-click the mouse to end the curve. You can go back and select the curve to display handles, and then move the handles to edit the curve.
	Freehand Lines	Using the mouse, draw a line in any direction. Click and drag the tool as if the mouse were the pencil. Release the mouse button to end the line.
	Draw a section of an ellipse	Draw arcs that are sections of an ellipse. Drag the tool to begin the arc. Release the mouse button to complete the arc.

Tip #204 from
Trudi Reisner

You can constrain types of line objects with the Shift key. When you constrain a line, for example, you can draw only a vertical, horizontal, or 45-degree line.

MODIFYING LINES

You can change line attributes such as line style, line width, and line color by clicking the appropriate button on the Property Bar. To change line attributes:

1. Change the line style by selecting the line, clicking the Line Style button on the Tool Palette, and choosing a line style from the pop-up Line Style palette, as shown in Figure 30.2.

Figure 30.2
Change the line style from the pop-up Line Style palette.

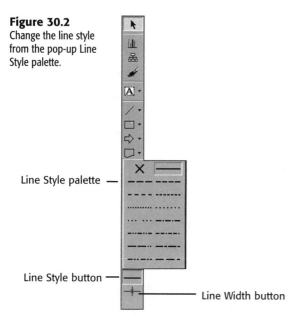

Line Style palette —

Line Style button —

Line Width button

2. Similarly, click the Line Width button on the Tool Palette, and then select a line width from the Line Width palette. Notice the <u>M</u>ore button, which takes you to the Object Properties dialog box (we'll get back to this in a moment).

3. Change the line color by selecting the line, and then clicking the Fill Attributes button on the Property Bar. Click the Outline tab, click the <u>C</u>olor button, and choose a color from the pop-up color palette in the Object Properties dialog box.

Tip #205 from *Trudi Reisner*	You can invert certain types of line objects with the Alt key while still holding down the mouse button. When you invert an arc, for example, the arc you are drawing changes from an upward-facing arc to a downward-facing arc.

You also can change line width, style, and color, along with other properties, by using the menu. Follow these steps:

1. Select the line, and choose Fo<u>r</u>mat, <u>O</u>bject Properties, <u>L</u>ine; or right-click the line and choose <u>O</u>bject Properties from the QuickMenu. You can also click the Fill Attributes button on the Property Bar. The Object Properties dialog box appears (see Figure 30.3).

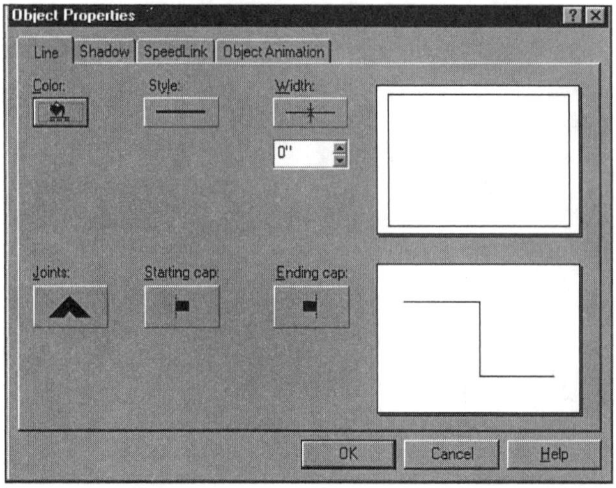

Figure 30.3
Change line attributes for the selected line in the Object Properties dialog box.

Tip #206 from *Trudi Reisner*

If you don't select a line before going into the Object Properties dialog box, the only way to get to the Object properties is to choose Format, Object Properties, Line. The new settings that you choose will become the default for all new lines you draw for the rest of that editing session.

2. On the Line tab, select from the following options. Notice the sample box updated to show you how your line will look.
   - Color—If the color you want doesn't appear on the palette, click More to create a custom color.
   - Style—Notice that selecting the large X means the line does not display at all.
   - Width—Select a predefined width, or in the edit box type the exact measured width you desire.
   - Joints—Choose to join two line segments with a Bevel, Miter, or Round edge.
   - Starting Cap or Ending Cap—The starting end of your line is where you began drawing. Choose the cap type you want from the palette that appears (see Figure 30.4). Cap types include round, flat, or square ends, and a variety of arrowheads and tails.

Tip #207 from *Trudi Reisner*

The sample box shows you how the line will look as you change its formatting attributes. Joints, ends, and arrowheads are more noticeable when the line thickness is greater than .05 inch.

Figure 30.4
You can add arrow-
heads to lines, as well
as specify how line
segments are connect-
ed and how lines end
on the Line tab of the
Object Properties
dialog box.

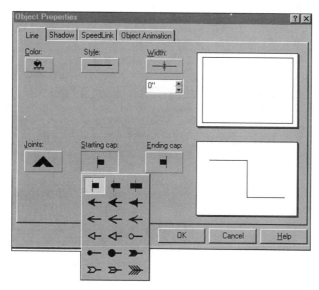

3. When finished with setting the line attributes, choose OK to close the dialog box.

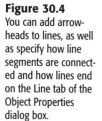 If you drew a Freehand line, but it turned out too angled and rough, see "Drawing the Perfect Line" in the Troubleshooting section at the end of this chapter.

If you drew a line, but can't see it on the screen, see "Choosing a Line Style" in the Troubleshooting section at the end of this chapter.

CREATING SHAPES

There are over one hundred shapes you can draw on your slides to give your presentation an artistic flair. You can choose from the following shapes: basic, arrow, flowchart, star, callout, and action. Use the shape tools on the Tool Palette to draw shapes on your slides.

DRAWING THE SHAPE

To draw a shape, click the shape's down-arrow button on the Tool Palette to display the various shapes. After drawing a shape, you then can drag one of its handles to change the shape. Table 30.2 describes the shape tools.

TABLE 30.2 THE SHAPE TOOLS

Tool	Tool Name	Description
◇ ▾	Basic Shapes	Click the tool and drag to create any of these basic shapes: rectangle, rounded rectangle, ellipse, parallelogram, trapezoid, diamond, octagon, triangles, hexagon, cross, pentagon, can, cube, and so on.

continues

TABLE 30.2 CONTINUED

Tool	Tool Name	Description
	Arrow Shapes	Click the tool and drag to create any of these arrow shapes: right arrow, left arrow, up arrow, down arrow, left-right arrow, up-down arrow, quad arrow, and so on.
	Flowchart Shapes	Click the tool and drag to create any of these flowchart process symbols: process, alternate, decision, data, predefined, internal storage, document, and so on.
	Star Shapes	Click the tool and drag to create any of these star shapes: 4-point star, 5-point star, 6-point star, 8-point star, ribbons, waves, and explosions.
	Callout Shapes	Click the tool and drag to create any of these callout shapes: rectangular, rounded rectangular, elliptical, cloud, 1-line with and without a border, and 2-line with and without a border.
	Action Shapes	Click the tool and drag to create any of these action button shapes: custom, home, help, information, back or previous, forward or next, and many others.

The shapes do not include circles or squares, but you can draw perfect circles or squares by holding down the Shift key while dragging diagonally to draw an ellipse or rectangle.

Tip #208 from
Trudi Reisner

Hold the Shift key while dragging to create a perfect square, circle, or 45-degree angle.
Hold the Alt key while dragging to create the object from a center point instead of the edge.

Figure 30.5 shows an example of each of the shapes.

Figure 30.5
You can use any of these eight shapes.

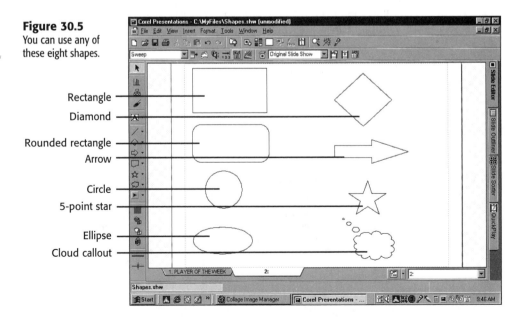

MODIFYING THE SHAPE

By default, shapes appear with a solid color fill. When drawing a shape, you can choose a fill color and pattern before drawing the object, or draw the object, select it, and then choose the fill and pattern. Additionally, you can change the border line style, color, and thickness before or after drawing the object.

You can create a shape with no fill, so the shape's border line is all you see onscreen and its inside is transparent. Alternatively, you can create the shape with a fill color or pattern and make the fill transparent or opaque. If the fill is transparent, you can use color and still see what's behind the closed shape; if the fill is opaque, it blocks out what is beneath it.

To select a fill or change the fill to None with the Tool Palette:

1. Select the object.

2. Click the Fill Pattern button on the Tool Palette. You see the fill pattern pop-up palette shown in Figure 30.6.

Figure 30.6
Use the fill attributes palette to change the fill type.

3. Choose a fill type, or choose the X to turn off the object's fill.

Tip #209 from
Trudi Reisner

Set the color of an object's fill by clicking the Foreground Fill Color button on the Tool Palette, and then choosing a color from the pop-up palette of colors.

To set the fill to a color or pattern:

1. Select the object, and then choose Format, Object Properties, Fill or right-click the object and choose Object Properties from the QuickMenu. The Object Properties dialog box now appears with the Fill tab selected, as shown in Figure 30.7.

Figure 30.7
You can set all Fill types and colors from the Object Properties dialog box.

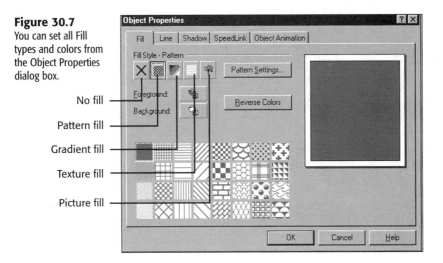

2. In the Object Properties dialog box, choose the X button to remove any fill. Alternatively, choose the Pattern, Gradient, Texture, or Picture buttons. Pattern creates a solid color or pattern, whereas Gradient produces a blend of two colors. Texture and Picture provide you with a selection of textures and pictures with which you can fill your objects.

3. If you chose Pattern, choose the fill pattern from the palette of choices, and then choose the Foreground and Background Colors.

4. If you chose Gradient, choose a gradient pattern, and then choose the Foreground and Background Colors.

5. If you chose Texture or Picture, select the Category you want to choose from, and then select a specific texture or picture.

6. Click OK to close the dialog box.

Figure 30.8 demonstrates various borders and fills.

Note

You can move a border (actually, a closed object with no fill) by selecting and dragging it to a new location. Additionally, you can select two or more items, such as a text box and a border, by holding the Shift key as you click the items.

Figure 30.8
Use borders with fills and patterns to attract attention.

Pattern fill

No fill

Gradient fill

Picture fill

Texture fill

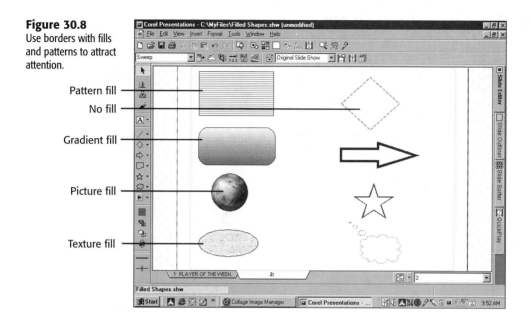

ENHANCING SHAPES

With the new image tools on the Property Bar, you can apply special effects to shapes. These image tools include Brightness, Contrast, Watermark, Gray Scale, Invert Colors, Silhouette, Outline, Coloring Book, Outline All, and Transparent. Experiment with these image tools to get the special effect you want for a shape. If some of the image tools are not on the Property Bar, choose Tools, Image Tools, and pick the tool you need.

To help you experiment with enhancing shapes, Presentations 9 now has a Real Time Preview feature, which lets you experiment with formatting and preview formatting before you apply it to the shape on your slide. When you point to choice in an image tool drop-down menu on the Property Bar, Presentations Pro gives you a preview of your selection right in the object on the slide. Each time you select an option, the change is shown on the slide before you apply it.

There are a host of wonderful new tools that can help you convert closed shapes to polygons and add special effects to shapes you've already drawn. To convert closed shapes to polygons, select the closed shape and choose Tools, Convert to Polygon.

You can add 3D effects to shape by using Tools, Quick 3-D. In the Quick 3-D dialog box (see Figure 30.9), on the Rotation tab, select a rotation, specify how much you want to rotate the image, and adjust the color. On the Perspective tab, choose from Linear, Parallel, or Inverse, and specify the depth.

Figure 30.9
Use the Quick 3-D dialog box to add rotation and perspective to a shape.

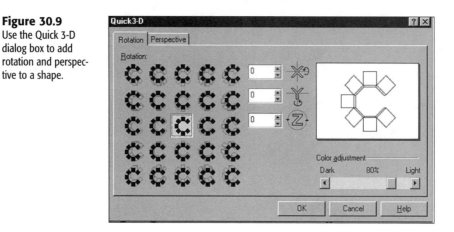

To contour text to a shape, use Tools, Contour Text.

The new Tools, QuickWarp feature is used to bend or twist a text created with the Text Box and Text Line tools. The QuickWarp dialog box contains numerous shapes for warping a text, as shown in Figure 30.10.

Figure 30.10
Use the QuickWarp dialog box to bend and twist text created with the Text Box and Text Line tools.

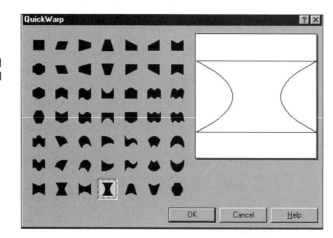

To combine a polygon with another object, select the objects you want to combine, and click the Combine tool on the Property Bar. To separate the combined object, select the object, and use the Separate tool on the Property Bar.

CREATING TEXTART

TextArt provides predesigned special text effects by adding designs and shapes to plain text. TextArt changes fonts in various ways by squeezing them, bending them into shapes, stretching them, and adding shadows, borders, and many other text effects. Using TextArt is an excellent way to create desktop publishing effects, especially for making logos.

To create TextArt, follow these steps:

1. Click the Text Object Tools down-arrow button on the Tool Palette, and choose Create Text with Special Effects. The Corel TextArt 9.0 dialog box opens, as shown in Figure 30.11.

Figure 30.11
You can create logos and desktop publishing text effects with the Corel TextArt 9.0 dialog box.

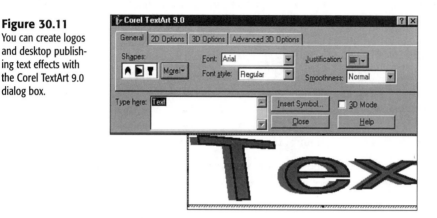

PART

IV

CH

30

2. Type the text for the TextArt image in the Type Here box, replacing the word *Text*.

3. Choose a shape for the text in the Shapes palette. If you want to see more shapes, click the More button and choose a shape from there.

4. Choose a font, font style, and justification to format the text.

5. Change any of the following TextArt options on the 2D Options, 3D Options, or Advanced 3D Options tab to custom tailor the TextArt image:

   • The 2D Options tab lets you change the pattern, shadow, outline, rotation, text color for the TextArt image. You can activate 2D mode by turning off the 3D check box.

   • The 3D Options tab gives you options for changing the lighting, bevel, depth of the bevel, and rotation for the TextArt.

   • The 3D Advanced Options tab offers options for specifying the texture for the face and bevel of the image, texture size, texture lighting, and color quality.

6. Click Close. The TextArt appears where you positioned the insertion point.

Note

If you no longer want the TextArt image on your slide, select the image by clicking it and pressing the Delete key.

ADDING PICTURES

You can add pictures or clip art from the Corel WordPerfect 9 suite of applications, or from other sources. Pictures help illustrate text and make a presentation more attractive. Corel Presentations 9 includes a Scrapbook that provides various categories of clip art, such as animals, architecture, arrows, and so on. Alternatively, you can insert a file from another program, such as a bitmap or Designer file.

INSERTING A PRESENTATIONS PICTURE

The Presentations Scrapbook provides a limited number of graphics that is installed on your computer when you install WordPerfect Office. In WordPerfect's Scrapbook, you can search and preview the images, drag and drop, and copy and paste them. Scrapbook organizes the images by category. You can even create your own category; view automatic updates of thumbnails; as well as preview sounds, movies, and bitmap images.

If you have a CD-ROM drive and the WordPerfect Office 2000 CD is in the drive, you also have access to an additional, very extensive collection of clip art.

 Note

If you want more clip art to choose from, you can buy packages of clip art (in black and white or color) from software stores and mail-order catalogs. These clip art "libraries" are packaged by topics such as animals, business, holidays, music, people, and so on. If you want more professional artwork, look for photo collections, which are usually sold on CDs.

To insert a Presentations clip-art picture:

1. Choose Insert, Graphics, ClipArt, or click the Clipart button on the toolbar. The Scrapbook dialog box appears (see Figure 30.12).

Figure 30.12
Insert a picture using the Scrapbook collection of clip art.

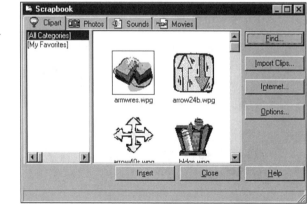

2. The Clipart tab displays the preinstalled clip-art figures. Choose a category and scroll through the scrapbook to find a picture you want to use.

3. If you don't find the image you need, you can access the CD clip art if you have the WordPerfect Office CD in your CD-ROM drive. Click the CD Clipart tab, and you see several folders of categories of clip art. Double-click folders to open them. Click the Return button at the upper-right corner of the dialog box to close a folder.

Tip #210 from
Trudi Reisner

To display more images at once on the screen, right-click the viewing screen and choose View, Large Icons to remove the check mark next to Large Icons.

4. Select a picture and drag it onto the Presentations editing screen or click the Insert button. Alternatively, you can right-click the image and choose Copy; then you can paste the image into your Presentations drawing or slideshow.

MODIFYING A PRESENTATIONS CLIP ART IMAGE

You can move, resize, cut and paste, add a border, and otherwise manipulate the picture as you would any object. In fact, when you drag an image onto your screen, more than likely the resulting image will be too large. You need to reduce the image by dragging sizing handles on the box until you have the size you want.

Tip #211 from
Trudi Reisner

To maintain the original proportions of an image, drag the corner handles. If you drag the sides of the image, it will not retain its proportions.

Besides changing its size, you also can modify just parts of the image. Suppose you have an image of a sign and a flower, but you want only the flower. To edit individual sections of the image, follow these steps:

1. Click the image to select it.

2. Click the Graphics button on the Property Bar, and choose Separate Objects. Alternatively, you can double-click the image, which temporarily separates the various parts of the image.

Note

If you are used to earlier versions of Presentations, you need to look on the Property Bar or on the Tool Palette, not on the menu, for many Graphic menu options.

3. Edit the parts of the image as desired. For example, you could select the parts of the sign and delete them, or even change the color of the flower.

4. Choose the Select tool from the toolbar and drag an area that encompasses the remaining objects of the image. Click the Graphics button on the Property Bar or on the Tool Palette and choose Group. If you double-clicked the image to edit it, click outside of the image edit box to regroup the remaining objects.

Separating images and editing them gives you virtually unlimited flexibility in creating the exact image you want without having to create your own original artwork.

INSERTING A PICTURE FROM ANOTHER PROGRAM

If you have clip art, drawings, or other pictures you want to use from another program, you can insert them into a presentation slide.

To insert a picture from another program or other clip-art collections:

1. Choose Insert, Graphics, From File. The Insert File dialog box appears.

2. In the dialog box, select File Type if you want to narrow the search to a particular type of file (for example, .pcx or .wpg).

> **Note**
>
> It is usually not necessary to specify the file type. Presentations automatically interprets the file type for you. You will normally use the file type function only when you want to save your file in a format other than .shw (for slideshows) or .wpg (for drawings).

3. Select the correct folder and then choose the file. Click the Insert button, and the file is inserted into your work area.

ADDING PICTURES FROM THE WEB

You can also add pictures that you find on Web pages to your Presentations drawings or slideshows. The Web has many sites that have public domain images, and as you surf the Web, you might find that you can easily increase your clip-art library with these graphics.

> **Caution**
>
> Although copying images from the Web is technically easy to do, you will usually be in violation of copyright laws if you take images from a public site without permission. Although many people do not know it, you cannot reuse photographs or clip art that you find in public sources without the permission of the creator.
>
> Be sure to email the administrator of the site where you found clip art and ask his or her permission prior to using the images.

You can take images from a Web site to incorporate into your drawings or slideshows by saving them to your local computer using Netscape. To do so, take the following steps:

1. Using Netscape, browse to the site containing the image you want to use.

→ For more information on browsing the Web, **see** "Browsing the Web from WordPerfect," **p. 592**

2. Right-click the image to be saved, and choose Save Image As. You see a Save As dialog box.

3. Navigate to the folder in which you want to save the image, and choose Save. The image is saved to your local computer.

To import the image, use the procedure outlined in the previous section "Inserting a Picture from Another Program." You then can manipulate the JPG or GIF image as you do other bitmapped images (see "Working with Bitmap Images" later in this chapter).

INSERTING AND FORMATTING TABLES

You can create a table within Presentations that enables you to display data in rows and columns. Organizing numerical information into a table format makes it easier to read and comprehend. Additionally, you can display any chart data in table format by choosing Table as the chart type; you can change the table back to a chart when it better suits the presentation.

PART

IV

CH

30

Tip #212 from
Trudi Reisner

You can also copy a Corel WordPerfect 8 table to the Clipboard and paste it into a Presentations slide.

When creating a table in Presentations, you can choose from six table formats, including outlined, shaded, and plain table designs. Presentations enables you to add titles, subtitles, and range colors, and otherwise format the data within the table.

ADDING A TABLE

You can create a table within Presentations into which you can enter, edit, and format the text, data, labels, and titles. You can also copy a table or table data from another program, such as Corel WordPerfect 9. After copying the table to the Clipboard, you can paste it into a Presentations slide.

To copy a table from another program, follow these steps:

1. Create the table in the other program (for example, in WordPerfect 9). You can format the table text and alignment; however, Presentations does not retain the formatting when it is pasted into a slide.

2. Select the entire table and choose Edit, Copy.

3. Switch to the Presentations program and display the slide into which you want to paste the table.

4. Choose Edit, Paste, and the table is embedded on the slide.

Note

When you embed a table in this way, it is created as an OLE 2.0 object in your slideshow or drawing, which means you can easily update the table. To find out more about OLE 2.0 objects (including how to edit them), see the section "Learning Techniques for Linking and Embedding" in Chapter 35.

To create a table within Presentations, follow these steps:

1. Choose the Chart button from the toolbar or from the Tool Palette. The mouse pointer changes into a hand holding a square.

2. Drag the hand across the slide page to define the area for the table.

Note

The area required for a table is much larger than the table itself. Instead of dragging an area for the table, you might find it easier to single-click the editing screen, which gives you a full screen table. You then can size the table later as needed.

3. Release the mouse button. The Data Chart Gallery dialog box appears.

4. In Chart Type, choose Table. Six table formats appear from which you can choose, as shown in Figure 30.13.

Figure 30.13
Choose Table as the chart type in the Data Chart Gallery dialog box to view various table formats.

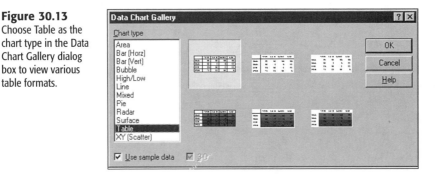

5. Choose a table format and click OK. The dialog box closes, and the datasheet window appears next to the table in your slide, as shown in Figure 30.14.

Figure 30.14
Use the datasheet to define a table's contents in Presentations.

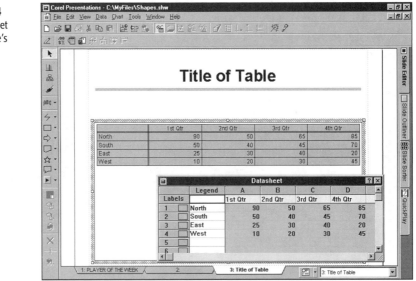

6. Enter the data into the datasheet as you did when creating charts in Presentations.

→ For more information on entering data in a datasheet, **see** "Entering Data," **p. 524**

7. Close the datasheet by clicking outside the hatch border that surrounds the chart object. The table appears in the designated area (see Figure 30.15).

Figure 30.15
The table appears in the slide or drawing when you close the datasheet after entering your data. The table object displays handles, indicating that it is selected.

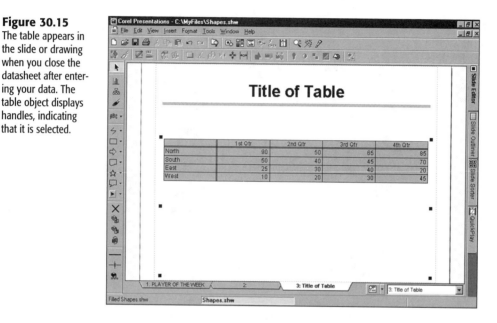

EDITING A TABLE

You can edit the information in a Presentations table at any time by editing the data in the table's datasheet. To edit the data in a table, ensure that the table is not selected, and then double-click the table to activate it. When active, the table's defining box displays a hatch border, and you may see the table's datasheet.

If the datasheet is not displayed, you can view it by clicking the View Datasheet button on the toolbar. The datasheet then appears. When you are finished editing, click outside the table editing area to close the datasheet, as well as the Chart Editor.

ENHANCING A TABLE

You can format the text and data in a table so that the text is large enough to easily read during a presentation. When you format the text or data within the table, all the text within the table reflects the formatted changes.

Additionally, you can add titles and subtitles to the table, and you can change the color of the table lines, background, font, and so on.

To format the text in a table, follow these steps:

1. Double-click the table to activate it, and then click the View Datasheet button to close the datasheet, if you prefer to have it out of the way.

2. Choose Chart, Layout/Type from the menu bar. The Table Properties dialog box appears, as shown in Figure 30.16.

Figure 30.16
Use the Table Properties dialog box to change the font and other table options.

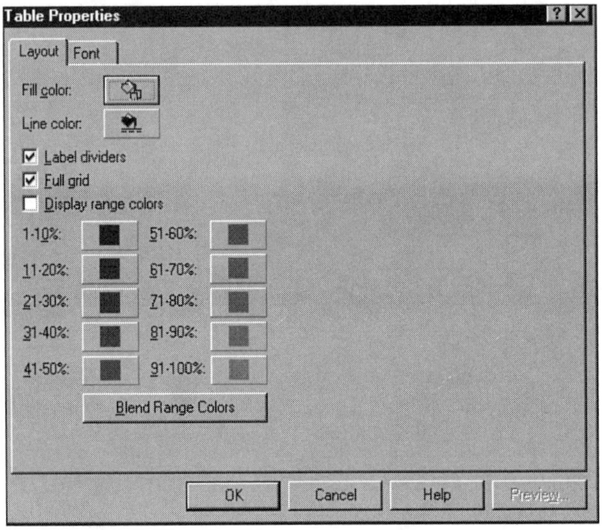

3. In the Layout tab, choose options as described in Table 30.3.

4. Choose font options by selecting the Font tab, and then choosing the font face, style, size, color, and appearance attributes. The Sample box shows you how your fonts will look.

Tip #213 from
Trudi Reisner

Change the type size to at least 36 points or even larger so it can easily be read in the presentation slide.

5. Click OK to close the Table Properties dialog box; alternatively, you can choose Preview to view the change before accepting it.

TABLE 30.3   TABLE/SURFACE OPTIONS

Option	Description
Display Range Colors	Shows or hides the selected colors to the table cells; this option fills each cell with the selected colors in the Range Colors area of the dialog box (see the "Applying Range Colors" section).
Blend Range Colors	Allows you to blend a color chosen for the minimum with a color chosen for the maximum of the range (see the "Applying Range Colors" section).

Option	Description
Label Dividers	Shows or hides the table's formatted gridlines in a table.
Full Grid	Shows or hides all gridlines in the table.
Fill Color	Choose one color to use for the table background.
Line Color	Choose one color to use for all gridlines.

APPLYING RANGE COLORS

Presentations includes a useful feature that enables the reader to quickly discern the data in a table: range colors. Each range color represents a different value in the table; the range color is applied as background color for each cell. The lowest values, for example, might be represented in a red cell, whereas the highest values could be represented in a yellow cell. Using range colors enables the viewer to quickly see the number of high and low values on the table.

Tip #214 from
Trudi Reisner

Use grays if you are printing in black and white; use colors if your presentation is onscreen.

You choose the range colors in the Table Properties dialog box from among the various shaded percentage buttons. You can blend colors or select specific colors for each range.

To blend colors, click the 1-10% box and a palette appears; choose the color to represent the first range in the table. Similarly, choose a color for the 91-100% box. Click the Blend Range Colors button to automatically fill in the remaining ranges with a blend of the two colors you selected.

Tip #215 from
Trudi Reisner

Don't use too many colors on a slide, because it clutters and obscures the information you're trying to convey. Be careful of dark colors that will hide the text/numbers in each cell of the table.

Figure 30.17 shows the table with a blend of grays applied to the ranges. Note that you must turn on the Display Range Colors option.

Alternatively, you can choose a color for each range block by clicking the block and choosing a color from the palette.

Tip #216 from
Trudi Reisner

Keep the colors light enough so that you can read all the data in the table cells. Try making the text bold if it's hard to read. Also, keep the text style simple; stay away from italic and other fancy styles, especially if you will be using the tables in a presentation.

Figure 30.17
Blend colors in the Table Properties dialog box to create the variation of grays shown in this table.

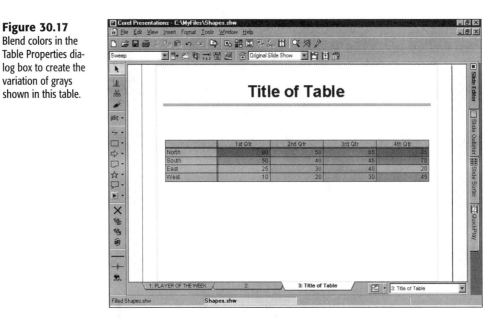

ADDING TITLES

Presentations enables you to add titles to your table. You can even format the title, if you want. Using the Title Properties dialog box, you can enter your own title or delete the title text altogether.

To add a title, follow these steps:

1. Double-click the chart to open the Chart Editor.
2. Double-click `Title of Chart`. The Title Properties dialog box appears (see Figure 30.18).

Figure 30.18
Use the Title Properties dialog box to add titles.

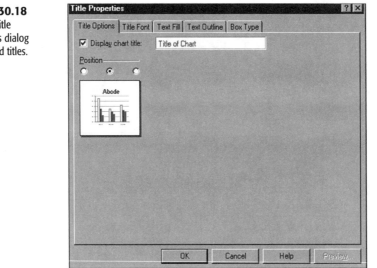

3. Enter the title in the Display Chart Title text box.

4. To format the title font, ensure that you are in the Title Font tab, and then choose the appropriate font options.

5. Choose the Text Fill or Text Outline tab to change the fill from solid to a pattern, or to specify the outline around the title letters. In the Text Outline tab, you need to choose a Line Style before other controls have any effect.

6. Choose the Box Type or Text Fill tab to change the type of box, or the pattern, gradient, fill, or texture that will fill the box. You need to deselect the No Box check box in the Box Type tab before other controls become available. The Box Type tab is shown in Figure 30.19.

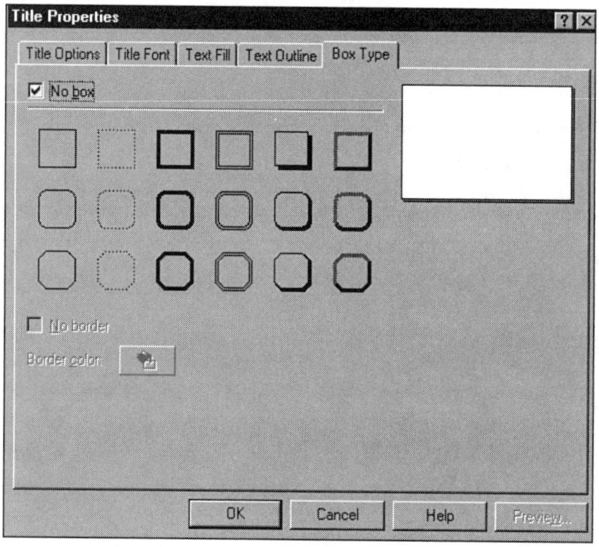

Figure 30.19
Choose from a variety of boxes for your title in the Box Type tab of the Title Properties dialog box.

7. On the Position tab, choose whether to put your title at the top, left, center, or right of the chart.

8. Click OK to close the Title Properties dialog box; then click the slide outside of the selected chart area to deselect the chart and close the datasheet.

WORKING WITH BITMAP IMAGES

You can incorporate two types of graphic images in your documents: vector images and bitmap images.

A vector image is stored as a formula. For instance, a circle might be stored as several codes that specify the shape (a circle), the location of the center point, the diameter, the line width, style, and color. Vector images can be stored efficiently because there is little information to store. They can also be resized and moved easily because you merely need to alter one or two elements in the stored formula. All the drawing objects you have worked with in this chapter so far are vector images, and vector images are the only type of images that many popular presentation packages can work with.

A bitmap image is stored as a series of dots (technically called pixels). When you scan a photograph into your computer, you are scanning (and saving) dots, not formulas. Therefore, scanned images are stored as bitmaps. Although bitmaps are important to be able to work with, they have limitations. They take up much more space, and resizing them is much more problematic because they're not stored as a formula.

Programs that manipulate bitmap images are often called paint programs; programs used to manipulate vectors are often termed drawing programs. The types of tools used in paint programs are different from the ones in drawing programs. For instance, paint programs contain tools such as paintbrushes, which spread a swatch of color on your image (by changing the color of the pixels that you use the tool on). Other tools include airbrushes that let you smooth colors gradually on an image—for instance, to "air brush" a smooth complexion on a scanned image of a face.

The default drawing type in Presentations is the vector drawing. However, you can create and edit both vector and bitmap images, and even change your bitmap image to a vector image with a function that traces the bitmap and creates formulas that describe it.

CREATING A BITMAP IMAGE

To add a bitmap image to a slide, click the Bitmap Image button Tool Palette. The mouse pointer changes into a hand. Drag the hand across the slide work area to create a box for the image. (If you single-click, the bitmap editing area fills the whole screen.) The view changes to Bitmap Editing view (see Figure 30.20), and the toolbar, Tool Palette, and Property Bar all have different tools on them.

Use the Text, Shapes, and Line tools to create your bitmap image just as you use them to create a vector image. In addition, you can use Paint and Eraser tools to enhance your bitmap images.

To paint a swatch of color in your image, select the Paintbrush tool. Select a color with the Foreground Fill color button, and change the brush shape and brush width with buttons on the Bitmap Property Bar, if desired. Your mouse pointer looks like the shape of the brush you have selected. Click and drag the paintbrush over the area of the slide to be painted.

Use the Airbrush tool in a way similar to that used with the Paintbrush. Choose the tool, select the appropriate color, and change the brush shape and width, if desired. Repeatedly swipe the airbrush over the area to be colored to apply the color, just as you would with a real can of spray paint.

Use the Roller tool to flood-fill an entire area of one color with the selected color. For example, you can replace a white background with a blue background.

Figure 30.20
Presentations includes a complete bitmap editor where you can work with graphics at the pixel level.

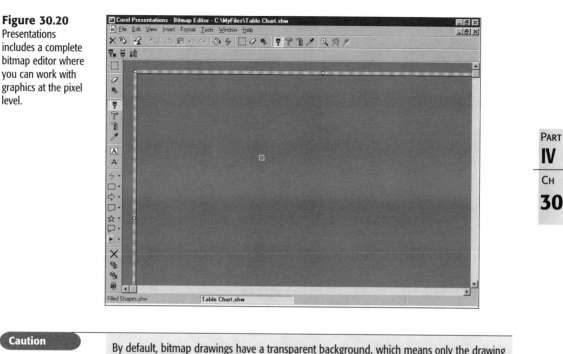

Caution

By default, bitmap drawings have a transparent background, which means only the drawing itself covers other objects in your slide. If you fill the background with a color, then the entire bitmap image, including the rectangular background, covers other images.

Tip #217 from
Trudi Reisner

You can choose Edit, Undo to undo your last action. If you want the action you undid to come back, you can then choose Edit, Redo.

Use the Eyedropper tool to "dip into" a color to make it the active color. To use this tool, select it, and then click an area of the drawing that has the color you want to duplicate. The color becomes the active foreground color, and you can use one of the other tools to apply it to other areas of your drawing.

The Erase tool erases the parts of the image that you drag it over.

When you are finished with your bitmap image, choose File, Close Bitmap Editor; or right-click the image and choose Close Bitmap Editor from the QuickMenu. Your bitmap image is inserted into your slide or drawing.

EDITING AN EXISTING BITMAP IMAGE

To edit an existing bitmap, double-click it. If the image was created in Presentations, you will see the same bitmap editing screen that you saw when you created the image.

TRACING A BITMAP IMAGE

You can trace a bitmap image to transform it into a vector image. This can be useful when you want to be able to size the image, as you might with a scanned signature.

To trace a bitmap image, click it once in the drawing or slide to select it. Choose Tools, Trace Bitmap. The image is transformed into a vector drawing.

SAVING GRAPHIC OBJECTS AS SEPARATE FILES

Until this point, we have explored the use of graphic objects as they add to or enhance a slide presentation. On occasion, you might need to save a specific object for use in other situations—in another slideshow or as part of a Web page, for example.

Presentations makes it easy to select the image you want to save, and then to save it in a native WPG (WordPerfect Graphics) format, or to export it (convert it) to some other format such as BMP (Windows bitmap), GIF (CompuServe Graphics Interchange Format), or JPG (Joint Photographic Experts Group).

Suppose you create a graphic image that you want to post on your own home page. To do so, it must be saved in a GIF or JPG format. To do this, follow these steps:

1. Select the object you want to save.

2. Choose File, Save As; indicate in the dialog box that you want to save the selected item(s); and choose OK.

3. In the Save As dialog box, supply the desired filename in the File Name box, and then change the File Type to .gif or .jpg. Presentations adds the appropriate filename extension to the filename. Choose Save.

4. Presentations displays the Export dialog box (see Figure 30.21). Unless you really need to change anything, such as the size of the image, choose OK and Presentations exports the image to the format you chose.

Figure 30.21
By using the Save As option, Presentations enables you to export graphic images you create to Web-ready formats, such as JPG and GIF images, and to determine their exact size and resolution.

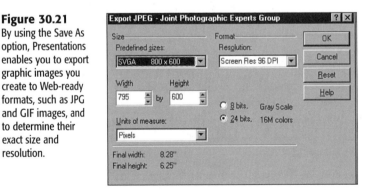

Caution

> Exporting an image does not save that image in the WPG format. If you intend to use Presentations to edit this image again in the future, you should also save the image as a WordPerfect Graphic.

PRACTICAL PROJECT

The PerfectExpert sales flyer project contains a combination of TextArt, pictures, and text. Figure 30.22 shows the Flyer, Sales PerfectExpert project you start with, but you can add your own graphics, a chart, shapes, and text to embellish the original flyer.

Figure 30.22
PerfectExpert sales
flyer project

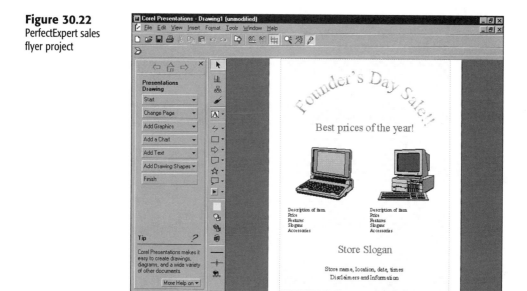

TROUBLESHOOTING

DRAWING THE PERFECT LINE

You drew a Freehand line, but it turned out too angled and rough.

Freehand lines are hard to draw smoothly; try using the Bézier Curve Line tool instead. After you draw the curve, double-click it to edit it, and then select a point (the mouse pointer turns into a crosshair when it's over a point). Move the handles associated with that point by dragging them.

CHOOSING A LINE STYLE

You drew a line, but can't see it on the screen.

Click the Line Style button on the Property Bar and make sure that a line style, rather than the x, is selected.

CHAPTER 31

PRINTING AND DISPLAYING YOUR PRESENTATION

In this chapter

UNDERSTANDING PRINTED SLIDESHOW OPTIONS

Whether you decide to print your presentation, make transparencies or slides, or present it as an electronic slideshow, you might want to have Speaker Notes, handouts, or audience notes to accompany it. Speaker Notes are pages that have one or more slides, along with notes that remind you of what you want to say while the slide is displayed. Audience notes are similar pages, but instead of notes, they display blank lines. Handouts are merely pages with one or more slides printed on them.

Audience notes and handouts can be printed at any time after you have created your slides. Because Speaker Notes have additional text, you need to create them as a separate operation. To create Speaker Notes:

1. Open your presentation and choose Format, Slide Properties, Speaker Notes, or click the Speaker Note button on the Property Bar. The Slide Properties dialog box appears (see Figure 31.1).

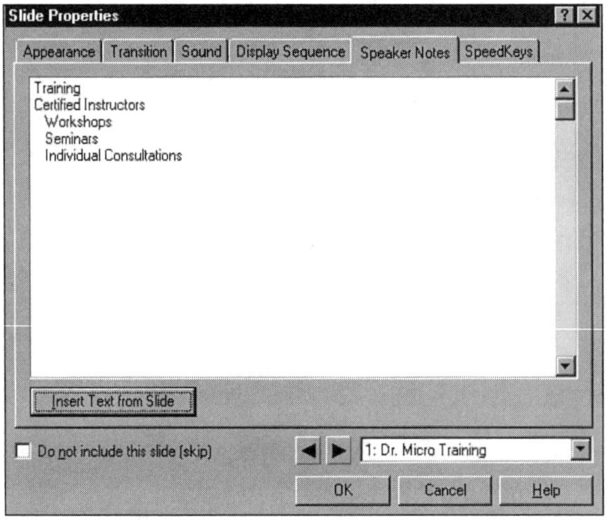

Figure 31.1
Enter comments and notes on the presentation in the Speaker Notes tab of the Slide Properties dialog box; click Insert Text from Slide for quick Speaker Notes.

2. Using the drop-down list in the lower-right corner of the dialog box, select the slide to which you want to add notes.

3. In the text box, enter the notes. Check the Insert Text from Slide button if you want to include the text of the slide in your notes.

4. Repeat steps 2 and 3 to enter notes to additional slides without closing the dialog box.

5. When you are finished, choose OK to close the dialog box.

PRINTING THE PRESENTATION

When you are ready to print, you can choose which presentation element you want to print—such as slides, Speaker Notes, and so on—and you can choose the number of copies, binding offset, and other options before printing. With Presentations' new PerfectPrint feature, you can enlarge or reduce a presentation to fit any paper size without changing the format of the page. PerfectPrint also lets you print on both sides of a page.

To choose printing options:

1. Choose File, Print, and ensure the Print tab is selected. You see the Print dialog box shown in Figure 31.2.

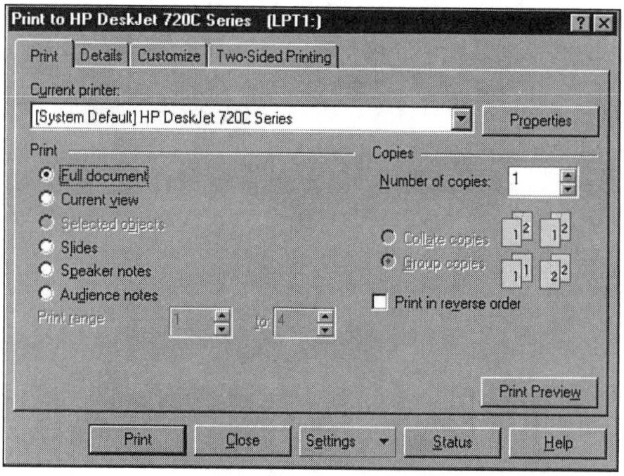

Figure 31.2
Choose print options in the Print dialog box.

Tip #218 from
Trudi Reisner

Choose Print Preview in the Print dialog box as you select options to see how your printout will look. Press the Esc key to return to the Print dialog box.

2. Begin by choosing the printer you want to print to and change the printer properties, if necessary.

3. In the Print area, choose the element you want to print:

   - Full Document—Prints the full document.
   - Current View—Prints only what you see onscreen; for example, if you are in a magnified view (zoom), Current View prints only that which is showing.
   - Selected Objects—Prints only those objects you have selected from a slide.
   - Slides—Prints all or part of the slideshow.
   - Speaker Notes—Prints thumbnails, or small pictures, of each slide with any notes you entered as Speaker Notes (choose Format, Slide Properties, Speaker Notes).
   - Audience Notes—Prints thumbnails along with lines so that the audience can take notes as you talk.

4. Select how much of your slideshow you want to print (the range of slide), the number of copies, and (for more than one copy) whether you want to collate or group the copies, and whether to print in normal or reverse order. The options to collate or group copies appear only if you specify more than one copy.

5. If you are printing handouts or Speaker Notes, choose how many slides to print per page.

6. On the Details tab, choose to Print Slide Title, or Print Slide Number as a footer or caption beneath the printed slide.

7. If you want, you can click Print Preview to see how your document will look when it is printed.

You can also set other printing options from within the Print dialog box. By selecting the Details tab, you can choose from among these options:

- Choose the printer and printer port you want to print to, or add a new printer.

- Choose the Resolution—whether to print in high, medium, or low quality.

- Choose whether to Print in Color or black and white. If you don't have a color printer, you can't choose that option. You can choose to let your printer try to guess how to print the colors in black and white, or let Presentations Adjust the image to print black and white. On black-and-white printers, it often helps not to print the background of the slide.

The new Customize tab in the Print dialog box lets you select PerfectPrint options for fitting the presentation to the paper size. By choosing the Customize tab, these options are available:

- Off—Turns off the PerfectPrint Customize option.

- Poster—Prints the presentation on poster-size paper. You can specify a poster size such as 2×2, 3×3, and so on, and the Poster option shows how many pieces of paper will be used when you print in the sample box.

- Enlarge/Reduce—Lets you enlarge or reduce your document by specifying a percentage.

- Scale to Fit Output Page—Enables you to scale your printed document to fit the page size. Click the Output Page button to view and modify the page size.

- Thumbnails—Prints the slideshow as thumbnails on handout pages so that viewers can make notes as they watch the show. Choose the number of slides you want on each page in the Thumbnails grid (3×4 is the default number of slides per page). You can have a maximum of 64 thumbnails on a page.

The Two-Sided Printing tab in the Print dialog box gives you options for printing on both sides of a page. If your printer supports two-sided (duplex) printing, you can set options for this here. If it doesn't, you can still manually print two-sided documents by specifying that the printer print the odd, and then the even pages. Also use this tab to set options for binding offsets (the whitespace on the inside margin of the document).

⚠️ *If you want to stop the print job after you choose Print in the Print dialog box, see "Canceling a Presentations Print Job" in the Troubleshooting section at the end of this chapter.*

If you cancel a print job from Presentations that is partially completed, you aren't able to delete it from the print queue, and a partial print job comes out of the printer, see "Purging Presentations Print Jobs" in the Troubleshooting section at the end of this chapter.

If your color graphics and text appear as an overall gray when you print to a black-and-white printer, see "Adjusting the Image for Black-and-White Printing" in the Troubleshooting section at the end of this chapter.

> **Note**
>
> If you have an HPGL plotter or a film recorder connected to your printer, you can print to either of them the same way you print to a printer. Using the Print dialog box, select the Print tab, and then choose the printer you need from the Current Printer drop-down list. Choose any other options as you did before and click Print.

CREATING AN ELECTRONIC SLIDESHOW

With Corel Presentations 9, you can create a slideshow and display that show on your computer's screen—or project it from your computer via a data display panel or projection device—for customers, employees, or students.

Electronic slideshows provide you a much greater opportunity to enhance the presentation by adding transitions between slides, having bullets appear one at a time, animating slide elements, or including sound and video to create a multimedia presentation.

ARRANGING YOUR SLIDES

When you print your slideshow, the arrangement of slides is not critical. You can shuffle your slides around and print them in any order that you desire. For electronic slideshows, however, you will need to ensure that your slides are arranged in the order that you intend to show them.

> **Tip #219 from**
> *Trudi Reisner*
>
> If you have an initial slide that lists all your topics, consider copying this slide so that it is displayed before you start each new topic. This way, the audience will see how each topic fits into the presentation as a whole.

To rearrange your slides, switch to Slide Sorter view by clicking the Slide Sorter tab at the right side of the screen. You see thumbnails of each of the slides in your slideshow. Select a slide by clicking it, or select several adjacent slides by clicking the first, and then holding down the Shift key while you click the last. Drag the slide(s) you want to move to their new location. As you drag them, you see a vertical line that indicates where the slides will be placed, as shown in Figure 31.3.

Figure 31.3
Rearrange slides by dragging them in Slide Sorter view.

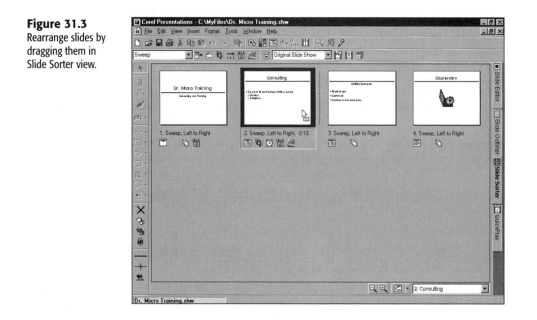

ADDING SLIDE TRANSITIONS

The first option you will probably want to set for your electronic slideshow is the transition you will use from one slide to another. You can specify that Presentations should go from one slide to the next when you press a key or click the mouse; or you can set Presentations to move from one slide to another after a specified amount of time. You can set transitions and timing for all slides or separately for each slide, if you like.

To set transitions:

1. Open your presentation and choose Format, Slide Properties, Transition; or right-click the slide and choose Transition from the QuickMenu. The Slide Properties dialog box appears (see Figure 31.4). (If you select the Slide Appearance toolbar button, you need to then select the Transition tab.)

Figure 31.4
In the Slide Properties dialog box, you can choose from a variety of transition effects that govern how one slide moves to the next.

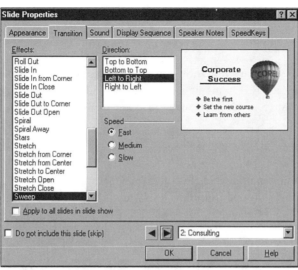

Tip #222 from
Trudi Reisner

A quick way to select just the transition you want is to click the <u>D</u>irection drop-down list from the Property Bar. As you point with the mouse at each transition type in the list, Presentations displays an animated preview box to show what the transition looks like.

2. From the list at the lower right of the dialog box, select the slide for which you want to set options, or check <u>A</u>pply to All Slides in Slideshow.

Tip #223 from
Trudi Reisner

If you have multiple slides selected before displaying this dialog box, then the right/left arrows don't appear to the left of the slide number.

3. Select the transition type from the <u>E</u>ffects list. You see how the effect works in the Preview window. Depending on the transition you select, you might also choose the <u>D</u>irection that it will occur. Also, choose the speed for the transition.

4. Move to the next slide to which you want to add a transition, and then repeat step 3 as needed.

5. When you are finished setting transitions, choose OK to return to your slideshow.

→ For more information on playing a slideshow, **see** "Playing Your Slideshow," **p. 583**

Tip #224 from
Trudi Reisner

If you are using Slide Sorter view, Presentations displays the type of transition you have set for each slide, as well as other icons to indicate timing, sound, Speaker Notes, and so on.

ADDING SLIDE TIMINGS

Normally, you want to manually advance from one slide to another so that you can spend as much or as little time needed on each slide.

Sometimes, however, you will want to have your slides advance automatically after a specified number of seconds. You might even want your slideshow to loop continuously, as when you play it at a store entrance or convention table to advertise a product or service.

In this case, you will want to set timings for your slides. You can do so as follows.

To set timings:

1. Open your presentation and choose Format, Slide Properties, Display Sequence; or right-click the slide and from the QuickMenu choose Display Sequence. You can also click the Display Sequence tool on the Property Bar. The Slide Properties dialog box appears with the Display Sequence tab selected (see Figure 31.5).

Figure 31.5
You can have your slides advance from one to the next automatically after a specified number of seconds by setting options in the Slide Properties dialog box on the Display Sequence tab.

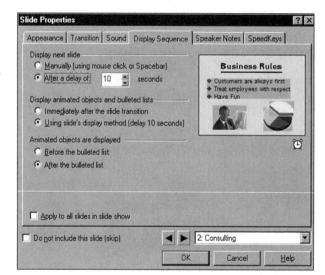

2. From the list at the lower-right corner of the dialog box, select the slide for which you want to set options, or check Apply to All Slides in Slideshow.

3. If you want to automate the slide timing, choose After a Delay Of, and specify the number of seconds between slides.

4. Choose options for any animated objects you have on your slide. If you select Immediately After Slide Transition, the animated object appears immediately after the slide has been drawn onscreen. If you choose Using Slide's Display Method (Manually), the animations and bullets are displayed manually or after a delay, depending on the option you selected.

5. Move to the next slide to which you want to add a slide timing, and then repeat steps 3 and 4 as needed.

6. When you are finished setting timings, choose OK to return to your slideshow.

Tip #225 from
Trudi Reisner

Set the seconds to delay higher for slides with a lot of information on them, so the viewer is sure to have enough time to read the information.

Note

You can add sound to a slideshow by using MIDI, digital audio, or CD audio sound files to one or more slides, if you have the sound hardware for the job. See the section "Including Multimedia Effects" later in this chapter.

ANIMATING SLIDE ELEMENTS

You can animate your slides further by having bullets appear one by one, with old bullets becoming dim. You can also have drawing objects fly in from the side, giving an animated appearance to your slideshow.

To animate your bullets in bullet slides:

1. Choose Slide Editor view by choosing View, Slide Editor, or by clicking the Slide tab at the right side of the screen. (You cannot animate bullets unless you are in Slide Editor view.)

2. Choose a slide that has bullets you want to animate, and click the bulleted list to select it.

3. Choose Format, Bulleted List Properties, and in the Bulleted List Properties dialog box choose the Bullet Animation tab. Alternatively, you can choose Format, Object Properties, Object Animation to see the dialog box shown in Figure 31.6.

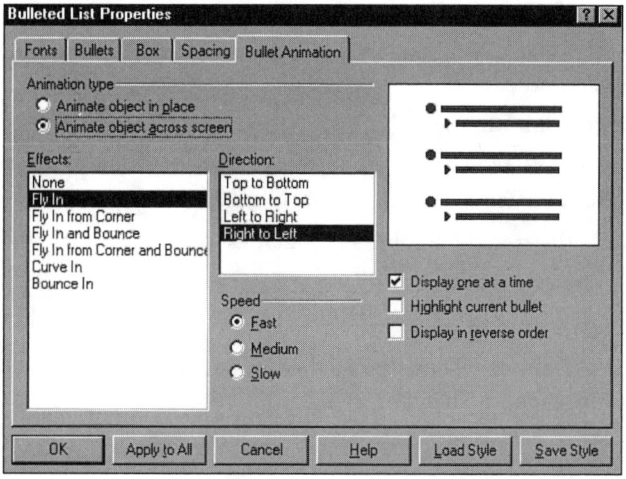

Figure 31.6
Animate bullets with special effects to add pizzazz to your presentation.

4. Select the type of animation you want to use from the Effects list, and set the Direction and Speed. If you want previous bullets to become dim, choose Highlight Current Bullet. You can also choose to display one bullet at a time, and to do so in reverse order if you like.

5. Click OK to exit the dialog box.

If you want to animate drawing objects or QuickArt that you've placed on your slide, do the following:

1. Select the first object to be animated—the object which should appear first after the slide displays.

2. Choose Format, Object Properties, Object Animation; or right-click the object and choose Object Animation from the QuickMenu. You see the Object Animation Properties dialog box shown in Figure 31.7.

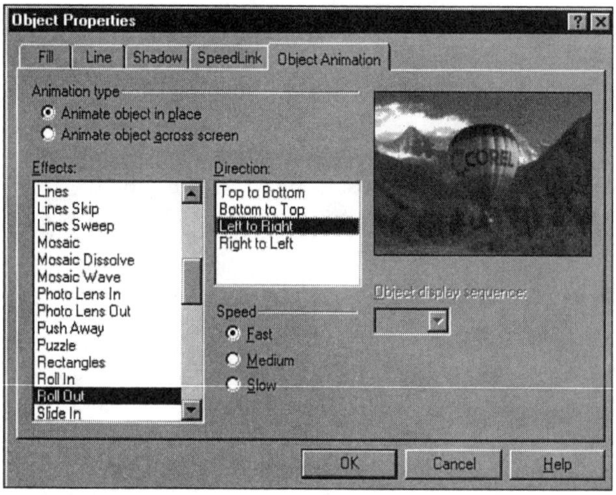

Figure 31.7
In the Object Animation tab of the Object Properties dialog box, you can animate objects on your slide to have them fly onto the slide.

3. Choose the specific animation or transition effect you want to use, and the direction and speed, if needed.

4. Click OK to return to the slide.

5. Select the next object to be animated, and repeat steps 2 through 4. If you need to reorder the animated object, change its Object Display Sequence number.

6. Continue with this until all objects are animated.

INCLUDING MULTIMEDIA EFFECTS

You can take your slideshow one step further by adding sounds to it, or even video files (if your hardware supports sound or video).

INSERT SOUNDS ON YOUR SLIDE

You can add short bursts of sound, such as clapping hands, or longer melodies that you can play during the entire slideshow, or during the display of one or more specific slides.

To add sound to your presentation, do the following:

1. Open your presentation and choose Format, Slide Properties, Sound; or right-click the slide and choose Sound from the QuickMenu. The Slide Properties dialog box appears with the Sound tab selected, as shown in Figure 31.8.

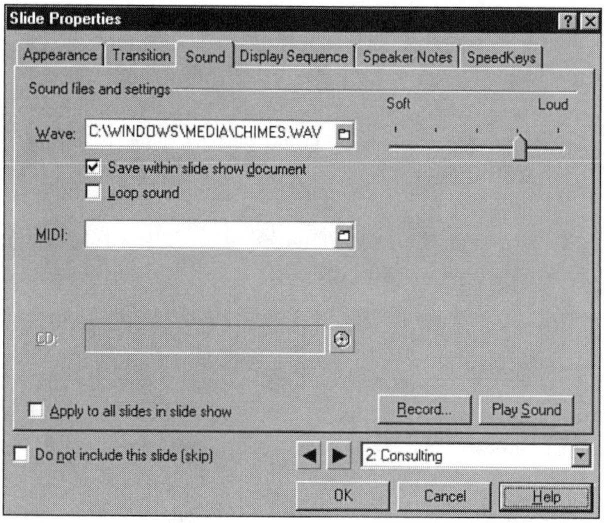

Figure 31.8
You can add sound to your slides to make a multimedia presentation by using the Sound tab of the Slide Properties box.

2. From the list at the lower-right corner of the dialog box, select the slide to which you want to attach the sound.

3. Select the type of sound you want to use, and then click the folder button to browse the folders and find the right sound file.

   Sound options include

   - Wave—Digitized sound files. Usually, they are quite large when saved to disk, but can be recorded and even edited with standard Windows audio tools.
   - MIDI—Considerably smaller and have much higher-quality sound, but also require special equipment to record. However, most Windows systems play MIDI files without any problem.
   - CD—Use any sound recording on CD to play along with your slideshow. You can even specify which track to play and where to begin and end on that track.

4. If you want the sound to loop and keep repeating, choose Loop Sound. You can set the volume (for example, louder for the introductory slide, but softer for the slide on which you'll be speaking). Click Play Sound to preview how it will sound.

5. If you have a microphone attached to a sound board in your computer, you can choose Record and add your own narration to your slides.

6. Choose OK to close the dialog box and return to your slideshow.

Tip #226 from
Trudi Reisner

To play a sound throughout your presentation, attach the sound to slide 1 and loop the sound.

ADD VIDEO CLIPS TO YOUR SLIDESHOW

You can use two methods to insert video clips into a Presentations slideshow. The first uses Corel's method and works better with some of its Internet-publishing capabilities. The second method depends on OLE (Object Linking and Embedding), and although it's more limited in what it can do, generally it works with a wider variety of movie file types.

To add a video clip to your slideshow using Corel's method, do the following:

1. Switch to Slide Editor mode by clicking the Slide Editor tab, and click the tab of the slide you want to attach your video clip to.

2. Choose Insert, Movie. Browse to find the movie file you want and choose Insert.

If you get an error message with the preceding method, try using OLE. The movie might insert without errors, but might not run when the slideshow is run. If that's the case, you need to use the OLE method, too. To insert a movie using the OLE method, follow these steps:

1. Switch to Slide Editor mode by clicking the Slide Editor tab, and click the tab of the slide you want to attach your video clip to.

2. Choose Insert, Object. You see the Insert Object dialog box (see Figure 31.9).

Figure 31.9
Use the Insert Object dialog box to add a movie clip or other multimedia object to your presentation only if Insert, Movie doesn't work.

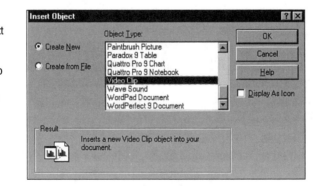

3. Choose Create from File, and then click the Browse button. You see the Browse dialog box.

4. Navigate to the movie clip file you want to use, and then double-click it. You return to the Insert Object dialog box. Click OK to return to the slideshow.

Using either method, the movie clip appears as an object on the appropriate slide. You can position and size the clip just as you do any other object. When the slideshow reaches that slide, click the movie clip to play it.

PLAYING YOUR SLIDESHOW

When you're ready to play your slideshow, Presentations offers you options for moving from slide to slide, using mouse pointers and highlighters to draw attention to aspects of your slide, and saving your show as a Quick File to eliminate pauses in your slideshow.

Caution

In the first release of Presentations 9, a dialog box appears if you do not have DirectX installed. This dialog box suggests that you go to the Corel Web site and download DirectX, a program from Microsoft that can assist in making slide transitions faster and smoother. Unfortunately, DirectX can also cause some rather severe problems by not interacting properly with your video hardware. Furthermore, once installed, you cannot remove DirectX from your system.

You can ignore this message each time by choosing Continue, or you can download and install the DirectX program. If DirectX does cause problems, you can disable DirectX in Presentations 9 by choosing Tools, Settings, Display, and then unchecking Take Full Advantage of Video Memory for Smoother Transitions.

PLAYING A SLIDESHOW

When you run the slideshow, Presentations clears the screen of tools, windows, menus, and everything except each slide.

To play a slideshow:

1. Open the slideshow. Choose View, Play Slideshow, or click the Play Slideshow button on the Property Bar. The Play Slide Show dialog box appears, as shown in Figure 31.10.

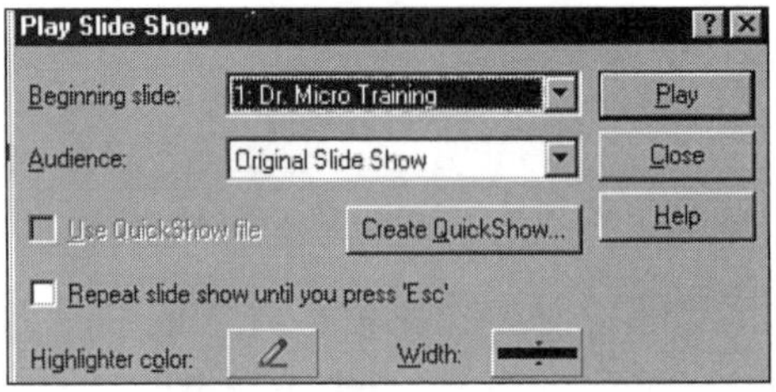

Figure 31.10
Choose to play the
slideshow, and
Presentations offers
you options as to
how you can present
your slideshow.

2. From the Beginning Slide list, choose the slide you want to start the presentation with.

3. You can use the mouse to highlight slides as you present them. Choose the Color and the Width of the marker you want to use during the presentation.

Tip #227 from
Trudi Reisner

Draw on the slide by clicking and dragging with the mouse. Don't just click the mouse, because that will cause the slideshow to advance to the next slide.

4. Choose Repeat Slideshow Until You Press 'Esc' if you want the show to run continuously.

5. Choose Play to start the show.

PLAY OPTIONS

While you are playing your slideshow, you have several options.

If the show is set to Manually Advance the Slides:

- Click the left mouse button, or press the right arrow or down arrow to advance to the next slide.

- Press Esc to cancel the show at any time.

- Click the right mouse button for a QuickMenu that enables you to jump to the first, last, next, or previous slide; end the sound; or increase or decrease the volume. Keystroke equivalents also are listed on the QuickMenu.

To show the cursor during your slideshow, move the mouse pointer. The cursor appears on your slide.

To highlight an area of your slide with an underline, move the mouse pointer to where the underline should start, and then drag the mouse pointer to draw an underline.

CREATING A QUICKSHOW FILE

Create a QuickShow file of your slideshow to speed up the display. When you create a quick file, you save the slideshow as a bitmap and thus the display is much quicker; however, the file is much larger than a slideshow, so be sure you have enough room for the show on your disk.

To create a quick file, choose View, Play Slideshow. The Play Slideshow dialog box appears. Choose Create QuickShow. If you haven't saved your file, you will be prompted to do so before the QuickShow is created. You see a Making QuickShow dialog box as the file is created.

When you play your slideshow in the future, you can choose to use the QuickShow file by checking the Use QuickShow file box in the Play Slideshow dialog box.

⚠️ *If you made a change in one of the slides, and now the slideshow seems slower, see "Saving As a Quick File" in the Troubleshooting section at the end of this chapter.*

If you're saving a copy of the slideshow to a floppy disk, but you're worried that the show is too large to fit on one disk, see "Saving Presentations to a Floppy Disk" in the Troubleshooting section at the end of this chapter.

MAKING A RUNTIME SLIDESHOW

PART

IV

CH

31

Making a runtime slideshow means to copy the show with all necessary program files to a disk so you can run the show on another computer that does not have Corel Presentations 9 installed.

To make a runtime file:

1. Open the slideshow or save the current show.

2. Choose File, Show on the Go or click the Show on the Go button on the Property Bar. The Show on the Go welcome screen appears (see Figure 31.11). The options that appear may be those from the last time a Show on the Go file was created.

Figure 31.11
The Show on the Go option allows you to copy your presentation to a disk so that it may be run from a computer that does not have Corel Presentations 9 installed.

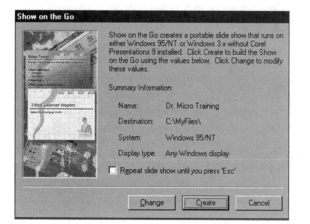

3. Choose <u>C</u>hange. You see the second step of the Expert shown in Figure 31.12. Select the drive (floppy, or any writable drive that has removable media, such as Zip, Jazz, or SparQ) or folder where you want to create the Show on the Go file, and then choose Next. (If you choose a folder that does not exist, you are asked whether you want the Expert to create it.)

Figure 31.12
Choose whether to save your runtime slideshow to a floppy disk or to a folder on your hard drive.

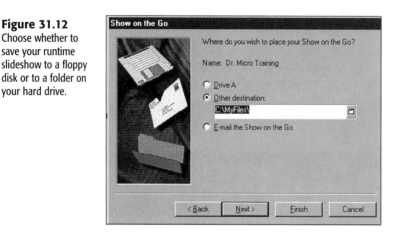

4. In the third step of the Expert, select whether your show will be played on a Windows 95/NT system or on both Windows 3.x and Windows 95/NT systems (see Figure 31.13). Choose <u>N</u>ext.

Figure 31.13
Tell Presentations on what kind of system you plan to play your slideshow.

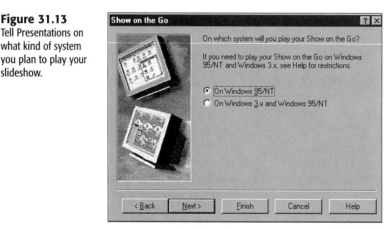

5. In the fourth step of the Expert, select whether the display of the system you will play your slideshow on matches yours (see Figure 31.14), or whether it should be able to be played on any Windows display. Choose <u>F</u>inish.

Figure 31.14
Tell Presentations on
what kind of display
you plan to show
your slideshow.

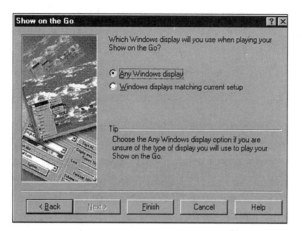

6. The final step shows the choices you have made. If any are incorrect, choose Change Again to revisit previous steps. If they are correct, choose Create. You see the Making Runtime dialog box as your show is converted, and then you return to the main Presentations window.

Note

If you choose to save the show so that it can be played both in Windows 95 or Windows 3.1, you will experience certain limitations. All transitions are immediate, and animation is removed. Slides with cascading bullets, however, still play normally. Quicklinks and OLE objects also do not work.

PRACTICAL PROJECT

Create a slideshow and play it with animation effects such as Blinds, Burst In, Circles Small, Dissolve, Mosaic Wave, Roll In and Roll Out, Sweep, Triangles, and/or any other Slide Transition effect.

TROUBLESHOOTING

CANCELING A PRESENTATIONS PRINT JOB

You want to stop the print job after you choose Print in the Print dialog box.

Presentations displays the Printing dialog box until the print job leaves the print buffer in Presentations. You can cancel the print job by clicking the Cancel button in this dialog box. After that, you can return to the Print dialog box (choose File, Print) and choose Status. From the list of current and past print jobs, click the document you want to cancel and choose Document, Cancel Printing.

PURGING PRESENTATIONS PRINT JOBS

If you cancel a print job from Presentations that is partially completed, and you aren't able to delete it from the print queue, a partial print job will come out of the printer.

Alternatively, you can click the Printer icon on the taskbar to display the Printer dialog box after the print job has spooled to Windows, and then highlight the print job and choose Printer, Purge Print Jobs.

ADJUSTING THE IMAGE FOR BLACK-AND-WHITE PRINTING

Your color graphics and text appear as an overall gray when you print to a black-and-white printer.

Choose the Details tab in the Print dialog box, and then choose the Adjust Image to Print Black and White option. If you are still unhappy with the results, return to the presentation and select the colored graphics you want to change. From the color palettes, you can choose from a variety of grays to assign text, chart markers, lines, fills, patterns, and so on. You might need to experiment with the grays to get the results you want.

SAVING AS A QUICK FILE

You made a change in one of the slides, and now the slideshow seems slower.

If you saved the slideshow as a quick file and then made a change to the show, you must create a quick file again to speed up the display.

SAVING PRESENTATIONS TO A FLOPPY DISK

You're saving a copy of the slideshow to a floppy disk, but you're worried the show is too large to fit on one disk.

You can usually fit one slideshow onto a high-density 3 $1/2$" or 5 $1/4$" floppy disk; however, if your show file is larger and fills up the disk, Presentations prompts you to insert a second disk.

Web Publishing with Corel WordPerfect Office 2000

CHAPTER 32

INTEGRATING COREL WORDPERFECT 9 WITH THE WEB

In this chapter

BROWSING THE WEB FROM WORDPERFECT

The first way that you can extend your desktop is by browsing the Web from WordPerfect. Whenever you want to access the Web, click the Change View button on the WordPerfect toolbar. You see the Internet Publisher toolbar shown in Figure 32.1.

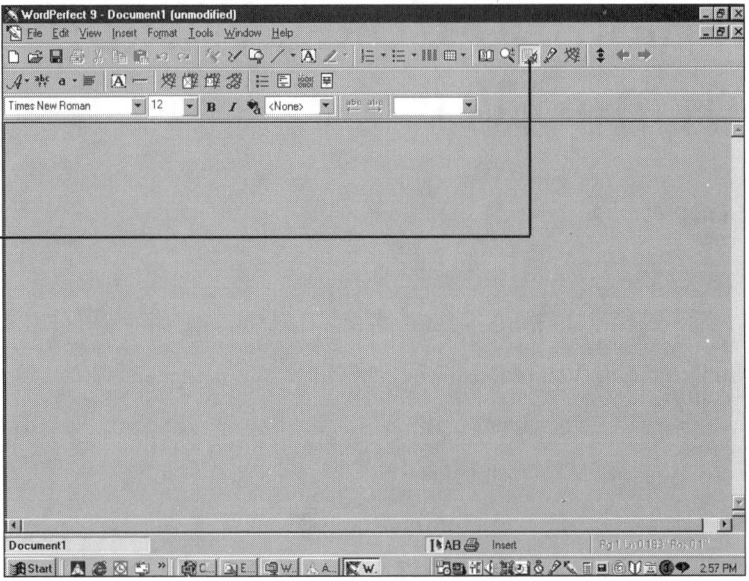

Figure 32.1
The Internet Publisher toolbar has buttons for browsing the Web and for converting your current document to a Web page.

Change View button ———

Be sure you're connected to your Internet service provider (ISP) and then click the Browse the Web button. You are taken into Netscape (or your default browser) and from there automatically to Corel's site. From there, you can obtain assistance with Corel products, or jump to anywhere else on the Internet.

USING INFORMATION FROM THE WEB IN YOUR DOCUMENTS

You not only can reach out to the Web from WordPerfect, but you can also bring information from the Web into your WordPerfect documents.

Whether it's recipes, technical support instructions, or IRS instructions, you will find it useful to be able to capture text from Web sites to integrate into WordPerfect documents you create.

Of course, if your Web is a corporate intranet, you may find many documents that are stored on your Web expressly for your use. Sections from corporate capability statements, résumé information, or the annual report can easily be incorporated into proposals or other documents you create in WordPerfect.

> **Caution**
>
> The information contained on Web sites is often copyrighted and will in any case be protected by relevant copyright laws. Always attribute quoted text, and strongly consider establishing a company policy regarding use of information obtained from the Internet after advice from legal counsel.

You can incorporate text from Web pages into your documents in three ways:

- Save Web documents to your local disk, and then convert them to WordPerfect.
- Copy information from a Web page to your WordPerfect document.
- Create a link from your WordPerfect document to information on a Web page.

SAVING AND CONVERTING WEB DOCUMENTS

The first way to incorporate information from the Web into your WordPerfect document is to save and convert the Web document. You can do this by first browsing to the document using Netscape, and then choosing File, Save As to save it to your local disk.

You can then convert the Web page into a WordPerfect document. After the document is converted into WordPerfect, you can edit it or copy or move sections of it into another WordPerfect document you are working on.

COPYING WEB INFORMATION INTO A DOCUMENT

Alternatively, you can copy selected text directly from a Web document into your WordPerfect document. To do so, use Netscape to browse to the document you want to copy text from.

When you are looking at the desired document, drag with your mouse over the text you want to select, and then choose Edit, Copy to copy the text to the Clipboard. Switch to Corel WordPerfect, click where you want the text to appear, and then choose Edit, Paste.

> **Caution**
>
> Viruses can be downloaded in program, data, and macro files. Be careful about indiscriminately downloading files from the Web. Some viruses can make every single file on your computer unusable. Practice "safe computing" by getting a virus protector (for individual machines or on a network) before getting set up to go out on the Web.

USING HYPERTEXT WEB LINKS

You can create links in your WordPerfect document that will take you to specific sites on the Web when you click them. For example, you might have a WordPerfect document on the network that discusses current industry trends. As you make points in your report, the supporting evidence can be links that readers can follow to see the Web-based data that led you to your conclusions.

PART

V

CH

32

If your Web link doesn't work, see "Editing a Web Link" in the Troubleshooting section at the end of this chapter.

→ To learn more about links and bookmarks, **see** "Adding Links and Bookmarks," **p. 600**

 Web sites change frequently. If you are responsible for WordPerfect documents that contain links to Web pages, be sure to check the links regularly to ensure they still work.

UNDERSTANDING WEB PUBLISHING

Everyone who has electricity has heard about the Internet by now, and most people in business are sure it's a "good thing." But many people still do not honestly know why they might want to create Web documents.

There are two types of webs that you might publish documents to, and they each have different purposes: the World Wide Web, which is part of the Internet; and private, corporate webs called intranets.

PUBLISHING TO THE WORLD WIDE WEB

The World Wide Web is part of the global Internet. Information published on it is available to the public. There are many types of WordPerfect documents you might want to put where the public can see them.

Individuals create personal Web sites that are a little bit like a telephone "white pages" listing, except that they tell the public more about you. Personal Web sites often contain information about your interests, your family, your work, and ways to contact you. Personal Web sites can be created using WordPerfect templates.

Companies create corporate Web sites on the Internet as a matter of public relations. They not only can establish a corporate presence on the Internet, they can sell products, deliver technical information, or provide white papers on topics of interest to their industry. WordPerfect is not the best software to create a sophisticated home page (the initial page you see at a company's site, often with sophisticated graphics). It is excellent, however, for creating the other Web pages, because technical information, white papers, and more, often already exist in WordPerfect.

A key to Web publishing is understanding that it is a public pronouncement. It's like standing on a box in the middle of Times Square and telling passersby what your opinions are. You don't know who is going to read it, and it may be more permanent than you think. Even if you change what's on a Web page, someone else may well have saved the original version to his or her disk.

PUBLISHING TO A CORPORATE INTRANET

Corporations are increasingly using intranets as the method of choice to publish internal documents. The nature of the intranet means that only corporate employees can access it.

The nature of the Web, however, also implies that employees with many different types of computers can see Web documents with all their formatting, allowing for inexpensive cross-platform integration.

For these reasons, corporations are publishing WordPerfect documents to their intranets, such as

- Internal Corporate Documents—All sorts of corporate documents, such as employee manuals, insurance application instructions, corporate policies, and the like are being published to intranets from their original WordPerfect format. Often, they are no longer being produced in hard copy to save money.

- Knowledge Bases—Because search tools can search the text of all documents published to the intranet, more technical files, résumé files, and historical documents are being published to internal webs to create searchable "knowledge bases" that can be accessed by personnel.

WordPerfect lets you publish your documents by creating HTML Web documents that can be uploaded to the Internet or a corporate intranet.

CREATING WEB DOCUMENTS

The Web is a part of the Internet that supports graphic and multimedia files written in HTML format. What's this all about?

The Internet supports the transmission only of text files, not the complex binary files that make up applications and data files and contain complex format coding (such as WordPerfect documents).

To get around this shortcoming, complex coding systems have been developed to translate programs and data files into plain text. One of these mechanisms is the Hypertext Markup Language (HTML). Using HTML, bold text is denoted by tags—ASCII codes that denote <b> as the beginning of bold and </b> as the end of bold. Similarly, <H1> denotes the Heading 1 style and </H1> denotes the end of it.

> **Note**
>
> ASCII is a fancy name for the characters on a typewriter keyboard—A–Z, 0–9, and a few others. When you read ASCII, you can generally substitute "plain text."

In the past, you had to learn HTML codes to create documents that could be published on the Web. Now, the Internet Publisher takes care of this for you, and you merely need to format your document using familiar WordPerfect commands.

Internet Publisher is a part of the WordPerfect program. It is a set of functions that allows you to create Web documents, save them in HTML format, and even convert existing WordPerfect documents to HTML and vice versa. You can create an empty Web document or use PerfectExpert to create a simple Web home page for yourself. In addition, the

Internet Publisher allows you to add and format text, create links, insert graphics, and add tables to your Web document.

When you publish a series of interlinked HTML documents on the Web, they become a Web site, and each document is called a Web page. The main page on your site that a person would usually go to first is called the home page.

For ease of writing, however, the following terms are used in this chapter to mean identically the same thing: HTML document, Web document, and Web page.

MAKING A BASIC WEB DOCUMENT

To start making a Web page, do the following:

1. Choose File, Internet Publisher. You see the Internet Publisher dialog box (see Figure 32.2).

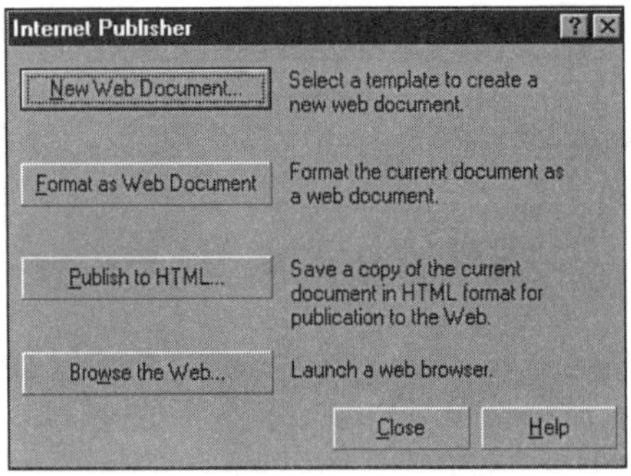

Figure 32.2
You can click the New Web Document button in the Internet Publisher dialog box to create Web documents, such as home pages for yourself or your business.

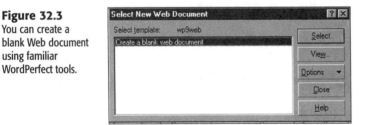

2. Click the New Web Document button. You see the Select New Web Document dialog box shown in Figure 32.3.

Figure 32.3
You can create a blank Web document using familiar WordPerfect tools.

3. Select Create a Blank Web Document.

4. Choose Select. You see a blank editing screen.

From here, you can add text, graphics, tables, styles, and other elements to the Web page. After you save your document in HTML format, you can then upload it to the Web. These steps are described in the following sections.

ADDING AND FORMATTING TEXT

After you have created a Web page, you will want to add text to it and format the text so that it appears attractive when seen in a Web browser such as Netscape. With the Internet Publisher, you not only can do this easily, but you can also copy text into your Web page from other WordPerfect documents.

ADDING TEXT

To add text to your Web page, type it in as you would in any other WordPerfect document. All the normal editing commands are available to you, just as they are in any other WordPerfect document. Move around the document with your mouse or keyboard, insert and delete text as you normally would, and even cut and paste text from one part of the document to another.

COPYING TEXT

To copy text into your Web document, open the document containing the text, select the text, and then choose Edit, Copy. Switch back to your Web document, place your insertion point where you want the text to appear, and choose Edit, Paste. The text is copied into your Web document, just as if you had copied it into any other WordPerfect document.

FORMATTING TEXT

When you are in the Internet Publisher, only the formatting features supported by HTML (the underlying "language" that Web documents are written in) are available to you. Notice that the toolbar and Property Bar change, as shown in Figure 32.4. Menu items that are not supported in HTML are removed as well.

Figure 32.4
When you create Web pages, your toolbar and Property Bar change to provide you with specialized options for your Web document.

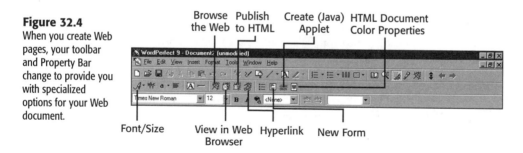

Format your text as you normally would, recognizing that not all the *formatting* commands you are accustomed to will be available. To bold a sentence, for instance, you highlight it and click the Bold button. To create a bulleted list, click the Bulleted list button at the beginning of a new line, and then type the bulleted items.

INSERTING HORIZONTAL LINES

The simplest graphic element that you can use to spice up your Web page is a horizontal *line*. To insert a horizontal line into your Web page, position your insertion point where you want the line to appear, and then click the Horizontal Line button on the Internet Publisher toolbar. You see a line in your Web document.

You can also edit the appearance and attributes of horizontal lines. To do so, select the line to be edited, right-click it, and choose Edit, Horizontal Line. You see the Edit Graphics Line dialog box (see Figure 32.5).

Figure 32.5
Specify the position, length, and thickness of horizontal lines in your Web document.

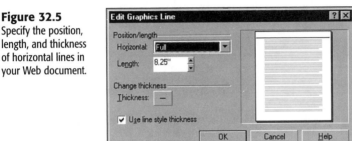

Specify the Horizontal position of the line (left, center, right, or full), the line's Length, and the Thickness of the line, and then click OK.

Many Web pages contain other types of graphic elements—either clip art or fancy bullets, buttons, and the like. You can import all of these into your Web pages with the Internet Publisher.

INSERTING CLIP ART

To insert *clip art (page 628)* into your Web page, click the Clipart button on the WordPerfect toolbar. You see the Scrapbook window.

Select the Clipart tab, navigate to the folder containing the image you want to use, and drag the image to your WordPerfect editing window. You see the image in your document (see Figure 32.6). Close the Scrapbook window.

Figure 32.6
Images appear in your document when you select them, and they are automatically converted to GIF format when you save your document as an HTML file.

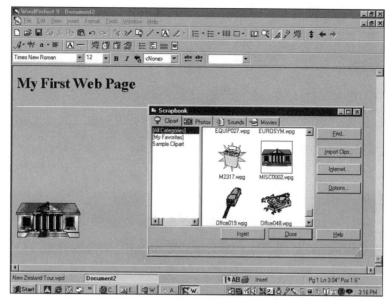

Note

The Web supports images saved in only two formats: GIF and JPG. Your image will be converted to GIF format when you publish your work as an HTML document.

PART

V

CH

32

To move your image, select it by clicking it so that you see handles around it. Position your mouse pointer inside the image; the pointer changes into a four-way arrow. Drag the image to its new location. HTML format limits where you can place the images. You can move an image to the center or to the edges of the page.

Similarly, you can size the image by selecting it, and then positioning your mouse pointer on one of the handles. The mouse pointer becomes a two-way arrow. Drag the handle to resize the image.

Tip #228 from
Trudi Reisner

You can't wrap several lines of text around a graphic like you can in a WordPerfect document. The box moves with the words in the line. You can change the position of the box on the line, but you can't change how several lines of text wrap.

⚠ *If the graphics box moves with the words in the line, see "Wrapping Text Around a Graphic" in the Troubleshooting section at the end of this chapter.*

To edit the image, you can double-click it. You see the Presentations menu options in your WordPerfect document (unless you are using a different default graphics editor for this type of file). Alternatively, you can right-click it to bring up the QuickMenu and use the same image-editing tools you use for other images in WordPerfect documents.

When those browsing the Web are in a hurry, they sometimes choose the option to have their browser not automatically load graphics. This can decrease the amount of time it takes for their system to load the information on the page so that they can view more pages faster. Additionally, some users do not have a browser that will permit the viewing of graphics of any sort, so they can see only text.

If you want to specify text that will display when users do not use a graphical browser, or when users do not choose to automatically load graphics, do so as follows:

1. Select the image, and then right-click it. You see the QuickMenu.

2. Choose HTML Properties. You see the HTML Properties dialog box shown in Figure 32.7.

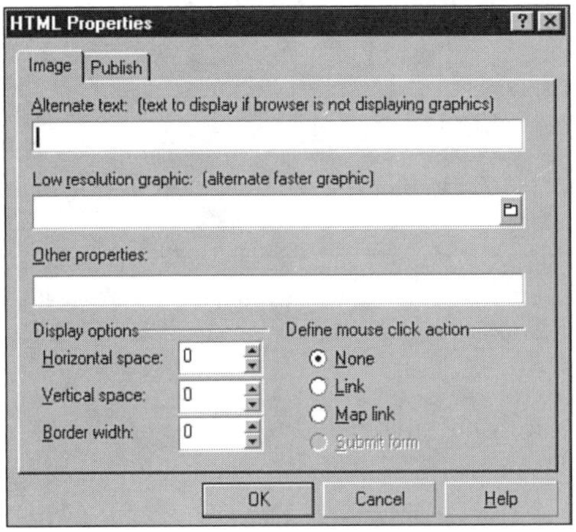

Figure 32.7
In the HTML Properties dialog box, you can specify text that will display in place of the image box if a user is not using a graphical browser.

3. Type the text in the Alternate Text box, and then click OK.

Note

Users who are familiar with HTML documents can also use this box to add ISMAP images—images that activate links when a specific part of the image is clicked by selecting the Map Link option.

Adding Links and Bookmarks

Your document becomes a full-fledged member of the Web when it provides links to other documents. You can easily add links to other documents, or to specific bookmarks within these documents. The links can be highlighted terms, or they can be small graphics that the user will click.

The link feature is used most often in conjunction with the Internet Publisher. It is, however, a part of WordPerfect itself. Therefore, you can create links from any WordPerfect document using the procedures described in this section.

CREATING AND EDITING LINKS

To create a link to a document on your disk or the Web, follow these procedures:

1. Open the document where you want the source of the link to be located.

2. Select the term that should be displayed for the text link or included in the link button.

3. Click the Hyperlink button on the toolbar, and choose Create Link. You see the Hyperlink Properties dialog box (see Figure 32.8).

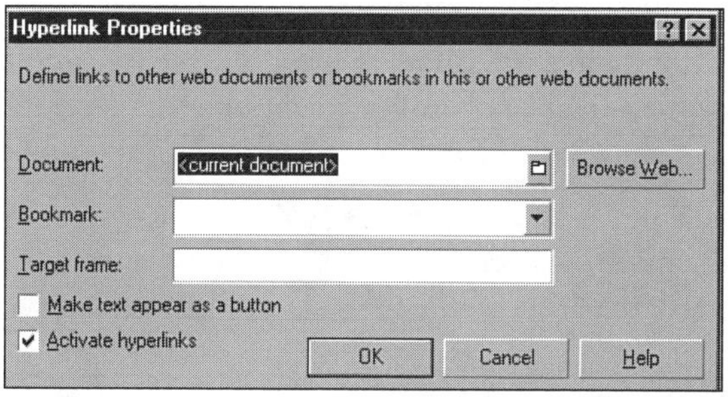

Figure 32.8
In the Hyperlink Properties dialog box, you can quickly create hypertext links to documents on your disk, your local intranet, or the Internet.

```
Hyperlink Properties                              [?][X]

Define links to other web documents or bookmarks in this or other web documents.

Document:      <current document>              [ ]   Browse Web...

Bookmark:                                        [v]

Target frame:  [                              ]

[ ] Make text appear as a button

[x] Activate hyperlinks        [  OK  ]  [ Cancel ]  [ Help ]
```

4. In the Document box, type the name of the file you want to link to. If it is a document on the disk, use the full path to the document, such as C:\Myfiles\Web\Index.htm. If it is a document on the Web, then you should use a complete URL, such as `http://www.corel.com/index.htm`.

   Alternatively, click the Browse Web button. Your default browser is launched, and you can navigate to the Web site to which you want to link. When you switch back to WordPerfect, the URL for the Web site appears in the Document box.

Be careful about using links to Internet documents that you don't control. You may link to a URL that is here today and gone tomorrow, so you need to think about how long the document created with a link will be available. You also need to be willing to check regularly to be sure that links in your documents are still working.

5. If you want the link to take you to a specific bookmark in the destination document, type the name of the bookmark in the Bookmark box. (Creating bookmarks is discussed in the next section.)

6. If you want the link to be a button, click the Make Text Appear As a Button option button.

7. Click OK. You return to your Web page and see the link term in blue; or you see the link button.

Tip #229 from
Trudi Reisner

Many Internet servers are case sensitive. To get to a URL on these servers, you must type in the link with the correct case. Because you don't know which servers are or are not case sensitive, it's a good practice to always use the exact case that you see.

You can edit the link after it's created by right-clicking it and choosing Edit, Hyperlink. You see the Hyperlink Properties dialog box, which has identical functionality to the Create Hyperlink dialog box discussed earlier.

CREATING BOOKMARKS

A bookmark is a specific position or section of text in a document that has a name. You can use bookmarks to go directly to a specific place in a document. You can create bookmarks in your Web documents—or in regular WordPerfect documents—so that links can take you to a specific place in your document, rather than merely to the beginning of the document.

In Web page design, a long Web page often has a table of contents at the top, and bookmarked positions throughout the document. Clicking the table of contents link terms takes you to specific sections of the document.

Tip #230 from
Trudi Reisner

You can go to a bookmark in a document by pressing the GoTo shortcut key, Ctrl+G, and specifying the bookmark you want to go to.

To create a bookmark, do the following:

1. Open the WordPerfect document or Web page that you want to put a bookmark in.
2. Click at the position you want to bookmark, or select the text you want to bookmark.
3. Click the Hyperlink button, and then choose Insert, Bookmark. You see the Create Bookmark dialog box shown in Figure 32.9.
4. Type the name of the new bookmark in this dialog box, and then click OK. You return to the document.

To use the bookmark, create a link to the appropriate file, including the bookmark, as was discussed in the previous section.

Tip #231 from
Trudi Reisner

There is no visible prompt that a bookmark has been created. However, you can press Alt+F3 to see the bookmark in Reveal Codes, if you like.

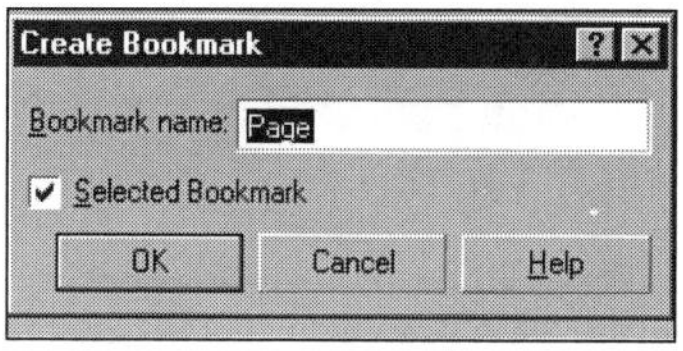

Figure 32.9
Web documents are even more friendly when you create bookmarks so that links can take the user to a specific place in the document.

INCLUDING TABLES

Web pages increasingly are being used to provide data to clients, customers, and employees. Catalogs and similar informational pieces are often best displayed in a *table*. With WordPerfect's Internet Publisher, you can insert a table into your Web page in the same way you would insert a table into a document.

To insert a table into your Web document using Internet Publisher, do the following:

1. Open the Web page and position your insertion point where you want the table to appear.

2. Click the Table QuickCreate button on the WordPerfect toolbar, and drag down to the appropriate cell for the number of rows and columns you want in your table. You see the table in your document, as shown in Figure 32.10.

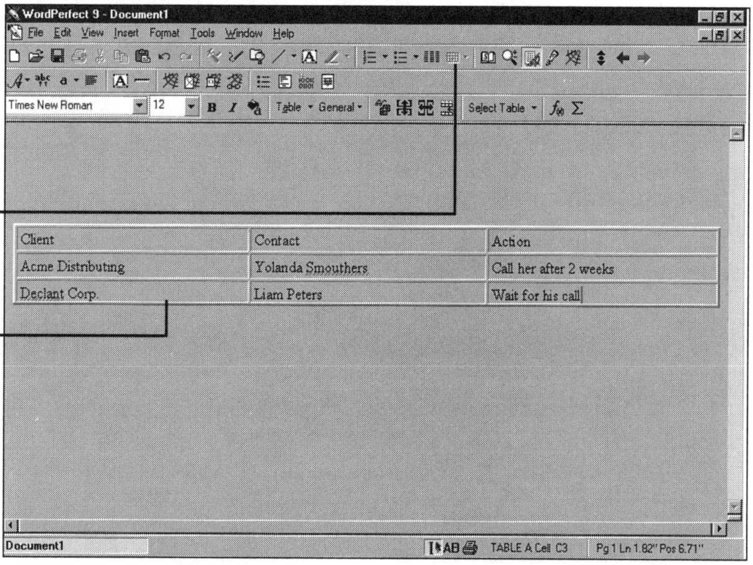

PART

V

CH

32

Figure 32.10
With the Internet Publisher, you can put tables in your Web page to display a variety of information.

Table QuickCreate button

Client	Contact	Action
Acme Distributing	Yolanda Smouthers	Call her after 2 weeks
Declant Corp.	Liam Peters	Wait for his call

Table that has been inserted into the Web page

3. Enter data in the table. Press the Tab key to advance to the next cell and Shift+Tab to go to the previous one. If you press the Tab key at the last cell in the table, a new row is created.

4. To format your table:

- Select the appropriate cells or columns, click the Table button on the Property bar, and then choose Format.

- Alternatively, right-click in the table and choose Format.

You see the HTML Table Properties dialog box (see Figure 32.11).

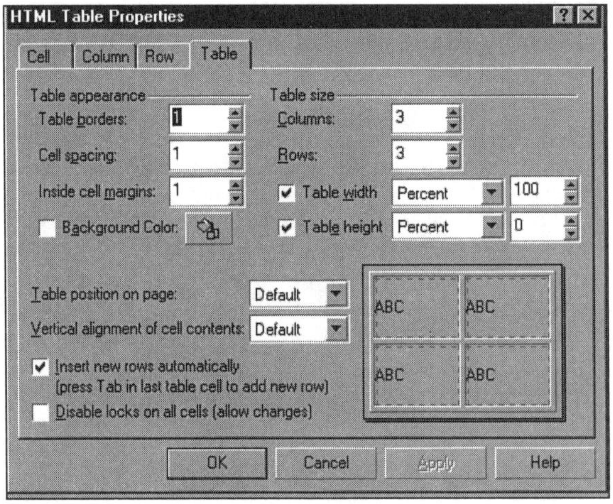

Figure 32.11
In the HTML Table Properties dialog box, you format your table by cell, column, or entire table.

ADDING FORMS

You might want to insert a form into your Web page to collect information from people who browse to your Web site. The Internet Publisher allows you to do this quickly and easily.

To create a form, click in your Web page where you want the form to appear, and then click the New Form button on the Property Bar. You see two yellow icons—the Form Begin and Form End icons—with your insertion point positioned between them. The Property Bar changes to display form tools, as shown in Figure 32.12.

Insert form fields by clicking the appropriate button. You can find out more about what each type of field does by looking up Forms, Web Document in the WordPerfect Help system.

Note

You will also need to specify how the form transmits information to you or to a database. This is done through an Action URL or Mime Script, which can be specified by clicking the Form Properties button. Discuss how to fill in this dialog box with your system administrator or Internet service provider, because the requirements depend on your specific system.

Figure 32.12
Internet Publisher provides a variety of tools to enable you to quickly create forms in your Web pages.

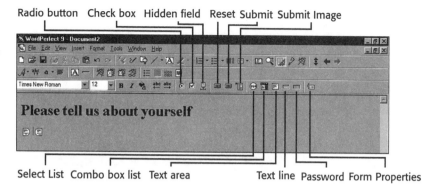

Radio button Check box Hidden field Reset Submit Submit Image

Select List Combo box list Text area   Text line Password Form Properties

PUBLISHING HTML DOCUMENTS

After you have created and edited your Web page using WordPerfect's Internet Publisher, the result is still a WordPerfect document, not an HTML (or Web) document. To publish it on the Web, you need to save it as an HTML document. You may also want to save another version of it as a WordPerfect document, so you can more quickly open it and edit it, without needing to convert it from HTML into WordPerfect when you open it.

PART

V

CH

32

> **Note**
>
> The term "publish" has two meanings. The normal usage of the term—for example, "publish a Web document"—means to place a document on the Web where people can see it. However, WordPerfect uses the term "publish" in a different sense, to mean converting a WordPerfect document to HTML.
>
> When used in this latter sense, the document still resides on your disk rather than on the Web, and you still need to copy it to the Internet so that people can see it.
>
> The meaning of the term in this book can be derived from the context in which it's used.

In any case, publishing your document means saving it as HTML. When you do this, the Internet Publisher converts the binary WordPerfect file into an ASCII text file with HTML codes in it.

Before you do that, however, you might want to see how the HTML document will look in a real Web browser. (Remember, what WordPerfect shows you is close to, but not necessarily exactly, how the document will look in a browser.)

VIEWING YOUR DOCUMENT

You can view your document whenever you want to, as you build it up and add more features to it. When you view your document, the Internet Publisher converts it to HTML and saves it as a temporary file, and then opens the file in your default Web browser.

To view your document, click the View in Web Browser button. Netscape (or your default browser) opens, and you see your Web page as it will look when it is published (see Figure 32.13).

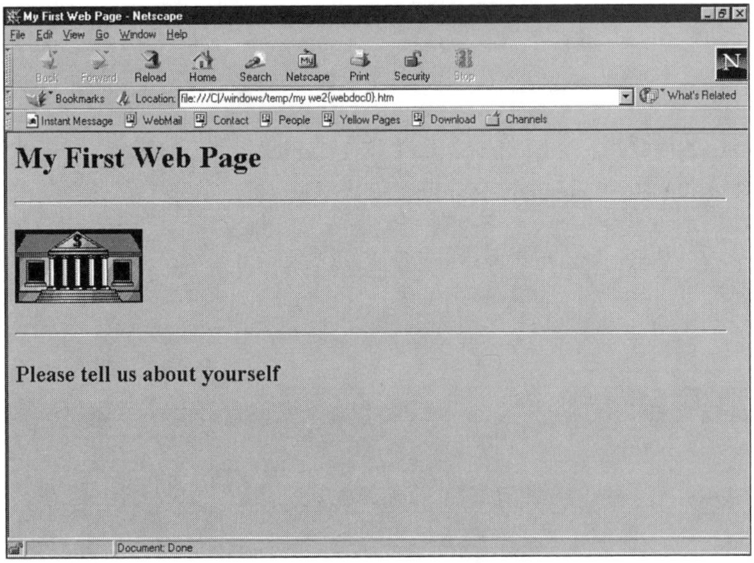

Figure 32.13
You can view your Web page in your default browser before you publish it to ensure that it looks the same in the browser as it does in the Internet Publisher.

Web documents can appear differently, depending on the browser used to access them. For instance, some earlier versions of standard browsers would not recognize a center code or an underline code. Many problems such as this have been cleared up in the later browser versions, but some people still have earlier browsers that have been purchased secondhand or passed down to them when new equipment was purchased for others. It is important to know who your most important customers are and the level of technology they have, and then set up pages to that standard.

SAVING DOCUMENTS AS HTML

Saving your document as HTML creates a new file with an .htm extension. It is an ASCII text file with HTML codes in it. If you have figures in your document, a folder is created with the same name as the document, and the figures are stored in that folder.

When you are satisfied with the Web page you have created, and you want to convert it to an HTML document, do the following:

1. Save the document as a WordPerfect document so that you can more easily edit it by opening the original WordPerfect document later, and so that you will have a backup of the file in case something happens to the version you will be putting on the server.

2. Click the Publish to HTML button on the Internet Publisher toolbar. You see the Publish to HTML dialog box (see Figure 32.14). If you have previously saved your document, you see the same document name, but with an .htm extension rather than a .wpd extension as the default choice.

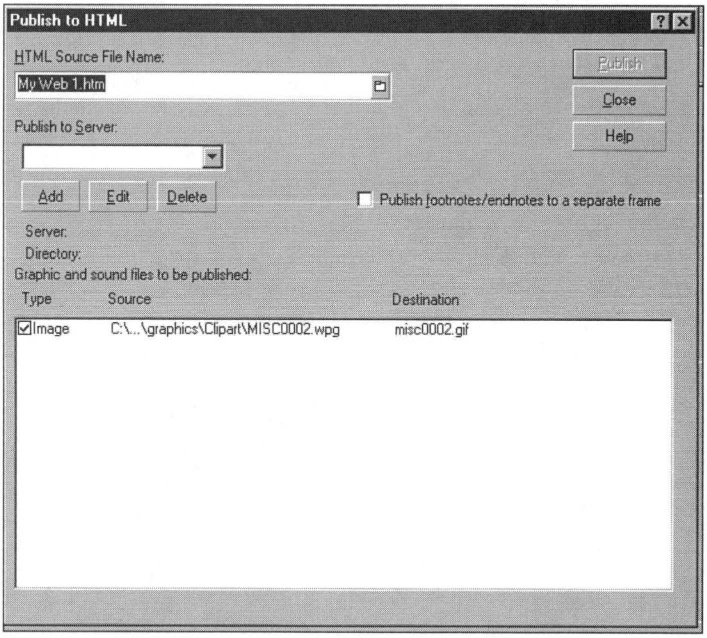

Figure 32.14
Use the Publish to HTML dialog box to save your document in HTML format.

> **Note**
>
> The Publish to HTML dialog box also has a text box in which you can specify where graphics and sound files will be saved.

3. Edit the name that appears in the Publish To box or accept the default name, and click OK. A copy of the document is saved as an HTML file, with the extension .htm.

Interestingly, you do not see the HTML file on your screen. You still see the WordPerfect version of the file, as you can see by examining the title bar, which still shows the WPD file.

COPYING DOCUMENTS TO YOUR WEB SERVER

The last step in publishing your Web page is to copy it to the Web server where it will reside.

Uploading Files to the Internet

An Internet server is often a UNIX-based computer that you cannot copy files to directly. Because UNIX is a different operating system than Windows, it is likely that you cannot use a tool such as Windows Explorer or WordPerfect's File, Save As and specify the disk drive of your Internet server as a destination for your files.

You might want to talk to your Internet service provider, your System Administrator, or your Webmaster about the best way to upload files to the Internet. At the least, these individuals will need to tell you where to upload them, and what permissions are needed.

⚠ *If you're not sure how you're going to upload files to the Internet, see "Uploading Files to the Internet" in the Troubleshooting section at the end of this chapter.*

A common way to upload files to the Internet is to connect to the location of your Web site via File Transfer Protocol (FTP), which you can do through Netscape. If this protocol is supported, then you can upload files to the appropriate workspace on the Internet Server.

To view the list of existing files and folders of your FTP site, type FTTP:// in front of the URL location in your Web browser (you can obtain the URL for your site from your system administrator). Figure 32.15 shows an example of an FTP site as seen through a browser.

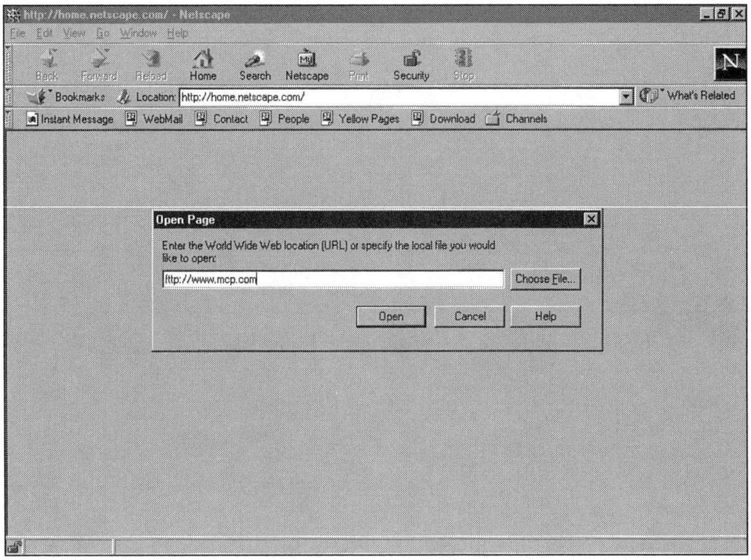

Figure 32.15
By connecting to an FTP site through your browser, you can see the names of the files and folders located at the site.

To upload your files to the server, do as follows:

1. Open Netscape.
2. Choose File, Open, Location, and specify the FTP address of the location to which you want to upload your files. (You will probably need to get the FTP address from your system administrator.) You see a list of files in your FTP directory.

3. Choose File, Upload File. You see the File Upload dialog box.

4. Navigate to the folder containing the file to be uploaded, and then double-click the file. You return to the main Navigator screen, and the file is uploaded to the specified directory.

5. After the upload is complete, you see the file listed in that directory by typing your FTP site URL as you did previously to view the list of existing files and folders of your FTP site.

UPLOADING FILES TO AN INTRANET

Similarly, if you are publishing to a corporate intranet, the intranet might be running on Windows 95, but more likely it is running on Windows NT, Novell NetWare, or UNIX. Directories where Web pages are located usually have limited access. You will want to talk to your system administrator about the best way to upload files to the intranet server. If you have sufficient permissions, you might be able to merely save your document to the intranet server with WordPerfect; or Netscape's File, Upload command (as discussed in the previous section, "Uploading Files to the Internet") might work in your particular situation.

CONVERTING HTML INTO WORDPERFECT

WordPerfect's Internet Publisher not only helps you create new Web documents, but you can also convert HTML documents into Corel WordPerfect documents and edit them.

To convert an HTML document into a WordPerfect document, you first need to save it from the Web to your network or local computer. Just do the following:

1. Open Netscape.

2. Choose File, OpenLocation, and specify the URL of the Web document you want to copy, as shown in Figure 32.16.

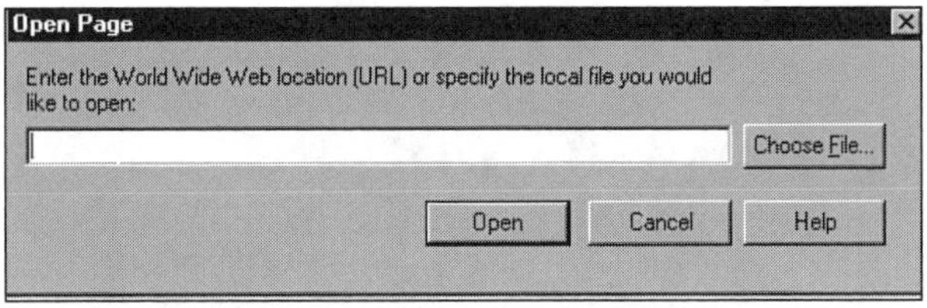

Figure 32.16
Use Netscape to save files from the Internet or a corporate intranet to your local computer.

Open Page

Enter the World Wide Web location (URL) or specify the local file you would like to open:

Choose File...

Open   Cancel   Help

3. Choose File, Save As. Navigate to the folder in which you want to save the document, and then click the Save button. The file is saved to your local computer or network drive.

After the file has been saved to a local drive, you can convert it to WordPerfect format by opening it as you would other documents:

1. In WordPerfect, click the Open button. Navigate to the folder containing the Web document to be opened.

Tip #232 from
Trudi Reisner

Web documents have an icon to the left of them that represents your default Web browser.

2. Double-click the HTML file to be opened. You see the Convert File Format dialog box, and HTML appears in the Convert File Format From box. If another format appears in the box, scroll through the list to find HTML.
3. Click OK. The file appears on your screen. You can now edit the file using the Internet Publisher as described earlier.

Note

Using the preceding procedure, your document is still formatted using only WordPerfect functions supported in HTML. If you want to format the document as a true WordPerfect document, choose File, Internet Publisher, Format as WP Document.

CONVERTING WORDPERFECT INTO HTML

WordPerfect's Internet Publisher not only helps you create new Web documents, you can also convert your present WordPerfect documents into HTML.

To do this, open the WordPerfect document, and then choose File, Internet Publisher, Format As Web Document.

You see the menus and toolbars of the Internet Publisher, and your document loses any formatting features that are not supported in HTML.

You can now publish your document in HTML by clicking the Publish to HTML button as described previously, so you can upload it to the Web.

PUBLISHING DOCUMENTS WITH THE WEB PUBLISHING WIZARD

The new Web Publishing Wizard in WordPerfect 9 guides you through the process of publishing your Web pages and other Web files on a Web server. The Web Server can be your Internet service provider or the server located on your local area network (LAN).

The Web Publishing Wizard prompts you to enter information about your Web page, support files, and Web server. To obtain this information, confer with your ISP, network administrator, or Webmaster.

Note

> Corel's Web Publishing Wizard is a Windows 98 product. Windows 95 also has a Web Publishing Wizard but it looks a lot different. You have to enable the Windows 98 version through Control Panel, Add/Remove software, and then click the Windows Setup tab. Find the Internet option, check the Web Publishing Wizard, and then install it from the Corel WordPerfect Office 2000 software CD.

To use the Web Publishing Wizard, follow these steps:

1. Choose File, Send To, Web Publishing Wizard to display the Web Publishing Wizard introduction dialog box (see Figure 32.17).

Figure 32.17
The Web Publishing Wizard allows you to publish documents to the Web.

2. Click the Next button. The Name the Web Server dialog box appears.
3. Type a name for the Web server.
4. Click the Next button. The Specify the URL and Directory dialog box appears. Type the URL (provided by your network administrator or ISP) in the URL or Internet Address text box. This is the Internet address where you'll access your personal Web pages (for example, http://www.mcp.com/treisner).
5. In the Local Directory text box, enter the local directory on your computer that corresponds to the URL you specified (for example, C:\MyFiles).
6. Click the Next button. Enter the rest of the information requested by the wizard and click the Finish button.

To see how your WordPerfect document appears when it has been set up for the Web server using the Web Publishing Wizard, choose File, Open to look at the file on your hard disk.

For more details on using the Web Publishing Wizard, refer to your Windows 98 reference book.

PRACTICAL PROJECT

Create a Web document in WordPerfect that contains a family newsletter with photographs. Then publish the Web document to the Web using the Web Publishing Wizard.

TROUBLESHOOTING

EDITING A WEB LINK

You created a hyperlink to a Web page from your document and it doesn't work.

You might link to a URL that is here today and gone tomorrow, so you need to think about how long the document created with a link will be available. You also need to be willing to check regularly to be sure that links in your documents are still working. You can edit the link by right-clicking it and choosing Edit Hyperlink. In the Hyperlink Properties dialog box, change the URL, ensuring it is spelled correctly and in the proper case.

WRAPPING TEXT AROUND A GRAPHICS BOX

You moved a graphics box and the box moves with the words in the line.

You can't wrap several lines of text around a graphic as you can in a WordPerfect document. You can change the position of the box on the line, but you can't change how several lines of text wrap.

UPLOADING FILES TO THE INTERNET

You aren't sure how to upload files to the Internet.

Talk to your ISP, your System Administrator, or your Webmaster about the best way to upload files to the Internet. At the least, these individuals will need to tell you where to upload them and what permissions are needed.

INTEGRATING COREL QUATTRO PRO 9 WITH THE WEB

In this chapter

PUBLISHING COREL QUATTRO PRO SPREADSHEET DATA

Let's start by looking at the ways you can share, or publish, your Quattro Pro files on the Internet. By doing so, you can provide easy access to information in your Quattro Pro notebooks.

Note

Technically, Quattro Pro cannot publish files on the Internet. In fact, not even WordPerfect can really publish files on the Internet. For that, you'll need a Web server—the combination of a computer connected to the World Wide Web (commonly just called the Web) plus the Web Publishing Wizard that enables users to access the information. The Web Publishing Wizard is available on the File menu in WordPerfect and Quattro Pro.

Fortunately, you usually don't have to worry about setting up your own Web server. If your company has its own Web server, you also have someone who administers the Web server. If an outside company provides your Internet connection, they probably also administer the Web server. If you do have to create and administer your own Web server, you'll find these Que books useful: *Running a Perfect Web Site with Windows* and *Webmaster Expert Solutions*.

SAVING SPREADSHEET DATA IN HTML FORMAT

One reason the Internet has become so popular is that standards have developed that enable people using different types of computers and different types of software to all view the same information. HTML—Hypertext Markup Language—is one of those standards. By saving documents in HTML format, you can make certain that other Internet users are able to read your documents.

→ For additional information on creating Web documents, **see** "Creating Web Documents," **p. 595**

In addition to the many standard spreadsheet formats it supports, Quattro Pro can save notebooks in HTML format with its Publish to Internet feature. When you've saved your Quattro Pro spreadsheet data in HTML format, you can then send the HTML file to your Web site administrator to be included on your Web site.

When you attempt to save Quattro Pro spreadsheet data in a format other than a Quattro Pro QPW v9 file, features that are unique to Quattro Pro 9 can be lost. This is certainly true when you try to save Quattro Pro spreadsheet data in HTML format. Therefore, you must always be sure to save any changes to a file as Quattro Pro QPW v9 before saving the file as an HTML file with Publish to Internet.

 If features unique to Quattro Pro 9 are lost in your Web page, see "Saving Quattro Pro Features" in the Troubleshooting section at the end of this chapter.

Tip #233 from
Trudi Reisner

Save your Quattro Pro notebook in Quattro Pro 9 format first to be certain you save all the formatting and features unique to Quattro Pro 9.

To save Quattro Pro spreadsheet data in HTML format, perform these steps:

1. Choose File, Publish to Internet, and select HTML in the Publish As section (see Figure 33.1).

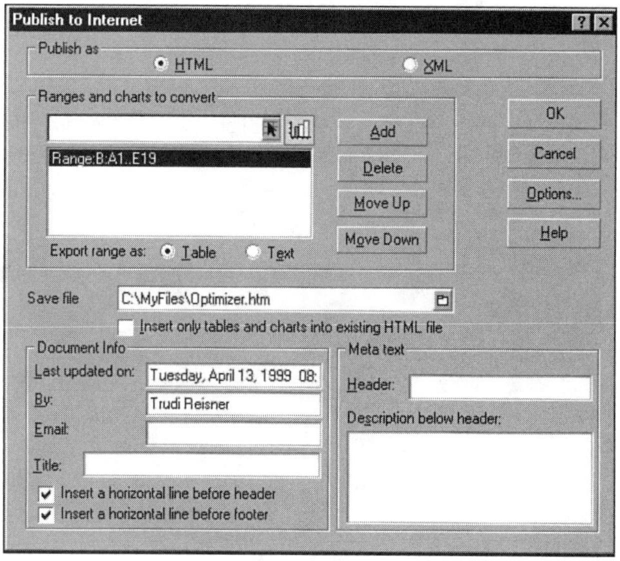

Figure 33.1
Select HTML in the Publish As section to save your Quattro Pro notebook in HTML format for publishing on the Internet.

2. In the Ranges and Charts to Convert list box, you should see the range of cells for all the spreadsheet data. In the example in Figure 33.1, the entire range for the spreadsheet data is B:A1..E19. If you want to select a different range of cells, click the Pointer button next to the Ranges and charts to convert box, and select a range of cells on the spreadsheet. Then click the Maximize button to expand the dialog box. The selected range appears in the Ranges and Charts to Convert box.

3. Click the Add button to add the range to the list box.

4. Choose either of two options to export your data in HTML format: Table or Text. Notice that the Internet Publisher displays the path and filename with the file type .htm in the Save File text box. If necessary, enter the correct filename in the Save File text box or click the Browse button and choose the path and filename.

5. Choose OK to save the Quattro Pro spreadsheet data in HTML format.

PART

V

CH

33

Note

When saving files for use on the Internet or on a company server that may not be able to correctly handle long filenames, be sure to use filenames that follow the DOS 8.3 filename conventions. This will help prevent any confusion that may result if the server shows only shortened filenames.

VIEWING YOUR HTML FILE

View your HTML files by opening them in your Web browser (such as Netscape Navigator or Internet Explorer) to see how they'll appear on the Internet. To do so, click the Open button in your Web browser, and then specify the path of the HTML file that you saved while in Quattro Pro (see Figure 33.2). You don't need to connect to the Internet to view your HTML files.

> **Note**
>
> If you use the Open button in your Web browser and it doesn't offer a dialog box with the browse option, you can choose File, Open File and use the Browse option in the dialog box to find the HTML file.

Figure 33.2
A Quattro Pro HTML file as it appears in Netscape Navigator.

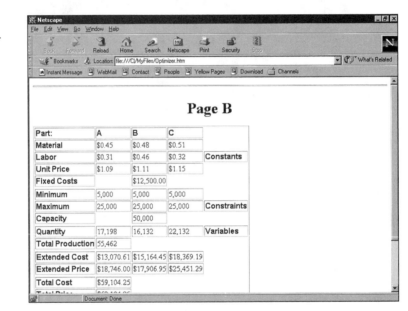

USING THE WEB PUBLISHING WIZARD

Quattro Pro's new Web Publishing Wizard steps you through the process of publishing your Web pages, support files (charts and tables), and other Web files on a Web server. The Web Server can be your Internet service provider (ISP) or the server located on your local area network (LAN).

The Web Publishing Wizard prompts you to enter information about your Web page, support files, and Web server. To obtain this information, confer with your ISP, network administrator, or Webmaster.

Perform these steps to use the Web Publishing Wizard:

1. Choose File, Send To, Web Publishing Wizard to display the Web Publishing Wizard introduction dialog box (see Figure 33.3).

Note

If you don't see the Web Publishing Wizard on the Send To menu, you'll need to install the Web Publishing Wizard. To do so, click the Start button, select Control Panel, Add/Remove Programs, and click the Windows Setup Tab. Choose Internet tools and put a check in the box for Web Wizard. Use your WordPerfect Office 2000 software CD and follow the rest of the onscreen instructions to install the wizard.

Figure 33.3
Use the Web Publishing Wizard to publish your Quattro Pro notebooks to a Web server.

2. Click the Next button. The Name the Web Server dialog box appears. Type a name for the Web server and click the Next button. The Specify the URL and Directory dialog box appears (see Figure 33.4). Type the URL (provided by your network administrator or ISP) in the URL or Internet Address text box. This is the Internet address where you'll access your personal Web pages. For example, http://www.mcp.com/treisner.

3. In the Local directory text box, enter the local directory on your computer that corresponds to the URL you specified. For example, C:\MyFiles.

4. Click the Next button. Enter the rest of the information required by the wizard and click the Finish button.

To see how your Quattro Pro notebook appears when it has been set up for the Web Server using the Web Publishing Wizard, choose File, Open and look at the file on the hard disk.

For more information on using the Web Publishing Wizard, refer to your Windows 98 documentation.

PART
V
CH
33

Figure 33.4
Specify the URL and directory to indicate where you'll access your personal Web pages.

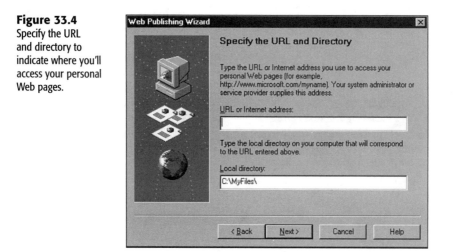

USING INTERNET FILES

Although sharing your information is useful, at some point you'll probably have the desire to get information from other people, too. In this section, we'll look at how you can use Internet files in Quattro Pro.

Note

You must be connected to the Internet before you can open files on the Internet or update links to Internet files. If you connect to the Internet through a dial-up connection, be sure to open that connection before you attempt to use Quattro Pro to open or link to Internet files.

 If you cannot open files on the Internet or update links to Internet files, see "Opening Files and Updating Links" in the Troubleshooting section at the end of this chapter.

OPENING FILES ON THE INTERNET

You can easily open Quattro Pro notebooks that are on the Internet. Suppose, for example, that your company has a master Quattro Pro notebook containing the current pricing for all your products. By making this notebook available on the Internet or a corporate intranet, your sales representatives could easily open the current file when they're visiting a customer and be certain that the pricing they're using is correct.

Caution

Unless your Web site administrator implements security measures limiting access to authorized users or implements a corporate intranet, anyone in the world who is browsing the Internet can access files you make available.

To open a Quattro Pro notebook file located on the Internet, you must know the correct
Uniform Resource Locator (URL) for the file. After you know the URL, you enter it in the
File Name text box of the Open File dialog box instead of entering the name of a local file.
For example, to open a Quattro Pro notebook located on a Web page:

1. Choose File, Open.

2. Enter the URL of the notebook file in the File Name text box. For example,
   `http://www.mcp.com/treisner/optimizer.htm` (see Figure 33.5).

3. Choose Open to open the notebook file. The notebook looks just like a file you might
   have opened from your local hard disk.

Figure 33.5
Specify the URL of the
notebook file in the
Open File dialog box.

SAVING FILES FROM THE INTERNET

You cannot save Quattro Pro notebook files to Internet locations. If you attempt to save a
notebook, Quattro Pro advises you that the file is read only and offers to save the file on
your computer. After you save the file on your system, you can use it just like any other
local file, but you should remember that the local file will not be automatically updated
when the Internet file is updated. To update your local copy, you must once again open the
copy located on the Internet and then save it on your computer.

LINKING TO INTERNET FILES

Rather than opening a complete Quattro Pro notebook file on the Internet, you may want
to create a link to a cell in a notebook file located on the Internet. You may find this a better choice if you need to both save data you've added to the notebook and still be certain
that you are always using the current information from a central source. For example, suppose you need to track how many pieces of several different items each customer orders, but
your pricing is volatile. If your home office maintains a master price list file in an Internet-
or intranet-accessible Quattro Pro notebook file, you can link the pricing column to that
file and simply update the links when you enter an order.

Tip #234 from
Trudi Reisner

> You may find that security is easier if your users link to cells in a master Quattro Pro notebook file on the Internet rather than opening an entire file on the Internet. This is because the master linking file can be considerably more obscure and contain data without any identifying labels.

In addition to linking to a Quattro Pro notebook on the Internet, you can create links to Internet information that is not in Quattro Pro format. Suppose that you want to create a notebook you can update periodically with the latest stock quotes from the Internet. You would first open the Internet file into a Quattro Pro notebook, using the procedure discussed in the earlier section titled "Opening Files on the Internet." Then, find the cell in the notebook where the information you want to link to appears. Switch to the notebook where you want the link to appear (or open a new notebook). Finally, type a link formula in the notebook that specifies the Internet site, and the sheet and cell reference. The syntax for this linking formula is

> +[URL]sheet:cell

The URL is the Internet address containing the information you want to link; sheet: cell is the sheet name and cell reference where the information appeared when you opened it in the notebook. Of course, you may need to update the URL or the sheet and cell reference in the link formula from time to time, if this information changes.

After this linking formula is in place, you can update the link at any time by choosing Edit, Links, Refresh Links. In addition, Quattro Pro gives you the option to update the link whenever you open the notebook file containing the link.

USING QUICKBUTTONS TO DISPLAY INTERNET DOCUMENTS

Sometimes you want to view information on the Internet rather than using that information within a Quattro Pro notebook. In some cases, a particular Web site (document) might contain information that would be useful in your Quattro Pro notebook, but is not contained in a Quattro Pro notebook.

For example, suppose someone has a Web site where they show the current prices for computer memory, but the Web site is an HTML file. You might want to visit this Web site often while you are working within Quattro Pro, and then manually add the current pricing to your Quattro Pro notebook. One way to automate this process is to use a QuickButton to open the document (see Figure 33.6).

To create a QuickButton to open an Internet document, do the following:

1. Choose Insert, Form Control, Button.
2. Point to an empty place on the notebook sheet and click the left mouse button.
3. Right-click the new QuickButton and choose Button Properties from the QuickMenu.
4. On the Macro tab, choose Link to URL.
5. Type the URL in the URL text box and then click OK.

6. Select the Label Text tab.

7. In the Enter Text text box, enter a short descriptive label for the QuickButton.

8. Click OK to complete the dialog box and return to the notebook.

9. Click a notebook cell to deselect the QuickButton.

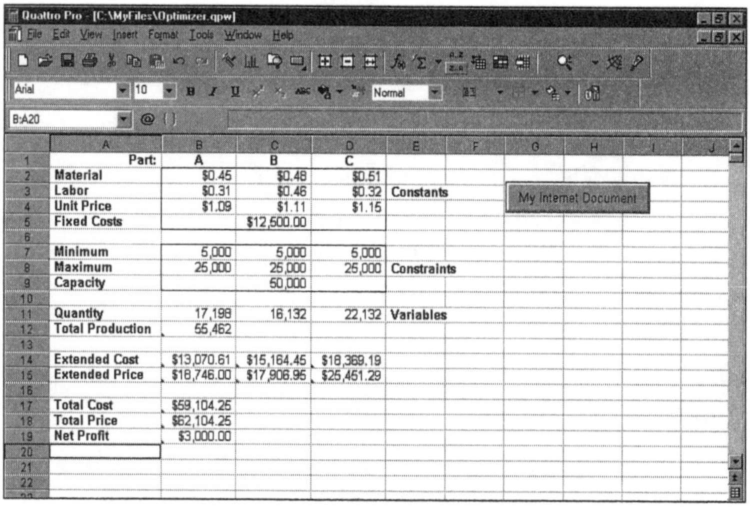

Figure 33.6
A QuickButton is used to open an Internet document.

To test your QuickButton, first be certain your Internet connection is open and then click the QuickButton. Your Internet browser opens and displays the document specified in the URL text box. You might need to switch to your Internet browser to see the document.

Note

If your default browser is set to Microsoft Internet Explorer, this is the browser that will automatically start, even if you have Netscape open. If this happens, start Netscape manually.

Tip #235 from
Trudi Reisner

Don't forget that information you copy to a Quattro Pro notebook from an Internet document is static. You might want to update the information just before creating a report.

After the document is displayed in your Internet browser, you can copy information to your Quattro Pro notebook. The exact technique you'll need to use will vary according to which Internet browser you use, but the general steps are as follows:

1. Select the information.

2. Use the Edit, Copy command in the Internet browser to copy the information to the Clipboard.

3. Switch to Quattro Pro and choose Edit, Paste to add the information to the notebook.

IMPORTING WEB DATA

Suppose you want to compile statistics on the amount of rainfall in the northwestern part of the United States and enter the data into a spreadsheet. You can find weather information on the Web and use Quattro Pro's new Web Query tool to create and run Web queries and import the Web data directly into your spreadsheet. After you run a Web query, you can update the query manually or automatically at a specified time interval.

CREATING A WEB QUERY

Here's how you can create a Web query:

1. Choose Tools, Internet, Create Web Query.

2. In the Create Web Query dialog box (see Figure 33.7), enter the URL and a search text string in the URL text box, such as `http://quote.pathfinder.com/weather/qc?rainfall=["rainfall","Enter one or several rainfall amounts separated by spaces:"]`.

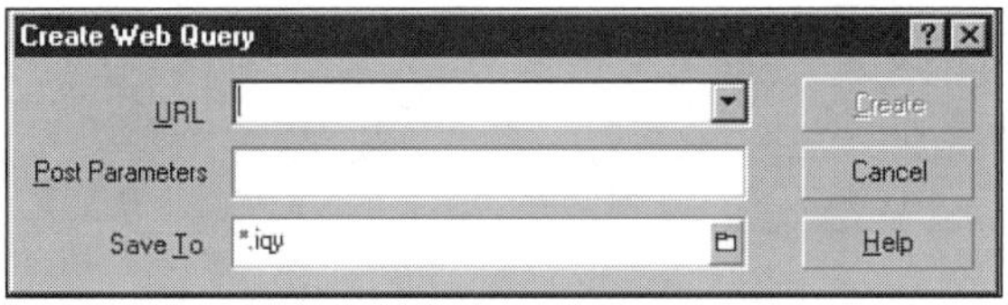

Figure 33.7
The Create Web Query dialog box is used to create a Web query.

3. Click the Browse button next to the Save To text box.

4. Choose the drive in the Look In list box and the folder in which you want to save the file.

5. In the File Name text box, type the filename and click the Open button.

6. Click the Create button in the Create Web Query dialog box. Quattro Pro saves your Web query as an IQY file.

RUNNING A WEB QUERY

When you're ready to run a Web query, be sure you're connected and online. Then follow these steps:

1. Choose Tools, Internet, Run Web Query. The Run Web Query dialog box opens, as shown in Figure 33.8.

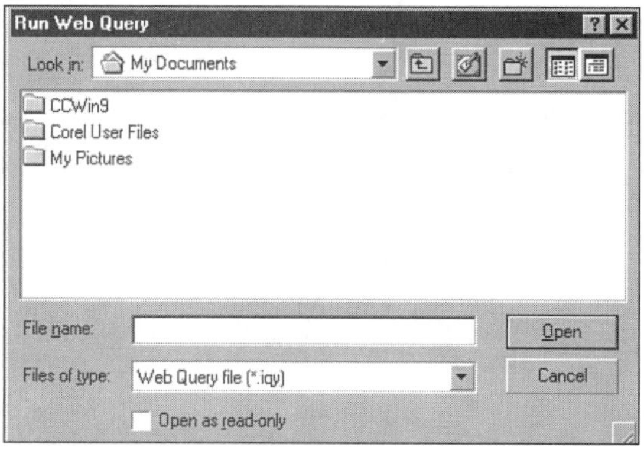

Figure 33.8
Run a Web query from the Run Web Query dialog box to import Web data into a spreadsheet.

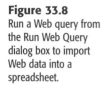

2. Choose the Web query you want to run, and click Open.

3. Click the Data tab. Choose New Notebook to import the data into a new notebook or choose Existing Notebook to use the current notebook.

4. Click OK.

5. If you are asked to enter a parameter value, type the value in the text box, and click OK. If the Web Query Preview dialog box appears, check the retrieved data, and click OK. The Web data is imported into your spreadsheet.

UPDATING A WEB QUERY MANUALLY

If you prefer to update a Web query manually, you can set this option when you run the Web query. Run the query, click the Options button, and choose the Refresh Data on File Open option. Each time you open the file, Quattro Pro runs the Web query and updates the data in your spreadsheet, providing you're connected and online.

UPDATING A WEB QUERY AUTOMATICALLY

You can set up your Web query to run automatically at a specified time. To do so, run the Web query, and in the Web Query Preview dialog box, click the Link button. Change any of the options in the Refresh Interval group to specify a time interval.

PRACTICAL PROJECT

Import data on one of your favorite topics from the Web by using the Web Query tool. After the Web data is in your spreadsheet, use the Publish to Internet feature to convert the data into a Web page. Then use the Web Publishing Wizard to publish that Web page on the Web.

TROUBLESHOOTING

SAVING QUATTRO PRO FEATURES

You saved a Quattro Pro spreadsheet data in HTML format and features unique to Quattro Pro 9 are lost in your Web page.

When you attempt to save Quattro Pro spreadsheet data in a format other than a Quattro Pro QPW v9 file, features that are unique to Quattro Pro 9 can be lost. This is certainly true when you try to save Quattro Pro spreadsheet data in HTML format. Therefore, you must always be sure to save any changes to a file as Quattro Pro QPW v9 before saving the file as an HTML file with Publish to Internet.

OPENING FILES AND UPDATING LINKS

You couldn't open a file on the Internet or update links to Internet files.

You must be connected to the Internet before you can open files on the Internet or update links to Internet files. If you connect to the Internet through a dial-up connection, be sure to open that connection before you attempt to use Quattro Pro to open or link to Internet files.

CHAPTER 34

INTEGRATING COREL PRESENTATIONS 9 WITH THE WEB

In this chapter

USING PRESENTATIONS WITH THE WEB

Corel Presentations is no longer merely a desktop application. It allows you to browse the Web and download material, such as clip art, into your slideshows or drawings.

Note

Most of the procedures you learn in this chapter apply only to slideshows created in Corel Presentations 9. To integrate drawings, you first must add them to a slideshow.

USING THE WEB BROWSER BUTTON

Log in to your ISP and then when you click the Corel Web Site button on the toolbar, you launch Netscape (or your default Web browser) and go automatically to Corel's Web site. You can browse this site for information on Presentations or proceed to somewhere else on the Internet.

USING SPEEDLINK TO LINK SLIDES TO THE WEB

If you are fortunate enough to have an Internet connection available when you play your slideshow, you can create links from text or graphics objects in your slideshow that jump to specific Web locations in your Web browser.

Suppose, for example, that you have a particular Web site that illustrates one of the points in your bulleted slide. Follow these steps:

1. Open your slideshow and go to the slide where you want to create the link.
2. If you are linking to any object other than an item in a bulleted list, skip to step 3. To create a link to a single item in a bulleted list, you must first create a closed object to cover the bulleted item. For example, select the Basic Shapes tool, and draw a rectangle over the text area you want to link. You might want to change the fill of the object to None so that you can see the text it covers.
3. Right-click the object you want to link and choose SpeedLink. The Object Properties dialog box appears showing the SpeedLink tab (see Figure 34.1, which shows the link already filled in).
4. Choose Action, and then choose Browse Internet from the drop-down list. Fill in the Location (URL) for the Web site you want to jump to.
5. Give the SpeedLink a unique name, and indicate whether the object should be invisible when you play the slideshow. This is handy if you're using an object laid over another object such as an item in a bulleted list.

Now, when you play the slide, the mouse pointer turns into a hand when positioned over the SpeedLinked object. Clicking the object takes you to your browser and the Web site you specified.

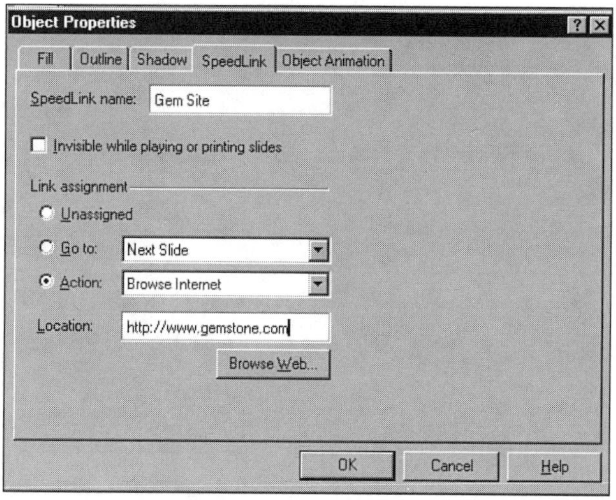

Figure 34.1
Using SpeedLinks, you can create areas on your slides that jump to specific Web sites when you click them.

USING SPEEDKEYS TO LINK SLIDES TO THE WEB

You also can jump to Web sites directly from your slides by defining SpeedKey links. For example, you have four items listed on your slide, each referring to a Web site on the Internet. You can assign Web addresses to any alpha or numeric key, and even to many function and control keys. When you press these defined keys, Presentations jumps to your browser and to the address linked to that key.

Suppose you want to jump to the Corel Web site, and you want to press C to do so. Follow these steps:

1. Open your slideshow and go to the slide where you want to create the SpeedKey link.
2. Choose Format, Slide Properties, SpeedKeys. Presentations displays the Slide Properties dialog box with the SpeedKeys tab selected (see Figure 34.2).
3. In the Keystrokes list, click the key you want to assign.
4. Choose Browse Internet from the Action drop-down list, and then fill in the Location (URL) for the Web site to which you want to jump.
5. If you choose Apply to All Slides in Slide Show, the SpeedKey works while viewing any slide. If not, the SpeedKey works only with the current slide, thus enabling you to assign the same key to a different Web site in another slide.
6. When you have made the changes you want, choose OK.

Now when you play your slideshow, pressing the SpeedKey takes you directly to the Web site you specified.

PART
V

CH
34

Figure 34.2
Using SpeedKeys, you can assign keys that jump to specific Web sites when you press them.

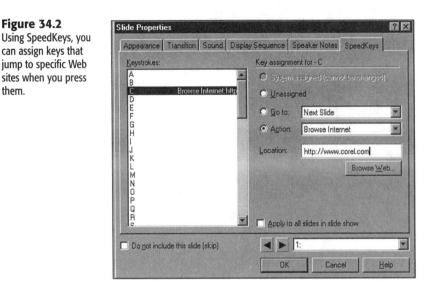

USING CLIP ART FROM THE WEB

The Internet can be a rich source for clip art to include in your slideshows. Using Netscape, it's easy to find and save clip art on your local computer, and then import it into Presentations.

Caution

Images on Web sites are often copyrighted, and are, in any case, protected by relevant copyright laws. Be sure to obtain permission from the copyright owner before using images from Web sites, and strongly consider establishing a company or institutional policy regarding use of information obtained from the Internet after advice from legal counsel.

You can find free public domain *clip art (page 598)* on the Internet. The easiest way to do so is to search for the term clip art using any of the popular search engines.

After you've found an image you like and have obtained permission to use it, you can copy a Web image into a Presentations slideshow easily by following these steps:

1. Open Netscape and browse to the Web site containing the image.

Note

If you access the Internet through a dial-up service, you first must connect to that service before you can use Netscape or any other browser.

2. Right-click the image. You see a pop-up QuickMenu.
3. Choose Save Image As. You see the Save As dialog box.
4. Specify a folder and filename for the image, and then choose Save. The image is saved to your local computer.

From Presentations, you can insert this image into your slideshow as you do any other image on your disk. The format of the graphic image, whether GIF or JPEG, converts automatically to a bitmap graphic image in your drawing or slideshow.

→ To learn more about inserting pictures, **see** "Adding Pictures," **p. 556**

CONVERTING SLIDESHOWS TO WEB PAGES

A slideshow can be an effective sales tool by presenting your company's mission to the public. Used as a simple type of computer-based training, slideshows can also be a learning tool. It can supplement other text-based Web pages by illustrating points with charts, diagrams, and tables.

Presentations includes a feature that enables you to convert your slideshow quickly and easily to one or more Web pages, so you can publish it on the Internet or on a corporate intranet.

Presentations offers two methods for publishing your pages to the Web, each with its strengths and limitations:

- HTML—This is the standard for Web pages, and all graphics-based browsers can display such pages without special additions or setup.
- Show It!—This method actually enables users to view slides with sounds, animations, and transitions, just as if you played the slideshow yourself. However, this also requires that users have Corel's free ShowIt! plug-in added to their browser.

UNDERSTANDING HTML WEB PAGE FORMATS

The most common method for publishing Web pages is by converting your slides to standard HTML. You can use HTML to publish your slideshow in four different ways. If your readers will be using a browser that supports frames (such as versions 2.0 or later of Netscape Navigator, or Microsoft Internet Explorer), you can create Web pages such as the one shown in Figure 34.3.

Note

The term publish has two meanings. The normal usage of the term—for example, "publish a Web document"—means to place a document on the Web where people can see it. Presentations uses the term publish, however, in a different sense, to mean converting a slideshow to HTML, preparatory to placing it on the Web.

When used in this latter sense, the document still resides on your disk rather than on the Web, and you still need to copy it to the Internet so that people can see it.

The meaning of the term in this book can be derived from the context in which it's used.

Table of Contents frame   Slide Controls frame

Figure 34.3
You can publish your
slideshow in Web
pages that have
frames, if your read-
ers' browsers support
this.

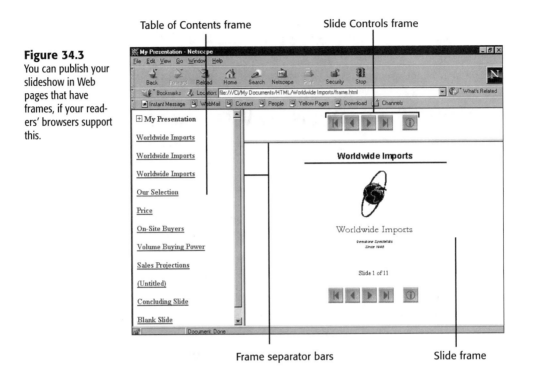

Frame separator bars   Slide frame

When frames are used, each slide has its own frame that is accessed from the Table of Contents frame or from the Slide Controls frame. In the Table of Contents area, bulleted slides are listed in a collapsible outline format: Click the + to the left of the slideshow title to expand the outline and see the slide bullets. In the Slide Controls frame, you have several useful controls for navigating through your slideshow (see Figure 34.4). These include

■ Download—Clicking this button enables viewers to download the original Presentations slideshow. This is particularly useful if they have the Presentations program.

■ Direction Buttons—These buttons take you to the start (beginning), previous, next, and end slides.

■ Play—If during setup you choose to make the slideshow self-running, the AutoPlay button enables the viewer to start playing the slideshow.

■ Table of Contents—Click this button to hide the Table of Contents frame, or to make it reappear.

If you want people to be able to read your slideshow even if their browser doesn't support frames, you can publish in multiple Web pages, with each slide on its own page, as shown in Figure 34.5.

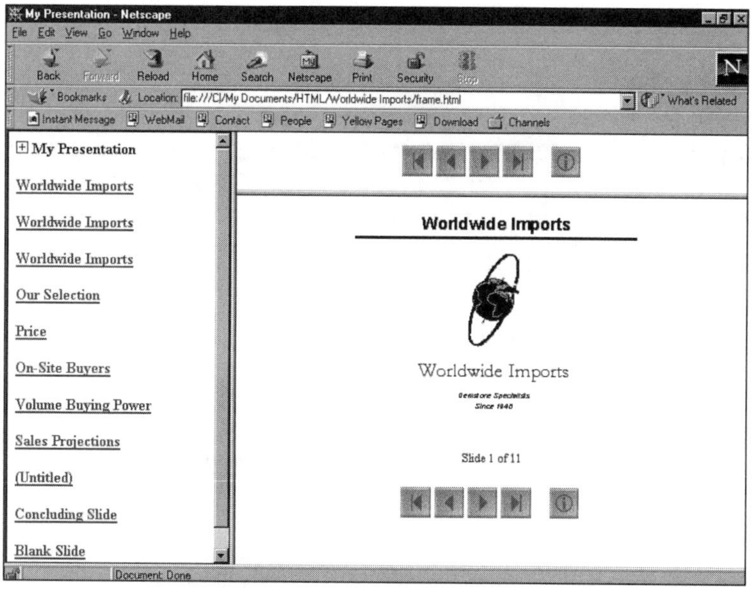

Figure 34.4
Using the frame version of the Web-based slideshow includes several handy tools for helping people browse through your show.

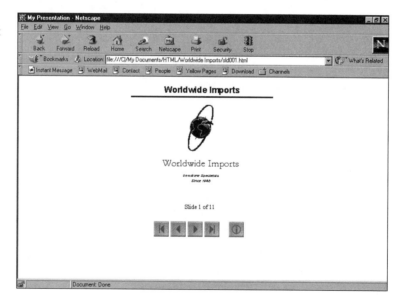

Figure 34.5
If you are not sure that everyone's browser supports frames, you might want to publish your slideshow with individual multiple pages.

With this type of setup, the viewer can click the slide title in the Table of Contents and return to the Table of Contents after viewing each slide. You also can set up the slides so that the viewer has the choice of using next or previous buttons to go on to the next slide without returning to the Table of Contents.

You can also publish your slideshow in one long Web page, with all the slides in the same page one after another, like the example shown in Figure 34.6. In this method, the viewer just uses the scrollbar to view one slide after the other.

Figure 34.6
If you prefer, you can put all your slides on one Web page.

Finally, you can publish thumbnails of your slideshow in one Web page. You can set this up so that viewers just have access to the thumbnails, or so that the thumbnails are buttons that the viewers can click, which will take them to a separate page with a larger version of the slide.

CONVERTING YOUR SLIDESHOW TO HTML

When you convert your slideshow, Presentations creates a series of files in a folder you specify. You should not try to save more than one slideshow in a particular folder, because many of the filenames might be duplicates.

To convert your slideshow to Web pages, ensure that your slideshow has been created, finalized, and saved. Then follow these steps:

1. With the slideshow onscreen, choose File, Internet Publisher, or click the Internet Publisher button on the Property Bar. You see the Internet Publisher dialog box shown in Figure 34.7.

2. Click the Next button. This is where you select a layout. The Create a New Layout option is already selected, which is the one you want to use.

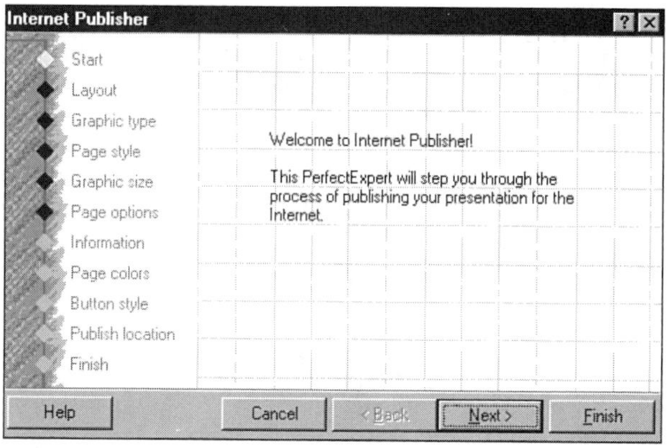

Figure 34.7
The Internet Publisher dialog box enables you to publish your slideshow to the Web using standard HTML and the ShowIt! plug-in with full sound and animation support.

Note

The option to create a custom layout allows you to customize any of the four styles discussed earlier and to save the style with a unique name.

3. Click the Next button, and specify whether to publish graphics using GIF, JPEG, or PNG (Portable Network Graphics) formats. You can also choose Show It to publish graphics with full animation, transitions, and sound.

4. Click the Next button, and choose the page style by selecting one of the four layout options described earlier: Browser Frames, Single Page, Multiple Pages, or Thumbnail Page (see Figure 34.8).

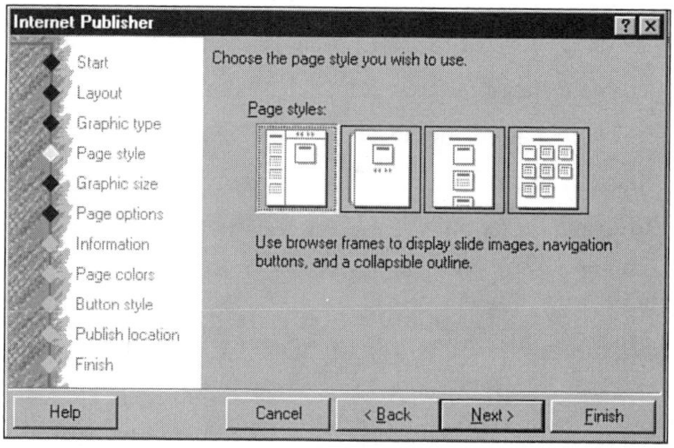

Figure 34.8
The Internet Publisher dialog box presents several screens to help you publish your slideshow to the Web. Here, you can specify the page layout you want to use.

PART

V

CH

34

5. Click the Next button, and select the display and size options for your graphics. Have Presentations create the size slide that looks best on the type screens most viewers will use.

Caution

If you choose a high screen resolution, the slides will appear much too large in many viewers. When in doubt, use the lowest common screen size, such as 640×480.

6. In the next step of the Internet Publisher dialog box, you can change your choice of the particular page options you want. Your selections in this screen determine your available choices in the next screens. For example, if you chose the Browser Frames page style, you have a whole series of navigational tools from which to select (see Figure 34.9).

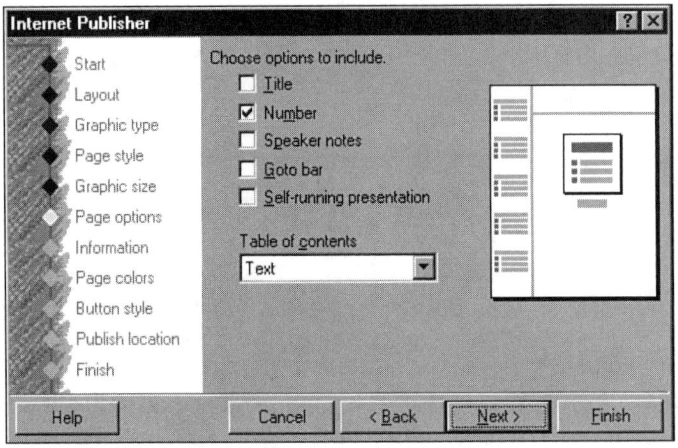

Figure 34.9
Presentations offers many choices for customizing just how your slideshow will appear when you place it on the Web.

Slideshow page customization options shown in Figure 34.9 include

- Title—Put the title of the presentation on each Web page.
- Number—Put page numbers on each Web page.
- Speaker Notes—Add the Speaker Notes to the bottom of each Web page.
- Goto Bar—Add a navigation slide bar to the bottom of each slide.
- Self-Running Presentation—Create a self-running slideshow, rather than one with manual advances. The viewer clicks the Play button and the show proceeds automatically to the end.
- Table of Contents—Add a table of contents page (for multiple-page slideshows) or frame (for frame-enhanced slideshows) that includes either Text (based on the title of each slide) or Graphic Thumbnails.

Note

As you make your choices, click the Next button to advance to the next screen, and see more options, or the Back button to review and change earlier choices. You can click Finish at any time to accept the normal default settings and create your HTML-based slideshow.

By default, the main slideshow file is named Index.html; all other page files have the .html extension, and image and sound files are stored in subfolders. To change any of these defaults, click the Advanced button.

As you click Next and advance to the various Internet Publisher screens, you see several other options, including

- Information—Indicate the location of your email address and your own home page, and any other information, such as the date the page was last updated, and Corel Presentations copyright information. The Include Link to Download Original Presentation File is another option. If you mark this check box, a copy of the Corel Presentations 9 slideshow file is also saved in the folder, and a link is created to the file. In this way, people who visit this Web site and who own Presentations 9 can click the link to download the file to their computer, where they can view it with Presentations.

- Page Colors—Use your browser's default colors, or specify colors for text, links, and so on. Set background colors or use a background wallpaper file.

- Button Style—Choose a button style for use on your page.

7. In the last dialog box called Publish Location, you can change the title of the presentation. Specify the location you want to publish the presentation to (see Figure 34.10).

PART

V

CH

34

Figure 34.10
Specify the location you want to publish the presentation to.

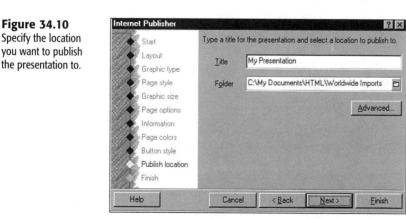

8. Choose <u>F</u>inish when you are done setting options. You see a dialog box showing the process as each slide is converted, and the files are created in the folder you specified. Presentations then asks whether you want to launch your browser and view your slideshow.

> **Note**
>
> After you've published your slideshow as HTML, you should view it with your browser prior to uploading it to your Web site to ensure that everything is as you want it to be. If the presentation is not right, it's easier to fix it in Presentations and republish it, but you can edit the HTML files themselves if you need to. You might want to refer to Que's *Special Edition Using HTML* for further information on editing Web pages.

If your slides appear much too large in your viewer, see "Specifying Screen Size for Slides" in the Troubleshooting section at the end of this chapter.

USING THE WEB PUBLISHING WIZARD

Corel Presentations incorporates a new feature called the Web Publishing Wizard that allows you to publish your presentations to a Web server.

→ For further information on how to use the Web Publishing Wizard, **see** "Publishing Documents with the Web Publishing Wizard," **p. 610**

→ For in-depth coverage of the Java language, **see** Que's *Special Edition Using Java.*

PUBLISHING COREL PRESENTATIONS WITH SHOWIT!

An exciting method for publishing your slides to the Web is Corel's ShowIt! program, which actually enables viewers to see your slideshows with animations, sounds, and transitions. You could even present your slideshow at a conference or meeting using nothing more than your browser and an Internet connection to your slideshow's Web site.

The method for preparing a ShowIt! slideshow for the Web is similar to the standard HTML method described earlier in this chapter. You can choose the filenames and locations, any additional information you want to add (such as your email address), the size of the display, and the color settings.

Presentations also automatically adds information about how viewers can obtain the free Corel ShowIt! plug-in to add to their Web browser.

After you create the ShowIt! slideshow, you play it just as you do a regular slideshow (see Figure 34.11).

While viewing a slide in your browser, you can do the following:

- Click the left mouse button on the slide to advance to the next slide, the next bullet, or an animated object.

- Have sound and video files play at their assigned times and locations.

- Click SpeedLinks to jump to other Web sites (however, SpeedKeys will not work).
- Click the Reload button (or equivalent) in your browser to start the slideshow over from the beginning.

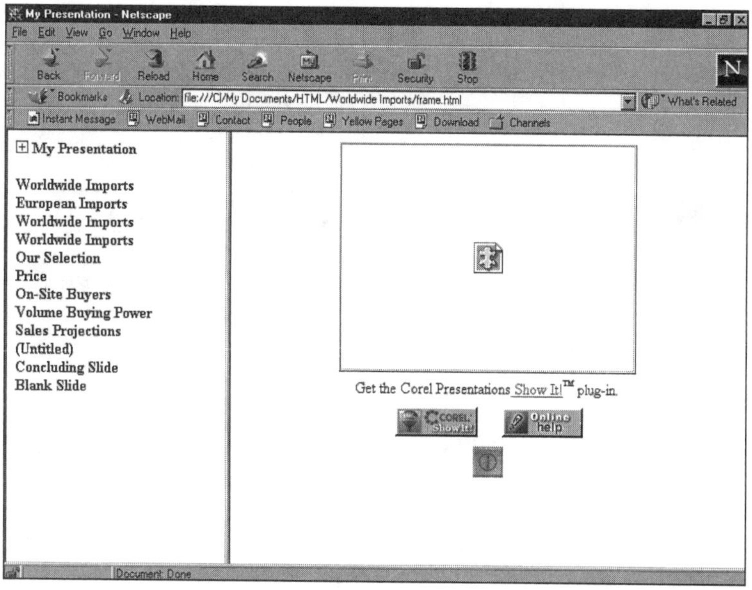

Figure 34.11
When you publish to ShowIt!, you can play the slideshow from your Internet browser just as you usually play your slideshow.

UPLOADING YOUR PRESENTATION

Before others can see your presentation, you need to copy it onto the Internet or your corporate intranet. You can use a few different applications to do so.

COPYING YOUR PRESENTATION TO THE INTERNET

To copy the presentation to the Internet, you need to use programs not included with Corel WordPerfect Suite 9. Therefore, this book cannot tell you how to do this; however, it is possible to specify what needs to be done.

To copy the presentation to the Internet, you must do the following:

- Know the address of the file area to which you will copy the presentation on your Internet server.
- Have sufficient access permission to copy the files.
- Create a subfolder on the Internet server for the presentation. You might also need to create additional subfolders for image and sound files, if you used them in your slideshow.
- Copy all files in your Web presentation folder to the appropriate subfolder(s).

PART

V

CH

34

If you cannot copy your presentation to the Internet, see "Copying a Presentation to the Internet" in the Troubleshooting section at the end of this chapter

You can also create a link from another Web site to your presentation. The link should be of the form:

```
http://www.server.com/folder/subfolder/index.htm
```

where server is the name of your Internet server, folder is the name of your main folder on that server, and subfolder is the name of the new subfolder you created for your presentation.

> **Caution**
>
> If you have changed the name of your table of contents page, that is the name that should be entered where it says index.htm in the preceding URL. Also, some servers are picky about filenames. Some require .html rather than .htm as filename extensions. Some are sensitive to upper- and lowercase (Index.html, INDEX.HTML, or index.html could be three different filenames).

Copying Your Presentation to a Corporate Intranet

Copying your presentation to a local Web site can entail any number of different methods, depending on how your site is set up. The basic procedure, however, is the same as the procedure to copy your presentation to the Internet.

You must create a specific subfolder on your Web server exclusively for the presentation, and copy all files from the folder in which you saved your Web presentation to this subfolder.

If files on your Web site are accessible via your Windows 95, Windows NT, or Novell network, you might be able to create the directory (folder) and copy the files via Windows Explorer. More often, you have to copy the files to a public workspace on your network, and your network administrator or Webmaster takes care of copying them to the appropriate locations on the Web server.

Emailing Your Presentation

As you are developing your presentation, you might want to email it to reviewers or your supervisor prior to finalizing it.

If you are using a mail system that supports an email standard called Simple MAPI, such as Novell's GroupWise, you can choose File, Send To, Mail Recipient and email your slideshow from within Presentations.

> **Note**
>
> Networks that use compatible email programs sometimes are not configured correctly, and the Send To, Mail Recipient option appears grayed. Ask your system administrator to check if the Send item does not appear on your menu.

To email your presentation, have the slideshow you want to send on the screen. Choose File, Send To, Mail Recipient. You are taken into your email system, and see a Send To dialog box with the slideshow automatically included as an attachment to your (blank) message. Fill in the recipient(s), a subject, and a message, and send your message!

If the mail option is not available, go into your email system and use the method appropriate for your system for attaching a file to an email.

PRACTICAL PROJECT

Create a slideshow for a marketing strategy presentation using the PerfectExpert project. Then work with the Internet Publisher to convert the slideshow for use on the Internet. Publish the slide to your Web server. Open your browser and run the slideshow that you placed on the Internet for everyone to see.

TROUBLESHOOTING

SPECIFYING SCREEN SIZE FOR SLIDES

Your slides appear much too large in your viewer.

If you choose a very high screen resolution, the slides will appear much too large in many viewers. When in doubt, use the lowest common screen size, such as 640×480.

COPYING A PRESENTATION TO THE INTERNET

You cannot copy your presentation to the Internet.

Check the address of the file area to which you will copy the presentation on your Internet server. Be sure you have sufficient access permission to copy the files. Create a subfolder on the Internet server for the presentation. You might also need to create additional subfolders for image and sound files, if you used them in your slideshow. Be sure to copy all files in your Web presentation folder to the appropriate subfolder(s).

Using the Bonus Applications

CHAPTER 35

USING DRAGON NATURALLYSPEAKING

In this chapter

What Is Dragon NaturallySpeaking?

Dragon NaturallySpeaking is a speech recognition and dictation application. Dragon matches the words you dictate with its stored vocabulary. It does not spell phonetically because the words you dictate would be misspelled. For example, if you say "relation" and it's not in Dragon's vocabulary, Dragon interprets the word as "relay shun."

Setting Up Dragon NaturallySpeaking

Before you set up Dragon NaturallySpeaking, be sure that you have a microphone or a headset connected to your computer. You'll be speaking into the microphone so that Dragon can recognize the words you speak and enter them in a document in written form.

Setting up Dragon NaturallySpeaking is a matter of defining user information. A user is a set of speech file and Registry settings. You need to set up user information before you begin using Dragon. The user information includes

- Audio system settings selected by the Audio Setup Wizard
- Acoustic information about your voice gathered during initial product training (General Training) and when you train specific words
- Vocabulary words and language model information
- Options dialog box settings
- Custom voice commands you create

The Dragon NaturallySpeaking Wizard helps you set up all the user information you'll need to work with Dragon. The wizard steps you through a series of dialog boxes to perform the following tasks:

- Create user speech files
- Run the Audio Setup Wizard
- Train Dragon NaturallySpeaking
- Run Vocabulary Builder
- View Quick Tour

After you install Dragon NaturallySpeaking, open WordPerfect 9. A new command called Dragon NaturallySpeaking should appear at the far-right end of the menu bar.

The first time you use Dragon, choose Dragon NaturallySpeaking, Use Natural Word. The Open User dialog box appears. Click New. The New User Wizard dialog box appears, as shown in Figure 35.1.

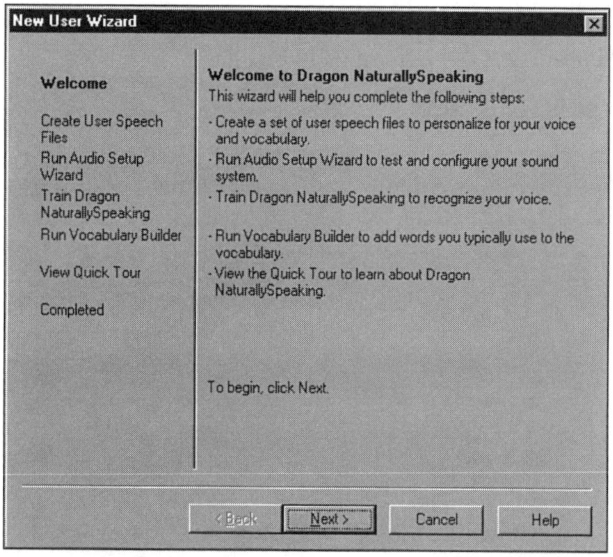

Figure 35.1
The New User Wizard helps you set up user information for Dragon NaturallySpeaking.

The Dragon NaturallySpeaking Wizard takes about 45 minutes to finish (15 of those minutes is for computer processing time). If you exit the wizard by clicking Cancel, the wizard remembers which steps you have completed, and the next time you open the wizard, you can pick up where you left off. If you click the Back button in the wizard, you return to the previous step.

CREATING USER SPEECH FILES

You need to set up and personalize a set of user speech files for Dragon to work properly. These speech files contain acoustic information about your voice that Dragon uses to recognize your speech. The speech files also contain any changes you make to the standard Dragon vocabulary (for example, any special words, names, acronyms, and abbreviations you add to its vocabulary).

To create user speech files, do the following:

1. In the Welcome to Dragon NaturallySpeaking dialog box, click the Next button.
2. For this step, type a name in the box for the user speech files.
3. Click the Next button. Dragon creates and loads the vocabulary. The asterisk next to Create User Speech Files in the left column of the New User dialog box indicates the task has been completed.

The next step in setting up Dragon is to run the Audio Setup Wizard screen, described in the next section.

PART
VI

CH
35

RUNNING THE AUDIO SETUP WIZARD

The Audio Setup Wizard enables you to adjust and optimize audio settings for Dragon.

Perform these steps to run the Audio Setup Wizard:

1. In the Run Audio Setup Wizard screen, click the Run Audio Setup Wizard button. The Dragon Systems Audio Setup Wizard dialog box appears, as shown in Figure 35.2.

Figure 35.2
Adjust and optimize your audio system with the Audio Setup Wizard.

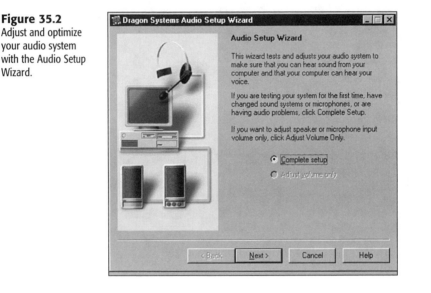

2. Choose Complete Setup.

Tip #236 from
Trudi Reisner

If you want to adjust the speaker or microphone input volume only, choose Adjust Volume Only. This option is available after you perform a complete setup.

3. Click the Next button. If necessary, connect your speakers to the speaker output jack on your sound system or computer.

4. Click the Next button. Then click the Start Test button to test your speaker connection. Use the volume slider at the bottom of the dialog box to adjust the volume. When you're finished testing the speakers, click the Stop Test button.

5. Click the Next button to save the volume setting. Now choose your input sound system, as illustrated in Figure 35.3. If you're unsure which one to use, click the Default button to choose the default sound system.

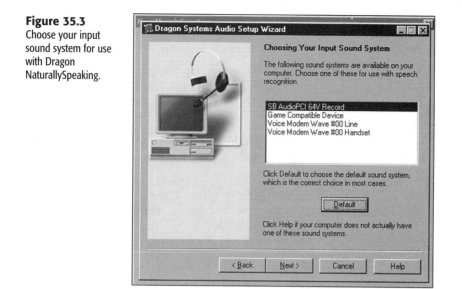

6. Click the Next button to save the input sound system. If necessary, connect your microphone to the microphone jack on your sound system or computer.

7. Click the Next button. Position your microphone so that it's a thumb's width from your mouth and a little to the side as shown in the photograph in the dialog box (see Figure 35.4). Be sure the face of the microphone mouthpiece points directly at your mouth.

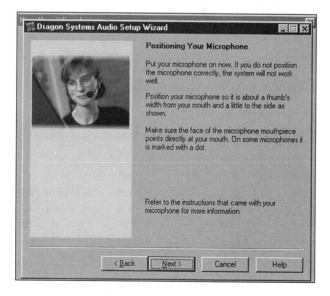

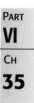

PART

VI

CH

35

8. Click the Next button. To test your microphone, click the $\underline{S}$tart Test button and speak into the microphone. When you hear a beep and see the `Sound Was Detected` message, it means that the microphone connection is working properly.

9. Click the Next button. The next step is to adjust your input volume. Click $\underline{S}$tart Test and read the paragraph that appears in the box, as if you are dictating. (Dragon adjusts the input volume, you will hear a beep, and the paragraph disappears. The volume is set.)

10. Click the Next button. You should see the Sound Level and Sound Quality set up for use with Dragon in the green region.

Note

If the sound quality is unacceptable, adjust the position of your microphone and run the entire Audio Setup wizard again. Move closer to the microphone, too. You can click the Help button to read about improving sound quality.

11. Click the Finish button. An asterisk appears next to the Run Audio Setup Wizard in the left column of the New User dialog box, which means you have completed the step.

In the next section, you learn how to train Dragon NaturallySpeaking for your voice.

TRAINING DRAGON NATURALLYSPEAKING

For Dragon NaturallySpeaking to adapt to the sound of your voice, you need to train Dragon and run the training program. There are two stages to the training procedure. First, you read aloud a few paragraphs and Dragon makes some minor adjustments. Second, you read aloud for at least 30 minutes and Dragon adapts to your voice.

Caution

Be sure you complete the second part of the training where you read aloud for 30 minutes because it will greatly increase recognition accuracy and dictation speed.

To train Dragon, follow these steps:

1. In the Train Dragon NaturallySpeaking for Your Voice screen, click the $\underline{R}$un Training Program button. The General Training Instructions dialog box opens. Read the instructions, and then click Continue to begin the first stage of the training.

2. Click $\underline{D}$emo to listen to an example of how to speak. Click the $\underline{R}$ecord button and say the sentence that appears in the box. Then read the text in the box as Dragon displays it. Click $\underline{P}$ause to pause reading the text, click $\underline{B}$ack Up to go to the previous text, click $\underline{N}$ext to go to the next text, or click $\underline{S}$kip Word to skip over a word for which Dragon doesn't recognize your voice.

3. Choose the type of text you want to read. Then read the text in the box as Dragon displays it. A yellow arrow displays next to the text you need to read. A yellow bar indicates that you must read the text again for Dragon to recognize your voice. A green bar means that Dragon recognized your voice for the text you're reading. A timer tells you how many minutes are remaining for you to read the text.

> **Note**
>
> For those of you who are susceptible to attacks of the "giggles," the Dave Barry text is very funny. As a result, you might have had to reread many of the paragraphs, which slows down the Training session. You might opt for different text if you want to speed up the Training session.

4. While you're reading the text, you can click Pause to pause reading the text, click Back Up to go to the previous text, click Next to go to the next text, or click Skip Word to skip over a word for which Dragon doesn't recognize your voice.

5. When you're finished reading all the text, you can either click Train More to read some more text or click Finish to end the training session. After you click Finish, Dragon takes several minutes to adapt the speech files to your voice and save the speech files. An asterisk should appear next to Train Dragon NaturallySpeaking in the left column of the New User dialog box, indicating the task is complete.

> **Note**
>
> If you choose to train more, be sure to save the training session when you finish. Click Finish to exit the training session properly and Dragon saves your speech files.

The next section shows you how to increase Dragon's speech recognition accuracy by personalizing your vocabulary.

RUNNING VOCABULARY BUILDER

For increased speech recognition accuracy, you need to run vocabulary builder. Read your own documents that represent your writing style for more accuracy. This is a way to personalize your vocabulary and add special words that are particular to the subject areas you work with. Adding vocabulary from your own documents reduces mistakes that Dragon makes.

Follow these steps to run vocabulary builder:

1. In the Run Vocabulary Builder screen in the New User Wizard dialog box, click Run Vocabulary Builder. The Vocabulary Builder dialog box appears, as shown in Figure 35.5.

2. Click Add Document. In the Add Documents dialog box, choose the drive in the Look In list, then choose the folder, and select a document.

3. Repeat step 2 to add each document to Vocabulary Builder.

4. When you're finished adding the documents, click Begin to process the document(s).

5. When Vocabulary Builder is finished, you see the New Words from Documents dialog box shown in Figure 35.6.

PART

VI

CH

35

Figure 35.5
The Vocabulary
Builder dialog box lets
you use your own
documents to build
vocabulary in Dragon.

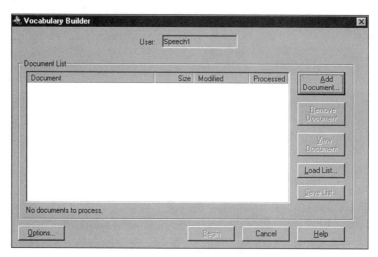

Figure 35.6
The New Words from
Documents dialog
box shows the words
and their context,
extracted from the
documents you ran
in vocabulary
builder.

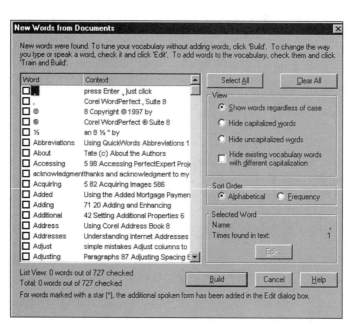

6. If you don't want to add these words, click <u>B</u>uild. If you want to edit a word, click in the check box next to the word, and click <u>E</u>dit. Change any options in the View and Sort Order sections. If you want to add words to the vocabulary, check them and click Train and <u>B</u>uild.

7. If you chose Train and <u>B</u>uild, the Train Words dialog box appears. Click the <u>R</u>ecord button and say each word that appears in the box at the top of the dialog box. When you're finished, click <u>D</u>one. Dragon builds the language model for the speech files and updates the speech files.

8. Choose <u>Y</u>es to save the changes. Then click OK.

The Quick Tour is the last task you can perform in the wizard, which is discussed in the following section.

VIEWING QUICK TOUR

If you've never used a speech recognition and dictation application or you don't how to run Dragon, it is strongly recommended that you take the Quick Tour. This tour shows you how to start using Dragon and covers the basic dictation and correction techniques you need to know. The tour takes about 15 minutes and should be viewed after you've gone through all the steps to set up Dragon.

To start the tour, click View Quick Tour in the New User Wizard dialog box. Figure 35.7 shows the screen you'll see in the Dragon NaturallySpeaking Quick Tour window.

Figure 35.7
The Quick Tour shows you how to get started using Dragon NaturallySpeaking and covers the basic dictation and correction techniques you need to know.

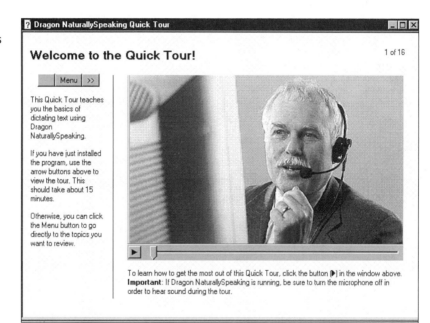

Follow the onscreen instructions to go through the Quick Tour. When you're done with the tour, click the Close (X) button to close the Quick Tour window. Then click the <u>F</u>inish button to close the New User Wizard dialog box. Now you're ready to give dictation.

PART
VI

CH
35

GIVING DICTATION

The important basic dictation techniques include using the microphone, speaking to dictate, giving voice commands, and using editing commands to correct the dictation. You also need to know how to save your speech files and restore speech files from the last backup.

USING THE MICROPHONE

For Dragon to hear you accurately when you speak into the microphone, be sure to position the microphone at the corner of your mouth, about a thumb's distance from your lips.

To turn the microphone on and off, click the Microphone icon in the tool tray on the Windows taskbar or press the plus key (+) on the numeric keypad on your keyboard.

If you need to answer the phone or talk to someone who walks into the room, it's a good idea to deactivate the microphone temporarily. To do so, say the voice command, "Go to Sleep." To reactivate the microphone, say the voice command "Wake Up." Be sure to pause before and after a voice command, so Dragon doesn't interpret the commands as words for dictation.

The program window into which you want to dictate must be active for Dragon to hear you. Just click anywhere in the window to activate it. The window's title bar will be highlighted indicating the window is active.

 If you give the voice command "Go to Sleep" and Dragon enters those words into your document, see "Giving Voice Commands" in the Troubleshooting section at the end of this chapter.

SPEAKING TO DICTATE

Before you dictate, you need to know a few important things. As you dictate, Dragon previews your words in a small yellow window called the Results box. Your dictation is recognized and processed phrase by phrase, not word by word. The Results box gives Dragon a chance to adjust its interpretation of your words and their context before entering them in your document.

To dictate, turn on your microphone, adjust the microphone, get comfortable, and think about what you want to say. Click in the document where you want to start dictating. Speak in your normal voice, at a normal pace, and pronounce each word clearly without overenunciating. Don't whisper, mumble, or slur your words. Pause after each phrase, not after each word. For punctuation, say "comma," "semicolon," and so on. To start a new line, say "New Line." To start a new paragraph, say "New Paragraph," as shown in Figure 35.8. Dragon capitalizes the first word of a new sentence and inserts the correct number of spaces after a punctuation mark.

You can correct recognition errors as you dictate. For example, if you say an unusual name such as Ritzo, Dragon will enter the word as "Writ so." This is different from revising text, which is explained later in this chapter. When Dragon doesn't recognize a word and enters an incorrect word into your document, you can correct that mistake with the Correction dialog box (see Figure 35.9). After you see an error, say "Correct That." The Correction dialog box appears with a list of suggested words. If one of the suggested words is correct, say that word by spelling it out loud, and click OK. Otherwise, spell out loud the correct word and click OK. Dragon corrects the word in the document. That way, Dragon will recognize the word the next time you say it.

Figure 35.8
A document that contains text entered by Dragon NaturallySpeaking dictation.

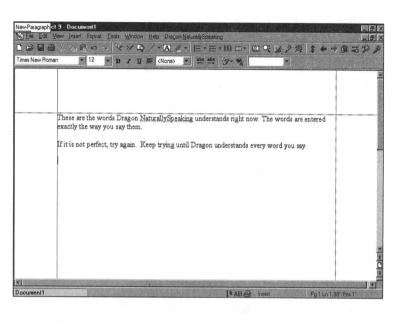

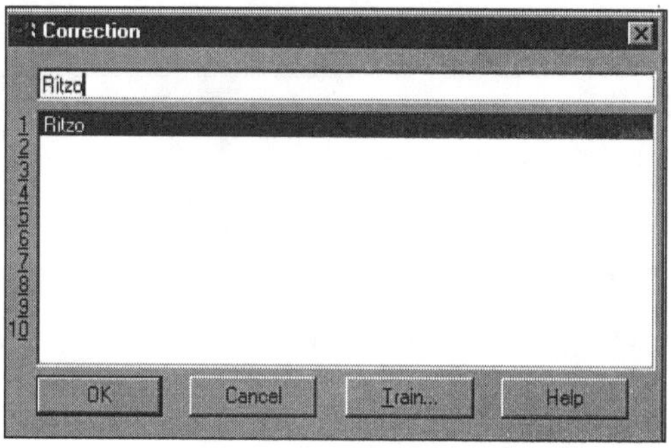

Figure 35.9
The Correction dialog box lets you correct recognition errors as you dictate text.

When you're finished dictating, turn off the microphone by clicking the Microphone icon in the tool tray on the Windows taskbar.

GIVING VOICE COMMANDS

When you give a voice command, such as "Go to Sleep" or "Wake Up," you must pause before and after the command. Otherwise, Dragon interprets the words as dictation and enters them into your document.

To move the insertion point in the document by voice, you need to say the following voice commands:

- "Go to Top" or "Move to Top"
- "Go to Bottom" or "Move to Bottom"
- "Move Left One Character" or "Move Right One Character"

PART

VI

CH

35

- "Move Left Three Words" or "Move Right Three Words"
- "Move Up One Line" or "Move Up Two Lines"
- "Move Down One Line" or "Move Down Two Lines"
- "Move to Beginning of Paragraph" or "Move to End of Paragraph"
- "Move to Beginning of Document" or "Move to End of Document"

If you give a voice command to move the insertion point and it doesn't move in the document, see "Moving the Insertion Point" in the Troubleshooting section at the end of this chapter.

Using Editing Commands

Dragon provides voice-editing commands for revising your text. To use these commands, first think about what you want to say to revise your text. Then use "Select-and-Say" to select the text in the document and say the new words. To select text, say "select" immediately followed by the words in the document that you want to select. Then dictate the new words.

To delete text immediately after saying it, say "Scratch That." To delete text you already dictated, say "Select" and what text you want to delete to select the text. Then say "Delete That."

Note You can say "Scratch That" a maximum of 10 times to delete the most recent phrases.

Formatting text can be done as you dictate or after you dictate. You can change the font size and add boldface, italic, or underline to your text.

To format text as you dictate, say "Set Font" and then say "Times New Roman." Say "Format That" and then say "18 Point," "Arial 12," or "Courier 18 Bold." Say "Format That" and then say "Plain Text" to remove formatting. Say "Set Font Bold," "Set Font Italics," or "Set Font Underlined."

To format text after you dictate, first say "Select" and say the text you want to format to select the text. To change font size, say "Change Font Size to 12"; to boldface text say "Bold That"; to italicize text, say "Italicize That"; to underline text say "Underline That."

Saving Current Speech Files

To save all the vocabulary you entered in the document in the current speech file, choose Dragon NaturallySpeaking, Users, Save Speech Files. You are asked to save the changes, so choose Yes.

To *save* your document that contains the dictation, save it as you normally would in WordPerfect.

WORKING WITH VOCABULARY

After you've built your vocabulary with the New User wizard and saved words in your document to the speech file, you can continue to add words to Dragon's vocabulary. You can train words manually, find new words in your document and add them to vocabulary, and use Vocabulary Builder and the Vocabulary Editor.

TRAINING WORDS

To train words manually, complete the following steps:

1. Choose Dragon NaturallySpeaking, Tools, Train Words. The Training dialog box opens as shown in Figure 35.10.

2. Enter the word or phrase in the box and choose OK. The Train Words dialog box appears.

3. Click Record and say the new word(s).

4. Click Done. Dragon adds the word to vocabulary.

Figure 35.10
The Training dialog box lets you train a new word manually.

FINDING NEW WORDS

Dragon can automatically find any new words you added to your document that vocabulary doesn't contain. To locate new words in your document to add to vocabulary, complete the following steps:

1. Choose Dragon NaturallySpeaking, Tools, Find New Words. Dragon searches for new words in your document and displays them in the Find New Words dialog box.

2. Click the check box next to the words you want to train.

3. Click the Train button to display the Train Words dialog box.

4. Click Record and say each word as it appears in the box.

5. Click Done. Dragon adds the new words to Vocabulary Builder.

USING VOCABULARY BUILDER

To increase speech recognition accuracy, add your own documents to the Vocabulary Builder that represent your writing style. This procedure personalizes your vocabulary and adds special words that are particular to the subject areas you work with. Dragon will make fewer mistakes if you add vocabulary from your own documents.

To add more documents to Vocabulary Builder, complete the following steps:

1. Choose Dragon NaturallySpeaking, Tools, Vocabulary Builder.

2. Click Add Document, and choose each document you want to use.

3. When you're finished adding the documents, click Begin to process the document(s).

When Vocabulary Builder is finished, you see the New Words from Documents dialog box that shows the words and their context, extracted from the documents you ran in Vocabulary Builder.

If you don't want to add these words, click Build. If you want to edit a word, click in the check box next to the word, and click Edit. Change any options in the View and Sort Order sections. If you want to add words to the vocabulary, check them and click Train and Build.

If you chose Train and Build, the Train Words dialog box appears. Click the Record button and say each word that appears in the box at the top of the dialog box. When you're finished, click Done. Dragon builds the language model for the speech files and updates the speech files. Choose Yes to save the changes. Then click OK.

USING VOCABULARY EDITOR

Vocabulary Editor lets you add and delete words in vocabulary.

To use Vocabulary Editor, choose Dragon NaturallySpeaking, Tools, Vocabulary Editor. The Vocabulary Editor dialog box opens, as shown in Figure 35.11.

To add a new word, click in the Written Form box, type the new word, and click Add. To add the spoken form of the new written word, choose the written form of the word. Next, click Train, click Record, say the word, and click Done.

To delete a word, type the new word in the Written Form box, or scroll through the Written Form list to find the word you want to delete. Click the word. Click Delete.

To close Vocabulary Editor, click Close.

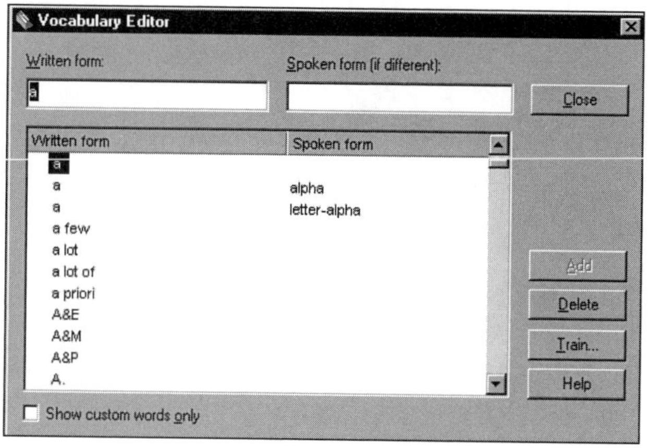

Figure 35.11
The Vocabulary Editor enables you to add and delete words from the vocabulary.

Written form	Spoken form
a	
a	alpha
a	letter-alpha
a few	
a lot	
a lot of	
a priori	
A&E	
A&M	
A&P	
A.	

Vocabulary Editor

Written form:

Spoken form (if different):

Close

Add

Delete

Train...

Help

☐ Show custom words only

PRACTICAL PROJECT

Use Dragon NaturallySpeaking to dictate an annual report, documents for a special project, a performance review, a memo, a letter, a résumé, or any document you would normally type up.

TROUBLESHOOTING

GIVING VOICE COMMANDS

You gave the voice command, "Go to Sleep," and Dragon enters those words into your document.

Be sure to pause before and after a voice command, so Dragon doesn't interpret the commands as words for dictation.

MOVING THE INSERTION POINT

You gave the voice command to move the insertion point and it didn't move the insertion point in the document.

First check the position of your microphone. Be sure you're speaking directly into the microphone. Be sure to pause before and after a voice command, so Dragon doesn't interpret the commands as words for dictation. Be sure you're saying the correct voice command for moving the insertion point.

CHAPTER **36**

USING CORELCENTRAL 9

In this chapter

WHAT IS CORELCENTRAL?

CorelCENTRAL is a personal information manager (PIM) that comes with the Corel WordPerfect Office 2000 suite of applications. CorelCENTRAL 9 functions as a three-ring binder you might tote around during your business day.

You can jot down appointments and events on a calendar, write names and addresses in an address book, keep a to-do list, record your daily activities in a journal book, and write on notes; however, CorelCENTRAL makes entering data, managing information, and printing the results much easier. You can use CorelCENTRAL to computerize your daily appointments and events, contacts, tasks, projects, journal entries, sticky notes, and much more. You can create almost anything in CorelCENTRAL that involves managing information.

You'll find the following in CorelCENTRAL:

- *Calendar* enables you to schedule and keep track of appointments, events, holidays, and tasks. You can find and view information in your schedule. Calendar helps you better manage the way you control your own time.

- *Day Planner* enables you to schedule and view events and tasks at a glance and is integrated with Calendar. When you schedule tasks or events in Calendar, you can view them in Day Planner as well.

- *Alarms* enables you to set up a reminder—an alarm that plays a ding sound and displays the CorelCENTRAL Alarms window to remind you of an event at the time the event occurs or before the event.

- *Card File* assists you with building a contact list that contains names, addresses, phone numbers, fax numbers, and email addresses. You can sort and store the addresses in various ways. You can even set up an address list with a group of frequently used addresses. All the details you need on Address Book are explained in Chapter 37, "Using Corel Address Book 9."

- *Memos* are the electronic version of paper notes. You can use notes to jot down ideas, reminders, questions, instructions, and anything else that you may write as a note on paper. You can organize the notes by category.

- *Address Book* assists you with building a contact list that contains names, addresses, phone numbers, fax numbers, and email addresses. You can sort and store the addresses in various ways. You can even set up an address list with a group of frequently used addresses. All the details you need on Address Book are discussed in Chapter 37.

To start any of these CorelCENTRAL applications (except for Day Planner), just click Start, choose Programs, WordPerfect Office 2000, Utilities, and choose a CorelCENTRAL application. Start Day Planner by clicking Start, and then choosing Programs, WordPerfect Office 2000, CorelCENTRAL 9. Alternatively, you can click the CorelCENTRAL Alarms, CorelCENTRAL 9, or CorelCENTRAL Address Book icon in the DAD tool tray on the Windows taskbar.

UNDERSTANDING HOW CALENDAR WORKS

Do you tote around a calendar during the day? Do you have a desk or wall calendar at home marked up with events, birthdays, anniversaries, holidays, meetings, and so on? What if you lost your calendar? Unfortunately, you could lose it, and you might be totally lost without it. Why not track your schedule electronically with CorelCENTRAL Calendar to computerize your business and personal schedule in one location?

PART

VI

CH

36

> **Note**
>
> Be sure to back up any information you enter into CorelCENTRAL to prevent data loss.

With Calendar, you can schedule and keep track of all your daily activities. You can fill in daily and weekly events in your schedule. For example, you might want to track interviews, meetings, conferences, doctor and dentist appointments, birthdays, and anniversaries.

To start Calendar, click Start, choose Programs, WordPerfect Office 2000, Utilities, CorelCENTRAL Calendar. Or just click the CorelCENTRAL Calendar icon in the DAD tool tray on the Windows taskbar. The CorelCENTRAL Calendar window appears, as shown in Figure 36.1.

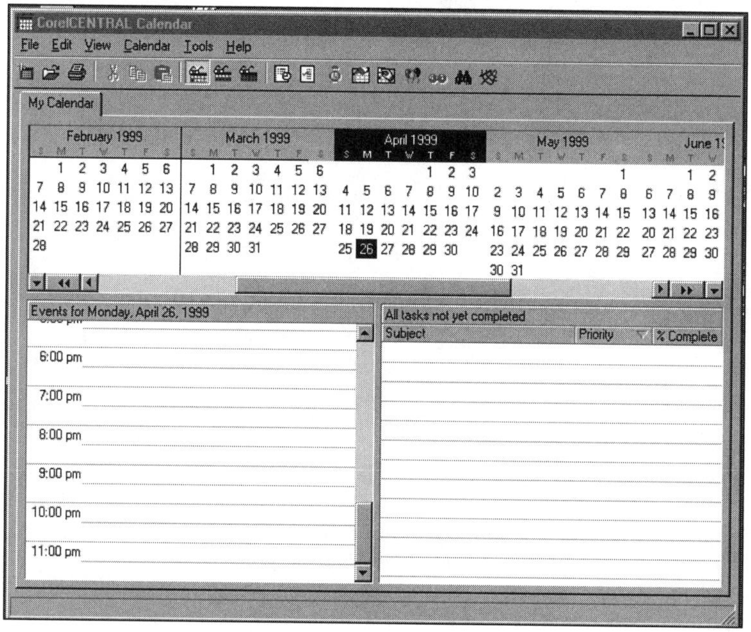

Figure 36.1
Calendar is used to set up events such as appointments and meetings, as well as tasks such as work assignments and projects.

SETTING UP AN EVENT

How does Calendar define an event? An event is an occurrence, such as an appointment and meeting. It is an activity for which you specify a block of time in Calendar.

To add an event to the schedule in Calendar, follow these steps:

1. In the Calendar window, choose Calendar, New Event. The New Event dialog box appears, as shown in Figure 36.2.

Figure 36.2
The New Event dialog box lets you add an event to the Event list in Calendar.

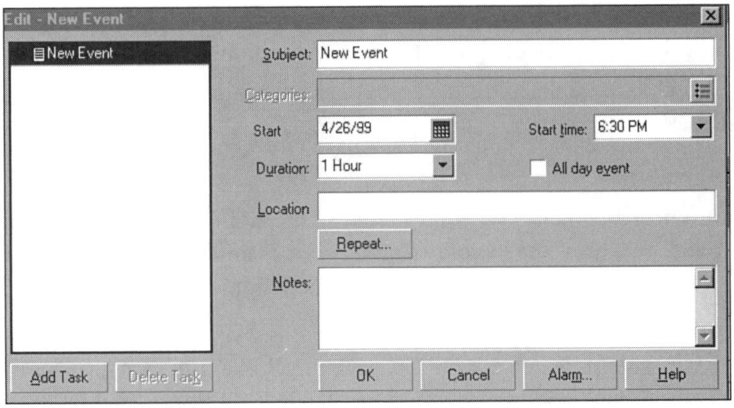

2. In the Subject box, enter a name for the event.
3. In the Start Date box, click the Mini-Calendar button. The Mini-Calendar appears.
4. Click the left and right arrows at the bottom of the Mini-Calendar to choose the year.
5. Click a month, and then click a day in the Mini-Calendar.
6. In the Start Time list box, choose a time.
7. In the Duration list box, choose a duration.
8. Click OK. The event appears in the Event list.

Note

An event can be an activity that lasts 24 hours or longer. For example, you can schedule an event such as a three-day conference, your summer vacation, or a seminar. To make an event an all-day event, check the All Day Event check box. A repeating event is an activity you schedule at a specific time for a specified time interval until you tell Calendar to stop scheduling the event.

If you have a weekly staff meeting and want to repeat this event, see "Repeating an Event" in the Troubleshooting section at the end of this chapter.

CREATING A REPEATING EVENT

Calendar also lets you schedule recurring events. You can repeat an event to remind you of birthdays, anniversaries, weekly meetings, and writing your weekly status report. For example, if you have a weekly staff meeting on Monday at 1:00 p.m., Calendar can schedule that meeting as a repeating event on that weekday and time slot into the near future or for as long as you like.

With a repeating event, each meeting is scheduled week after week until you tell Calendar to stop scheduling them. That way, you won't have to manually add this meeting to your schedule every week, one at a time.

If you need to add a repeating event, you can do so as follows:

1. Right-click the event you want to repeat in the Event list, and choose Edit Event. Or create a new event.

2. Click the Repeat button in the Edit or Create Event Dialog Box. The Repeat Event dialog box appears.

3. Choose one of the following to specify a repeating pattern for repeating the event:
   - Click the Weeks of Month tab to repeat an event by the week of the month.
   - Click the Days of Month tab to repeat an event by the day of the month.
   - Click the Weeks tab to repeat an event by week.
   - Click the Days tab to repeat an event by day.

4. In the Event Repeats Every box, type a number to specify the time interval.

5. In the From box, click the Mini-Calendar button, and click the arrows at the bottom of the Mini-Calendar to choose the year, and then click a month and a day.

6. In the To box, click the Mini-Calendar button, and click the arrows at the bottom of the Mini-Calendar to choose the year, and then click a month and a day.

7. In the On Day(s) group, found on all but the Days tab, choose one or more day check boxes.

8. In the During section, found only on the Weeks of the Month tab, choose one or more week check boxes.

9. Click OK to add the repeating event to the Event list.

EDITING AN EVENT

Sometimes you'll want to change an event. Frequently, you'll need to change the start and end time for an event or reschedule it to a different date and time.

Before you edit an event, it's helpful to know how to find the event you want to change in the Event list. To quickly search for the event, choose Edit, Find or press Ctrl+F. The Find dialog box opens. In the Find box, type the characters, word, or phrase you want to search for and click OK. When Calendar locates the event based on your search criteria, the event appears highlighted in the Event list.

To edit an event, right-click an event in the Event list, and choose Edit Event. Make any necessary changes and click OK. The changes you made to the event are reflected in the Event list.

If you no longer need an event, you can delete it by right-clicking the event, and choosing Delete Event from the QuickMenu.

Caution

> Be sure you want to delete an event because there is no Undo command to reverse the deletion of an event.

SETTING A REMINDER ALARM FOR AN EVENT

CorelCENTRAL Alarms gives you two ways to set a reminder alarm:

- Quick Alarm lets you set a reminder to ring an alarm at the time the event occurs.
- Alarm allows you to set a reminder to ring an alarm at a specific time interval before an event, such as a few minutes, or one day.

If you want to set a quick alarm for an event, right-click the event in the Events list, and choose Alarm. The alarm will sound at the time that the event was scheduled.

To set an alarm with a time interval for an event, follow these instructions:

1. Right-click the event in the Events list, and choose Edit Event.
2. Click the Alarm button. The Alarm dialog box appears, as shown in Figure 36.3.

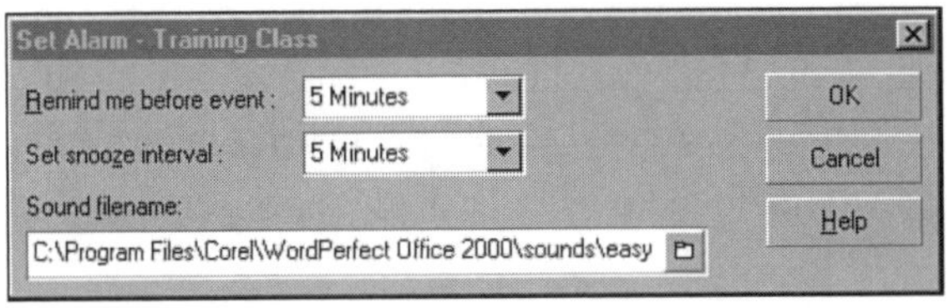

Figure 36.3
The Alarm dialog box is used for setting an alarm with a time interval.

3. In the Remind Me Before Event box, choose or type a time period.

Note

> CorelCENTRAL alarms don't use seconds for time intervals. If you type "seconds," "s," or "sec" into a text box, Alarms converts the seconds into minutes.

4. If desired, in the Snooze Interval list box, choose a time period. The snooze time interval is the amount of time between when you click the snooze button and when the alarm sounds again, just like the 10-minute snooze on your alarm clock at home.
5. Click the Browse button (small button at the end of the drop-down list), choose a .wav file, and click OK to specify the alarm sound that plays.
6. Click OK to set the alarm.

You should see an alarm icon next to the event in the Events list in Calendar and Day Planner (Day Planner is discussed later in this chapter). When the alarm sounds, click OK to turn the alarm off. If you set a snooze alarm, click the Snooze button to turn the alarm off, and the alarm will sound again after the specified period of time.

When you no longer need the alarm for an event, you can delete it. Right-click the event that has an alarm, and choose Alarm. Keep in mind that a check mark next to Alarm on the menu signifies that the alarm is set.

ADDING HOLIDAYS TO CALENDAR

By default, holidays do not appear in CorelCENTRAL Calendar or Day Planner (discussed later in this chapter in the section "Using Day Planner"), but you can add them to Calendar whenever you want. To add holidays, choose Calendar, Holidays. Put a check mark next to the holidays of various countries you want to display, and click OK. The holidays appear in the Events list and are recognized as all-day events in Calendar and Day Planner (see Figure 36.4).

Figure 36.4
Holidays can be displayed in the Events list in Calendar.

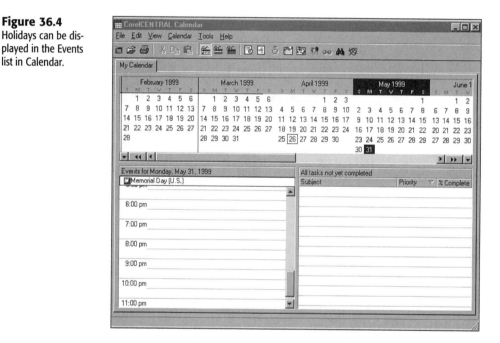

HIDE HOLIDAYS ON CALENDAR

Holidays can take up a lot of space in the Events list and slow the display time of Calendar and Day Planner. Be sure to display only the holidays you really need to reference. You can hide categories of holidays to speed up the display time.

To hide holidays, choose Calendar, Holidays. Remove the check marks from the check boxes next to the countries whose holidays you want to hide, and click OK. CorelCENTRAL removes those holidays from the Events list in Calendar and Day Planner.

VIEWING CALENDAR

By entering all your events in Calendar, you create a professional-looking schedule. The next logical step is to find out what you've scheduled and where things are. With Calendar's viewing options, you can quickly and easily find and view information in your schedule. You can view events assigned to a date, return to the default or current date, and view events by date, week or month.

If you want to view a specific date, choose Calendar, Go To Specific Date. In the Pick a Date box, click the Mini-Calendar button, and click the arrows at the bottom of the Mini-Calendar to choose the Year, and then click a month and a day. The Calendar displays the date you asked for. Figure 36.5 shows a specific date in Calendar.

Figure 36.5
Viewing a specific date in Calendar.

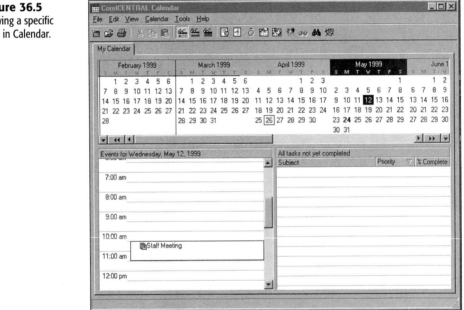

To view today's date, choose Calendar, Go To Today.

If you prefer to see events by day, choose View, Day. Calendar displays a day at a time in the Events list.

To view events by week, choose View, Week. You should see a week at a time in the Events list, as shown in Figure 36.6.

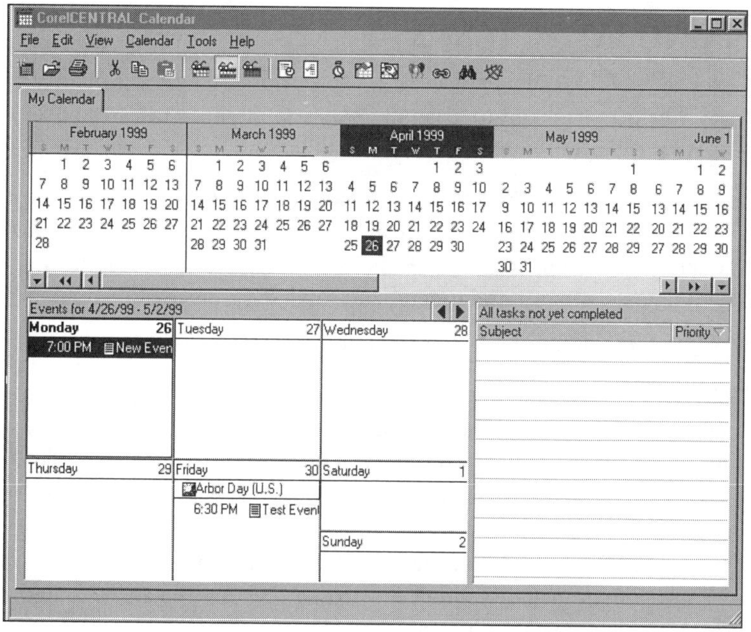

Figure 36.6
Viewing a week at a time in the Events list in Calendar.

If you need to view events by month, choose View, Month. Calendar shows you a month at a time in the Events list, as shown in Figure 36.7.

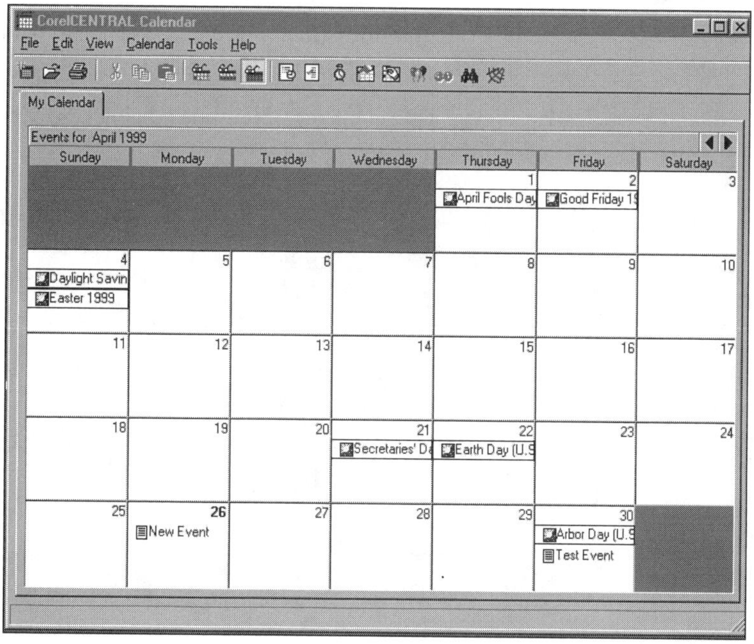

Figure 36.7
Viewing a month at a time in the Events list in Calendar.

WORKING WITH TASKS

CorelCENTRAL Calendar can help you stay focused during the day by managing your tasks. The tasks you add to Calendar help you organize tasks and projects that are significant to various dates and events on your schedule.

You can add tasks for daily things you need to do and items you must work on to complete a work assignment or project. Any duties that you accomplish are called tasks. Some good examples of tasks include completing a form every month, making a phone call to a contact, scheduling a doctor's appointment, and servicing a piece of equipment.

Just like the repeating events in Calendar, you can have repeating tasks that recur at a specified time interval.

A project is a larger goal that you need to complete and can include several tasks and subtasks. Duties that are attached to tasks and events are called subtasks. For example, reviewing the budget, preparing an annual report, giving a performance review, writing a book, and designing a brochure are some projects that you might need to accomplish. These projects can be broken down into tasks and subtasks. For example, when you design a brochure, your tasks might include writing the text and getting the artwork, and your subtasks might include ordering paper and selecting ink color.

In this section, you learn how to add tasks, add repeating tasks, and edit, delete, and move tasks and subtasks.

ADDING TASKS

Tasks can be organized by category for easier viewing. You can assign a task to one or more categories and specify the start date for the task. To add a task, follow these steps:

1. Choose Calendar, New Task. The Edit - New Task dialog box opens, as illustrated in Figure 36.8.

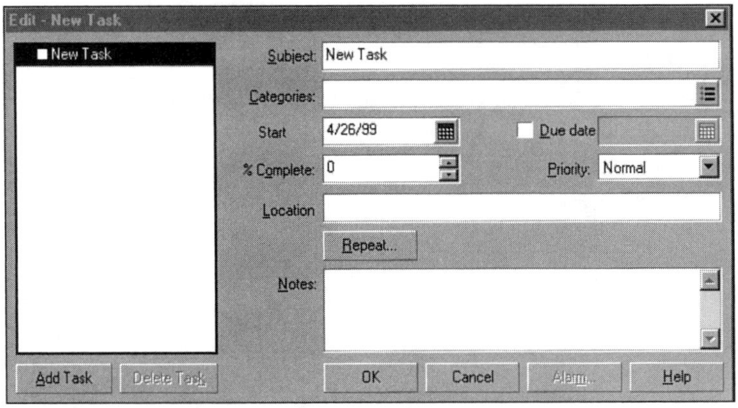

Figure 36.8
The Edit - New Task dialog box lets you add tasks to the Task list in Calendar.

2. In the <u>S</u>ubject box, enter a name for the task.

3. Click the <u>C</u>ategories button, and choose one or more categories in the <u>C</u>ategories list.

4. In the Start date box, click the Mini-Calendar button, and click the arrows at the bottom of the Mini-Calendar to choose the Year, and then click a month and a day.

5. Choose OK to add the task to the Task list in Calendar.

Adding Subtasks

A *subtask* is a small task that must be done before a task is completed. For instance, a subtask of a task might be a meeting you must attend before designing a brochure. The subtask of an event might be an email you must send when an employee has a birthday. A subtask is added to tasks and events. To add a subtask, follow these steps:

1. Right-click in the Task list and choose <u>A</u>dd Task or <u>E</u>dit Task, or right-click in the Event list, and choose <u>A</u>dd Event or <u>E</u>dit Event. Then click the <u>A</u>dd Task button. The New Subtask dialog box opens.

2. In the <u>S</u>ubject box, enter a name for the subtask.

3. Click the <u>C</u>ategories button, and choose one or more categories in the <u>C</u>ategories list.

4. In the Start date box, click the Mini-Calendar button, and click the arrows at the bottom of the Mini-Calendar to choose the Year, and then click a month and a day.

5. Choose OK to add the subtask to the Task list in Calendar.

Moving Subtasks

You can move a subtask by dragging it to another task, event, or subtask. Remember you can move only one subtask at a time.

Adding Repeating Tasks

If you have a recurring task that needs to be done repeatedly, you can add a repeating task to the Task list. For example, if you have to complete a quarterly budget on the last day of the quarter at 3:00 p.m., Calendar can schedule that task as a repeating task on that weekday and time slot into the near future or for whatever duration you like.

A repeating task, such as the quarterly budget, is scheduled quarter after quarter until you tell Calendar to stop scheduling them. That way, you won't have to manually add this budget to your schedule every quarter, one at a time.

Perform these steps to add a repeating task:

1. Right-click the task you want to repeat in the Task list, and choose <u>E</u>dit Task.

2. Click the <u>R</u>epeat button on the toolbar. The Repeat Task dialog box appears, as shown in Figure 36.9.

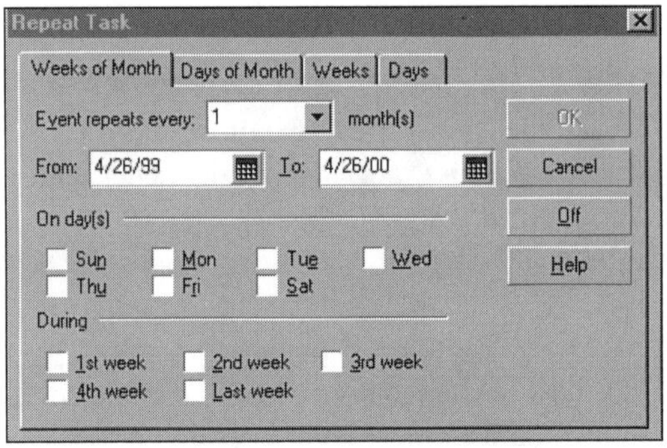

Figure 36.9
The Repeat Task dialog box enables you to add a repeating task to the Task List in Calendar.

3. Choose one of the following to set a repeating pattern:
   - Click the Weeks of Month tab to repeat a task by the week of the month.
   - Click the Days of Month tab to repeat a task by the day of the month.
   - Click the Weeks tab to repeat a task by week.
   - Click the Days tab to repeat a task by day.

4. In the Event Repeats Every box, type a number to specify the time interval.

5. In the From box, click the Mini-Calendar button, click the arrows at the bottom of the Mini-Calendar to choose the year, and then click a month and a day.

6. In the To box, click the Mini-Calendar button, click the arrows at the bottom of the Mini-Calendar to choose the year, and then click a month and a day.

7. In the On Day(s) group, found under all tabs except Days, choose one or more day check boxes.

8. In the During section, found only on the Weeks of the Month tab, choose one or more week check boxes.

9. Click OK to add the repeating task to the Task list.

EDITING A TASK

Sometimes you might need to modify a task or subtask. Often, you'll need to change the start and end time for a task or reschedule it to a different date and time.

When you have a lot of tasks and subtasks in your Task list, you might find it helpful to use the Find feature to locate the task you want to change. To quickly search for the task, choose Edit, Find or press Ctrl+F. The Find dialog box opens. In the Find box, type the characters, word, or phrase you want to search for and click OK. When Calendar locates the task based on your search criteria, the task appears highlighted in the Task list.

To edit a task or subtask, close the Find Dialog box, right-click a task or subtask in the Task list, and choose Edit Task. Make any necessary changes and click OK. The changes you made to the task or subtask appear in the Task list.

If you don't need a task or subtask any more, delete it by right-clicking the task or subtask, and choosing <u>D</u>elete Task from the QuickMenu.

> **Caution**
>
> Be sure you really want to delete a task before you do it because there is no Undo command to reverse the deletion of a task.

CHANGING THE PRIORITY OF A TASK

You can assign a priority to a task to show its level of importance. Priority is useful when you want to sort tasks by how important they are.

You can choose from five priority levels for tasks and subtasks: Highest, High, Normal, Low, and Lowest. To change the priority of a task or subtask, right-click the task or subtask in the Task list, and choose <u>P</u>riority. Choose a priority and click OK.

 If you need to change the priority for a task, see "Changing the Priority for a Task" in the Troubleshooting section at the end of this chapter.

CONVERTING TASKS, SUBTASKS, AND EVENTS

CorelCENTRAL lets you convert tasks and subtasks into events, and convert events into tasks and subtasks. You can covert only one task, subtask, or event at a time.

To convert a task or subtask into an event, drag the task or subtask from the Task list to the Event list. If you want to convert an event into a task, drag the event from the Event list to the Task list. To convert an event into a subtask, drag the event from the Event list to a task in the Task list. Or drag the event to an event in the Event list. You can also drag the event to a subtask in the Task list.

RECORDING PROGRESS ON TASKS

Calendar lets you record the progress on tasks by specifying the percentage of work that you have accomplished for each task or subtask. To do so, right-click a task or subtask in the Task list, choose Percent <u>C</u>omplete, and choose a percentage.

If you want to mark a task complete, check the check box next to the task or subtask name in the Task list.

VIEWING TASKS

The Task list is located in the lower-right side of the Calendar desktop. You can change the tasks and columns shown in the Task list.

You can view tasks in three ways: by category, by completion status, or by time period. Subtasks are filtered by the task to which they are attached. For instance, if you mark a subtask completed, but the task to which it is attached is not, both the task and the subtask are displayed when you filter the Task list by the Not Complete status.

To filter the task list by category, completion status, or time period, choose View, Filter Task List. In the Category list box, choose a category. In the With Status section, choose Complete or Not Complete or both options. In the From Time Period list box, choose a time period. Click OK. The tasks appear in the list, organized by the filters you selected. Figure 36.10 shows a Task list filtered by completion status.

Figure 36.10
You can create a filter that shows tasks by completion status.

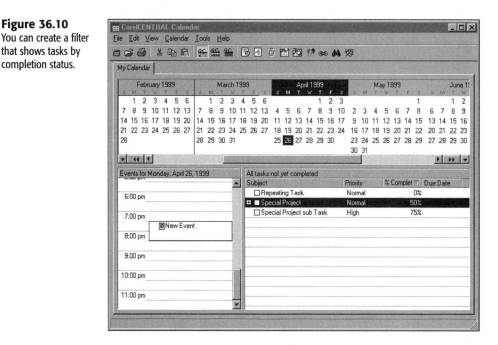

If you want to change the columns shown in the Task list, you can hide and display columns. To hide a column, right-click the Subject column title, and remove the check mark next to the column you want to hide. To display a column heading, right-click the Subject column title, and put a check mark next to the column you want to display.

USING DAY PLANNER

Calendar and Day Planner are integrated applications in CorelCENTRAL. The events and tasks you schedule in Calendar appear in Day Planner, too. You can schedule and view events and tasks in Day Planner.

Day Planner is called CorelCENTRAL 9 and can be started by clicking Start, and then choosing Programs, WordPerfect Office 2000, CorelCENTRAL 9. An alternative way to start Day Planner is to click the CorelCENTRAL 9 icon in the DAD tool tray on the Windows taskbar.

An Event list and Task list appear in Day Planner, just as they do in Calendar (see Figure 36.11). Any changes you make to events and tasks in Calendar are updated in Day Planner and vice versa.

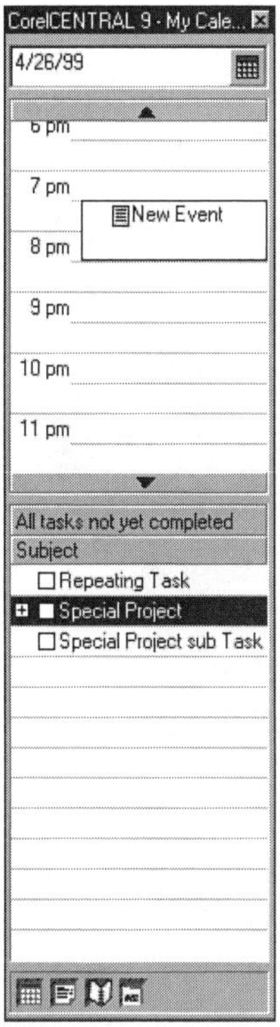

Figure 36.11
CorelCENTRAL Day
Planner lets you
schedule and view
events and tasks, just
as you would in
Calendar.

MANAGING CARD FILES

CorelCENTRAL Card File is your information assistant that keeps track of any information you want to record and store. For example, you can create a card file for reference material, inventory, projects, employees, and anything else you can think of. Card File is like a mini database application that lets you group the cards together in a card file. For instance, you can create a card file of your CD collection and create a group within that card file called "Classical" for your classical music CDs.

Start Card File by choosing Start, Programs, WordPerfect Office 2000, Utilities, CorelCENTRAL Card File, or if the Calendar is open, choose Tools, Card File, or click the CorelCENTRAL Card File icon in the DAD toolbar if it appears there.

CREATING CARDS

The first step involved in creating cards is to create a new card file. To do so, choose File, New; or click the New Card File icon; or press Ctrl+N, and type a name for the card file in the Name to Display on Tab box. In the Filename for Card File Box, type a path for the card file. Click OK.

To add a card, choose Cards, New Card to add the fields that will be on the cards. Then type the information in each field. The card appears in a list, as shown in Figure 36.12.

Figure 36.12
Cards you create appear in the Card File list.

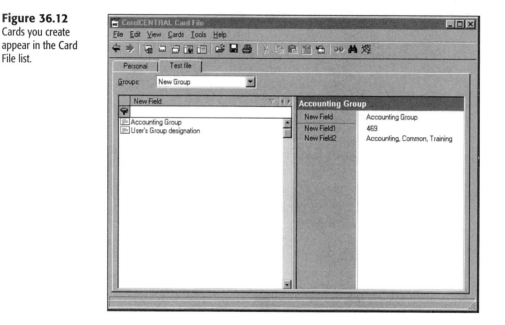

ADDING FIELDS

After you add cards to your card file, you can add either of two types of fields to cards: a global field or a local field. A global field is added to all cards in the card file. A local field is added to the selected only. A field can be a specific piece of information you want to include in your card file. In the CD collection card file example, you might want to add a global field called "Artist" and a local field called "Dance" on the cards for each CD that has music you can dance to.

A field can be formatted in various ways. The formats you can choose from include Alpha/Numeric, Check Box, Currency, Date/Time, Email Address, Internet URL, Mailing Address, Numeric, Radio Button, and Separator.

To add a global field to all cards, choose Cards, New Global Field, and enter a name for the field.

To add a local field to a particular card, choose the card in the Cards list, choose Cards, New Local Field, and enter a name for the field.

You can duplicate a field by choosing a field in the fields list, and then choose Cards, Duplicate Field.

To delete a field, click a field in the list of fields. If prompted, choose Yes in the Delete Field dialog box.

EDITING CARDS

After you add cards to your card file, you can duplicate, cut, copy, paste, and delete cards.

To duplicate a card within the same card file, click a card in the card list, and choose Cards, Duplicate Card. An exact copy of the card appears in the same card file.

You can edit a card by using any of the typical editing features to change the information in any field on the card. Highlight the information and type over it, use insert, delete, copy and paste, and cut and paste to edit the information.

To cut or copy a card within a card file or between card files, follow these steps:

1. Click a card in the card list.
2. Choose Edit, Cut or Edit, Copy.
3. Right-click a card in the card list where you want the card to appear, and choose Paste. If you want to paste the card into a different card file, be sure to click the tab of the card file where you want to paste the card.

To delete a card, click the card you want to remove, and choose Cards, Delete Card. The card no longer appears in the card list.

GROUPING CARDS

If you want to organize your cards in a card file, you can use the Group feature. For instance, in a card file with music CDs, you can create a group for classical, and another group for jazz. If you have a card file to track upcoming employee performance reviews, you can create a group for each month to diary when a performance review is due.

To create a group, complete the following steps:

1. Choose Cards, New Group.
2. In the Name box, enter a name for the group. You have three options for adding cards to the group: Empty, Include Selected Cards, and Include All Cards from Group. Choose one of these options.
3. Then, put a check mark in the Include Fields from New Group check box. This option includes the fields from the selected group.
4. Click OK to create the group in the card file. The group name appears in the Groups list box.

Then you can add existing cards to the group. To do so, click a card in the Cards list. Choose Cards, Assign Card to Group. Then click a group.

To delete a group, choose the group in the Groups list box, and choose Cards, Delete Group.

> **Caution**
>
> Be sure you want to delete a group because there is no Undo command to reverse the deletion of a group.

To rename a group, choose the group in the Groups list box, choose Cards, Rename Group, and in the Enter New Group Name box, type a new name for the group.

To view a group, choose a group in the Groups list.

SAVING A CARD FILE

To save a card file, complete the following steps:

1. Click the tab for the card file you want to save.
2. Choose File, Save As.
3. Choose the drive in the Save In list box, choose the folder, and enter a filename in the File Name box.
4. Click OK to save the card file.

To delete a card file, follow these steps:

1. Click the tab for the card file you want to remove.
2. Choose File, Delete. In the Available Card Files list, click the file you want to delete.

You can rename a card file by doing the following:

1. Click the tab for the card file you want to rename.
2. Choose File, Rename and in the New Tab box, type a new name for the card file.
3. Click OK to save the new name.

OPENING A CARD FILE

To open a card file, choose File, Open. Choose the drive in the Look In list box, choose the folder, and choose Card Files (*.ccf) in the File Type list box. Double-click the filename to open the card file.

When you're ready to close a card file, choose File, Close.

VIEW CARD FILES

If you want to view a card file, click the tab of the card file you want to view. To see the previous card file, choose View, Previous. To see the next card file, choose View, Next.

You can change the order of the file cards name on the tabs in the Card Files box. To do so, complete the following steps:

1. Choose View, Reorder Card files.

2. Click the card file name in the Card File box.

3. Choose Move Up to move the card file up one position in the list or choose Move Down to move the card file down one position in the list.

4. Repeat these three steps until the card files are shown in the order you want in the Card Files box.

Note

You can print your card files. First set up the pages for printing by choosing File, Page Setup. Select the options you want, and click OK. Choose File, Print, click the Print tab, choose your printing options, and click the Print button.

MAKING USE OF MEMOS

CorelCENTRAL Memos enables you to create the electronic version of paper notes and keep them organized by category. With Memos you can write down your brilliant ideas, reminders to yourself and others, questions you want to ask, instructions, directions, and anything you would normally jot down on a paper note.

After you work with Memos, you'll probably be able to reduce the number of notes that you keep on your desk or post all over your computer monitor.

To start CorelCENTRAL Memos, click Start, choose Programs, WordPerfect Office 2000, Utilities, and choose CorelCENTRAL Memos. An alternative way to start Memos is to click the CorelCENTRAL Memos icon if it appears in the DAD tool tray on the Windows taskbar. You can also click the CorelCENTRAL Memos icon at the bottom of the Daily Planner.

WRITING MEMOS

To write a memo, choose File, New. Enter a name for the memo, and press Enter. In the Type in the Memo Text Here box, type the text for the memo. The memo appears as a memo icon on the CorelCENTRAL Memos desktop, as shown in Figure 36.13.

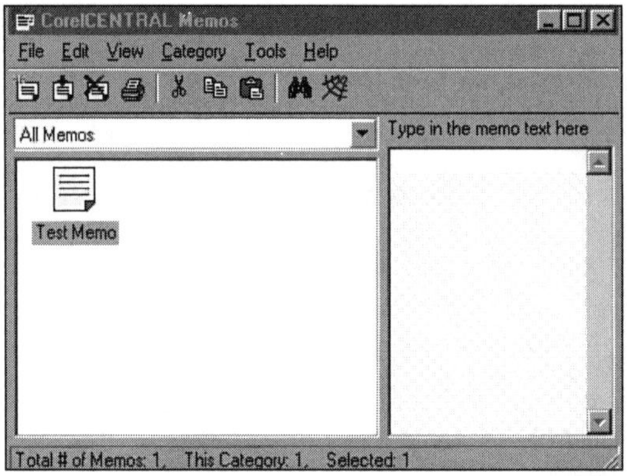

Figure 36.13
Memo icons on the
CorelCENTRAL Memos
desktop.

EDITING MEMOS

To make changes to a memo, select the text in the memo, and type over the text.

You can cut, copy, and paste text in memos by selecting the text, choose Edit, and choose Cut or Copy. Position your insertion point where you want to paste the text, and choose Edit, Paste.

To find text, choose Edit, Find. In the Text box, type the text you want to locate, and click the Find Now button.

To rename a memo, click on a memo, choose File, Rename, type a new name for the memo, and press Enter.

To delete a memo, click on a memo, and choose File, Delete.

> **Caution**
>
> Be sure you want to delete a memo because there is no Undo command to reverse the deletion of a memo.

VIEWING MEMOS

Memo icons come in two sizes: large and small. To choose a memo icon size, choose View and either Large Icons or Small Icons.

To view memo icons in a list or in detail, choose View, and List or Detail.

To arrange memo icons, choose View, Arrange Icons, and choose By Name or Auto Arrange.

To line up memo icons in a grid, choose View, Line Up Icons.

To refresh the memos on the CorelCENTRAL Memos desktop, choose View, Refresh.

PRACTICAL PROJECT

Enter your schedule in Calendar for business and personal use. Be sure to add your family and friends' birthdays, anniversaries, and special events.

Enter tasks for a project to track the work assignments necessary to complete the project. Use Day Planner to check off the completed tasks and view the completion status of the outstanding tasks.

Set up card files using Card File for your favorite hobbies. Print the cards to have a hard copy of the records for your hobbies.

Use Memos to write memos for your appointments, things to do, or special dates. For example, write a memo to remind yourself or others about meetings, shopping lists, and work projects.

TROUBLESHOOTING

REPEATING AN EVENT

You have a weekly staff meeting and want to repeat the event.

Set up the event as a repeating event. To do so, create a new event. Click the Repeat button in the Create Event Dialog Box. Choose your options and click OK.

CHANGING THE PRIORITY FOR A TASK

You need to change the priority for a task.

Right-click the task in the Task list, choose Priority, select a priority level, and click OK.

CHAPTER 37

USING COREL ADDRESS BOOK 9

In this chapter

UNDERSTANDING HOW ADDRESS BOOK WORKS

Address Book interfaces closely with Microsoft Exchange, and to understand how Address Book works, you need to understand a few things about Exchange.

> **Caution**
>
> If Exchange is installed after Address Book, then Address Book can show an error on start-up. This occurs because Exchange overwrites information that Address Book modifies on its installation. If you have problems integrating the two, try uninstalling Address Book and then reinstalling it (after Exchange has been installed).

⚠ *If you installed Exchange after Address Book, and Address Book reflects an error on startup, see "Installing Exchange and Address Book" in the Troubleshooting section at the end of this chapter.*

UNDERSTANDING MICROSOFT EXCHANGE PROFILES

Exchange is the universal Inbox in Windows that provides a central point for services, including your faxes, Microsoft Mail messages, Internet email, and Microsoft Network email. If you have installed Exchange, you will have one or more of these services installed as well.

These services use address lists. Microsoft Mail uses a Postoffice Address List. The other services can access the Postoffice Address List, but because it doesn't maintain much information; you will usually use the Personal Address Book that is created for you when you install Exchange.

Because more than one person might use a given computer, Exchange supports profiles. The Microsoft Exchange help system describes a profile as

> "…a set of configuration options used by Microsoft Exchange and other messaging applications that contains essential information, such as which information services you are using. This information includes the location of your Inbox, Outbox, and address lists, and the personal folder files available to you for storing and retrieving messages and files."

In short, you can think of a profile as the information needed to support an individual user of Exchange services.

UNDERSTANDING HOW ADDRESS BOOK USES PROFILES

When you install Address Book, a new Exchange profile—the Corel 9 Settings profile—is created. By default, the service that is set up in this profile includes the Address Book. Depending on how Exchange was configured when Address Book was installed, the profile might also include your Exchange Personal Address Book, and/or your Microsoft Mail Postoffice Address List.

When you open Address Book, it looks at the last profile you specified. The address books you see depend on the profile you use. If you create profiles for several people who use the same computer, each person sees only their own address books.

You usually use just the default Corel 9 Settings profile. If you need to add a profile, or add services to an existing one, you can do so as follows:

1. Right-click the Inbox icon in the Windows desktop, and then choose Properties. You see the MS Exchange Settings Properties dialog box.

2. Choose Show Profiles.

3. Choose Add to create a new profile or Copy to copy an existing one to a new one. (If you choose Add, you need to use the Inbox Setup Wizard to configure the different Exchange services you want to include in the new profile.)

4. To add a service to an existing profile, select it, and then choose Properties. You see the Corel 9 Settings Properties dialog box. Select the service you want to add.

5. Click OK to add the service.

PART
VI
CH
37

Tip #237 from
Trudi Reisner

Use this procedure to add the Personal Address Book service to your Corel 9 Settings profile, if you do not see the Microsoft Exchange Personal Address Book as one of your address books in Address Book.

To use a different profile with Address Book 9, check with your system administrator for instructions on how to change the profile for Address Book.

CREATING ADDRESS BOOKS

You can use just one address book if you prefer, or create as many address books as you like. You may find it useful, for example, to have one address book for personal addresses and another for business contacts.

To create a new address book from the main Corel Address Book window, complete the following steps:

1. Choose File, New or click the Create a New Address Book button on the toolbar. You see the New Address Book dialog box.

2. Select an address book type, such as CorelCENTRAL, and click OK. The New Address Book Properties dialog box appears, as shown in Figure 37.1.

3. Enter the name of your new address book and click OK. You see a new address book name with its icon in the Tree view on the left side of the Address Book window.

After you have created more than one address book, you can select the appropriate one by clicking its name in the Tree view in the Address Book window.

Note

Address Books from previous versions of CorelCENTRAL update automatically when CorelCENTRAL 9 is installed.

Figure 37.1
You can create separate address books for your personal and business addresses.

New Address Book Properties

Address Book | Security

Name:

OK   Cancel

ADDING CONTACT INFORMATION

Address Book maintains two types of records: records for individuals and records for organizations. When you create a record for an individual, you can include their organization as one piece of information about them. If you enter an organization name that is not in the Address Book, a record for that organization is created automatically, containing only the organization name. If, when you create a record for an individual, you specify an organization that is in the Address Book, the person's record is linked to the record for that organization.

To add an organization to your address list, do the following:

1. From the main Address Book window, choose Address, New or click the Create a New Address Entry button. You see the New dialog box.

2. Select Organization and click OK. You see the Organization Properties dialog box shown in Figure 37.2.

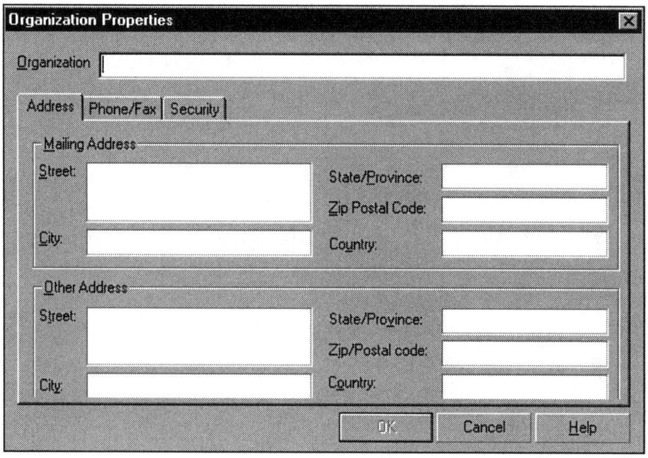

Figure 37.2
Insert the main number and address for the organization in the Organization Properties dialog box.

Organization Properties

Organization

Address | Phone/Fax | Security

Mailing Address
Street: State/Province:
                                Zip Postal Code:
City: Country:

Other Address
Street: State/Province:
                                Zip/Postal code:
City: Country:

OK   Cancel   Help

3. Enter information in each field. Press Tab to move to the next field; press Shift+Tab to move to the previous one.

4. When you've finished, click OK to return to the main Address Book window.

Use a similar procedure to enter a new person into the address book:

1. From the main Address Book window, choose Address, New or click the Create a New Address Entry button. You see the New dialog box.

2. Select Person and click OK. You see the Person Properties dialog box, which is similar to the Organization Properties dialog box.

3. Enter information in each field. Press Tab to move to the next field; press Shift+Tab to move to the previous one.

4. When you've finished, click OK to return to the main Address Book window.

PART

VI

CH

37

You can edit an existing contact in a similar manner. Select the person or organization whose record you want to change, and then click the Edit an Address Entry button. You see the Properties dialog box that has the same functionality as the dialog box used to create the record. Make changes in the appropriate fields, and then click OK.

CREATING CUSTOM FIELDS

You can also create custom fields that are maintained for each person or organization. For instance, you might want to have a field called Web Site for organizations, in which you can record the URL for the contact's organization's Web site. To do so, complete the following steps:

1. Select the Address Book in the Tree view.

2. Choose Edit, Custom Fields from the main Address Book window. You see the Custom Fields dialog box (see Figure 37.3).

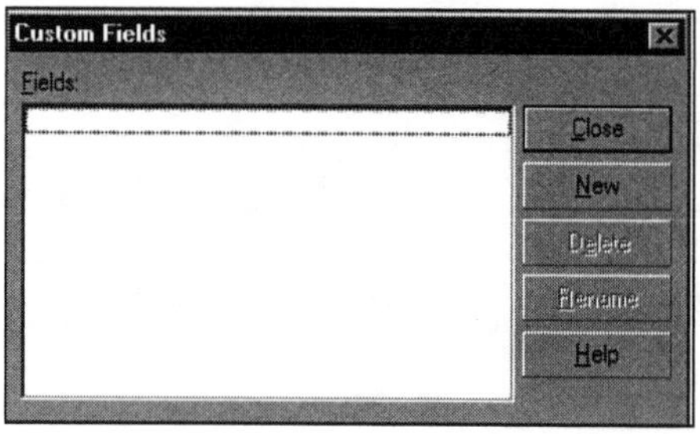

Figure 37.3
The Custom Fields dialog box allows you to add new fields for persons or organizations.

3. Choose New. You see the New Custom Field dialog box.

4. Put the name of the new field in the New Field Name box and click OK.

To use custom fields, create or edit a record. You see the Properties dialog box. Click the Custom tab. You see the new fields that you have added. Fill in information as needed.

IMPORTING CONTACTS

You can also import your contact list from another application. This can be especially handy when you have already created a contact list in another application, and you don't want to have to manually reenter your entire address list.

The first step is to save your address list in comma-separated value (CSV) format. (Corel calls this format ASCII-Delimited Text.) The commands you will use for this differ, depending on the program, but commonly there is a File, Export command. Occasionally, you instead will use File, Save As, and specify CSV as the Save As Type. Check the documentation for your particular program for details.

Note

CSV format puts each record on a separate line, with each field contained in quotation marks and separated by a comma, as shown here:

"Smith","Joe","555-1212"

"Jones","Mary","666-1313"

The CSV format is a "lowest common denominator" that most address list programs can all export to and import from.

After you have saved your information as a CSV file, you can import it into Address Book as follows:

1. Select an address book in the Tree view.

2. Choose File, Import, and ensure that ASCII Text (*.txt) is selected in the File Type box. You see the Import dialog box, shown in Figure 37.4.

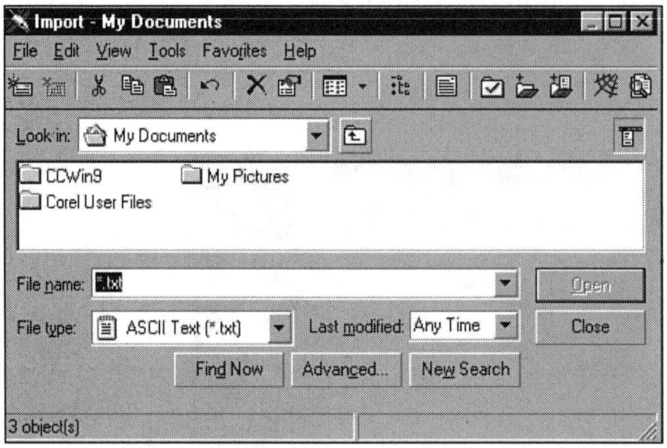

Figure 37.4
You can import text from other address books by saving them in a common format such as comma-separated value.

3. Choose the drive where the ASCII file is stored from the Look In list box. Then choose the folder in which the file is stored. Double-click the ASCII filename.

4. In the ASCII Delimiter Setup dialog box, shown in Figure 37.5, specify the Field Delimiter character as a comma and the Record Delimiter as a carriage return Line Feed. Click OK.

Figure 37.5
Specify what character separates fields (usually a comma), and which encapsulation characters should be stripped out of the file (usually carriage returns).

5. In the Field Mapping dialog box, shown in Figure 37.6, you see a list of fields in the database being imported, and you can associate (map) them to the Address Book fields. Fields with the same name are mapped together automatically; fields that don't have a corresponding Address Book name have IGNORE FIELD, indicating that they will be ignored unless you specify which field they correspond to. To specify a field that doesn't have a corresponding name, select it in the left column, and then click the field in the middle column containing the Address Book fields.

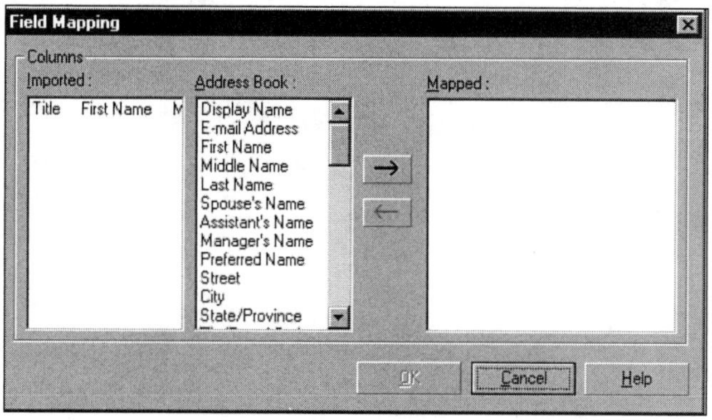

Figure 37.6
Map fields between the two databases. If fields have the same name, they are mapped together automatically.

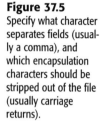

6. Choose OK. The database is imported, and you return to the Address Book main window.

CREATING ADDRESS LISTS

You can create address lists, which are groups of persons or organizations contained in the address book. These groups are part of the address book, and can be created, deleted, edited, or renamed when necessary.

To create an address list, follow these steps:

1. In the Tree view, click the address book to which you want to add an address list.

2. Choose Address, New or click the Create a New Address Entry button on the toolbar. You see a new text box at the right of the Corel Address Book window.

3. Choose Group and click OK. You see the Group Properties dialog box, as shown in Figure 37.7.

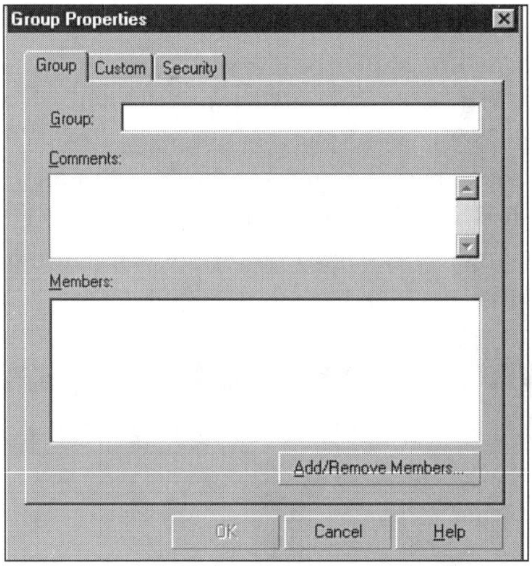

Figure 37.7
You can create address lists to easily send mail to several people.

4. Enter a name in the Group box and click OK.

5. Click the Add/Remove Members button and select one or more names you want to add to the new address list. To select multiple names, click the first name, and then hold down the Ctrl key while clicking additional names.

6. Click the Add button. You see the selected names in the Group Members list box at the right side of the Add/Remove Members dialog box.

7. Click OK. You return to the Group Properties dialog box. The selected member names appear in the Members list box.

8. Click OK. The group is added to the Address Book list, denoted by a group icon, as shown in Figure 37.8. You can use a group just as you use any other name in the address list.

Figure 37.8
Groups and organizations are denoted by special icons in the address list.

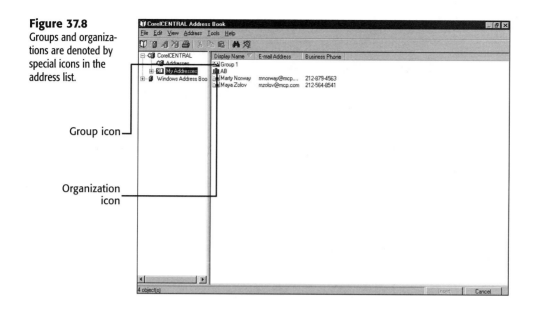

Group icon

Organization icon

USING ADDRESS BOOK

You can use Address Book to access appropriate records, and edit, delete, or copy them. You may also want to use Address Book in conjunction with WordPerfect, to dial phone numbers from Address Book, or to use Address Book for email addresses.

FINDING AND FILTERING RECORDS

You can arrange the records in Address Book by last name, first name; or by first name, last name. To do so, click the column heading button for the column you want to sort. A down arrow appears on the button. Click the button to sort in ascending order and click the button again to sort in descending order. Your list is re-sorted by the desired field.

If you want to change the order of the columns, click a column heading button and drag it to the desired location in the row of column headings. The column appears in its new position in the address book.

If you want to look up a name by text that exists in any field, click in the column heading of the field in which the text exists, choose Edit, Find or press Ctrl+F. Type the text in the Find box and click Find Now. The first name matching the typed letters is selected.

You can also create a filter for your address list that shows only the records meeting specified criteria.

To do so, choose View, Filter. You see the Filter dialog box (see Figure 37.9).

Figure 37.9
You can create a filter that shows only specified records.

Choose the field you want to filter the list by from the drop-down list, and then choose the operator (by default, it is the equal sign). Type the criterion text in the right text box. If you want to add another criterion, click the End button, change it to And or Or, and enter additional criteria. Click OK when you're finished. You see the filtered list.

EDITING, DELETING, OR COPYING RECORDS

After you have located the appropriate record, you can edit, delete, or copy it. To edit a record, select it, and then double-click it; or right-click the record, and choose Edit, or choose Address, Edit. You see the appropriate Properties dialog box, where you can make the appropriate changes.

Tip #238 from
Trudi Reisner

Be sure your filter is turned off by choosing View, Remove, Filter.

To delete a record, select it, and press the Delete key; or click the Delete an Address Entry button; or choose Address, Delete, and then click Yes in the verification dialog box. The record is removed from the address list.

Caution

Be careful when you delete records because Address Book doesn't have an Undo feature, so deleted records are permanently lost.

To copy a record, select it and choose Edit, Copy. Switch to the desired address list, if needed, and then choose Edit, Paste. If the operation creates a duplicate record, you are warned; then the duplicate record is created. You can also use the Copy and Paste buttons on the toolbar to copy and paste records.

Tip #239 from
Trudi Reisner

You may find this to be an easy way to create records for related persons, or persons in the same organization who share many fields of information.

Note

If you have a modem attached to your computer and a telephone on the same line, you can use Address Book to dial a phone number. You also need to ensure that the Windows Phone Dialer application is loaded. To dial a person, highlight his or her entry and click the Dial button.

SYNCHRONIZING AN ADDRESS BOOK WITH PALMPILOT

If you have a 3Com PalmPilot, you can synchronize an address book with it. In other words, when you add addresses to Address Book in CorelCENTRAL 9, they are added to Address Book in PalmPilot; when you add addresses to Address Book in PalmPilot, these addresses are automatically added to Address Book in CorelCENTRAL 9.

When you want to synchronize PalmPilot and CorelCENTRAL 9 Address Books, you need to do two things: Enable the CorelCENTRAL Address Book PalmPilot conduits and then perform a HotSync in PalmPilot as you normally would.

To enable CorelCENTRAL Address Book PalmPilot conduits, choose Tools, PalmPilot Conduits. The Enable/Disable Pilot Conduits dialog box opens.

Put a check mark in the Address Book check box and click OK. Next, perform a HotSync in PalmPilot by clicking Start, and choosing PalmPilot Desktop, HotSync Manager. Be sure your PalmPilot is in its cradle. Then, click the HotSync button on the PalmPilot. After you HotSync, reopen the CorelCENTRAL Address Book to reflect the changes you made.

To disable the CorelCENTRAL Address Book PalmPilot conduits, choose Tools, PalmPilot Conduits. In the Enable/Disable Pilot Conduits dialog box, remove the check mark in the Address Book check box and click OK. Restart your HotSync Manager in PalmPilot to reflect the conduit you disabled in CorelCENTRAL Address Book.

PRINTING ADDRESSES FROM ADDRESS BOOK

You can print one or more names and addresses and choose any columns you want to print. The new PerfectPrint feature lets you print the addresses exactly the way you want them to appear on different paper sizes.

You can print your addresses from the Print dialog box and set up your print options from there. But if you have already set up your print options and are back to the Address Book window, you can click the Print button on the Address Book toolbar and then click Print to print your address book.

If you use the Print dialog box to print your addresses, you can choose from several print options, such as printing the current record, selected records, or all records.

Corel's new PerfectPrint feature offers two printing options. Click the Customize Tab and choose Poster to print your addresses on huge poster-size paper. The Enlarge/Reduce feature lets you enlarge or shrink an Address Book list to fit any paper size without changing the format of the page.

The Scale to Fit Output Page option adjusts the printed document to fit the selected page size. Click the Output Page button to view or change the page size.

Finally, the Thumbnails option lets you print up to 64 miniature versions of the addresses, like Rolodex cards, on one piece of paper. Click the Output Page button to change the page size.

You can also print page borders and page number on your address book pages.

When you are finished choosing your print options, click the Print button in the Print dialog box. Corel Address Book prints your addresses.

INTEGRATING ADDRESS BOOK WITH WORDPERFECT

You might find that you access Address Book more from WordPerfect than you do as a standalone application after you get used to its easy functionality.

INSERTING NAMES AND ADDRESSES INTO WORDPERFECT

Your address books can be used to quickly insert a name and address into a WordPerfect document, or to serve as the data source for merge operations.

To insert a name and address in a WordPerfect document, open WordPerfect and create or open the document. Position your insertion point where you want the name and address to be inserted, and then choose Tools, Address Book. You see the Corel Address Book window (refer to Figure 37.8).

Choose the appropriate address book, and then select the desired person or organization. Click Insert. You see his or her name and address in your WordPerfect document.

Tip #240 from *Trudi Reisner*	If you select an address group, all the names and addresses will be brought into your document.

If you like, you can specify which fields will be imported into your WordPerfect document. In the Format Address dialog box (see Figure 37.10), pick from the four default formats, or add a format that includes just the fields you want by choosing Custom and creating a new format.

Figure 37.10
Choose the fields you want to use from the Address Book from the Format Address dialog box.

→ For details on the Merge feature, **see** "Using Merge," **p. 282**

You can also use your address books as data sources for merge operations. When you choose Tools, Merge or press Shift+F9 in WordPerfect, you see the Merge dialog box shown in Figure 37.11. From this dialog box, you can click the Address Book button to view, edit, or add entries to an address book.

Figure 37.11
Address books can be used as the data source for WordPerfect merges.

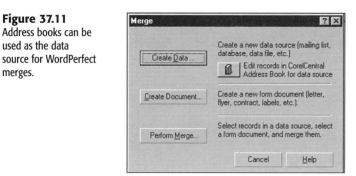

To use an address book as the data source, do not click the Create Data button; this is used to create a data source. Instead, choose Create Document. After you choose whether to create the merge file in the active window or a new window, you see the Associate Form and Data dialog box (see Figure 37.12). Select Associate an Address Book, and then choose from existing address books in the drop-down list box that becomes active.

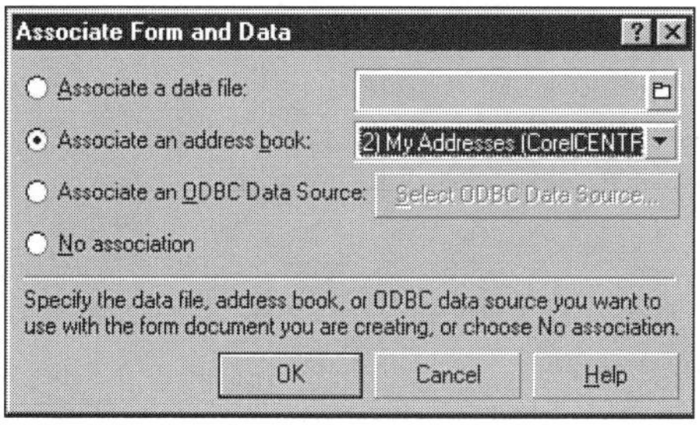

Figure 37.12
You are given the option of using an address book as the data file when you create the form file.

If you entered your personal information the first time you used a template in WordPerfect, and now you want to change it, see "Changing Personal Information" in the Troubleshooting section at the end of this chapter.

PRINTING AN ENVELOPE

WordPerfect's Envelope feature automatically formats and addresses your envelope. If you have already typed the inside address into a letter, and you want an envelope for the letter, just choose Format, Envelope.

To address an envelope after typing a letter, follow these steps:

1. Choose Format, Envelope to open the Envelope window and display the Envelope toolbar shown in Figure 37.13.

2. Click the Return Address button on the Property Bar. Choose Address Book and select your address for the return address.

3. To change the font face or size used in the return address, choose a font or size from the Property Bar.

Figure 37.13
WordPerfect's Envelope feature automatically formats and addresses your envelope.

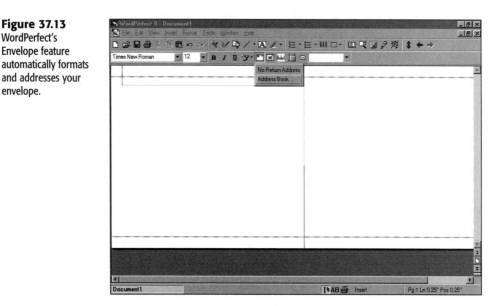

 4. To enter or add a mailing address (if the mailing address is not automatically selected), click the Mailing Address button on the Property Bar. Choose Address Book and select your recipient from Address Book, or type the recipient's name in the Mailing Address area of the envelope.

5. As with the return address, you can change the font or point size used in the mailing address.

6. If you want a USPS bar code printed on the envelope, click the Bar Code button on the Property Bar, and select whether you want the bar code printed above or below the address.

7. To print the Envelope immediately, click the Print button on the toolbar.

> **Note**
>
> The font on an envelope is automatically taken from the document initial font (File, Document, Default Font). To save the document text in the Envelope window, be sure that the document initial font is what you want both for the letter and the envelope.

PRACTICAL PROJECT

It's convenient to have a printout of the phone directory near the phone when you're making phone calls to your contacts in the address book. You can also give this phone directory to colleagues. To print the contacts in a phone directory style, choose File, Print. In the Print Format list box, choose Address List.

TROUBLESHOOTING

INSTALLING EXCHANGE AND ADDRESS BOOK

You installed Microsoft Exchange after you installed Address Book, and Address Book shows an error on startup.

This happens because Exchange overwrites information that Address Book modifies on its installation. Uninstall Address Book and then reinstall it (after Exchange has been installed).

CHANGING PERSONAL INFORMATION

You entered your personal information the first time that you used a template in WordPerfect, and now you want to change it.

Choose File, New from Project, click Options, Personal Information in the Options menu, and then click OK. Select your entry in the Address Book, and then click the Edit button. Edit the entry, and then click OK to return to the Address Book. Click Cancel or Insert (if data is to be inserted) to return to the WordPerfect New Projects dialog box, and then click Close to return to the main editing window.

INDEX